Amherst in the World

Edited by

Martha Saxton

DOI: https://doi.org/10.3998/mpub.11873533

Print: 978-0-943184-20-3

Open access: 978-0-943184-21-0

Library of Congress Control Number: **TK**

Orra White Hitchcock (1796-1863), one of the first American women artists of science, drew all the images on the front cover: a world map indicating volcanic areas, a mastodon maximus skeleton, and the shift of stone obelisks at a convent in Calabria, Italy caused by an earthquake. The colors on the spine are from her graphic representation of valleys. She made 61 illustrations in all for her husband Edward Hitchcock's classes on geology and natural history.

Contents

Introduction

Amherst in the World

Martha Saxton

This volume celebrates the two hundredth anniversary of Amherst College. A group of historians, many alumni, and others with expertise on the college have written chapters on the school's substantial and far-reaching past. Amherst's unique history intersects and parallels those of fellow institutions. The histories in this volume illuminate the events, crises, and transitions that many educational institutions have confronted, including slavery; wars; the relations among religion, science, and the curriculum; the interplay of town and gown; the changing population of students; struggles over college governance; and funding.[1] The chapters implicitly, and sometimes explicitly, affirm both the vitality—and the utility—of a liberal arts education and Amherst's continual debates to improve that education to suit and sometimes challenge the historical eras through which is has passed.

Amherst is not the oldest liberal arts school in the country—that honor goes to Washington College in Chestertown, Maryland (established in 1782), but it is one of the most respected. Among the approximately two hundred and fifty-five liberal arts colleges in the United States, on a variety of indices, Amherst regularly scores at or near the top.[2]

This collection of essays helps explain Amherst's path to prominence. It also illuminates Amherst's two hundred years as a center of commitment to the liberal arts.

At its founding in 1821, Amherst per force entered into an ongoing controversy over what knowledge was worth having in the young republic. After the American Revolution, Benjamin Franklin criticized Harvard for a curriculum designed to identify and decorate a ruling class, not to produce well-informed citizens capable of practical thinking and innovation. He founded an academy—later to be the University of Pennsylvania—and took a utilitarian stand in the debate over what constitutes a useful education.[3] But Washington College, founded in 1782, offered a limited version of Harvard's curriculum, declaring its intention to educate citizens who would create the businesses and shape the institutions of the United States. Three years later, the New York Board of Regents founded Union College in Schenectady, New York. It was nondenominational and offered a classical curriculum initially, but in the early nineteenth century, its president, the reverend Eliphalet

Nott, responded to pressure for practical training. Union began offering a degree for its new science program, an alternative to the liberal arts curriculum.

Shortly after the Revolution, the second great awakening Protestant revivals began rolling over the East Coast and accompanying western settlers. Its converts produced Sunday schools, magazines, bible societies, and reform campaigns as well as schools: notably, Amherst College.

The college founders wished to prepare young men to evangelize the sin-ridden world, but it did not offer a religious curriculum. Amherst's admission requirements, not so different from Harvard's, required knowledge of Greek and Latin and "vulgar arithmetic." Like its competitors and peers, the college offered mathematics, philosophy, geography, and chemistry. The college adhered to what Yale's president Jeremiah Day articulated in 1828 as the recipe for liberal arts schools: "The two great points to be gained in intellectual culture, are the discipline and the furniture of the mind." Of these two, he thought, the first was undoubtedly the most important, as it would "throw the student upon the resources of his own mind. . . . The scholar must form himself by his own exertions. . . . We doubt whether the powers of the mind can be developed, in their fairest proportions, by studying languages alone, or mathematics alone, or natural or political science." He thought the differing demands required to master a variety of disciplines would train student minds in flexibility and self-reliance, giving them tools adequate to confront life's problems. [4]

In 2017, Cullen Murphy, a trustee of the college, wrote that a liberal-arts education at Amherst "means understanding that our diversity and our values are complementary ingredients."[5] This volume illustrates the college's deliberations over these issues from its earliest years. Debate has reflected the changing historical and economic circumstances of the college, and students, faculty, alumni, and administrators have all participated.

Fredrick L. Hoxie's essay on Amherst graduates and their relationships with indigenous people also provides an example of the evolution of college teachings on the rights of nations and their responsibilities toward others. Early nineteenth-century imperialism blended with evangelical Christianity to shape the expansive "civilizing" goal of Amherst missionaries toward Native Americans. Amherst missionaries (like those from other schools) urged conversion to Protestantism as well as cultural assimilation as steps along the road to eventual statehood for indigenous people. As the juggernaut of manifest destiny made this increasingly unlikely, Amherst faculty began teaching a more free-market approach to political economy, which imposed a sink or swim attitude toward people who resisted capitalism or remained at its margins. The policies, which Amherst graduates helped craft, included forced assimilation through the now-notorious boarding schools for Native Americans and allotment of reservation land, including bringing white settlers onto large territories previously reserved for native peoples and support for the coup that toppled Hawaii's native monarchy.

Toward the turn of the twentieth century, Amherst students seeking to illuminate the world with evangelical Christianity became rarer, while those wishing to make careers in finance, business, government, and law became more numerous. Around the same time, some students, faculty, and local activists, like Helen Hunt Jackson, began challenging some of the colonialist practices of the nineteenth century and sharing in a growing sympathy for indigenous people as well as others who were not benefiting from the expanding economy.

Before 1945, the curriculum and the college's admissions policies changed slowly and with reverses. In 1912, Amherst hired Alexander Meiklejohn as president, a political progressive. He opposed prejudicial admissions policies and hired a number of young, like-minded faculty members to replace more conservative professors. Meiklejohn reorganized the curriculum to engage students with contemporary social and economic problems. Strikingly, doctor Charles Eastman, a Dakota and advocate for Native Americans, spoke on campus the year after Meiklejohn was hired. The reasons for his abrupt and well-publicized firing in 1923 are disputed, but his liberal views did not characterize his next three successors.[6] Conflict over the curriculum and diversity among students and faculty was part of the landscape at the college.

Amherst adopted new scientific theories and advances after passionate back and forth.[7] The same president, Julius Seelye, who opposed the Chinese Exclusion Act of 1882 as discriminatory, also opposed teaching geology, as its newer findings potentially supported an evolutionary rather than a biblical history of the world. Amherst incorporated new disciplines like sociology and anthropology in the early and mid-twentieth century, and later it incorporated African American studies, women's and gender studies, Native American studies, and Hispanic studies.[8] In the latter cases, activist students and some faculty advocated for new fields of knowledge that were relevant to the expanding student body, pushing against resistance from those who understood these disciplines as having a stronger political than intellectual basis.

Over the years, Amherst, like its fellow liberal arts schools, including Franklin's University of Pennsylvania, Harvard, and Yale, have arranged, polished, reupholstered, added to, and sometimes discarded the furniture that Jeremiah Day spoke of. The search for the providential *feng shui* of courses—to stimulate students to intellectual discovery and continuing curiosity—remains a constant and defining liberal arts project.

These chapters portray two centuries of Amherst graduates, professors, and community members tied to the college. A significant number wound up in intellectually, economically, and politically rarefied circles. For most, a liberal arts education was not a useless luxury but a vital tool in continuing to educate themselves—in reasoning, in making decisions, and in participating in the world.

Humanistic inquiry, careful research, critical analysis, and precise writing betray the liberal arts training of the contributors to this volume. Their stories about Amherst tell us about changes in the college's populations, its economic fortunes, and the school's avowed purposes. We meet students, graduates, administrators, employees, faculty, and community members whose lives affected and were affected by the college.

Three groups of chapters follow. The first part, titled "Student Bodies and Souls," concerns the identity of Amherst students: who they were, how they lived, and how their beliefs influenced their purposes. (Clearly, questions about the soul of the students and the college pervade the whole volume, but the later works have other significant commonalities.) The articles unfold the evolution of the college's changing assumptions about itself, its rightful flock, and its goals.

The first three chapters explore the college's founding Christian ambitions, as they became reality. Collectively, missionaries produced considerable global ferment. They did not necessarily reap the religious and moral rewards they hoped for, but they established schools, made some converts, encouraged literacy among both men and women, spread ideas about capitalism and free labor, and made remarkable advances in philology. Gary Kornblith sees Amherst fulfilling its founding promise to "illuminate the lands" with Christianity, among other things. A full half of the first generation of graduates became ministers. (For the post-Civil War generation, it would be 17 percent.)

Edward Jones (class of 1826), unusual in background but not vocation, was the first African American to enroll at the college. He became one of its earliest missionaries, as principal from 1841 to 1856 of the Anglican mission and school in Fourah Bay, in what is now Sierra Leone. David W. Wills pieces together Jones's somewhat hesitant journey from his undergraduate days to his successful years in Sierra Leone. Wills pays particular attention to what Jones's experience reveals about the significance of race in the college's early years.

Native people, on this continent and in Hawai'i, intersected with the college nearly from its founding. Fredrick L. Hoxie marks three periods in Amherst's involvement with native people, beginning with the college's support for the national goals of "civilizing" them. A second period distinguished by rapid dispossession, paternalism, and forcible assimilation followed. Gradually and unevenly, a period of reckoning with the costs of earlier policies emerged. This more reflective era continues to the present, as native students and faculty push for a more historically aware and inclusive institution.

Born and raised in Japan, Niijima Jō arrived at the college in 1867, having stowed away on a Yankee merchant ship owned and piloted by evangelical Christians. Niijima earned degrees from Amherst and Andover Theological and returned to Japan where he founded the Dōshisha in Kyoto, a liberal arts college modeled on Amherst but that included Christian study. Trent Maxey explains how Niijima created an intellectually and theologically rigorous educational center for the small-but-growing number of Christians in Japan.

The next two chapters discuss the arrangements that accommodated student appetites for nourishment and companionship. During its first century, Amherst College, as a residential college, provided some rooms but no meals for students. Consequently, students dined with local families until the 1930s. As Daniel Levinson Wilk shows, administrators, worrying about the centrifugal force of fraternities and scattered lodgings, looked to give students a unifying experience. Beginning in the Great Depression, college dining halls and new fraternity dining facilities supplanted the boarding houses, removing students from these long-standing commercial and social relationships with townspeople. Eventually Valentine, which opened in 1941, fully centralized campus eating.

Fraternities, as Nicholas Syrett relates, began attracting students from the 1830s on. Members—mainly wealthier students, not bound for the ministry, whose ideas of manhood contrasted sharply with those of their more pious classmates—sought out the companionship of others like themselves. The growing strength of fraternities during the late-nineteenth century and their insistence on their right to exclude became, after World War

II, hard for Amherst faculty and administrators to reconcile with the college's liberal principles. The slow and painful abolition of fraternities paralleled other cascading changes at the college, some of which are detailed in the last three chapters of this section.

Young Jewish men began studying at Amherst in the very early twentieth century. Their welcome fluctuated with both the reputation of Jews in US culture and the attitudes of Amherst's admissions officers. Wendy Bergoffen judges Amherst's admission policy toward Jews as similar to that of many other schools. She singles out, however, a few administrators like Eugene Wilson for challenging traditional bars to the admission of Jews and Rabbi Yechiael Lander for encouraging Jewish students to enjoy a rich religious life at Amherst.

Matthew Randolph recounts the remarkable story of the Dunbar School in Washington, DC, that produced a stream of extraordinary African American students who started attending Amherst at the turn of the twentieth century. Dunbar graduates included some of the most prominent thinkers and reformers of the century, including Dr. Charles Drew, Charles Hamilton Houston, and William Hastie. College rules, racism, and the pressure on these young men to blend in isolated them. It was not until the 1960s that the admission of more African Americans from a variety of schools and backgrounds made it possible for black students to create a fuller community and work openly to improve their college lives.

Amherst held off going coeducational until 1975 to 1976—late compared with similar schools. Saxton's essay documents some of the social and intellectual barriers women faculty and students fought in trying to find equality at the college. Integrating women into a previously all-male school uniquely challenged the school's identity. It not only required rethinking educational offerings and teaching methods, but also providing a safe environment for all students.

Professor Rick Lopez tracks Latinx activism in search of equality and acceptance at the college. Lopez illuminates the pressures on Lantinx men and women to integrate into the dominant culture, to be responsible for educating others about themselves, and to refrain from retreating into the comfort of the company of other similar students. Their difficulties parallel those of many minorities trying to find a comfortable existence at the college.

The second part, "College and Beyond: Views and Refractions," offer oblique angles on the college and those attached to it. Some chapters portray the quests of people associated with the college. Others reflect on changes in the school that would affect its standing and image in the world. K. Ian Shin picks up the missionary theme in his study of Amherst's complicated relationship with nineteenth-century China. Amherst's few missionaries to China exerted a disproportionate influence on its forced opening. Despite the imperialism bound up with the missionary project, religious sympathies contributed to Amherst's president Julius Seelye's outspoken opposition to the Chinese Exclusion Act of 1882. In Shin's chapter, we learn about Amherst in China, as well as about the experiences and perceptions of the rare Chinese men who came to the college.

Emily Dickinson, tied to the college through her male relatives and to the town through convention and circumstance, nevertheless traveled the world imaginatively. David S. Reynolds portrays the surprising combination of her familiar appreciation of the exquisite details of the natural world with her less-familiar enthusiasm for the sordid exploits of drunks and criminals. That she could satisfy her catholic curiosity in Amherst provides a complex, mid-century view of the town, praised by the college founders only four decades earlier for its distance from urban temptations.

Amherst's faculty, like others, confronted Charles Darwin's unsettling ideas and evidence in the aftermath of the Civil War. The debates, as Jane F. Thrailkill shows, infused scientific work while making a shadowy appearance in Nathaniel Hawthorne' s novel *The Marble Faun*. At the college, geologist Edward Hitchcock and his son Edward "Doc" Hitchcock Jr. both believed that science and religion could coexist, and Hitchcock Sr. pursued research that potentially substantiated the claims of Darwin. President Seeley, however, cancelled geology classes in 1880 for just that reason.

In Julie Dubrow's study of David, Mabel, and Millicent Todd, Amherst, both the town and the college, exerted a centripetal force that helped hold that increasingly chaotic family together. Mabel Loomis's marriage to David Todd, professor of astronomy, endured despite her thirteen-year affair with Austin Dickinson, brother of Emily. Millicent Todd Bingham, Mabel and David's daughter, sacrificed a career as a geologist teaching in New York City, returning to assist her mother in Amherst, collecting and publishing Emily Dickinson's poetry. Millicent made sure the poems and papers ended up with the college.

In investigating the abrupt and widely publicized firing of president Alexander Meiklejohn in 1923, Richard Teichgraeber III attributes its remarkable newsworthiness to the underlying growth of wealth and power among the college's graduates over the previous generation. Marking this striking change, two men representing the greatest fortunes of the country—Standard Oil and Phelps Dodge mining—joined the three-man board of trustees in 1890. Joining them was a partner at J. P. Morgan.

Debby Applegate's search for the typical Amherst man of the roaring twenties provides a literary and historical backdrop for the trustees' distrust of Alexander Meiklejohn's intellectual and social idealism. Applegate finds the Amherst man's image in popular books "starchy" and unimaginative. In tracking down the Amherst graduates who became the power brokers to elect Calvin Coolidge (class of 1895) to the presidency in 1923, she unearths Amherst's contributions to the underlying economic conservatism of the Jazz Age. Meiklejohn's liberal views contrasted markedly with those of the business-friendly conservatives characterized in roaring twenties fiction.

The chapters in the final part, "Emergencies," examine the interplay among the college, political conflict, and war. Michael E. Jirik analyzes the pre-Civil War disagreements between student abolitionists and the more conservative colonizationists, largely made up of Amherst faculty, with presidential support. Amherst administrators and faculty had the example of the 1834 antislavery disruptions at Lyman Beecher's Lane Seminary in mind, which caused fifty students to leave and go to Oberlin. The college, not wishing to provoke such a crisis, did not prohibit debate on campus as Beecher had. Students and faculty disagreed with one another but preserved their mutual respect and affection. Eventually, when the student abolitionists turned from William Lloyd Garrison's insistence on moral suasion to politics, they took the debate largely off campus.

The advent of the Civil War compelled most southern students to return home and graduates to enlist in the Union army. Bruce Laurie reveals a range of motives among Amherst soldiers, tracing their evolving views as the war progressed. A few started out as abolitionists, but the majority fought initially to preserve the Union. Encounters between freed African Americans and Amherst-educated soldiers persuaded a number of the latter to embrace black freedom. Many from the college fell in the war, including the son of the college's president.

Two authors consider student and community responses to the injustices of the 1960s; most prominently, the war in Vietnam and racism. Christian G. Appy describes the radicalization of many faculty, administrators, and students. Using the views of Amherst's famous liberal historian, Henry Steele Commager, Appy charts the rise of campus dissent against the Vietnam War and racism. He uses the experience and testimony of numerous students to describe the growing antipathy to the war, including the voice of an Amherst GI who resisted the war on the battlefield in Vietnam. Appy also makes the point that the intimacy and respect prevalent in the Amherst community kept it from the most violent ravages of political and social disagreement that occurred on other campuses, paralleling Jirik's findings on the containment of disagreement in the years before the Civil War.

Molly Michelmore looks at tax resistance that two Amherst students recommended as an antiwar tactic. She opens up its history and its brief popularity with war protestors in the 1970s. It was not particularly effective in that fight, but she found that the practice and philosophy remained tools of resistance against arbitrary government for decades in the Amherst community.

This volume only concerns a few of the people, disputes, crises, and achievements that have emanated from or enveloped Amherst College in its two hundred years. These chapters recount stories of students of the liberal arts engaging coherently in the debates and projects animating their communities. They display the strong bonds of affection and respect that develop between students and faculty, as they struggle to understand together. And, bracingly, they often show students of the liberal arts taking their college to task for not living up to its ideals.

Cullen Murphy's inspirational description of Amherst's ambition pertains to its past as well as its future. He writes of the college as "a place where all three words in the phrase 'diverse intellectual community' have as much meaning as the middle one has always had.... The task is educational, and it is cultural. It means sending graduates into the world who can be effective across boundaries of every kind in an increasingly global environment. It means equipping them with respect for diversity in many forms, including points of view and modes of argument, and with a bedrock commitment to critical thinking and freedom of expression." The college has been engaging in this pursuit for two hundred years. These chapters help illuminate moments along that unfinished trail.

PS

As we finish the last preparations for this volume, Amherst College, like schools and institutions across the country, has closed to keep us safer from the menacing pandemic. I am most thankful for the work of the participants and all the people involved in editing and producing this volume, completed under conditions we could scarcely have imagined when we set out.

Professor and contributor Richard Teichgraeber has written about the College in World War I, observing that for reasons of geography and timing, it was fortunate to lose only fifteen people associated with Amherst to the influenza outbreak of 1917–18. It will require another group of historians in another volume to describe and analyze what, if any, marks COVID-19 will leave on Amherst.

Martha Saxton
April 8, 2020

Notes

1. Cullen Murphy, "Statement of Board of Trustees' Meeting," January 26, 2016, http://arial2.amherst.edu/CT00365403MDEyMzg0LTAwNTQ2NjQ=.HTML?D=2016-01-26.

2. William Smith, "An Act Founding a College at Chestertown [in Maryland]," www.washcoll.edu/centers/starr/revcollege/firstcollege/index.html; Victor Ferrall Jr., *Liberal Arts at the Brink* (Cambridge, MA: Harvard University Press, 2011), 15; Amherst College is number 2 in the National Liberal Arts ranking.

3. Michael Roth, *Beyond the University: Why Liberal Education Matters* (New Haven, CT: Yale University Press, 2014), 95–100, 103; Christina Elliot Sorum, "'Vortex, Clouds, and Sun': New Problems in the Humanities?" *Distinctively American: The Residential Liberal Arts Colleges*, eds. Steven Koblik and Stephen Graubard (New Brunswick, NJ: Transaction Publishers, 2000), 241.

4. Hugh Hawkins, "The Making of the Liberal Arts College Identity," in *Distinctively American*, eds. Koblik and Graubard (New York: Routledge, 2000), 2; Sorum, "'Vortex, Clouds, and Tongue,'" 245.

5. Murphy, "Statement," 74.

6. See Teichgraeber and Applegate in this volume.

7. See, in particular, Thrailkill and Dobrow in this volume.

8. See Appy, Saxton, Lopez, and Hoxie in this volume.

PART I

Student Bodies and Souls

Fulfilling the Founders' Purpose

The Religious Careers of Early Amherst College Graduates

Gary J. Kornblith

The founders of Amherst College were men on a mission. As Noah Webster explained at the laying of the cornerstone of the school's first building on August 9, 1820, the college's overriding purpose would be "educating for the gospel ministry young men in indigent circumstances, but of hopeful piety and promising talents." This objective, in turn, was part of a larger evangelical enterprise: "Extending and establishing the Redeemer's empire—the empire of truth." "Blessed be *our* lot!" Webster exclaimed. "We live to see a new era in the history of man." But alongside feelings of excitement was a sense of peril. Righteous Christians comprised only a small portion of humankind while the number of sinners was vast and growing. In "a sermon delivered on the same occasion," Reverend Daniel A. Clark emphasized the need for additional ministers to spread the gospel. "It is impossible not to see that the Christian churches have neglected their duty too long," he explained. "We must be more thoroughly awake soon, or nothing but a boundless desolation stares us in the face." Amherst College would promote spiritual deliverance near and far. Clark predicted that "this institution will collect about it the friends of the Lord Jesus . . . and will yet become a fountain pouring forth its streams to fertilize the boundless wastes of a miserable world." The result would be nothing less than "the salvation of perishing millions."[1]

In its first two decades, Amherst College largely achieved the founders' goal of preparing young men of modest means for careers spreading the Christian faith. Of the 663 men who received degrees from Amherst through 1840, 382 (58 percent) went on to serve as ministers, missionaries, Christian educators, and the like.[2] No other college in New England—and probably no other college in the United States—graduated as high a proportion of religious professionals in the early nineteenth century.[3]

At its inception, Amherst represented what one historian has termed "the anti-Harvard."[4] In 1806, the Harvard Overseers named Unitarians to serve as Hollis Professor of Divinity and as president of Harvard College. To orthodox Congregationalists, these appointments marked a betrayal of the school's Puritan heritage. The establishment of Amherst College was part of a conservative reaction against Harvard's perceived heretical tendencies. Although Amherst was never formally affiliated with any particular denomination, Congregationalists, Presbyterians, and Dutch Reformed dominated the faculty and student body during the college's early years.[5]

In keeping with the founders' intentions, early Amherst students tended to be notably less genteel than their Harvard counterparts. Not that every Amherst student was truly "indigent." As a condition for leaving Williams to become Amherst's first president, Zephaniah Swift Moore insisted that Amherst admit affluent as well as impoverished applicants.[6] Yet a survey conducted in 1830 to 1831 indicates that during that academic year, 51 percent of Amherst students received financial aid from either the college's charity fund or an outside educational society—a higher percentage than at the other sixteen American colleges and universities that supplied relevant data. (Harvard did not bother.)[7]

The reminiscences of Warren Harrison Beaman (class of 1837) convey what it was like to grow up in modest circumstances in early nineteenth-century New England. The fifth of eight children, Beaman was born in Wendell, Massachusetts, on January 7, 1813. His father was a farmer and carpenter. The house where Warren spent his childhood was "one story, about square, having two square rooms in front, a door, a vestibule in the center, and long kitchen, and bedroom, pantry, cellar-way and chamber-way back." "Only one room was plastered," he recalled, and "no part of the house was painted, either in or outside." Furnishings were basic. The kitchen boasted "a tall clock, table, chairs, bed, trundle bed, dresser and cupboard," as well as a sizable open fireplace with "a brick oven at its side." "I never saw a cooking stove till I was twelve years old," Beaman noted in his memoir. "There were not many, if any, in Wendell, before that time."[8]

The family's "farm consisted of 40 acres of wood land, about 100 acres of mowing and pasturing." While the Beamans raised much of their own food, they also participated in small-scale trading networks. "Neighbors made exchanges, frequently, when an animal was slaughtered," and the family purchased "salt fish" and other supplies on a periodic basis. Youngsters made do with a rather plain, monotonous diet: "Bread or Indian pudding and milk were the common food of children for supper, often for breakfast. Chestnuts, and cherries were among our luxuries."[9]

Religion was an essential aspect of Beaman's upbringing. His parents "belonged to the church" and "maintained family worship" at home. On the Sabbath, the whole family attended both morning and afternoon services at the local Congregational meetinghouse. "Most of the people went to meeting, summer and winter," Beaman explained. "The[y] expected to go to meeting as much as they expected to eat at regular meal time."[10]

Warren Beaman's boyhood typified the youthful experiences of early Amherst graduates who went on to religious careers. Three-fifths grew up in New England communities with fewer than twenty-five hundred residents.[11] Many were farmers' younger sons who could not expect to inherit land. Collegiate education offered a way to escape the material constraints of New England's stagnating agricultural economy.[12]

To gain entrance to Amherst College, young men had to demonstrate a command of Latin and Greek, English grammar, and "vulgar" arithmetic.[13] While some studied classical languages with their hometown ministers or other local men of learning, over three-quarters of those admitted in the early years were "fitted for college" at privately operated academies. The college's most common feeder school was Amherst Academy, which had been founded in 1814. Though separate institutions, Amherst Academy and Amherst College shared a common set of trustees until the college obtained its state charter in 1825.[14]

Somewhat surprisingly, religious faith was not a formal condition for admission to the college, and the original curriculum did not include coursework in the bible. Yet Christian values permeated Amherst's institutional culture from the start. In his classic *History of Amherst College during Its First Half Century*, William S. Tyler (class of 1830) observed:

> The usual religious meetings of the week at this time, besides the public services of the Sabbath, were the religious lecture on Thursday evening, conducted by the President and the preaching Professors in rotation, the meetings of the several classes [i.e., freshmen, sophomores, etc.] by themselves on Friday evening, the meetings of the church, and sometimes of all the professors of religion [i.e., confirmed Christians] on Saturday evening, and the prayer meeting for all the students, during the hour immediately preceding public worship Sabbath morning.

In 1827 a "weekly Bible exercise" was added to the extracurricular schedule.[15]

Most potent were the religious revivals that punctuated the college's early decades, part of a larger historical phenomenon known as the Second Great Awakening. Compared to the raucous, outdoor camp meetings in the Trans-Appalachian West, Amherst revivals were rather tame affairs.[16] Yet, in later life, participants remembered them as wondrous manifestations of the Holy Spirit that produced a profound sense of spiritual rebirth. Justin Marsh (class of 1824) wrote enthusiastically about the revival of 1823: "At no time in the day . . . could a person go into an entry and pass up to the fourth story without hearing the voice of prayer from some room. The work of God's grace seemed to go right through the College."[17] With similar fondness, Leander Thompson (class of 1835) "loved to recall the incidents of the revival" that took place during his senior year. "To a certain little band of students . . . it was *especially* welcome," he explained. "Day after day and night after night, they had been praying . . . for just such a blessing." When it finally arrived, they "felt like mounting on wings and praising God DAY AND NIGHT forever."[18]

In the farewell address he delivered upon stepping down as Amherst's second president in 1845, Heman Humphrey recited the dates of seven religious revivals that had taken place at the college since its founding: 1823, 1827, 1828, 1831, 1835, 1839, and 1842. "By comparing these dates," he noted, "it will be seen that no class has ever yet graduated without passing through at least one season of spiritual refreshing."[19] What made this record especially impressive was that, while religious revivals could be hoped for and actively encouraged, they were, in Humphrey's view, the work of God, not of the faculty or other college officers.[20]

After receiving their BA degrees, early Amherst graduates with ministerial ambitions either studied theology under the supervision of an established clergyman or entered a school of theology—sometimes after teaching at an academy for a few years or tutoring at the college level to raise necessary funds. The most popular place to pursue a postgraduate religious education was Andover Theological Seminary, followed by the East Windsor (Connecticut) Theological Institute, the Auburn (New York) Theological Seminary, and

Princeton Theological Seminary. The average time between college graduation and ordination was five years. The average age at ordination was thirty.[21]

For analytical purposes, the religious careers of early Amherst graduates can be grouped into four broad categories: (1) settled ministers who pastored to a given congregation for an extended period of time, (2) home missionaries and other clerics who by design circulated frequently from place to place, (3) educators and officers of benevolent societies who promoted religion as a central part of their jobs, and (4) foreign missionaries who spread the gospel among peoples outside the United States—and also among Native Americans, who were deemed "foreign" despite their indigenous roots. The boundaries between these categories were not always sharp, and many graduates transitioned from one category to another over the course of their careers. A handful of case studies illustrate the wide range of career paths that Amherst men pursued in service to God.

Settled ministers comprised three-fourths of the early Amherst graduates who entered religious professions.[22] To be settled was not necessarily to be stable or secure, however. With the disestablishment of churches following the American Revolution, settled ministers no longer enjoyed the financial assurance of tax-supported salaries, from which most of their colonial forebears had benefitted. Consequently, they grew increasingly dependent on the active approval of their congregants.[23] Many early Amherst graduates served successively as pastors to a series of congregations during their prime adult years, and later they often functioned as acting pastors or "stated supply"—in effect, as substitute preachers employed by churches on a temporary basis.

John Whitney (class of 1831) is a case in point. Following his graduation from Amherst at age twenty-seven, Whitney pursued graduate studies at Andover Theological Seminary, and in 1834, he was ordained as minister of the First Church of Boxford, Massachusetts. After preaching there for three years without great success, he was dismissed. (Only one new member joined the church during his tenure.) In 1837, Whitney assumed the pulpit of the Trinitarian Congregational Church in Waltham, Massachusetts, where he pastored for the next two decades. Upon his discharge from that post in 1858, he successively supplied churches in Dunstable, Westford, and West Boylston, Massachusetts, and in Robbinston, Maine. In 1863, he relocated to Canaan, New York, where he served as acting pastor to local Congregational and Presbyterian churches until 1867. That year he retired from the ministry and moved to Newton, Massachusetts, where he took up horticulture. He died in 1879, at age seventy-four, leaving a widow and five children.[24]

Of all the early Amherst graduates who became settled ministers, none was more renowned than Henry Ward Beecher, reputedly "the most famous man in America."[25] Beecher's achievements as a preacher, author, and public figure were little foreshadowed by his mediocre academic record at Amherst. Nor did he enjoy a meteoric rise to evangelical stardom. After graduating from Amherst in 1834, he studied at Lane Theological Seminary in Cincinnati under the critical eye of his distinguished father, Lyman Beecher, a leader of the Second Great Awakening and Lane's president. In 1837, at age twenty-four, Henry accepted an invitation from the fledgling Presbyterian Church in Lawrenceburgh, Indiana. He also married Eunice Bullard, an Amherst classmate's sister, to whom he had become engaged five years before. Although he struggled at first in the pulpit, he gradually honed his oratorical skills and gained local popularity as a congenial fellow who enjoyed socializing with ordinary townspeople Yet Henry was also ambitious. In 1839, when offered a better paying position in Indianapolis, the state capital, he jumped at the chance to move on and to move up.[26]

Beecher served as minister of the Second Presbyterian Church of Indianapolis for seven years. Under his auspices, the congregation grew in size and prestige, prompting his parishioners to construct a new church building to showcase his rhetorical talents and to advertise their own respectability. In contrast to his father's stern Puritanical teachings, he emphasized Christ's love rather than God's wrath and offered his listeners the prospect of both earthly prosperity and heavenly salvation. His sermons were joyful and entertaining. As one contemporary later remembered, Henry Ward Beecher "believed in mixin' happiness and a good time with religion."[27]

Soon Beecher's reputation reached well beyond Indiana. In 1844, he published *Seven Lectures to Young Men*, which attracted nationwide attention.[28] In 1847, leaders of the Plymouth Church of Brooklyn, New York, offered Beecher a starting salary of $1500 if he would relocate.[29] He made the move, and he stayed at Plymouth Church until his death; for forty years his fame and salary increased in tandem.

During the 1850s, Beecher incited controversy by suggesting that the force of arms might prove more effective than religion in the struggle against the Slave Power. Rifles shipped to antislavery settlers in "Bleeding Kansas" gained the nickname "Beecher's Bibles."[30] But compared to many other northern evangelicals, Beecher came to his antislavery convictions rather late. When Amherst students debated remedies for slavery in the early 1830s, he favored colonization over immediate abolition.[31] He began his studies at Lane Seminary just as Theodore Dwight Weld and the other "Lane Rebels" decided to withdraw from the school rather than cease agitating for black rights, as demanded by its board of trustees. Like his father, Henry remained loyal to Lane; he derided the rebels as "a little muddy stream of vinegar that went trickling down to Oberlin."[32] Only after passage of the Fugitive Slave Act of 1850 did Henry recognize the nation's continuing attachment to slavery as a grave moral crisis.[33] Yet, by the end of the decade, he was identified in the public mind with the cause of the slave almost as firmly as his sister, Harriet Beecher Stowe, the author of *Uncle Tom's Cabin*. He supported the Republican Party and celebrated Abraham Lincoln's election in 1860. When Confederate forces attacked Fort Sumter, Beecher called for "war redder than blood and fiercer than fire" to suppress the slaveholders' unconscionable rebellion.[34]

Once the Civil War and slavery came to an end, however, Beecher lost interest in black rights. He opposed radical Reconstruction and promoted instead the reconciliation of northern and southern whites on the basis of their religious and racial affinities.[35] His public influence continued to grow as he lectured extensively and published prolifically. His sentimental novel *Norwood* appeared in 1867, and he subsequently produced nineteen volumes of *Plymouth Pulpit*—a collection of his sermons—as well as a host of other books. Beecher was a pervasive presence in postwar American popular culture.[36]

In October 1872, Beecher's reputation came under siege when feminist Victoria Woodhull charged him with having carried on an adulterous affair with one of his parishioners,

Figure 1. Henry Ward Beecher, class of 1834. Courtesy of Amherst College Archives and Special Collections.

Elizabeth Tilton, who happened also to be the wife of a former protégé. Beecher himself claimed feminist credentials—he served as the first president of the American Woman Suffrage Association—but that failed to protect him from the ensuing uproar. For three years, the salacious Beecher-Tilton scandal captured public attention like few other stories of the era. While the members of Plymouth Church exonerated their minister of any wrongdoing, a civil trial initiated by Tilton's husband ended in a hung jury.[37] Beecher kept his job and escaped legal punishment, but, according to a contemporary, he "never recovered his old buoyancy" in the scandal's aftermath.[38]

On February 4, 1887, Beecher appeared at the annual dinner of Amherst College alumni, held at Delmonico's in lower Manhattan. "It was the first Alumni dinner he had attended since he was involved in trouble," reported the *New York Times*, which added that "at least half a dozen [alumni] had refused to come on Mr. Beecher's account." He arrived after the meal was over but in time to hear remarks by the college's president, Julius H. Seelye, who took note of Beecher's presence. "Mr. Beecher knows very well that we have positive convictions at Amherst," Seelye observed,

> and yet he knows very well and has illustrated it supremely that we are a great deal more careful at Amherst to teach a man how to think rather than what to think. I not unfrequently find pupils of mine—Mr. Beecher himself perhaps—going off in direc-

> tions [laughter] that we are not pleased to find wholesome [laughter], but we have confidence sufficient in truth to come to this conclusion—that if a man will think clearly and closely he will come out to the truth no matter through what roundabout method he may approach it.

Beecher replied affectionately, "I can't forget Amherst until I become unconscious of my own personality." "If [ever] there were a set of men who believed in religion it was the Faculty of Amherst College," he declared. "There was old Dr. Humphreys [*sic*], a grand old Puritan. I've forgotten his instructions if I ever heard them [laughter]. But him I have never ceased to feel in all my after life."[39] A month later, Beecher died of a stroke at the age of seventy-three.[40]

Like Henry Ward Beecher, Ezra Fisher, Amherst class of 1828, went west as a young man. Again, like Beecher, he spent time ministering in Indianapolis. But unlike Beecher, Fisher then went further west, and he served for most of his career not as a settled minister but as a home missionary. Hundreds of his letters to the secretary of the American Baptist Home Mission Society offer insight into the experience of promoting religion in "frontier" regions of the United States during the middle decades of the nineteenth century.[41]

A restless as well as pious individual, Fisher once remarked that his "health would not admit of a sedentary life."[42] In April 1845, after a decade spent preaching in the Mississippi Valley, he, his wife Lucy, and their four children set out from Illinois for the Oregon territory—a distance of approximately twenty-five hundred miles.[43] In early December, they reached Oregon's Tualatin Plains, where they were "kindly received into the cabin of Br[other David T.] Lenox." Over the ensuing winter, the six Fisher family members, thirteen Lenox family members, plus "almost every night, one, two or three travelers" lived cheek by jowl in "but one room, about 18 feet by 22, without a single pane of glass."[44]

Fisher faced daunting challenges in launching his Oregon mission. The few Baptist settlers in the territory were widely dispersed so that "all efficiency by church organization is lost," he explained to the Home Mission Society's secretary. Basic supplies were scarce and expensive.[45] It hardly helped that in the mid-1840s, sending mail and cargo between Oregon and New York took six months in each direction.[46]

Although he did not employ the term, Fisher firmly believed in the idea of Manifest Destiny. In an 1847 letter, he wrote, "Whatever God has in store for our majestic River [presumably the Columbia] and our spacious and safe harbors on the Pacific, one thing is now reduced to a demonstration: We must become a part of the great North American Republic."[47] Yet he worried that Baptists back east did not adequately appreciate the precarious spiritual condition of Oregon's population. He considered most of the territory's Euro-Americans as well as Native Americans to be "heathen," and he feared that the better-organized Roman Catholic Church would quickly surpass the Baptists and other Protestant denominations in making converts.[48]

In the spring of 1848, Fisher reported glimmers of hope that his efforts were beginning to bear fruit. "Last Lord's day we organized a little feeble church in Clatsop Plains consisting of seven members, three males and four females," he wrote on March 24. A week later, he rejoiced, "We still see increasing evidence that the Spirit of the Lord is over us."[49]

Yet, by the fall of 1848, the spiritual outlook had darkened. "Our whole community has been perfectly convulsed with the rumor of much gold in the valleys and hills of California," Fisher explained. "Our congregations are fast waning. . . . Numbers of our brethren have gone to spend the winter at the gold mines and others will go in the spring."[50] With deep ambivalence, Fisher himself joined the rush to California in March 1849, leaving behind his wife and children, including a one-year-old son.[51] In the space of two months, he extracted "about $1000 worth of gold" and headed back to Oregon.[52]

Upon his return, Fisher used his newfound wealth to advance the Baptists' missionary agenda by helping to purchase land on which to build a college for educating future ministers. He also took charge of a secondary school in Oregon City. In 1851, he assumed the role of "exploring agent" for the entire Oregon territory. In this capacity, he traveled hundreds of miles each quarter—sometimes by boat, other times by horse, and frequently on foot.[53] Yet the results were modest. At the close of 1852, he reported, "We have but eleven or twelve feeble churches in the territory and they together number less than 200 members—men, women and children."[54]

Ever a true believer in his cause, Fisher persisted. Finally, in February 1854, he dispatched news of "the first revival of religion that Oregon City has witnessed."[55] Soon, revivals swept through several nearby communities as well, and in April, Fisher wrote that during the previous three months, "one hundred and two hopeful converts have been added by baptism."[56] Fisher's joy was mixed with personal sadness, however. The catalyst for this religious awakening was the death of Lucy, his wife of thirty-four years. Fisher grieved at the same time that he took satisfaction in the upsurge of conversions.[57] With four children still living at home, he also looked for a new wife. He married the widow Amelia Mallard on June 27, 1854.[58]

The following spring, Fisher announced his intention to retire from his position with the American Baptist Home Mission Society. "In view of the gradual decline of my physical, not to say mental powers," he explained, "I feel that I have a right to ask for a more limited field which will call for less exposure in winter rains and the inconveniences of a frontier life."[59] In November 1855, he accepted an invitation to serve as the pastor of a small church in the Willamette Valley, and he subsequently took up farming on the side.[60] In 1861, he and his wife moved to The Dalles, on the southern bank of the Columbia River, where—except for a year's stay in Southern California—he preached for the remainder of his life. He died at the age of seventy-four on November 1, 1874.[61]

Asa Bullard graduated from Amherst College alongside Ezra Fisher in 1828, and seven years later, Bullard became Henry Ward Beecher's brother-in-law when Beecher married his younger sister. Yet Bullard pursued a different kind of religious career than either Beecher or Fisher. For forty years, he served as the corresponding secretary and general agent of the Massachusetts Sabbath School Society. His passion was preparing young people to lead pious lives.[62]

Born the son of a country doctor in 1804, Bullard grew up in comfortable circumstances in West Sutton, Massachusetts. He underwent conversion at age seventeen, and at age twenty, he followed his older brother, Artemis, to Amherst College.[63] In *Incidents in a Busy Life: An Autobiography*, published in 1888, Bullard reported that while he was at

Amherst, he formed a bible class for "the colored people in town, of whom there were quite a number." "My interest in this class of people," he added, "was such that for two or three years my heart was very much set upon spending my life in Africa."[64]

After graduating from Amherst, Bullard taught for a year in Maine and then studied for two years at Andover Theological Seminary. By 1831, he wanted to go west, not to Africa, but Artemis persuaded him instead to return to Maine to become general agent of the Maine Sabbath-School Union.[65] In January 1832, Bullard "was ordained as an evangelist" in Portland, and four months later, he married Lucretia G. Dickinson, whom he had met while boarding at her father's house during his college years.[66] After the wedding, Lucretia joined Bullard "in the work, pleading the Sabbath-school cause with the mothers and children at home, while I was holding meetings and laboring among the people outside."[67] By the end of 1832, "one hundred new schools had been organized"; another 189 schools were added the following year.[68]

Yet the West still beckoned. In the fall of 1833, Bullard decided to sign on as chaplain of the American Seamen's Friend Society in Cleveland. Before he could depart for Ohio, however, he received an offer from the Massachusetts Sabbath School Society to serve as its corresponding secretary and general agent. "After very serious and prayerful consideration, and much marveling at the manner in which providence had several times so obviously disposed of what I proposed," Bullard wrote in his autobiography, "I accepted the invitation and entered upon the service for the Society March 1, 1834."[69] A half-century later, he had no regrets.

Among the first tasks Bullard assumed in his new job was editing the *Sabbath School Visiter*, a monthly periodical that published a wide array of articles for a diverse audience, including both adults and children. From the start, Bullard had high ambitions for the magazine: "It may rouse to new zeal and engagedness many a teacher; break the deep slumbers of indifference, which have settled down upon many a parent; and trace upon the characters,—the hearts of thousands of our youth, those lineaments, which the fires of the last great day, and the ages of eternity can never, never efface."[70] Within three years of Bullard's taking charge, the magazine's circulation roughly doubled, reaching almost nine thousand in 1837.[71]

Bullard also supervised the publication of books and pamphlets for the Massachusetts Sabbath School Society, lectured throughout the state, recruited and counseled legions of volunteers, provided curricular materials to hundreds of schools, helped with fundraising, and compiled the society's annual reports. He took special pride in a campaign to rekindle young people's study of the Westminster Shorter Catechism.[72]

In 1844, the Massachusetts Sabbath School Society replaced *The Sabbath School Visiter* with two new periodicals: *The Congregational Visiter*, a monthly aimed at adults, and *The Well-Spring*, a weekly aimed at children. While the former title lasted only five years, the latter title proved an enduring hit under Bullard's editorial command. Juvenile readers appreciated not only *The Well-Spring*'s content, which was curated exclusively for youngsters, but also its frequency—arriving at a child's house "just as often as father's paper does." At its peak, *The Well-Spring* boasted "a circulation of over sixty thousand copies a week."[73]

In later life, Bullard loved to tell anecdotes about meeting adults who would thank him for enlivening and enlightening their childhoods.[74] After his death on April 5, 1888, a colleague in the Sabbath school movement observed, "He never was installed over a local parish, but perhaps there is not a minister living who has spoken to so many people at such impressible periods in their lives as he. Think of it! a whole generation has grown to maturity who can remember him in their childhood as the tall man with a kindly countenance crowned with snow-white hair."[75] Asa Bullard was, in effect, the Fred Rogers of nineteenth-century America.

While they comprised less than one-tenth of all early Amherst graduates who pursued religious careers, foreign missionaries were among the most extraordinary.[76] Perhaps nobody exemplified the intellectual brilliance, religious dedication, and moral conundrums of these remarkable men better than Justin Perkins (class of 1829).[77] Born in West Springfield (Holyoke), Massachusetts, in 1805, Perkins grew up in a Christian household and experienced a spiritual rebirth at age eighteen. In 1825, he entered Amherst College, where he earned the nickname "the twenty-four-hour boy" for his unflagging diligence. After graduation, he taught at Amherst Academy for a year, spent two years studying at Andover Theological Seminary, and tutored for a year at Amherst College.[78] He planned to return to Andover for another year of study when, in January 1833, the American Board of Commissioners for Foreign Missions (ABCFM) asked him instead to initiate a mission among the Nestorians in Persia, whose plight as oppressed Christians in a Muslim-dominated country attracted the board's attention.[79]

Before he could embark on this assignment, Perkins had to be ordained and, as advised by the board's secretary, he had to get married. Heman Humphrey preached at Perkins's ordination in June, and in July, Perkins wed Charlotte Bass of Middlebury, Vermont, whose pastor assured the ABCFM that she possessed the virtue required of a missionary wife.[80] The couple sailed from Boston on September 21. After stopping in Malta, southern Greece, Constantinople, and Trebizond, and making an arduous overland trek across much of Turkey as well as a small patch of Russia, they reached Tabreez (Tabriz) in northwestern Persia on August 23, 1834. Three days later, Charlotte, though gravely ill, gave birth to a baby girl.[81]

Once Charlotte's health began to improve, Perkins set out for Oroomiah (Urumia), the projected location of the Nestorian mission. During the one-hundred-and-forty-mile journey, he chanced upon Mar Yohannan, a Nestorian bishop who agreed to teach him Syriac, the Nestorians' native language. While in Oroomiah, Perkins met the Persian governor of the province, who welcomed the prospect of a Christian mission so long as it focused its efforts solely on the Nestorian minority and left the Mohammedan majority alone. The regional patriarch of the Nestorian church also gave his approval. With Mar Yohannan at his side, Perkins returned to Tabreez optimistic about prospects for success.[82]

He waited a year before launching the mission in Oroomiah, however. One reason for the delay was personal tragedy: Perkins and Charlotte lost their infant daughter in January 1835.[83] Another factor was the desire for additional personnel to staff the mission—particularly a physician. In response, the ABCFM sent out Dr. Asahel Grant and his wife Judith, who arrived in Tabreez in mid-October.[84] By the end of November, the Perkinses and the Grants had relocated to Oroomiah and commenced missionary work among the Nestorians.[85]

Perkins's gift for languages allowed him to master Syriac with impressive speed. Shortly after settling in Oroomiah and establishing a seminary for boys, he began "reducing this language to a written form, and translating parts of the Scriptures for reading cards."[86] But Perkins's linguistic proficiency did not enable him to engage with Nestorian culture on its own terms. Instead, he approached the people he wished to inspire with an attitude of righteous condescension that bordered on contempt. "They are, as a people, very degraded," he observed, "and even the best of them are *morally* as weak as infants, and must be treated with great patience and forbearance, 'as a nurse cherisheth her children.'"[87] He found the Nestorian version of Christianity profoundly deficient. "Of the meaning of regeneration, even their most intelligent ecclesiastics seemed to know little or nothing," he complained. "The plain commandments of the decalogue,—those against falsehood and the violation of the Sabbath, for instance, were wantonly and almost universally broken. . . . Profaneness prevails among them . . . to an extent that astounds an American ear."[88]

Notwithstanding his arrogance, Perkins and his American colleagues attracted followers among the Nestorians by energetically promoting education. The mission added a boarding school for girls in 1838 and a printing press in 1840. It also established primary schools and Sabbath schools in villages surrounding Oroomiah. But various segments of the local population pushed back against the American missionaries, as did French Jesuit competitors. Relations with civil authorities and leaders of the Nestorian church fluctuated considerably over time.[89]

The greatest obstacle confronting the Oroomiah mission was epidemiological. Cholera and plague swept through the area repeatedly. Perkins observed on one occasion, "we find some relief in the evidence we have that God has used, and is using, these terrific scourges . . . to shake down the fabric of Muhammedism."[90] But Christian devotion did not confer immunity. In January 1839, Mrs. Grant died after a brief but violent illness.[91] Most devastating were the deaths of children. In April 1840, Perkins wrote despondently, "Our youngest son, a fine boy of a year old, died last July, and our oldest son, almost 4 years old, died in February. Thus is our home left unto us *desolate*.—We, however, mourn not alone. Of six children of our mission, five died in the short space of *one month*."[92]

Charlotte Perkins took the loss of her children especially hard. Though in the summer of 1840 she gave birth to a healthy new daughter—named Judith after the late Mrs. Grant—Charlotte's own health worsened; by fall, she was suffering from seizures as well as depression. Seeking relief, the family left Oroomiah in July 1841 and traveled back to the United States. Accompanied by Mar Yohannan, they landed in New York City on January 11, 1842.[93]

The Perkinses remained in the United States for nearly fourteen months, during which time Charlotte recuperated at her parents' homestead in Vermont while Perkins preached and lectured across much of the Northeast and as far south as Virginia.[94] He also prepared his five-hundred-page tome *A Residence of Eight Years in Persia, among the Nestorian Christians*.[95] On March 1, 1843, the Perkinses, Mar Yohannan, and four Americans newly assigned to the Nestorian mission boarded a vessel at Boston and headed again across the Atlantic. Benefiting from major improvements in transportation since the Perkinses' first trip to Persia, they reached Oroomiah on June 14.[96]

Figure 2. Justin Perkins, class of 1829, and Charlotte Perkins. Courtesy of Amherst College Archives and Special Collections.

Over the next decade, Perkins focused on translating the bible and other religious texts for publication in modern Syriac.[97] He moved the family's primary residence from Oroomiah to nearby Mount Seir in the hope that Charlotte's health would benefit from the higher elevation. She subsequently gave birth to three more children, but only one of them—Henry—lived beyond infancy. Charlotte found personal fulfillment in homeschooling the precocious Judith, who dazzled adults with her keen intelligence, compassion for others, and "maturity of character."[98] Then, on September 3, 1852, twelve-year-old Judith was stricken by cholera. Within less than twenty-four hours, she was dead.[99]

Grief overwhelmed Charlotte and undermined the Perkinses' marriage. In 1857, with young Henry in tow, Charlotte returned to the United States. Justin followed in 1858, but he was unprepared to give up his religious calling in order to tend to the needs of his ailing wife. In the summer of 1862, he traveled back to Persia to resume his duties at the Oroomiah mission.[100] Before departing, he arranged for Charlotte's admission to the McLean Asylum for the Insane, in Somerville, Massachusetts.[101] She was still residing at McLean's in 1865.[102]

In the summer of 1869, for reasons of "failing health" and "a strong desire again to meet the loved ones of his own household," Justin Perkins bid farewell to Persia for the last time.[103] After growing increasingly sick in transit to the United States, he spent the fall convalescing at a nephew's residence in Brooklyn and then at another nephew's house in Chicopee, Massachusetts. No longer confined to McLean's, Charlotte came to his bedside and cared for him in his final illness. On New Year's Eve, he died peacefully at the age of sixty-four.[104]

Considered as a whole, the first generation of Amherst graduates was remarkably faithful to the purpose of the college's founders. More than half pursued religious careers, and they promoted the Christian gospel in places ranging from frontier outposts to major metropolises, from the East Coast to the western edge of North America, and in remote locations on other continents, including Africa and especially Asia. Besides preaching innumerable sermons, members of this dedicated brigade wrote, translated, and published books and other texts on an amazing scale. Impressive as these accomplishments were, however, at the end of the nineteenth century, the Christian millennium appeared no closer to realization than it had at the century's start.

Amherst students adjusted their career aspirations accordingly. In the second iteration of his *History of Amherst College*, published in 1895, William S. Tyler observed that the proportion of graduates who went into the ministry stood at only 17 percent during the period of 1866 to 1889. Tyler offered a mixed assessment of the college's changing character. On the one hand, he opined, "we cannot but regret that more of our graduates do not become ministers." On the other hand, he declared, "we cannot but rejoice that so many of them are Christian laymen, workers for Christ in business, in the professions, in all the common walks of life." Yet he worried that contemporary Amherst students spent too much time on "foot-ball . . . and base-ball . . . and the junior promenade and the like social pleasures" and too little time on the "spiritual truths and eternal realities" that really mattered.[105] Amherst College, it seemed, was at risk of losing its moral compass. The founders' purpose had been fulfilled, but not forever.[106]

Notes

1. Noah Webster and Daniel A. Clark, *A Plea for a Miserable World: I. An Address, Delivered at the Laying of the Corner Stone of the Building Erecting for the Charity Institution in Amherst, Massachusetts, August 9, 1820, by Noah Webster, Esq.; II. A Sermon, Delivered on the Same Occasion, by Rev. Daniel A Clark, Pastor of the First Church and Society in Amherst; III. A Brief Account of the Origin of the Institution* (Boston, MA: Ezra Lincoln, 1820), 7, 8, 19, 28–29. For secondary accounts of the founding of Amherst College, see W. S. Tyler, *History of Amherst College during Its First Half Century, 1821-1871* (Springfield, MA: C. W. Bryan, 1873), 13–72; Claude Moore Fuess, *Amherst: The Story of a New England College* (Boston, MA: Little, Brown, and Co., 1935), 8–50; Theodore P. Greene, "Hopeful Piety," in *Passages of Time: Narratives in the History of Amherst College*, ed. Douglas C. Wilson (Amherst, MA: Amherst College Press, 2007), 3–9.

2. These figures are derived from entries in W. L. Montague, ed., *Biographical Record of the Alumni of Amherst College during Its First Half Century, 1821–1871* (Amherst, MA: J. E. Williams, 1883), 9–180; *Amherst College Biographical Record 1973*, sesquicentennial ed. (Amherst, MA: Trustees of Amherst College, 1973), 1–43.

3. Edward Hitchcock, *Reminiscences of Amherst College, Historical, Scientific, Biographical and Autobiographical: Also, of Other and Wider Life Experiences* (Northampton, MA: Bridgman & Childs, 1863), 191.

4. Roger L. Geiger, *The History of American Higher Education: Learning and Culture from the Founding to World War II* (Princeton, NJ: Princeton University Press, 2015), 185.

5. Geiger, *History of American*, 141, 185; Hitchcock, *Reminiscences of Amherst*, 191; Montague, *Biographical Record*, 9–180.

6. Tyler, *History of Amherst*, 70; Fuess, *Amherst*, 46.

7. "View of the American Colleges, 1831," *American Quarterly Register*, May 1831, 294.

8. Warren Harrison Beaman, *Reminiscences in the Life of Warren Harrison Beaman, Written in the Year 1900 at the Age of 87* (Amherst, MA: n.p., 1900), 1, 3, 6, 7.

9. Beaman, *Reminiscences*, 7, 9, 10.

10. Beaman, 8, 14.

11. Montague, *Biographical Record*, 9–180; Jesse Chickering, *A Statistical View of the Population of Massachusetts, from 1765 to 1840* (Boston, MA: C. C. Little and J. Brown, 1846); Vermont Historical Society, "Census by Towns," Vermont History Explorer, accessed February 17, 2018, http://vermonthistory.org/explorer/discover-vermont/facts-figures/census-records/census-by-towns; *Fifth Census or Enumeration of the Inhabitants of the United States, 1830* (New York: Norman Ross Publishing, [1832] 1990).

12. David F. Allmendinger Jr., *Paupers and Scholars: The Transformation of Student Life in Nineteenth-Century New England* (New York: St. Martin's, 1975), 13–18. On the evolution of the New England economy in the early nineteenth century, see Christopher Clark, *The Roots of Rural Capitalism: Western Massachusetts, 1780–1860* (Ithaca, NY: Cornell University Press, 1990).

13. *Catalogue of the Officers and Students of the Collegiate Institution, Amherst, Mass., Oct. 1822* (Greenfield, MA: Denio & Phelps, 1822), 10.

14. Montague, *Biographical Record*, 9–180; Fuess, *Amherst*, 23–25; Frederick Tuckerman, *Amherst Academy: A New England School of the Past, 1814–1861* (Amherst, MA: Trustees of Amherst Academy, 1929), 1–5, 11–62.

15. Tyler, *History of Amherst*, 196–97.

16. On varieties of revivalism during the Second Great Awakening, see Sydney E. Ahlstrom, *A Religious History of the American People* (Garden City, NY: Image Books, Doubleday & Co., [1972] 1975), 1:504–70; William G. McLoughlin, *Revivals, Awakenings, and Reform: An Essay on Religion and Social Change in America, 1607–1977* (Chicago, IL: University of Chicago Press, 1978), 98–140.

17. Quoted in Tyler, *History of Amherst*, 85.

18. Tyler, 212–13.

19. Quoted in Tyler, 273.

20. For an insightful discussion of revivals at Amherst College, see Susan Margaret Metzger, "Upon This Rock: A History of Religion at Amherst College" (BA honors thesis, Amherst College, 1994), 25–46, Amherst College Archives and Special Collections, Amherst College, Amherst, MA.

21. Montague, *Biographical Record*, 9–180.

22. Montague, 9–180.

23. Ann Douglas, *The Feminization of American Culture* (New York: Avon, 1977), 23–35.

24. Montague, *Biographical Record*, 83; "Family: Whitney, John (1803–1879)," Whitney Research Group, accessed March 9, 2018, http://wiki.whitneygen.org/wrg/index.php/Family:Whitney,_John_(1803-1879); Sidney Perley, *The History of Boxford, Essex County, Massachusetts: From the Earliest Settlement Known to the Present Time: A Period of about Two Hundred and Thirty Years* (the author, 1880), 294–95; *Obituary Record of Graduates of Amherst College for the Academical Year Ending July 3, 1879*, 2nd

printed series 7 (Amherst, MA: McCloud & Williams, 1879), 156; Charles Alexander Nelson, *Waltham, Past and Present; and Its Industries. With an Historical Sketch of Watertown from Its Settlement in 1630 to the Incorporation of Waltham, January 15, 1738* (Cambridge, MA: J. Ford & Son, 1879), 112–14; John Whitney, "Response to Questionnaire" (1874), Whitney, John, Class of 1831, Alumni Biographical Files, Amherst College Archives and Special Collections, Amherst College, Amherst, MA; *Fitchburg Sentinel*, June 3, 1879, 2.

25. Debby Applegate, *The Most Famous Man in America: The Biography of Henry Ward Beecher* (New York: Doubleday, 2006).

26. Applegate, *Most Famous*, 75–161.

27. Quoted in Applegate, 172.

28. Applegate, 184. See also Clifford E. Clark, "The Changing Nature of Protestantism in Mid-Nineteenth Century America: Henry Ward Beecher's *Seven Lectures to Young Men*," *The Journal of American History* 57 (March 1971): 832–46.

29. Applegate, *Most Famous*, 195.

30. Applegate, 281–82.

31. Robert J. Brigham, "Amherst College: A Pious Institution's Reaction to Slavery, 1821–1841" (BA honors thesis, Amherst College, 1985), 87–88, 116–19, Amherst College Archives and Special Collections, Amherst College, Amherst, MA.

32. Quoted in Paxton Hibben, *Henry Ward Beecher: An American Portrait* (New York: George H. Doran, 1927), 69.

33. Applegate, *Most Famous*, 239–54.

34. Quoted in Applegate, 327.

35. William G. McLoughlin, *The Meaning of Henry Ward Beecher: An Essay on the Shifting Values of Mid-Victorian America, 1840–1870* (New York: Alfred A. Knopf, 1970), 221–42; Edward J. Blum, *Reforging the White Republic: Race, Religion, and American Nationalism, 1865–1898* (Baton Rouge: Louisiana State University Press, 2005), 91–97.

36. Clifford E. Clark, "Beecher, Henry Ward," in *American National Biography Online* (New York: Oxford University Press, 2000), https://doi.org/10.1093/anb/9780198606697.article.0800112.

37. Applegate, *Most Famous*, 410–53. On the Beecher-Tilton Scandal, see also Richard Wightman Fox, *Trials of Intimacy: Love and Loss in the Beecher-Tilton Scandal* (Chicago, IL: University of Chicago Press, 1999).

38. Quoted in Applegate, *Most Famous*, 456.

39. "Amherst Alumni's Feast," *New York Times*, February 5, 1887, 2.

40. "The Late Henry Ward Beecher," *Brooklyn Eagle*, March 8, 1887, 2.

41. Ezra Fisher, *Correspondence of the Reverend Ezra Fisher: Pioneer Missionary of the American Baptist Home Mission Society in Indiana, Illinois, Iowa and Oregon*, eds. Sarah Fisher Henderson, Nellie Edith Latourette, and Kenneth Scott Latourette (Portland, OR: n.p., 1919).

42. Fisher, *Correspondence*,71.

43. Fisher, 158–66.

44. Fisher, 166.

45. Fisher, 168.

46. Fisher, 17.

47. Fisher, 189.

48. Fisher, 187.

49. Fisher, 222, 227.

50. Fisher, 230–31.

51. "1850 United States Federal Census for Ezra Fisher," Ancestry.com, accessed March 29, 2018.

52. Fisher, *Correspondence*, 259–61.

53. Fisher, 19–21, 266–329, 346–61.

54. Fisher, 363.

55. Fisher, 426.

56. Fisher, 432.

57. Fisher, 423–26.

58. Fisher, 23; "Amelia Avery Millard Fisher—LifeStory," Ancestry.com, accessed March 30, 2018.

59. Fisher, *Correspondence*, 463–64.

60. Fisher, 24–25, 481.

61. Fisher, 27–28.

62. Asa Bullard, *Incidents in a Busy Life: An Autobiography* (Boston, MA: Congregational Sunday-School and Publishing Society, 1888).

63. Bullard, *Incidents*, 11, 15, 38, 72, 86, 88.

64. Bullard, 90–91.

65. Bullard, 99–111.

66. Bullard, 115, 117.

67. Bullard, 122.

68. Bullard, 114.

69. Bullard, 126–27.

70. Asa Bullard, "Sabbath School Visiter," *Sabbath School Visiter*, April 1834, 94.

71. *Annual Report of the Massachusetts Sabbath School Society, Presented at the Annual Meeting*, vol. 3 (Boston: Massachusetts Sabbath School Society, 1835), 10; *Annual Report of the Massachusetts Sabbath School Society, Presented at the Annual Meeting*, vol. 5 (Boston: Massachusetts Sabbath School Society, 1837), 7.

72. Bullard, *Incidents*, 129–33.

73. Bullard, 9.

74. Bullard, 9–10, 138, 187.

75. Quoted in Bullard, 225.

76. Montague, *Biographical Record*, 9–180; Hitchcock, *Reminiscences*, 193–99.

77. My understanding of Perkins has been greatly enhanced by Martha Saxton's essay "Justin Perkins: False Prophets" in *The Transformation of This World Depends Upon You*, ed. Wendy Ewald et al. (Göttingen: Steidl, 2014), 43–55. For a valuable general study of Amherst missionaries in the Middle East during the nineteenth century, see Paul H. Younger Jr., "*Terras Irradient*: A Study of Amherst College Missionaries in the Near East in the Nineteenth Century" (BA honors thesis, Amherst College, 1959), Amherst College Archives and Special Collections, Amherst College, Amherst, MA.

78. Henry Martyn Perkins, *Life of Rev. Justin Perkins, D. D.: Pioneer Missionary to Persia* (Chicago, IL: Woman's Presbyterian Board of Missions of the Northwest, 1887), 9–10.

79. Justin Perkins to Rufus Anderson, February 20, 1833, ABC 6, vol. 11, p. 39, American Board of Commissioners for Foreign Missions Archives, Houghton Library, Harvard University. On the early history of the ABCFM, see Clifton Jackson Phillips, *Protestant America and the Pagan World: The First Half Century of the American Board of Commissioners for Foreign Missions, 1810–1860* (Cambridge, MA: Harvard University Press, 1969); Emily Conroy-Krutz, *Christian Imperialism: Converting the World in the Early American Republic* (Ithaca, NY: Cornell University Press, 2015).

80. Justin Perkins to Rufus Anderson, February 20, 1833, June 13, 1833, ABC 6, vol. 11, p. 39, Ameri-

can Board of Commissioners for Foreign Missions Archives, Houghton Library, Harvard University, Cambridge, MA; "Missionary Ordination," *New York Observer and Chronicle*, July 13, 1833; H. M. Perkins, *Life of Rev. Justin Perkins*, 11; Thomas A. Merrill, "Testimonial Respecting Mrs. Charlotte Perkins," July 23, 1833, ABC 6, vol. 11, p. 39, American Board of Commissioners for Foreign Missions Archives, Houghton Library, Harvard University, Cambridge, MA.

81. Justin Perkins, *A Residence of Eight Years in Persia, among the Nestorian Christians: With Notices of the Muhammedans* (Andover, MA: Allen, Morrill & Wardell, 1843), 27–142 passim; Justin Perkins, *Missionary Life in Persia: Being Glimpses of a Quarter of a Century of Labors among the Nestorian Christians* (Boston, MA: American Tract Society, 1861), 11–28.

82. Perkins, *A Residence*, 165–97.

83. Perkins, 204.

84. Gordon Taylor, *Fever and Thirst: An American Doctor Among the Tribes of Kurdistan, 1835–1844* (Chicago, IL: Chicago Review Press, 2007), 7–13.

85. Perkins, *A Residence*, 227–33.

86. Perkins, *Missionary Life*, 44.

87. Perkins, *A Residence*, 205.

88. Perkins, 247.

89. Perkins, 336–37; Perkins, *Missionary Life*, 48–78; Justin Perkins and Thomas Laurie, *Historical Sketch of the Mission to the Nestorians and of the Assyria Mission* (New York: American Board of Commissioners for Foreign Missions, 1862), 15.

90. Perkins, *A Residence*, 218.

91. Taylor, *Fever and Thirst*, 22, 25; Perkins, *A Residence*, 370–71.

92. "Rev. Justin Perkins," *Hampshire Gazette*, October 28, 1840.

93. Perkins, *A Residence*, 462–64, 477, 491.

94. Joseph G. Cochran, *The Persian Flower: A Memoir of Judith Grant Perkins, of Oroomiah, Persia* (Boston, MA: American Tract Society, 1853), 9; Justin Perkins, "Journal of a Visit in America," Justin Perkins (AC 1829) Papers, Ser. 5, Sub-series A, Box 5, vol. 2, Amherst College Archives and Special Collections, Amherst College, Amherst, MA.

95. Perkins, *A Residence of Eight Years in Persia*, v–vi.

96. Perkins, "Journal of a Visit in America"; H. M. Perkins, *Life of Rev. Justin Perkins*, 31.

97. Perkins, *Missionary Life in Persia*, 75; H. M. Perkins, *Life of Rev. Justin Perkins*, 47–49.

98. Cochran, *Persian Flower*, 17-52; H. M. Perkins, *Life of Rev. Justin Perkins*, 39.

99. Cochran, *Persian Flower*, 110–11, 114, 132.

100. H. M. Perkins, *Life of Rev. Justin Perkins*, 39, 56–61.

101. For reports on Charlotte's condition from McLean's director and his wife, see Augusta M. D. Tyler and John E. Tyler to Justin Perkins, September 16, 1862, Justin Perkins (AC 1829) Papers, Ser. 1, Sub-series A, Box 2, Folder 4, Amherst College Archives and Special Collections, Amherst College, Amherst, MA; Augusta M. D. Tyler and John E. Tyler to Justin Perkins, November 16, 1862, Justin Perkins (AC 1829) Papers, Ser. 1, Sub-series A, Box 2, Folder 4, Amherst College Archives and Special Collections, Amherst College, Amherst, MA; Augusta M. D. Tyler to Justin Perkins, February 14, 1863, Justin Perkins (AC 1829) Papers, Ser. 1, Sub-series A, Box 2, Folder 4, Amherst College Archives and Special Collections, Amherst College, Amherst, MA. I am deeply grateful to Mimi Dakin and Chris Barber for bringing these materials to my attention.

102. "Massachusetts State Census, 1865," Ancestry.com (online database), 2014, https://www.ancestry.com/search/collections/9203/.

103. H. M. Perkins, *Life of Rev. Justin Perkins*, 72.

104. H. M. Perkins, 73, 76.

105. W. S. Tyler, *A History of Amherst College during the Administrations of Its First Five Presidents: From 1821 to 1891* (New York: F. H. Hitchcock, 1895), 291, 290.

106. On the evolution of Amherst College in the half-century after the Civil War, see Thomas Le Duc, *Piety and Intellect at Amherst College, 1865–1912* (New York: Columbia University Press, 1946).

Remembering Edward Jones

First Black Graduate, Missionary Hero, "Genteel Young Man of Excellent Disposition"[1]

David W. Wills

When Edward Hitchcock (1793–1864)—clergyman, noted geologist, and third president of Amherst College—published his *Reminiscences* in 1863, he recorded with pride the school's record in producing foreign missionaries. Reporting that the young college, in its first four decades, had produced a total of sixty-three, he named them all and provided a brief synopsis of the career of each. Clearly, he thought the list an impressive one—and suspected it might be unrivaled by any other college.[2] There were among the first fifteen names on his list—all of them graduates of the 1820s—a number of very well-known and highly regarded American Protestant missionaries. Among them, for example, was Henry Lyman (1809–1834), much remembered as "the martyr of Sumatra" who died in 1834 at the very start of an early effort at missionary work among the Batak of Sumatra, killed (and apparently eaten) by the people he meant to evangelize.[3]

The fifth name on the list, falling between two lesser luminaries, was that of Edward Jones (c. 1808–1865)—as notable as any other, but for very distinctive reasons. A free man of color from Charleston, South Carolina, Jones was one of the first African American graduates of an American college. Only one other, Alexander Lucius Twilight (1793–1857), a free black from Vermont, who graduated from Middlebury College in 1823, is said to have preceded Jones—though it appears that the very light-skinned and quite aptly named Twilight was not known to be of African descent during his Middlebury years. No such ambiguity surrounded a second African American, John Brown Russwurm (1799–1851), who received his BA from Bowdoin College just weeks after Jones graduated from Amherst. Twilight, though also at times a preacher or pastor, made his career primarily as an educator, serving for many years as the principal of Brownington Academy in northern Vermont, near the Canadian border.[4] Russwurm, the best-known of the three, emigrated to Africa, and for a time was an educator there, but his primary labors were as governor of the Maryland Colony at Cape Palmas in Liberia.[5] Jones, by contrast, made his greatest mark as a missionary educator in West Africa. Ordained to the Episcopal priesthood in 1830, Jones is most remembered for his fifteen-year term (1841–1856) as principal of Fourah Bay College. A school in Sierra Leone sponsored by the evangelical Anglican Church Missionary Society, Fourah Bay was both a pioneering attempt at Western-style education and an important institutional base for the spread of Protestant Christianity in West Africa.[6] In his years at Fourah Bay, Jones was associated with Samuel Ajayi Crowther (c. 1807–1891) who became the first African bishop ordained by the Church of England, and Jones's students there included such notable figures as James Africanus Beal Horton (1835–1883) and James "Holy" Johnson (c. 1836–1917). When one meets someone from Fourah Bay, they generally know about Edward Jones and keep alive a memory of his role in this history.[7]

By contrast, when Jones is remembered in contemporary Amherst, it is not so much because of anything in particular that he did, but rather because he was the college's first African American graduate. Amherst today is very much about the promotion and celebration of its diversity—albeit diversity of a very specific sort. The emphasis falls on race, ethnicity, gender, and sexual orientation, and from this point of view, the college's history is not a happy one. Yet even when the college's past is set in sharp negative contrast to its increasingly diverse present, an exception is sometimes made for Amherst's past role in educating African American men. That story begins with Edward Jones of the class of 1826.[8] Contemporary Amherst takes pleasure and pride in the memory that, in the fall of 1822, the very second year of the college's existence, before it had even secured a charter from the state legislature, it had enrolled a black student.

But in Edward Jones's own lifetime, when Amherst called him to mind, it was generally to celebrate his role as a missionary hero. The importance of his race was minimized. When his years at Amherst were recalled, it was said that his race really had not mattered. It was claimed that he had been treated like other Amherst students. Addressing members of the alumni at the commencement of 1853, Heman Humphrey (1779–1861), who served the college as president from 1823 to 1844, observed that "some of you remember Edward Jones of the Class of 1826." "Though his skin was darker than your own," Humphrey continued, "I rejoice to testify here, that you treated him as a brother student; & it was with no ordinary satisfaction, that when you graduated we gave him his diploma with the rest."[9] A student in one of the classes ahead of Jones later ventured a similar opinion. Writing in the *Amherst Student*, long after the fact, nearly a half-century after Jones's graduation, this anonymous alumnus recalled that "notwithstanding the disadvantages of his color . . . he was well received by both teachers and pupils,—passing through college without encountering any serious impediments or mortifications."[10] Though he must have arrived at Amherst with sufficient education to meet the entrance requirements in the classical languages, Jones did not do well enough in course to win himself a "Commencement appointment"—a place on the extensive commencement program that was regarded as an important measure of academic success. Decades later, Edward Hitchcock opined that the failure of Jones—and several other notable Amherst missionaries—to distinguish themselves at graduation "must make any reasonable Christian man feel how ridiculous is his plea that he must give up the idea of being useful in the world, because he failed to obtain a Commencement appointment." He particularly singled out Jones's subsequent career as telling evidence for his point. "It is not probable," Hitchcock concluded, "that many of our highest missionary appointees will get ahead of President Jones in rank and dignity."[11] Jones's missionary career had by then made him an outstanding alumnus, and he seems to have been a source of considerable institutional pride. "Who of you, if Edward Jones were here today," Heman Humphrey asked the assembled alumni in 1853, "would not be proud to grasp his hand and call him brother?"[12]

*

Could Jones's experience at Amherst really have been as racially unproblematic as these accounts suggest?[13] Two unanswered question are why Jones applied to Amherst and why the college admitted him. There is nothing in the college's archives about his admission. Presumably, at some point in the late summer or early fall of 1822, he turned up in Amherst, armed with letters of recommendation from educators and clergymen whose names the college would have recognized, was satisfactorily examined in Greek, Latin, and arithmetic by the president or one of the faculty of the college—the customary procedure of the time—and was admitted. But what led him to Amherst? This remains a mystery. As an Episcopalian and a Charlestonian, let alone an African American, it might seem odd that Jones would end up in a small town in western Massachusetts at a fledgling college run by Congregationalists. But there were more Episcopalians than one might have expected at Amherst in the 1820s and more people with ties to Charleston as well.[14] Though as yet unchartered and housed in a single hilltop building in a town of around two thousand inhabitants when Jones arrived, Amherst College was also a node on a wide-ranging set of networks.[15] Along exactly which of those networks Jones came to Amherst is unclear, but it may well have been anchored at the one end by whoever taught him the classical languages, perhaps an Episcopal priest.[16]

There is one source from the 1830s that purports to tell a more detailed story of Jones's admission. It appeared in an early black newspaper, the *Colored American*. It says that when Jones applied for admission to the college's first president, Zephaniah Swift Moore (1770–1823), "the President, actuated by a mixture of compassion and novelty, thought he would like to receive the young man." But when he proposed the idea to the faculty and students, students voiced "decided opposition"—shouting racial epithets, saying they would not attend class with him, and so forth. The president, the story continues, overcame this opposition by assuring the students that Jones was different, that he was "NOT AT ALL LIKE OUR NEGROES. Gentlemen, he is a-w-a-y from the South." Supposedly, this turned the tide, and the story concludes: "Our Charlestonian brother entered the college, enjoyed its privileges and received its honors, whilst a Northern colored man would hardly witness its commencement, or visit its halls, without being abused and insulted."[17] The story this newspaper article tells has clearly lost nothing in the telling, and its author just as clearly has his own axe to grind. None of the story's details, moreover, can be confirmed elsewhere. But its claim that Jones indeed "enjoyed [the] privileges" of the college (as Amherst sources claimed), but did so because he was not a typical northern black, that he was different—different in a way that had to do with his Charleston origins—is a claim to which we will return later.

What do we know directly about Jones's experience, not as it was later remembered, but as it registered on the contemporary records of the college? Where, for example, did he live? John Brown Russwurm lived off campus during his years at Bowdoin, as did Theodore Wright, the first African American to attend a Protestant divinity school, while at Princeton Theological Seminary in the late 1820s.[18] What was Jones's experience at Amherst? The slender catalogues that Amherst published during the years of Jones's residence list the name, hometown, and rooming arrangements of each student.[19] Throughout his college career, Jones lived on campus, in South College, Amherst's original building, and roomed every year with a white classmate.[20] Over the course of four years, he had three roommates, all from western Massachusetts. During his first year and again in his third year, Jones roomed with Robert Cutler (1808–1890), who had been born and raised in Amherst. In his sophomore year, his roommate was Calvin Washington Babbitt (1798–1869), from the hill town of Goshen, to the northwest of Amherst. In his senior year, he roomed with Artemas Thompson (1800–1839), from the Berkshire County town of Hinsdale.[21] Nothing about Jones's general rooming arrangements seems odd or out of line with the patterns evident among other students, at least as these are documented by the catalogues.

But is there a fuller story that can be squeezed out of these bare records? Roommates at Amherst in the 1820s were apparently not usually assigned to each other, but entered into the arrangement by mutual agreement, sometimes before they arrived at Amherst.[22] But it seems likely that Jones might not have been able to select his first-year roommate. Someone else probably brokered the initial assignment. Perhaps the key was the age of the two young men. It is not known exactly when Jones was born, but it was very likely in either 1808 or 1809, which means he was only thirteen or fourteen when he entered Amherst. Robert Cutler, Jones's first-year roommate, was thirteen when he entered the college and seventeen when he graduated. Only one other student in their class was that young. This was a period, moreover, when the age span among the student body as a whole was especially wide. Twelve of the graduating members of their class were born before 1800, making them as much as ten or eleven years older than their youngest classmates. Calvin Washington Babbitt, Jones's second-year roommate, was at the older end of the age spectrum, entering Amherst at twenty-four and graduating at twenty-eight. Unlike Cutler, who eventually made his career as a builder—first in Amherst, then later in Grand Rapids, Michigan—or Artemas Thompson, who became a lawyer and died in his late thirties of yellow fever "on a business trip" to Mobile, Alabama, Babbitt was the only one of Jones's three roommates to pursue a ministerial career. Perhaps someone thought that Jones, who had come through the college religious revival of his freshman year with no signs of being "hopefully converted," needed an older and religiously more earnest roommate. Or did Jones and Babbitt simply hit it off? And why did he go from Babbitt back to Cutler, then on to Thompson?

It can also be asked where Jones ate his meals—and whether this figured into his rooming decisions. Amherst, through its early history, did not have a refectory. Some especially frugal students seem to have taken their meals in their dormitory rooms, but most apparently boarded somewhere in town. Was finding Jones a place to board a racially charged issue? Robert Cutler, Jones's first- and third-year roommate, lived in Amherst. Did he board at home? Did Jones join him? Jones's senior-year roommate, Artemas Thompson, was from out of town, but his mother was the sister of John Leland, the college's treasurer, who lived in Amherst and apparently sometimes boarded large groups of students. Did Jones board there his senior year? One also wonders how Jones, a South Carolinian, endured trooping to the village through the snow three times a day for his mid-winter meals or what he made of the Amherst cuisine.[23]

An Amherst student of Jones's era later recalled that he "freely associated" with white students in "all their exercises and amusements."[24] Is there any hard evidence of this? Yes—in the record of Jones's activities as a member of the Athenian Society, one of early Amherst's two student "literary societies." Initially, the Alexandrian and Athenian Societies were considered two branches of the same "United Fraternity," the incoming class being equally divided between them—not by choice, but rather alphabetically or by lot. They split in the fall of 1825, early in Jones's senior year, with the Alexandrians claiming that the Athenians were breaking the rules and trying to recruit some of their rival's assigned members. Thereafter, the allotment system was abandoned, but it was apparently the mechanism by which Jones found himself an Athenian.[25]

The Athenian Society's records for the first three years of Jones's time at Amherst are apparently missing, but the minutes for his senior year exist (probably because of the separation of the societies) and provide an outline sketch of his involvement in its activities.[26] Like the Alexandrian, the Athenian Society elected its own officers and ran its own affairs, which included a number of activities. Its main business, however, was holding meetings on alternate Wednesdays to debate some contemporary issue, and occasionally sponsoring "special meetings" or "exhibitions." These special meetings, open as well to members of the Alexandrian Society and the faculty, had a more extensive program of "orations," "essays," "conferences," "colloquies," and "dialogues." (Classroom time in that era, especially during the first three years, was largely a matter of drill work in the classical languages and mathematics, so a good deal of student creativity and intellectual energy was channeled into student societies.)

If Jones were ever elected an officer of the Athenian Society, it was not at the elections recorded in the existing minutes. Since there were five other senior Athenians besides Jones who were not elected to any office, his omission is not clear evidence of discrimination.[27] The minutes show, moreover, that Jones participated in the debates within the society, and the public exhibitions that the society sponsored, more prominently than some of the other members. Each debate was typically conducted by four students. Between mid-October, when the minutes begin, and early March, when participation in the debates was voluntary (later on, the debaters were appointed in alphabetical order), ten debates were held. Jones, who volunteered three times, was among the most frequent participants. Only one student participated more often. There also seems nothing odd or out of the ordinary about the other society members with whom Jones was associated in these debates. The debate questions for which he volunteered were all questions of political practice or principle, as most of the debate questions were: "Would the acquisition of foreign territory be beneficial to the United States?"; "Ought the possession of property in our country be made a prerequisite for holding the right of suffrage?"; "Ought representatives to be bound by the will of their constituents?" By contrast, the debate to which he was appointed, in

June, was on the altogether atypical question of whether a "system of gymnastic exercises" should be introduced into the college.

During the time covered by these minutes, there is only one question of unambiguous and very direct reference to African Americans. It occurs on August 2, not long before commencement. The question put was: "Does the scheme of colonizing in Africa the free blacks of our country merit general support?" Note that the question was about free blacks, not slaves, so it was very directly relevant to Edward Jones, but he was not among the debaters. The question was decided in the affirmative. One would very much like to know what Jones made of this, but there is a good chance he was not even there.[28]

Probably the closest we come to hearing Jones's voice in these minutes is in the tantalizingly spare record of the Athenian Society's public "exhibition"—in the spring of Jones's senior year. These exhibitions were planned well in advance and must have required more extensive preparation than the nearly weekly debates. Jones's responsibility was to produce a "Dialogue"—the concluding item on the program. No text or description of this dialogue is known to exist. It may have been improvised, rather than scripted. We have only the title and a list of the characters. Entitled "The Culpepper Family," the dialogue involved six characters. There were two Culpeppers: "Old Culpepper," the family patriarch (portrayed by George Washington Boggs, another South Carolinian, and later missionary to India), and his son "Young Culpepper" (Jones's roommate, Artemas Thompson). Additionally, there was a friend of young Culpepper; another character whose name, Tightfist Holdfast, makes clear he was the heavy of the piece; and two "servants"—Richard, a servant of the Culpeppers, and Moses, a servant of Tightfist Holdfast. One is inclined to read servant as slave and take the name Moses as a sign that Tightfist Holdfast was a kind of Pharaoh and that the dialogue had a clear political point, but there is nothing to go on beyond the simple list of characters, and it seems these presentations were not always intended seriously.[29]

In addition to these formal records about Jones's rooming arrangements and his participation in the life of the Athenian Society, there are also a few reminiscences from fellow students about Jones's career at Amherst. Scattered over time, differing in circumstances and motivation, these brief accounts convey a memory of Jones that is consistent with the formal record, but nuanced in interesting and, in some respects, surprising ways.

The best known is a "Reminiscence" that appeared in the *Amherst Student* in 1875, nearly a half-century after Jones's graduation.[30] The anonymous alumnus who supplied it seems to have been a class or two ahead of Jones. At some point during his college years, this fellow student had come into possession of the published text of a funeral sermon delivered in an English country church in the 1700s. The sermon is scarcely a homiletic masterpiece. In praising the virtues of the recently deceased, for example, the preacher mixes unsurprising mention of his subject's good deeds with curious attention to seemingly extraneous detail, telling his listeners, for example, that as a "beggar boy" this man had come "into this country on the back of a dun cow; it was not a black cow, nor a brindled cow, nor a white cow, it was a dun cow."[31] Clearly, the upperclassman found the sermon highly amusing and thought it extremely well suited for a larger comic stratagem. As he later recalled:

> It was then customary to have the Wednesday afternoon exercise of declamation conducted in the presence of the Faculty and before the entire body of students; and it

> occurred to the writer to suggest to Jones the idea of reciting, on one occasion, for his part the quaint sermon here given. He committed it to memory, and arraying himself in black, even to his gloves and stockings, went through the performance with great solemnity, and, as supposed, to the immense edification of his audience. He was not suffered, however, to take his seat without a mild rebuke from the President, Dr. Humphrey, for the choice he had made of the piece spoken, which the reverend doctor said savored too much of trifling with serious things.

As Hugh Hawkins observed in a biographical essay on Jones written in the late 1970s: "Whether the incident shows Jones's inclusion in the college ethos or his specialness can be debated."[32] Perhaps it should be read simply as a typical instance of an upperclassman making an underclassman the youthful agent of his mischief-making. But why did the originator of the prank think that Amherst's one black student was the best person to carry it out?

There is evidence from Jones's time at Amherst that the college's stock of comic tropes included that of the ignorant black preacher as the peak of the ridiculous. Jacob Abbott (1803–1879), subsequently a bestselling author, was a tutor during Jones's junior year, then professor of mathematics until 1829.[33] In the 1830s, he published an account of the religious life of the college, reporting that, in what was Jones's senior year, a promising revival had been broken up by the aggressive tactics of a half-dozen students who presented themselves as "the most bold, hardened, notorious enemies of religion." (At their head was another one-day missionary hero, Henry Lyman. Later remembered as the "martyr of Sumatra," Lyman, as an unregenerate freshman, apparently was a terror to the godly.) Not satisfied with attempting to break up the meetings of their more pious schoolmates by "brow-beating intrusions," these students set up their own antimeeting, excluding "every friend of religion" among their peers and inviting the officers of the college, one by one, to try their luck at preaching down their militant resistance to any work of grace. Strikingly, the students' studied defiance eventually acquired a racial dimension. According to Abbott, when the students had run through all of the college officers, "the few who remained, conducted the meetings themselves, with burlesqued sermons and mock prayers, and closed the series at last, as I have been informed, by bringing in an ignorant black man whose presence and assistance completed the victory they had gained over influences from above."[34] Who the "ignorant black man" might have been, and whether he was a knowing or innocent accomplice in this enterprise, is unknown.[35] Unknown as well is what Edward Jones made of this use of an "ignorant black man" as the *ne plus ultra* of a farcical assault on the reigning evangelical ethos. Was he deeply offended by it? Maybe. But maybe not.

There is an exceptionally interesting document, previously overlooked, that tells us how at least some of Jones's fellow students remembered him, not a half-century later but within a decade of his graduation. The context—very political—was a meeting of the New England Anti-Slavery Convention. The motion on the floor was whether to endorse the Oneida Institute in upstate New York as "the only literary institution, east of Ohio, where it is officially announced that colored students can enjoy equal privileges with others." Oneida was, at the time, beleaguered, and the motion's proponents wished to rally abolitionists to its support. But some of those present thought the resolution cast too negative a light on the racial policies and practices of other northern colleges. As the following selections from the published *Proceedings* make clear, Jones's experience at Amherst came to figure importantly in the debate.

> Rev. Mr. Thurston, of Maine—Wished to inquire, if it were strictly true, that Oneida Institute was the only college east of Ohio, in which colored pupils could be received? . . .
>
> Rev. Mr. Thatcher of Mass., said—That prejudice must be taken into the account. The New England colleges might not exclude colored students, but they encouraged a prejudice which created an atmosphere in which a colored student could not live. He could not be on equal terms with his classmates, and at every step in improvement was compelled to drag the heavy chain which prejudice had bound to him. . . .
>
> *A young gentleman* in the broad aisle (whose name we could not learn) said—That he was a student at Amherst College, in Mass., a few years ago. One of his classmates was a colored young man, of the name of Jones. He was admitted to the friendship, intimacy, and kindness of the whole College. He roomed with the white students, and in all their exercises and amusements freely associated with them. They treated him as cordially as they did any fellow student, and he knew of no reason why colored students would not be received at Amherst, and treated as kindly as any others.
>
> Mr. E. WRIGHT, of New York, said—He knew of a formal application made to the Trustees of Amherst College, whether they would receive men of color. They refused to publish any such notice to the world. It was true, that individuals might be received there, and treated kindly, but the institution would not keep open its doors as the Oneida College had done. . . . Amherst will not open its doors, publicly, to colored pupils. . . .
>
> Rev. Mr. Pratt, of Medford said—He was . . . connected with Amherst College, when Jones was educated there. Jones was a person of decided influence in the College. He doubted if any one exercised more influence with the students. He surpassed one third of the class in his studies, and it was a matter of deep regret, that he did not come up to the highest point, in the severer studies. He believed that the very circumstance of Jones' color gave him more privileges and more sympathy. Mr. Pratt said, he wished the facts might be fairly stated . . . [Mr. Pratt was asked how black Jones was.] He described him as a very light mulatto. That made no difference. He was every where known as a person of color. Amherst, he said, did not advertise that they would receive colored pupils, neither did they advertise that they would receive pupils with red hair, but none who applied had ever been rejected.
>
> A gentleman said—He knew Jones. He was nearly white. Was a young man of remarkable talent for ingratiating himself—The speaker was a member of the College with Jones. His father possessed immense wealth . . . and that gave him the influence spoken of. He was also a genteel young man, and of excellent disposition.[36]

Immense wealth? A genteel young man of excellent disposition with a remarkable talent for ingratiating himself?

The Jones family's wealth may not truly have been immense, but from the standpoint of a college significantly populated by young men from the rocky hillside farms of western

Massachusetts, it would nonetheless have been impressive. Charleston, South Carolina, was one of two North American cities (New Orleans being the other) where racial stratification came closest to West Indian patterns of privileging a distinct class of free persons of mixed race. Though his father, Jehu Jones (c. 1769–1833), had been born a slave, by the time of Edward's childhood, he was becoming a well-established member of Charleston's brown—not black—elite.[37] Jehu Jones and his second wife, Abigail Deas, ran the Jones Hotel, which was, at the time, *the* place to stay for the traveling white elite, both domestic and foreign. The most vivid account of Jones comes from F. Colburn Adams's "thinly fictionalized" antebellum novel *Manuel Pereira, or, The Sovereign Rule of South Carolina, with Views of Southern Laws, Life, and Hospitality*. A white Charlestonian says of him:

> Jones was almost white, a fine portly-looking man, active, enterprising, intelligent, honest to the letter, and whose integrity and responsibility was never doubted. He lived in every way like a white man, and, I think, with few exceptions, never kept company with even *bright folks*. His house was unquestionably the best in the city, and had a widespread reputation. Few persons of note ever visited Charleston without putting up at Jones's, where they found not only the comforts of a private house, but a table spread with every luxury the country afforded.[38]

Living "in every way like a white man" included owning slaves. William Cooper Nell, the antebellum African American historian whose father, he said, had known Jones, claimed that "Mr. Jones often exerted his influence and contributed his means to redeem persons from slavery," and it is possible that Jones's holding of these slaves was a legal formality to secure these persons their freedom. Yet slaveholding of the more customary sort was scarcely an unknown practice among Charleston's brown elite, and there is evidence indicating that the prosperous Joneses participated in it, putting slaves to work in their hotel.[39] In any case, they were far from poor. One reason Edward Jones may have been admitted to Amherst was that his family could pay the bills.

Zephaniah Swift Moore, we were told by the *Colored American*, persuaded a reluctant student body to accept Jones because he was a different kind of Negro. Indeed, he was. If we have imagined Amherst's first black graduate as an earnest young man rising from the bottom, a young African American of limited means and narrow experience struggling to find his footing in the wider world of Amherst College, we have imagined wrongly. Whatever may have been going on inside his head and heart (which remains an elusive question), this was clearly not his persona during his college days, and not the way he was first remembered at Amherst. As noted above, Jones's roommates were all from Amherst or the hill towns of western Massachusetts. One does not want to exaggerate their provinciality. But it seems fair to say that, in spite of his relative youth, Jones's experience of the world had been wider and surely more cosmopolitan than that of most of his schoolmates. As his fellow students remembered him in the 1830s, he comes across as something of a budding urban sophisticate—impious, irreverent, affluent, genteel, graced with exceptional social skills, a young man of influence.

How did Edward Jones, thus remembered, turn into a missionary hero? Jones arrived at Amherst on the heels of the Vesey Conspiracy, an alleged plan by African Americans in Charleston, under the leadership of the free black Denmark Vesey (1767–1822), to violently overturn the white regime. Historians are still arguing about whether or not the conspiracy was in fact real or an elaborate frame-up.[40] Either way, there were trials and hangings of the alleged conspirators—three dozen were hanged—in the months immediately before Jones was admitted to Amherst. About what Jones made of all this one can only speculate. It is not uncomplicated. The revolt, if actually real, was not hatched in the social environs of the Jones Hotel. But the aftermath of the affair did impose very serious constraints on Jones's present life and future prospects. A law was passed restricting free persons of color who left South Carolina from returning to the state. After he came to Amherst, Jones literally could not go home again. Neither could part of his family, including his mother, who had gone to New York. In the Amherst catalogues after his freshman year, New York is listed as his residence and that seems to be where he went after his graduation.[41]

There, he became a close friend of John Brown Russwurm, Bowdoin's black graduate of the class of 1826. A decade older than Jones, Russwurm was clearly the senior partner in this friendship. In 1827, Russwurm joined Samuel Cornish in launching the first African American newspaper, *Freedom's Journal*, and Jones at some point became involved with that project, perhaps when Cornish resigned and Russwurm took over as editor in September 1827.[42] The following summer, Russwurm put Jones in touch with the American Colonization Society about the possibility of going to Liberia, under its auspices, as a doctor—his medical education in the United States to be arranged by the society. Jones was ready to sign on, but the deal was undone by a negative letter from Solomon Peck (1800–1874), a member of the Amherst faculty. (A Baptist, Peck added something to the "diversity" of the Amherst faculty of the 1820s.)

What Peck had to say about Jones's student days seems generally consistent, though not identical, with the recollections of his fellow students. After consulting "with the faculty respecting the character of Edward Jones," as well as drawing on "what fell under [his] own observation during [Jones's] last year's residence in this place," Peck told the Colonization Society that he could scarcely recommend him. "I am compelled to state," Peck wrote, "that while he indicated some degree of talent, he manifested an utter destitution of literary ardour & of moral principle." Further, he had "seriously injured the interests of the College not only by his example, but more especially by his direct efforts to spread the contamination of his impurity & infidelity among his fellow students." Exactly what "impurity" Peck had in mind he does not say, but a fondness for alcohol was probably part of it.[43] In any case, Peck, too, saw Jones as influential, and in a very worldly way.[44] Disappointed in his hopes to become a doctor, Jones seems to have become involved, in late 1828 and early 1829, with a black school in Philadelphia.[45]

Up to this point, his postgraduation course seems meandering and uncertain—though one must remember that he was still very young and that making one's way in American society as a college graduate was an untrodden path for African Americans. Early in 1829, however, a clear direction emerges. In February, he was admitted to the African Mission School in Hartford, a small and short-lived effort by the Episcopal Church to educate black missionaries for Africa. During the year and a half he was associated with this school, he spent a good deal of his time studying Arabic at Andover Theological Seminary.[46] In the summer of 1830, he was ordained to the Episcopal priesthood, with the expectation that he would go to Liberia as a clergyman, more or less under the joint auspices of the Episcopal Church and the American Colonization Society. At some point in the fall of 1830, Jones backed out of this arrangement and went instead to England. From there, he made his way to Sierra Leone, where he eventually made his mark as a missionary educator.[47]

What accounts for this seemingly abrupt change of direction early in 1829? David Agnew Wilson (1821–1912), a Presbyterian minister who had served as a missionary to Liberia in the 1850s, met Jones on his travels to and from his mission field and found him an interesting and impressive figure. After he returned to the United States, he met an Amherst graduate of Jones's era who told him more about Jones's life. Eventually, Wilson published his reflections, and this is what he said about how the man Solomon Peck wrote off turned into a missionary hero. Jones's family, he stressed, had indeed been very well-off: "Wealth flowed in upon him," he said, "in a full stream. . . . . Funds without stint were placed at his disposal." But then "his father's pecuniary affairs became seriously embarrassed and the resources of the son at once kept short." Here is his full account of what happened next:

> His hopes disappointed, his prospects blighted, and his spirit no doubt chafed at the occasion of his calamity, he was tempted to drown his sorrows in the bowl, and the boa was beginning to wrap him in its fatal folds. It was then he met a friend of better days, who, seeing his danger, spoke faithful words of warning and of hope. They were not in vain. The whole man changed. With new views of life and duty he resolved to devote himself to the ministry.

Edward Jones's evangelical conversion experience came late, but it came. Or at least that's the story an unnamed alumnus told the Presbyterian missionary.[48]

Jones's career in Sierra Leone cannot be examined here, though doing so might shed additional light on his Amherst years. For one thing, as an educator, he seems to have been tenaciously committed to a curriculum not unlike what he had experienced at Amherst. It was not just his family's resources but his knowledge of Greek and Latin that got him into Amherst. He resisted pressures to turn Fourah Bay, and the grammar school associated with it, toward a less academic and more "practical" curriculum. There is also evidence that the genteel charmer of his student days did not entirely disappear from the missionary priest. Jehu Hanciles, who has written very perceptively about Jones's African career, quotes a Church Missionary Society colleague who said of Jones: "The charm he throws around so many, the way in which he fascinates most persons, is remarkable." Some also doubted the depth of his piety. Most strikingly, Hanciles also reports that Jones had a reputation in Sierra Leone for being "hot tempered"—something which does not appear in the Amherst record. Was he simply less angry in his student days? Or did he keep it hidden? Or do the Sierra Leone accounts of his "hot temper" reflect the biased views of white authorities there, with whom he had more than a few quarrels, both civil and ecclesiastical? One historian of Sierra Leone has said that Jones, in his early years at Fourah Bay, "represented the heritage of protest against racial oppression, otherwise almost absent from the Colony at [that] time."[49] If one wishes for a more overtly militant Edward Jones than the Amherst version, this would seem the place to look.

Notes

1. This essay is part of a larger and ongoing study of Edward Jones and of related subjects in the early history of Amherst College, the relation of blacks to the early American Protestant missionary movement, and the experience of early-nineteenth-century African Americans with exceptional educations. An earlier version was delivered as the Inaugural Lecture of the John E. Kirkpatrick 1951 Professorship at Amherst College, September 19, 2014. During the nearly two decades of work on this larger project, I have received much assistance from the Archives and Special Collections staff at the Amherst College Library, particularly, at the start, from Daria D'Arienzo and Floyd Merritt, and, more recently, from Margaret Dakin, Jennifer Bolmarcich, and Mariah Leavitt. Samuel Keaser 2017, my student research assistant for much of his Amherst career, dug in many archival corners for me in search of overlooked material on Jones. I am also much indebted to Randall K. Burkett for sharing with me his unpublished pioneering research on Edward Jones and other black Episcopal clergy. Most especially, I would like to thank Scott Sessions for his extraordinarily generous, resourceful, and wise assistance at every stage of this project.

2. Edward Hitchcock, *Reminiscences of Amherst College, Historical, Scientific, Biographical, and Autobiographical: Also, of Other and Wider Life Experiences* (Northampton, MA: Bridgman & Childs, 1863), 203–4. Hitchcock also provided a chart showing the varying rate at which Amherst itself had graduated missionaries between 1821 and 1860. I have not attempted to recalculate Hitchcock's figures from the college's modern alumni records. The work of Clifton Jackson Phillips provides a table listing the primary collegiate sources from which the ABCFM drew its foreign missionaries (and its domestic ones to Native Americans) up to 1840. See Phillips, *Protestant America and the Pagan World: The First Half Century of the American Board of Commissioners for Foreign Missions, 1810–1860* (Cambridge, MA: Harvard University Press, for the Asian Research Center, 1969), 29. For foreign missionaries, the six leading institutions were Yale (20), Amherst (19), Williams (18), Dartmouth (15), Middlebury (14), and Union (14). Since Amherst was the youngest of the schools, launched only eleven years after the ABCFM was founded, these figures suggest that it was the single largest source of ABCFM foreign missionaries in the decades of the 1820s and 1830s. Phillips's data is drawn from "Statistical View of the Officers, Missions, and Missionaries of the Board," *Missionary Herald* (Boston, MA), 36, no. 1 (January 1840): 17–38.

3. There is a joint biographical sketch of Lyman and his colleague Samuel Munson in William B. Sprague, *Annals of the American Pulpit, or, Commemorative Notices of Distinguished American Clergymen of Various Denominations, from the Early Settlement of the Country to the Close of the Year Eighteen Hundred and Fifty-Five*, 9 vols. (New York: Robert Carter, 1858–1869), 2:747–52. See also William Thompson, *Memoirs of the Rev. Samuel Munson, and the Rev. Henry Lyman, Late Missionaries to the Indian Archipelago, with the Journal of Their Exploring Tour* (New York: D. Appleton, 1839). *The Martyr of Sumatra: A Memoir of Henry Lyman*, ed. Hannah Lyman Willard (New York: Robert Carter, 1856) was prepared by Lyman's sister, with copious extracts from his diaries and letters. Lyman also figures prominently in the chapter on early Amherst missionaries in Theodore Baird, *The Most of It: Essays on Language and Imagination* (Amherst, MA: Amherst College Press, 1999), 12–42. See also Wendy Ewald, Thomas Keenan, Martha Saxton, and Fazal Sheikh, *The Transformation of This World Depends upon You: Voices from Amherst and Beyond* (Göttingen: Steidl, 2014), 57–61.

4. Having previously studied for six years at the Orange County Grammar School in Randolph, Vermont, Twilight entered Middlebury as a junior in 1821, just a year before Jones began at Amherst.

After his graduation in 1823, he taught school in Peru, New York, for four years and studied theology. He was licensed as a preacher by the Champlain Presbytery in 1827 and then preached to two area congregations while teaching for a year in Vergennes, Vermont. When he went to Brownington to serve the Orleans County Grammar School in 1829, he also became acting pastor of the town's Congregational Church and was ordained there in 1829. He served the church from 1829 to 1834 and again more briefly in the mid-1840s and early 1850s. Ambitious to make the school a serious academy, he saw to the building of a four-story granite structure, today open to visitors as the Old Stone House Museum of the Orleans County Historical Society. He also served in the Vermont state legislature in the 1836 to 1837 term. From 1847 to 1851, because of issues with the school's trustees and the church's deacons, Twilight left Brownington and taught across the border in Quebec, returning to head what had become Brownington Academy for the last years of his life. Scholarly biographical studies of Twilight are limited: Gregor Hileman, *The Iron-Willed Black Schoolmaster and His Granite Academy* (Brownington, VT: Orleans County Historical Society, 1974), reprinted from the *Middlebury College Newsletter* (Spring 1974), a brief but careful assessment, remains useful. "Alexander Twilight," a short biographical statement on the website of the Old Stone House Museum (http://www.oldstonehousemuseum.org) provides some additional details, as well as access to some of Twilight's sermons. The most extended account is a short, popular work, aimed primarily at young readers. See Michael T. Hahn's *Alexander Twilight: Vermont's African American Pioneer* (Shelburne, VT: New England Press, 1998). For a recent biographical synopsis, see Sholomo B. Levy's "Alexander Lucius Twilight," in *African American National Biography*, ed. Henry Louis Gates Jr. and Evelyn B. Higginbotham, 8 vols. (New York: Oxford University Press, 2008), 7:275–77.

5. Born in Jamaica to a white American father and black slave mother, Russwurm was educated early on in Quebec and then at Hebron Academy (and perhaps elsewhere) in Maine. He entered Bowdoin as a third-year student in 1824. In the late 1820s, he collaborated with the Presbyterian clergyman Samuel Cornish in launching *Freedom's Journal*, the first African American newspaper. In 1829, he controversially broke with Cornish on colonizationism, publically embraced the American Colonization Society, and departed for Liberia. There he served, for a time, as the superintendent of public schools, editor of the *Liberian Herald*, and colonial secretary, in addition to engaging in trade. From 1836 until his death in 1851, he was governor of the colony in Liberia established by the Maryland Colonization Society. There is considerably more literature on Russwurm than on Twilight or Jones. Basic biographical information can be found in an entry by W. E. B. Du Bois in the *Dictionary of American Biography*, 22 vols. (New York: Charles Scribner, 1928–1958), 16:253, and another by Penelope Campbell in *American National Biography*, ed. John A. Garraty and Mark C. Carnes, 24 vols. (New York: Oxford University Press, 1999), 19:117–18, also reprinted with a revised bibliography in *African American National Biography*, 7:50–51. General biographical studies, with sharply differing points of view, are provided by Sandra Sandiford Young, "A Different Journey: John Brown Russwurm, 1799–1829" (PhD diss., Boston College, 2004), and Winston James, *The Struggles of John Brown Russwurm: The Life and Writings of a Pan-Africanist Pioneer, 1799–1851* (New York: New York University Press, 2010). Amos Jones Beyan reviews his early life before focusing primarily on his years in Africa. See Beyan, *African American Settlements in Africa: John Brown Russwurm and the American Civilizing Efforts* (New York: Palgrave Macmillan, 2005). Russwurm's religious beliefs and associations have received limited attention in the scholarly literature about him. James (*Struggles*, 26–27) suggests he "had little time for revealed religion," was thought to be a Deist, and joined the Protestant Episcopal Church only toward the end of his life. Little also has been said about his ties to Edward Jones, although James refers to him as a "close friend" (66).

6. Founded in 1814, the name and nature of the school changed over time. A general history, with an entrée into the considerable prior literature on the subject, is provided by Daniel J. Paracka Jr., *The Athens*

of West Africa: A History of International Education at Fourah Bay College, Freetown, Sierra Leone (New York: Routledge, 2003).

7. No scholarly biography of Jones has been published and shorter biographical studies are limited and often inexact. "Edward Jones," in *Obituary Record of Graduates of Amherst College, for the Academical* [sic] *Year Ending July 11, 1872* (Amherst, MA: H. M. McCloud, 1872), 18–19, which "regretted that so little information in regard to his early life can be obtained" was inaccurate about his post-Amherst theological education and focused primarily on his years in Africa—an enduring pattern. An important early biographical essay by Clarence G. Contee had less impact on subsequent scholarship than it might have because of its lack of documentation. See Contee, "The Reverend Edward Jones, Missionary-Educator to Sierra Leone and 'First' Afro-American College Graduate, 1808(?) to 1865," *Negro History Bulletin* 38 (1975): 356–57. A renewed interest in Jones at the college is marked by Stephen N. Keith, "The Life and Times of Edward Jones: Sower of the African Diaspora" (BA thesis, Amherst College, 1973), Amherst College Archives and Special Collections, Amherst College, Amherst, MA. The most important of Amherst historian Hugh Hawkins's publications on Jones is "Edwards Jones, Marginal Man," in *Black Apostles at Home and Abroad: Afro-Americans and the Christian Mission from the Revolution to Reconstruction*, ed. David W. Wills and Richard Newman (Boston, MA: G. K. Hall, 1982), 243–53. Michael Crowder, who also taught briefly at Amherst College, surveys Jones's early life with an emphasis on his education, hoping to illuminate his career as an educator in Sierra Leone. See Crowder, "From Amherst to Fourah Bay: Principal Edward Jones" (unpublished typescript essay, spiral-bound with others in *Bicentenary of the Founding of the Colony of Sierra Leone, 1787–1987*, International Symposium on Sierra Leone, Miatta Conference Center, Brookfields, Freetown, May 19–21, 1987). Nemata Amelia Blyden focuses almost entirely on his African career, which is also discussed in more general works about education and Christian missions in West Africa. See Blyden "Edward Jones: An African American in Sierra Leone," in *Moving On: Black Loyalists in the Afro-Atlantic World*, ed. John W. Pulis (New York: Garland, 1999), 159–182; and, for example, Jehu Hanciles, *Euthanasia of a Mission: African Church Autonomy in a Colonia Context* (Westport, CT: Praeger, 2002). Other brief biographical synopses include Donald M. Lewis, "Edward Jones," in *The Blackwell Dictionary of Evangelical Biography, 1730–1860*, ed. Donald M. Lewis, 2 vols. (Cambridge, MA: Blackwell, 1995), 1:619; Donald S. Armentrout, "Edward Jones," in *American National Biography*, 12:191–92; and Cheryl Dudley, "Edward P. Jones, Sr." in *African American National Biography*, 4:649–50. See also note 37, below.

8. It has sometimes been suggested, for example, in Harold Wade Jr., *Black Men of Amherst* (Amherst, MA: Amherst College Press, 1976), 5, 10–12, that Robert Purvis also attended the college around the time Jones did. There is, however, no evidence in the college's records, or in the standard sources and authorities about its early history, to support this claim. Strong circumstantial evidence suggests that Purvis instead attended Amherst Academy, the secondary school to which the college was then closely related, and there is direct evidence that his younger brother Joseph did so. See Margaret Hope Bacon, *But One Race: The Life of Robert Purvis* (Albany: State University of New York Press, 2007), 22, 219nn22–23; Amherst Academy, *Catalogue of the Trustees, Instructers [sic], and Students, November 1828* (Amherst, MA: J. S. & C. Adams, [1828]), 5, and Amherst Academy, *Catalogue of the Trustees, Instructors, and Students, November 1829* (Amherst, MA: J. S. & C. Adams, [1829]), 7, Box 1, Folder 9, Early History Collection, Amherst College Archives and Special Collections, Amherst College, Amherst, MA.

9. Heman Humphrey, "An Address before the Alumni of Amherst College. Delivered in the Chapel at Commencement, August 1853," unnumbered p. 12, President's Office Records: Heman Humphrey, Amherst College Archives and Special Collections, Amherst College, Amherst, MA. A typescript copy of the full paragraph of this speech in which Humphrey discusses Jones, lacking only the few words he had crossed out, is located in the Alumni Biographical Files (Edward Jones 1826), Amherst College Archives and Special Collections, Amherst College, Amherst, MA.

10. "A Reminiscence," *Amherst Student* 9, no. 5 (December 4, 1875): 34.

11. Hitchcock, *Reminiscences*, 330, 331.

12. Humphrey, "Address before the Alumni of Amherst College," unnumbered p. 14.

13. On Russwurm's experience at Bowdoin, see Young, "A Different Journey," 60–70, and especially James, *Struggles*, 16–24. There is also a discussion of Russwurm's time at Bowdoin and a treatment of his later life, with special attention to the ongoing role of his Bowdoin education and connection in Margaret Sumner, *Collegiate Republic: Cultivating an Ideal Society in Early America* (Charlottesville: University of Virginia Press, 2014), 160–63, 165–78.

14. Jones was only one of ten Amherst students in the 1820s who eventually entered the Episcopal priesthood (or died so intending): George Champlin Shepard 1824, Caleb S. Henry 1825ng, Chauncey Colton 1826, Eleazer Hutchinson 1827ng, Henry Adams 1828, Andrew Murdock Brown 1828, Levi Corson 1828ng, Chester Newell 1829ng, and Frederick Daniel Goodwin 1829ng—all of whom were at Amherst at some point during Jones's years. While Adams was a Congregationalist pastor for two decades before becoming an Episcopalian, most of the others entered the Episcopal priesthood within a few years of their graduation from Amherst. There were also apparently a few students at Amherst who were or became lay Episcopalians, though they are harder to identify. Jones's fellow students at Amherst included another Charlestonian, Samuel Haslet (who died in 1825), and three other South Carolinians—John Brevoort Van Dyck 1826, George Washington Boggs 1827, and Edward V. Monroe 1820ng. In 1825, during Jones's third year at the college, there were also three Charlestonians at nearby Amherst Academy—William Kunhardt, Ralph Middleton, and Edward Swinton (who had been there since 1823). Joel Wyman 1825 and Alonzo Chapin 1826 followed up their work at Amherst College with medical educations in Charleston. Charles Upham Shepard 1824, brother of Episcopal priest George Champlin Shepard, would later teach at the Charleston Medical College from 1834 to 1861 and again from 1865 to 1869—years when he concurrently held teaching positions at Yale and then at Amherst. When Amherst was inaugurated and dedicated in September 1821, the sermon was given by Aaron W. Leland, a Presbyterian pastor from Charleston and younger brother of the college's treasurer, John Leland. His son James was an Amherst student in the late 1820s. Solomon Peck, who joined the Amherst faculty at the start of Jones's senior year, had spent a few months in 1824 as a home missionary in Charleston. There were no Episcopalian faculty members at Amherst, but the school tried in the spring of 1824 to appoint one—Jasper Adams, at the time president of the College of Charleston. For the graduates and nongraduates (ng) cited above, see J. Alfred Guest, *Amherst College Biographical Record, 1973: Biographical Record of the Graduates and Non-Graduates of the Classes of 1821–1971 Inclusive* (Amherst, MA: Trustees of Amherst College, 1973), 2 (C. U. Shepard, G. C. Shepard), 4 (Chapin, Colton, Henry, Wyman), 5 (Van Dyck), 6 (Haslet, Boggs), 7 (Hutchinson, Adams), 8 (Brown), 9 (Corson), 11 (Goodwin), 12 (Monroe, Newell), and 20 (Leland). On Kunhardt, Middleton, and Swinton, see *Catalogue of the Trustees, Instructors, and Students of Amherst Academy, during the Quarter Ending November 13, 1823* (Wendell, MA: J. Metcalf, 1823); *Catalogue of the Trustees, Instructors, and Students of Amherst Academy, during the Quarter Ending November 10, 1824* (Northampton, MA: H. Ferry at the Oracle Office, 1824); and *Catalogue of the Trustees, Instructors and Students of Amherst Academy, during the Quarter Ending August 9, 1825* in a bound volume of Amherst Academy Catalogue Broadsides, 1816–1825, Box OS1, Folder 7, Amherst College Early History Collection, Amherst College Archives and Special Collections, Amherst College, Amherst, MA. On Aaron and John Leland, see William Seymour Tyler, *History of Amherst College during Its First Half Century, 1821–1871* (Springfield, MA: Clark W. Bryan, 1873), 71, 240–41; Sherman Leland, *Leland Magazine, or, A Genealogical Record of Henry Leland and His Descendants, Containing an Account of Nine Thousand, Six Hundred and Twenty-Four Persons, in Ten Generations, and Embracing Nearly Every Person of the Name of Leland in America from 1653 to 1850* (Boston, MA: Weir & White, 1850), 219–21, 241–46. On Peck, see *General Catalogue of the Theological Seminary, Andover, Mass., 1880* (Andover, MA: Warren

F. Draper, 1880), 40. For the seldom-mentioned attempt to appoint Adams, see Tyler, *History*, 160n1, and one of several press reports announcing it at the time, "Literary and Philosophical Department," *The Gospel Advocate: Conducted by a Society of Gentlemen* 5, no. 5 (May 1825): 164. For biographical information on Adams, see Harris Ellwood Starr, "Jasper Adams," in *Dictionary of American Biography*, 22 vols. (New York: Charles Scribner's Sons, 1928–1958), 1:72; and *Religion and Politics in the Early Republic: Jasper Adams and the Church-State Debate*, ed. Daniel L. Dreisbach (Lexington: University Press of Kentucky), 163–64.

15. The United States Census reported an Amherst population of 1,917 for 1820 and 2,631 for 1830. Figures for 1765 to 1895 are provided in Edward W. Carpenter, *The History of the Town of Amherst, Massachusetts* (Amherst, MA: Carpenter & Morehouse, 1896), 604. Census data in James Avery Smith, *The History of the Black Population of Amherst, Massachusetts 1728–1870* (Boston, MA: New England Historic Genealogical Society, 1999), indicate there were twenty-six African Americans in Amherst in 1820 (14) and fifty in 1830 (20). I have found no evidence regarding Jones's interaction with the black population of the town..

16. Though it is possible that Jones, like Twilight and Russwurm, studied at a precollegiate grammar school or academy, I have yet to find evidence of this. If not, his preparation from Amherst, beyond the elementary level, would have come through private instruction. A plausible hypothesis, as yet unconfirmed, is that he was taught by one or more of the Episcopal priests of Charleston. Charles W. Thomas, a Georgia Methodist who encountered Jones in Sierra Leone in the 1850s, reported that Jones "had received his first lessons in religion and letters from Mr. Pine, formerly rector of the Episcopal church in Charleston," in his *Adventures and Observations on the West Coast of Africa and Its Islands: Historical and Descriptive Sketches of Madeira, Canary, Biafra, and Cape Verd Islands, Their Climates, Inhabitants, and Productions* (New York: Derby & Jackson, 1860; New York: Negro Universities Press, 1969), 100. As is not uncommon in such accounts, this information seems garbled. I have identified no priest named Pine serving an Episcopal parish in Charleston during the pertinent years, but Jones was likely referring to Smith Pyne (1803–1876). Pyne was ordained only in the late 1820s, never served a parish south of Washington, DC, but lived in Charleston from his early childhood until he was sent to study at Eton in England at the age of fifteen. He might, as a teenager, have given a young Jones his "first lessons in religion and literature." More speculatively, and less plausibly, if Jones, who it seems is generally thought to have come directly from Charleston to Amherst, instead first went to New York for a time, he might have studied there with Pyne who was a student at Columbia College, from which he graduated in 1823. I have seen no evidence, apart from Thomas's report, tying Jones to Pyne, but this too remains under investigation. On Pyne, see John Vaughan Lewis, *In Memoriam, the Reverend Smith Pyne* ([Washington, DC]: [St. John's Church], 1876]); and Frederick Wallace Pyne, *The John Pyne Family in America, Being the Comprehensive Genealogical Record of the Descendants of John Pyne (1766–1813) of Charleston, South Carolina* (Baltimore, MD: Gateway, 1992), 40–44.

17. See "National Inconsistencies of Character," *The Colored American* 1, no. 44 (November 4, 1837): 3 (original punctuation preserved). The senior editor of the paper was Samuel Cornish, who had known Jones since the 1820s and might well have written the story, although I have found no direct evidence to confirm this. Whoever the author was, he appears to have visited Amherst, attended Jones's commencement, and been badly treated. On the editors of the *Colored American*, see David E. Swift, *Black Prophets of Justice: Activist Clergy before the Civil War* (Baton Rouge: Louisiana State University Press, 1989), 82–85. This work of continuing importance has much to say about the paper, and even more about Cornish, but does not mention any relation to Jones.

18. On Russwurm's residence at Bowdoin, see Young, "A Different Journey," 64, and James, *Struggles*, 18. Both of these works appear to rely for this point, directly or indirectly, on Horatio Bridge's view that

Russwurm "lived at a carpenter's house, just beyond the village limits." See Bridge, *Personal Recollections of Nathaniel Hawthorne* (New York: Harper, 1893), 30. James H. Moorhead, in his *Princeton Seminary in American Religion and Culture* (Grand Rapids, MI: Eerdmans, 2012), says that Wright did not live in Alexander Hall, the seminary's dormitory, but "found lodging off campus, possibly with an African American widow" (83). According to Wright himself, during his years at Princeton, "it was my happiness to board and room in a very respectable and pious colored family." See his letter (390–95) in the appendix of the *Memoir and Select Remains of the Late Rev. John R. M'Dowell, the Martyr to the Seventh Commandment, in the Nineteenth Century* (New York: Leavitt, Lord, 1838), 392.

19. For Jones, see *Catalogue of the Officers and Students of the Collegiate Institution, Amherst, Mass., Oct. 1822* (Greenfield, MA: Denio & Phelps, 1822), 8; *Catalogue of the Officers and Students of the Collegiate Institution, Amherst, Mass., November 1823* (Hartford, CT: P. B. Goodsell, 1823), 8; *Catalogue of the Officers and Students of the Collegiate Institution, Amherst, Mass., November 1824* (Northampton, MA: H. Ferry, 1824), 6; and *Amherst College Catalogue of the Corporation, Faculty, and Students, October 1825* (Amherst, MA: Carter & Adams, 1825), 5. Unless otherwise noted, the information provided above on the general and specific rooming arrangements of Amherst students during these years comes from these catalogues (5–9, 2–10, 5–9, 5–10, respectively).

20. Jones's successive rooms were 10, 26, 9, and 25 in South College. Late nineteenth- and early twentieth-century renovations preserved the exterior design of the building but substantially changed its interior, thus the rooms are not configured as they were in Jones's time. See Stanley King, "*The Consecrated Eminence*": *The Story of the Campus and Buildings of Amherst College* (Amherst, MA: Amherst College, 1951), 13–14, 112, 310–11; "North and South Colleges," in the "College Activities" section, *Amherst Alumni News* 6, no. 2 (October 1953): 13; and Amherst College Buildings and Grounds Collection, Series 1, Sub-Series A: South College, Box 1, Folder 5, Amherst College Archives and Special Collections, Amherst College, Amherst, MA. There is a brief description of the early rooms in South College in Tyler, *History*, 73. That all of Jones's rooms at Amherst were on the east-facing side of the building is made clear in "Diagram of rooms in South College with names of occupants, 1821–1822," Amherst College Early History Manuscripts and Pamphlets Collection, Box 1, Folder 6, Amherst College Archives and Special Collections, Frost Library. A second dormitory and classroom, North College, was put into use in the middle of Jones's first year. See Tyler, *History*, 74–75.

21. Basic biographical information on Jones's roommates can be found in Amherst College, *Biographical Record of the Alumni of Amherst College, during its First Half Century, 1821–1871*, ed. William L. Montague, with Edward P. Crowell and William E. Biscoe (Amherst, MA: J. E. Williams, 1883), 26 (Babbitt), 29 (Cutler), and 34 (Thompson); and Guest, *Amherst College Biographical Record*, 4–5. Unless otherwise indicated, the information on these individuals discussed in the text above is drawn from these sources.

22. I have not come across any general statement of Amherst's policy about the selection of roommates. But for evidence that they were self-chosen, see, for example, Asa Bullard to William S. Tyler, "Letter to Prof. Tyler about Class of 1828," n.d., Alumni Biographical Files (Asa Bullard 1828), Amherst College Archives and Special Collections, Amherst College, Amherst, MA. These comments occur in Bullard's page about Asaph Boutelle, with whom he roomed during his first three years. David F. Allmendinger Jr. cites the recommendation in Asa Dodge Smith's student advice books of the 1830s, that Christian students select only other Christians as roommates, which suggests student selection was a general practice. See Allmendinger, *Paupers and Scholars: The Transformation of Student Life in Nineteenth-Century New England* (New York: St. Martin's, 1975), 106; and Smith, *Letters to a Young Student* (Boston: Perkins & Marvin, 1832), 156–58.

23. Allmendinger provides a general discussion of boarding arrangements in American colleges, including Amherst, during the early nineteenth century. See Allmendinger, *Paupers and Scholars*, 81–86.

A glimpse of those during Jones's era is provided by William S. Tyler, who was an Amherst student in the class of 1830, in *Autobiography of William Seymour Tyler, D.D., LL.D., and Related Papers, with a Genealogy of the Ancestors of Prof. and Mrs. William S. Tyler*, ed. Cornelius B. Tyler (privately printed, 1912), 27: "I boarded four terms . . . in a club at Mr. Green's, an old house . . . half way down to Mill Valley, and my board never cost me more than seventy-five cents a week. . . . Many of the best students in the college then boarded at about the same rate, and in a style of simplicity and frugality, of course, to correspond, dispensing with tea and coffee and all luxuries, but having an abundance of wholesome and nutritious food." See p. 37 above, for Jones's prior dining environment in Charleston.

24. *Proceedings of the New England Anti-Slavery Convention, Held in Boston, May 24, 25, 26, 1836* (Boston, MA: Isaac Knapp, 1836), 57.

25. George R. Cutting, *Student Life at Amherst College: Its Organizations, Their Membership, and History* (Amherst, MA: Hatch & Williams, 1871), 13–16. This book, by an 1871 Amherst graduate, provides the standard account of these early societies, but there is other relevant material in the college's archives. See, for example, the unsigned and untitled history, written with good-natured partisanship from the standpoint of the Alexandrian Society, in Clubs and Societies, Series 3: Alexandrian Society, Box 5, Folder 2, Amherst College Archives and Special Collections, Amherst College, Amherst, MA. A pencil annotation on the first page of the manuscript, in a different hand, says "by John Stebbins Lee '45."

26. "Athenian Society of Amherst College: Constitution, Minutes, Lists of Members," Clubs and Societies Collection, Series 7: Athenian Society I, Box 12, Folder 11, Amherst College Archives and Special Collections, Amherst College, Amherst, MA. This bound, handwritten volume is identified as "Volume 2." Volume 1 seems to be missing. Volume 2 begins with the constitution. The minutes follow, starting on October 12, 1825, but the entry for that date stops after a few words. If this were in fact the chaotic night both societies attempted to conduct their business simultaneously, this would explain the incompleteness of these minutes. At the very back of the volume are two lists of members, grouped by class, which—as they begin with the seniors of Jones's class then run through the three successive classes—seem to give the membership for Jones's senior year. While they largely overlap, however, they are not entirely consistent.

27. The list of officers elected on October 26 and March 15, respectively, are given in "Athenian Society of Amherst College: Constitution, Minutes, Lists of Members," Clubs and Societies Collection, Series 7, Athenian Society I, Box 12, Folder 11, pp. 30, 35. Amherst College Archives and Special Collections, Amherst College, Amherst, MA. An additional election was held on July 5, 1826 (p. 41), but no seniors were elected.

28. I have come across, but have been unable to confirm, the suggestion that seniors were sometimes absent from campus during the summer term before commencement. If so, Jones would presumably have missed the August meeting.

29. "Order of Exercises at the Exhibition of the Athenian Society, on Wednesday Evening, April 6, 1826," Clubs and Societies Collection, Series 7, Athenian Society I, Box 13, Folder 2, Amherst College Archives and Special Collections, Amherst College, Amherst, MA.

30. "A Reminiscence," *Amherst Student* 9, no. 5 (December 4, 1875), 34–35.

31. The entire text of the sermon as appended at the end of "A Reminiscence."

32. Hawkins, "Jones, Marginal Man," 244.

33. Sources for general information on Abbott include Edward L. Lach Jr., "Jacob Abbott," in *American National Biography*, 1:27–28, and Carol Gay, "Jacob Abbott," in *American Writers for Children before 1900*, ed. Glenn E. Estes, Dictionary of Literary Biography, 42 (Detroit, MI: Gale, 1985), 3–11. Abbott was the father of the noted Congregational liberal preacher and editor Lyman Abbott (1835–1922).

34. Jacob Abbott provides an extended account of the "College Revival," focusing on April 1827 (the year after Jones's graduation), but briefly discusses the failed revival of the year before as background. See

Abbott, *The Corner Stone, or, A Familiar Illustration of the Principles of Christian Truth* (Boston, MA: William Pierce, 1834), 313–38. Tyler quotes from Abbott's account, but draws on other sources as well. See Tyler, *History*, 197–203. Quotations from Abbot: "enemies of religion" (325), "friend of religion" (325), "ignorant black man" (326), and from Tyler: "brow-beating intrusions" (201). Tyler identifies Lyman as the leader of the opposition to the revival of 1826 (202).

35. "Sambo Coon," an African American who became "a friend and servant" of Amherst College students from the classes of 1828 through 1854, was said to have once been "a preacher of the Methodist persuasion to his colored brethren in slavery." He reportedly came to town, however, only after the final abolition of slavery in New York, in the summer of 1827, too late for Jones's era. See the published reminiscence in Charles H. Sweetser, *Annals of Amherst College: The Soil, the Seed, the Sowers, the Presidents and Professors, Together with a Popular Guide to the College Buildings and Various Cabinets* (Northampton, MA: Trumbull & Gere, 1860), 58–59. It is affectionate but thoroughly patronizing and notes his "unsurpassed comicalities" (58).

36. The broad discussion over the Oneida resolution is reported in *Proceedings of the New England Anti-Slavery Convention* (1836), 54–59. Comments about Jones occur on 57 and 58. The Revered Pratt of Medford was Levi Pratt, Amherst College class of 1826, a fellow member of the Athenian Society with Jones. I have not been able to identify the other speakers who claimed to have overlapped with Jones at Amherst. I am indebted to Scott Sessions for calling this important document to my attention.

37. Jehu Jones and his family have long been discussed in the standard sources on free persons of color and other African Americans in South Carolina, albeit sometimes very briefly. See, for example, E. Horace Fitchett, "The Traditions of the Free Negro in Charleston, South Carolina," *Journal of Negro History* 25, no. 2 (April 1940): 143–44; Marina Wikramanayake, *A World in Shadow: The Free Black in Antebellum South Carolina* (Columbia: University of South Carolina Press, 1973), 58n37, 77, 79, 103, 106, 110–11, 177; Michael P. Johnson and James L. Roark, *Black Masters: A Free Family of Color in the Old South* (New York: Norton, 1984), 252; and Bernard E. Powers Jr., *Black Charleston: A Social History, 1822–1885* (Fayetteville: University of Arkansas Press, 1994), 43–44, 47. In the late 1980s, the South Carolina Department of Archives and History issued two public program packets of documents on Jehu Jones and his family: Roberta V. H. Copp, *Jehu Jones: Free Black Entrepreneur*, ed. Judith M. Brimelow (1989), and Roberta V. H. Copp, *Jones: Time of Crisis, Time of Change*, ed. Judith M. Brimelow (1989). There is considerable information about the Jones Hotel in an extended study of the building in which it was housed, in Harriett P. Simons and Albert Simons, "The William Burrows House of Charleston," *Winterthur Portfolio* 3 (1967): 172–203, republished in revised form "without the architectural drawings and descriptions" in *South Carolina Historical Magazine* 70, no. 3 (July 1969): 155–76. The prominent Sierra Leonean Davidson Nicol (1924–1994) had apparently written a substantial account of the Joneses but seems only to have published "The Jones Family of Charleston, London, and Africa," in *Sierra Leone Studies at Birmingham, 1988: Proceedings of the Fifth Birmingham Sierra Leone Studies Symposium 15th–17th July 1988 Fircroft College, Birmingham*, ed. Adam Jones, Peter K. Mitchell, and Margaret Peil (Birmingham: Centre of West African Studies, University of Birmingham, 1990), 89–90.

38. F. Colburn Adams, *Manuel Pereira, or, The Sovereign Rule of South Carolina, with Views of Southern Laws, Life, and Hospitality* (Washington, DC: Buell & Blanchard, 1853), 88–89. For a recent discussion of the novel, which characterizes it as "thinly fictionalized" (111), see Anthony Szczesiul, *The Southern Hospitality Myth: Ethics, Politics, Race, and American Memory* (Athens: University of Georgia Press, 2017), 111–16. But while Adams's portrait of Jehu Jones quoted above appears to be consistent with other evidence, his treatment of the Jones family in other respects seems much less historically reliable. Edward Jones does not appear in the novel.

39. William Cooper Nell provides a very brief and largely derived discussion of Jehu Jones. See Nell, *The Colored Patriots of the American Revolution, with Sketches of Several Distinguished Colored Persons, to*

Which Is Added a Brief Survey of the Condition and Prospects of Colored Americans (Boston, MA: Robert F. Wallcut, 1855), 244–45. After reproducing, without attribution and with silent omissions, the passage quoted above from Adams, *Manuel Pereira*, and more, he praises Jones's efforts to "redeem" slaves, mentioning that his father, William G. Nell, had been one of Jones's apprentices when, before he became a hotel owner, he ran a tailoring establishment. Nell does not mention Edward Jones, though he does briefly refer to his older brother, Jehu Jones Jr., who was ordained in 1832 to the Lutheran ministry. See Karl F. Johnson and Joseph A. Romeo, "Jehu Jones (1786–1852): The First African American Lutheran Minister," *Lutheran Quarterly* 10, no. 4 (Winter 1996): 425–43. For the evidence that Jones employed slave labor at both his tailoring business and at the Jones Hotel, see Larry Koger, *Black Slaveowners: Free Black Slave Masters in South Carolina, 1790–1860* (Jefferson, NC: McFarland, 1985), 147, 153–54, 263nn30–31, 264–65nn53–55.

40. The present phase of the ongoing debate over the nature of the Vesey Conspiracy was inaugurated by the work of Michael P. Johnson, as presented and debated in the two-part "Forum: The Making of a Slave Conspiracy," *William and Mary Quarterly*, 3rd ser., 58, no. 4 (October 2001): 915–76, and 59, no. 1 (January 2002): 135–202.

41. Information concerning which members of Edward Jones's family moved to New York, when they moved, and how long they remained there, is scattered and incomplete and therefore a matter of continuing investigation. But New York clearly seems to have been his home at least from 1823 to 1828.

42. The fullest account of the paper does not mention Jones's role. See Jacqueline Bacon, *Freedom's Journal: The First African American Newspaper* (Lanham, MD: Lexington, 2007). The evidence that Jones worked there seems to come from a single source—a traveler in Africa who, again, garbled what Jones had told him. According to George W. S. Hall, "Jones was for some time a contributor to or assistant editor of the *Liberator*, an abolition paper published by the Rev. J. Cornish, also a colored man, and the late John B. Russwurm" (211). See Hall, "Sierra Leone: Chapter Third," *African Repository* 35, no. 7 (July 1859): 204–13.

43. Before the college had been opened, the trustees voted to prohibit "the students from drinking ardent spirits or wine, or any liquor of which ardent spirits or wine should be the principal ingredient, at any inn, tavern, or shop, or keeping ardent spirits of wine in their rooms, or at any time indulging in them." See Noah Webster's "Origin of Amherst College in Massachusetts," in his *Collection of Papers on Political, Literary, and Moral Subjects* (New York: Webster & Clark, 1843), 225–54, at 250.

44. John B. Russwurm to R. R. Gurley, June 23, 1828; Edward Jones to R. R. Gurley, July 5, 1828; and Solomon Peck to R. R. Gurley, July 19, 1828, Incoming Correspondence, American Colonization Society Papers (microfilm), Reel 4. See also entries for June 23, 1828, and July 25, 1828, Board of Managers Minutes, pp. 631, 638, American Colonization Society Papers (microfilm), Reel 289.

45. From October 17, 1828, until its last issue on March 28, 1829, *Freedom's Journal* carried an advertisement for "the Academy in Morris' Alley, under the care of Messrs. Gloucester and Jones," which, in addition to "all the common branches of a good English education," offered instruction in Latin and Greek, as well as needlework and drawing for girls. Additionally, an article explained that the Academy had previously been headed by Jeremiah Gloucester, but was now "opened under the superintendence" of Stephen H. Gloucester and Edward Jones, "lately of this city," that is, New York. See "Education in Philadelphia," *Freedom's Journal* 2, no. 29 (October 10, 1828): 226. Jeremiah and Stephen Gloucester were the sons of John Gloucester, the initial minister of Philadelphia's first black Presbyterian church. After the death of Jeremiah, who had been educated at the African School of the Synod of New York and New Jersey (Presbyterian). Stephen, who lacked comparable formal education, would not have been able to offer advanced instruction on his own. On the Gloucester brothers, see Andrew E. Murray, *Presbyterians and the Negro* (Philadelphia, PA: Presbyterian Historical Society, 1966), 34–35. I am indebted to Scott Sessions for bringing to my attention these items from *Freedom's Journal*.

46. There appears to be no adequate scholarly study of the African Mission School. It opened in the fall of 1828, but Jones reportedly became connected with it only in February 1829. He seems to have spent some time in Hartford, studying Hebrew, among other things, but then arrangements were made for him to study Arabic at Andover Seminary "for a few months." See "African Mission School Society," *Episcopal Watchman* 3, no. 22 (August 15, 1829): 175, and *Report of the Board of Directors of the African Mission School Society, Presented at a Meeting of Said Society Held in Christ Church Hartford, on the 6th of August, 1830* (Hartford, CT: G. F. Olmstead, 1830), 4. Though it has generally been said in the limited biographical literature on Jones that he attended Andover Theological Seminary for "two years," or from 1828 to 1830, this seems inconsistent with the chronology emerging from African Mission School publications, as well as with his teaching in Philadelphia into early 1829. But the published records of Andover Seminary are inconsistent. The earliest listing in its catalogues that I have found for Jones comes only in 1857, when he is identified along with two others as a "resident student" (not a regular member of the class) in association with the class of 1830. His name is followed by "1—," meaning he was there for less than one year. He is also listed in a "Supplement" to the "Alphabetical Catalogue," which appears to list all such nongraduates, in the *Triennial Catalogue of the Theological Seminary, Andover, Massachusetts, MDCCCLVII* (Andover, MA: Warren F. Draper, 1857), 37, 94, and in the *General Catalogue of the Theological Seminary, Andover, Mass., 1880* (Andover, MA: Warren F. Draper, 1883), 333, 350. He is listed among other graduates of the class of 1831 with "1828–1830" after his name in *General Catalogue of the Theological Seminary Andover, Massachusetts, 1808–1908* (Boston, MA: Thomas Todd, [1909?]), however, 122–23. Although this is a matter of continuing investigation, I believe the 1857 record is accurate, as it is consistent with the other sources. During his time at Andover, he roomed on campus with Bela Bates Edwards, Amherst College class of 1824. See Edwards A. Park, *The Life and Services of Professor B. B. Edwards: A Discourse Delivered in the Chapel of Andover Seminary, June 25, 1852* (Andover, MA: Warren F. Draper, 1852), 17–18.

47. The circumstances surrounding his withdrawal from the Liberia plan and decisions to go from there to England and then on to Sierra Leone—a subject of continuing investigation—are too complex to narrate or document here. It does appear, however, that the claim he went first to Liberia and then on to Sierra Leone, which one finds in some of the literature and even in some nineteenth-century sources, is mistaken.

48. "Reminiscences of Sierra Leone," *Hours at Home: A Popular Monthly of Instruction and Recreation* 5, no. 4 (August 1867), 320–26, quoting from 325. Another version of the piece is published with significant silent omissions in the *African Repository* 45, no. 11 (November 1869): 327–33. It names "Rev. D. A. Wilson, formerly a missionary to Liberia," as author. Wilson does not identify the "classmate" of Jones with whom he spoke, except to say that he was "a worthy minister of New Hampshire (now no more)." Milton Kimball (1799–1865) seems to be the member of the class of 1826 who best fits this description, but Wilson may have used "classmate" simply to mean schoolmate. Heman Humphrey, who had "entirely lost sight" of Jones after his graduation, also met Wilson and learned from him about Jones's post-Amherst career, including that he had "made a profession of religion." He cited Wilson's admiring statements about Jones's work in Africa in his "Address before the Alumni of Amherst College" (1853), unnumbered pp. 13–14. As with others who met Jones in Africa and later wrote about him, some of Wilson's information about Jones seems garbled. On Wilson, see his obituary in Joseph H. Dulles, *Necrological Report Presented to the Alumni Association of Princeton Theological Seminary at Its Annual Meeting, May 6th, 1913*, Necrological Reports and Annual Proceedings 4, no. 4, Princeton Theological Seminary Bulletin 7, no. 2 (August 1913), 211–12.

49. On the connection of Jones's educational philosophy at Fourah Bay to his education at Amherst, see Keith, "Life and Times," 114; Hawkins, "Marginal Man," 248; and Crowder, "From Amherst to Fourah

Bay," 21. In *Euthanasia of a Mission*, Hanciles provides a discussion of the Fourah Bay Institution during Jones's years there (72–81) and a general assessment of Jones's career in Sierra Leone (96–103) and mentions his charm (98), doubtful piety (78), hot temper (98), and heritage of protest (153). For the last of these, Hanciles cites Christopher Fyfe, *Africanus Horton, 1835–1883: West African Scientist and Patriot* (New York: Oxford University Press, 1972), 26.

Amherst and the Native World

Frederick E. Hoxie

It should not be surprising to find an essay on Native Americans and Native Hawaiians in a book about the history of Amherst College. Amherst, after all, was inspired by missionary zeal, and Native Americans and other indigenous peoples were early objects of evangelism. The college's founders had set their sights on bringing Christian civilization to the world, but Native Americans were never far from their minds. "There is scarcely a town in the valley," the college's first historian wrote, "whose soil was not sprinkled with blood in the early wars with the Indians." [1] Another college chronicler wrote: "The forests were haunted by unseen foes," and local residents "could never be free . . . from fear of catastrophe." [2]

Professor W. S. Tyler reported, in his 1873 history of the college, that its early leaders sought "to commemorate the sufferings and sacrifices by which our fathers won this valley to civilization, learning and religion." Trustee Noah Webster celebrated that victory and assured those gathered to launch the new institution that they would find their generosity rewarded as Amherst graduates became "the instrument of converting a family, a province, perhaps a kingdom of Pagans and bringing them within the pale of the Christian church."[3] Transforming "kingdoms of Pagans" was a central ambition of early Amherst; that goal was reflected in the institutional seal, designed by professor of Latin and Greek Nathan Welby Fiske and stamped on all official documents: "*Terras Irradient*" ("They Shall Enlighten the Lands").

The handiest lands to "enlighten," in 1821, were the indigenous territories in North America and the islands of Hawai'i. "Pagan kingdoms" in the Middle East and Asia attracted missionary attention, but in the 1820s, the Natives of North America and the Pacific were most immediately accessible.[4] In its early decades, Amherst's missionaries were uniformly committed to converting the "pagans" in these areas to Christianity and "raising up" their nations to civilization. By spreading the gospel, Amherst's ministers expected to create a world of Christian communities. Over time, however, the graduates who traveled to the accessible indigenous communities in North America and Hawai'i dropped that second task. As the United States expanded across the continent and incorporated native peoples in North America and the Pacific within its boundaries, ministers from Amherst abandoned "raising" the nations and turned their attention to persuading their congregations to assimilate into the general American population. By 1900, promoting "American-

Figure 1. The "Bloody Brook" monument in South Deerfield, MA, erected in 1835 to commemorate a battle that took place during the Massachusetts Colony's seventeenth century war with "King Philip" (Metacom). Many Amherst students and college leaders attended the monument's dedication. Courtesy of the Newberry Library.

ization" had become the unifying goal for both the college's graduates in the native world and for the college itself.

In the twentieth century, Amherst's ambitions regarding indigenous peoples shifted yet again. Across the globe, the protestant churches that had traditionally supported Amherst began to question using the gospel alone to uplift "pagan" peoples. Progressive churchmen and women asked if it might be more important that missionaries adapt to foreign cultures to better promote economic development, education, and modern health care. At the same time, advocates of "Americanization" within the United States questioned their nationalistic rhetoric and began exploring the contributions of cultural traditions that were not European—or even Christian—to national life. At the college, a more diverse student body—as well as the decline of religious education and a classical curriculum—encouraged a more cosmopolitan outlook. Amherst faculty and students engaged in contemporary issues and were less enamored of the traditional curriculum. By the 1990s, both global cultures and indigenous traditions within the United States had become subjects of study—native peoples were no longer objects of conversion. By the time of its bicentennial, a college founded in a valley "won for civilization" had made a place within its curriculum, its community, and its history for the peoples who earlier had been viewed as agents of violence and targets of dispossession. They had become partners in inquiry and fellow agents of enlightenment.[5]

The story of Amherst's engagement with the native world can be sketched here in three parts: the mission era, the era of expanding US nationalism, and the era of rising cosmopolitanism. In each section, we can witness Amherst's engagement with native peoples and the resonance of that engagement on campus.

MISSIONARIES

At its founding, the college's curriculum reflected its evangelical vision. Classical learning was fundamental for an institution committed to carrying Christian civilization to the world, but from the start, modern thinkers were also featured among the students' required texts. Thus, in addition to exploring the political ideas of the ancient Greeks, Amherst students read Enlightenment thinker Emer de Vattel's eighteenth-century treatise on international relations.

Vattel's *Law of Nations* was written as European nations struggled to move beyond religious warfare of the Reformation Era and extend their empires across the globe.[6] Vattel proposed a new world order based on international trade and stable diplomatic relationships. This vision, Vattel wrote, required "a just and rational application of the Law of Nature to the affairs and conduct of nations."[7] He argued that in a civilized world, "states . . . may acquire rights . . . by pacts and treaties."[8] Treaties, like foundational agreements within a single state, would be the source of stability and order. While Vattel did not imagine that stateless indigenous peoples would participate in this new world, he did recognize that "pagan" nations such as those in the Middle East and Asia could be diplomatic and economic partners of Europeans.[9]

From Vattel's perspective, the most important divide in the world was between those who cultivated the earth and those who did not. "The whole world," he wrote, "is appointed for the nourishment of its inhabitants. . . . Every nation [is therefore] obliged to cultivate the ground that has fallen to its share." Those who fulfilled that obligation should be recognized as nations, while "those people . . . who having fertile countries, disdain to cultivate the earth . . . deserve to be exterminated as savage and pernicious beasts." Such "idle" communities, he argued, must eventually give way to enterprising states.[10] But, he added, "idle" communities could save themselves by learning to "cultivate the earth." Missionaries could be pivotal instruments in that economic conversion.[11] Vattel's view fit neatly with the missionary outlook of the Protestant leaders who participated in Amherst's founding. They were enthusiastic supporters of the American Board of Commissioners of Foreign Missions (ABCFM), the protestant society headquartered in Boston that, by 1821, had already embarked on an ambitious campaign to bring the gospel to the world. ABCFM missionaries agreed with Vattel, that individual conversion need not subvert the rule of local rulers. The goal should be individual conversion and the eventual "raising up" of the "pagan" nation through trade and diplomacy. As a consequence, the ABCFM strategically targeted communities where trade and diplomatic activity had already begun. Its missionaries would encourage this enterprise and guide the pagan nations towards Christianity. The ABCFM sent its first missionaries to India and Hawai'i because those places were already engaged with European powers. These same considerations caused ABCFM officials to focus their North American efforts on tribes like the Cherokees and the Iroquois groups in upstate New York, whose leaders had already demonstrated an openness to literacy, treaty-making, and the market economy.[12]

The Amherst graduates who became missionaries among Native Americans and in

Hawai'i were agents of the ABCFM. They pursued the twin goals of Christian conversion and the uplift of "pagan" societies into civilized nations. As an early chronicler of the college declared, "The American Board was calling so loudly for laborers ... it [is] absolutely necessary that some new effort should be made to secure an adequate supply."[13] Most clergy who attended Amherst chose "home" missions within the settled communities of the United States, but several dedicated graduates answered the ABCFM's call. In December 1829, for example, on the eve of his departure for Hawai'i, Reuben Tinker (1827) announced that "four hundred millions of immortals ... are resting this day on our hands." Their salvation, he added, "must be accomplished ... by our individual exertions, charities and prayers."[14]

Tinker was among the first to join the missionary effort in the islands that would eventually come under American rule. He would soon be joined in Hawai'i by Isaac Bliss and Benjamin Wyman Parker (both of the class of 1828). His contemporaries who served Native American communities on the continent included Hiram Smith (1823), Nathaniel Fisher (1826), and Asher Bliss (1829)—all assigned to Iroquois tribes in upstate New York. (Matthew Scovell, a nongraduate, left Amherst in 1826 to serve as a missionary to the Cherokees.)[15] By the 1840s, these early missionaries would be augmented with two additional graduates: Daniel Dwight Hitchcock (1844), who had been born at the ABCFM Cherokee mission in Georgia and who returned to the tribe as a physician, and Sereno Bishop (1846), another missionary son who was born in the Hawaiian islands, educated in the United States, but who returned "home" in 1853 following his ordination.

These nine represent the first generation of American missionaries who devoted their "exertions, charities and prayers" to the salvation of native peoples. They focused the bulk of their attention on religious instruction and literacy. Tinker, for example, edited a Hawaiian language mission newspaper, *Ke Kumu Hawai'i* ("The Hawaiian Teacher"), that published translations of bible texts, along with letters from church members and short pieces on the world beyond the islands. Benjamin Parker and his young wife opened a mission on rural Oahu Island. There, their granddaughter later recalled, "they found a loyal body of simple, industrious and exceedingly lovable people to whom they brought the message of Jesus Christ."[16]

Asher Bliss and Daniel Hitchcock followed similar careers in North America. Bliss was "warmly welcomed" at the Cattaraugus reservation in western New York, when he and his wife arrived there in 1832.[17] The pair ministered to a congregation of Christian Senecas and established a network of primary schools in the community. The ABCFM reported in 1839 that, under Bliss's leadership, the tribe had "gone forward cultivating their ground, erecting new buildings and manifesting more industry and enterprise generally than at any former period." The missionary leaders looked forward to a new spirit that would encourage the tribe to "commune together at the Lord's Table."[18] Hitchcock began his service a decade later in Indian Territory where the Cherokees had been moved after being expelled from Georgia. He took up his post immediately after graduation, married the daughter of Samuel Worcester (a renowned ABCFM missionary to the tribe), and continued on until his death in 1867.[19]

While the North American missions attracted a number of early graduates, they found the tribes at the center of their efforts were soon embroiled in conflicts with the United

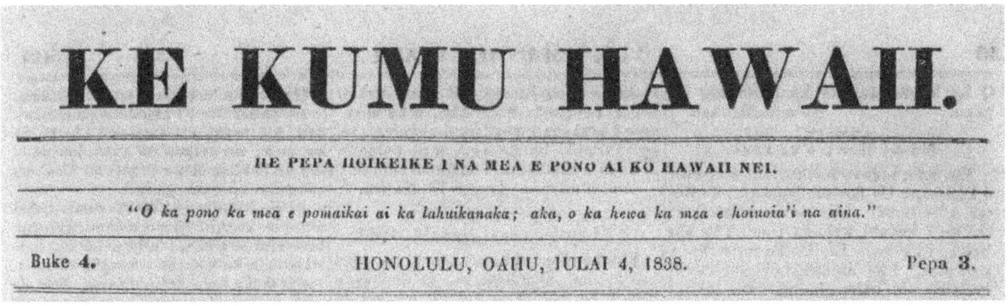

KE KUMU HAWAII.

HE PEPA HOIKEIKE I NA MEA E PONO AI KO HAWAII NEI.

"O ka pono ka mea e pomaikai ai ka lahuikanaka; aka, o ka hewa ka mea e hoinoia'i na aina."

Buke 4. HONOLULU, OAHU, IULAI 4, 1838. Pepa 3.

Figure 2. *Ke Kumu Hawai'i* ("The Hawaiian Teacher," a newspaper edited by Amherst graduate Reuben Tinker (1827). The masthead reads: "A messenger of justice and good life in Hawai'i," and below that: "The justice and good fortune enjoyed by the nation, along with the sins and wickedness in the land." Courtesy of the Newberry Library.

States. Both the Senecas in western New York and the Cherokees in Georgia were targets of the "removal" policy advocated by Andrew Jackson. Jackson declared (falsely) that settlers and Indian tribes were incapable of living together peacefully and that native peoples must therefore relocate west of the Mississippi. Tribes like the Cherokees and Senecas had lived alongside Europeans for more than a century, but the expansion of cotton agriculture in the South and commercial expansion that accompanied canal building in New York made removal popular among voters. Jackson's program was fiercely opposed by ABCFM missionaries, who argued that these enterprising nations deserved to have their treaties honored and to be treated according to the law of nations. The secretary of the ABCFM, Jeremiah Evarts, was removal's most outspoken opponent. He argued that removing these increasingly Christian tribes from their homes would be a national sin.[20] As a petition submitted by church leaders to the Massachusetts legislature in 1830 argued, removal "would probably bring upon us the reproaches of mankind and would certainly expose us to the judgements of Heaven."[21]

But Jackson prevailed. By 1840, the bulk of the native population in states east of the Mississippi had been forced west, delivering the affected tribes both physical suffering and a stunning blow to their national identity.[22] The ABCFM reported in 1840 that removal had thrown the New York tribes "into great distress and despondency.... The whole transaction," the report added, "is characterized by falsehood, dishonesty and oppression."[23] This defeat also shook the confidence of missionaries. As the board reported the following year, "The circumstances of the Indians ... for ten years past ... [has] created in the Christian community extensively and especially among candidates for missionary employment, an unhappy despondency respecting Indian missions and an aversion to engaging in them ... The prospects for a change in the political atmosphere were poor," the report added, deepening the "impression ... that the Indians are doomed to speedy extinction."[24]

In the aftermath of the disastrous removal era, the ABCFM urged missionary training grounds like Amherst to make "special efforts" to "awaken the missionary spirit in young men pursuing a course of liberal education."[25] But the college's gospel evangelists now set their sights elsewhere. Only Daniel Dwight entered the North American mission field after

1840—and he returned to the Cherokee community that had been his boyhood home—and those who had earlier chosen Native American missions gradually moved away. Hiram Smith, Nathaniel Fisher, and Matthew Scovell appear to have ended their Indian ministries by midcentury, while Asher Bliss, laboring amidst a shrinking community of Senecas at Cattaraugus, was reassigned in 1851 "to the duties of ministry among the whites."[26]

The Hawaiian missions followed a similar path. At first, Reuben Tinker, Benjamin Parker, and the other ABCFM clerics had great success with individual conversion and efforts to extend literacy to the Hawaiian nation. At the same time, the missionaries remained loyal to the local monarchs who were often pressured by visiting ship captains to surrender their chiefly authority or ally themselves with foreign powers (particularly Great Britain and France).

The most prominent missionary ally of the Hawaiian government was William Richards, a Williams College graduate who arrived in the islands in 1823. Soon fluent in Hawaiian, Richards served as an effective counselor to island rulers until 1838 when he resigned from the mission and became a full-time political advisor to King Kamehameha III. In that post, he participated in the drafting of the kingdom's first written constitution. In 1842, he and Native Hawaiian Timothy Ha'alillio were named special envoys to the United States.[27] By 1850, the ABCFM leadership in Boston concluded that the Hawaiian mission's success justified its closure. This young Christian nation could proceed alone. The formal closing of the Hawaiian mission came in 1863, when the Boston headquarters ended its financial support of pastors in the islands and supervised a reorganization of the Hawaiian churches that placed native ministers in charge of local congregations. "We see," the ABCFM declared, "a Protestant Christian nation in the year 1863, in place of a nation of barbarous pagans only forty years before—self-governing in all its departments, and nearly self-supporting. . . . We regard this Christian community . . . as demonstrating the triumphant success of the gospel of our Lord and Savior Jesus Christ."[28]

While it appeared that the Hawaiian nation had been successfully "raised up," the resident American missionary community shifted its focus from nationhood to the quality of the islands' "civilization," expressing growing skepticism regarding the abilities of the islands' native peoples. This negative view grew more prominent after 1850, following the annexation of California to the United States. Honolulu suddenly came within the commercial orbit of San Francisco and its booming community of merchants and as a consequence, the American population of the islands rose sharply. These new residents began calling for closer commercial and military ties to the United States. Sereno Bishop (1846) was among the most outspoken advocates of that position. While he had been born in the islands and had ministered there for decades, shifting circumstances altered his loyalties. After serving several native congregations in the 1850s and 1860s, he moved to Honolulu, became involved in real estate development, and edited the Hawaiian Evangelical Association's newsletter *The Friend*. From this position, he wrote critically of the monarchs who struggled to defend Hawaiian sovereignty, claiming that local Christianity was not "self-sustaining." Native leaders, he wrote, were "actively sapping and breaking down the feeble honesty and imperfect probity of the native people." He argued that corrupt local monarchs were incapable of leading a civilized nation. They were sure to produce "[a] general lapse away from civilized and constitutional government back toward the license and despotism of the heathen past."[29]

NATIVES AND THE AMERICAN NATION

At its founding in 1821, Amherst was an obscure frontier institution, struggling to bring Christian learning to the world. Thirty years later, the territory of the United States extended to the Pacific, and the nation referred to itself as an "empire," whose Manifest Destiny appeared obvious: to settle the North American continent and "civilize" the lands beyond. This transformation of American national identity had a profound impact on the public's view of the indigenous peoples living under its expanding sphere of influence. Once viewed as distant, "pagan" nations, North American native communities had become internal residents of the United States who were either doomed to extinction or, at best, destined for years of "tutelage" before they could join the modern nation. As America's influence in Hawai'i grew, native people there came to be viewed in a similar way.

At midcentury, the Amherst College campus was also affected by the bursting size and power of the United States. Enrollment grew, the college began attracting students from beyond rural New England, and the intense religious atmosphere of the missionary era faded from prominence. Campus-wide evening prayers were abandoned and revivals became "less frequent and less powerful."[30] Secular fraternities became a fixture of social life, athletic competition began, and, despite the persistence of a classical curriculum, a growing proportion of Amherst graduates chose careers outside the ministry. At the celebrations surrounding the college's fiftieth anniversary in 1871, for example, a survey revealed that while nearly 50 percent of all living alumni were ministers, only 25 percent of the graduating class planned to follow that precedent.[31] Amherst presidents and most board members continued to be clergymen, but new ideas appeared. Instruction in the sciences and mathematics expanded with the construction of Walker Hall in 1868, and among the faculty, there was general acceptance of evolution and new secular approaches to philosophy. Student perceptions of politics and economics were no longer dependent on the diplomatic vision of Vattel's *Law of Nations*; during the 1830s, that text was replaced in the senior curriculum by Jean Baptiste Say's *Political Economy*, a celebration of free-market manufacturing and global trade.[32]

As the college's graduates and faculty became more reflective of the expanding American nation-state, attitudes toward native peoples also shifted. Students appeared sympathetic to the conditions of indigenous people, but they also adopted the popular idea that Native Americans were doomed to extinction. In 1857, for example, students presented a program to celebrate "Ye Birthday of Pocahontas." It consisted of a number of humorous pieces celebrating "ye wild Indians" and "ye days when ye salvages lived in ye land." It concluded with songs celebrating the students' devotion to local hard cider and expressing their disdain for the college's prohibition rules. (Amherst had banned alcohol at its founding; the first college in the United States to do so.) They sang of Pocahontas's father: "Powhatan never interfered, nor cooling drinks denied her, Then why should Profs make such a fuss

And growl 'cause we drink cider?"[33] No longer "pagans" eager for the gospel, the Natives in this performance were simply backward drunkards. An article in the student-run *Amherst Magazine*, five years later, underscored that view. In a short story set in frontier Wisconsin, the unnamed authors described how a group of Winnebago Native Americans performed their dances for local settlers in exchange for liquor. At the end of the day, "the tired spectators repose comfortably in their homes," they wrote, "but the poor red man wraps his blanket about his weary and intoxicated body . . . utters a little drunken gibberish, gives a wild howl . . . and is lost in his sleep of inebriety."[34]

The shift in the college's view of Native Americans can be seen in the career of Francis Amasa Walker of the class of 1860. Walker served in the Civil War before going on to a distinguished career as a government statistician, economist, and, later, president of the Massachusetts Institute of Technology (MIT). In his early years in Washington, DC, however, Walker's reputation as an efficient administrator won him an appointment as Commissioner of Indian affairs. Walker was inexperienced, but not shy about announcing his view of the Natives' predicament. He argued that it was impractical to view Native American tribes as nations or to take their treaties seriously. Native people required substantial rehabilitation before they could participate in American society. Without government assistance, he wrote in 1872, Native Americans would soon be swallowed up by the progress of the nation: "The westward course of population is neither to be denied or delayed for the sake of the Indians . . . the Indians must yield or perish." The government's duty was simple: "To snatch the remnants of the Indian race from destruction." With an eye to the dwindling group of religious leaders who defended treatymaking, he declared that the Natives' friends should "exert themselves in this juncture and lose no time."[35]

Francis Walker was likely aware that one of the best known "friends" of the Native Americans of his day had spent her childhood in the town of Amherst. Helen Hunt Jackson (1830–1885), a poet and polemicist, was the daughter of Nathan Welby Fiske, the designer of the college seal and author of its motto "*Terras Irradient*." In the 1870s, she turned to "the Indian Question" in the hopes of encouraging sympathy for native communities too often dismissed as "savages." The ultimate product of her efforts was *A Century of Dishonor*, a powerful chronicle of the American government's mistreatment of the Native Americans. Published in 1881, Jackson's indictment was delivered in a blood-red binding to every member of Congress.

When it appeared on legislators' desks, Jackson's call for the humane treatment of Native Americans featured an introduction by Amherst president Julius Seelye, a former professor of philosophy at the college and the first alumnus to become campus chief executive. Seelye had also served a term in Congress as a Republican representative from western Massachusetts and had sat on the Indian Affairs Committee where he had observed, firsthand, both the bloody consequences of frontier conflict (Custer's defeat at the Little Big Horn occurred during his term) and the legendary corruption in the Interior Department's Office of Indian Affairs. Seelye's prominence made him a logical choice to promote Jackson's book.

In his introduction, Seelye argued that conversion to Christianity was only the starting point of native uplift. Whether the "pagan" in question was one of the "cannibals of the

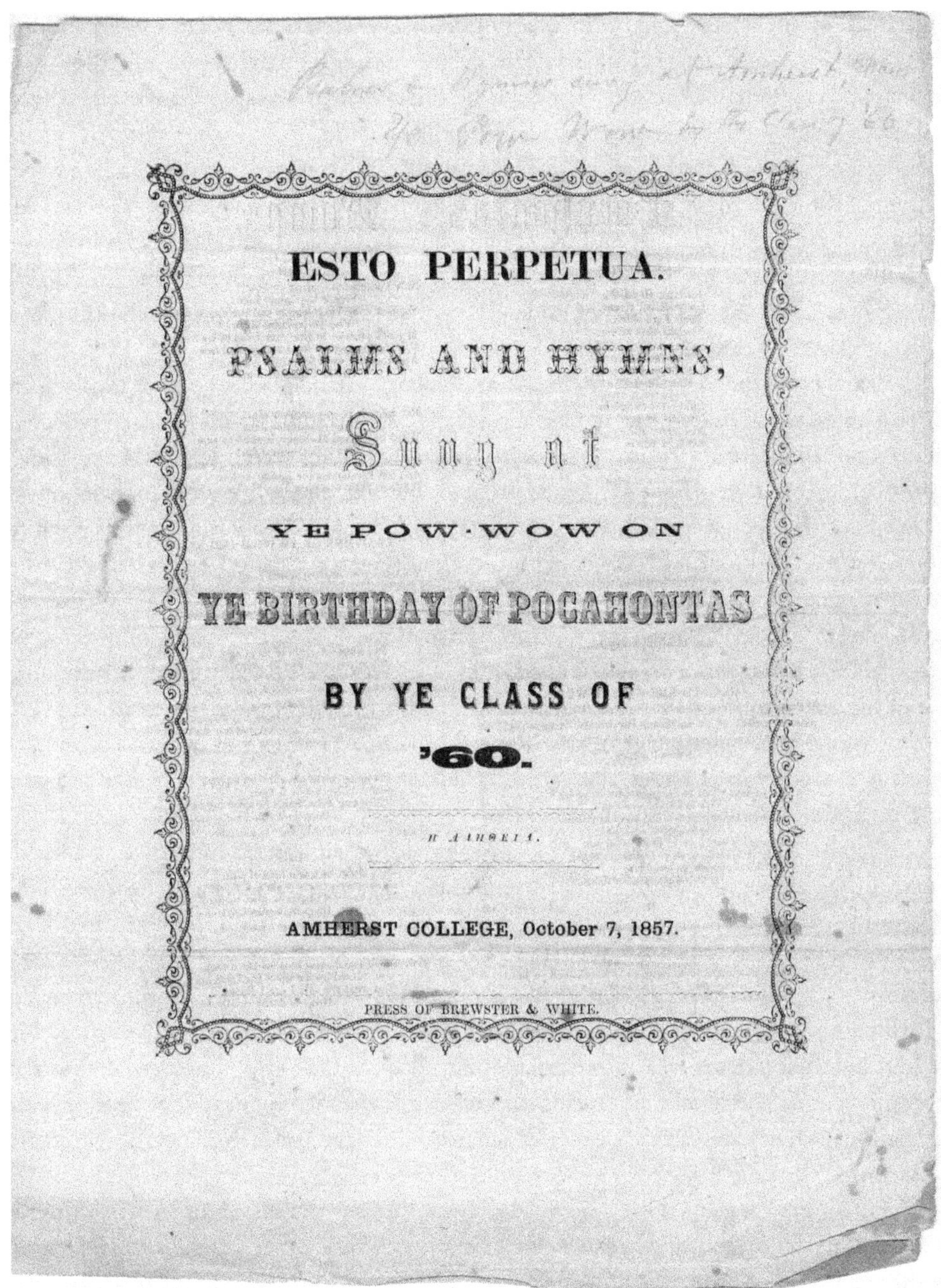

ESTO PERPETUA.

PSALMS AND HYMNS,

Sung at

YE POW·WOW ON

YE BIRTHDAY OF POCAHONTAS

BY YE CLASS OF

'60.

Η ΑΛΗΘΕΙΑ.

AMHERST COLLEGE, October 7, 1857.

PRESS OF BREWSTER & WHITE.

Figure 3. Sheet music for the student celebration, "Ye Pow Wow on Ye Birthday of Pocahontas By Ye Class of '60." Courtesy of Amherst College Archives.

South Seas" or "the wildest and most savage of the North American Indians," Seelye wrote, he required "a spiritual gift" that "quickens his desires and calls forth his toil." But a spiritual gift was not enough. "Christianized though he might be, [the Native American] would need, for a longer or shorter time, guardianship like a child."[36] In Seelye's view, the guarantees enshrined in Indian treaties were based on the "false view . . . that an Indian tribe, roaming in the wilderness . . . is a nation. . . . Indian tribes are not a nation," he observed, and humanitarians like himself and Ms. Hunt should oversee their progress. "It becomes us wisely and honestly to inquire," he added, "whether in order to give the Indian his real rights, it may not be necessary to set aside prerogatives to which he might technically and legally lay claim."[37]

The careers of the Amherst graduates and college officials who became involved in Native American affairs in the remaining decades of the nineteenth century reflected Walker's and Seelye's paternalism. Samuel Augustus Stoddard (1862) served as a missionary in Native American territory from 1874 to 1883. He, like his predecessors in the removal era, left his native congregation when conflicts arose between local tribes and the white "sooners" who called for an end to tribal protections. George Waldo Reed (1882) served a mission congregation at Little Eagle, South Dakota, on the Standing Rock Sioux Reservation from 1887 to 1927. Like Stoddard, Reed pursued the goal of converting native people to Christianity while deferring to the expansion of US controls. Reed argued that the purpose of his plains mission was "to stand firmly against heathen practices and to teach . . . people wisdom and righteousness." He devoted himself to training indigenous preachers as well as to traditional pastoral duties.[38] But he also endorsed the government's effort to bring "discipline" to the reservations.

The final—and perhaps best known—Amherst "humanitarian" in Native American affairs in the nineteenth century was Merrill Gates, who succeeded Julius Seelye as college president in 1890. Gates had been named to lead Rutgers University at the age of thirty-four. He was neither an alumnus nor a minister, but he shared his predecessor's commitment to paternalism in Native American affairs.[39] Gates supported the expansion of government boarding schools—institutions based on the assumption that separating children and their parents was an essential aspect of education—and the forced division of reservations into individual homesteads (a project spearheaded by President Seelye's congressional colleague, representative—later senator—Henry Dawes from nearby Pittsfield, Massachusetts).

Amherst's engagement with Native Hawaiians during the last decades of the nineteenth century followed the paternalistic trajectory of Walker, Seelye, and Gates. During the late nineteenth century, the kingdom of Hawai'i was in a state of almost perpetual crisis. An 1875 free-trade agreement with the United States removed all tariffs on Hawaiian sugar and brought unprecedented prosperity to the realm. But this new wealth fell almost entirely into the hands of the foreigners who owned the major sugar plantations in the kingdom and quickly deepened Hawai'i's entanglement with the United States. (Agreements with the United States during this period also granted it exclusive rights to Pearl Harbor.) Powerful businessmen like California's Claus Spreckels were able to use their

Figure 4. Julius Seelye (1824-1895), professor of philosophy and member of congress (1875-77), who served as Amherst's President from 1876 to 1890. Seelye wrote the introduction to Helen Hunt Jackson's polemic attack on the U.S. government's treatment of Indians, *A Century of Dishonor* (1881). Courtesy of Amherst College Archives.

sugar profits to expand their land holdings in the kingdom and erode the power of the local monarchs.

Sereno Bishop argued that Hawaiians were doomed to extinction unless they could bring American immigrants into the Kingdom. Their "only hope," Bishop wrote, "physically, socially and politically, is in renouncing the corroding vices of heathen life" and accepting in turn the fact that "Anglicized civilization . . . is inevitably to prevail. Their only good prospect," he continued, "is heartily to fall in line with it."[40]

While provocative and popular among local whites, *The Friend*'s opinions were inconsequential for Hawaiians until January 1893, when Queen Liliuokalani was forced to abdicate her throne by a group of white businessmen aided by US troops. When President Cleveland rejected the insurgents' request for immediate annexation, the rebels declared Hawai'i a Republic and dispatched lobbyists to Washington, DC, to plead their case. Bishop and his colleagues enthusiastically endorsed these actions. *The Friend*'s editor declared that Liliuokalani's "caprice and arrogance" had called forth "the wrath and power of the . . . long suffering whites."[41] Bishop was quick to cast the conflict as a struggle between civilization and barbarism. "Hawai'i is the final outpost of occidental civilization in the western hemisphere," he later wrote. "It immediately confronts the inferior but tenacious civilization of the Orient. Here the two forms meet and grapple."[42]

The annexation issue remained unresolved until 1898, when the outbreak of the Spanish-American War—and the acquisition of the Philippines—pushed Congress to make the island nation a US territory. Bishop was overjoyed—and unconcerned—that annexation would take place over the objections of the native community and without a democratic plebiscite. For him, the conflict with Spain was "the harbinger of the coming Kingdom of God."[43] And his friends back at Amherst seemed to agree; the college awarded him an honorary degree in 1896, a time when Queen Liliuokalani was actively campaigning for the restoration of her throne. Support for annexation was also strong among Bishop's Amherst colleagues who had emigrated to Hawai'i. These included Frank Alvan Hosmer (class of 1875) who, in 1890, left Great Barrington High School to assume the presidency of Oahu College (now Punahou School), an institution created in 1841 by Hawaiian missionaries for the education of their children.[44] Hosmer shared Bishop's disdain for the Hawaiian monarchy and his enthusiasm for annexation. Other Amherst graduates with similar views included Oliver Taylor Shipman (class of 1879), who became a rancher on the island of Hawai'i, and Arthur Burdette Ingalls (class of 1890), who taught briefly at Punahou before becoming a Honolulu customs officer following the imposition of American rule.

NATIVE PEOPLE AND AMHERST'S SECOND CENTURY

By the turn of the twentieth century, Amherst had aligned itself firmly with America's national institutions and global aspirations. College leaders had replaced the founding dream of bringing "pagan" nations to the gospel with a vision of Amherst graduates occupying the front ranks of the nation's professions and business enterprises. In their view, the native peoples under American rule, whether in North America or Hawai'i, were not citi-

Figure 5. Queen Liliuokalani (1838-1917). Liliuokalani was overthrown by American settlers and U.S. troops in January, 1893. This image from the frontispiece of *Hawaii's Story by Hawaii's Queen*, a plea for the restoration of her throne, published in 1898. Courtesy of the Newberry Library.

zens of nations ready to be "raised" to civilization, but backward folk in need of discipline and uplift.

But despite the fervent convictions of Francis Walker, Julius Seelye, and Sereno Bishop, progress and civilization are not static concepts. History continues. Definitions of progress evolve, as do ideas surrounding the meaning of conversion and civilization. And native peoples persist. Despite the United States' conquest of North America and Hawai'i, the indigenous peoples of those places sustained their communities and rejected the marginal roles assigned to them. Amherst's engagement with the native world during its second century illustrates these facts.

On September 28, 1913, the Dakota physician Dr. Charles A. Eastman came to Williston Hall to speak to the Amherst College Christian Association on the topic "Some Experiences Among the Indians of the Northwest." The most famous Native American of his day, Eastman had been born into a Minnesota Dakota band in 1858. His family converted to Christianity when he was a child and enrolled him in mission schools at an early age. A star student, he ultimately found his way to Dartmouth College (class of 1887) and Boston University Medical School, where he received his medical degree in 1890. Eastman began his career as a physician (he attended the victims of the Wounded Knee massacre in 1890), but he soon shifted to lecturing on Native American affairs.[45]

In 1903, Eastman, his wife Elaine Goodale, and their six children moved into a house on Belchertown Road in Amherst. "During his residence in Amherst," the *Boston Globe* reported, the Dakota physician "entered into the social and educational life of the town and his children have taken high rank in the school. His wife," the article noted, was "president of the Amherst Indian Association, composed of leading women of the different churches."[46] During his nearly two decades in Massachusetts, Eastman published memoirs and commentaries on native life and traveled widely as a speaker and advisor to organizations such as the YMCA, the Boy Scouts, and the US Office of Indian Affairs. Handsome, articulate, and deeply engaged with the task of defining Native Americans' place in modern American life, Eastman embraced the "civilization" promoted by Julius Seelye and Sereno Bishop, but he rejected the idea that Indian people lacked a rich cultural tradition. In a speech to the Harvard Union in 1906, for example, he declared, "The Indian is a true philosopher, and as such has never been surpassed by any representative from civilization."[47] His family's presence in the town of Amherst and his public career were tangible reminders of dispossession's legacy. And they demonstrated that native people were not backward, and had not disappeared.[48]

Eastman's appearance in Williston Hall may well have marked the beginning of a shift in Amherst College's view of the native world. The Dakota physician conceded that he had learned a great deal from "civilization," but he insisted in his lectures that Native American culture was "imbued with the spirit of worship." Jesus's humble and virtuous life, he often noted, suggested to many native people that the Christian savior must have been a Native American.[49] Claims like these occurred randomly and unpredictably in Amherst classrooms during the early years of the twentieth century, but they multiplied in number and intensity over the decades, as others questioned the fixed assumptions underpinning the public's faith in "Americanization."

Figure 6. Charles A. Eastman, the Dakota physician who lived with his family in Amherst in the early twentieth century and lectured on the college campus in 1913. Courtesy of the Newberry Library.

One thread of this process of reexamination can be traced through the career of the Amherst student who likely invited Dr. Eastman to campus: the president of the Christian Association Theodore A. Greene. The son of an Amherst-educated pastor (Frederick William Greene, 1882), Greene was an idealistic Christian activist. Soon after graduation, Theodore A. joined the staff of the Broadway Tabernacle, a Manhattan church founded by abolitionist Lewis Tappan that had long advocated progressive causes such as bringing women into the clergy, promoting world peace, and ending racial segregation. Greene went on to lead the First Church of Christ in New Britain, Connecticut, where he supported progressive causes and became active in the new ecumenical organizations such as the Federal Council of Churches (forerunner of the National Council of Churches) and the World Council of Churches. At the time of his death in 1951, he had just been appointed director of the Washington, DC, office of the National Council of Churches of Christ in the U.S.A.[50]

Reverend Greene's career ran parallel to the course of liberal Protestantism in the twentieth century. When he was its leader, the Amherst Christian Association encouraged students to work in schools and settlement houses to address the needs of immigrants and the poor. Over the ensuing decades, social justice issues drew the college's students and faculty away from orthodox religion. In the process, liberal Protestant leaders like Greene and others of his generation began to argue (as Charles Eastman had in his lectures and essays) that mission work either in the United States or overseas should focus on alleviating poverty and illiteracy rather than focusing solely on the gospel. Greene attended the World Council of Churches' founding congress in Amsterdam in 1948, and was also an early leader of Church World Service, an ecumenical organization dedicated to promoting economic self-help across the globe.[51]

Amherst's curriculum in the twentieth century also came to reflect this liberal Protestant approach to social progress. College catalogues indicate that courses of study gradually shifted from the fixed, classical curriculum of the late nineteenth century and toward disciplinary-focused programs that explored issues of economic injustice, international trade and politics, and racial and cultural differences, both inside and beyond the United States. As the number of academic departments grew, they began offering new majors in the social sciences—economics, political science, psychology—and encouraging explorations of literature and history that addressed the American past. In 1930, for example, a course in international relations covered the workings of the League of Nations, the World Court, and the Pan-American Union. Anthropology courses on human origins and the evolution of culture appeared in 1939, and in 1950, the history department offered its first course on westward expansion, one that proposed to trace the "influence of the frontier" and the "growth of American nationalism." Cultural anthropology was added in 1960, promising students an opportunity to develop projects on "the dynamics of culture change in modern times." These areas of study offered windows onto indigenous experiences and opportunities for reflection on the nature of the native world.

None of the curricular shifts in the twentieth century would have occurred without a corresponding shift in the community of students and teachers who shaped and experienced them. Over the first half of the twentieth century, the college became less identified with its sectarian Christian roots. Amendments to the college charter removed the requirement that clergymen sit on the board of trustees. Chapel services became less frequent, and then shifted to nondenominational topics before becoming nonreligious "assemblies" and then being dropped altogether. Changes in the size and composition of the faculty and student body occurred slowly before World War II, but in the prosperous decades following the conflict, growth and increased diversity came quickly. Enrollment grew from less than eight hundred in the 1920s to nearly two thousand by century's end. Most of these students came to Amherst from beyond New England, and a steady (and expanding) stream of them came from African American, Jewish, and Catholic families. After 1975, half of Amherst's students were female, and over the ensuing forty years, the college was led by Catholic, Jewish, and female presidents.[52]

As Amherst grew more cosmopolitan and its curriculum opened doors to student learning about contemporary events and a variety of cultural traditions, a place opened on campus for native people. That opening took place first in the classroom, as student interest and faculty curiosity introduced the native world to the college curriculum. During the 1960s, humanities and social science offerings addressed American racial minorities and issues of social justice, but it would take several years for courses on Native American subjects to be taught. Barry O'Connell, a member of the English faculty, first introduced native authors into his survey of American literature, and then in the early 1980s, he began offering courses focusing exclusively on indigenous topics. During that same decade, O'Connell and colleagues from Smith and the University of Massachusetts joined forces to organize a committee that, by the 2000s, had become the Five College Native American and Indigenous Studies Program.[53] The expanding presence of indigenous topics in the college curriculum also inspired the Robert Frost Library to acquire a major collection of books by Native American authors and to promote research in its archives.[54]

At the same time, Amherst sought to recruit members of previously under—or un—represented groups to Amherst. Two Native American scholars were appointed to the faculty in 2012, and the admissions office worked to bring Native Americans and Native Hawaiians to the student body. The presence of senior indigenous faculty members insured that native topics would continue to be present in the curriculum and that underrepresented students would continue to find themselves reflected in the life of the college. The numbers of native students remained relatively small, and their experiences were sometimes difficult, but the effort to make the college a welcome place for people from diverse backgrounds would continue.

AMHERST AND THE NATIVE WORLD

The story of the college's engagement with the native world reminds us that for Americans, indigenous history and United States history are deeply interwoven; neither thread can be fully understood without reference to the other. As an institution whose history extends back to the era of the nation's founding, Amherst College has been part of this interweaving process. The college's students, faculty, and administrators have encountered Native Americans and Native Hawaiians—both real and imagined—since the day of its found-

Figure 7. Amherst College Rare Book School, 2018. Drawing on the Amherst College Library's extraordinary Kim-Wait/Eisenberg Native American Literature Collection, a dozen scholars from institutions across the United States explored a variety of research and scholarly topics in a program led by Michael Kelly, head of Archives and Special Collections, and Professor Kiara Vigil of the Department of American Studies. Courtesy of Amherst College.

ing. And, as they sought to bring "enlightenment" to the lands, they discovered the reality of the native world, grasping eventually both its complexity and its potential.

NOTES

1. W.S. Tyler, *History of Amherst College During the First Half Century, 1821–1871* (Springfield, MA: Clark W. Bryan, 1873), 18. I am grateful to Michael Kelly, head of Archives and Special Collections at Amherst's Robert Frost Library, for his many suggestions and frequent help. I have also benefited from the editorial suggestions provided by fellow authors in this volume, especially Richard Teichgraeber III.

2. Claude Moore Fuess, *Amherst: The Story of a New England College* (Boston, MA: Little Brown, 1935), 12. The specter of past conflict was also reinforced by living local memories. In particular, Tyler refers to the college "officers" involvement with the dedication in 1835 of a monument to Englishmen killed near South Deerfield in King Philip's War (p. 19). In addition, the Abenaki family of Deerfield captive Eunice Williams visited the area—perhaps regularly. The latest report indicates a visit in the spring of 1838, which involved a meeting with "ten or twelve" Amherst students. See Elizabeth Huntington to Edward Huntington, May 20, 1838, Porter-Phelps-Huntington Papers, Porter-Phelps-Huntington House Museum, Hadley, Massachusetts. I am grateful to Lisa Brooks for sharing this document, which was transcribed and annotated by Amherst student Christine Miranda.

3. Ibid., Fuess, *Amherst*, 19. For more on the memory of Native American warfare in New England, see Christine DeLucia, *Memory Lands: King Philip's War and the Place of Violence in the Northeast* (New Haven, CT: Yale University Press, 2018), especially chpt. 5.

4. For an account of the American Protestants' global ambitions at this time, see Emily Conroy-Krutz, *Christian Imperialism: Converting the World in the Early Republic* (Ithaca, NY: Cornell University Press, 2015).

5. For more on the idea of "making room" for native history in the American past, see Philip J. Deloria, K. Tsianina Lomawaima, Bryan McKinley Jones Brayboy, Mark N. Trahant, Loren Ghiglione, et al., "Unfolding Futures: Indigenous Ways of Knowing for the Twenty-First Century," *Daedalus* 147, no. 2 (Spring 2018): 14.

6. See W. S. Tyler, *History*, 77–79. Vattel was Swiss. The first English edition of *Laws* appeared in 1760, but interestingly, an American edition was published in Northampton in 1820.

7. Emer de Vattel, *The Law of Nations* (Northampton, MA: S. Butler, 1820), 3.

8. Vattel, *Law of Nations*, 12. Vattel explained: "To establish on a solid foundation the obligations and laws of nations, is the design of this work. The *law of nations is the science of the law subsisting between nations and states, and of the obligations that flow from it*" (emphasis in original), 46.

9. Vattel, 13.

10. Vattel, 99.

11. Vattel, 218.

12. See Conroy-Krutz, *Christian Imperialism*, especially 19–29. Native American communities were never uniform in their outlook. There were dissenting groups within the Cherokees, Senecas, and others who opposed the missionaries' message.

13. *Annals of Amherst College: The Soil, The Seed, The Sowers* (Northamphton, MA: Trumbull and Gere, 1860), 3.

14. Reuben Tinker, *Ought I To Become a Missionary?* (Dedham, MA: L. Powers, 1831), 1.

15. Rev. Samuel Chenery Damon (class of 1836) also served in Hawai'i from 1842 until his death in 1885 but was not an AABCFM missionary. As pastor of the Seaman's Chapel in Honolulu, Damon devoted himself to temperance causes and preaching to a largely white congregation.

16. Caroline Parker Green, "Benjamin Wyman and Mary Elizabeth Parker," *The Friend* (May 1933), 106.

17. *Memoirs of American Missionaries Formerly Connected with the Society of Inquiry Respecting Missions in the Andover Theological Seminary* (Boston, MA: Pierce and Parker, 1833), 189.

18. *Annual Report of the ABCFM* (Boston, MA: Crocker and Brewster, 1839), 153; and *Memiors of American Missionaries*, 187.

19. "Daniel D. Hitchcock" file, Amherst College Archives, Amherst College, Amherst, MA.

20. For a description of Evarts and his campaign against removal, see Francis P. Prucha, *The Great Father* (Lincoln: University of Nebraska Press, 1983), 200–8.

21. *Boston Christian Register* 9, no. 5 (January 30, 1830).

22. For a recent overview of the removal process in both the North and the South, see Jeffrey Ostler, *Surviving Genocide: Native Nations and the United States from the American Revolution to Bleeding Kansas* (New Haven, CT: Yale University Press, 2019), chpts. eight and nine.

23. ABCFM, *Annual Report*, 1840, 188.

24. ABCFM, *Annual Report*, 1841 (Boston, MA: Crocker and Brewster), 48.

25. ABCFM, *Annual Report*, 1843 (Boston, MA: Crocker and Brewster), 56. The pleas for more North American missionaries continued. Among the most poignant came in 1849 when the ABCFM leadership noted that "the melancholy fact that [the Native Americans] are melting away . . . urges us to

evangelize the wasted and wasting tribes as quickly as possible. We owe them a great debt; and if, in the inscrutable providence of God, they must perish from off the earth, those who have entered into their inheritance are surely bound to do everything in their power to prepare them for, and aid them on their way to that rich and glorious inheritance of the saints in light, from which they can never be expelled." See ABCFM, *Annual Report*, 1849 (Boston, MA: T. R. Marvin), 69.

26. ABCFM, *Annual Report*, 1851 (Boston, MA: T. R. Marvin), 163.

27. For a fuller treatment of Richards's career and the complexities of Hawaiian national politics in the early nineteenth century, see Noelani Arista, *The Kingdom and the Republic: Sovereign Hawai'i and the Early United States* (Philadelphia: University of Pennsylvania Press, 2019).

28. Rufus Anderson, *The Hawaiian Islands: Progress and Condition Under Missionary Labors*, 3rd ed. (Boston, MA: Gould and Lincoln, 1865), 325–26, 328. The local churches became self-supporting, but the ABCFM supported the pensions of retired Hawaiian missionaries.

29. *The Friend* 47, no. 10 (1889), 79; and 45, no. 9 (1887), 71.

30. See Fuess, *Amherst*,151–55.

31. W. S. Tyler wrote in his *History* that "if they only carry their Christian principles with them into the secular professions and the high places of influence in the state as well as the church, . . . it is a result which would gladden the hearts even of those good men who founded the institution in prayer and faith chiefly for the education of ministers" (645).

32. Jean Baptiste Say, *A Treatise on Political Economy* (Philadelphia, PA: John Gregg, 1830). Say shared Vattel's belief in the benevolent effects of increased trade, but he was not concerned with international law or the advancement of justice. "Wealth," he wrote, "is essentially independent of political organization" (ix).

33. Thanks to Michael Kelly for discovering "Esto Perpetuia. Psalms and Hymns Sung at Ye Pow Wow on Ye Birthday of Pocahontas By Ye Class of 1860," Amherst College, October 7, 1857. For debates on campus, see "Hitchcock Society of Inquiry," March 14, 1890: "Has the treatment of the Indian by the U.S. been more inhuman than that of the Irishman by England?" "The Mountain Meadow Massacre," 1877.

34. "The War Dance," *Amherst Magazine*, May 1, 1862, 408.

35. *Annual Report of the Commissioner of Indian Affairs*, 1872, reprinted in F. P. Prucha, *Documents of United States Indian Policy*, 3rd ed. (Lincoln: University of Nebraska Press, 2000), 139.

36. Julius Seelye, "Introduction," *Helen Hunt Jackson, A Century of Dishonor* (New York: Harper Brothers, 1881), 1, 2, 3.

37. Seelve, "Introduction," 4, 5. It is striking that Seelye's reasoning followed so closely the rationale for removal that had been put forward by Andrew Jackson and his supporters.

38. Rev. G. W. Reed, "Among the Indians: Missionary Work in Out-Stations," American Missionary Association, Congregational Rooms, Fourth Avenue and Twenty Second Street, New York, n.d., 6. Amherst College Special Collections, Amherst College, Amherst, MA. Amherst College Special Collections also contains a remarkable letter from Reed to his classmate W. H. Thompson, written in the immediate aftermath of the killing of Sitting Bull on the Standing Rock Sioux Reservation. Reed observed that the elimination of "the old rascal" had prevented a wider Native American war. See George W. Reed to W. H. Thompson, December 31, 1890.

39. Despite his meteoric rise, Gates had a troubled tenure at Amherst. He became embroiled in conflicts with both the faculty and student body and eventually lost the confidence of the board of trustees. He resigned in 1899, replaced by alumnus (and minister) George Harris of the class of 1866.

40. *The Friend* 45, no. 8 (1887), 63.

41. *The Friend* 51, no. 2 (1893), 9.

42. *The Friend* 55, no. 10 (1897), 76.

43. *The Friend* 56, no. 5 (1898), 33. The undemocratic aspects of the annexation are explored in James L. Haley, *Captive Paradise: A History of Hawai'i* (New York: St. Martin's, 2014), chpt. 19. See also Noenoe Silva, *Aloha Betrayed: Native Hawaiian Resistance to American Colonialism* (Durham, NC: Duke University Press, 2004).

44. While the school was not officially restricted to whites (it admitted a small number of children of Hawaiian elites), its students were largely drawn from Protestant families and the children of the American business community.

45. See *Annual Report of the Amherst College Christian Association*, 1913–1914, 10. The previous year's report thanked "Dr. C. E. Eastman" for speaking at one of the association's Sunday evening meetings. The report added that its Sunday gatherings were "thrown into open discussion" after presentations by speakers (one of whom was President Meiklejohn). It also noted that based on the success of these lively meetings, the group would devote one Sunday per month in the coming year to "a forum on religious and ethical questions appertaining to college life." Presumably, Eastman's formal lecture in September 1913 came as a result from his earlier appearance before the group. See *Annual Report*, 1912–1913, 7.

46. "Dr. Eastman Returns," *Boston Globe*, October 25, 1910, p. 2.

47. "Talks of the Real Indian," *Boston Globe*, October 24, 1906.

48. See the *Hartford Courant*, February 15, 1908, "Training of the Young Indians," p.2.

49. See Charles Eastman, "Civilization as Preached and Practiced," quoted in Frederick E. Hoxie, *Talking Back to Civilization: Indian Voices from the Progressive Era* (New York: Bedford/St Martin's, 2001), 76.

50. "Rev. Dr. T. Greene Is Dead in Capital," *New York Times*, June 10, 1951.

51. The shift in Protestant thinking during the decades encompassed by Theodore A. Greene's career is cogently summarized in David A. Hollinger, *Protestants Abroad: How Missionaries Tried to Change the World but Changed America* (Princeton, NJ: Princeton University Press, 2017). Hollinger's survey traces the powerful role of missionaries and missionary children in the twentieth century's reexamination of America's role in the world. These Protestant church men and women were among the leading critics of US policy in Asia, Latin America, and the Middle East, often putting them at odds with political interests, military officials, and more conservative evangelical Christians. While Theodore A. Greene traveled below Professor Hollinger's radar, he was sympathetic to the cosmopolitan trend the historian describes. At the time of his death, Greene was involved in a number of ecumenical Protestant organizations, among them the ABCFM, the organization that had dispatched missionaries to Native American communities and to Hawai'i in the first decades of the nineteenth century, which was increasingly engaged with social justice and economic reform as well as evangelism.

52. One of the faculty members who enthusiastically supported the growing diversity of the Amherst campus and student body in the second half of the twentieth century was Theodore P. Greene (class of 1943), the son of Charles Eastman's campus host, Theodore A. Greene.

53. In 1992, Professor O'Connell became the first Amherst faculty member to make a significant scholarly contribution to the field of Native studies when he published *On Our Own Ground: The Complete Writings of William Apess, A Pequot* (Amherst: University of Massachusetts Press). Presented as an edited collection of Apess's writing, the volume includes extensive annotations and an introduction that offers a comprehensive view of the author's life.

54. The Kim-Wait/Eisenberg Native American Literature Collection is housed in Amherst's Robert Frost Library and contains works produced from the eighteenth century to the present.

Niijima Jō, the Dōshisha, and the Christian Liberal Arts in Meiji Japan

Trent Maxey

Amherst graduates from 1909 onward will have seen the portrait of Niijima Jō hanging in Johnson Chapel.[1] A gift from his graduating class of 1870, the portrait commemorates the first Japanese student to have graduated from a Western institution of higher education. It has also connected Amherst College to its sister institution in Kyoto, Dōshisha University. Founded by Niijima in 1875, the Dōshisha[2] began with eight students, and today enrolls over thirty thousand students in fourteen undergraduate divisions and eighteen graduate programs. This does not include the separate Dōshisha Women's College and twelve other secondary and primary schools. From its founding to this day, the Dōshisha has remained a Christian school in a way Amherst College has not.

In part, the Dōshisha returns us to the context of Amherst College's early relationship to Christian missions. As Gary Kornblith and David W. Wills point out in this volume, Amherst produced a significant number of foreign missionaries during its first half-century. According to *The Amherst Student* in 1879, "A quarter of all the foreign missionaries sent out by the American Board are graduates of Amherst College."[3] Niijima Jō found his way to Amherst in part because of alumni like Elija Coleman Bridgman, the first missionary sent to China by the American Board of Commissioners for Foreign Missions. (See K. Ian Shin's chapter in this volume.) There he oversaw the translation of English-language books into Chinese, including his own *Short Account of the United States of America*, the very book that first sparked a young Niijima's interest in the United States and Christianity.[4]

The evident role Christian missions played in linking Niijima to Amherst College should not suggest, however, that he and the school he established in Japan were mere products of American missionary zeal. Rather, the fact that the Dōshisha maintains its Christian identity more clearly to this day than Amherst does tells us less about American Christian missions than it does about private higher education as it took shape in Meiji-era Japan (1868–1912). Niijima labored to introduce the liberal arts to Japan because he believed them to be vital for educating men and women capable of independent thought and guided by moral conscience. The avowedly Christian character of Niijima's vision ensured that his endeavor faced significant opposition in Japan, but it was precisely the distance and therefore independence that Christianity created between Dōshisha and state-sponsored forms of education that mattered to Niijima and his successors. The liberal arts sustained academic independence in Meiji-era Japan precisely because it was Christian, not in spite of it.

TO AMERICA

Arthur Hardy's *The Life and Letters of Joseph Hardy Neesima* (1891) and Jerome Davis's *A Sketch of the Life of Rev. Joseph Hardy Neesima* (1894) both provide vivid accounts, often in Niijima's own hand, of his life.[5] Rather than poorly imitate the oft-told story of Niijima's dramatic decision to stow away on an American merchant ship in pursuit of Western education, the focus here is on the context that motivated Niijima to risk capital punishment and escape Japan in 1864. Niijima Shimeta was born in 1843, the eldest son of a retainer to the daimyo lord of Annaka and part of the 8 percent or so of the population that belonged to the samurai estate. He was ten when Commodore Matthew Perry and a squadron of American naval ships steamed into Edo Bay in 1853 to demand an end to the Tokugawa shogunate's strict limitations on foreign contact. The so-called unequal treaties exchanged in 1858 between the shogun and Western powers opened a number of ports, including Yokohama, Nagasaki, and Hakodate granting extraterritoriality to foreign nationals. The West's intimidating technological power and the ensuing influx of new information quickly cast doubt upon the viability of the two-and-a-half-century-old Tokugawa polity, organized around predominantly hereditary status distinctions and designed to resist any threat to stability.

Niijima belonged to a generation of young samurai galvanized by the apparent weakness of the Tokugawa shogunate. He and others like him sought knowledge about the wider world in order to reform and strengthen Japan against the threat of colonization. At the age of thirteen, Niijima took up *Rangaku*, or Dutch studies, and was reading texts on astronomy and physics in Dutch by age seventeen. When the shogunate opened its own naval academy, Niijima enrolled, spending time in the company of John Manjirō, a castaway who had been rescued by an American whaler, and spent his youth in Fairhaven before returning to Japan in 1851. In 1863, Niijima abandoned his study of Dutch in favor of English.[6]

In his thirst for knowledge, Niijima encountered not only the Chinese translation of Bridgman's *Short Account of the United States of America*, but also Christianity. Newly opened treaty ports facilitated a largely unregulated influx of information, including Christian evangelical literature. By one estimate, over eight hundred Christian titles written in Chinese made their way into Japan by 1867. Bridgman's volume introduced the history of the United States, its Constitution, and social institutions, including public education and correctional institutions. Strikingly, the list of young samurai who read and were influenced by Bridgman's *Short Account* is a veritable who's who of late-Tokugawa activists.[7] The proposition that all were created equal and therefore the United States rejected hereditary rule and elected its president crystalized Niijima's frustration with the Tokugawa order, especially his hereditary obligations to his *daimyo*—what he later referred to as "my prince's square enclosure."[8] Even though breaking the proscription against foreign travel remained a capital offense, and leaving the service of one's lord without leave was also punishable, Niijima chose to risk not only his own life but also the livelihood of his family in order to escape. He secreted himself, with the captain's blessing, aboard an American merchant ship in Hakodate.[9] By the time he arrived in Boston a year later, he had his English name, Joe, and had exchanged one of his two swords for a Chinese New Testament.[10]

Niijima was not the only young samurai to study abroad. The Tokugawa shogunate sent students to the Netherlands in 1862, the domains of Satsuma and Chōshū each sent students to Britain between 1863 and 1865, and the new Meiji government sent significant numbers of students abroad after 1868. In each case, the students were expected to acquire the expertise to rapidly transform Japan's institutions, economy, and, above all, military. These students received government funds in exchange for their loyalty and commitment to state priorities; they promised not to convert to Christianity and studied only the subjects identified by their superiors as priorities. Niijima, by contrast, struck out on his own and, though supported by benefactors in the United States, was completely independent of authorities in Japan. He studied what he wanted without answering to anyone back in Japan. Keenly aware of and proud of this distinction, Niijima would later draw on it to argue for the importance of private higher education in Japan.

Niijima reached Boston in July 1865, just three months after Abraham Lincoln's assassination. The ship's owner, Alpheus Hardy and his wife, moved by Niijima's letter in poor but fervent English declaring his desire for an education, decided to sponsor his education, first at Phillips Academy and then at Amherst College, where Hardy was a trustee.[11] Niijima adopted the name Joseph Hardy Neesima. During his nearly two years at Phillips Academy, Niijima drank deeply from the well of Puritan pietism, even as it was about to fade in Gilded Age America.[12] Phillips Academy reinforced this influence with its strict code of conduct, which prohibited playing cards, dancing, smoking, and even the reading of novels.[13] Niijima was baptized in the chapel of Andover Theological Seminary on December 30, 1866.

Nijjima deepened his close association of education with Christian spiritual formation during his time at Amherst College, beginning in the fall of 1867. Though focusing his studies on the sciences, Niijima was deeply influenced by Julius Seelye, then-professor of mental and moral philosophy and an ordained minister. Amherst had witnessed the last of its great Christian revivals in the academic year prior to Niijima's matriculation, and the growth of one's Christian faith was still emphasized on campus.[14] Of the 247 students at the college during the 1868 to 1869 school year, eighty-nine were preparing for ministry and twenty-four were "looking forward to [the] mission field."[15] Niijima immediately joined the "missionary band."[16] The pietistic brand of Christianity that Niijima imbibed emphasized a moral individualism that would shape his subsequent educational vision. Texts like Brown University president Francis Wayland's *The Elements of Moral Science* (1835) taught Niijima that "the individual and his intensions, rather than the group, bore the onus of social responsibility."[17] The fundamental purpose of education, therefore, was to shape the moral character of individuals so that they could serve the common good. Seelye summarized this perspective in his response to a solicitation from the Japanese diplomatic representative in Washington, DC. Asked for advice regarding the best form of education a reforming Japan should adopt, Seelye wrote: "Indeed, morality will only spring from some sort of a religious inspiration, and, unless our schools and educational influences can be penetrated by a religious spirit, they will not make men virtuous, however extensive their culture."[18] Niijima, who suffered from frequent illness, spent a considerable amount of his time recuperating in the Seelye household, and counted Seelye as a lifelong mentor. Influenced by Seelye, among others, Niijima came to individual self-reform through Christian education as the answer to the challenge of reforming Japan into a civilization capable of surviving as an independent nation.[19] A merely technical education would not suffice.

TO A NEW JAPAN

A new oligarchic government, ruling in the name of a restored emperor, replaced the stifling Tokugawa polity that Niijima had escaped following the so-called Meiji Renovation (*Meiji Ishin*) of 1868. The new government declared its principal aims in April of that year with a five-article charter oath issued in the emperor's name:

1. Deliberative assemblies shall be widely established and all matters decided by open discussion.
2. All classes, high and low, shall be united in vigorously carrying out the administration of affairs of state.
3. The common people, no less than the civil and military officials, shall all be allowed to pursue their own calling so that there may be no discontent.
4. Evil customs of the past shall be broken off and everything based upon the just laws of Nature.
5. Knowledge shall be sought throughout the world so as to strengthen the foundation of imperial rule.[20]

Though vague, the promise to dismantle the hereditary constraints on occupations, the rejection of "evil customs of the past," and the global pursuit of knowledge answered the frustrations of a generation of young samurai who had, like Niijima, felt stymied by the old order. A tangible expression of the new government's willingness to radically reform Japan came in the form of the Iwakura Embassy in late 1871. Having successfully dismantled the last institutional vestiges of daimyo autonomy, the new government dispatched a full one-half of its leadership, accompanied by a large number of students, to the United States and Europe. The mission's firsthand observations of Western institutions and technologies shaped the direction of government reforms in Japan for a generation.[21] The arrival of the Iwakura Embassy in the United States afforded Niijima an opportunity to legalize his status as a Japanese subject and to forge close personal ties with the new political leadership. Niijima aided the mission's investigation of Western systems of education. That experience, while valuable in itself, also foregrounded the distance between Niijima's nascent conception of a private Christian education and the vision of a centralized public education that the mission took away from its travels.

Having graduated from Amherst College with a bachelor of science degree in 1870, Niijima had commenced his seminary training at Andover when Mori Arinori, the Japanese chargé d'affaires in Washington, DC, summoned him to assist the Iwakura Embassy. While he complied, Niijima was intent on preserving his independence as a practicing Christian. The new government had formally inherited the Tokugawa-era proscription of Christianity within Japan, and the embassy met with considerable protest over the persecution of underground Catholics who had resurfaced in the Nagasaki region in the late 1850s.[22] Japanese students sponsored by the government were required to promise not to convert to Christianity.

For Niijima, the ability to serve the higher moral cause of his faith was the goal of the independence and freedom, which mattered so much to him.[23] His famous decision not to bow when introduced to Tanaka Fujimaro, the commissioner of education with the Iwakura Embassy, expressed his demand to be treated as an equal and free individual.[24] During the year he spent accompanying Tanaka and the embassy, Niijima refused to travel on the sabbath and made no secret of his desire to evangelize in Japan.[25] Even though they had formed a close working relationship, when Tanaka pressed him to abandon his theological studies and enter government service, Niijima firmly declined.[26]

Tanaka's formal report on the education systems of the United States and Europe was written with Niijima's assistance and shaped educational policy through the 1870s in Japan. Tanaka stressed the need for a practical and rational education, separated from religion and publicly controlled by the state. For example, Tanaka observed at the outset his general conclusion regarding the role of religion in education: "Countries that leave the method of education in the hands of commoners and priests (*heimin sōryo*), leaving the government outside of it, have lost the primary path to developing human knowledge, speeding the progress of civilization, and placing their country ahead of others."[27] Tanaka underscored the lesson that clergy impeded the proper purpose of education—advancing knowledge in the service of progress—by citing specific examples he observed in the United States and Europe. New England, for example, placed the administration of its schools in the hands of the government, thus progressing beyond the "shame of slavery." British education, by contrast, had been held back by the dominance of the clergy and divisions based on sectarian affiliation. Hence, the 1870 education law introduced fundamental changes intended to strengthen nonclerical control over education.[28] Niijima's belief in a private Christian education would have to contend with this secularist approach to education.[29]

Having completed his service to the Iwakura embassy, Niijima Jō graduated from Andover Theological Seminar in 1874 and was ordained in the Congregational Church. He was also made a corresponding missionary with the American Board of Commissioners for Foreign Missions, among the first and the largest Protestant mission organizations in the United States.[30] The first hint that Niijima's vision of Christian service in Japan would focus on education came at the American Board's annual meeting in Rutland, Vermont, that year. Niijima wanted to ask for support in building a Christian school in Japan but was discouraged from doing so, even by Alpheus Hardy, his benefactor and a member of the American Board. The board had long prioritized evangelism and the training of evangelists over broader educational enterprises.[31] Niijima nonetheless persisted and made an impassioned appeal: "The church in Kobe has no educational institution, but she must have something of the kind. It is repulsive to the Japanese mind to beg, but I fear we must beg for that, for Christ says, ask and ye shall receive. Therefore I ask you to give help enough to start this training institution, to raise up teachers and preachers to help some 33,000,000 people."[32] Those in attendance were moved to pledge nearly $5,000 in support of Niijima's school. An important ambiguity existed as to precisely what kind of school Niijima envisioned in his appeal; was it a liberal arts college on the model of Amherst College or closer to the evangelical training schools the American Board were accustomed to supporting?[33] The gloss of his speech quoted above refers to a "training school," which was the term the American Board would use until the late 1880s, indicating that the mission conceived of the school as an institution dedicated to training clergy and evangelists. Niijima would later claim that he envisioned something different, a school that harnessed Christianity in the service of a broader educational mission. The imprecision would create friction between Niijima and the American Board in the years ahead, but also created room for him to maneuver on the ground in Japan.

When Niijima landed in the treaty port of Kobe in late 1874, a little more than ten years after his illicit escape from Japan, he confronted two challenges. One the one hand, he would be introducing Christian education to a country with strong anti-Christian sentiments and a government intent on centralizing educational regulations. On the other hand, he would have to contend with the American Board and its missionaries, who did not share his vision for an expansive, and expensive, form of Christian liberal arts. Even though these challenges caused tremendous difficulties for Niijima, and certainly exacerbated his already poor health, one could argue that Niijima succeeded in laying the foundation for the Dōshisha by playing one off of the other.

TO KYOTO

To be clear, Niijima was a fervent evangelist as well as an educator, and the Congregational Church in Japan, the *Kumiai Kyōkai*, grew to be one of the largest Protestant denominations in Japan, in part through his efforts. He spent, for example, his first three weeks back in Japan visiting his parents in Annaka, Gunma Prefecture, on the northwest edge of the Kantō Plains, where he planted the seeds of what would become the Annaka Congregational Church and one of the most thoroughly evangelized regions in Japan.[34] Open and direct evangelism was still difficult in the early 1870s, however. Although the government had ceased openly prohibiting Christianity in 1873, administrative and social resistance continued to frustrate missionary activities.[35] Education provided one path for evangelism. Some missionaries accepted teaching posts in public educational institutions, relying on proximity to indirectly expose young students to Christianity. Other missionaries opened their own modest, private language schools to achieve the same ends. Niijima and his American Board colleagues attempted to do the same by opening a school in Ōsaka, near the foreign settlement, but the governor refused to grant permission for fear of anti-Christian agitation. Kyoto, the former imperial capital, surfaced as an alternate location for the school when Niijima made the acquaintance of one Yamamoto Kakuma.

A man of considerable intellect, Yamamoto had risen to be a consultant to the governor of Kyoto, Uemura Masanao, despite having fought against the new government during the brief civil war that preceded the Meiji Renovation. A Chinese text on Christianity had drawn Yamamoto to Christianity and paved the way for his support of Niijima's educational vision.[36] Without Yamamoto, the Dōshisha would never have been founded, and it would not have been located in Kyoto. The combined influence of Yamamoto with Governor Uemura in Kyoto, and Niijima's direct appeals to Tanaka, then serving in the Ministry of Education in Tokyo, ultimately secured the permission he needed to found a private English school in Kyoto, a center of Buddhist opposition to Christian evangelism.[37]

Despite its distance from the legal security of the treaty ports, Kyoto promised Niijima and his missionary colleagues a base of operations in the cultural heart of Japan. Founded in 794, the ancient capital hosted head temples for most Buddhist sects as well as prominent Shinto shrines. The symbolic value of locating a Christian school there escaped no one. Consequently, resistance, overt and covert, was palpable, and receiving dispensation for American Board missionaries to reside in Kyoto as faculty of the new school proved tremendously difficult. Foreign citizens needed special permission to reside outside the treaty ports, and it took all of Yamamoto and Niijima's combined influence with officials to finally secure permission for Jerome Davis and his family to reside in Kyoto. Legal restrictions on property ownership by foreign entities were circumvented by forming a holding company, named the Dōshisha, which means "the company of shared purpose," with Niijima and Yamamoto as the nominal trustees.[38] To this company, Yamamoto arranged the sale of 5.5 acres of land for $550. This land, formerly the grounds of the Kyoto estate of the lord of Satsuma and located adjacent to Sōkokuji, a major Rinzai Zen temple, stood in the heart of Kyoto, directly north of the former imperial palace grounds. The American Board, still skeptical about the viability of a training school in the old capital, did not immediately release funds to build on those grounds. Still, by the fall of 1875, Niijima and Davis were ready to open the Dōshisha English School in rented buildings.

The Dōshisha English School formally opened on November 9, 1875, with eight students (it would grow to forty students by the next spring).[39] The school promised to teach a wide range of subjects, including English, Chinese studies, mathematics, surveying, geography, astronomy, physics, anatomy, chemistry, geology, world history, international law, economics, and ethics.[40] From its inception, the school was caught between the American Board's focus on Christian evangelism over education and the demands of government regulations. For example, when Niijima sought approval to hire two additional American Board missionaries as faculty for the school that year, the governor resisted, citing ongoing protests from Buddhists in the city. The governor relented only when Niijima promised that the school would not teach Christianity except "under the name of moral science." Although the missionaries were to be allowed to preach in their private homes, the removal of Christianity from the curriculum of the school from the outset precipitated a crisis between Niijima and the American Board.[41]

On the one hand, in the spring of 1876, the American Board missionaries voted to erect two buildings that combined the function of dormitory, classrooms, chapel, and library.[42] But even when the buildings were complete, some missionaries still wanted to reject Niijima's compromise with the governor, even if that meant being driven out of Kyoto altogether. Niijima weathered this storm by deciding to dedicate the new buildings with a Christian service in the chapel and to begin teaching theological courses, except for biblical exegesis, on campus.[43] The deep trust that the American Board felt toward Niijima, who was nearly one of their own, allowed him to weather this and similar storms. That trust also endowed the Dōshisha with an important measure of independence from the board that meant the school was never fully a "mission school" under the control of foreign missionaries.[44]

The arrival of a group of students in the fall of 1876 dramatically impacted the character and future direction of the Dōshisha and furthered its development of the Christian liberal arts. The so-called Kumamoto Band was a group of young men, almost all former samurai, who had studied under captain Leroy Lansing Janes, an American army veteran hired to teach at the Kumamoto Yōgakkō, a school created in 1871 to teach Western military science. Thirty-five students, drawn to Christianity by Janes's moral discipline, famously climbed Mount Hanaoka on Sunday January 30, 1876, to hold a service and sign a declaration of their faith.[45] This public act of Christian conversion led to the immediate closure of the Kumamoto school. Janes reached out to Davis to secure the students' admission to the Dōshisha, where they could continue their education with their Christian faith preserved.[46]

The significance of this influx of students for the future of Niijima's school is difficult to exaggerate. Its members included four future presidents of the Dōshisha, future financiers and industrialists, educators, and prominent Protestant Christian leaders.[47] Tokutomi Sohō is most famous for his long and prominent career as a journalist while Miyagawa Tsuneteru, Ebina Danjō, and Kozaki Hiromichi are counted among the founding fathers of the Congregational Church in Japan, and were prominent public intellectuals in their own right.[48] The students were, however, less than impressed with the school that greeted them. Kozaki Hiromichi famously recalled their first impressions of the Dōshisha when they arrived:

> The school consisted at that time of only two small houses, with no equipment to speak of, and, if the Yōgakkō boys and four or five others be excepted, the rest were all more or less transient students. With no fixed rules or regulations, without a fixed course of study, and with little order or discipline, the school was in a condition exactly similar to the old-time private schools for the study of Chinese. Among the students were found ex-policemen, blind masseurs, and many others with no preparatory education of any sort, who had flocked to the school through the introduction of missionaries. [As they formed the larger part of the students,] their disorderliness and irregularities were beyond imagination, and we who had been trained at the Yōgakkō where order was kept, could not help being surprised and disappointed.[49]

Keenly independent and strong-willed, the young men of the Kumamoto Band took Janes's admonition to heart to "make it the perfect place you desire," and set about fashioning the Dōshisha in their image.[50] They introduced strict rules, requiring all students to abstain from alcohol, tobacco, and gambling. Mandatory chapel attendance was enforced. These standards emphasized self-regulation, equality, and independence among the students, ideals that Niijima shared but could not enforce by himself.

Improving the academic standards of the Dōshisha proved more challenging for the Kumamoto Band. They chafed at the low quality of instruction and frequently challenged the faculty in class, including Niijima. Tokutomi, who left the Dōshisha prior to graduation but maintained close ties to Niijima and the school, later observed that Niijima was a man of heart if not of intelligence.[51] Theological instruction was a particular bone of contention. A course of theological studies was created separate from the English school to accommodate the Kumamoto Band's interest in entering the ministry.[52] They resented, however, the naïve, literalist interpretation of the Bible and the plain pietism taught by the American Board missionaries. The Kumamoto Band were more interested in liberal theological currents, especially higher criticism. This openness toward Unitarianism and the embrace of evolutionary theory created an important fault line separating many Japanese Christian leaders, including Kozaki Hiromichi and Ebina Danjō, from their missionary counterparts. It also brought into relief the diverging visions of Christian education at the Dōshisha. The Kumamoto Band amplified Niijima's commitment to a broad educational institution by demanding a version of Christianity that was open to scholarly inquiry.[53]

The Dōshisha bore the stamp of the Kumamoto Band by the time they graduated as its first class in 1879. Christian service had become a prominent element of campus life; traveling between school terms, members of the Kumamoto Band had planted a number of Congregational churches in Okayama, Nara, Hikone, Ōtsu, Osaka, and Annaka.[54] The anniversary of the Kumamoto Band's conversion on Mount Hanaoka was celebrated by the Dōshisha student body, at least until Niijima's death.[55] They had also collaborated with Niijima to establish a clear program of secular studies modeled after the Yōgakko. The first year was devoted solely to the study of English, and the following four years were given over to a balanced study of the sciences and humanities.[56] Abe Isoo, later a prominent Christian socialist, recalls that when he arrived at the Dōshisha in 1879, its residential character distinguished the school from others in Japan. The one hundred and twenty to one hundred and thirty students lived a life strictly regimented by rules they voluntarily adopted. Classes were held in the mornings, five days a week. This allowed students significant amounts of independent study. Upper-classmen tutored the under-classmen, and Abe boasted that the level of English mastery among Dōshisha students was impressively high.[57]

1879 also proved a pivotal year in redefining the relationship between the Dōshisha and the American Board. The new governor of Kyoto reported to the Ministry of Education in Tokyo that the school was not in fact under Niijima's control, but was rather a thinly disguised front for a foreign mission.[58] To deflect this threat, Niijima pressed the American Board in Boston for a permanent endowment that the Dōshisha would control. The board granted an annual appropriation of $8,000 directly to the school in November 1879, with the stipulation that the funds be expended in consultation with the mission.[59] In his letter to the Prudential Committee of the American Board explaining the need for this change, Niijima took the opportunity to lay out why the Dōshisha had also become something more than a training school for ministers and evangelists:

> In this connection I must mention the standard of our school. Our people are making a bold strike in educational affairs. The government institutions of learning as well as some private schools are advancing above us. If we do not strive to improve we shall be left in lower strata of educational system, and fail to lay hold of the best class of students. Our good missionary friends have thus far tried to teach the Bible too much and neglected scientific teaching. Numbers of promising boys were much disappointed and have left us to go to the schools in Tokyo, where they will have no Christian influence.[60]

The problem stemmed, in Niijima's view, from too narrow a conception of what a Christian education should produce: "If I were in the place of Dr. Clark I should put all my effort in founding a strong Christian university in Japan, in order to raise up Christian ministers, Christian physicians, Christian statesmen, and even Christian merchants. Christians must not be charged with being ignoramuses, or we shall not get the respect of the people. We shall be ridiculed for our ignorance as well as for our faith."[61] Niijima echoed the Kumamoto Band's frustrations, and his decision to hire three members of the graduating Kumamoto Band (Yamasaki Tamenori, Ichihara Morihiro, and Morita Kumando) as faculty marked a clear effort to strengthen the educational scope of the school.

SEEKING A UNIVERSITY

Aided in part by the influx of the Kumamoto Band and by its growing fiscal and curricular independence from the American Board, Niijima's school entered the 1880s more confident in its vision to become a comprehensive Christian university built on a liberal arts foundation. Niijima's efforts to turn the Dōshisha into a university began in earnest in 1882 and persisted until his untimely death in 1890.[62] Room does not permit a thorough account of his efforts and the gradual evolution of his vision for a university. Crucially, Niijima appealed for support to a wide audience, not just Christians, repeatedly arguing that a private higher education based on Christian principles would benefit Japanese society as a whole. He organized local support in Kyoto, and traveled to Tokyo to appeal to elite politicians and industrialists.[63] His appeal was aided, in part, by the government's efforts through the 1880s to revise the unequal treaties. Elites in Tokyo calculated that publicly supporting a private Christian school would curry favor with the treaty powers.

The highwater mark of Niijima's efforts was the publication of an appeal in November 1888. Carried in most major newspapers and magazines, the appeal summarized the history of the Dōshisha and laid out Niijima's argument that a private university, voluntarily supported, was vital to educating individuals willing to and capable of serving the common good: "We do not believe that it is a good plan to leave the work of education entirely in the hands of the government. We ourselves as citizens are duty bound to educate our children, and we can accomplish this with greater thoroughness, energy, and economy, because we are carrying out our own ideas."[64] Relying solely on the government to define the object and character of education, Niijima argued, betrayed "a spirit of indifference and lack of initiative," the opposite of the sense of independence and autonomy he sought when he escaped his hereditary obligations. Government education, he continued, focuses almost entirely on utility and not on developing the character of the student, with the result that students emerge with narrow competences and outlooks: "Their method is coercion and suppression rather than training up men of open mind, men of self-discipline who are free and independent, self-reliant, working out their own destiny."[65] Out of this critique of state-controlled education comes Niijima's full-throated appeal for a Christian university in Japan: "Some may say that it is a scheme for propagating Christianity or for training evangelists. Such objections do not at all understand what we have in mind. Our aim is not so narrow. We are making Christianity the basis of our education because we believe that its principles alone have a vital power to mold the character of young men. And in addition to the theological course, already in operation, we plan to establish regular university courses in politics, economics, philosophy, literature, and law."[66] Niijima had arrived at the mature definition of a Christian liberal arts in Japan, a definition that owed as much to his understanding of the dominance in Japan of state-controlled education as to his experiences in New England. His vision for a Christian education differed, on the one hand, significantly from what his missionary colleagues sought and, on the other hand, was openly critical of the ideological bent of state education.

The nearly incessant travel for fundraising rapidly undermined Niijima's already poor health, and he finally succumbed in January of 1890 at the age of forty-seven. His final wishes for the future of the Dōshisha were dictated from his deathbed:

1. The work of the Dōshisha will consist hereafter of three inseparable ideals; that is, moral education based upon the Christian religion, literary and political development of the nation, and scientific progress of the people.
2. The object of the Dōshisha will be in the teaching of theology, politics, literature, science, etc. Nevertheless, every endeavor should be used in the making of men who will be possessed of an energetic spirit and active force to be devoted to their country and who will love true liberty.
3. The members of the Dōshisha will treat the students with appropriate courtesy and consideration.
4. Students of a free and independent disposition shall not be restrained in their acts but guided in conformity with their original nature to the end that their character be fully developed.
5. With the growth of the institution there is a tendency of its turning into a machine. Serious care should be taken to guard against this.[67]

Although a gift of $100,000 from Jonathan Harris of New London, Connecticut, promised in late 1888 for the purpose of creating a school of science at the Dōshisha, boosted

Niijima's hopes for expanding his school into a university, the decade following his death was a difficult one for his successors and for the Dōshisha.[68]

Japan in the 1890s turned from relatively open and pragmatic approaches to education toward an increasingly nationalistic conservatism. With the Imperial Rescript on Education, issued just seven months after Niijima's death, the state claimed control over moral education in the name of the emperor, and schools like the Dōshisha struggled to maintain their avowed dedication to a Christian education.[69] The Japanese government constructed an educational system with imperial universities at the pinnacle, relegating private institutions of higher education to a vulnerable and supplemental role. Private schools came to depend on privileges conferred by the state, especially conscription deferrals, which rendered them vulnerable to ideological pressure. The need to compromise with those pressures would culminate in a substantial crisis in 1896, over the whether the Dōshisha would remove its commitment to a Christian education in article one of its constitution. The affair further divided the school from the American Board and led president Kozaki Hiromichi to resign.[70] It was a painful reminder of the precariousness of private education, especially a Christian one, in an increasingly imperialistic Japan.

The question of when the Dōshisha realized Niijima's original vision is difficult to answer. Its current status as a formally recognized private university dates from 1948, but it can be argued that the school moved toward its current shape through incremental recognition by the Japanese state in 1912 and 1920. The 1920s also marked the moment when Amherst College alumni ceased teaching at the Dōshisha as American Board missionaries. From James Jenkins in 1921 onward, Amherst College came to forge a more direct and secular connection with its sister institution in Japan. Student representatives were sent from 1922 onward, until John Whitney Hall returned in 1941. Those ties were renewed after the Second World War and continue to this day.[71] Even as Amherst College and the Dōshisha forged new and stronger ties through the twentieth century, the Christian liberal arts have remained central to the Dōshisha mission and self-definition.

For over a decade, every graduating class of the Dōshisha Elementary School has visited Amherst College in June as the concluding piece of their six years of elementary education. Those students begin their weeklong stay in Amherst with a Christian service in Johnson Chapel. They pray, sing hymns, and listen to their school principal remind them of the founding ideals of Dōshisha—ideals that Niijima formed during his time at Amherst College. Long after Johnson Chapel ceased to be a place of regular Christian services, those who celebrate Niijima's founding vision return to Amherst to consider what he meant by a Christian liberal arts education. While their visits may remind the college that Christianity was once central to the way it first engaged with the wider world, the students may find the significance of Niijima's legacy closer to home.

Notes

1. Niijima's names are rendered in a number of ways in the sources, owing to the shifting conventions of Romanizing the Japanese language and to Niijima's own informal adoption of American names. American sources from the nineteenth century frequently identify him as Joseph Hardy Neesima, Hardy being the surname of his chief benefactor. For the sake of consistency, I will use the modern Japanese rendering of his name, Niijima Jō 新島襄. All Japanese names are rendered surname first, per convention.

2. Originally a holding company for foreign mission property, the Dōshisha, whose board of trustees govern Dōshisha University and all other affiliated schools, is conventionally written with the definite article.

3. *The Amherst Student* 12, no. 12 (March 29, 1879): 138.

4. Ueno Naozō, ed., *Dōshisha hyakunenshi tsūshi-hen*, vol. 1 (Kyoto: Doshisha, 1979), 21.

5. Arthur Sherburne Hardy, *The Life and Letters of Joseph Hardy Neesima* (Boston, MA: Houghton Mifflin, 1891); J. D. Davis, *A Sketch of the Life of Rev. Joseph Hardy Neesima* (New York: Fleming H. Revell, 1894).

6. Ueno, *Dōshisha*, vol. 1, 31–32.

7. Ueno, 31–32. These include Sakuma Shōzan, Yoshida Shōin, and Yokoi Shōnan.

8. Hardy, *Life and Letters*, 29.

9. The details of Niijima's flight from Hakodate to Shanghai, and thence to Boston aboard the *Wild Rover*, make for good reading, and Gavin Campbell provides an excellent exploration of Niijima's time at sea in the broader context of transpacific shipping links between the United States and Asia. See Gavin Campbell, "'We Must Learn Foreign Knowledge': The Trans-Pacific Education of a Samurai Sailor, 1864–1865," *Japanese Journal for American Studies*, no. 25 (2014): 1–26.

10. Hardy, *Life and Letters*, 40.

11. You can read Niijima's letter to the Hardys in Davis, *Sketch*, 3–10.

12. Davis, 50–59.

13. Ueno, *Dōshisha*, vol. 1, 43.

14. Irwin Scheiner, *Christian Converts and Social Protest in Meiji Japan* (Berkeley: University of California Press, 1970), 148.

15. Kitagaki Muneharu, *Niijima Jō to Āmosuto Daigaku* (Kyoto: Yamaguchi shoten, 1993), 293.

16. Davis, *Sketch*, 75.

17. Scheiner, *Christian Converts*, 153.

18. See Julius Seelye, *Education in Japan: A Series of Letters Addressed by Prominent Americans to Mori Arinori* (New York: D. Appleton and Co, 1873), 70. For a broader discussion of Seelye and the place of pietism at Amherst College, see Thomas Le Duc, *Piety and Intellect at Amherst College 1865–1912* (New York: Columbia University Press, 1946).

19. As Irwin Scheiner's succinctly puts it, "secular and religious were identified; national aims became identical with the objective of the pious"; Scheiner, *Christian Converts*, 154.

20. William De Bary and Arthur Tiedemann, eds., *Sources of Japanese Tradition*, vol. 2: *1600 to 2000*, 2nd ed. (New York: Columbia University Press, 2005), 672.

21. For an English translation of the official record of the embassy's travels, see Graham Healey and Chushichi Tsuzuki, eds., *The Iwakura Embassy, 1871–73: a true account of the ambassador extraordinary & plenipotentiary's journey of observation through the United States of America and Europe*, 5 vols. (Princeton, NJ: Japan Documents, 2002).

22. Trent Maxey, *The "Greatest Problem": Religion and State Formation in Meiji Japan* (Cambridge, MA: Harvard University Asia Center, 2014), 55–92.

23. Niijima reportedly worried that the Japanese government would offer to repay Alpheus Hardy for his educational expenses and wrote to Orilla H. Flint in March 1871 that he hoped Mr. Hardy would decline to be reimbursed; Nishida Takeshi, "'Bushidō-teki kirisuto-sha' Niijima Jō: Takahira Kogorō no Amāsuto enzetsu," *Kirisutokyō shakai mondai kenkyū*, no. 55 (December 21, 2006): 37.

24. Davis, *Sketch*, 37–38.

25. The records of Niijima's time with the embassy are found in Niijima Jō zenshū henshū iinkai, ed., *Niijima Jō zenshū*, vol. 7 (Kyoto: Dōmyōsha, 1983), 37–86.

26. Davis, *Sketch*, 40.

27. Tanaka Fujimaro, *Riji kōtei*, vol. 1 (Tokyo: Monbushō,1873), 7.

28. Tanaka Fujimaro, *Riji kōtei*, vol. 3 (Tokyo: Monbushō, 1875), 21.

29. Niijima would later summarize the lesson of his time with the Iwakura Embassy in the following way: "In addition came the belief that if my country desires to rival Western civilization, it must do more than imitate their external material culture; it must seek to attain to what is essential and fundamental in the West. As I pondered thus, I made a vow that on my return to Japan I would establish a private university and so do my best for the advancement of my country." Niijima Jō, *The Founding of the Doshisha and Doshisha University*. (Kyoto: Doshisha, 1960), 12–13.

30. Davis, *Sketch*, 40.

31. When missionary D. C. Greene sought permission from the board to engage in educational work, he was told: "You know well how strongly averse the Committee are to mere literary and education missions, and I am sure you will make the subject one of much thought and much prayer before you settle down in the belief that Christ sent you there not to preach the Gospel but to study, teach, and write books." Quoted in Paul V. Grisely, "The Dōshisha, 1875–1919: The Indigenization of an Institution" (EdD diss., Columbia University, 1973), 77.

32. Ueno Naozō, ed., *Dōshisha Hyakunen shi: shiryō-hen*, vol. 2 (Kyoto: Dōshisha, 1979), 63–64.

33. Kōno Hitoaki, "Niijima Jō no daigaku setsuritsu undō (1)," *Dōshisha Dansō*, no. 9 (March 1989): 2–3.

34. For a recent study of Congregationalist Christianity in Japan centered in Annaka, see Emily Anderson, *Christianity and Imperialism in Modern Japan* (London: Bloomsbury Academic, 2014).

35. Maxey, *Greatest Problem*, 77–81.

36. Aoyama Karin, *Yamamoto Kakuma* (Kyoto: Dōshisha, 1928), 177–78; Ueno, *Dōshisha*, vol. 1, 75–78

37. Aoyama, *Yamamoto*, 174–86.

38. Davis, *Sketch*, 54–55.

39. Ueno, *Dōshisha*, 90–91.

40. Niijima, *Niijima Jō zenshū*, 4; Ueno, *Dōshisha*, vol. 1, 84–85.

41. Davis, *Sketch*, 57; Ueno, *Dōshisha*, vol. 1, 88–90.

42. Ueno, *Dōshisha*, vol. 1, 91–92.

43. Ueno, 93.

44. For a brief discussion of the Dōshisha in relation to mission schools established in Meiji-era Japan, see Dohi Akio, *Nihon Purotesutanto Kirisutokyō-shi* (Tokyo: Shinkyō shuppansha, 1980), 77–83.

45. See, F. G. Notehelfer, *American Samurai: Captain L. L. Jane and Japan* (Princeton, NJ: Princeton University Press, 1985). The declaration is reprinted in Ueno, *Dōshisha*, vol. 1, 16–18.

46. Hardy, *Life and Letters*, 207–12.

47. Of the thirty-five who signed the pledge on Mount Hanaoka, eighteen enrolled in Dōshisha.

48. Takamichi Motoi, "Kumamoto Band to shoki Dōshisha," in *Kumamoto Band Kenkyū*, ed. Dōshisha Daigaku jinbun kagaku kenkyūjo (Tokyo: Misuzu hobo, 1965), 234–58.

49. Quoted in John D. Pierson, *Tokutomi Sohō 1863–1957: A Journalist for Modern Japan* (Princeton, NJ: Princeton University Press, 1980), 56–57.

50. Pierson, *Tokutomi*, 57.

51. Tokutomi Sohō, *Sohō jiden* (Tokyo: Chūō Kōron sha, 1935), 124.

52. Ueno, *Dōshisha*, vol. 1, 100.

53. For a survey of the theological divisions between missionaries and Japanese Christians, see John F. Howes, "Japanese Christians and American Missionaries," in *Changing Japanese Attitudes Toward Modernization*, ed. Marius Jansen (Princeton, NJ: Princeton University Press, 1967), 344–46.

54. Ueno, *Dōshisha*, vol. 1, 143.

55. Ueno, 149.

56. Pierson, *Tokutomi*, 57.

57. Abe Iso'o, *Shakaishugi-sha to naru made: Abe Iso'o jiden* (Tokyo: Kaizōsha, 1932), 43, 51–52, 55–56, 58, 64–65.

58. Hardy, *Life and Letters*, 225–27.

59. Hardy, 231, 233.

60. Hardy, 227–28.

61. Hardy, 228–29.

62. See, for example, Okita Yukiji, "Niijima Jō no 'shigaku' shisō," *Doshisha Dansō*, no. 7 (February 1987): 1–26.

63. Itō Yahiko, *Niijima zenshū wo yomu* (Kyoto: Kōyō shobō, 2002), 47–54.

64. Niijima, *Founding*, 19.

65. Niijima, 21.

66. Niijima, 22–23.

67. Ueno, *Dōshisha*, vol. 1, 709.

68. Ueno, *Dōshisha*, vol. 1, 369–93.

69. Kenneth Pyle calls this moment a "major watershed in modern Japanese history." See Kenneth Pyle, *The New Generation in Meiji Japan: Problems of Cultural Identity, 1885–1895* (Stanford, CA: Stanford University Press, 1969), 188.

70. Ueno, *Dōshisha*, vol. 1, 433–57.

71. Kitagaki Muneharu, "Āmosuto-kan gojyūnen no ayumi," in Ā*mosuto daigaku to Dōshisha daigaku no kankeishi*, ed. Doshisha Daigaku jinbunkagaku kenkyūjo (Kyoto: Shōyō shobo, 2013), 1–68

Exclusivity, Segregation, and Democracy

Amherst College and Its Fraternities

Nicholas L. Syrett

In the early 1940s, Amherst College administrators convened two committees—one composed of faculty, the other of alumni—to investigate life at Amherst and make recommendations for the college's future. Among the topics for investigation were student activities—fraternities, in particular. As the United States entered into war after the bombing of Pearl Harbor, the investigations were temporarily put on hold, but the war and the questions it raised, especially about democracy and citizenship, ended up playing a major role in the two reports' findings. At colleges across the country, the absence of large numbers of male students for the duration of the war allowed administrators to consider what changes they might like to make when a new student body arrived on campus at the close of the war. Perhaps no college took that opportunity for reflection more seriously than Amherst.

The faculty report, which was completed in January of 1945, explained: "The fraternities represent an entrenchment of the world without inside the college community. They are the center of a kind of social education that reinforces the conventional values of our society in an environment where those values are being analyzed. Hence, there is a real and natural antagonism, which anyone at all acquainted with them will recognize, between the fraternities and the college." The committee, with one dissenting opinion, voted to abolish fraternities at Amherst. The majority of the alumni committee, which issued its report the next month, concurred.[1]

The two committees were unsuccessful. A group made up of fraternity alumni convened itself into what it called the Fraternity Business Management Committee and produced its own report, arguing that fraternities should be allowed to remain on campus if they made certain reforms, among them an end to racial discrimination and a new policy that allowed any interested student to join a Greek-letter organization. That report ultimately proved persuasive with Amherst's board of trustees, which voted to allow fraternities to remain on the postwar campus in June 1945.[2]

While Amherst faculty had lost this fight, about four decades later—in 1984—they ultimately did prove successful in having the trustees ban fraternities, even if that policy change proved only partially fulfilled till the early twenty-first century. Over the course of that period, some, though certainly not all, Amherst fraternity men fought to make their organizations fundamentally more egalitarian by breaking with national organizations that banned the initiation of women, nonwhite, or non-Christian members.

Throughout this period, many Amherst College faculty, students, and administrators who argued against fraternities framed their arguments in language that contrasted campus life with a changing world outside campus gates. They spoke of democracy as fundamentally opposed to segregation. As in the report quoted above, they contrasted the purpose of a college education with the values of exclusivity and snobbishness enacted by their fellow students in fraternities. In short, some Amherst community members chose to change, and eventually eradicate, their fraternities. Amherst College remains one of only a handful of colleges—most of them also small, liberal arts colleges in the Northeast—to eliminate fraternities from campus.[3] In so doing, reformers at Amherst and similar colleges were attempting to construct a collegiate world that was increasingly welcoming women, people of color, working-class people, and religious minorities into more facets of American life. They did not want to perpetuate a collegiate model that reified the sort of privilege that moneyed white men had long enjoyed on college campuses. This impulse was at times utopian—especially as they met with resistance from fraternity men at Amherst—and remains unfulfilled, just as it does in the US society more broadly, but it demonstrates many of Amherst's students' and administrators' desire to transform the college in response to the world beyond campus.

*

If Amherst's post-World War II abolition of fraternities makes it close to unique among US colleges and universities, its nineteenth- and early twentieth-century fraternal history is much more typical. Fraternities were born out of literary societies at Amherst, as they were at most other colleges. At Amherst, these were the Athenian and Alexandrian, begun soon after the college's founding in 1821.[4] Because literary societies were open to everyone, students on some campuses began to form more secretive societies that could regulate membership for a certain level of exclusivity: fraternities.[5]

Looking backward, we can see that the first fraternity founded at Amherst was Alpha Delta Phi in 1836. But it is only in hindsight that Alpha Delta Phi and others of its ilk—like Psi Upsilon (founded at Amherst in 1841), Delta Kappa Epsilon (1846), and Chi Psi (1864)—can be differentiated from the other secret societies named for Greek letters that were proliferating on antebellum college campuses. What eventually distinguished fraternities from these other societies was that they were exclusive and competitive, often about the recruitment of members. They also provided a means for students to defy the faculty by joining what were usually outlawed societies (though not at Amherst), groups that often broke other college rules prohibiting drinking and gambling. During the antebellum era, when large numbers of poorer men already in their twenties were attending college to train for the ministry, fraternities tended to seek out younger, wealthier men who were more able to flout college rules. College fraternities served a social function for the men who joined, men who wanted to surround themselves with others of their kind.[6]

William Gardiner Hammond, who entered Amherst in the fall of 1846, was recruited by both Alpha Delta Phi and by Psi Upsilon; he chose the latter. Within a year of initiation, his diary describes how fraternities were combining to defeat one another—and anyone unaffiliated with a Greek-letter society—in the elections for leadership of the literary societies: "Electioneering for tomorrow night is abundant. Our prospects are dark; the 'base compound' are working hard. If we *are* defeated, it will be no dishonor; the pure and aristocratic Alpha Delts must feel somewhat ashamed of their company." Alpha Delta Phi was colluding with Delta Kappa Epsilon in order to secure the election. Amherst's president, Edward Hitchcock, identified another problem with these early fraternities: competition for members. As he explained, "There would be a desperate struggle amongst the students to obtain the leading men in the classes for the different societies, and they would ere long come to regard this matter as one of the most important interests in college." But what of the student over whom no fraternity competed? He was not only shut out of fraternities but increasingly of the life of the college itself.[7]

Even though many college presidents shared these worries about fraternities, by the 1870s and 1880s, most colleges and universities had incorporated fraternities into the fabric of college life. Boards of trustees and administrations, including Amherst's, were now peopled by men who had belonged to fraternities as undergraduates. Edward Hitchcock the elder gave way in 1861 to president Edward Hitchcock Jr., who had been a member of Alpha Delta Phi. Fraternities grew in number, alongside the growth of colleges themselves. The more established fraternities simply became more exclusive, relying on wealth in order to make decisions about membership. This trend was wholly in keeping with the growing concentration of wealth among an elite beyond the college gates during the Gilded Age. As fraternities and their alumni built large and elaborate dwellings on or near college campuses, membership dues also increased, meaning that only the richest were able to join the organizations and self-segregate around their wealth. In October 1890, the *Amherst Record* published a carefully detailed drawing of a large mansion, the new home of Alpha Delta Phi: "The handsomest building of this character in Amherst and will rank well with any in the New England States. The estimated cost of the building was $40,000, and the money has been so expended as to produce a building that is not only an architectural ornament to the town, but one that furnishes a comfortable and elegant home to members of the fraternity during their sojourn at Amherst." It was, of course, to be a home only for those who could afford to join. This meant also that competition for new members continued apace, which led to new rules for rushing and pledging. At Amherst in 1903, for instance, administrators made its fraternities abide by the resolution "that we make no appointments or pledges with prospective members of Amherst College before they leave trains upon their arrival in Amherst, or before getting off the electric cars at the corner of Northampton Road and Pleasant Street, or the Amherst terminal." These rules aimed to create a level playing field for all the fraternities, and also attempted to curb the worst excesses of the process.[8]

By the late nineteenth century, fraternities also tightened their grip on the extracurriculum. Fraternity men not only combined to ensure that only Greek-letter men were elected to campus offices, but they also used these "combines" to occupy the ranks of the yearbook and musical organizations, and they actively recruited star athletes. It had gotten so bad at Amherst that even its "Non-Fraternity Association" had a baseball committee to "look out for the baseball interests of the society." At the same time, fraternity members had become the students least likely to care about academics and most likely to break rules about drinking, hazing, and other pranks. Through the 1920s, fraternity brothers at many colleges, Amherst among them, styled themselves as high-toned collegiate gentlemen by day though they broke rules with abandon at night. They controlled the social scene as well, not just excluding their poorer classmates, but now formally barring the small number of immigrants, including Jews and Catholics as well as African and Asian Americans, who attended colleges. The national organizations wrote addenda to their constitutions excluding such "undesirables," a step largely unnecessary in the antebellum period when such men had been so few in number.[9]

This was the situation facing Amherst administrators when they convened committees to consider the future of Amherst's fraternities in 1941. The Great Depression had weakened fraternities' power on campus, as fewer men joined, and the war itself temporarily depleted the number of men attending college. It was an ideal time to consider what place fraternities might have at postwar Amherst College. Even fraternity members themselves expressed some reservations at the state of affairs, with 68 percent of surveyed brothers still supporting their existence on campus, but a majority believing that fraternities were too expensive and that the organizations had no need to be affiliated with nationals.[10]

The faculty committee documented a number of disturbing trends. First, fraternities controlled student government. While there had previously been rules in place trying to limit the power of fraternities to secure power via elected campus office, in 1938, the interfraternity council effectively replaced student government as such; the independents were collectively accorded one seat on this council, with each fraternity also granted one seat. This system did not accord with the proportion of students at Amherst, and it funneled the structure of governance through fraternities. More importantly for faculty, "it would be no exaggeration to say that the fraternities dominate the social life of the college." Significantly, the organizations continued to exclude based on race, religion, social class, and also on nebulous characteristics like physical appearance, charisma, and ability to get along well with present members. "Good looks, good clothes, an air of premature sophistication, and athletic prowess would seem to be some of the criteria that are most influential in determining the students' choices. Scholarship, beyond the minimum ability to qualify for initiation by attaining passing grades, is rarely an important qualification." Nonfraternity men, for instance, won academic honors far out of proportion to their presence on campus. Nonfraternity men were also much more likely to have attended public schools, an indication that they were less privileged than fraternity men. Because fraternities controlled so much of social life and extracurricular activities on campus, "admission to college is not tantamount to admission to all of the rights and privileges that the life of an undergraduate affords. This is a fundamental inconsistency," the faculty committee wrote. They further explained that "the fraternities, which may once have helped students to mature, now more often help to breed social irresponsibility and emotional regression. They do this by putting a premium on mediocrity in the literal sense of the term."[11]

In their report, the alumni had a different set of worries: "We believe that the sense of exclusiveness and social preferment which thus arises is hurtful to the young men who are in the fraternities because it gives them a false and undemocratic sense of superiority. And it hurts the students who are outside the fraternities by giving them a wholly unwarranted sense of being inferior and of being social outcasts." They particularly noted that those who might be "of the minority racial or religious groups in American society" and those who might be "too poor" would be the most likely to be excluded. Both the faculty and the alumni objected not only to the power that fraternities wielded on the Amherst campus, but they also pointed to fundamental inconsistencies between what Amherst, as a college, was trying to do for its students and the values that were inculcated by Greek-letter organizations. They saw the college's role as helping students question social distinctions that led to discrimination, whereas fraternities themselves discriminated. The Amherst faculty and alumni on these committees believed that this kind of discrimination was not something that the college could continue to countenance.[12]

While these two reports ultimately proved unsuccessful at convincing Amherst's board of trustees to abolish fraternities, the board did mandate that no fraternity could be permitted to continue at Amherst if its national charter contained a clause barring nonwhite and non-Christian men from membership.[13] They set a deadline of February 1, 1949, as the date by which Amherst fraternity chapters had to report to the administration that their national organizations had eliminated such clauses (if they had ever had them); they later extended that deadline by four years. Fearing admission of a nonwhite brother, the national office of Delta Tau Delta immediately denied Amherst's chapter permission to reopen after the war. In response, the chapter issued a statement claiming that they had "gone through a war where the ideals of democracy were tested under fire," and thus began operating as a local fraternity.[14]

In March 1948, Amherst's chapter of Phi Kappa Psi pledged freshman Thomas Gibbs, who was African American, a member of the track team, and a class officer. They pledged him with full knowledge that their decision to do so would likely be met with some resistance. While the Phi Kappa Psi constitution did not actually contain an explicit racial exclusion clause, members nevertheless consulted with their own chapter alumni, who were largely supportive of the decision. Someone must have leaked the information, however, because within a few weeks, they began to receive letters from other chapters and from the national organization. One of the chief benefits of fraternity life is that one gains access to a network of men across the country who have joined brother chapters. National fraternities have traditionally controlled membership precisely so that a man in any one chapter can know that all of his brothers, no matter where they might be located, exemplify the ideals of the fraternity—ideals that often have to do with wealth and pedigree. Amherst's Phi Kappa Psi chapter was about to disrupt this tradition, and many of its brothers, both active and alumni, were worried that this would have consequences, not just for the men at Amherst, but also for the reputation of all in Phi Kappa Psi.

The initiation of Gibbs was scheduled for discussion at the annual meeting in the summer of 1948. In preparation for the conference, the Amherst brothers took the unusual step of sending a letter to fifty-four other chapters asking their opinion about initiating Gibbs. Of the one-third that responded, about half were opposed, a third were in favor, and the rest noncommittal. The chapter decided to go ahead with its plan to make Gibbs a brother, quoting Phi Kappa Psi's former president in the letter explaining their decision: "Phi Kappa Psi seeks to assist men to lift their eyes to wider horizons, to become tolerant, to question all things in the light of reason; and finally to develop the moral courage to follow those paths that have been illuminated unto them and without regard to external consequences." The Amherst chapter simultaneously released a statement to the press via the Amherst College News Bureau, which included its letter to the national office, and a Boston newspaper reported on the story, which was soon picked up by newspapers nationwide. The national office of Phi Kappa Psi promptly yanked the charter from Amherst's chapter, and it reconstituted itself as a local fraternity called Phi Alpha Psi. Gibbs was initiated as a brother.[15]

Racial integration would continue on haltingly over the next decade at Amherst, and well beyond that at some schools that still have traditionally white fraternities that have yet to initiate a man of color. Some nationals were willing to comply with the removal of discriminatory clauses from their constitutions, but they then wrote discrimination into rituals or encouraged it in secret ways. In 1951, a Bowdoin College fraternity chapter was suspended for doing this, a fraternity that also had a chapter at Amherst. This prompted a writer for the Amherst *Student* to ask: "How many other fraternities are there on campus who have no clause of discrimination in their charter but who would have difficulty if they 'stepped out of line'? How many houses have gentleman's agreements with their national organizations?" In 1959, Amherst student Ralph Young explained that of the thirteen houses on campus, seven had "pledged Negroes," and three were expelled by their nationals. By 1952, Amherst had finally moved to a system whereby any student who wanted to join a fraternity was guaranteed admission to at least one: 100 percent membership. Amherst was the first college to make this pledge, a blow to antidemocratic exclusivity in and of itself, but also particularly significant for the issue of racial segregation.[16]

In order to make the 100 percent membership clause possible, Amherst relied on the Lord Jeffrey Amherst Club (or Lord Jeff Club), which had been founded in 1935 by members of the class of 1939, to provide some sort of social club for those Amherst students unwanted by fraternities. The club was not exclusively Jewish in the 1930s, though Jews did predominate; African Americans and some white students otherwise too poor to pay fraternity dues also joined. When, in the 1940s, Amherst officials considered what to do with those who no established fraternity would pledge—for any reason, not just skin color or religion—the Lord Jeff Club seemed the perfect solution because anyone could join. The board of trustees voted to give the Lord Jeff Club an endowment and a house that would put it on par with the established fraternities. In theory, it would also be treated similarly to the fraternities. In practice, however, the Lord Jeff Club ended up serving a mixed group of students: both those who rejected fraternity life outright as well as those who were not given bids to the fraternities. For a time, this included most of Amherst's Jews. As Jacob Nabatoff has shown, the Lord Jeff Club allowed Amherst to abide by the principle of 100 percent membership, while at the same time no particular old-line fraternity was actually forced to admit people of color or Jews. The Lord Jeff Club enabled Amherst to maintain a policy of "separate but equal." By the mid-1950s, however, while the majority of affiliated Jews were still in the Lord Jeff Club, other fraternities had begun to pledge them. By the end of the decade, religious discrimination in Amherst's fraternities seems to have ceased, and the Lord Jeff Club itself had disbanded. Jews, at least those who were interested in joining a fraternity, had been integrated into Amherst's Greek scene.[17]

During the 1950s and 1960s, the college continued to evaluate the presence of fraternities on campus. A 1957 report recommended that fraternities remain on campus, in part because a large majority of undergraduates in a 1956 survey favored their retention. Because of financial difficulties, in the early 1960s, the fraternities deeded their properties over to the college, and the alumni corporations leased them back for a small annual fee, continuing to operate them as before. In one way, the fraternities benefited from this because they were no longer responsible for paying the property taxes or upkeep. The college, however, was also poised to be able to exercise greater control over the eventual fate of fraternities because it now owned their homes. At the same time, by the mid-1960s, interest in fraternities among Amherst students was lessening. By 1965, only 74 percent of eligible men were in fraternities—this number not including freshmen. Only 36 percent of students lived in fraternity houses, others opting for dormitory life. A 1965 report by a committee charged with investigating student life minced no words in their evaluation of the organizations: "We came unanimously to the conclusion, then, that the fraternities at Amherst had become an anachronism, that the possibilities for their reform had been exhausted, and that they now stood directly in the way of exciting new possibilities for student life.... The fraternities have made their points, but they seem to have no more points to make. It is now they who are behind the times." This committee's language is important because its members did not just note fraternity misbehavior, which was quite common, but instead framed their major concerns around fraternities being an "anachronism" and "behind the times," not just with other students on campus, but with the world beyond campus as well. This committee was evaluating what was best for the campus using standards outside the bounds of the college itself, and they found the fraternities to be wanting.[18]

And yet the fraternities remained, continuing to misbehave and sow dissent. In 1967, for instance, a Yale student named Alan Boles published an exposé of Amherst's fraternities and their rush system in the *Yale Daily News*. He documented a persistence of discrimination, despite official prohibitions against it. He claimed that fraternities were responsible for various stunts involving humiliation of their fellow students and damage to property. And despite the 100 percent membership policy, many freshmen deemed less desirable by fraternities during rushing season were well aware that they were not wanted as members. In another incident from the mid-1970s, Chi Phi brothers, as part of a mandated ritual, vandalized college property, disrupted other student activities, and repeatedly interrupted a guest lecture on tai chi sponsored by the Asian Studies Committee. As the dean of students put it in a letter to the college, "Many of the Asian-American students sensed in the incident and the applause a cultural rebuff, a kind of racism, that they had not expected and find it hard to tolerate." Fraternities continued to exert an outsize and distinctly negative influence on campus life.[19]

In the midst of this long-term trend, in 1974, the board of trustees voted to admit women beginning in 1975. Five fraternities voluntarily began to admit women, either as residential or as social members. In 1980, the board mandated that women also be admitted to the remaining fraternities. The trustees believed that Amherst could no longer support a system that discriminated based on sex. As the Select Committee on the Quality of Undergraduate Life, which was made up of both student and faculty representatives, reported in January 1980, there were still "several all-male fraternities, which control some of the most desirable housing and social space." Women and racial minorities continued to feel excluded on Amherst's campus, and fraternities very much contributed to that exclusion. Many student respondents complained that fraternities had the choicest spaces and continued to dominate the social scene on campus. The committee found that the men in the single-sex fraternities—now down to five—exhibited narrower attitudes toward women, while the residents of mixed-sex dormitories and fraternities reported livelier socializing and more egalitarian relationships between the sexes. Finally, the committee objected to the basis upon which fraternities selected members and thus eligibility for living in preferred housing: "We have come to believe that the invitational method of deciding membership in fraternities is detrimental to the quality of student life." No matter the group being excluded—nonwhites, Jews, women, or simply the unpopular, however defined—the fundamental problem was that one group of undergraduates was able to choose the next cohort of students who would receive preferential treatment and housing at Amherst.[20]

The decision to mandate that all fraternities admit women met with mixed results. Chi Psi, for instance, chose to become dormant (at least for a time) rather than initiate women. For many men, gender exclusivity is at the heart of the fraternity experience; admitting women would have defeated the purpose of joining a fraternity. Other fraternities seem to have complied with the mandate, some of them dissociating from their national organizations (which would not allow women as members). But even in some of these chapters, brothers who lived with women continued to exhibit sexist attitudes, and some vandalized and trashed the women's bedrooms.[21]

In part because of this continued discrimination, only four years later, in February 1984, the board of trustees voted to discontinue the fraternity system altogether. The trustees were cognizant of the fact that fraternities had weakened over the course of the 1970s and that some of those that did remain had committed what their report called "unacceptable acts" and "gross social behavior." By 1984, of the twelve national fraternities that had existed in 1946, only two remained. Six others had become local organizations "with varying degrees of insolvency." Unequal access to housing remained a key issue. The fraternities occupied valuable real estate, and the board of trustees was interested in making Amherst a truly residential college, where all students could live on campus. The 1980 report quoted above had also found that women students' primary complaint about the transition to coeducation was housing reform; for men, it was the second most common complaint. The elimination of fraternities was thus part of an overall reorganization of housing and student life that also included the building of a new student center.[22]

The resolution of 1984 went only partially fulfilled. Amherst banned the fraternities from campus and transformed the houses into dormitories. The college could also easily choose not to recognize them as official campus organizations, which meant they had no designated place in college governance. What the Amherst administration came to realize, however, was that this did not stop students from joining the organizations themselves, which could meet off campus and continue to initiate new members. They could also reorganize as single-sex organizations; because they were no longer governed by the college itself, they were also no longer governed by its rule mandating mixed-sex membership. As the Chi Psi fraternity explained in an annual report, "Interestingly enough, this final step [the 1984 ban] in fact removed the chief obstacle to a reactivated Alpha Chi." In the summer of 1985, Chi Psi's national delegates unanimously granted (for the second time) a charter to Amherst's chapter of Chi Psi, and the fraternity was reestablished at Amherst, albeit off campus, as a single-sex fraternity. Other fraternities at Amherst pursued similar strategies, meaning that the ban on fraternities actually had the unintended consequence of allowing single-sex organizations to regain ground. Some fraternities also persisted in their misbehavior, former members living together in particular dorms, whose residents were kept up at night by their antics and who were charged for fixing their vandalism: broken light bulbs, a severed water pipe, smashed windows, and stolen fire extinguishers.[23]

This state of affairs persisted for thirty years beyond the 1984 ban, the administration cognizant of the fact that students continued to join the organizations, which "exist but simultaneously do not exist." The death knell for fraternities at Amherst came in the mid-2010s, when fraternities across the nation were almost constantly in the news for breaking rules related to hazing, binge drinking (the two sometimes leading to deaths), misogyny, racism, and sexual assault. In May of 2014, Amherst's administration once again banned fraternities, this time at the recommendation of a 2013 report by Amherst's Sexual Misconduct Oversight Committee. That committee found that despite the fact that fraternities did not officially exist on campus, their members combined together to advance their own interests in student government, noting that the Association of Amherst Students boasted a severe gender imbalance (twenty-five men and seven women), and that men in positions of power often traded on social capital to coerce sex from unwilling women. Fraternities, however underground they might be, did not foster an environment of inclusion on the Amherst campus.[24]

Amherst aimed to combat underground fraternities using its Honor Code, which was rewritten to prohibit membership in any fraternity, sorority, or fraternity- or sorority-like organization. At the time of the ban, there were only three fraternities in operation off campus: Chi Psi, Delta Kappa Epsilon, and another called OT; one of these (Chi Psi) boasted a majority nonwhite, but still all-male, membership. While Amherst president Biddy Martin explained that the ban was not in reaction to sexual assault, the fact that the committee charged with investigating sexual assault had recommended the ban makes this explanation less believable. The press garnered by a former student's open letter to the Amherst administration about her experience after a sexual assault on campus in 2012 had led to the committee report in the first place and an investigation by the Department of Education. In this instance, Amherst was once again reacting to pressures from beyond campus in making good on its ban thirty years prior. Amherst's actions came not just because of reflection and introspection, as in past cases involving fraternity policy, but rather because of outside pressure and negative attention. That said, Amherst remains one of only a handful of campuses to ban fraternities outright, including their underground iterations.[25]

Fraternities have a long and troubled history on US college and university campuses.

The last decade's coverage of hazing deaths, binge drinking, and sexual assault make that amply clear, but these are only the latest manifestations of what have been long-term trends. As exclusive organizations with nebulous membership criteria, fraternities have always discriminated in one way or another. On questions of race, class, and sex, this has been obvious, but in the case of hazier characteristics like attractiveness, charisma, and lineage, this discrimination has been no less persistent. Amherst College has been one of the few colleges to recognize that the fundamental nature of fraternities ran counter to the goals of the education it sought to provide to its students. While Amherst's commitment to rethinking, and ultimately banning, fraternities has varied over the past seventy years, ultimately it has taken a step that few other institutions have even contemplated, let alone enacted. I argue here that Amherst did so not just because of the problems that almost all schools have encountered with their fraternities—those that disrupt student life and cause headaches for administrators—but also because Amherst administrators and some students (even occasionally those in fraternities themselves) were taking cues from the world beyond the campus itself, and were envisioning the ways that Amherst might learn and grow in concert with the society around it.

Notes

1. *Amherst College, Report of the Faculty Committee on Long Range Policy*, January 1945, 116; "A Report of the Alumni Committee on Postwar Amherst College," *Amherst Alumni Council News*, vol. 18, no. 3, February 1945, 124, both in "Fraternities Opening After the War" folder, Amherst College Archives (hereafter ACA), Amherst College, Amherst, MA.

2. "The Amherst Fraternity," Report of the Committee on Postwar Fraternities by the Fraternity Business Management Committee of Amherst College, February 1945, "Fraternities Reopening After the War" folder, ACA; Nicholas L. Syrett, *The Company He Keeps: A History of White College Fraternities* (Chapel Hill: University of North Carolina Press, 2009), 235.

3. Others include Colby, Bowdoin, Middlebury, and Williams Colleges, and Wesleyan University.

4. See David W. Wills's chapter in this volume.

5. George R. Cutting, *Student Life at Amherst College: Its Organizations, Their Membership and History* (Amherst, MA: Hatch & Williams, 1871), 13-43, 159, 169, 180, 189.

6. Cutting, *Student Life*, 159, 169, 180, 189; Syrett, *Company He Keeps*, chpts. 1 and 2, for background on the founding of fraternities and their antebellum members. On college students in the antebellum era, see David F. Allmendinger, *Paupers and Scholars: The Transformation of Student Life in Nineteenth-Century New England* (New York: St. Martin's, 1975); Colin B. Burke, *American Collegiate Populations: A Test of the Traditional View* (New York: New York University Press, 1982).

7. William Gardiner Hammond, *Remembrance of Amherst: An Undergraduate's Diary, 1846–1848*, ed. George F. Whicher (New York: Columbia University Press, 1946), 46, 127; letter from Edward Hitchcock to "the boys," November 5, 1846, "Miscellaneous" folder, Delta Kappa Epsilon, General Files, ACA; Edward Hitchcock, *Reminiscences of Amherst College, Historical, Scientific, Biographical, and Autobiographical: Also, of Other Wider Life Experiences* (Northampton, MA: Bridgman & Childs, 1863), 320.

8. *Amherst Record*, October 29, 1890, 1; Clarence Birdseye, *Individual Training in Our Colleges*

(New York: Macmillan, 1907), 218; See also Syrett, *Company He Keeps*, chpt. 4; George E. Peterson, *The New England College in the Age of the University* (Amherst, MA: Amherst College Press, 1964); Thomas LeDuc, *Piety and Intellect at Amherst College, 1865–1912* (New York: Arno Press, 1969).

9. Syrett, *Company He Keeps*, 160; "Non-Fraternity Association Constitution and Minutes, 1900–1904," Folder 2, Box 2, Clubs and Societies Collection, ACA.

10. "Dissatisfaction on Fraternities Shown by Poll," *Springfield Union*, March 9, 1938; Fraternities/Newsclippings Folder 1, ACA.

11. *Report of the Faculty Committee*, 111, 113, 114, 115, 116, 117. See also Ralph Young, "Discrimination and the Amherst Fraternity," *Amherst Student*, May 1959, 1–2, "Regulation and Discrimination, 40s–50s" folder, ACA.

12. "A Report of the Alumni Committee," 114–15.

13. A handful of Jews had already been admitted to Amherst fraternities with no perceptible reaction from national organizations, but no student of color had yet been initiated. See Syrett, *Company He Keeps*, 357n27.

14. Howard Whitman, "The College Fraternity Crisis," *Collier's*, January 8, 1949, 65; Syrett, *Company He Keeps*, 248; Anthony James, "The College Social Fraternity Antidiscrimination Debate, 1945–1949," *The Historian* 62, no. 2 (Winter 2000): 303–24.

15. Letter from Frederick D. Greene II to Howard L. Hamilton, November 7, 1948, "Regulation and Discrimination, 40s–50s" folder, ACA; Syrett, *Company He Keeps*, 248–49; James, "College Social Fraternity"; Whitman, "College Fraternity Crisis."

16. *Student* quoted in Young, "Discrimination," 3–4.

17. Jacob Nabatoff, "Jews and Fraternities: The 100% Rushing Rule as a Progressive Step Forward for Amherst College" (undergraduate student paper, Amherst College, May 11, 2017), 4, 8, 11.

18. "Report of the Committee to Restudy Fraternities at Amherst College," *The Amherst Student*, supplement to October 3, 1957, vol. 87, no. 4, 5–6; "Fraternities at Amherst Deed Property to College," August 8, 1963, Folder 39, Box 1, Fraternities Collection, ACA; "Fraternities at Amherst," *Amherst Reports*, vol. 2, no. 4, June 1963, 20; "A Report to the Committee on Educational Policy from the Subcommittee to Study Student Life," *Amherst Alumni News*, Special Issue, Winter, 1965, 8–9. See also Alan Boles, "Amherst's Gentlemen Rush," *Yale Daily News*, April 14, 1967, 6–9.

19. Boles, "Amherst's Gentlemen's Rush"; letter from David Drinkwater to the Amherst Community, November 3, 1975, Folder 39, Box 1, Fraternities Collection, ACA.

20. "Report of the Select Committee on the Quality of Undergraduate Life," January 11, 1980, 17–19, 64–65, ACA; "Coeducation Timeline," ACA.

21. "Chi Psi Annual Report, 2008–2009, Alpha Chi," June 3, 2009, 42, http://c.ymcdn.com/sites/www.chipsi.org/resource/collection/a0e1e7b1-1be8-4074-9597-436585f08f3b/08-09AnnualReport_Chi_V2.pdf?hhSearchTerms=Spencer+and+song; Christopher Bohjalian, "Last All-Male Fraternities at Amherst Admit Women," *Daily Hampshire Gazette*, April 24, 1981, 11, Folder 39, Box 1, Fraternities Collection, ACA.

22. "Final Report of the Ad Hoc Committee on Campus Life," February 21, 1984, General Files: Fraternities, ACA, Amherst College, Amherst, MA, https://www.amherst.edu/system/files/1984%2520Final%2520Report%2520on%2520Campus%2520Life.pdf; "Report of the Select Committee," 62. For the statements by the trustees and the college council, see Board of Trustees, "Trustees Statement, February 1984," Amherst College, https://www.amherst.edu/offices/student-affairs/community-standards/college-standards/fraternity-policy.

23. "Chi Psi Annual Report," 42; "Burning Down the House: Dissension at Mayo-Smith," *The Amherst Student*, February 18, 1985, 6, Folder 39, Box 1, Fraternities Collection.

24. "Oversight Committee Releases Report on Sexual Misconduct," *The Amherst Student*, May 14, 2014, http://amherststudent.amherst.edu/?q=article/2013/02/05/oversight-committee-releases-report-sexual-misconduct.

25. Sophie Murguia, "Board Bans Off-Campus Fraternities," *The Amherst Student*, May 7, 2014, http://amherststudent.amherst.edu/?q=article/2014/05/07/board-bans-campus-fraternities. For more on the thirty-year period of off-campus fraternities, see Steve Pfarrer, "Frats Get Qualified nod at Amherst," *Daily Hampshire Gazette*, December 1, 1997, 1, 7.

Jewish Experience at Amherst College

Wendy H. Bergoffen

The history of Jewish experience at Amherst is not exceptional. The college was not markedly restrictive, nor was it especially welcoming—at least in the earliest years, when Jewish students struggled to gain entrance to elite schools in the Northeast. What distinguishes this story are a few individuals who possessed the courage of their convictions and challenged longstanding traditions. At distinct moments over one hundred years, these men—one outsider, one insider, and one religious adviser—readied Amherst for a greater Jewish presence. The curricular changes marshaled by Alexander Meiklejohn in the 1910s, accompanied by his intellectual rigor, put Amherst on the map for Jewish students. When the dean of admission, Eugene "Bill" Wilson (class of 1929), denounced snobbery by casting his net in public schools, he transformed postwar student demographics. Years later, rabbi Yechiael Lander called upon Jewish men and women to join together in spirituality and for social justice. This story traces Jewish experience at the college and highlights two interdependent forces: trends in US history affecting the perception and treatment of Jewish people and the bold actions taken by administrators to shape Amherst College with and against these tides.

EARLY SOCIAL BOUNDARIES

Across the nation, relatively few Jewish students pursued higher education in the nineteenth century, and those who did hailed from wealthy families. They cut a cultivated figure and could mix in the club-like atmosphere of small New England schools, with their fraternities, secret societies, and sporting cultures. But they were not especially drawn to Amherst College, with its founding mission to train young men for the Christian ministry. Jewish families were not especially drawn to the town of Amherst either. The total population was five thousand in 1900, and until the First World War, the Labrovitz clan was the only Jewish household. No synagogue, no kosher butcher, and no *mikveh* (ritual bath). The Labrovitz family haberdashery, situated on the corner of Amity and Pleasant Streets, "rented caps, gowns, and tuxedos," as well as "clothing geared to the tastes of male students" at State Agricultural College (later the University of Massachusetts) and Amherst College.[1] Not until the closing of the century did Amherst welcome its first Jewish notables on campus.

Jacob Henry Hollander may have ambled past the Labrovitz establishment during his extended stay in the fall of 1894. Hollander studied at Johns Hopkins University, later assuming a distinguished position on its faculty. His colleague, Herbert Baxter Adams (class of 1872), professor of American and institutional history, was a classmate of Amherst College professor John Bates Clark (class of 1872). That fall term, Clark had lectured at Johns Hopkins and, in exchange, Hollander visited the Amherst campus. His five-week series of lectures received a warm reception in the *Amherst Student*: "The department of Political Economy is to be congratulated on having secured the service of so able an economist and teacher as Dr. J.H. Hollander." The article declared, "He is well known among economists and has contributed many able works to the literature of Political Economy." That he was likely the first Jewish academic to lecture at Amherst goes unremarked. Notably, Herbert Baxter Adams played a vital role in the founding of the American Jewish Historical Society in 1892. Of these efforts, Adams was eulogized as "a staunch supporter and interested participant in the Society's work," who showed "the keenest interest and most cordial sympathy" for the preservation of the American Jewish past. Adams taught courses on Jewish history at Johns Hopkins and described, in 1900, lecturing "to young men and young women of the Hebrew faith in the class-room of their own synagogue." A thoroughly Amherst man, Adams broadened his intellectual scope in Baltimore and helped to bring a wider world of ideas to the Amherst campus by facilitating Hollander's visit.[2]

Mortimer Loeb Schiff missed Hollander's lectures by a few months. Though Schiff identified with the class of 1896, he only attended Amherst from 1892 to 1894. His name bespeaks the joining of two powerful German Jewish banking families from New York: the Loebs and the Schiffs. Although Schiff wanted to attend Harvard, his father chose Amherst. As a leader of the US Jewish establishment, Schiff the elder felt a smaller college would insulate his son from "the many temptations a young man is subject to with so many students around."[3] At the closing of the Gilded Age, fraternities shaped the Amherst scene, and most fraternities did not admit Jews, African Americans, or other "undesirable elements." That Schiff easily pledged Beta Theta Pi suggests the enormous influence the Loeb Schiffs enjoyed.

But such bonds offered little protection from the harassment of his classmates. Alfred Stearns (class of 1894) recalled that "his favorite pastime" in French class "was to eject Mortimer Schiff from the room." As Schiff proceeded with his recitations, "the only serious student in the group," Stearns and his pals would approach "their victim, pick him up in their arms, carry him to the door and deposit him outside, while Schiff, when he had had time to gather his breath, would sneak back to his place." Other stunts included pinning Schiff's chair and desk to the wall.[4] Despite his abbreviated course of study and the goading he endured, Schiff gave generously to the college throughout his life. In the early 1900s, his gifts resulted in new squash courts, and years later, he bequeathed $50,000 to the college.[5] Schiff was likely the first Jewish student to attend Amherst College. Jews became increasingly less rare on college campuses in the decades to come.

NEW VISIONS FOR AMHERST

With an influx of immigrants around the turn of the century—fleeing political and religious persecution in Eastern Europe—the US Jewish community lost its sturdy bourgeois profile. It was a period when Jews marked the boundaries between upstanding wealthy members of the community and working-class greenhorns. It would take time and access to public education before the children of this immigrant generation could take their seats beside other college students, an ascent that proved difficult as institutional gatekeepers sought to limit their access. The more Jews pursued higher education the more elite schools developed "weapons to repel an invasion."[6] Rather than relying on the old standbys of tests and recommendations to safeguard admission, administrators increasingly looked to character: a flexible term that could mean anything from status and popularity to athleticism and leadership.

An elegant education was reserved for those who could pass for gentile in looks and comportment. A host of monikers emerged to parse these distinctions, including "professional" Jews and "chip-on-the-shoulder-Hebrews." Most troublesome were the "greasy grinds," who poured over their studies—in the Converse library and elsewhere—hungry for high grades and eager to show off. "You can't expect to hang around with the scum of New York," carped one observer of the period, "and expect to be respected." "New York Jew" became synonymous with "obnoxiousness." Administrators hoped to quell anxieties over such "Jewish problems" by limiting the number of Jewish students in their midst and, thereby, lessening the tensions between Jews and non-Jews. There could be no Jewish problems, they reasoned, if there were no (or very few) Jews. By the "tribal twenties," a period marked by heightened xenophobia, Harvard, Princeton, Columbia, and Yale had openly or covertly adopted quotas to address these concerns. Restrictive quotas became the sine qua non for schools in the Northeast, where a majority of Jewish Americans lived and initially chose to apply. In this cultural crucible, it took chutzpah, or guts, for a Jewish student to choose Amherst and enter its consecrated eminence.[7]

Philip Brisk (class of 1921) did just that. The Gardiner, Maine native earned the esteem of his classmates as a crack athlete, playing skillfully on the varsity football and baseball teams as well as some club sides. Though Brisk remained unaffiliated during his four years at Amherst, he served as vice president for his class and, in 1921, gave the class toast. Brisk took a first job coaching football at Thornton Academy in Saco, Maine, then solicited recommendations from Paul C. Phillips, professor of physical education and hygiene, and President Meiklejohn for a teaching position at Mercersburg Academy in Pennsylvania. There ensued a telling exchange, documenting the prejudice Jewish alumni faced in seeking employment, even with an Amherst diploma.

By all accounts, Brisk was well liked and well assimilated at Amherst. His Jewishness did not negatively mark him as an outsider, as evidenced by articles in the *Amherst Student* and his *Olio* blurb. During this "golden age of sport," when Americans embraced physical culture after the war, Brisk's profile embodied the masculine ideal. Except for his Jewishness, Brisk bore the markings of muscular (Christian) Amherst. Mercersburg headmaster

William Irvine had sent Phillips a letter in early January 1922, criticizing Amherst faculty for endorsing Brisk without noting "that he is a Hebrew." Mercersburg was "not able to use a Hebrew young man as a regular member of our faculty," and Irvine "felt a little sore" for not receiving "the full particulars." Interestingly, Irvine's letter begins by offering praise for the contributions of a Mr. Frank Glick, former football coach at Mercersburg: Glick "is one of the most skilled coaches that we have had" and "is all right in personality and character. He is, as you probably know, a Hebrew but this fact does not seem to be a handicap to him in his work." Brisk may have received a warmer reception at Mercersburg had he applied for a coaching position. Irvine's letter was subsequently forwarded to the president's office, and Meiklejohn offered a terse rejoinder: "I think I need hardly say that it had not occurred to me that you would need information on that point. . . . I am very sorry that you were misled by what we failed to say."[8]

Though athletes and well-heeled Jewish students adapted more easily at Amherst and elsewhere, the college did admit a Russian Jewish immigrant during the 1910s whose family had settled in Northampton. Son of a highly regarded Hebrew scholar and social worker from Vilna, Elhanan Hirsch Golomb (class of 1919) did *not* personify the Amherst Man.[9] His *Olio* entry records no sports, class, or other student activities, only the provisional tolerance of his peers. Alternately deemed a "yokel" and "ouija board gone wrong," classmates describe Golomb delivering "Palestinian monologues at great length" (likely proto-Zionist tracts) that fell on dumb ears, as "nobody can understand him." One wonders if he and Brisk ever crossed paths, as the latter raced from one athletic field to the other. After graduation, Golomb earned a master's degree at the University of Pennsylvania, then a PhD at Dropsie College for Hebrew and Cognate Learning, and rabbinical ordination at the Jewish Theological Seminary. His long teaching career included positions with the Hebrew Orphans Home in Philadelphia, Johns Hopkins University, and Baltimore Hebrew College before he retired in Israel. Golomb translated the Amherst mission of enlightening the lands—with Hebrew rather than Christian teaching—and was a forerunner in a century-long tradition of Amherst Jewish alumni becoming rabbis.[10]

In fostering an academic and intellectual environment, his oft-memorialized "place of the mind," Meiklejohn tempered, however subtly, the prevailing criteria for exclusion in higher education. If "education was revolution, a never-ending experiment," then ambitious Jewish students were poised to take full advantage. This story of Jewish experience at Amherst offers a somewhat different view of the turbulent Meiklejohn era. Amid the flow of discriminatory quotas at other institutions, Amherst offered at least a partly open door, judging from statistics compiled by national Jewish organizations in the 1910s. Of primary concern to the Union of American Hebrew Congregations was outreach: discerning how many Jewish students engaged with religious life during their college years. Its report of 1916 indicates ten Jewish students from Amherst College met with "Rabbi Samuel Price" of Springfield, who also spoke with the president and dean. The *Menorah Journal*, a publishing arm of the Intercollegiate Menorah Society, seemed most interested in counting the heads of self-identifying Jewish students. For the 1915 to 1916 academic year, its census lists a total of fourteen Jewish students at Amherst; the following year, the number dropped to twelve students. Interestingly, the counting performed by the Bureau of Jewish Social

Research (BJSR) focused entirely on "Jewish names" in college directories. (Jewish naming and claiming has a long history, a practice known colloquially as "Jew-hooing.") For the 1918 to 1919 academic year, the BJSR report identifies only eight Jewish students at Amherst. It is difficult to know if Brisk (son of Jacob Samuel) was counted. That a range of Jewish-identified groups began charting Jewish student enrollments in the 1910s suggests that changes were underway across the nation, as well as at Amherst.[11]

Jewish students did not choose Amherst because of Meiklejohn; they were increasingly choosing college, and his focus on academics rather than religious training made Amherst a more attractive school than it had been a decade earlier. Though the number of Jewish students was not especially high in these early years, the college showed increases during Meiklejohn's tenure. In 1923, he opined: "We may not keep ourselves apart either from persons or from cultures not our own. We dare not shut our gates to fellow-citizens nor to their influence. So we must welcome boys of other stocks. And if they do not come, we must go out and bring them in." Meiklejohn may have rattled the chains of tradition, but the bonds did not entirely break as his view of fellow citizens was not shared by all. When Otto Glaser, professor and chair of biology, sought to hire Herbert Friedman in 1926 as an instructor, he was told to consult with an influential alumnus and trustee. Accepting Jewish students was one thing; appointing Jewish faculty was another. The story, as relayed by Herman Greenberg (class of 1930), details how Frederick Woodbridge (class of 1889), dean and professor of philosophy at Columbia, reportedly "came on like a truck driver" to the suggestion and told Glaser, "Over my dead body!" Friedman was hired and taught at Amherst from 1927 to 1929, before accepting a position with the Smithsonian National Museum of Natural History, which he held for decades. Anti-Semitism increased in college and university settings, as well as across the nation, during the 1920s and 1930s. In 1924, president Calvin Coolidge (class of 1895) signed the Johnson-Reed Act, codifying immigration quotas based on national origins and barring entry to most southern Italians and Eastern European Jews. It was a time when Henry Ford popularized Jewish conspiracy theories, such as those detailed in *The Protocols of the Elders of Zion,* and circulated them widely in the *Dearborn Independent.* And across the airways, Father Charles Coughlin decried the rise and exploitative powers of Jewish capitalists.[12]

For their part, Jewish students found Amherst a lonely and isolating place during the interwar years. Fraternities shaped life outside the classroom, including where students studied, dined, and slept. With national charters barring membership to Jews, African Americans, and other nonwhite and non-Christian students, local members did little to challenge norms of exclusion. And despite the proliferation of Jewish fraternities across the country in the 1930s, no chapters ever appeared on the Amherst campus. To address this deficiency, a group of students—Jewish and non-Jewish—formed the Lord Jeffrey Amherst Club (or the Lord Jeff Club) in 1935. Conceived as a "non-selective, democratic social organization," the club offered unaffiliated students "equal opportunity to the intellectual and social facilities" on campus, free from discrimination based on "race, creed, personality clashes, or economic barriers." The group was lauded by faculty for its dedication to democratic principles, commitment to Amherst's educational mission, and loyalty to the college community. Its social justice ethos suggests how deeply students felt excluded by their peers. Alumni recalled the sting of social rejection for decades. Stanley Marcus, of the Neiman-Marcus department store, attended Amherst from 1921 to 1922 and described his status after freshman rushing, "a member of a group of six 'barbarians' including two other Jews, one Chinese, and two blacks," highlighting the "discriminatory social system" that compelled him to transfer to Harvard. It took fifty years for members of the Amherst class of 1936 to offer a formal apology to their Jewish peers.[13]

E. Ernest Goldstein (class of 1939), a founding member of the Lord Jeff Club, also experienced social exclusion. He recounted that Amherst "provided the sole, and unforgivable, experience in my life of being treated as a second-class citizen, thereby providing my incentive to combat prejudice and discrimination." Before embarking on an exemplary career dedicated to just those pursuits, and shortly after graduation, Goldstein wrote to then-professor Charles Cole (class of 1927) to ask about Jewish acceptance to Amherst. Cole's reply, dated January 12, 1940, outlines an informal policy of limiting the number of Jewish students. "The whole matter seems to be shrouded in a good deal of mystery," Cole concedes. "I think it is a college policy to admit about 8 or 9 a year.... But I think that if one of the eight or nine admitted fails to turn up his place is filled sometimes with a non-Jewish boy—which if you admitted only very top-notch men apt to go off to Harvard, Yale, etc. might serve in some years to cut the number well below 8 or 9." Bright and ambitious young men sought this shining college on a hill. But as intellectual doors opened to them, social doors closed. This was true for most students, but not all. Robert M. Morgenthau (class of 1941), who pledged Alpha Delta Phi, was certainly an exception. And in 1941, Eustace Seligman (class of 1910) began his long tenure on the board of trustees, earning high praise for his good offices.[14]

TRANSFORMATIONS IN THE POSTWAR ERA

Whereas the college brooked social discrimination in the decade leading up to the war, the Holocaust made casual anti-Semitism untenable in its aftermath. The Amherst campus felt different when it resumed operations in the fall of 1946. The GI Bill brought an older set of students to the quad, with altered perspectives on college and life. Fraternities had been put on notice: be inclusive or risk extinction. The institution of 100 percent rushing meant every student who wanted to join a fraternity could do so. Hierarchies still separated the highly sought-after students from the unenviable "leftovers," but no students could be roundly excluded. Though it would take years to reach full compliance, the rule symbolized a "progressive step forward." For Jewish students, social opportunities could extend beyond the Lord Jeff Club. Neighboring schools such as Wesleyan and Williams struggled to integrate or reform their fraternity systems well into the 1950s.[15]

Changes in fraternity customs at Amherst prompted the questioning of other traditions, such as mandatory chapel. For decades, the only two requirements—outside of coursework—were compulsory chapel and athletics. Edward "Doc" Hitchcock (class of 1849), professor of physical education and hygiene, had advocated the interdependence of mind, body, and spirit, echoing other New England reformers, such as Sylvester Graham and William Alcott. Hitchcock believed his program, the "Amherst Plan" of calisthenics, strength training, and hygiene courses, would preserve the health of the student body. His influence extended well into the twentieth century, as academics, athletics, and chapel shaped student experience. In the 1950s, students enjoyed the competition of Chapel Dash, whereby contenders tried to see how late they could leave Valentine Dining Hall and still make it to chapel on time. More subversive was Chapel Flashing, described as "arriving a bit early to check in at the door, walking around to the other door, waiting until the monitor there seemed preoccupied, and then quickly exiting." Such playful expressions were countered with protests over requirements to attend religious services. Ultimately, a compromise was reached: secular assemblies would be held in addition to religious services, and students could attend two chapel meetings of their choice. Clearly, the culture and composition of Amherst was changing from its nineteenth-century roots, training poor but talented men for the ministry.[16]

Bill Wilson sparked many of these changes. The conscientious objector, Quaker, and "former boatman, who understood the currents of the times" accepted the offer to serve as dean of admission with one condition: "no race, creed, or color restrictions of any sort." Charles Cole, who had sympathized with Jewish students in the past and assumed the presidency after the war, guaranteed no interference. Wilson's view of admissions was practical as well as principled: "There are very able, interesting Jewish students around this country, and if they're going to be excluded from some places," he reasoned, "this would be a good field to fish in." The skilled angler adjusted his cast, visiting public schools in New York and establishing a professional relationship with Abraham Lass, principal of Abraham Lincoln High School in Brooklyn. They partnered in 1965, to write the *College Student's Handbook*, and created new pathways for bright public school students. Wilson took Meiklejohn's aspiration seriously: if students did not come to Amherst, then Amherst must seek them out. To this end, Wilson used all tools available to achieve a diverse class. Admissions photographs had been weaponized for decades to exclude students, especially at small colleges. Wilson saw things differently. Anecdotally, he claimed he could not knowingly accept a wide range of students without being able to see them. His continued use of admissions photographs landed him in hot water in the late 1950s, when the Massachusetts Commission against Discrimination threatened to sue the college for defying the 1949 Fair Educational Practices Act. A January 1958 editorial in the *Student* outlines Wilson's broadminded position, accompanied by a cartoon depicting an applicant with a bag over his head. Wilson relented, foregoing photographs, and maintained his commitment to selecting a balanced class and working with alternative feeder schools.[17]

Wilson's approach was part art, part science. The art, as many alumni recall, included his deft use of personal interviews to gauge an applicant's potential. Skeptical of test scores as an index of aptitude, Wilson met with students one-on-one and often extended offers before candidates left campus. From his first year in office, this "dean of deans" compiled data on entering classes to share with prospective students, their families, and school counselors. The "Annual Report to Headmasters and Principals" included occupational intentions, prior school activities, a breakdown of public and private schools represented, and, for a number of years in the 1950s, religious "distribution." In 1954, Wilson reported the group included sixty-three Jewish students among the 306 admitted, likely one of the largest-percentage Jewish classes in college history.

So many alumni of the postwar era offer a similar refrain: Dean Gene changed my life. Martin Seham (class of 1954) recalled "a wonderful, insightful man who addressed every boy as a man and every man as a friend." He was known to take a young man under his wing, steering him to a favorite fishing hole where they could discuss life or not talk at all. Wilson inaugurated the Green Dean position, offering a recent graduate the opportunity to learn the practice of counseling students and selecting a class. Robert Ward (class of 1957) was one such student, who eventually chose a career in education. Years later, after the memorial service for Cole, Ward described Wilson's contributions to Amherst: "Prejudices that had once been operative were shelved and even Jews and rough-edged Catholics were judged on some equal basis. And a guy named Eugene S. Wilson brought that change about."[18] With Cole's blessing, Wilson upended traditions and profoundly changed Amherst College—many say for the better and for the future. And he did so with grace and a wonderful sense of humor.

Across the country, and at Amherst, opportunities also expanded for Jewish faculty in these years. The town's leafy pathways welcomed the legendary city walker Alfred Kazin, who taught for several years in the American studies department. Lauded for his "unorthodox teaching style," students appreciated his focus on "the feeling you get from a book," which resulted in "everybody really reading." Looking back on his years at Amherst, Kazin described rambles down "a long, long street: you just get out and start walking and trust to luck. . . . Just one long street up and down, for miles it goes, and always named Pleasant." Other notable Americanists and wordsmiths followed. Leo Marx joined the English department in 1958, later welcoming Allen Guttmann, also from Minnesota, to the faculty, and inviting Tillie Olsen to teach for a year. She developed a revolutionary women's literature curriculum and radicalized a number of faculty wives. Remembered as "the toughest scientific mind in the room," Joseph Epstein commenced a long and celebrated career in the philosophy department in 1952. Much as students of the era described the 1950s as "assimilationist times," an ever-enlarging Jewish faculty helped pave the way for changes on campus in the decades to come. By the late 1960s, sociologists Jan Dizard and Norman Birnbaum took forceful political positions in their work and on campus, just as students Marshall Bloom and Ted Rosengarten (both class of 1966) fought prejudice and worked for social justice.[19]

HILLEL AND SPIRITUAL CONNECTIONS

Whereas only a small portion of US Jewish students entered college at the turn of the twentieth century, by the late 1970s, one sociologist estimated "80–90% of Jewish youth" were pursuing higher education. As US Jews achieved social mobility and faced significantly less discrimination, communal leaders questioned how such openness affected Jewish faith and religious practice. Once young people left the structure and expectations of home life, would they continue to identify and worship as Jews? These worries were not new. A primary goal of B'nai B'rith Hillel, a college student organization founded in the 1920s at the University of Illinois, was to inculcate basic Jewish values in young men and women during "the most plastic period of their development." As these students readied for leadership positions after college, Hillel hoped to inspire them to become "leaders of their Jewish communities" as well. Student self-governance offered practical skills, but more importantly it taught students "to become serving Jews."[20] The proliferation of Hillel chapters across the country corresponded with the growth of Jewish Greek culture, offering spiritual, intellectual, and social camaraderie for a growing number of Jewish college students.

Hillel came to Amherst, perhaps surprisingly, in the midst of World War II. Rabbi Arthur Hertzberg arrived in 1943, ready to serve Jewish students in the valley. With few men on campus, save for those in residence for military training, there was little work, and Hertzberg left after one year. The next two decades were relatively quiet, with some students not recalling the presence of any Jewish adviser or activities on campus. Rabbi Louis Ruchames chartered Hillel through the 1950s, when Jewish students primarily sought to blend in with their peers. His scholarly temperament eventually drew him to academic work in the history department at the University of Massachusetts Boston.

As a student organization on campus, Hillel came alive when rabbi Yechiael Lander assumed leadership in 1967, bringing an ambitious vision to his work, "engaging Jewish students in worship, learning, and social activism." Lander encouraged students to conduct religious services, schedule events, and shape Jewish involvement on campus. In an annual program report from 1977 to 1978, Lander highlighted student volunteers tutoring Russian Jews in Springfield, as well as "speeches, public vigils, and a good deal of letter writing" on behalf of Soviet Jewry.[21] As Jews across the country had moved decidedly into the mainstream, Hillel offered a Jewish framework to engage meaningfully with members of the community: Hillel students shined a Jewish light on the world.

Most beloved and fondly remembered by alumni of the 1980s and 1990s were cooking meals together on Friday nights and welcoming the Sabbath bride. "Roommates, friends, boyfriends, and strangers" gathered to enjoy dinners of "Kraft macaroni," pulled together on shoestring budgets and prepared in the Garman House kitchen. For many, Friday night meals exemplified "Jews doing Jewish with other Jews." Non-Jews joined as well. Here was an opportunity to shape the contours of Jewish experience at Amherst and create a "secular synagogue." Jewish education enlivened the mind, weekly and holiday worship bolstered the spirit, and Sabbath meal preparation sustained the social body. The group eventually outgrew Garman Lounge, and members sought a permanent site for Jewish congregation on campus.[22]

With confidence and determination, board members advocated for a designated Jewish space. The October 1994 proposal highlighted Hillel's growth as one of the largest student organizations, with over two hundred and fifty members, and its rich programming, which created "a more diverse and intellectually stimulating environment for the entire Amherst community." To support and sustain this work, Hillel needed a kosher kitchen, Jewish sanctuary, and room enough for offices and meeting areas. Beyond such practical needs, a Jewish space would bolster recruitment: "Faced with the choice between Amherst" and other schools, "Jewish students may choose to attend a school where there is a visible commitment to the sustenance of Jewish life." Students envisioned a Jewish site in the center of campus, easily accessible for all members of the community. After a lengthy process, whereby administrators and students voiced competing interests, the quest for a Jewish-specific site ended with the establishment, in 1998, of the Cadigan Center for Religious Life, a multifaith center located in the hinterlands of Woodside Avenue and faculty housing.[23]

This was also the era of coeducation, which engendered a new set of pressures, as Jewish women navigated longstanding (and unspoken) college traditions within a Christian and male institution. For some in the early 1980s, their experiences intersected with "the last years of the fraternities," which extended membership to women. Some experienced gender as the salient category of difference, as they were "focused on being equals in the classroom and on the sports fields" with their male peers. Athletics did not always offer a level playing field, however. One Jewish student recalls a crushing choice: observing a high holy day or taking the annual photo with the rest of her squad. Students and visitors to campus can scan the walls of LeFrak Gymnasium to find a picture of the 1984 women's volleyball team holding a teddy bear and sign with the name of their missing teammate.[24]

Today, Amherst is one of the most diverse liberal arts colleges in the nation, a legacy of president Anthony Marx (2003 to 2011). Jewish students contribute to this diversity, as they have for decades. Except now students on campus identify as Asian Jewish, black Jewish, and much else. Their Jewishness may seem different from their Amherst forebears. But like the Jewish classes beginning in the 1950s, these students are changing the college and its culture: they embody transformations in twenty-first century US Jewish experience. Over the last hundred years, a few key figures had the courage to effect reforms demanded by the times and to push for institutional change. The Amherst mission will continue to evolve in this century, with new students—Jews among them—enlightening and serving a wider world.

Author's Note

My sincere gratitude to all the Jewish alumni who shared their experiences and stories. To members of my Jews at Amherst seminar, Delancey King (class of 2018), Talia Land (class of 2020), Jesse Levitin (class of 2019), Jacob Nabatoff (class of 2017), Gabby Rose (class of 2019), and Mikayla Gordon Wexler (class of 2019), your curiosity, enthusiasm, and diligence produced excellent works of institutional history. The exceptional staff of the Amherst College Archives and Special Collections supported and enlivened our work. A special thanks to Peter Berek (class of 1961), a Jewish alumnus, colleague, and generous mentor. As I embarked on this work, Peter pushed me to ask all the right questions and seek all the right people.

Notes

1. On early New England campus life, see Benjamin A. Wurgaft, *Jews at Williams: Inclusion, Exclusion, and Class at a New England Liberal Arts College* (Williams, MA: Williams College Press, 2013) and David Potts, *Wesleyan University, 1831-1910: Collegiate Enterprise in New England* (New Haven, CT: Yale University Press, 1992). On the Landis family, see Edward Landis, "An Immigrant's Boyhood," in *Essays on Amherst's History*, ed. Theodore P. Greene (Amherst, MA: Vista, 1978), 273; and Joan Jacobs Brumberg, "The 'Me' of Me: Voices of Jewish Girls in Adolescent Diaries of the 1920s

and 1950s," in *American Jewish Women's History: A Reader*, ed. Pamela Nadell (New York: New York University Press, 2003), 226.

2. *Amherst Student*, September 22, 1894, 1; J. H. H., "Necrology: Herbert Baxter Adams," *Publications of the American Jewish Historical Society* 10 (1902): 173, 174; Herbert Baxter Adams, *The Church and Popular Education* (Baltimore, MD: Johns Hopkins University Press, 1900), 33.

3. Qtd. in Naomi W. Cohen, *Jacob H. Schiff: A Study in American Jewish Leadership* (Hanover, MA, and London: Brandeis University Press/New England University Press, 1999), 4. By the 1890s, New York alumni played an important role in the direction of the college. This coterie of bankers and others may have influenced Jacob Schiff's decision to send Mortimer to Amherst; see Richard Teichgraeber III's chapter in this volume.

4. Nicholas Syrett, *The Company He Keeps: A History of White College Fraternities* (Chapel Hill: University of North Carolina Press, 2009), 172.

5. *Amherst Graduates' Quarterly* 5, no. 17 (November 1915): 160; *American Jewish Year Book* 8 (1906–1907), 211; Mortimer Schiff, Biographical File, Amherst College Archives, Amherst College, Amherst, MA. On Schiff's financial contributions to the college, see Stanley King, *A History of the Endowment of Amherst College* (Amherst, MA: Amherst College, 1950) and *"The Consecrated Eminence": The Story of the Campus and Buildings of Amherst College* (Amherst, MA: Amherst College, 1951).

6. Harold Weschler, "The Rationale for Restriction: Ethnicity and College Admission in America, 1910–1980," *American Quarterly* 36, no. 5 (Winter 1984): 644.

7. Irwin Edman, "Reuben Cohen Goes to College," *Menorah Journal* 12, no. 2 (April–May 1926): 130; Daniel Greene, "Reuben Cohen Comes of Age: American Jewish Youth and the Lived Experience of Cultural Pluralism in the 1920s," *American Jewish History* 95, no. 2 (June 2009): 158. On disparaging notions of New York Jews, see Jonathan Pollock, "Jewish Problems: Eastern and Western Jewish Identities in Conflict, University of Wisconsin, 1919–1941," *American Jewish History* 89, no. 2 (June 2001): 171; Syrett, *The Company He Keeps*, 169–70; Stephen Steinberg, *The Academic Melting Pot: Catholics and Jews in Higher Education* (Berkeley, CA: Transaction Books for the Carnegie Foundation, 1979), 15, 8; and Marianne Sanua, "'We Hate New York': Negative Images of the Promised City as a Source for Jewish Fraternity and Sorority Members," in *An Inventory of Promises: Essays on American Jewish History*, eds. Jeffrey Gurock and Marc Lee Raphael (Brooklyn: Carlson, 1995). On quotas in the 1920s, see Marcia Synnott, *The Half-Open Door: Discrimination and Admissions at Harvard, Yale, and Princeton, 1900–1970* (Westport, CT, and London: Greenwood, 1979), and Jerome Karabel, *The Chosen: The Hidden History of Admissions and Exclusion at Harvard, Yale, and Princeton* (New York and Boston, MA: Mariner, 2006). On the "tribal twenties," see John Higham, *Strangers in the Land: Patterns of American Nativism, 1860–1925* (New Brunswick and London: Rutgers, 1988).

8. Jesse Levitin, "Jews and Athletic Culture at Amherst College at the Beginning of the Twentieth Century" (Jews at Amherst seminar essay, Amherst College, Amherst, MA, May 2018), 9–10. Philip Brisk, Biographical File, Amherst College Archives, Amherst College, Amherst, MA; Delancey King, "Muscular Amherst: The Experience of Jewish Student Athletes during the 'Golden Age of Sport'" (Jews at Amherst seminar essay, Amherst College, Amherst, MA, May 2017), Meiklejohn Collection, Box 7, Folder 1, Amherst College Archives, Amherst College, Amherst, MA.

9. For a discussion of the Amherst man, see Debby Applegate's chapter in this volume.

10. *Olio*, volume 62, 1919, 161, Elhanan Hirsch Golomb, Biographical File, Amherst College Archives, Amherst College, Amherst, MA.

11. Robert Thomas Brennan, "The Making of the Liberal College: Alexander Meiklejohn at Amherst," *History of Education Quarterly* 28, no. 4 (Winter 1988): 584. "Annual Report of the Union of Hebrew Congregations," Department of Synagog and School Extension, January 1916, 8047; *Menorah Journal* 2, no. 1 (February 1916): 261; *Menorah Journal* 3, no. 1 (February 1917): 253; Bureau of Jewish Social Research,

qtd. in Alfred Jospe, *Jewish Students and Student Services at American Universities: A Statistical and Historical Study* (Washington, DC: B'nai B'rith Hillel Foundations, 1963), 5. On "Jew-hooing," see Susan A. Glenn, "In the Blood? Consent, Descent, and the Ironies of Jewish Identity," *Jewish Social Studies* 8, nos. 2/3 (Winter/Spring 2002): 139–52. Also see Abraham D. Lavender, "Studies of Jewish College Students: A Review and a Replication," *Jewish Social Studies* 39, nos. 1/2 (Winter–Spring 1977): 37.

12. Alexander Meiklejohn, *Freedom and the College* (New York and London: Century, 1923), 135; qtd. in Brennan, "The Making of the Liberal College," 589. Notably, when Meiklejohn established Experimental College at the University of Wisconsin, Madison, the majority of out-of-state students were Jewish; Pollack, "Jewish Problems," 172. For more on the Meiklejohn era, see Richard Teichgraeber III's chapter in this volume. On faculty hiring, see Herman A. Greenberg (class of 1930), "Reminiscences on Prof. Herbert Friedman (at Amherst 1927–29)," May 6, 1982, Amherst College Oral History Project Collection, Box 2, Folder 31, 1, Amherst College Archives, Amherst College, Amherst, MA. Charles Cole hired Isaiah Frank in 1939 for a two-year position as an instructor of economics. President King applauded Frank's work but told him "they had never had a Jew as a member of the faculty," and therefore "there would be no prospect of a job." Family memoir, courtesy of Robert Frank (class of 1964). On anti-Semitism during the Depression era, see Marcia Synnott, *Student Diversity at the Big Three: Changes at Harvard, Yale, and Princeton since the 1920s* (New Brunswick, NJ, and London: Transaction, 2017), 66, and Leonard Dinnerstein, *Anti-Semitism in America* (New York and Oxford: Oxford University Press, 1995), esp. chpt. 6.

13. On the proliferation of Jewish-Greek life nationally, see Marianne R. Sanua, *Going Greek: Jewish College Fraternities in the United States, 1895–1945* (Detroit, MI: Wayne State University Press, 2003); "Lord Jeffrey Amherst Club 1935–1950," club pamphlet, Club and Society Collection, Box 23, Folder 7, Amherst College Archives, Amherst College, Amherst, MA; Stanley Marcus, *Minding the Store: A Memoir* (New York: Little, Brown, 1974), 33. On the apology, I appreciate the suggestion from Dick Klein (class of 1966), email communication to author, December 15, 2016. Also see Bill Ellis, *Class of 1936 50th Reunion Book*, 166–67, Amherst College Archives, Amherst College, Amherst, MA.

14. *Class of 1939 50th Reunion Book*, 45, Amherst College Archives; Letter from Charles Cole to E. Ernest Goldstein, January 12, 1940, courtesy of Dan Goldstein (class of 1969).

15. On Amherst fraternities, see Nicholas L. Syrett's chapter in this volume. On Jewish rushing, see Jacob Nabatoff, "Jews and Fraternities: The 100% Rushing Rule as a Progressive Step Forward for Amherst College" (Jews at Amherst seminar essay, Amherst College, Amherst, MA, May 2017); David Potts, *Wesleyan University, 1910-1970: Academic Ambition and Middle-Class America* (Middleton, CT: Wesleyan University Press, 2015), 250; Wurgaft, *Jews at Williams*, chpt. 3, esp. 116–26.

16. On compulsory requirements, see Levitin, "Jews and Athletic Culture," 8–9, and Mikayla Gordon Wexler, "Chapel Calls: Religious Culture at Amherst in the Postwar Period" (Jews at Amherst seminar essay, Amherst College, Amherst, MA, May 2017). On Hitchcock and the Amherst Plan, see Robert T. Hayashi, "The Student Body: Doc Hitchcock and Physical Education in the Connecticut River Valley" (Amherst College Reunion Presentation, Amherst, MA, 2015). On chapel "flashing," see Bill Weisberger (class of 1959), email communication to author, March 13, 2017. Also see Joseph "Joel" Andrews, "On Being an Amherst Student and Jewish in the 1950s," *Class of 1959 50th Reunion Book*, 40–44, Amherst College Archives, Amherst College, Amherst, MA.

17. Letter from Robert A. Ward to Bill Wilson, February 13, 1978, Eugene S. Wilson Papers, Correspondence Folder, Amherst College Archives, Amherst College, Amherst, MA; Eugene S. Wilson, January 17–18, 1979, Amherst College Oral History Project Collection, Box 2, Folder 31, 9, Amherst College Archives, Amherst College, Amherst, MA; "Massachusetts Tells Amherst 'No Pictures,'" *Amherst Student*, January 30, 1958, 1, 3; "Applicant X," editorial, *Amherst Student*, February 3, 1958, 2. I appreciate the suggestion from Leonard Gordon (class of 1959), email communication to author, January 2, 2017.

18. Mark Gerchick, "Bill Wilson: 'The Dean of Deans,'" *Amherst Student*, June 5, 1971, 6; "Looking Backward, and Forward," *New York Times*, March 4, 1981, A26'; Bill S. Wilson, "Admission to Amherst College in 1954," Annual Reports to Secondary Schools, 1947–2012, Admission Office Collection, Amherst College Archives; Martin Seham, personal memoir, courtesy of Lee Seham (class of 1984); Fishing Packet Folder, Eugene S. Wilson Papers, Amherst College Archives, Amherst College, Amherst, MA; letter from Ward to Wilson, February 13, 1978. Other perspectives on Ward have surfaced in recent years.

19. On Jewish faculty nationally, see Edward S. Shapiro, *A Time for Healing: American Jewry since World War II* (Baltimore, MD, and London: Johns Hopkins University Press, 1992), 100–1, and David A. Hollinger, *Science, Jews, and Secular Culture: Studies in Mid-Twentieth Century American Intellectual History* (Princeton, NJ: Princeton University Press, 1998), 7–9; "Amherst Teaching Debut Made by American Studies' Kazin," *Amherst Student*, October 10, 1955, 3, 6; Richard M. Cook, ed., *Alfred Kazin's Journal* (New Haven, CT, and London: Yale University Press, 2011), 194; note that Olsen taught in the English Department from 1969–70; Annemarie Iker and Katie Allyn, *Tillie Olsen and Amherst College: Conversations* (self-published, 2011). On Epstein, see Tim Clegg, email communication to author, December 16, 2016; Peter Strauss (class of 1958), email communication to author, December 15, 2016. See also Norman Birnbaum, *From the Bronx to Oxford and Not Quite Back* (Washington, DC: New Academia, 2018). On Marshall Bloom, see Martin Dobrow, "A Life in Full Bloom; 50 Years Ago, This Amherst College Student Embodied Turbulent Times," *Hampshire Gazette*, May 25, 2016, and "The Shaping of Marshall Bloom at Amherst College in the 1960s," May 26, 2016. Also see Christian G. Appy's chapter in this volume.

20. Lavender, "Studies of Jewish College Students," 37; Abram L. Sachar, "The B'nai B'rith Hillel Foundations in American Universities," *American Jewish Year Book* 47 (1945–46), 142; Deborah Dash Moore, *B'nai B'rith and the Challenge of Ethnic Leadership* (Albany: State University of New York Press, 1981), 141, 145.

21. Gabby Rose, "Shaping a Jewish Community: The Changing Role of Hillel in Jewish Life at Amherst" (Jews at Amherst seminar essay, Amherst College, Amherst, MA, May 2017), 4–5, 9; Rabbi Yechiael Lander, "Annual Program Report—B'nai B'rith Hillel Foundation, Smith College–Amherst College, 1977–78," Hillel Collection, Amherst College Archives, Amherst College, Amherst, MA

22. Talia Land, "Hillel at Amherst: An Analysis of Its Food, Friends, and Future" (Jews at Amherst seminar essay, Amherst College, Amherst, MA, May 2018); Lila Corwin Berman (class of 1998), personal essay shared with Talia Land, March 21, 2018; Rabbi Brenner Glickman, email communication to Talia Land, March 25, 2018. On "Jews doing Jewish," see Mark Rosen, "The Remaking of Hillel: A Case Study on Leadership and Organizational Transformation," Brandeis University, Fisher-Bernstein Institute for Jewish Philanthropy and Leadership, 2006, 41. On Hillel as "secular synagogue," see Moore, *B'nai B'rith*, 148.

23. Itai Grinberg, Sara Gubins, Michal Podell, and Ryan Senser, "Proposal for Amherst Hillel Center for Judaic Life," October 1994, 1, 3, Hillel Collection, Amherst College Archives, Amherst College, Amherst, MA. Also see Rose, "Shaping a Jewish Community," 7–9.

24. Jody Shapiro (class of 1983), email communication to author, December 16, 2016; Deb Vogel Kenney (class of 1982), email communication to author, December 20, 2016; Sharyn Stein (class of 1986), email communication to author, December 31, 2016. Also see Martha Saxton's chapter in this volume.

Coeducation

The Unanticipated Revolution

Martha Saxton

> [Coeducation] was a revolutionary event in the College's life in ways that few at the time foresaw.
>
> CULLEN MURPHY

President Martin, installed in 2011 as the first woman president of Amherst College, arrived when it had weathered more than four decades of coeducation. Her cordial welcome confirms Amherst's pride in the achievements and willingness to struggle with the challenges produced by men and women learning together.

Martin took the job with the ambition of helping the school's extraordinarily diverse student body make the very most of the college's academic, athletic, and social riches. Her administration is working to help identify and clear as many different paths to academic success as the college's diverse student body might need.[1] This project focuses on much more than coeducation, but its origins lie within the 1975 commitment to opening Amherst to women.

Actively helping faculty and students get the best out of one another consolidates a long-term change in the college's sense of its responsibilities to its students. At the time that Amherst first admitted women, there was little proactive thinking about what, if anything, women might need to help them learn in a very male-dominated environment. The college was not unique in this, but it had an embedded male, white Anglo-Saxon Protestant (WASP) mid-twentieth-century intellectual and social culture that proved frustratingly difficult to change. In describing that culture as WASPy, which many of the people I spoke to do, one must bear in mind that Jews have a long and important history at Amherst.[2] No longer subject to quotas, Jewish students entered the college in increasing numbers in the post-World War II years. Rather than a WASP culture, perhaps a socially and intellectually elite culture, which had recently been WASP is a better way to describe Amherst's ethos at the time. The keepers of Amherst traditions never doubted that their ways represented the best in US education and fiercely resisted change. Many unhappy women faculty and students in the first fifteen or so years of coeducation suffered with educational methods that worked well with only a small group of largely male, privileged students.

In a broader context, Amherst's experience with coeducation is both unique and tied to national developments. At this writing, women slightly outnumber men at the college. Nationwide, for many decades, the pool of qualified women applicants for higher education has been larger than the pool of qualified men. Ironically, male educators in the early twentieth century found coeducation in the public schools "defective . . . [because] girls did better than boys." Worry about boys' academic performance in the early twentieth century spurred some educators to separate the sexes to protect boys in classes where girls had the edge. Administrators brought sports into the curriculum, hoping to keep boys in school longer. Until the 1960s, educators invoked a "boy problem" with coeducation to explain boys' relatively poor academic performance compared with that of girls' and their significantly higher rates of infractions and dropping out.[3] However, coeducation was cheaper and more popular than segregation, so single-sex education remained the exception.

By the 1970s, educators and feminists began taking stock of coeducation's harmful effects on girls, like lessons from sexist textbooks, teachers' disproportionate attention to boys, gender discrimination in sports, sex-stereotyped activities, and advice steering female students away from science, math, and generally male-associated professions and activities.[4] In recognition of these findings, Congress passed Title IX (one of the educational amendments of 1972).[5]

With this national conversation in the background, formerly all-men's schools discussed admitting women. As with public school education, economics rather than principles largely drove decisions. Debts from recent expansion projects in the uncertain financial future of the seventies contributed to administrators' anxieties. But more immediately worrying to administrators was a nationwide decline in the overall size of the college-applicant pool and the rising number of young men who were applying to coeducational schools. Yale president Kingman Brewster summed it up: being an all male school was "a real handicap to getting the best men."[6]

Yale, first among the Ivies, accepted women applicants in 1968. Princeton, which had lost to coeducational schools 39 percent of the men admitted to the class of 1972, went next.[7] Dartmouth stepped late and slowly along the others' path. Its president, John Kemeny, new in 1968 and faced with the coeducation issue, worried that Dartmouth was "turning out a generation of male chauvinist pigs who would not be able to work with women in the professions." Dartmouth's traditional male culture made the transition notably difficult. (The title of Nancy Malkiel's book *Keep the Damned Women Out* came from a disgruntled Dartmouth alumnus.)[8]

Many trustees at Amherst cherished its masculine ethos. They also worried that the costs of expanding the student body and hiring more faculty would be prohibitive while potentially diluting the quality of an Amherst education.[9] It was not immediately evident that these fears would be baseless. However, one scholar summarized later: "The admission of women to the remaining all-men Ivy League colleges, as well as to such prestigious men's colleges as Amherst and Williams, maintained or improved these institutions' finances and academic standings."[10]

In January 1968, in the wake of Yale's admission of women, Amherst's president Calvin Plimpton met with the presidents of Vassar, Williams, Smith, and Wesleyan to discuss facilitating coeducational cooperation among them.[11] In the fall of 1969, Plimpton's Long-Range Planning Committee endorsed coeducation. The board voted it down. To delay things, they and newly appointed president John William "Bill" Ward (1971–1979) mounted the Select Committee to study the matter further. The committee included the first woman hired as a professor at Amherst, Rose Olver (1962). (She recalled that the experience on that Committee made a feminist out of her.[12]) It also included Ellen Ryerson in American studies. Between them, they constituted 50 percent of the women on a faculty of 135.

In November 1972, the Select Committee made its report in favor of coeducation to the board and president at the Century Club. The Century, perhaps the most exclusive club in New York City, excluded women until the Supreme Court forced it to admit them in 1988. The women serving on the Select Committee had to wait in a little lobby inside the entrance to the club, as Olver remembered, being "smuggled up" in the service elevator when it was time to make their presentation. The board rejected the Select Committee's recommendation despite agreeing in January 1973 to the principle that "a place of learning is built upon qualities of mind and imagination. Sex religion, ethnic origin, and race do not enter into it. . . . There is no principled reason against the inclusion of women in an environment of learning."[13]

After an election bringing some new and younger members on the board, it agreed in 1975, not unanimously, to admit women. (As one member said, "A good deal of the trustees feel that they have been pressured into this co-ed idea."[14]) It announced its decision with a toneless description of the numbers of women who would enter and when.[15] Bill Ward, who had been ambivalent about coeducation, echoed the flat statement. He said for some time afterward, he "felt no pleasure, either with the decision or with the fact it finally had been made. . . . I was simply empty." Perhaps he did not really consider it a victory. In professor Kim Townsend's study of Ward, he displayed little sympathy with the women's liberation movement and did not think an increased presence of women in public life would necessarily improve it, but instead make it more impersonal and contractual. Townsend calls this view possibly "prescient."[16]

These drawn-out and often acrimonious deliberations occurred during the social and political movements of the 1960s and '70s, as many institutions, including Amherst, were slowly diversifying their undergraduate bodies. Amherst faculty committees and administration, particularly after Martin Luther King Jr.'s murder and the terrible summer that followed, shared "the urgency" felt by black students in bringing "meaningful change" to the college."[17] Simultaneously, the brutal war in Vietnam produced protests at Amherst and across the country.[18] At the same time, students were protesting colleges' paternalistic behavior toward them and demanding more social and academic freedom.

However, feminism did not power the shift to coeducation, which was notable for its rocky implementation at most schools. As Nancy Malkiel, a scholar of coeducation, observes, "powerful men" took the decision to admit women, not women who were demanding their rights. As a result, "women and their needs were largely left out of the equation."[19]

In these vertiginous times, the Amherst College Council (January 6, 1969) had the task of developing new regulations for women visiting men at the college, to reflect changing attitudes about both sexual activity and student autonomy. President Plimpton's references to rules regarding "entertaining ladies" suggests how much ground the College Council had to cover to arrive at a vocabulary—much less a consensus—on the conduct of undergraduate men and women.

The council, astonishingly, seems to have been the only group in the college formally grappling with changing social and sexual attitudes, and it was surprised to find it time-consuming and laborious: "No subject has demanded as much time and thought . . . over the last three years as the question of what is the institutional context for women visitors to Amherst . . . an issue which many thought of peripheral concern to a liberal education." Professor and alumnus Frederick L. Hoxie, along with his classmate Robert Fein, met with the distinguished alumnus John J. McCloy at the University Club in New York City to discuss coeducation. Hoxie admits that the conversations were naïve but probably "unprecedented. . . . At least McCloy thought so."[20] If so, it underlines Malkiel's point that this educational transformation was made from the top down.

The council reported on two prevailing and equally unhelpful views: one, that premarital sex was immoral and should not happen or be facilitated; the other, that sex should be treated as a teaching opportunity. Professor Theodore Greene, articulating an impressive, not to say cosmic, ambition, wrote that the college should adopt "those procedures [in the college residences] which lead . . . toward a . . . serious discussion of the relations between the sexes and to clarify and question and develop appropriate moral standards for coming generations."[21]

The expectation at several campuses was that women would have, as James Fairchild, Oberlin's president, had argued a century earlier, a "civilizing influence" on men. Professor Olver remembered being pained to hear clichéd responses to the Select Committee's report, such as, "The presence of women would . . . tame the savage beasts in [the] dining hall, dorms, fraternities."[22]

Meanwhile, the uncivilized behavior of some Amherst men persisted despite students having set their own rules for women visitors. The College Council admonished students to "go out of their way to see to it that the personal integrity and sensibilities of visitors, in particular women guests, are respected."[23] Soon after a fall 1973 board of trustees' meeting with students to discuss coeducation, an infamous article called "Sleazing" appeared in the *Amherst Student*, which set out guidelines for extorting commitment-free sex from local college women. Its authors argued that Amherst was already as coeducational as was necessary: "I mean, when was the last time a Holyoke broad made a significant contribution in your English class?" asked the protagonist.[24]

Preparation for admitting women students meant hiring women faculty as well as living up to Title IX requirements. Although Rose Olver would be a welcoming and helpful presence for the twenty-seven junior faculty women whom Amherst hired between 1973 and 1978, the majority did not stay long.[25]

Marguerite Waller, hired from Yale in 1974, remembered being told by a male student (the only kind there were in 1974) that his father had paid a lot of money to go to Amherst, and he did not expect his son to have a female professor.[26] Young women faculty, some of whom looked younger than they were, had to work hard to be taken seriously and endured hostility and disrespect from their colleagues, no less their students.[27] Perhaps more significantly, in the long term, tenured Amherst men hired women in specialties new to the college, but often decided later that their initially intriguing fields, like Brazilian film, had no enduring value. Waller had studied critical theory, which actively repelled her new colleagues in the English department. Waller remembers a senior member of her department stating in a department meeting that he didn't see that what she taught contributed anything to anyone's general education."[28]

The English department, which arguably dominated the college's intellectual life and tone at the time, was composed mainly of men from Harvard, committed to rewarding professors who possessed "quality of mind," a hard-to-define and rare intellectual distinction whose ambiguity made evaluations and tenure decisions opaque. These professors made no secret of disliking critical theory and scholarship about gender—intellectual pursuits that, on other campuses, "[were transforming] the subjects studied there."[29]

Hoping to support struggling women faculty, the college, under president Julian Gibbs, hired anthropologist Mary Catherine Bateson as dean of faculty. Dean Bateson, who had just returned from revolutionary Iran, arrived at Amherst as five young women professors publicly announced that they would not stand for tenure. Some believed that they would not be judged fairly. As Kate Hartford remembered, "We'd seen another slightly more senior colleague rejected . . . largely, it appeared . . . because they couldn't accept the feminism in her scholarship." But Hartford herself left because she "found the College irredeemably racist, sexist, and elitist."[30]

Mary Catherine Bateson thought that Amherst's senior male faculty had replicated sexist stereotypes by hiring a cohort of very young, untenured women faculty, and that the setup was ripe for "bullying and patronizing." Hiring many women of similar age also meant that they came up for tenure at the same time and inevitably were pitted against each other. Among her recommendations was to bring two senior, tenured women to campus to have some strong female voices in decision-making roles.[31] She also recommended the appointment of "additional women to the board" and the "abolition of fraternities." The board adopted these proposals. Bateson wrote later that she thought that she "brought Amherst to a turning point in its treatment of women."[32]

New women faculty at all levels found the prevailing Amherst classroom style distressing. As Olver described it, she would deliver a lecture and then "engag[e] in hand to hand mental combat with the students." She noted that if students liked you, you were seen as insufficiently rigorous. (She later abandoned this kind of pedagogy with relief, but it served her well as the only woman on the Amherst faculty for some years.[33]) Cullen Murphy, of the class of 1974 and chairman of the board of trustees, reflected that "a lot of male students at Amherst would have been . . . learning from, this [style of teaching and coaching from men] all their lives." He thinks it served "that particular group of male students . . . creating a bit of a boot-camp atmosphere."[34]

The 1984 "Report on the Conditions of Work for Faculty Women at Amherst College" that Bateson had initiated set out to account for the fact that up until then, "more women faculty have left than remain."[35] The report stated that women found men's ways of teaching "abrasive, competitive and conflictual, showy, brash, sarcastic, rough and challenging."

Younger women who did not teach this way got poor evaluations. In addition to their classroom discomfort, junior women were forced to postpone their own research to serve in disproportionate numbers on committees. They found themselves expected, as women, to spend hours nurturing a stressed and unhappy student body,[36] while male teachers were seen as the ones providing intellectual guidance.[37] Few senior faculty members were interested in, or capable of, mentoring the research of women faculty members. Finally, the college still assumed one-career families and operated like a paternalistic family, rather than an equitable institution. Women faculty were expected to get tenure before getting pregnant; women who commuted faced discrimination; generally, college expectations for women faculty overlapped broadly with the traditional roles of faculty spouses.

As the first classes of women students entered the college (transfers in 1975 and first-years in 1976), problems surfaced right away. Many, who had been motivated to be pioneers of change at elite schools, suffered high levels of stress and lowered self-confidence due to hostility to their presence and lack of adequate advanced thought of their needs.[38] Arlene Stein was one of the first one hundred and fifty women admitted to Amherst's class of 1980, entering a college of fifteen hundred. Stein, who now heads the Interdisciplinary Center for Women's Studies at Rutgers, was excited at the prospect of being a trailblazer, but found herself very unhappy and out of place.

It was plain to Stein that most of the men were having a better time than the women because the college reflected them positively, particularly if they were "gentlemen jocks" and fraternity members. The women found no warm reflections of themselves. Years later, she found that most of her women classmates had been miserable like her but had blamed themselves and did not talk about their unhappiness with one another. She coped by excelling at her studies and spending her junior year at Brown. Stein found it impossible to separate class, ethnicity, and gender in understanding her deep discomfort at the college. She felt that the college made no effort to accommodate undergraduates who were not male, privileged, WASP, and athletically inclined.[39] In this, she anticipated President Martin's understanding that more than gender affects how students can thrive and therefore learn. Stein's critique was not unique, but there were, of course, women students in the early years of coeducation who thrived at Amherst. They were likely to be self-confident and able to fit in socially with the dominant culture. As women's athletic facilities improved, Amherst women increasingly enjoyed the egalitarian atmosphere of competitive sports.

However, women students transferred out. In the March 19, 1978, faculty meeting, a professor warned of a "potential exodus" of women seeking to transfer from Amherst. One woman gave as her reason: "To get away from the kind of college Amherst is."[40]

Amherst's "Report to the New England Association of Schools and Colleges" in March 1978 noted that the fraternities manifested a "degrading attitude toward women," and that there was an "increase in incidents of exhibitionism and voyeurism" requiring heightened security in the dorms.[41]

Many professors and administrators agreed that fraternities posed a threat to women's well-being. Materially, fraternities made it hard for women to find decent housing, thus violating Title IX. The fraternities, which dominated college social life, also dominated $5 million dollars' worth of real estate: the college's best living quarters. In 1980, fraternities were instructed to admit women, but the fraternities would admit no resident counselors (upper-level students living in dorms who advised other students on problems), and the college was generally in "police mode," trying to rein in fraternity brothers, with incidents that regularly included "vandalism [and] personal humiliation of students."[42] Former dean of students Ben Lieber recalled that a young woman student whose mother was helping her move into her room in a fraternity house was confronted with a pornographic mural in the laundry room.[43] Even after the trustees pushed the fraternities off campus, they still dominated college social life. Dean Lieber remembers that for two years, the juniors and seniors most affected by the demise of the campus fraternities behaved "horribly—that it was a pretty awful time."[44] Meanwhile, it would be ten years before the dorms were renovated with proper bathroom facilities for women

Peter Pouncey, from Columbia, assumed the presidency in 1982. He had no previous connection with Amherst and no nostalgia for an all-male environment. He had advocated for coeducation at Columbia in 1975.[45] He and his administration and several departments worked to hire women faculty members. In the academic year 1982 to 1983, Amherst had 157 male faculty and thirty-two women. (By comparison, Oberlin had 159 men and forty-seven women, and Smith had 223 men and 147 women.[46]) Between 1983 and 1988, fourteen women were hired who remained and got tenure at the college.[47]

Women faculty, continuing to find few to mentor and support their research, believed that the absence of a women's and gender studies department implicitly devalued their chosen fields.[48] The women's and gender studies department came up for discussion and a vote in September 1986. Objections to its formation came from male faculty who did not see it as a legitimate field of study but as the product of "political frustration and political need, connected with the change to coeducation and the changing position of women at the College." Professor Eve Sedgwick responded to these objections by pointing out that throughout the humanities and social sciences, there was "a flat distaste for unnecessary subordination," referring to the subordination of women and knowledge pertaining to them.[49] The faculty voted to found women and gender studies (WAGS; later SWAGS).

Meanwhile, coeducation clearly had not civilized some Amherst men. About two hundred women students and faculty occupied President Pouncey's office in the spring of 1985, to protest, among other things, harassment and assaults on women and gay people and what protestors saw as a perverse and ineffectual disciplinary system that forced students into mediation and almost never punished perpetrators. Women would not report offenses because they saw the mediation process as just further harassment. They asserted that the college accepted men's drunkenness "as mitigating any action, no matter how . . . destructive." They charged that three cases of "serious violence" were never even adjudicated, despite the fact that administrators knew about them."[50] Women spoke of "daily catcalls, obscene and abusive signs . . . anonymous phone calls late at night" that most had simply learned to tune out. But women were also withdrawing from seeking public offices on campus, to avoid further harassment.

Pouncey, the College Council, and students failing to get a fair hearing all pushed to reform the disciplinary system.[51] In 1987, the faculty condemned the old system as "deplorable" and created a new one without mandatory mediation.[52] (Despite these remedies, survivors of assault continued to see that system as a deterrent to reporting and unsupportive of their well-being. Under President Martin, Amanda Vann, and others, it has been revised so that reporting is much more frequent.[53])

Pouncey tried to put into Amherst's code of conduct a prohibition on faculty-student sexual relations, but the closest he was able to come was the statement that "many faculty at Amherst College believe that a sexual relationship between a student and a teacher betrays a teacher's deepest obligations."[54] Some faculty objected that such a prohibition would extinguish the essential "erotic" component of teaching. The college only voted in 2020 to prohibit sexual relationships between faculty and students.

For women students of color, racism intersected with the sexism they encountered. They found themselves working "in the classroom to educate classmates and professors that there were valid views outside that of white mainstream America." And they engaged with each other "as black students [who] mirrored every societal conflict concerning 'race,' identity, class and gender."[55] Barbara Liggon Smoot (class of 1984) reflected that "dealing with socio/economic/class differences as well as racial/ gender differences meant that I had to develop an inner strength to make it through Amherst. Today I can tell you I am one tough cookie!"[56]

The Pouncey administration, college students, and faculty in the 1980s fought and won some important battles in the service of greater equity on campus. When Tom Gerety and Lisa Raskin took over in 1994, as president and dean of faculty, respectively, Raskin was the first woman in this position who had been at the college since the very early days of coeducation. Although she had made it through her graduate school years as the only woman in the psychology department at Princeton, where porn movies were a common form of entertainment, she "didn't know she was a woman and different" until she arrived at Amherst. Hired in 1979 at age twenty-five, she was often mistaken for a student. Like Marguerite Waller, Kate Hartford, and other women faculty, she found Amherst debilitating, a social and psychological "pressure cooker."

But by the time she took up the duties of dean of faculty, turmoil and dissatisfaction among women professors had diminished compared to her early years at Amherst. Male and female assistant professors and associate professors were of equal numbers now. Of the full professors, 95 percent were men, but the growing number of tenured women had begun to alter faculty decision-making. She observed that the college had very strong individual departments and that they changed at uneven rates. During her years, three faculty women sued the college for discrimination in departments that were slow to change: mathematics, biology, and economics.[57] They were very happy with their settlements, she recalled, with wry satisfaction.

Younger faculty—not only women—were using less caustic teaching styles. Perhaps as a consequence, students felt empowered to ask faculty for what they needed. As professor Pat O'Hara in the chemistry department remembered, she was "haunted" by the plea of Ashanti Brown and her sister Amani (both class of 1997) to establish a quantitative-skills support center. Many entering students, hoping to be doctors, found themselves unprepared for boot-camp chemistry at Amherst and had to change their career goals. O'Hara was moved by the plea that students did not want to lower Amherst's standards but wanted to have the "tools to be able to tackle this . . . rigorous science curriculum."[58]. O'Hara had already begun offering extra courses (on her own time) to alleviate the problem.

The Moss Quantitative Center, which provides institutional support for students, emerged from these students' activism and the commitment of O'Hara and others. The Quantitative Center joined the Summer Science Program initiated in 1989, to give interested students a leg up when they encountered Amherst's rigorous science and mathematics offerings.[59]

On the social plane, the hook-up culture joined sexual assault as a problem, but not one susceptible to college regulation. Beth Slovic (class of 1997), a journalist and teacher, steered around it, and many other women—and men—did as well but refrained from openly criticizing it. She now believes that implicit acceptance of hooking up had the effect of enforcing heterosexuality: "I think I may have avoided talking about how I was not hooking up with random guys every weekend as a way to avoid suspicion that I was gay."[60] Slovic observes in her own classes now that her students are far more comfortable with varieties of sexuality—their own and others'—than her classmates at Amherst were. Decades before, Arlene Stein had felt that WASP jockness permeated Amherst culture. Hooking up expressed aspects of that culture. Meanwhile, sports teams replaced fraternities as the centers of social life. Hooking up also capitalized on the way the mythology of sexual freedom had largely been decoupled from women's liberation. Hook-ups of course are not unique to the college, but without coeducation, their consequences and embarrassments would be invisible on the Amherst campus.

Dean of faculty Greg Call and president Tony Marx presided over the greatest change in the composition of the student body since coeducation. Amherst began welcoming substantially increased numbers of students who were the first in their families to go to college, increased numbers of international students, and ethnically, economically, and geographically diverse students. While the tradition of boot-camp teaching was becoming rare on campus, the varieties of new students hastened its demise. President Martin recalls that in discussions during and after the 2015 Amherst Uprising, when students of color and others supporting them occupied Robert Frost Library, nontraditional students often pointed to the college's unpreparedness for the very diversity it invited. The criticism recalls the first women students finding only bathrooms with urinals when they arrived, symbolic of the college's obliviousness to the many changes needed to facilitate coeducation.[61] This history of lack of forethought suggests an ongoing, unspoken conviction that the college did not need to change.

But some professors *were* prepared. Professor Call of the mathematics department had dreamed of opening the curriculum up to all students for thirty years, believing that proficiency in math would do just that. In 1988, against his colleagues' judgment, he started a math club. Since leaving the deanship, Call has worked with the mathematics faculty to make the department one of the largest and most welcoming in the college. It now has an unprecedented seventy-five majors, of whom, a majority—thirty-nine—are women. The department has introduced an array of supportive initiatives that have boosted its remarkable expansion. Half the math faculty are women, and the department "is making strides in minority hiring." Professor Call says the transformation really found traction in the last ten to fifteen years, when national educational changes helped. Students now all arrive at the college with some calculus, starting out with more familiarity and less fear of math than students two decades prior. Professor Call currently hosts a Math Table (actually, three are needed to accommodate everyone) at Valentine Dining Hall every Monday. "Young and old go every week," he said, properly delighted with its success.[62]

Like Professor O'Hara, President Martin understands that students want to succeed on Amherst's academic terms, but sometimes need support along the way. She encounters alumni who remember with fondness the harsh teaching styles of their professors and wish it had never changed, but she reflects that the college has shifted from reverence for "quality of mind" to an equally demanding insistence on rigor.

President Martin and her colleagues are working with faculty observations and findings in cognitive science to identify and accommodate "learning differences" that go beyond gender, and can be influenced by generation, race, nationality, economic background, and degrees of ableness. On a more intimate level, she keeps open-office hours for students who want to come and talk to her. She offers individual strategies for students to find their way toward classroom comfort and recognition.

Cullen Murphy summarizes coeducation's role in the dramatic changes that he has observed at Amherst College since graduating in 1974. Amherst had long admitted "untraditional" students, but in small numbers, and those students adapted to Amherst—or not.[63] "The admission of women on a 50–50 basis upended this regime. For the first time, the institution as a whole had to change fundamentally. . . . I think coeducation permanently broke the mold ever after when it came to Amherst's thinking about *everything*—to the benefit of everyone."

Hailing the triumph of coeducation and its absorption into the wider pedagogical project of supporting diverse students, however, may be premature. There has recently been a sharp upturn in applications, and more importantly, yield—or students actually enrolling—at many women's colleges, including Smith, Mount Holyoke, Bryn Mawr, Barnard, and Agnes Scott. Admissions officers at women's schools, for the first time, are using the value of single-sex education as a selling point instead of trying to minimize it. Called by journalists the Trump Bump, this development may have to do with the behavior and language of our president and the actions of his administration. It may have something to do with the #metoo movement, or the increasing numbers of reports of sexual misconduct in the last several years on campuses across the country.[64] In an increasingly competitive world, it may have to do with the persistent findings that women educated with other women in their college years do better academically, and professionally. Whatever the combination of reasons for many women's growing interests in single-sex education, it seems that the debate about coeducation, abruptly interrupted by the financial and demographic concerns of the 1960s that underlay elite male schools' transition to coeducation, is resuming.

Notes

1. Carolyn Biddy Martin, personal communication with the author, August 20, 2018.
2. See the chapter in this volume by Wendy Bergoffen.

3. David Tyack and Elizabeth Hansot, *Learning Together: A History of Coeducation in American Public Schools* (New Haven, CT: Yale University Press, 1992), 166–70, 198–99.

4. Tyack and Hansot, *Learning*, 246–51.

5. Tyack and Hansot, 258.

6. Nancy Malkiel, *"Keep the Damned Women Out," The Struggle for Coeducation* (Princeton, NJ: Princeton University Press, 2017), 61.

7. Malkiel, *Damned Women*, 123–24.

8. Malkiel, 450, 461.

9. Alice S. Rossi, "Coeducation in a Gender Stratified Society," in *Educating Men and Women Together; Coeducation in a Changing World*, ed. Carol Lasser (Chicago: University of Illinois Press, 1987), 15; Malkiel, *Damned Women*, 468.

10. Leslie Miller-Bernal and Susan L. Poulson, eds., *Challenged by Coeducation: Women's Colleges Since the 1960s* (Nashville, TN: Vanderbilt University Press, 2006), 8.

11. Amherst College Faculty Minutes, 1967–68, p. 2313, Dean of Faculty, Robert Frost Library, Archives and Special Collections, Amherst College, Amherst, MA.

12. Kim Townsend, John William, *Ward, An American Idealist* (Amherst, MA: University of New England Press, 2014), 119–26; Board of Trustees Minutes, January 27, 1968, January 25, 1969, November 6, 1971, pp. 2318, 2369, 2513, Office of the Board of Trustees, Amherst College, Amherst, MA.

13. Minutes Trustees, January 27, 1973, Office of the Board of Trustees, Amherst College, Amherst, MA.

14. Townsend, *Ward*, 130, 126, 128, 133, 135; Minutes Trustees, January, 23, 1973, pp. 2566–71, Office of the Board of Trustees, Amherst College, Amherst, MA.

15. Minutes Trustees, January 27, 1973, Office of the Board of Trustees, Amherst College, Amherst, MA.

16. Townsend, *Ward*, 119–26.

17. Rosalind Rosenberg, *Changing the Subject: How the Women of Columbia Shaped the Way We Think about Sex Politics* (New York: Columbia University Press, 2004), 250; Beth Bailey, *Sex in the Heartland* (Cambridge, MA: 1999), 82, 85, 91.

18. Faculty Minutes, Dec. 21, 1967, January 8, 1968. Faculty Meeting Minutes (combined with CO6 and CEP and College Council) Minutes, March 10 and 12, 196, Robert Frost Library, Archives and Special Collections, Amherst College, Amherst, MA.

19. Malkiel, *Damned Women*, xxi, 170.

20. Frederick L. Hoxie, personal communication with the author, July 2019.

21. Faculty Minutes, January 4, 1969, under "Propositions for Possible Vote by the Faculty," Robert Frost Library, Archives and Special Collections, Amherst College, Amherst, MA.

22. Elizabeth Aries, Rose Olver, and Jane Taubman, *Gender Matters: The First Half-Century of Women Teaching at Amherst* (Amherst, MA: Amherst College, 2014), 102.

23. Faculty Minutes, April 24, 1972, Folder 29, Robert Frost Library, Archives and Special Collections, Amherst College, Amherst, MA.

24. "Sleazing," *Amherst Student*, November 8, 1973.

25. Aries, Olver, and Taubman, *Gender Matters*, 212–14.

26. Marguerite Waller, personal communication with the author, September 15, 2018.

27. Kate Hartford, personal communication with the author, September 17, 2018.

28. Marguerite Waller, personal communication.

29. Rosalind Rosenberg, *Changing the Subject*, 311.

30. Kate Hartford, personal communication, July 4, 2019.

31. Mary Catherine Bateson, personal communication with the author, July, 11, 2018.

32. Mary Catherine Bateson, *Composing a Life* (Boston, MA: Atlantic Monthly Press, 1989), 222–23.

33. Aries, Olver, and Taubman, *Gender Matters*, 99–101.

34. Cullen Murphy, personal communication with the author, November 17, 2018.

35. "Report of the Ad Hoc Committee on the Conditions of Work for Faculty Women at Amherst College," III, 36, Office of the Dean of Faculty, Amherst College, Amherst, MA.

36. The faculty and the College Council discussed the slowness of the college to "meet the needs of a student body consisting of men and women." The council further noted that "the racial and ethnic climate of the College is not ideal." The chair of the College Council reported on May 31, 1978, that "perhaps the unsatisfactory condition of student life is in part a result of the fact that Faculty members such as myself have shown total unconcern about nonacademic affairs. My present judgment is that when 'quality of life' gets to be in such a poor state as it is now, it does have an effect on the academic life of the College." See Notes of the College Council, Robert Frost Library, Amherst College Archives and Special Collections, Amherst College, Amherst, MA, 1978.

37. Notes of the College Council, 61.

38. Malkiel, *Damned Women*, 162, 221.

39. Arlene Stein, personal communication with the author, May 14, 2018.

40. Erica Poor, "AC '98 Homecoming '95, Remembering '75," *The Student*, from "File on Coeducation," Robert Frost Library, Archives and Special Collections, Amherst College, Amherst, MA.

41. "Amherst College Report to the New England Association of Schools and Colleges" (self-evaluation in preparation for the Visiting Committee, March 12–14, 1978).

42. Faculty Minutes, September 1979, September 5 1980, November 3, 1981, November 29, 1983, Robert Frost Library, Archives and Special Collections, Amherst College, Amherst, MA.

43. Ben Lieber, personal communication with the author, June 25, 2018.

44. Ben Lieber, personal communication.

45. Rosenberg, *Changing the Subject*, 267.

46. Alice S. Rossi, "Coeducation," 26.

47. Aries, Olver, and Taubman, *Gender Matters*, 216–17.

48. Aries, Olver, and Taubman, 41.

49. Faculty Minutes, September 29, 1986, Robert Frost Library, Archives and Special Collections, Amherst College, Amherst, MA.

50. "Ten Years of Coeducation," *The Student*, April 10, 1985, 8; "Report of College Council on the Judicial System, Robert Frost Library, Archives and Special Collections, Amherst College, Amherst, MA.

51. Peter Pouncey, personal communication with the author, 1997–2010. He continued to see the issue as an intractable "he-said/she-said problem," even with an improved disciplinary system.

52. Faculty Minutes, April 21, 1987.

53. The Clery statistics for 2017 to 2018 list twelve reported assaults, the highest number I have seen. See "Annual Security and Fire Safety Report," Clery Compliance Document, 2018, Amherst College, Amherst, MA, https://www.amherst.edu/system/files/ASR-Clery%2520Report%25202018_0.pdf.

54. Faculty Minutes, September 29, 1987, Robert Frost Library, Archives and Special Collections, Amherst College, Amherst, MA.

55. Mavis Campbell, *Black Women of Amherst College* (Amherst, MA, Amherst College Press, 1999), 153, quoting Karen Cole (class of 1985).

56. Campbell, *Black Women*, 77, 140.

57. Lisa Raskin, personal communication with the author, September 17, 2018.

58. Campbell, *Black Women*, 266–27.

59. Greg Call, personal communication with the author, September 17, 2018.

60. Beth Slovic, email communication with the author, July 7, 2018.

61. Arlene Stein, personal communication.

62. Greg Call, personal communication.

63. See chapters in this volume by Matthew Alexander Randolph and Rick Lopez.

64. Janet Zollinger Griele "Coeducation or Women's Education? A Comparison of Alumnae from Two Colleges: 1934–79" *Men and Women Together*, 118; Scott Jaschik, "Women's Colleges See Boost in Wake of 2016 Election," *Inside Higher Ed*, August 13, 2018. Barnard College had a similar experience, as did Bryn Mawr, Mount Holyoke, Wellesley, and Agnes Scott College.

Creating a Place for Latinidad *at an Elite Liberal Arts College*

Amherst College, the 1970s through Today

Rick López

Amherst College admitted its first cohort of working-class Latinos in 1972, inspired by the War on Poverty, the ongoing civil rights movement, and by its own mission to educate the best and the brightest students of all backgrounds. This small group of Latinos initiated a long struggle for inclusion within a student community that sometimes virulently rejected them. This chapter traces the process of diversification and cultural and economic inclusion at an elite college from the late 1970s to today. It also considers the dynamic between top-down and bottom-up initiatives.[1] The creation of space for *Latinidad* within Amherst has been inseparable from the role the college should play in the country and the world, and how the country and the world would be reflected within the campus community.

The surprisingly few studies of minority-student activism are based mostly on large universities in California or on K–12, and focus on ethnic studies programs and on repression that administrations deployed against student activists. While the findings of such studies reflect the general climate in which Amherst College students and administrators acted, Amherst's trajectory is different.[2] Elizabeth Duffy and Idana Goldberg's *Crafting a Class* remains one of the best studies of the interplay between minority admissions practices and social mission, yet it does not account for the agency of student activists nor campus climate, and twenty-five years have passed since it came out.[3] The lack of parallel case studies makes it hard to measure Amherst against other schools, but preliminary comparisons suggest that it was a leader, and remains so. This study attempts to explain how and why Amherst College emerged as a leader, along with the possibilities and limitations of its efforts.

PART I. CREATING A LATINO PRESENCE: FOUNDING LA CAUSA

When Les Purificación and Tomás Gonzáles (both class of 1976) entered Amherst College in 1972, as two of only five Hispanic freshmen, they were at the cusp of a transformation.

Together with Edmundo Orozco (class of 1974), who had arrived two years earlier, they created a Latino student organization called La Causa to foster community and help the college recruit Hispanic applicants.[4] Roderick Ferguson, studying student protests of the '60s and '70s, shows that elite institutions admitted minority students, but "at low numbers," deliberately staving off any potential challenge to the cultural and political status quo. Administrators felt enormous pressure to maintain the status quo by preventing minorities from impacting the culture of the campus, the epistemology of academic inquiry, or the power relations that sustained the existing model of higher education. This pressure came from multiple levels, ranging from the Nixon administration's 1970 "Report of the President's Commission on Campus Unrest" to the college's own influential alumni and affluent student families.[5] When Amherst College Latinos created La Causa, with its prescient commitment to recruiting working-class Latino applicants, they changed the future of Latinidad and set the course for the ways elite colleges could embrace economic and ethnic diversity.

It was Edmundo Orozco who initially led the way. He arrived at Amherst College in 1970 after being personally recruited by dean of admission Eugene Wilson (class of 1929 and dean from 1946 to 1972). Undeterred by the fact that he was one of only four Hispanics in the student body, the working-class Mexican American student from Carlsbad, New Mexico, enthusiastically immersed himself in the life of the college.[6] His freshman year, he served on the search committee that hired president John Ward (1971–1979), and by his junior year, he gained acceptance into Amherst's prestigious Independent Scholar Program to study US Latino entrepreneurship, mentored by the sociology professor Norman Birnbaum.

Dean Eugene Wilson is well known for moving beyond recruitment as a tool simply to "fill each entering class" and instead toward strategic recruitment and mindful admissions to shape the character of the college while fulfilling its mission. Wilson argued that Amherst's privileged position of having a low acceptance rate, a high retention rate, and strong financial resources gave it flexibility to lead in recruiting and educating a diverse student body. He engaged in "extensive recruitment both to make Amherst's name nationally known and to draw applicants of outstanding intellectual promise from every socioeconomic class and region of the country."[7] To this end, Wilson and his protégé and successor Edward "Ed" Wall (dean of admission from 1972 until 1982), hired Orozco at the start of his sophomore year to travel the country in search of promising Hispanic students from low-income backgrounds and lesser-known high schools.[8]

In the late 1960s, colleges and universities worked to attract the best black students to enhance their school's reputation and to establish it as an agent of progressive social change.[9] Amherst College was among the first to extend this same reasoning to US Hispanic and low-income students.[10]

Paying attention to economic class and cultural nuance, Wilson avoided lumping together Latin American students with its US Hispanics. This was important to the school's social mission because, while both groups contributed to student diversity, Latin American students at that time came largely from the white upper class, while US Hispanics tended to be poorer and had to overcome prejudice and inequality to achieve the academic preparation needed to gain admission to Amherst. Hence, Amherst and its peers saw Wilson's attention to US Hispanic and low-income students as an influential innovation.

Orozco saw the first fruits of his contribution to this endeavor at the start of his junior year, when Purificación (a working-class Latino from New York City who earned a reputation for political debate) and Gonzáles (a Mexican American son of a diplomat who had a reputation among his peers as a gifted and politically aware writer and orator) enrolled in Amherst. The three collaborated to found La Causa at the end of that same fall semester of 1972.[11]

Its charter stated: "La Causa shall have the following aims: the creation of a viable Latino social, cultural, and political body; also, the enlargement of Latino enrollment in Amherst College. La Causa shall be comprised of Latino students and concerned individuals." Toward these goals, it established the Central Committee, plus five subcommittees: *cultural,* to emphasize "the plurality" of "Latino culture within the United States"; *educational,* to develop resources in "areas concerning our academic interest"; *community affairs,* to encourage "socio-political ties to surrounding Latino communities, both in the Valley and" beyond; and, crucially, *recruitment,* to work closely with the admissions office to identify and recruit Latino students.[12]

According to Gonzáles, members knew that to create change, "you need numbers."[13] So, "one of the major things we did was get together with Dean Wall and go recruiting so that we could add to our numbers . . . to . . . be stronger." Katie Fretwell (class of 1981), who joined the admissions office in the 1980s and served as dean of admission from 2012 to 2018, describes Wall as "an outspoken advocate for coeducation and diversity at Amherst" who "orchestrated dramatic changes in the composition of the student body" and "[made] each student feel that he or she had been handpicked to play an important role in the life of the college."[14] Alumni from the era consistently express this view of Wall, who in turn respected them as agents of institutional change.

Juan X. Roca (class of 1975), from a prosperous South American family, found common cause with his working-class US Latino peers. In early December 1974, as cochairperson of La Causa, Roca sent a letter to high school students on La Causa letterhead stating that the group, "in conjunction with the Office of Admission and members of the faculty," was trying "to increase our enrollment of Latinos on campus." He announced that two Latino Amherst students, perhaps accompanied by a faculty member and an admissions officer, would soon visit their school to "speak with as wide a range as possible of both male and female" Latino "prospective applicants."[15] Such collaboration between Dean Wall and La Causa yielded seven Latino matriculants in the fall of 1975, a notable improvement over 1969, when the entering class lacked any Latinos.[16]

The seven working-class Latinos who started in 1975, along with nine white female transfer students (the vanguard for full coeducation the following year), introduced new kinds of students into the college, and some white male students made it clear to both groups that they were not welcome.[17] Ed Camacho (class of 1979) was a member of this 1972 cohort. Despite the small number of Latinos at Amherst, Camacho initially saw it as a huge improvement over his experience as a scholarship student in a New York City prep school, where he had been the only Latino in his graduating class and one of only three in the entire school. But Camacho recalls that faculty and administrators, and especially his fellow students, made him and other low-income Latinos feel like ethnic tokens and economic charity cases who, in exchange for an elite education, were expected to give up things that other students did not, such as connections to their family and culture.[18]

Soon after Camacho and his cohort arrived, the Student Allocations Committee (SAC) announced that it would no longer fund La Causa.[19] Previously, Orozco had used his connections in student government to gain fair funding for La Causa. But his graduation left Latinos without an experienced student advocate. SAC's actions taught Camacho and the other newly arrived Latino students that they would have to proactively demand a place within the Amherst community.

Struggling to adjust to life at Amherst College, they turned to the administration for support. Their interactions with Prosser Gifford, dean of the faculty from 1967 to 1979, left them dispirited. Though Gifford taught African politics, and seems to have been supportive of coeducation, Orozco and González, along with Camacho and other members of the new cohort, describe Gifford as hostile to African American and Latino students. A similar sense of Gifford's approach to students of color emerges from a 2011 interview, in which he claimed that the black student activists who occupied Converse Hall in February 1970, calling for the creation of a black studies department, were essentially saying, "'We want to be in control, we want to be in control of what we learn,' but ultimately it wouldn't work, and I think the better ones saw that."[20]

Orozco described Gifford as opposing the efforts of Wilson and Wall to diversify the student body. Camacho remembered that when he and other Latinos reached out to Dean Gifford in 1972 for support, he accused them of trying to separate themselves from the rest of the student body. Their multiple interactions with Gifford left Latino students with the impression that he would have preferred Amherst without the disruptive presence of working-class or minority students. Amherst administrators never reacted against student activists with the virulence seen at places such as Berkeley, where administrators cast minority student activists and ethnic studies as *threats* to diversity and institutional stability, and resorted to turning police powers against them.[21] Yet, Gifford's response demonstrates congruence with the paternalistic attitude that minority students encountered on other campuses.

Nevertheless, Wall persisted in his recruitment of Hispanic applicants. In 1975, Amherst accepted nineteen US Latinos (plus four Latin Americans). Ten of the fourteen initially accepted the offer, but, at the last minute, three of them decided not to enroll, leaving only seven US Hispanics to matriculate. As a consequence, Wall's office successfully deepened its collaboration with La Causa, involving its members not just in recruitment but also in encouraging Latino admitted students to enroll. The next year (1976) saw an increase to twelve US Latinos (2.9 percent of the entering class), the highest level that Amherst had achieved up to that date.

From 1976 through the 1980s, the office of admission continued to rely on La Causa members, openly sharing with them the names and contact information of Latino applicants and admits.[22] Institutional records show that between 1976 and 1985, Latino enrollment fluctuated between two and twelve new students per year, for an average of nine (just over 2 percent of each entering class). This small but relatively stable Latino community included a growing percentage who were female, working class, and from outside the Northeast.

Camacho recalls that the need for the sense of community that La Causa created was acute. La Causa welcomed "students who were white and who were black" and from all economic backgrounds, "anyone who was sympathetic to this notion that we needed to exist." But Latinos, in particular, saw La Causa as the only setting on campus where they could be themselves. It broadened their understanding of what it meant to be Latino while helping them feel enough of a sense of belonging on campus that they could focus on their studies.[23]

To create community while combatting negative stereotypes, La Causa members started with simple things like bringing a salsa band to campus and partnering with Valentine Dining Hall for Puerto Rican food night, serving *tostones*, *pernil*, and *arroz con gondules*. Luis Chaluisan (class of 1986), who was part of the cohort of working-class Latinos who started at Amherst in 1975, used theater and music to forge connections among people. He and Gonzáles each hosted a radio show on the college station, and, in 1975, Chaluisan founded Pa'lante, an annual dinner and talent show that brought together students from across the Five Colleges (the collaborative among Amherst College, Smith College, Mount Holyoke College, Hampshire College, and the University of Massachusetts, Amherst). Pa'lante continues today as one of Amherst's enduring student traditions.[24] Despite these initiatives, Latinos failed to convince the majority-white student body to accept them as equals within the Amherst community.

PART 2. THE FAYERWEATHER SIT-IN OF 1978 AND THE CREATION OF THE CENTRO CULTURAL JOSÉ MARTÍ

The chapters by Christian G. Appy (class of 1977) and Matthew Alexander Randolph (class of 2016) in this volume describe the long-standing expectation that nonwhite students should avoid gathering in groups larger than three, lest white students accuse them of separatism. This placed the burden for integration on minorities while absolving white students from any similar responsibility. Like Chicano activists across the country who rejected what they critiqued as the assimilationist politics of the preceding Mexican American generation, Amherst Latinos of the 1970s refused to abide the by the old rules. Instead, they congregated, increased their numbers, and demanded a two-way process by which whites and minorities shared the work of fostering an inclusive community.

On Wednesday, December 6, 1978, approximately thirty students walked into the Amherst College snack bar in Fayerweather Hall and began a three-day sit-in that swelled to one hundred activists. Three months earlier, Latino students had started the school year with high hopes. In his convocation speech, President Ward argued that the college needed to be a place "where differences . . . can be joyously sustained" rather than treated as supposed threats to the Amherst community.[25] The student government had ended the previous academic year with a plan to defund La Causa and other affinity groups. But, inspired by Wall's speech, Michael Barach (class of 1980) announced that the Student Activities Committee, which he chaired, would take into account that "minority groups can contribute as much to campus life as . . . [the radio station] WAMH and The Amherst Student" newspaper, and therefore deserved to be funded.[26]

In contrast to Barach's message of good will, the editors of the *Amherst Student* characterized the small number of Latinos as a threat to the college. They urged "the entire student body [to] maintain a close watch" to assure that these "special interest groups do not" engage in activities that might "undermine the sense of community."[27] With this, they dashed the hopes that President Ward had expressed.

Tensions spread from pages of the newspaper into a conflict over the airwaves. Minorities had complained for years about the fact that WAMH segregated soul, rhythm and blues, and other nonwhite music to specific hours during the weekend, prohibiting such music from being played on weekdays. Unable to convince WAMH to alter its policy, the Afro-American Society, La Causa, and an organization from the time called Straight Ahead sent a letter to the Federal Communications Commission (FCC), charging that the station was failing to "fulfill the FCC's charter which requires educational FM stations to take community interests into account," and therefore should be temporarily taken off the air.[28]

The groups that had drafted the letter to the FCC proposed a solution: add an official minority representative to the WAMH programming board. When the radio station balked, La Causa member Chaluisan threatened that if those in charge of WAMH refused to take minorities into account then, as "an absolute last resort," minority students might occupy the WAMH offices.[29]

The SAC supported minority students by threatening to withhold funding unless WAMH changed. Radio station leaders finally agreed to accept a minority representative on the programming committee, selected by their majority white staff. After prolonged negotiations, everyone finally agreed that the minority representative would be selected by the minority members of the staff.[30]

Revealing some students' sense of indignation, commentary in the *Amherst Student* charged that whites, out of a misguided sense of guilt, regularly allowed themselves to be steamrolled by minorities. A member of the class of 1980 complained that when white students called out minorities for infantile intransigence—comparing minorities to children throwing apple fritters in a dining hall and refusing to be corrected—they found themselves intimidated by accusations of racism. The student seized the opportunity to also denounce freshman orientation programs for African American students, not just as "useless, but actually harmful."[31]

Latino students recall how animosity from their white peers took a toll on their ability to focus on their academic and emotional well-being. Confronted by growing hostility, Camacho and Latinos requested from the dean of students a room where La Causa members could host events "as part of the campus experience and part of campus life." They met unexpected opposition. "I think his name was Dean [of students James] Bishop. . . . He was African American, but he didn't really understand why the Latino students and the black students" felt a need to meet together for community and to plan campus activities. "He perceived it as us . . . separating ourselves from the rest of the campus. His view was that we were all Amherst students, and that we shouldn't engage in that type of thing."[32] Even the editorial board of the *Amherst Student*, which instigated antagonism against minorities, expressed dismay at Bishop's refusal to acknowledge the existence of racial tensions on campus.[33]

La Causa members considered President Ward one of their few administrative supporters, but they became frustrated even with him. Reporter Emily Rubin (class of 1981) explained, in 1978, that in February 1976, Ward had promised La Causa members "all the help I can give" for a Latino cultural center. After almost two years of stalled negotiations, La Causa "quietly" occupied his office. Ward assured them that they would receive a Latino cultural center "in an accessible, visible, central location, not in a basement." But a week later, Ward wrote to Camacho, claiming it was "Dean Bishop's area to find 'a suitable solution.'" Bishop proposed three options: a room in Wilder Observatory more than a kilometer from the middle of campus, a small basement room in White Homestead that could accommodate only two folding chairs, or a basement storage room in Stone dormitory. Speaking to Rubin in 1978, Camacho said that "on a symbolic level the basement is the administration's way of shoving the cultural needs of La Causa underground. . . . The administration has an obligation to minorities to provide the means for developing and communicating cultural diversity."[34]

In mid-November 1978, President Ward abruptly announced his resignation, leaving Latinos worried that any hope of getting a cultural center was disappearing. They acted quickly. La Causa members found that "as long as you don't interfere with the process of learning according to the student Code of Conduct," it was "difficult to get suspended" for staging a sit-in. So "we decided to take over the snack bar at Fayerweather Hall."[35]

At that juncture, on Wednesday, December 6, 1978, students walked into the snack bar and art gallery in Fayerweather Hall and announced they would "remain . . . [there] until President Ward responds favorably" to La Causa's request for a meeting space. When administrators tried to force the protestors out by closing the snack bar, the students declared that if the administration refused to negotiate, they would claim part of the snack bar, Fayerweather room 102, as the Latino cultural center. President Ward finally met with the protestors, who assured him that they would leave the room as soon as they were offered a reasonable space.[36]

Student organizations, academic departments, and individual faculty across the Five Colleges sent letters supporting the sit-in to La Causa and to President Ward. One professor wrote that the fact that "Latino students at Amherst feel compelled to take over a building for something as simple as an adequate place to gather . . . speaks volumes about the College's lack of concern for the . . . needs of those students."[37]

However, editors of the *Amherst Student* chided Latino students, characterizing their occupation of the snack bar as "both unjustified and intolerable" intransigence by petulant minorities. The newspaper editors even created a "Dubious Achievement Award" to give to La Causa that they mockingly named "THE, 'HEY I HEAR YOU'VE GOT A SPECIAL ON TACOS TODAY' AWARD." [38] This award was combined with racist awards for other minorities. Camacho noted that "to his credit, President William Ward" recognized that these responses were "racist," "quite inflammatory," and "not the right thing for the white students" to be doing. They "proved the point that this is why this [cultural space for Latinos] was needed." [39]

President Ward apologized to La Causa for the newspaper's insulting award, and met with the one hundred protestors. Addressing them in the snack bar, Ward term the white students' insults "a minor strain of nastiness." He granted La Causa a former art classroom in Fayerweather Hall as a Latino cultural center, promising that when "a larger room should become available . . . , La Causa will have priority."[40]

The *Amherst Student* refused to back down, prompting other white students to defend their Latino peers. Emily Rubin (class of 1981), for example, criticized the "insensitivity and lack of recognition which the administration has shown toward Hispanic students, the insulting way the newspaper portrayed the protest . . . and the . . . many students who seemed more concerned with missing a few munchies than the important issues which were at the root of the occupation."[41]

The Latino cultural center opened in January 1979, and even the *New York Times* covered the students' success.[42] Steven Epstein (class of 1981) reported that La Causa "named the cultural center after [the famous Cuban essayist and poet] José Martí because he represents 'universal revolutionary struggle,' the same type of struggle which La Causa underwent last semester in securing the cultural center."[43] At the entrance to the Centro Cultural José Martí, they placed a plaque that read: "Conocer es Resolver," meaning "To Know Is to Resolve."[44] La Causa arranged a formal inauguration in March, with lectures by professors from Amherst and the other five colleges.[45] When Amherst constructed Keefe Campus Center in 1987, student activists held the administration to its promise to move the Centro Cultural José Martí to the new building. Disappointingly, however, the space they received was in the basement.[46]

PART 3. THE BACKLASH

After the Fayerweather sit-in of December 1978, Latinos found themselves confronted with backlash from some white students who viewed minorities as interlopers tearing at the foundation of Amherst culture. According to college records, at that time, there were only fifteen Latinos (eleven men and four women) out of 1,500 students, a mere 1 percent of the student body. There should have been twenty, but five had departed without completing their degrees. These fifteen Latino students contended with daily reminders that they were unwelcome. The editors of the *Amherst Student* even dampened Latinos' celebration of the Centro Cultural José Martí by warning them "not to let their cultural center become a place which fosters separatist attitudes and hostility to the majority culture."[47]

When individual minority students failed to convince the editors of the *Amherst Student* to offer balanced coverage, a group of student organizations drafted a joint letter to the newspaper criticizing its "shortsighted ignorance" and callous mockery of Latinos, blacks, and other groups. The authors asked: "Does *The Student* mean to say that minorities, in all aspects of the word, and their organizations are undesired . . . at Amherst College?"[48]

They argued that, for balanced coverage, the newspaper should give minorities a page in each issue to offer their own perspectives.[49] The editors accused minority organizations of trying to quash free expression. As the debate became increasingly acrimonious, the administration decided to step in to mediate.

The winter recess brought a short respite, but tensions reignited when a member of the class of 1979 accused minorities of taking advantage of white people's tolerance and posing a "separatist" threat:

> This is an unusually tolerant institution. [But] apparently, a minority of minorities have the attitude that this is a situation readily lending itself to short-term exploitation. . . . They seek special status as a group rather than fair treatment as individuals. They shy away from individual accountability and action. . . . A double standard exists. Minorities can coercively occupy buildings, slander the College, the student body, and society as a whole, but claim immunity from the fact [that] two plus two equals four, a la 1984. You'd better see five fingers or you're being insensitive and need to learn more about your own racism.

He concluded that blacks and Latinos "don't want equal treatment. It is abundantly clear that they want preferential treatment. . . . It's time to say, 'Enough!'"[50]

Tensions rose even higher after a member of the class of 1981 charged that "Black students cannot cry racism every time they are denied a whim, like the child who wails that his parents don't love [him] if they don't let him have an elephant or a ton of candy. Most students just laugh and say, 'no Mr Mtima [referring to Lateef Mtima (class of 1982), a black student leader], we aren't racists, we do love you, but this one piece of candy you just can't have."[51] In a cartoon that the newspaper initially tried to censor, John G. Russell (class of 1979) shot back by depicting a white, privileged Amherst student reclining in an armchair, paternalistically lecturing an adult-faced black child in his lap. He shakes his finger at the child, stating: "Now, repeat after me, my child: I have no rights that need to be recognized; I have never been abused; to be different is to be unequal."

Camacho also countered: "We want to be part of the College, but" without having to check our Latino culture at the door.[52] Responding to accusations of a supposed antiintellectual disdain for individualism, Walter Harris (class of 1979) wrote, "I certainly have never been accepted here as an individual. I am constantly reminded of my blackness, by whites in a hundred ways and on a daily basis. . . . The blunt reality is that we are perceived by the white community not as individuals, but as Blacks, Latinos, or Asians, i.e. collectively as members of a group. Racism at Amherst is a collective problem requiring a collective solution."[53] Even President Ward joined the conversation, arguing that "Latino and Black students wish to be part of Amherst College, and they wish to be perceived and treated with decency and respect, individually and collectively. Too often they are not."[54]

David O. Russell (class of 1981), of future film-making fame, argued that the real question is not why minorities might want a page in the *Amherst Student* to share their perspectives, but why some of his white peers reacted so vehemently against the idea that they should have a voice, and against the idea that La Causa should have a space within the Amherst community. "I am a white male from a relatively affluent background. . . . If I feel alienated, then one can imagine how the real minorities must feel." He asked: "Will students at Amherst give minorities an office and hope they'll shut up? Will students tell minorities, in more ways than one, to transfer? Or will the majority of affluent preppy whites at Amherst be receptive to different people and work to change and enlighten themselves socially, racially, sexually, and economically?"[55]

In the middle of February, President Ward convened an all-campus meeting to plea for greater acceptance of diversity.[56] The ideal, Ward said, was "the yearning for brotherhood and decency," but these "are not the reality of the College, and I'm sad to say they're not." He stated his greatest concern in the form of a question: "How do we honor . . . and I mean *honor* . . . the diversity among ourselves while asserting the value of our shared and common life together?"[57]

In the heated discussion that followed, Luis Chaluisan stood up to declare that being a minority at Amherst was to be treated like "a piece of shit," as though "[we are] against everything that Amherst stands for."[58] John G. Russell called out white peers who he claimed refused to accept him and other minority students as part of the Amherst community.[59] Clearly, the meeting had not gone as Ward had hoped.

But in the coming months, individual faculty and administrators offered personal support to besieged minority students, and the *Amherst Student* newspaper eventually brought in a new editorial board that was more accepting of diversity.

In the 1970s, the Office of Admission, under the direction of Eugene Wilson and Ed Wall, had established Amherst as a leader in student diversity and helped set the course that led to the creation of La Causa and the blossoming of Latino activism. However, under Ward's successor, Julian Gibbs (president from 1979 to 1983), those who felt uneasy about the presence of minorities on campus saw the tide shift in their favor.

LEGACIES, 1980S TO TODAY

The late 1970s through the 1990s saw gradual progress in how Amherst College presidential administrations thought about diversity and inclusion and how they responded to those who opposed the trend toward a diverse student body, but the path was not smooth. Wall and Ward were committed to diversifying Amherst but never managed to enroll a class of more than 2.9 percent Latinos. This dipped slightly under president Julian Gibbs, with a low of 1.6 percent, possibly to assuage certain conservative white students and alumni who were anxious about cultural change.[60]

After Gibbs died in office in 1983, he was replaced by Peter Pouncey (1984–1994). Pouncey and dean of admission Henry Bedford (1982–1986) increased the percentage of Latinos to a new high of 3.9 percent.[61] Linda Davis Taylor (1987–1989), Bedford's successor, accelerated this trend. Just three years later, when she handed the office to Jane Reynolds (1989–1998), she and President Pouncey had increased the number of Latinos from twelve to thirty-nine, establishing a new high of 9.3 percent for the class that entered in 1989. Initially, the Pouncey administration had recruited middle-class and high-income Latinos from prep schools but, for the class of 1989, Pouncey and Davis Taylor had shifted toward a much more difficult focus on working-class Latinos from urban and rural high schools.

Shifts that look small in term of statistics powerfully impacted the experiences of Latino students, particularly those from a working-class background. Under President Gibbs, as the number of Latinos, particularly those of working-class backgrounds, sagged, a rift emerged between the dwindling number of low-income US Hispanics and the more economically well-off Latin Americans. Uncomfortable with La Causa's ideals, a number of Latin American students created a splinter club called Hispaña in 1980, which was dedicated to hosting cultural receptions as a sort of extension of the Spanish department and competed against La Causa for funding from the student government. This split was difficult, because the number of Latino students was so small. By the late 1980s, the two groups had reunited, but at the price of La Causa abandoning most of its social or political ambitions.[62]

In May 1991, Aaron Greenman (class of 1993) correctly observed in the *Amherst Student* that La Causa had become so apolitical over the years that the organization had become "virtually non-existent."[63] He also noted that La Causa seemed poised for resurgence. The class of 1993 not only included the largest share of Latinos in the college's history, but it also was the most regionally and economically diverse and the most heavily low-income and first-generation group that the college had seen.

The new wave of Latino students resuscitated La Causa during the 1989 to 1990 academic year under the leadership of Anthony Wright, Michelle Duran, Jorge Armenteros, Nelson González (all class of 1993), and others, and then reclaimed a political consciousness and progressive agenda in 1991 under the leadership of myself (class of 1993) and Gilberto Simpson (class of 1994). Under a revitalized La Causa, Latino students became committed to fostering both mutual understanding and collective action.

Similar to what had happened in the 1970s under President Ward, the college's impressive recruitment efforts under President Pouncey came without a plan for how to create an inclusive environment. Students called for courses and epistemologies of knowledge that recognized the history and experience of minorities, pleaded with the administration to recruit faculty and staff of color, and to foster a culturally inclusive student climate.

In the spring of 1992, as riots broke out in Los Angeles in the wake of the acquittal of four policemen in the beating of Rodney King, La Causa joined with the Black Student Union (BSU) in a student takeover of the main administrative offices in Converse Hall.[64] They asked for better support for students of color, diversification of the faculty, and opening of the curriculum to diverse histories and experiences. Students won the support of a number of faculty, and their actions led to the hiring of a visiting professor in US Latino studies as well as a promise to work on diversifying the faculty. In a partial replay of 1979, this success was met by a backlash from segments of the Amherst community. Rather than give in to the backlash, Pouncey and Reynolds stood by their goal of diversifying the student body.

During the student takeover of Converse Hall in 1992, the *Amherst Student* picked up its role as mouthpiece for antidiversity voices, publishing articles such as "Force-Feeding Multiculturalism," "Diversity Seats do Little for Students," and "Ethnic Studies Department Unnecessary." But unlike 1978–1979, the newspaper now welcomed minority students' rebuttals, with articles such as "College Lacks Latino Studies Department" and "Diversity Seats Give Minorities Voice in Government," as well as letters to the editors defending the needs of minority students on campus.[65]

Pouncey and his administration had helped Latinos achieve a critical mass, and this made a difference for their campus experience. Whereas fifteen Latinos in 1979 had found themselves besieged, this time, there were around one hundred and twenty Latino students to support one another, respond to criticism individually and collectively, and maintain genuine debate.

The gains made by Pouncey slowed under his successor, president Tom Gerety (1994–2003). Under President Gibbs, Latinos averaged 2.25 percent of each entering class. Pouncey almost doubled this to an average of 4.38 percent in the first half his term, then almost doubled it again to 8.56 percent per year the second half of his term. Under Gerety, the percentage of Latinos in each entering class declined slightly to 7.74 percent per class during the first half of Gerety's term, then to 7.56 percent in the second half of his term, with a low of 5.3 percent (twenty-three students) in 1997, a figure not seen at Amherst since the mid-1980s. The hiring of Tom Parker as dean of admission and financial aid in 1999 led to improvements in 2000 and 2001, but the number of Latinos and other minorities dropped again and remained at that level for the remainder of Gerety's term.[66]

More significant than the stagnation of the numbers under President Gerety was the change Latino students felt in the campus climate, both from the administration and from white peers. La Causa members were well aware of the sagging or stagnating number of Latino and working-class students. They voiced their opposition when President Gerety cancelled minority orientation, refuting his claim that it encouraged minorities to engage in separatism. They also pushed back against the growing number of white peers who seemed to have become emboldened in their opposition to affirmative action and diversity efforts. The student government, meanwhile, slashed La Causa's funding, claiming that because not enough white students chose to attend its events, the organization was not serving the campus community. The tone of the school newspaper also turned decidedly negative. The lack of diversity among faculty and staff meant that minority students found few allies of color to whom they could turn for support at this moment when they felt that they had to contend with challenges on all sides.[67]

Yet, the outcome was not the same as it had been in the 1980s, because a group of students led by Lori Casillas (class of 1995) and others had formed an organization called the Chicano Caucus in 1993 and had created a US Latino cultural house called La Casa. The Chicano Caucus provided politically engaged Latinos (not just Chicanos) with a space in which to express their concerns and defend their political ideals on and off campus in collaboration with La Causa and the Black Student Union. And La Casa, the cultural house, gave students a place to find a sense of belonging within a campus on which they felt marginalized.

Latino students found relief when President Gerety was succeeded by Tony Marx (2003–2011). The new president made ethnic and economic diversity a priority for his administration and brought Latino enrollment to a new high of 13.7 percent (sixty-three students) by the end of his term. President Gerety had favored a hands-off approach regarding diversity and inclusion. President Marx, by contrast, took a personal interest in increasing the college's ethnic and economic diversity, while recruiting ever more academically competitive students. He brought his senior staff on board, offered sustained institutional support for these goals, and fostered student conversation. Marx partnered with Parker to develop the college's relationship with QuestBridge (a national organization that connected low-income students with selective colleges and universities) to recruit low-income students and to inaugurate a new policy that enabled them to graduate debt free. Marx and Parker added admissions staff to focus on the recruitment of nontraditional students, created a fly-in program for low-income prospective students to visit campus, and reached out to trustees, alumni, and other donors to win their enthusiastic backing.[68]

Marx's successor Carolyne "Biddy" Martin (2011–present) and her senior staff solidified diversity and inclusion as core elements of Amherst College's modern cultural identity. Dean of admission and financial aid Tom Parker was succeeded by Katie Fretwell (class of 1981) in 2015, and then by Matt McGann in 2019, each of whom devoted themselves to recruiting the best students of every ethnic and economic background. Except for a small dip in 2017, when Amherst lost students to Yale's effort to increase the size and diversity of its student body. Latinos comprised between 13 and 14.2 percent of each Amherst College entering class.

In the fall of 2017, President Martin supported the creation of the US Latinx and Latin American studies (LLAS) program, which grew out of years of planning by a group of faculty and students.[69] Through LLAS, Amherst has affirmed an institutional presence for diverse ways of experiencing and studying Latinidad. Through its curricular offering and institutional presence, LLAS welcomes US Latinx and Latin American students and faculty into the Amherst intellectual community while preparing *all* Amherst students to succeed in a changing world.

CONCLUSION

Reflecting on the impact of her time at Amherst, Mari Curbelo (class of 1980) proposes that perhaps it was the adversity she overcame at Amherst within an intimate community that led her to develop her political consciousness. It "was almost like an incubator for some of us to then move on and bring that sense of identity and community and social justice to the outside world."[70] The case of Amherst College suggests that the strength of its transformation results from the fact that its commitment to diversity and inclusion was forged through struggle and experimentation, advanced by ideal-driven leadership from above and committed student activism from below. This process has made the changes more enduring than if they had been merely rhetorical, or imposed from on high, or if they had been only tolerated or subtly undermined, as scholars have found has occurred too often within higher education.

The absence of similar case studies focusing on other elite campuses makes it difficult to draw definitive conclusions about how the success of Amherst College compares with other campuses, but existing studies, combined with a sense of the broad landscape of higher education, do allow for some tentative conclusions. Amherst did not resort to intensive policing or criminalization of student protesters, nor did it delegitimize student voices while casting the professionalized administrative bureaucracy as the true defender of diversity and inclusion. On the contrary, even as it has done so imperfectly, Amherst has prioritized intensive engagement among its students and among students, faculty, alumni, and administrators. By creating enduring change through leadership and sustained engagement, rather than by bureaucratic fiat, it has become a leader among its peers on economic and ethnic diversity.

Notes

1. Students from the US Latino history course taught by myself and professor Solsiree del Moral in the fall of 2016 located and organized these documents and deposited the collection into the Amherst College Archives and Special Collections. I want to thank the following student researchers for their work organizing the La Causa Papers and conducting interviews: Irma Zamora (class of 2017), Helen Burgueño (class of 2021), Joshua Hernández (class of 2020), Genesis Peña (class of 2020), Brittanie Lewis (class of 2017), and Diego Gómez (class of 2020). Thank you, also, to Mike Kelly and Rachel Jirka in the Archives and Special Collections; the many alumni who shared their stories through interviews; Jesse Barba in Institutional Research for his help with data; and the Latinx and Latin American studies program (inaugurated in fall 2017) for its ongoing support for research into the history of Latinx students at Amherst College; and to my colleagues who read the drafts of this essay and offered crucial feedback and advice.

2. Roderick Ferguson, *We Demand: The University and Student Protests* (Berkeley: University of California Press, 2017); Irum Shiekh, *On Strike! Ethnic Studies, 1969–1999* (Center for Asian American Studies, University of California Berkeley, 2008), documentary film; Carlos Muñoz Jr., *Youth, Identity, Power: The Chicano Movement* (New York: Verso, [1989] 2007); Suzanne Oboler, *Ethnic Labels, Latino Lives: Identity and the Politics of (Re)Presentation in the United States* (Minneapolis: University of Minnesota Press, 1995), 59–66; Kathryn Schumaker, *Troublemakers: Students' Rights and Racial Justice in the Long 1960s* (New York: New York University Press, 2019); Victoria-María MacDonald, *Latino Education in the United States: A Narrated History from 1513–2000* (New York: Palgrave MacMillan, 2004), 215–73.

3. Elizabeth Duffy and Idana Goldberg, *Crafting a Class: College Admissions and Financial Aid, 1955–1994* (Princeton, NJ: Princeton University Press, 1998).

4. Note that students at the time used the terms *Hispanic* and *Latino* interchangeably to individuals of Latin American heritage who grew up in the United States. On rare occasions, their use of the term *Latino* also encompassed individuals from Latin America. In this chapter, I will follow their practice of using *Hispanic* and *Latino* interchangeably to refer to individuals who grew up in the United States, and will try to clarify where I refer to international students from Latin America.

5. Ferguson, *We Demand*, 9–10.

6. Edmundo Orozco, interview by Rick López, May 15, 2018. Two Hispanics entered in 1968, zero in 1969, and two (including Orozco) in 1970, according to a data report from the Amherst College Department of Institutional Research.

7. Elizabeth Duffy and Idana Goldberg, eds., "Admission to Amherst College: The O'Connell Report," in *Crafting a Class: College Admissions and Financial Aid, 1955–1994* (Princeton, NJ: Princeton University Press, 1998), 25, 37, and 45.

8. Orozco, interview.

9. Duffy and Goldberg, "Admission," 141.

10. Minutes of the Faculty Committee on Admission and Financial Aid, March 18, 1970, Amherst College Archives, cited by Duffy and Goldberg, "Admission," 147. In her 2011 study of student recruitment at Amherst College, Rachel Rubin shows that the institution's success resulted from the fact that it had an unusually long-term commitment to diversity that transcended rhetoric. See Rachel B. Rubin, "Recruiting, Redefining, and Recommitting: The Quest to Increase Socioeconomic Diversity at Amherst College," *Equity & Excellence in Education* 44, no. 4 (2011): 512–31.

11. Orozco, interview; Ed Camacho, interview by Rick López, March 22, 2018; Les Purificación, interview by Diego Gómez, June 8, 2018; and Tomás Gonzáles, interview by Diego Gómez, May 16, 2018.

12. Constitution of La Causa, circa 1972/73, Box 1, Folder 13, La Causa Papers, Archives and Special Collections, Amherst College, Amherst, MA. The founders disagree about whether they chose the name "La Causa" in honor of the United Farm Workers' Union led by César Chávez, where, unbeknownst to the students, Jerry Cohen (class of 1963) served as general counsel starting in 1967. On Jerry Cohen and the United Farm Workers, see Jerry Cohen, "Gringo Justice: The United Farm Workers Union, 1967–1981" (unpublished manuscript, February 2008), and the rich holdings of the Jerry Cohen Papers, Archives and Special Collections, Amherst College, Amherst, MA.

13. Gonzáles, interview.

14. Katie Fretwell, "In Memorium: Ed Wall," *Amherst Magazine*, Winter 2004.

15. Juan X. Roca, "Co-Chairperson of La Causa to high schools," December 2, 1974, Box 1, Folder 9, La Causa Papers, Archives and Special Collections, Amherst College, Amherst, MA.

16. Data Report, Department of Institutional Research, Amherst College, Amherst, MA.

17. Helen Deutsch, "Women's Studies, Solitude and Struggle," *Amherst Student*, October 5, 1978. Deutsch writes: "When Women first arrived at Amherst in 1976, a Women's Studies major arrived with them," and in 1978, there were three students completing the major.

18. Ed Camacho, interview by Brittanie Lewis, June 25, 2017; and Ed Camacho, interview by Rick López, March 22, 2018.

19. Daniel Calvert, "La Causa: Siempre Pa'lante" (unpublished senior honors thesis, Amherst College, May 18, 2007).

20. Prosser Gifford, interview by Robert Townsend, June 8, 2011, Amherst College Oral History Project, Frost Library, Amherst College, Amherst, MA; "Blacks Seize Buildings," *Amherst Student*, February 18, 1970; "Black Demands in Brief," *Amherst Student*, February 19, 1970.

21. Ferguson, *We Demand*, 6–11; and Shiekh, *On Strike!*

22. Lists of Hispanic American students matriculating each year, 1976–1981, Box 1, Folder 7, La Causa Papers, Archives and Special Collections, Amherst College, Amherst, MA, and Data Report.

23. Gonzáles, interview; and Ed Camacho, interview, June 25, 2017.

24. Gonzáles, interview; Héctor Banegas, interview by Diego Gómez , January 5, 2019; Program for Pa'lante, inaugural year of 1975, in possession of Luis Chaluisan; quotated from Ed Camacho, interview, June 25, 2017.

25. Quoted in Martin Melaver, "Ward Opens Year," *Amherst Student*, September 11, 1978.

26. Quoted in "SAC Receives Record Requests," *Amherst Student*, September 25, 1978.

27. Editorial Board, "Funding Communal Plurality," *Amherst Student*, September 25, 1978.

28. "WAMH, Minorities, Airwaves Rippled," *Amherst Student*, October 9, 1978.

29. "WAMH, Minorities."

30. "WAMH modulates," *Amherst Student*, October 12, 1978.

31. Gib Hecker, "Racism, a Tragedy of Errors," *Amherst Student*, October 26, 1978.

32. Camacho, interview, June 25, 2017.

33. "A Dean for Students," *Amherst Student*, November 6, 1978.

34. Rubin, "Fayerweather Occupied." *Amherst Student*, White Homestead was later converted into the Wilson Admission Center. On the size of the rooms, see Tomás Gonzáles, interview by Diego Gómez, May 15, 2018; Juan X. Roca, interview by Brittany Lewis, August 6, 2017; and "Amherst Sets Protest Deadline," *Boston Globe*, December 8, 1978.

35. Camacho, interview; Héctor Banegas, interview by Diego Gómez, January 5, 2019; Emily Rubin, "Fayerweather"

36. Camacho, interview.

37. Roberto Márquez, professor at Hampshire College to John William Ward (Amherst College president), December 8, 1978, Box 1, Folder 10, La Causa Papers, Archives and Special Collections, Amherst College, Amherst, MA. La Causa's archives contain letters from student organizations at Amherst College, University of Massachusetts (UMass), Mount Holyoke College, Hampshire College, and several UMass academic departments and centers.

38. Editorial Board, "'The Cause' Celebre," *Amherst Student*, December 7, 1978.

39. Camacho, interview, March 22, 2018, and Calvert, "La Causa."

40. Emily Rubin, "La Causa Sit-In Successful," *Amherst Student*, December 14, 1978.

41. Anonymous, letter to the editors, *Amherst Student*, December 14, 1978.

42. "A Sit-In Ends at Amherst College after Accord on Hispanic Center," *New York Times*, December 9, 1978.

43. Steven Epstein, "*Centro Cultural* to Open," *Amherst Student*, March 8, 1979.

44. Camacho, interview, March 22, 2018.

45. Ginger Howard, "La Causa Center Opens," *Amherst Student*, February 1, 1979, and Epstein, "*Centro Cultural*."

46. Cesar Paulino (class of 1988) describes the conversations that led to the move to Keefe and the support of dean Ben Lieber. See Cesar Paulino, interview by Diego Gómez, December 22, 2017, and Ben Lieber, dean of students, to Cheng Gon Jon, January 23, 1987, Box 1, Folder 10, La Causa Papers, Archives and Special Collections, Amherst College, Amherst, MA.

47. Editorial Board, editorial, *Amherst Student*, December 14, 1978.

48. Third World Forum, Afro-American Society, La Causa, Gay Alliance, Women's Center, and Straight Ahead Committee, letter to the editors, *Amherst Student*, December 14, 1978.

49. Diane Oklandek, "Third-World Groups Demand Page," *Amherst Student*, December 14, 1978.

50. Eric Grover, "Chauvinistic Opportunists," *Amherst Student*, February 5, 1979.

51. David Bershtein, "Nihilistic Racism," *Amherst Student*, February 5, 1979.

52. John Rosenzweig, "Minorities Spurn E-Board," *Amherst Student*, February 1, 1979.

53. Walter Harris, "A Collective Problem," *Amherst Student*, February 8, 1979. See also *Going through College, a Perspective*, directed by John David Coles and Kim Farry, 1978, Archives and Special Collections, Amherst College, Amherst, MA.

54. Quoted in Harris, "Collective Problem."

55. David O. Russell, letter to the editors, *Amherst Student*, February 8, 1979.

56. "College Meeting," *Amherst Student*, February 5, 1979.

57. Quoted in Brad Justus, "Ward Report to Campus, Discussed Racial Climate," *Amherst Student*, February 12, 1979.

58. Justus, "Ward."

59. Ezekiel Emanuel, letter to the editors, *Amherst Student*, February 15, 1979. Emanuel describes Russell's comments in order to take issue with his accusations.

60. This observation emerged repeatedly among interview subjects, and is corroborated by institutional admissions data.

61. Rachel Rubin similarly notes the importance of presidential leadership in setting the agenda for the Amherst Office of Admission, as well as for the broader campus culture. Rubin, "Recruiting, Redefining, and Recommitting," 512–31.

62. María "Mari" Catalina Curbelo, interview with Diego Gómez, February 29, 2018; various, Box 1, Folder 3; La Causa Minutes, Meeting #2, September 21, 1980, Box 1, Folder 8, La Causa Papers, Archives and Special Collections, Amherst College, Amherst, MA.

63. Aaron Greenman, "Amherst Cultural Organizations Enliven Campus Life," *Amherst Student*, May 26, 1991.

64. Sarah Levesque, "Students List Demands, Amherst College Takeover Continues," *Collegian* (UMass), Wednesday, May 6, 1992, front page.

65. Walton Burns, "Diversity Seats Do Little for Students," *Amherst Student*, October 26, 1994; Nikhil Rao, "Ethnic Studies Department Unnecessary," *Amherst Student*, May 3, 1995; A. E. Sokol, "Force-Feeding Multiculturalism," *Amherst Student*, April 5, 1995; Jorge Armenteros, "Diversity Seats Give Minorities Voice in Government," *Amherst Student*, December 4, 1991; Luis Espinoza, letter to the editors, *Amherst Student*, September 30, 1992; Amanda Birmingham, "College Lacks Latino Studies Department," *Amherst Student*, March 2, 1994; and Susan Williams, "BSU Letter Addresses Black Enrollment," *Amherst Student*, November 6, 1996, front page.

66. "Amherst College Annual Reports to Secondary Schools" and Institutional Research Reports.

67. La Causa budget documents and letters, Spring 1998, Box 1, Folder 5, Archives and Special Collections, Amherst College, Amherst, MA; Antonio Martinez, La Causa Alumni Representative, letter to alumni, March 9, 1997, Archives and Special Collections, Amherst College, Amherst, MA; Rina Reyes and Seagram Villagomez, to E-Board La Causa Paper, Archives and Special Collections, Amherst College, Amherst, MA.

68. Tom Parker, interview by Diego Gómez, August 12, 2014.

69. During a spring 2014 dinner meeting at President Martin's home with faculty, students, and staff, President Martin, endorsed the proposal by La Causa member Carlos González Sierra (class of 2014) to explore the possibility of such a major. She appointed Rick López (class of 1993) chair of the ad hoc exploratory committee. Faculty and students (including Hugo Sánchez [class of 2017] and Irma Zamora [class of 2017]) met weekly for about a year (2014–2015) and consulted with colleagues at Amherst College and within the Five Colleges to consider all options, and then proposed a detailed plan. After a reorganization of the Spanish department during the 2015 to 2016 academic year, including the hiring of professor Paul Schroeder Rodríguez to chair Spanish, a group of faculty consisting of Rick López, Paul Schroeder Rodríguez, Solsiree del Moral, Leah Schmalzbauer, and Mary Hicks drafted a proposal for the new major during the 2016 to 2017 academic year. In light of the Amherst Uprising that had occurred during November 2015, and with strong support from the dean of the faculty Catherine Epstein, President Martin, the Committee of Six, and the Committee on Educational Policy, they proposed the new department to the faculty, which, on May 18, 2017, voted unanimously to endorse its creation.

70. Curbelo, interview.

Remembering Dunbar

Amherst College and African American Education in Washington, DC

Matthew Alexander Randolph

Charles Drew Memorial Cultural House, the only dormitory on Amherst College's campus named after a black alumnus, reminds passersby of Amherst's extensive African American history.[1] Charles Drew's lifesaving innovations in blood preservation contributed to the Allied effort during World War II, and Drew was also an unforgettable football and track legend during his Amherst days. In 1987, Charles Drew Memorial Cultural House officially became a themed residence hall at Amherst as a "testament to [Drew's] continuous inspiration and example."[2] Beyond Drew as an individual is the larger story of a long-standing connection between Amherst and his black public high school in Washington, DC.

Across the twentieth century, Amherst graduated more students from Paul Laurence Dunbar High School than any other college outside of Washington, DC.[3] Dunbar men frequently entered Amherst in pairs or larger cohorts. They included men who would go on to become household names in African American history such as William Hastie, a groundbreaking federal judge, and Montague Cobb, a president of the National Association for the Advancement of Colored People (NAACP).

For some class years, Dunbar students made up the majority, if not the entirety, of black students attending Amherst. Harold Wade (class of 1968) wrote in his posthumously published *Black Men of Amherst* that "the school's reputation was so great, it is reported, that Amherst College would accept any student recommended by the Dunbar administration without the student even having to take an entrance examination."[4]

As a black public high school in a separate and unequal school system, Dunbar upended the traditional notion of feeder schools as private, predominantly white institutions like Exeter, Deerfield, and Andover. The legacy of Dunbar students gave (and continues to give) Amherst an early twentieth-century precedent for black students' potential for success on its campus, an experiment in student diversity that predates the racial history of peer institutions of higher education.

Yet the question remains: Why and how did so many black students from Dunbar end up enrolling at Amherst during the first half of the twentieth century? What forces—both at Amherst College and in Washington, DC—enabled and sustained this academic pipeline?

Dunbar was the first black public high school in the nation, "the jewel in the crown of the black school system" in Washington, DC, during the age of segregation.[5] Dunbar's teachers included several notable experts in their fields such as Carter G. Woodson. Known as the "Father of Black History," Woodson balanced teaching at DC public schools with his doctoral studies.[6] In 1912, he became the second African American to earn a PhD from Harvard University after W. E. B. Du Bois. Not surprisingly, with teachers of such caliber, as one alumnus from the Dunbar class of 1957 recalled, Dunbar became "the place to go if you thought you were college material and wanted to be prepared to go."[7]

From 1870 until the Supreme Court finally ruled the segregation of public schools unconstitutional in 1954, Washington, DC, operated a dual school system. The black division of the school system operated with a notable degree of independence under the supervision of a black assistant superintendent. As George Derek Musgrove and Chris Myers Asch explain in *Chocolate City: A History of Race and Democracy in the Nation's Capital,* black Washingtonians adapted to the challenges of segregation by striving "for black autonomy and equated educational excellence with their ability to run their schools relatively free from white interference."[8]

Founded in 1870, the Preparatory High School for Colored Youth—Dunbar's original name—initially operated out of a Presbyterian church basement in Washington, DC. The school became M Street High School in 1892, when students moved to a building on M Street, which still stands today. M Street High School was renamed Paul Laurence Dunbar High School in 1916. The renaming anticipated yet another location change in 1917: this time to a castle-like brick building that was demolished in the 1970s, to be succeeded by more modern replacements in 1977 and 2013.[9]

It is difficult to discuss the connection between Dunbar and Amherst without also recognizing the radical origins and policies of Oberlin College in Ohio. In the 1830s, the trustees of Oberlin agreed that students should be admitted to the college "irrespective of color."[10] Unlike Amherst, Oberlin, from its inception, also accepted women as well as men. At a time when few American colleges educated either African Americans or women, Oberlin was responsible for training several black women who would become teachers and principals at Dunbar.

Mary J. Patterson, the first African American woman to receive a bachelor's degree in the United States, graduated from Oberlin College in 1862 and served as principal of Dunbar twice between 1871 and 1884.[11] She initiated a program of rigorous coursework, based on her experience at Oberlin.[12] Patterson was followed by the well-known educators and activists Anna Julia Cooper and Mary Church Terrell. Both Cooper and Terrell graduated from Oberlin and then headed to Washington, DC, to teach at Dunbar. These women, like other college-educated African Americans in the Jim Crow era, had limited opportunities to use their advanced credentials in higher education outside of historically black universities.

Teaching positions at black public high schools attracted black college graduates who dreamed of making a fair wage and applying their education to their careers. However, the bar for black teachers was set high, partly as a consequence of segregation.[13] Terrell, who taught at Dunbar from 1887 to 1891, described the struggles black women faced in seeking employment under Jim Crow:

> Unless I am willing to engage in a few menial occupations, in which the pay for my services would be very poor, there is no way for me to earn an honest living, if I am not a trained nurse or a dressmaker or can secure a position as a teacher in the public schools, which is exceedingly difficult to do. It matters not what my intellectual attainments may be . . . if I try to enter many of the numerous vocations in which my white sisters are allowed to engage, the door is shut in my face.[14]

Adding to black women's difficulties in finding work was the policy that married women could not be teachers in the nation's capital. Terrell left her position at Dunbar in 1891, when she married the school's principal at the time.[15] She would go on to lead the National Association of Colored Women in 1896, contributing to the suffrage movement and challenging racial segregation in Washington, DC, until she died in 1954.

Dunbar's teachers in the early twentieth century were brilliant, devoted, and creative, despite limited resources. Among the most extraordinary was Angelina Weld Grimké, who taught English courses at Dunbar even as she pursued a parallel career as a poet and playwright. Her father, Archibald Grimké, was born into slavery in antebellum South Carolina, and later rose to prominence as a leader of the NAACP. Inheriting Archibald's dedication to racial justice, Angelina built a reputation within the DC black community for her production of plays like *Rachel* in 1916, with an antilynching theme.[16]

Dunbar teachers not only encouraged students to apply to competitive colleges beyond Washington, DC, but also prepared them for entrance examinations. Amplias Glenn graduated from Oberlin in 1902 and served as both an educator and a counselor at Dunbar from 1904 until his retirement in 1927.[17] As a fellow teacher recalls, Glenn "conducted college guidance with no clerical aid for two decades," while simultaneously teaching Latin and heading the foreign language department.[18] Thanks to Glenn's efforts, Dunbar students received scholarships to northern colleges, including Bowdoin, Brown, Dartmouth, Harvard, and Yale, as well as Amherst.[19]

Dunbar graduates heading to institutions like Amherst were certainly a minority of college-bound students. It was much more likely that Dunbar students would attend local and historically black institutions, like Howard University and Miner Teachers College. Nonetheless, it is remarkable that even a small minority of early Dunbar graduates had the confidence and guidance to leave DC for predominantly white colleges.

Anna Julia Cooper deserves much of the credit for fostering an academic climate that prepared students equally for local universities as well as northern institutions far from home. Cooper was born into slavery in Raleigh, North Carolina, in 1858. Her father was probably her master, who also owned her mother, Hannah Stanley Haywood.[20] After studying at Oberlin in the 1880s, Cooper moved to Washington to teach at Dunbar and served as principal from 1901 to 1906. Given her ascent from slavery to higher education,

Cooper had full confidence that hard-working black students could succeed alongside their white peers at colleges beyond the nation's capital.

Cooper engaged actively in contemporary conversations on the future of education for black Americans. Given the unfulfilled promises of emancipation and Reconstruction, several prominent thinkers of the time debated what kind of education would best help black communities in the United States. Booker T. Washington, founder of the Tuskegee Institute in Alabama, believed blacks should strive for economic self-sufficiency and championed vocational education over classical learning.[21] He saw the best path forward for blacks as one that created the least resistance.

On the other hand, W. E. B. Du Bois often challenged Washington's educational philosophy. Du Bois was an intellectual, trained as a sociologist, and the first African American to acquire a PhD from Harvard. He opposed Washington's willingness to sacrifice "the higher education of Negro youth . . . and concentrate all their energies on industrial education and accumulation of wealth and the conciliation of the South."[22]

Cooper corresponded with Du Bois regularly and attended the 1900 World Exhibition in Paris with him and his wife. Later, she also contributed to *The Crisis*, the magazine Du Bois edited for the NAACP. Finding a kindred spirit in Du Bois, Cooper viewed classical education and lifelong learning as critical to black freedom and progress. Her vision also melded Du Boisian ideas with mindfulness of women's development. Cooper advocated for the inclusion of women in intellectual and academic life, "making it a common everyday affair for women to reason and think and express their thought."[23]

The friendship and solidarity between Du Bois and Cooper guided the trajectory of Dunbar's curricular development. Cooper insisted on a classical curriculum for Dunbar, an oddity for any public school in the United States at the time, and that curriculum persisted for decades after her tenure as principal. Without such a foundation, Dunbar students would not have met the particular requirements of northern colleges. Accordingly, the 1922 Dunbar student handbook included course offerings in both ancient and modern languages.[24] Amherst still required applicants to be proficient in Greek and Latin through the 1920s.[25]

Cooper triumphed in fashioning Dunbar as an educational institution in the tradition of Du Bois. However, her steadfast protection of the curriculum led to conflicts with the school board and her eventual removal as principal in 1906.[26] Cooper defended her record, claiming that, throughout her administration, "there have been boys to enter Harvard, Yale, Amherst, Brown, and other colleges from Dunbar without conditions . . . [and] there had never been any attempt to enter Harvard direct from the Dunbar High School previous to my administration."[27]

Cooper went on to get a PhD in history in 1924, from the Sorbonne in Paris, making her the fourth African American woman to earn a doctoral degree.[28] Cooper then returned to DC to teach at Dunbar until her retirement in 1930. More than thirty years after her principalship, Dunbar's 1944 philosophy echoed the ethos of the liberal arts colleges for which Cooper sought to prepare her students: "We believe that in a democracy free secondary education should be provided for all, regardless of race . . . the pupils should be prepared to meet effectively the changing situations in their present and future lives . . .

adapted to their capacities, the curriculum should be broad and modern enough to meet the requirements of all pupils."[29] Thanks to Cooper's leadership, Dunbar was uniquely positioned among public schools in DC, black or white, to sustain a pipeline to New England colleges for years to come.[30]

Under Cooper, the first Dunbar students to attend Amherst were Robert Mattingly and James Le Count Chestnut, who completed their degrees in 1905 and 1907, respectively. In the Amherst College yearbook, classmates remembered "Mat" as one of the "mighty few fellows in Amherst who can enjoy Mathematics."[31] Mattingly finished his college coursework in only three years and graduated Phi Beta Kappa, an honor that six other Dunbar-Amherst alumni would later claim.[32] After graduating, Mattingly and Chestnut returned to Washington, DC, to pursue lifelong teaching careers at Dunbar and other DC public schools.[33]

William Tecumseh Sherman Jackson, an African American Amherst graduate (class of 1892), succeeded Cooper as Dunbar's principal in 1906. Upon stepping down from the principalship in 1909, Jackson taught mathematics and coached sports through the 1920s. Although Jackson grew up in Virginia and did not attend Dunbar himself, as an Amherst College graduate, he was committed to maintaining and facilitating the pipeline from Dunbar to Amherst that had begun under Cooper's leadership.

In the fall of 1888, Jackson enrolled at Amherst alongside two other black students: William Henry Lewis, his classmate at the Virginia Normal School, and George Washington Forbes from Mississippi.[34] US Senator George Frisbie Hoar of Massachusetts covered Jackson's college tuition and was known for his progressive beliefs.[35] In spite of the inclusive politics of his benefactor, Jackson encountered classmates at Amherst with degrading perceptions of African Americans. While Jackson attended Amherst in the 1880s and 1890s, the college's athletic culture was infused with racism. The baseball team organized annual blackface minstrel shows as part of their fundraising efforts.

In April 1889, during Jackson's first year, an Amherst-orchestrated minstrel show took place in the city hall of nearby Northampton. In the promotional flyer, the baseball team even sold "round-trip [train] tickets including admission to minstrels" and proclaimed the racist comedy show as "all for base ball."[36] A few years later, in May 1893, student journalists reported in the *Amherst Student* that "their plantation melodies were received with hearty applause, and were repeatedly encored."[37]

One can only imagine the discomfort and disappointment, if not fear and outrage, that Jackson probably experienced as some white classmates mocked black people for profit. In spite of these dynamics in Amherst's athletic culture, Jackson excelled as a track athlete, and after graduation, he became an advocate for Amherst, encouraging students at Dunbar to attend his alma mater.

Probably the best-known Dunbar pupil that Jackson guided to Amherst was Charles Hamilton Houston, the legendary lawyer who participated in practically all of the civil rights cases leading up to the *Brown v. Board of Education* ruling. He mentored other lawyers who advocated for racial justice in courts across the country.[38] Through his faculty position at Howard, Houston encouraged talented graduates of the university's law school to join the NAACP's legal efforts, including his most famous protégé Supreme Court justice Thurgood Marshall.

Figure 1. The Amherst College track team in 1890 with William Tecumseh Sherman Jackson at the center. Courtesy of the Amherst College Archives.

Thanks to his academic aptitude and engaged parents, Houston completed middle school at the age of twelve and graduated from Dunbar in 1911, when he was only fifteen. Houston's parents, William, a law clerk, and Mary, a hairdresser, relocated from Kentucky to Washington, DC, in search of a better life. They worked hard to provide their only child with an upbringing that they had never received. Although he received a scholarship to the University of Pittsburgh, his parents wanted him to be educated at Amherst College, despite the greater expense.[39]

As the only black student in the Amherst College class of 1915, Houston faced daunting social hurdles. Amherst's unofficial policy of keeping black students housed apart from whites meant isolation. The white-only fraternity life further separated him physically and socially from his classmates. Out of solitude, Houston became more self-reliant, converting a vacant room in his dormitory into a study and focusing his time on excelling academically.[40]

Like Mattingly, Houston completed his courses at Amherst quickly, graduating as valedictorian at the age of nineteen. He then left western Massachusetts and headed across the state to attend Harvard Law School. The staff writers of the *Olio*, the Amherst yearbook, remembered "Charlie" as an academic star, deeming him "one of the hard workers of the class . . . [who] deserves anything that his scholarship may bring him."[41]

In the following decade, Dunbar alumni comprised the majority of the black men who received their Amherst College diplomas.[42] As a mathematics instructor and a track coach, Jackson taught these students both inside and outside the classroom. A gifted runner during his own Amherst days, he prepared several young Dunbar men to continue with athletics at the collegiate level. Lacking the appropriate facilities of its own, Dunbar relied on Howard University, the premier historically black university in the district, a little over a mile away, to share its athletic fields.[43] Nonetheless, in the spring of 1921, Dunbar won third place in the annual Penn Relays in Philadelphia, defeating high school track teams from around the country.[44]

Frederick Allen Parker from the Amherst class of 1920 was an unforgettable runner. *Olio* writers noted that "when he gets going his spikes are about the only things that keep him back."[45] The *Olio* also praised the athleticism of another Dunbar-Amherst track star, Robert Percy Barnes.[46] Barnes graduated Phi Beta Kappa in 1921, and the college appointed him as a chemistry instructor after his graduation. This would technically situate Barnes as the first African American member of the Amherst faculty. Amherst would not hire a black faculty member for a tenure-track professorship until the arrival of Dr. James Q. Denton in 1964.

Charles Drew (class of 1926), Montague Cobb (class of 1925), and William Henry Hastie (class of 1925) all made the Amherst College varsity track team in 1923. These three scholar-athletes had probably been warned about the slights they would experience as they traveled away from Amherst to less-welcoming venues for competitions. Even if they built some camaraderie with white students during Amherst track practices, the realities of racial difference quickly reasserted themselves off campus.

In 1925, Cobb, Drew, and Hastie ate alone at the Brown University dining hall while the rest of their team dined at the Narragansett Hotel. The hotel management heard there were "colored boys on the Amherst team and sent word that they would not serve them."[47] The ride back to Amherst from Providence was shrouded in silence.

Even if sports failed to connect them with their white peers, the Dunbar-Amherst men created spaces for themselves for bonding and solidarity. Drew organized a ukulele group, probably the first of its kind in Amherst history.[48] The ensemble necessarily included the musically gifted Will Mercer Cook, one of Drew's Dunbar classmates who also attended Amherst. Although Cook did not join Drew on the track team, he became an invaluable comrade when it came to the arts. When he was growing up, "Merc," as he was known by his Amherst classmates, had traveled with his father, Will Marion Cook, a violinist and composer, as he toured across the United States and Europe.

W. Mercer Cook composed a song called "Sweetheart of All My Dreams" that the ukulele group performed at their 1924 prom. It was so successful that Cook had to sue to get his royalties when it was plagiarized.[49] Nonetheless, his talents were not always recognized by the college at large. Cook's son Jacques recalls that his father told him that the head of the Amherst choir thought he had "the best voice on campus,"[50] yet the choir forbade blacks from joining.[51]

Figure 2. A group of African American students after an Amherst College church service in 1923, including several Dunbar-Amherst men. From left to right: Charles W. Lewis (class of 1923), W. Montague Cobb (class of 1925), William Henry Hastie (class of 1925), William B. D. Thompson (class of 1927), Gaius C. Bolin (class of 1925), and W. Mercer Cook (class of 1925). Courtesy of the Amherst College Archives.

Cook went on to earn a PhD in French from Brown University in 1936. His passion for the French language led him to become a professor at both Howard University and the University of Haiti. In the 1960s, Cook served as the US ambassador to three African nations: Niger, Senegal, and the Gambia. Both Amherst and Brown ultimately took note of Cook's accomplishments, granting him honorary degrees in 1965 and 1970, respectively. He encouraged his sons Mercer and Jacques to enroll at Amherst, and his grandchildren carried on the Amherst legacy as well.

William Hastie, another Dunbar-Amherst track star, studied at Harvard Law School after Amherst just as Charles Hamilton Houston had done. Hastie, who happened to be Houston's cousin, became a member of the Amherst College Board of Trustees.[52] Throughout his life, he used the law as a tool to fight racial injustice, first as a dean at Howard University Law School and later as the first black federal judge.

In the foreword to Harold Wade's *Black Men of Amherst*, Hastie speculated on the sharp decline in black students at Amherst in the two decades immediately after his own. Only nine black students attended Amherst in the 1930s and 1940s, including four young men from Dunbar who did not ultimately graduate.[53] According to Hastie, the roots of Amherst College's struggles with its black student graduation rates rested with the college leadership. He asserted that "the then President of the College [Stanley King, president from 1932 to 1951] adopted a practice of inviting successive groups of seniors to social evenings at the President's House until this hospitable gesture had been extended to all seniors who were not black."[54]

It is also true that black people suffered disproportionately more from the Great Depression than other groups, which deterred the pursuit or completion of higher education in general. Dunbar teacher Mary Gibson Hundley ascribed students' lack of admission to competitive northern colleges during this era to "the failure of the administration and faculty and because of the financial depression."[55] Amherst College would not experience a resurgence in black student enrollment until the late 1940s.

In 1946, Eugene Wilson (class of 1929) became the college's dean of admission, a position he held until his retirement in 1972. A 1971 interview in the *Amherst Student* noted that Wilson ultimately "reversed the percentages of public and private school graduates of the college."[56] Under Wilson's leadership, Amherst admission deans made efforts to diversify incoming classes, including organizing frequent trips down to Washington, DC, to meet with Dunbar students in person.[57]

Amherst faced competition from rivaling northern colleges for the best and brightest Dunbar seniors. Williams College, near Amherst, had its own history of recruiting Dunbar men going back to the early twentieth century, with about fifteen Dunbar students enrolling between 1909 and 1944.[58] In response, Wilson sought out local leaders in the black DC community who could identify talented young men who might be a good fit for Amherst.

Wilson strategically collaborated with the Drew family that embodied Dunbar's connection with Amherst. Nora Drew Gregory, Charles Drew's sister, served as a liaison between Amherst and the black Washington community. After her brother died in an automobile accident in 1950, Gregory diligently promoted his alma mater. (Gregory's father-in-law, James Francis Gregory, also graduated from Amherst in 1898 and was one of the first African Americans in the United States to be elected captain of a college baseball team.)[59]

Before his senior year at Dunbar in 1953, Harold Haizlip (class of 1957) simply remembered Nora Drew Gregory as his elementary school teacher. However, in Haizlip's senior year, Harvard, Yale, Williams, Amherst, and Dartmouth all accepted him. Gregory persistently advocated for Amherst to be his top choice. Haizlip recalled that she invited him to her home: "[There was a] very nice white gentlemen Eugene Wilson . . . the dean of admission! . . . This was at a time when it was unusual for college administrators, and white college administrators, to be so aggressive. . . . I'm sure they knew Nora Gregory's lineage. . . . Her son . . . became the first African-American astronaut, Frederick Gregory."[60] After Haizlip, Amherst recruited a cohort of three Dunbar seniors for the class of 1959, who happened to also be neighborhood friends: Lawrence Burwell, Robert Jason, and Raymond Hayes. Hayes remembered that "we were all interested in science and medicine and were encouraged by the opportunity to attend Amherst together."[61] Both Hayes and Jason received $700 each through an Amherst College scholarship, while Burwell received $500.[62] These were all relatively significant contributions at the time. Annual tuition at Amherst was $1,425 during the 1955 to 1956 school year.[63]

Like so many of his predecessors, Mansfield Neal (class of 1961), the last Dunbar-Amherst man in this story, received encouragement from a network of Dunbar-Amherst alumni. One of the men who encouraged Neal to attend Amherst was Chauncey Larry (class of 1927)). Larry followed the career trajectories of several Dunbar-Amherst predecessors like Jason, Mattingly, and Chestnut. He taught at many Washington, DC, public schools, including Dunbar, from 1944 to 1950.

Larry took action to ensure graduates of his high school could have the same opportunities that he did, all the way through his retirement in 1968. In the pamphlet for Larry's retirement celebration, a colleague remarked that "his extreme interest and dedicated service on the Amherst scholarship committee are manifest in the number of students, sponsored by him, who have since matriculated at that college and have entered public service."[64] As Neal remembered, earlier generations of Dunbar-Amherst men wanted to "make sure we were aware of Amherst, had information about Amherst, and considered Amherst."[65]

Dunbar alumni like Neal looked back on their high school days with gratitude. They cherished their memories of a building full of brilliant black teachers who looked like them, who believed in them, and who wanted them to change the world. Still, these same alumni also wished for a world where a segregated school system would not be necessary in the first place. Like Houston and Hastie, Neal became a lawyer to work against the legal and social regime that had made Dunbar a necessary countermeasure:

> My mom had taken me and my brother Stu, who was a year younger than me, to shop downtown. On our way back, it was rush hour and we took a trolley car. Here's my mom, with packages and two little boys (4 and 5 years old). She had to walk to the back of a trolley car to try to find a seat, walk past empty seats. And I said, "Mom, why can't we sit here?" And all she could do was cry. And that, if nothing else, really motivated me to say "I'm going to kill this system no matter what it takes."[66]

Ultimately, segregation and an ambitious African American community created Dunbar. In *First Class: The Legacy of Dunbar*, journalist Alison Stewart reminds us that although Dunbar stands out as a "winner" during the time of school segregation in Washington, students and teachers alike were making the best of a demeaning, cruel, and unconstitutional system that kept African Americans as second-class citizens and sought to limit their potential.[67]

The mission of Dunbar, predicated on what Hayes called a "selective college prep program for black students in a segregated system," became antiquated after the 1954 Supreme Court ruling.[68] *Bolling v. Sharpe* was part of a collection of court cases in 1954 that were considered along with the more well-known *Brown v. Board of Education* case. *Brown* declared state laws establishing separate public schools on the basis of race to be unconstitutional but specifically applied to states, not to a federal district like Washington, DC. After the *Sharpe* decision, doors opened to previously white-only private and public schools for both black students and teachers in Washington.[69] Opportunities expanded beyond Dunbar for black children in the district seeking a college preparatory education.

Although Dunbar remains predominantly black today, the reshuffling of the DC public school system quickly turned Dunbar and other institutions into neighborhood schools. While the principle of equal opportunity behind desegregation was noble, its implementation radically changed the educational landscape of Washington, DC, and the nation at large. Dunbar stopped taking promising black students from throughout the district and adapted to serve students in the immediate zone around it.[70]

As Dunbar's capacity to produce students academically prepared for elite liberal arts colleges faded, Amherst found alternative sites of recruitment in the 1960s. Dean Eugene Wilson worked with the guidance counselor at Andrew Jackson High School in New York to recruit Harold Wade and Cuthbert Simpkins for the Amherst class of 1968.[71] Simpkins and Wade cofounded the Afro-American Society (the predecessor to the contemporary Amherst College Black Student Union). The long-standing pattern of admitting no more than four black students per class gave way in the 1970s to classes with at least twenty entering black students.[72]

Since Amherst would not become coeducational until the 1970s, the relationship between Amherst College and Dunbar High School in the early twentieth century may seem like a story of men. However, many Dunbar women simultaneously attended prestigious liberal arts colleges throughout the country such as Smith, Mount Holyoke, Oberlin, and Spelman.[73] Moreover, as educators, mothers, and community leaders, black women in the nation's capital from Anna Julia Cooper to Nora Drew Gregory empowered both young men and women at Dunbar to shoot for the stars.

The Dunbar-Amherst men of the early twentieth century found community at Amherst but still did not always feel welcome. Their complicated experiences at Amherst connect to the contemporary tension of belonging and frustration that many students of color have felt toward Amherst. As Diane Lee writes in the *Amherst Student* regarding the Amherst Uprising of November 2016, "while it started as an hour-long moment of solidarity with black students facing violence at Yale and the University of Missouri, it expanded into a powerful weekend in which black, brown and other marginalized students shared their stories of institutionalized racism and oppression at Amherst."[74] A desire to belong at Amherst was at the heart of the Amherst Uprising—a continuation of the struggle that Dunbar-Amherst men of past generations knew all too well.

Not until their fiftieth class reunion would Hayes and Burwell call out the separatist housing practices that continued into the 1950s. At that point, Hayes reflected that "our requests for roommates were denied and single rooms in different dormitories were assigned to us." He recalled that there were also no black faculty, administrators, or mentoring programs. Hayes and Burwell "duly acknowledged" how Amherst encouraged their successes, but "so much could have been offered to ease the discomforts of those formative years."[75]

Today, Dunbar students typically do not attend liberal arts colleges after graduation, but the Amherst legacy lives on.[76] Near a banner with the school's motivational motto, "Keep A-Pluggin' Away," three alumni plaques honor graduates of Amherst: Houston, Hastie, and Cobb.[77] Perhaps as the story of Amherst College unfolds into its third century, the two institutions can revive the dormant connection and adapt to the contemporary realities of the public school system in Washington, DC.

Table 1. Paul Laurence Dunbar High School Students at Amherst College by Class Year, 1906–2005

1906
Robert Nicholas Mattingly
1907
James LeCount Chestnut
1909
James Blaine Hunter
1911
John Randolph Pinkett
1912
*Edward Gray
1915
Charles Hamilton Houston
1916
Francis Morse Dent
1920
Frederick Allen Parker
1921
Robert Percy Barnes
1923
*George Nolen Calloway
*Charles Dudley Lee
Charles William Lewis
1925

William Montague Cobb
*George Winston Harry
Will Mercer Cook
William Henry Hastie

1926
Charles Richard Drew
*Thurman Luce Dodson

1927
Chauncey Baker Larry

1928
Clarence Reed White

1929
Harold Over Lewis
David Utz
George Williams

1931
*Carl Curtis Beckwith

1934
*Harry Greene Risher

1940
*Highwarden Just

1943
*John Hurst II

1951
Mercer Cook

1956
Ralph Edward Greene
Karl Sinclair Atkinson

1957
Harold Cornelius Haizlip

1958
Edward David Crockett

1959
Lawrence Rogers Burwell
Raymond Lewis Hayes Jr.
Robert Stewart Jason Jr.

1961
Mansfield Castleton Neal Jr.

1962
*Frederick Drew Gregory

2005
Lynettra Artis

*Did not graduate from Amherst

Notes

1. Edward Jones was the first African American graduate of Amherst College. He received his diploma in 1826, five years after the college's founding in 1821.

2. Amherst College, "Charles Drew Memorial Cultural House Constitution," accessed August 7, 2019, https://www.amherst.edu/campuslife/housing-dining/residential-life/theme/drew/drew_const.

3. Evan J. Albright, "A Slice of History," *Amherst Magazine*, Winter 2007 edition, https://www.amherst.edu/amherst-story/magazine/issues/2007_winter/blazing/slice.

4. Harold Wade, *Black Men of Amherst* (Amherst, MA: Amherst College Press, 1976).

5. Jacqueline Moore, *Leading the Race: The Transformation of the Black Elite in the Nation's Capital, 1880–1920* (Charlottesville: University Press of Virginia, 1999), 89.

6. Pero Gaglo Dagbovie, *Carter G. Woodson in Washington, D.C.: The Father of Black History* (Charleston, SC: The History Press, 2014), 39.

7. Dalton Allen, personal communcation with the author at Dunbar High School, July 11, 2018.

8. Christ Myers Asch and George Derek Musgrove, *Chocolate City: A History of Race and Democracy in the Nation's Capital* (Chapel Hill: University of North Carolina Press, 2017), 216.

9. "D.C. Leaders to Celebrate New Dunbar High School Facility," *Washington Post*, August 18, 2013.

10. Robert Samuel Fletcher, *A History of Oberlin College from Its Foundation through the Civil War*, vol 1 (Oberlin, OH: Oberlin College, 1943), 170.

11. Other Oberlin graduates after Patterson would also serve as principal in years to come. In total, between 1870 and 1964, Dunbar recruited principals with degrees from a range of prestigious colleges, including three from Oberlin, two from Harvard, one from Dartmouth, and one from Amherst.

12. Alison Stewart, *First Class: The Legacy of Dunbar, America's First Black Public High School* (Chicago, IL: Lawrence Hill Books, 2013), 32.

13. Brent Staples, "Where Did All the Black Teachers Go?" *New York Times*, April 20, 2017.

14. Mary Church Terrell, "What It Means to be Colored in the Capital of United States," *Independent*, January 24, 1907.

15. Tyina Steptoe, "Mary Church Terrell (1863–1954)," Black Past, January 17, 2007, https://www.blackpast.org/african-american-history/terrell-mary-church-1863-1954/.

16. As a playwright, Angelina Weld Grimké hoped her play *Rachel* could convince white audiences of the immorality of lynching. The drama committee of the National Association for the Advancement of Colored People (NAACP) brought the play to the stage, sponsoring a production in Washington, DC, in March 1916.

17. Henry Robinson, "The M Street High School, 1891–1917," *Records of the Columbia Historical Society, Washington, DC.* (Washington, DC: Historical Society of Washington, DC, 1984), 127.

18. Mary Gibson Hundley, *The Dunbar Story, 1870–1955* (New York: Vantage Press, 1965), 69.

19. Robinson, "M Street," 127.

20. Mark Giles, "Special Focus: Dr. Anna Julia Cooper, 1858–1964: Teacher, Scholar, and Timeless Womanist," *Journal of Negro Education* 75, no. 4 (2006): 621–34.

21. In the 1895 "Atlanta Compromise," Booker T. Washington articulated his philosophy in one of the first African American speeches recorded in sound, arguing that blacks should focus on building self-sufficient communities through vocational trades: "In all things, purely social we can be as separate as fingers, yet one in the hand as all things essential to mutual progress." In Washington's compromise, Southern blacks would accept segregation to focus on their economic progress, postponing concerns for legal equality, civil rights, and integration.

22. W. E. B. Du Bois, "On Booker T. Washington," *Souls of Black Folk* (Bookbyte Digital, 1903), electronic edition (Apple Books).

23. Anna Julia Cooper, *A Voice from the South* (Chapel Hill: University of North Carolina Press, [1892] 2000), electronic edition (text scanned by Robin Roencker, Academic Affairs Library, University of North Carolina, Chapel Hill, NC), https://docsouth.unc.edu/church/cooper/cooper.html.

24. *A Handbook of Information* (Washington, DC: Paul Laurence Dunbar High, Hamilton Printing Company, 1922).

25. *Amherst College Catalogue*, 1921/1922 ed., Amherst College Digital Collections, Amherst College, Amherst, MA, 34, https://acdc.amherst.edu/view/asc:544979/asc:545166.

26. Stewart, *First Class*, 45–68.

27. "Opening of the Public Schools," *Evening Star*, September 17, 1906, 3.

28. Cooper lived a long life that spanned the scope of the emancipation of enslaved blacks to the struggle for civil rights in the United States. She passed away at the age of 105 in 1964 (living through the 1961 college graduation of the final Dunbar-Amherst man discussed in this essay).

29. Hundley, *Dunbar Story*, 22.

30. Other black public schools in DC would take different paths. Armstrong High School, where Booker T. Washington gave an address during the school's dedication ceremony in 1902, specialized as a vocational institution in the spirit of the Tuskegee movement. In 1928, Cardozo, the business department of Dunbar, originally organized in 1886, would become a separate high school in its own right.

31. *Olio*. 1906 ed., (Amherst, MA: Amherst College), 211.

32. Robert Mattingly, "Birth of M Street High School" (self-published pamphlet by the author, 1976), Amherst College Archives, Amherst College, Amherst, MA, 22.

33. "Chestnut, James Le Count," Amherst College Biographical Record, 1939 ed., Amherst College Archives, Amherst College, Amherst, MA.

34. "Albright, Evan J." Amherst College Biographical Records, 1939 ed., Amherst College Archives, Amherst College, Amherst, MA.

35. "Rights of the Chinese," *New York Times*, Thursday, March 2, 1882.

36. "Minstrels: Special Train to and from Northampton, April 26" (promotional flyer of the Amherst College baseball team from 1889), Amherst College Archives, Amherst College, Amherst, MA.

37. "The Minstrel Show," *Amherst Student*, May 20, 1893.

38. "NAACP History: Charles Hamilton Houston," NAACP, accessed August 8, 2019, https://www.naacp.org/naacp-history-charles-hamilton-houston/.

39. Genna Rae McNeal, *Groundwork: Charles Hamilton Houston and the Struggle for Civil Rights* (Philadelphia: University of Pennsylvania Press, 1983), 30–31.

40. McNeal, *Groundwork*, 31–32.

41. *Olio*, 1915 ed., Amherst College, Amherst, MA, 244.

42. Wade, *Black Men*, appendix 1.

43. *A Handbook of Information* (Washington, DC: Paul Laurence Dunbar High, Hamilton Printing Company, 1922), 56.

44. *Handbook*.

45. *Olio*, 1920 ed., Amherst College, Amherst, MA, 169.

46. *Olio*, 1921, ed., Amherst College, Amherst, MA, 183.

47. Spencie Love, *One Blood: The Life and Resurrection of Charles Drew* (University of North Carolina Press, 1997), 110.

48. Wade, *Black Men*, 44.

49. Wade.

50. Jacques Cook, email correspondence with the author, December 4, 2018.

51. *Olio*, 1925 ed., Amherst College, Amherst, MA, 199.

52. William H. Hastie Jr. (son of William H. Hastie), interview with the author, February 7, 2019.

53. Wade, *Black Men*, 112. Note that four Dunbar alumni did not graduate from Amherst College in

the 1930s and 1940s: Carl Curtis Beckwith (class of 1931), Harry Greene Risher (class of 1934), Highwarden Just (class of 1940), and John Hurst II (class of 1943).

54. Wade, *Black Men*, xvi.

55. Hundley, *Dunbar Story*, 70.

56. "Bill Wilson: The Dean of Deans," *Amherst Student*, June 3, 1971.

57. The Dunbar-Amherst pipeline was renewed with the arrival of a second Mercer Cook—Amherst class of 1951 and son of W. Mercer Cook—who graduated from Dunbar and enrolled at Amherst in 1947, just one year after Wilson's arrival.

58. In 1924, Allison Davis, a Dunbar alumnus, graduated summa cum laude from Williams College as valedictorian and pursued an illustrious career in anthropology and psychology. Davis was the first African American to secure a faculty position at a major university, earning tenure at the University of Chicago in 1947.

59. "James F. Gregory," *Washington Bee*, July 30, 1898, 4.

60. Harold Haizlip, phone call with the author, May 10, 2016.

61. Raymond Lewis Hayes, phone call with the author, May 14, 2016.

62. Hundley, *Dunbar Story*, 125.

63. *Amherst College Catalogue*, 1955/1956 ed., Amherst College Digital Collections, Amherst College, Amherst, MA. 35.

64. "A Tribute to Mr. Chauncey B. Larry upon His Retirement," December 31, 1968, Amherst College Archives, Amherst College, Amherst, MA.

65. Mansfield Neal, personal interview with the author in Vineyard Haven, MA, July 13, 2018.

66. Neal, interview.

67. Stewart, *First Class*, xii.

68. Raymond Lewis Hayes, email correspondence with the author, July 28, 2018.

69. Jeanne Rogers, "Dunbar High Plays a New Role: It's Now a Neighborhood School," *Washington Post*, January 23, 1957.

70. Rogers, "Dunbar High."

71. Cuthbert Simpkins, email correspondence with the author, June 28, 2019.

72. Wade, *Black Men*, appendix 1.

73. Otelia Cromwell served as head of Dunbar's English department in the 1920s and taught for many years. Cromwell forged a connection with the all-women's Smith College. She became the first African American graduate of Smith College in 1900 and inspired several young women at Dunbar to attend her alma mater.

74. Diane Lee, "In Honor of Amherst Uprising," *Amherst Student*, December 4, 2018.

75. Raymond Lewis Hayes, personal communication with the author, "Young, Gifted and Black at Amherst College, 1955–59," 2009. This reflection was originally written in 2009, when it was shared during Hayes's fiftieth reunion at Amherst College.

76. Since Mansfield Neal enrolled at Amherst College in 1957, Lynettra Artis was the only graduate from Dunbar to attend Amherst in 2005. Artis pursued a legal career attending Howard University's law school.

77. The motto is derived from "Keep A-Pluggin Away," a poem by Paul Laurence Dunbar, the school's namesake. Paul Laurence Dunbar, "The Complete Poems of Paul Laurence Dunbar" (New York: Dodd, Mead, and Company, 1913).

Feeding Amherst

Daniel Levinson Wilk

On a Thursday in 1847, the fourth division recited their compositions as usual. Root argued that Noah had built his ark in New York State, Seelye spoke on empiricism, and Stearns spoke on the Mexican war. "Flattest set I ever heard," wrote William Gardiner Hammond in his diary. "I fairly blushed for the class." George Frederick Walker read an essay about a dream he'd had recently. In the dream, he fell asleep for about two hundred years, awoke, "and then found things, as was natural, marvelously changed, traveled by telegraph, ate by machinery which propagated its own species, and saw 10,000 students in Amherst!"[1]

Rates of growth over the last two hundred years suggest we are not on track for ten thousand students by 2047.[2] Though we now stream video of ourselves instantaneously down distant wires and through the air, our bodies are not actually traveling by electric pulse. Amherst students are not yet fed by machines that reproduce, unless you count the plants and animals.

Forty years after Walker's dream, Edward Bellamy published *Looking Backward*, a novel whose protagonist, Julian West, falls asleep in 1887 and also wakes to a world transformed by technological innovation. Bellamy was from Chicopee Falls, a thirty-minute drive from Amherst today, but his novel takes place in Boston in 2000. The provision of food in this futuristic world has been systematized on a grand scale. Newspapers report what is for sale, families order their meals accordingly the night before, and industrial kitchens do all the cooking, with breakfast and supper home-delivered, and dinner (now we would call it lunch), the grandest meal of the day, taken in private dining rooms sequestered in another building. There is no advanced technology to feed people at table—not like the machine that smushes food into Charlie Chaplin's face in *Modern Times* (1936), just a waiter who had "the manner of a soldier on duty, but without the military stiffness." West has trouble believing that waiters in the year 2000 are treated with dignity, but his host Dr. Leete assures him that no waiter would feel more embarrassed to wait on him than he would feel to tend to their health. In the future, all work is treated with dignity.[3]

The two hundredth anniversary of Amherst College is also the eightieth anniversary of Valentine Hall, a moment of revolution in the relationship between Amherst students and the people who fed them. For the one hundred and twenty years prior to Valentine, Amherst students mostly ate off campus; for the first seventy years, almost entirely. At the beginning, when everyone slept in South College, the administration refused to provide meals and banned students from eating in their rooms. It forced them into town and countryside, onto the open market. A community of boardinghouse entrepreneurs grew up to meet them there—mostly women, many of them widows, just like boardinghouse keepers in the rest of the United States. As the size of the student body increased, boardinghouses' dining halls got bigger and bigger. By the twentieth century, some sat scores at a time. On the way to and from meals, the students of Amherst College coursed across the green and through town.

On March 1, 1847, in the same year that he recorded his classmate's dream of fully-automated eating at Amherst, William Gardiner Hammond wrote down his schedule for the entire day. Try to count the number of commutes to town and back—the PO is the post office, another trip.

> VI.30 Up and to prayers.
> 40. To recitation; called up.
> VII.30 To breakfast.
> VIII.20 Getting in wood.
> 45. Called on Seelye and Edwards to see about the catalogue.
> IX.45. Got mathematical lesson.
> XI. Recitation: called up.
> XII. Dinner.
> 45. Studying Greek.
> I.30 Went out to see about getting Crosby.
> II. Studying Greek.
> IV. Recitation.
> V. To the P.O.
> 10. Prayers.
> 30. Supper.
> VI.5. Talked with chum.
> 30. Studied Horace.
> VII.15. Went over for Crosby.
> 35. Called on Tutor Green.
> VIII.15 Psi Upsilon Meeting.
> XI. Studied Horace.
> 25. Wrote up journal.
> 45. Read, etc.
> XII. To bed.[4]

Hammond seems to have been living in a dormitory on campus at the time and was boarding with Mrs. Dwight, an "estimable lady" for whom Hammond developed respect, even affection, over the years he spent at her table.[5] He went to Mrs. Dwight's for breakfast at 7:30 a.m., at noon for dinner, and at 5:30 p.m. for supper. Meals gave structure to his day—he constantly marks other events as happening "after breakfast," "after dinner," "after tea," and "after supper."[6]

Having created this local economy of boardinghouse keepers, the college eventually tried to compete with it—campus cafeterias opened in the 1890s, and fraternities retrofitted their kitchens to prepare full meals in the 1930s. By the end of that decade, president Stanley King finally sold trustees and donors on a single dining hall sufficient to the needs of the whole student body, plus coercion to keep them there.

Valentine Hall changed student life at Amherst College profoundly, creating the college experience shared by most of us living graduates. We eat together, in small groups, but at the same time as an entire college of students. Valentine also changed the relationship of Amherst College students to their neighbors across the town/gown divide, as students' most intimate ties to citizens of Amherst were severed and forgotten. The community of boardinghouse keepers collapsed. In the work of feeding Amherst students, town entrepreneurs and their staff were replaced by employees of the college.

For the first one hundred and twenty years, a time when Amherst students followed a rigid course of study in their classes, they had considerable choice—limited by money, seniority, race, and market supply—in where to eat and sleep. The earliest students lived in doubles in South College and then North College and trudged three times a day, sometimes in the snow, to the homes of local people. Within five years, about a quarter of the student body (sixteen freshmen, eight sophomores, two juniors, and three seniors) were living in boardinghouses, and presumably eating in them too, some alongside other students who commuted in from campus.[7]

Students could choose to live on campus, and most did until the end of the nineteenth century, but they were banned from eating in the dorms. The rule was flouted, of course—students brought in crackers, peaches, coffee, oysters, bowls, and spoons. Sometimes they drank cherry rum or gin, or smoked cigars. Legends arose of secret banquets with turkeys and chickens roasting in the fireplace and even an underground apartment below a trapdoor in the dorms; the door was eventually left open by accident, so the story went, and the evidence was revealed to President Humphrey: a mess of wine kegs, bottles, and chicken bones.[8] And Amherst students ate in the fields. Charles U. Shepard (class of 1825) remembered that the "College grounds gave us all the chestnuts we wanted, and the hickory groves furnished boundless supplies of walnuts."[9]

But for regular meals, most students boarded with members of the community. This was common at the time—in the 1700s, campuses like Harvard and Yale had dining commons, but by the 1800s, the practice had fallen out of favor and boarding was the rule. At Amherst, some students slept in dorms on campus and ate in town; others slept and ate in town, sometimes in different houses. The choice to board was also common outside higher education, wildly popular among single men and women, widows and widowers, newly married couples starting out, congressmen when at Congress, and sailors when not at sea. References to them passed through the literature, theater, and jokes of their eras.[10]

At first, Amherst didn't feed students because it didn't have the money to buy, lease, or build and staff a dining hall. The school couldn't even pay to keep the place clean or the lights on. Students bought their wood from Pelham dealers who visited campus most days, then chopped it and built their own fires. They painted their rooms and lit them with candles or whale oil they procured themselves. On "Chip Day," they raked leaves across campus and, on "Gravel Day," they resurfaced the paths across campus. The outhouses were filthy; students sometimes burned down the stinking wooden urinals in protest, but the privy was built of brick. "Oh, the freezing of the defecating of students for the first 40 years of Amherst College life," wrote Doc Hitchcock, a student son of the school's president, and later a beloved professor of physical education.[11]

By 1830, the college could afford to pay a local farmer named Phinchas Warner to clean and cart away the ashes from its stoves and, in 1834, another farmer to sweep the floors. The first full-time custodial employee, the first proper "professor of dust and ashes," was "Professor Charley" Thompson.[12] His wife Eliza washed and mended students' clothes and cooked and waited tables at the president's house and elsewhere around campus, as the wives of janitors in all sorts of institutions were expected to do. In addition to cleaning up, raking leaves, and tending the fire in the chapel, Professor Charley helped drunk boys find their beds and found the college bible or replaced the college bell's tongue when students stole them. He returned Sabrina to her pristine state after every student prank dressing, painting, or relocating her, and when his boss ordered him to destroy the statue, Thompson hid it in his barn. Thompson kept his students' secrets. He refused to name students to administrators for infractions, but sometimes he discreetly passed word if a student needed help with food. Thompson regaled students with stories from his past life as a whaler and his visits to London, China, Java, Santiago, Siberia, and the Congo Free State. When alumni returned to campus, he generally remembered their names—so, at least, say the hagiographic and self-serving remembrances of Thompson written by old white people.

Spencer Haught (class of 2009) has persuasively argued that the relationship of administrators and students to service employees like Charley and Eliza Thompson was paternalistic. Professor Charley and Amherst students may have felt real affection, but not on a basis of equality.[13] Amherst was more democratic than Southern campuses like William & Mary, where students brought along house slaves, and less democratic than the dining hall in Bellamy's *Looking Back*.[14]

The earliest years of the school probably sustained more mutual respect among students and the people who fed them than later eras. Students lived on campus and boarded in the homes of professors, farmers, and townspeople. "The farmers were glad of a home market for their productions," Shepard wrote, "and their families made small charge for the preparation of our food, the Collegian then being a novelty in the village, and his society considered a pleasure." Edwards A. Beach (class of 1824) boarded in town in exchange for teaching music and leading the choir in the village church, and he and others found their relations with the townspeople who fed them "in the highest degree confidential and affectionate."[15]

As the school grew, the feelings of generosity and affection seem to have continued. Some boarded students out of charity. Many professors, presidents of the college, their wives (Mrs. Humphrey, Mrs. Hitchcock, Mrs. Fiske, and others), and some other members of the community fed students, especially poor ones studying to spread the gospel, for little or no money. Sometimes they housed them for free. Until the Civil War, the president of the school and his wife usually housed two or three people at a time—tutors, professors, and charity students. Some college wives formed a sewing society that made and mended student clothing.[16]

Others boarded Amherst students to supplement their income. The Reverend John Sanford and his family took in boarders, but it wasn't always enough. Writing his son to ask for an eight dollar loan, he continued, "What I want is, if we take boarders next term, to have money enough in hand to buy every thing we want without making a single debt."[17] Amherst House, the town's hotel, also earned a small share of its income from students who ate there occasionally or for the entire term. By 1855, a few students were also living in rooms at Amherst House, a practice that continued until about 1880.[18]

Other citizens of Amherst boarded students as their main stream of income. Mrs. Dwight was a widow who seems to have lived from her boarders' fees, including, for a time, William Gardiner Hammond. The business of boarding students was uncertain because students moved from place to place each semester in search of better or cheaper food, and because of the tradition at most colleges before the Civil War of arriving for the semester whenever one felt ready, sometimes weeks late.[19] A boardinghouse keeper never knew exactly how many mouths she would have to feed or incomes she could count on. Mrs. Dwight relied on students to encourage each other to board with her. Classmates pressed Hammond to switch to Dwight's when he was still boarding with Mrs. Ferry, and Hammond later brought in a student named Cook to the Dwight table for the fall 1847 semester.[20]

In his 1873 history of the college, professor W. S. Tyler wrote that many of these women, "most of them widows . . . have cared for their boarders as if they were their own sons, and whom their boarders, in turn, will always remember with not a little of the honor, affection, and esteem which they bear to their own mothers." Tyler especially remembered Mrs. Montague, Mrs. Merrill, Mrs. Linnell, and Mrs. Ferry, Hammond's first boardinghouse keeper: "The Christian homes which they have furnished to scores and hundreds of students are still remembered, by them at least, among the *institutions* of Amherst." Student Story Hebard wrote of Mrs. Montague's house: "It has been my lot to be placed in a family so agreeable that I scarcely know or perceive sometimes whether I am at home or among strangers." Mrs. Ferry kept table for thirty-six years and boarded nearly two hundred students over the course of her career; Doc Hitchcock remembered that when he was a student, she "always helped us to the 'provisions' and held her tongue" when he and his classmates snuck food into the dorms.[21]

These women (and sometimes men) also presided over conversational communities at the table. They and their daughters provided much of the female companionship Amherst students could expect. "Mrs. Dwight and her lovely daughters flourishing as usual when I went down to tea;" wrote Hammond on May 12, 1847, "apparently glad to see me."[22] "What do we talk of at table?" asked one anonymous student in the *Amherst Literary Monthly* of December 1887: the events of the day, the campus gossip, the essays that students recited aloud in recitation and how well the faculty and students performed in class, "personal jokes and amusing stories," and the day's news if anyone had read the paper.[23] And schemes were gotten up—schemes to rush fraternities, to best the rival literary society, to compete in baseball games, to paint slogans in red across the village sidewalks. Conversation was sparse at breakfast and generous at other meals.[24] Sometimes the conversation was dull; as Reverend John Sanford noted in 1852, "We have had a very quiet set of boarders this term, who, I suspect not high in scholarship."[25] The liveliest tables could be found at Professor

Snell's house in the first decade of the school and at Professor Hitchcock's after, as well as the house of Reverend Dr. David Parsons, who sometimes boarded students for free if they had no money to pay. "Not unfrequently," wrote one alumnus of the Parsons dining table, "he would keep the whole table, family and boarders in a roar of laughter."[26]

Some boardinghouses also offered students work, waiting tables in exchange for financial aid—wages or sometimes just food. In boardinghouses, a student waiter's important skill was drawing other students to board at the house.[27] Future dean of admission Bill Wilson focused on his former Deerfield classmates when he recruited a ten-man table at Ms. Peg Moore's boardinghouse. The popular dessert was pastry chef Brownie Robert's Merry Widows—cupcakes topped with hot fudge and whipped cream—and Wilson made sure that on Merry Widow days, each of the men at his table got three.[28] W. S. Tyler, later an Amherst professor and historian of the school, worked for two semesters as "the steward (purchaser and purveyor) of the club" run out of the house of Mr. Green, who lived halfway down to Mill Valley. In exchange for this work, Tyler's board "cost me almost nothing."[29] George A. Plimpton (class of 1876), grandfather of the famous journalist, *ran* a boardinghouse on South Pleasant to support himself in college and solicited classmates as customers for his own profit. He served a lot of cheap salt cod that he bought in the markets of Boston and shipped by the barrel to Amherst.[30] Other students organized eating clubs, though information on them is thin—it is unclear how much work the students actually did to procure and serve food and how much was delegated to boardinghouse keepers with whom they contracted.[31]

I have found no descriptions of table service in Amherst boardinghouses, aside from a passage in the *Amherst Literary Monthly* from 1889, which mentions that "ringing of knives on glasses, mild at first but with growing anger in its sound" brought the straying attention of the waiter back to the table.[32] Service was likely the common sort, what people sometimes called the *American Plan*, where waiters placed large platters and bowls on the table and everyone served himself. If there was a roast, it was carved by the person presiding over the table; it was possible to request a particular cut, and the knowledge that boardinghouse keepers soon gained of their customers' tastes could be used to show affection or hostility in the distribution of meat. The American Plan was common in boardinghouses, restaurants, and hotel dining halls throughout the nineteenth century, though *European Plan* places (with a la carte service and hotel rooms with no meal plan attached) competed throughout and came to dominate in the twentieth.[33]

Aside from their regular meals in boardinghouses, Amherst students found many places to eat and drink. On the way to campus at the beginning of each term, they stopped at the Delavan House in Albany, New York, the Exchange House in Springfield, Massachusetts, or Warriner's in the same town, where Hammond and five schoolmates "all fell in love with our waiter, a pretty βαθνκολπος [deep-bosomed] winning girl of sixteen or seventeen."[34] Back at school, they patronized an African American man named Fuller who sometimes rolled a big wheelbarrow onto campus to serve ice cream. Students could also drop by Fuller's house late at night for ice cream or biscuits and butter, or ask him over to their room with a jug of malmsey—a fortified Madeira wine—or hire him to host a banquet in his house, complete with roast turkey and pork, side dishes, pie, cake, ice cream, and plenty of alcohol.[35]

Students ate cake and apples and drank coffee and tea at gatherings and parties in town. When visiting young women at Mount Holyoke Seminary, it was necessary to take tea at the hotel in town because only water was allowed on campus, and sometimes students had to make the three-hour walk back to Amherst in the dark. When out for a walk or a ride, students could stop for meals or some mead in surrounding inns and restaurants, cider and apples from local mills, wild strawberries on the mountainside, or a glass of water or bowl of milk from a farmer's house. On one long stroll to Mount Holyoke (the mountain this time) in June 1847, Hammond and some classmates stopped at the Holyoke Hotel for pie, and again at the top of the mountain for more refreshments, and "were unmercifully jewed" on the bill in both places. Amherst House, the hotel in town, was always available for a fancy meal, a pail of lemonade, or breakfast when one's father was visiting campus.[36]

After the Civil War, choices expanded. Places like Frank P. Woods's, Hill's Restaurant, and Orient Springs House opened in town and advertised in the *Amherst Student* (which began publication in 1868) and the town paper. Students could visit for meals, baked goods, and ice cream, and arrange catering for parties, class suppers, and sleigh rides.[37] In those years, it became a tradition to hold class dinners and fraternity banquets in hotels and restaurants around the region, as far away as Springfield. At a senior dinner in 1884, the Windsor in Holyoke served little neck clams, green turtle soup, salmon, beef, chicken, deviled crab, plum pudding, salad, rice dishes, vegetables, desserts, and after-dinner drinks.[38] Students could also visit "Peanut John" Musante (sometimes "John Peanuta") and his unnamed but "buxom and jovial" wife, who sold peanuts and dispensed advice from the corner of campus.[39]

At the end of the century, the college finally tried to take a stronger responsibility for housing and feeding its students. In 1891, South College was renovated—steam heat and other amenities were added—and suites were carved out, each with three or four well-lit bedrooms and a common room.[40] The next year, the college purchased Boltwood House (standing where Converse Hall is today), renamed it Hitchcock House, and opened the first dining hall on campus, with seating for one hundred students and room for four or five students to live. Soon after, Boyden House was opened, with rooms for a few students and a dining hall that could feed eighty or a hundred. That made less than two hundred meals for a campus of more than four hundred students, not to mention faculty and staff. Neither Hitchcock nor Boyden House seems to have run close to capacity. Looking back on these developments half a century later, Stanley King pointed to the influence of Harvard University, which had opened a dining commons in 1878 that the Harvard Corporation found to be cheaper for students than boarding out, more convenient, and freighted with "moral significance."[41]

If the administrators of the college hoped that on-campus dining halls would create upstanding young men, they probably did not succeed. King, who was a student at the time (and would later be the president of the school and the foremost champion of building Valentine Hall), found that "student behavior in the dining room at Hitchcock was often deplorable."[42] At the same time, boardinghouses were losing their ability to instill a family feeling and moral sense in students, because they were getting too big. Photos from Amherst College Special Collections in the late 1800s show twelve students (circa 1864), eleven students (1892), and ten students at Mrs. Morse's house in the 1892 to 1893 school

Figure 1. Students on the porch of Amherst House, c. 1864. Amherst College Photographs Collection, Amherst College, Amherst, MA.

Figure 2. Boardinghouse portrait, 1892. Amherst College Photographs Collection, Amherst College, Amherst, MA.

Figure 3. Mrs. Morse's rooming house, 1892–1893. Number four is future president Calvin Coolidge. Amherst College Photographs Collection, Amherst College, Amherst, MA.

year, including future US president Calvin Coolidge; eight of these men also lived with Mrs. Morse, but Harry Barker stayed at Mrs. Avery's, and Coolidge roomed at the home of Mr. Trott.[43]

By 1911, we have evidence of much larger numbers: Brown's fed fifty-two students per meal, Perry's fed seventy-five, and Waite's lunch counter fed eighty-three students regularly.[44] Peg Moore, who ran a boardinghouse in the 1920s, fed about one hundred and twenty students three meals a day.[45] In this changed environment, the moral authority and personal touch of the boardinghouse keeper declined.

Students seemed to prefer boardinghouses, even as they grew, to food on campus. According to Stanley King, Hitchcock Hall's "elaborate menu served in uninviting surroundings [was] not appetizing." Finally, in his last semester, King moved his meals to a boardinghouse kept by Colonel Houghton, where the food was "excellent." It was possible to run a good campus dining hall—King found one when he went to Harvard Law School—but Amherst could not seem to manage it.[46] Hitchcock was torn down in 1916 to make way for Converse Memorial Library; by then, Boyden House had been converted into faculty housing. When Morrow Dormitory opened in 1926, named for patron Dwight Morrow, a powerful banker on Amherst's Board of Trustees, it also had a cafeteria, with similarly uneven results.[47]

Soon after Morrow opened, fraternity houses began to feed their members. In the 1870s, a series of fires in downtown Amherst destroyed buildings where fraternities had rented space, and they began to buy their own houses. Alumni committees for each fraternity chapter managed the property, raised money to pay the mortgage, and kept a watchful eye on the house to "see that the undergraduate standards of housekeeping were maintained at a satisfactory minimum." Like the college, fraternities often relied on African American men for custodial work—men like Perry Roberts, who evoked the same warm, affectionate condescension among the members of Delta Upsilon that Professor Charley did among the students living in the dorms.[48]

Unlike fraternities at other schools, Amherst chapters did not feed their members until the 1930s, when the tide quickly turned.[49] In 1933, five fraternities had dining rooms in their homes, and one or two others had exclusive arrangements with boardinghouses to feed their members.[50] As in boardinghouses and on-campus cafeterias, fraternities offered work for poorer students to wait upon the richer ones at mealtime. Two pamphleteering seniors in the class of 1938 claimed that waiting fraternity tables was the most lucrative student job on campus, so much so that it created "an unhealthy financial basis for the rushing season."[51]

When fraternities finally began to eat together in the 1930s, in their houses or in exclusive boardinghouses, they broke a longstanding tradition at Amherst. Until then, unlike members of other fraternity chapters across the country, Amherst students did not eat with their fraternities. Many Amherst students were proud of this tradition, and when it ended in the 1930s, some expressed concern. The pamphleteers of 1938 looked back wistfully to the era of small boardinghouses, a time that had ended, they say, a quarter of a century earlier. "Friends ate together in small groups, and there was no segregation even remotely resembling the fraternal herding which exists today."[52]

The fraternity house dining era was short. Even before it began, administrators had been mulling a greater commitment to on-campus dining. In 1911, a report surveyed the dining policies and facilities of Dartmouth, Harvard, Williams, Andover, Exeter, the Massachusetts Institute of Technology (MIT), nine boardinghouses in town, and Amherst House. It found that students everywhere considered on-campus cafeteria food "rotten." "Finding this word in common use everywhere," wrote the anonymous author of the report, "I conclude that it means nothing anywhere." There are no comments in the report on the quality of the food in the boardinghouses. Descriptions of food service at other schools suggested the decisions managers faced at on-campus cafeterias. How do you keep your ratio of labor-to-food costs low? Should you employ students or professionals as waiters? How big should the dining hall be, and what proportion of the student body should it aim to serve? Should food be served under the American or European plan? How do you keep students and dollars coming in?[53]

Reforms did not come in 1911, but the idea for a better dining hall persisted. Presidents George Harris (1899–1912) and Alexander Meiklejohn (1912–1923) recommended a student commons, but neither tried to raise the money.[54] A 1933 report framed the question of a central dining commons in terms of the health of its students: "Your Committee has unanimously come to the conclusion that the College should be responsible for the physical well-being of its students, and that the careful and scientific selection, preparation, and serving of food, as well as the condition under which it is prepared and served, is an important part of this responsibility."[55] Years later, Valentine manager William M. Golding laid it out a little more clearly: on-campus dining halls were needed because at fraternity houses "they would eat beans and frankfurts all week so they'd have the money to buy beer and booze."[56] Everyone started talking about that report in 1933—in conversations among friends, in columns of the *Student*, in letters from alumni to President King.[57] Fundraising stalled for fraternities still investing in new kitchens. Boardinghouse women took notice that they might be losing their livelihood.[58]

On campus, the committees grew thicker in 1938 and 1939,[59] and eventually President King raised the money for a central dining hall, named the building for admiralty lawyer Samuel H. Valentine (class of 1866) and his wife Eliza, persuaded the trustees to go along with the investment (despite war in Europe and uncertainty at home), and got the thing built.[60] Gordon Bridges was hired away from Bowdoin College to run the dining hall. His assistant, Ms. Coral Kenney, served as hostess of the dining rooms. There were eleven workers in the central kitchen, and nearly seventy-five students waiting tables and washing dishes on full and halftime shifts. The dean chose who received these jobs. Once boardinghouse matrons had decided which students deserved what we would today call work-study jobs; now administrators were consolidating power over who could and couldn't afford to stay in school.[61] British soldiers chased Native Americans around the edges of the dishware, a design that Stanley and Peg King approved on a visit to a Boston china company during their summer vacation—the designer was a Smith graduate and knew the fight song.[62]

Valentine Hall brought scale and central planning to the feeding of Amherst students. Since the 1820s, when each student had to buy their own wood from firewood dealers, the school had stubbornly refused to centralize purchasing and build the power to exact lower prices. Boardinghouses had purchased on a slightly greater scale. Fraternities went one further; when they began feeding themselves in the 1930s, some got together to purchase food and supplies collectively, at a discount (I have found no evidence that boardinghouse keepers created purchasing cooperatives). Still, even these attempts to buy bulk could not match Valentine. When the rationing of World War II came, fraternities that still cooked couldn't keep themselves in food, but Valentine, through the long-term Boston food market connections of professional manager Gordon Bridges, did just fine.[63]

Valentine differed from boardinghouse serving customs—there were menus and table service at first, but during the war, they were replaced with counter service in serving rooms off each of the three dining rooms. This is when tin trays came into use; after the war, the school tried to decommission the trays, but the students protested because they fit more food. Each dining room was staffed by students and managed by a student headwaiter. A few students worked in the kitchen alongside full-time employees.[64]

Fraternities still tended to eat with each other, congregating in different rooms—Dekes in East, Kappa Theta at the end of East, Psi Upsilon in West, AD downstairs—but the administration discouraged it. As the black student population grew after the war, they also sometimes congregated at particular tables, but women, when they finally arrived, did not seem to segregate themselves in any particular place. William M. Golding was manager of Valentine when Amherst went co-ed, and found that women's good decorum and the work ethic of female student employees improved Valentine; suddenly it was easy to staff the breakfast shift. Though seating patterns in Valentine sometimes reflected divisions in the student body, King argued that it was a force for unity. It put "emphasis on membership in the College rather than on membership in a fraternity" and created "a stronger sense of [students'] Amherst fellowship" than fraternity dining rooms.[65]

Was that stronger sense of fellowship the ultimate goal? Or was it also a diversion of fellowship from Christian charity to high capitalism, orchestrated by a new corporate elite? In this collection, chapters by Debby Applegate and Richard Teichgraeber III argue that the early twentieth century was a period of profound change for Amherst College. Wealthier students enrolled, graduated, and became still wealthier alumni. The student body and the curriculum became more secular, and the school lost its religious mission. A strong connection grew to New York City's corporate and financial sectors through alumni like George A. Plimpton (class of 1876, schoolbooks!), who had run a boardinghouse while he was a student, Charles M. Pratt (class of 1879, petroleum), Daniel Willis James (class of 1889, mining), Bruce Barton (class of 1907, advertising), and, most of all, Dwight Morrow (class of 1895), a partner at J. P. Morgan and eventually ambassador to Mexico. These men were crucial in shaping the modern US economy, making Calvin Coolidge (class of 1895) president of the United States and changing Amherst into the self-contained, secular institution of the twentieth and twenty-first centuries. See Teichgraeber's chapter, note 40, for a little more on Morrow, perhaps the most powerful man in the history of Amherst College.

Campus governance changed, shifting significant decision-making power to trustees and other wealthy alumni who kept bringing their money back to campus. That is the Amherst that existed for all of us alumni who are still alive, and exists today; remarkable are today's wealth, secularization, and the pipeline to Wall Street.

Is this shift the cause of the campus dining halls in the 1890s, the fraternity dining rooms of the 1930s, and ultimately Valentine? Did rich, relatively secular New York City alumni prefer that students eat on campus, and if so, why? Several fellow contributors to this volume have asked me if the slow shift toward eating on campus was part of secularization of the curriculum, or the changing class status of the students. I have developed hypotheses that answer these questions in the affirmative, but I have not been able to demonstrate them with evidence; sometimes, quite the opposite.

For example, it could be that Gilded Age industrialists and bankers, committed to the growth of large, vertically integrated, multidivisional firms, might also have urged Amherst to bring in-house certain functions that had been traditionally outsourced. Alternatively, the college had a broad pool of rich alumni, so it could finally afford to build a dining hall and more dormitories. Or, students could afford to pay more for food because they were richer, and the college saw opportunities for profit where they had not existed before. Or the decline of religious feeling meant administrators no longer needed students to eat in a family setting with a parental figure available to lead prayers, watch students' manners, and scold. Perhaps the new elitism of Amherst's leaders motivated the creation of a total school environment, following the lead of other elite universities that had built up their dorms and dining halls in recent decades. Maybe the new arrangements answered students' greater desire for luxury with a shorter walk and easier path to meals. I see no evidence to support these claims. But, whatever the reasons for building a central dining hall, it was not to make relations between students and servers more democratic.

Perhaps rich alumni thought their spoiled children would be more prone to bad behavior than past students and would need to be cloistered on campus whenever possible. But in the past, parents and professors made the opposite argument—that only living and eating as a boarder in a small home would instill discipline and morality in a young man. I would suggest that the middling-poor classes of the mid-1830s were among the worst behaved in Amherst history, what with Tennessee rising sophomore Robert C. McNairy beating abolitionist senior John L. Ashley with a cane at the commencement ceremony in 1835, and subsequent student unrest sparked by the expulsion of William O. Gorham.[66]

The stated purpose of building Valentine was to create a stronger sense of community on campus; provide better, healthier food; and perhaps to consolidate control over work-study jobs. It clearly did those things. Today, the food is great, the hum of conversation fills the rooms, all students who need financial aid receive it, and some work in Valentine.

After Valentine, Amherst boardinghouses went into decline. During the war, Peg Moore rented rooms to West Point instructors who were on campus training troops, and afterward to secretaries. She never completely lost her connection to the campus, though. In later years, she often walked with Robert Frost on the way to pick up the newspaper: "Never discussed his poetry. Indifferent about that. Just treated him as a human being."[67]

Notes

1. William Gardiner Hammond, *Remembrance of Amherst* (New York: Columbia University Press, 1946), 202–3.

2. "Catalogue of the Officers and Students of Amherst College," Amherst College, vol. 1847–1848, 14, https://www.amherst.edu/amherst-story/facts.

3. Edward Bellamy, *Looking Backward* (Boston, MA: Tickenor and Company, 1888), 214, 218.

4. Hammond, *Remembrance of Amherst*, 75.

5. Hammond, *Remembrance of Amherst*, 45, 50, 60, 132.

6. See, for example, Hammond, *Remembrance of Amherst*, 22, 24, 25, 27, 28, 98, 104, 107, 108, 143.

7. *Catalogue of the Officers and Students of Amherst College for the Academical Year 1825-6* (Amherst, MA: J. S. & C. Adams & Co, October 1854), 7–14, Amherst College Digital Collections, Amherst College, Amherst, MA, accessed December 17, 2018, www.amherst.edu/library/archives/college-history.

8. Edward "Doc" Hitchcock, "Wood Fires and Mud," *Amherst*, Fall 1991, 14-21, Student Housing—General, Buildings & Grounds Collection, Box 17, Folder 33, Special Collections, Amherst College, Amherst MA; Hammond, *Remembrance of Amherst*, 75, 85, 87, 100, 137, 194, 198, 238; Margaret Dakin, "An Ample Nation," *Consecrated Eminence* (blog), April 24, 2017, http://www.consecratedeminence.wordpress.com; George R. Cutting, *Student Life at Amherst College* (Amherst, MA: Hatch & Williams, 1871), 124.

9. W. S. Tyler, *History of Amherst College During the First Half Century, 1821–1871* (Springfield, MA: Clark W. Bryan, 1873).

10. Wendy Gamber, *The Boardinghouse in Nineteenth-Century America* (Baltimore, MD: Johns Hopkins University Press, 2007); David F. Allmendinger, *Paupers and Scholars: The Transformation of Student Life in Nineteenth-Century New England* (New York: St. Martin's, 1975), 81–85; Frederick Rudolph, *The American College and University* (New York: Alfred A. Knopf, 1962), 27, 101–2, 205.

11. The privy was "a series of brick stalls, with a door, and a plank perforated with an oval opening, say twelve by eight inches, [pitched] at a steep angle so that a subject must place himself on the orifice not by sitting but by bracing of himself by his feet in a crouching posture. There was also a projecting plank made to reach the back of the occupant so that he could not mount the seat and defile it." Hitchcock, "Wood Fires and Mud"; William Seymour Tyler, *History of Amherst College During Its First Half-Century: 1821–1871* (Springfield, MA: Clark W. Bryan, 1873), 79; Spencer Haught, "Lives of Consequence: A History of Service Employees at Amherst College" (undergraduate thesis, Amherst College, 2009), 8.

12. "Professor of Dust and Ashes" was a common phrase used to describe campus janitors. Sometimes he was an indigent student who worked for discounted tuition or rooming fees, sometimes an employee of the school; if the latter, often a black man. "Window Seat," *Amherst Literary Review* 2 182–84; Hammond, *Remembrance of Amherst*, 148, 293; Rev. M. M. G. Dana, *Western Colleges, Their Claims and Necessities*, reprint, *New Englander* (Congregational Club of Minnesota, November 1880), 17; Rev. C. B. Barton, *The Founders and Founding of Illinois College* (Jacksonville, IL: John K. Long, 1902), 24; Edward J. Bartlett, *A Dartmouth Book of Remembrance* (Hanover, NH: Webster Press, 1922); Melvin Gilbert Dodge, ed., *Fifty Years Ago: The Half-Century Annalists' Letters to the Hamilton College Alumni Association 1865 to 1900* (Kirkland, NY: Hamilton College, 1900), 20, 121–22, 240, 310; Leverett Wilson Spring, *A History of Williams College* (Boston, MA: Houghton Mifflin, 1917), 306; Tyler, *History of Amherst College*, 608; Haught, *Lives of Consequence*, 13–14.

13. Haught, *Lives of Consequence*, 18–29, Nicholas L. Syrett, *The Company He Keeps: A History of White College Fraternities* (Chapel Hill: The University of North Carolina Press, 2009), 69–70; Hammond, *Remembrance of Amherst*, 172; Roberts Walker, "Prof. Charley," in *An Amherst Book*, ed. Herbert E. Riley (New York: Republic Press, 1896), 102–5; John Dutton Wright, "Prof Charley," *Amherst Literary Monthly* 2, no. 4 (1887[?]), 183; A. E. L., *"Prof. Charley" A Story of Charles Thompson* (Boston: D. C. Heath, 1902), 17–22, 29; Haught, "Lives of Consequence," 7. Abigail E. S. Lee was the daughter of William A. Stearns, president of Amherst from 1854 to 1876. On Sabrina, see Max Shoop, *Sabrina: The Class Goddess of Amherst College* (Amherst, MA: Max Shoop, 1910); Winthrop H. Smith, Halyor R. Seard, and John G. Gibson, *Sabrina: Being a Chronicle of the Life of the Goddess of Amherst College* (Seward, Gibbon, and Smith, 1921); Eve Kosofsky Sedgwick, "Sabrina Doesn't Live Here Any More," *Amherst* 37, no. 5 (Spring 1985): 12–17, 21.

14. Craig Steven Wilder, *Ebony & Ivy: Race, Slavery, and the Troubled History of America's Universities* (New York: Bloomsbury, 2013), 136; Kelley Fanto Deetz, "Finding Dignity in a Landscape of Fear: Enslaved Women and Girls at the University of Virginia," *Slavery & Abolition* 39, no. 2 (2018): 254, 256. I haven't found evidence of students bringing slaves to northern schools, but plenty of northern colleges, college presidents, and college faculty owned slaves through the early nineteenth century, at Dartmouth, Queens College, Kings College (Columbia), the College of New Jersey (Rutgers), Yale, Harvard, the College of Philadelphia (founded by Benjamin Franklin during his slave master period), the College of Rhode Island, etc. And, as we have learned in recent years, higher education supported and profited from slavery in many, many other ways. Wilder, *Ebony & Ivy*, 119–28; Deetz, "Finding Dignity in a Landscape of Fear," 251–66; Syrett, *The Company He Keeps*, 74. Many schools now have active projects to recover and remember their legacies of slavery; see "The Lemon Project," William & Mary, http://www.wm.edu/sites/lemonproject/; "Steering Committee on Slavery and Justice," Brown University, [provide access

date], http://www.brown.edu/Research/Slavery_Justice/; "Yale Slavery and Abolition Portal," Yale University, http://slavery.yale.edu; "The Princeton and Slavery Project," Princeton University, Princeton, NJ, http://slavery.princeton.edu.

15. Tyler, *History of Amherst College*, 74, 80.

16. Tyler, *History of Amherst College*, 299–301; Hitchcock, "Wood Fires and Mud," 17; *Catalogue of the Officers and Students of Amherst College*, vols. 1821–22, 1825–26, 1830–31, 1835–16, 1840–41, 1845–46, 1850–51, 1855–56, 1860–61, 1865–66, 1870–71, 1875–76, 1880–81, 1885–86, 1890–91, 1895–96, Amherst College Digital Collections, Amherst College, Amherst, MA, accessed December 17, 2018, http://www.amherst.edu/library/archives/college-history.

17. Sanford saved other ways—he lit no fire in the eating room in January; the fires in the cook room on one side and the parlor on the other kept it warm enough for him, even if the boarders complained. Reverend John Sanford to John E. Sanford, January 14 and July 19, 1852, Sanford Collection, Special Collections, Amherst College, Amherst, MA.

18. Hammond, *Remembrance of Amherst*, 176, 210; *Catalogue of the Officers*, 1855–56, 1860–61, 1865–66, 1870–71, 1875–76, 1880–81.

19. Hammond, *Remembrance of Amherst*, 19; Rev. John Sanford to John E. Sanford, January 14, 1852, Sophia Sanford to John E. Sanford, May 24, 1852, Sanford Collection, Special Collections, Amherst College, Amherst, MA.

20. Hammond, *Remembrance of Amherst*, 45, 160.

21. Tyler, *History of Amherst College*, 301–2; Allmendinger, *Paupers and Scholars*, 99; Hitchcock, "Wood Fires and Mud," 19.

22. Hammond, *Remembrance of Amherst*, 79, 104–5, 220.

23. Editorial, *Amherst Literary Monthly* 2, no. 6 (December 1887): 329–30.

24. "Window Seat," *Amherst Literary Monthly* 4, no. 2 (May 1889): 82–84.

25. Reverend John Sanford to John E. Sanford, July 19, 1852, Sanford Collection, Special Collections, Amherst College, Amherst, MA.

26. Tyler, *History of Amherst College*, 106.

27. William Orr, "College Eating in the Early Eighties," *Amherst Record*, April 18, 1934, Amherst College Committees Collection—Eating and Housing, 1933–1938, Special Collections, Amherst College, Amherst, MA.

28. "Roast Beef and Merry Widows," *Amherst*, Fall 1989, 21–23, General Files—Housing—Off Campus Housing & Boardinghouses, Special Collections, Amherst College, Amherst MA.

29. William Seymour Tyler, *Autobiography of William Seymour Tyler* (private printing, 1912), 27.

30. King, *Consecrated Eminence*, 103.

31. See, for example, *Amherst College Olio*, 1866, 34–36; 1878, 88–99; 1887, 153.

32. "Window Seat," *Amherst Literary Monthly* 4, no. 2 (May 1889): 82–84.

33. Daniel Levinson Wilk, *Lives of the Service Sector* (forthcoming).

34. Hammond, *Remembrance of Amherst*, 21–22, 104.

35. Hammond, *Remembrance of Amherst*, 133, 148, 170, 250–51, 256–57.

36. Hammond, *Remembrance of Amherst*, 30, 36, 41, 77–79, 108–9, 114, 116–17, 121–22, 125, 135, 137, 140, 142–43, 148, 150, 157, 174, 191, 201, 207, 208, 226, 245, 271–75.

37. *Amherst Student*, February 1, 1868, 8, February 26, 1876, 1; *Amherst Record*, March 17, 1886, 1, Amherst College Committees Collection, Special Collections, Amherst College, Amherst, MA; "Window Seat," *The Amherst Literary Monthly* 2, no. 5 (November 1887): 235–36.

38. "Banquets," Amherst College Bound Memorabilia Series 1, Dramatic Programs, 1899–1908, vol. 14, Special Collections, Amherst College, Amherst, MA.

39. Stearns, *An American Boyhood*, 62–3l; Canfield, *Seed & Sowers*, 60; *Olio*, 1904, 215; Herbert Elihu Riley, *An Amherst Book* (Washington, DC: Republic Press, 1896), 134–37.

40. Frederick H. Hitchcock, *The Handbook of Amherst, Massachusetts* (Amherst, MA: Frederick H. Hitchcock, 1891), 135.

41. Stanley King, *"The Consecrated Eminence": The Story of the Campus and Buildings of Amherst College* (Amherst, MA: Amherst College, 1951), 103–4, 196, 318–19; *Catalogue of the Officers and Students of Amherst College*, Amherst College Digital Collections, accessed December 17, 2018, http://www.amherst.edu/library/archives/college-history. "By Order of Committee of College Trustees, Sept 7th, '92," Lucius Boltwood House (Hitchcock Hall)—General, Buildings & Grounds Collection, Box 2, Folder 40, Special Collections, Amherst College, Amherst, MA.

42. King, *Consecrated Eminence*, 103.

43. Four more students who are not in the photo are listed as living at Mrs. Morse's in the school catalogue; perhaps they ate elsewhere, or maybe they just missed the photo shoot, and there were fourteen or more people who ate there. A scrap of paper from sometime in the early 1890s shows that eleven men boarded at Mrs. Marsh's house one term. "Amherst House Student Group c. 1864," "Boardinghouse Group 1892 identifications," and "Mrs. Morse's Rooming House verso," General Files—Housing—Off Campus Housing & Boardinghouses, Special Collections, Amherst College, Amherst, MA; *Catalogue of Amherst College*, 1892–1893, 12–21.

44. The number of diners in boardinghouses were self-reported by the boardinghouse owners. The anonymous author who collected them for a 1911 report suspected they were unintentionally inflated because some students ate meals both in town and at Hitchcock Hall on campus. When their numbers were added to the number of students the college counted eating in Hitchcock, the total was 556 students, but the student body was only 464. "1911 Council Report on Dining Halls," Amherst College Catalogue, 1911–1912, 30, General Files, Special Collections, Amherst College, Amherst, MA.

45. "Roast Beef and Merry Widows," *Amherst*, Fall 1989, 21–23, General Files—Housing—Off Campus Housing & Boardinghouses, Special Collections, Amherst College, Amherst, MA.

46. "Dining Hall Regulations," Lucius Boltwood House (Hitchcock Hall)—General, Buildings & Grounds Collection, Box 2, Folder 40, Special Collections, Amherst College, Amherst, MA; King, *Consecrated Eminence*, 103–4.

47. Student Housing—Morrow Dormitory—General Files, Special Collections, Amherst College, Amherst, MA; King, *Consecrated Eminence*, 176–77, 196, 318–19.

48. At campuses across the country, black domestic workers in fraternities became a common object of ridicule, both in nostalgic memoirs and novels about college life. King, *Consecrated Eminence*, 148–51; Syrett, *Company He Keeps*, 30, 162, 165–68.

49. King, *Consecrated Eminence*, 225.

50. "Editorial Comment," *Amherst Graduates Quarterly* 22 (February 1933): 137.

51. "Amherst's Greatest Need: An Eating Union and Residence-Houses," 1938[?], Student Housing—General Files, Buildings & Grounds Collection, Box 17, Folder 33, Special Collections, Amherst College, Amherst, MA.

52. George O. Trenchard, "Eating in Fraternity Houses," *Amherst Graduates' Quarterly* 74 (February 1930): 101–3; "Amherst's Greatest Need"; "Report of Committee to Study."

53. "1911 Council Report."

54. King, *Consecrated Eminence*, 325; "Past Presidents," Amherst College, accessed January 3, 2019, http://www.amherst.edu/amherst-story/president/past_presidents.

55. "Report of Committee to Study," 3.

56. "Interview with William M. Golding, Manager and Walter R. Lucas, Assistant Manager of Val-

entine Hall, February 4, 1981," Amherst College Oral History Project, Special Collections, Amherst College, Amherst MA.

57. "Editorial Comment," *Amherst Graduates Quarterly* 23 (February 1933): 136–38.

58. King, *Consecrated Eminence*, 225–26.

59. "Report of Eating and Housing Committee," Amherst College Committees Collection—Eating and Housing, 1933–1938, 2–8, Special Collections, Amherst College, Amherst, MA.

60. King, *Consecrated Eminence*, 256–58; "Construction Is Begun on New Valentine Hall," Amherst College Catalogue, 1941/1942, 122, Student Housing—Valentine Hall—General, Buildings & Grounds Collection, Box 19, Folder 40, Special Collections, Amherst College, Amherst, MA.

61. "Valentine Hall at Amherst College," Student Housing—Valentine Hall—General, Buildings & Grounds Collection, Box 19, Folder 40, Special Collections, Amherst College, Amherst, MA.

62. "Interview with William M. Golding"; King, *Consecrated Eminence*, 260–61.

63. "Interview with William M. Golding," 22.

64. "Interview with William M. Golding," 22–23; "College Marks Official Opening of Valentine Hall This Afternoon," *Amherst Student*, October 29, 1941, 1–3, Student Housing—Valentine Hall—General, Buildings & Grounds Collection, Box 19, Folder 40, Special Collections, Amherst College, Amherst, MA; "Handbook for Headwaiters and Student Employees," Student Housing—Valentine Hall—General, Buildings & Grounds Collection, Box 19, Folder 43, Special Collections, Amherst College, Amherst, MA.

65. "Interview with William M. Golding," 19–20; King, *Consecrated Eminence*, 262–63.

66. Gorham had refused to give a prize speech because of conscientious objection to the giving of prizes and awards. This was a common ethical position among the student body—some thought it immoral to draw honorary distinctions among students, and others disliked the low level of distinction they had received. A standoff almost led to the expulsion of the entire junior class, and word of dissatisfaction spread, leading to lower enrollments for years to come. Allmendinger, *Paupers and Scholars*, 104–5; W. S. Tyler, *History of Amherst College During Its First Half Century 1821–1871* (Springfield, MA: C. W. Bryan, 1873), 250–59.

67. "Roast Beef and Merry Widows," 22.

PART II

The College and Beyond

"*The farthest West shakes hands with the remotest East*"

Amherst College, China, and Collegiate Cosmopolitanism in the Nineteenth Century

K. Ian Shin

"That 'westward the course of empire tends,' is to-day meeting its final fulfillment," Henry Davis wrote in 1868 while a senior at Amherst College. "The farthest West shakes hands with the remotest East, across the no longer 'wide Pacific.'"[1] While Davis celebrated closer relations between the United States and China, he did not realize just how important his alma mater had been in facilitating this handshake. Several pioneers of US–China relations claimed an Amherst connection: the first American missionary in China was Elijah C. Bridgman (class of 1826), and he and another nongraduate, missionary-physician Peter Parker (class of x1831), aided the negotiations of the first treaty between the two countries. Although the college, at the end of the nineteenth century, enrolled only about four hundred students in any given year, their collective impact on US–China relations far outweighed their numbers.

The dense connections between Amherst and China were sustained by the enduring attachment that its graduates felt for the college across the Pacific Ocean. To be sure, other aspects of their identity—especially their faith—also defined their views and experiences abroad. This chapter argues that the college affiliation of US travelers during the nineteenth century meaningfully shaped the links they forged between the United States and China—a phenomenon I call *collegiate cosmopolitanism*.

The collegiate cosmopolitanism of Amherst graduates in China manifested in three key ways. First, graduates like Bridgman, Stephen Johnson (class of 1827), James G. Bridgman (class of 1842), and Charles Hartwell (class of 1849) led the American evangelization of China and formed the vanguard of US–China relations alongside the merchants of the old China trade. Beyond proselytizing, collegiate cosmopolitans also cultivated social and intellectual ties between Amherst and China, strengthening the college's library and museum collections. Thus, Amherst participated in a Euro-American system of Christian and scientific imperialism, backed by the diplomatic and military power of Western countries, that eroded China's sovereignty over the course of the nineteenth century. However,

China was not simply a passive victim of foreign domination. In fact, Amherst graduates were intimidated by the prospect of living and working in China, and Chinese people who came to Amherst as early as the 1840s demanded to be seen on their own terms.

Migration emerged as a third theme in contacts between Amherst and China in the late nineteenth century, as the presence of Chinese people in the United States became an increasingly fraught political and social question. The issue challenged the cosmopolitan outlook of earlier decades and divided college leaders from students. Grounded in their republican and Christian convictions, leaders like Julius H. Seelye (class of 1849) opposed the restriction of Chinese immigration in the late 1870s, while many students embraced exclusion.

Amherst's first Chinese student arrived against this backdrop of xenophobia and racism, struggling to carry on the tradition of collegiate cosmopolitanism. By standing against the virulent politics of the era, Chinese students at Amherst and elsewhere embodied the college's motto to "give light to the world" when others failed.

FROM AMHERST TO CHINA: THE CHRISTIAN IMPERIALISM OF RELUCTANT EVANGELISTS

Amherst students and graduates during the first half of the nineteenth century were primarily interested in China to bring it to Christianity. Secondhand sources of information rather than personal encounters or travel experiences provided impressions of China and Chinese people. These sources painted for prospective missionaries an inviting but daunting picture of China: on one hand, the supposed backwardness of the Chinese justified the intervention of Christians; on the other hand, the scale of the challenge unnerved them. Protestant evangelists like Elijah Bridgman, Peter Parker, and Charles Hartwell went to China reluctantly. Once there, however, they built a multifarious missionary enterprise that had a lasting impact—both positive and negative—far beyond the walls of the church.

The accomplishments of American missionaries like Bridgman and Parker rested unquestionably on an unequal relationship between China and "the West"—what historian Emily Conroy-Krutz calls "Christian imperialism." Missionaries "presumed their right to come into foreign spaces and transform them, relying on their own values as they judged those around them."[2] Members of the Society of Inquiry, an Amherst student organization established in 1821 to "form a bond of union and sympathy between Christian men in college," gave clear voice to this presumption in 1849, when they debated the question: "Is it right to introduce the Bible into a Country in direct opposition to its Laws?" The society answered in the affirmative.[3] The student debaters almost certainly had China in mind, for the Qing government had steadfastly issued prohibitions against Christianity since the eighteenth century.[4] For students at Amherst, the divine imperative to spreading God's word overrode Chinese sovereignty.

Missionaries both enabled and relied on the military and political might of their home countries to advance their cause. Conroy-Krutz observes that missionaries promoted religion, but they also "were concerned with the spread of Anglo-American culture . . . seeing

Figure 1. Elijah C. Bridgman, Ca. 1826. Amherst College Archives and Special Collections, Amherst College Library.

governance as a tool in this larger project."[5] Expanding economic and political ties between the United States and other parts of the world, whether voluntary or not, would carry the gospel far and wide. Writing on the cusp of war over Great Britain's coercive importation of opium into China, Elijah Bridgman expressed his hopes that the conflict would open China for missionary work: "We have long mourned over the desolations around us. . . . And now, we trust, the God of nations is about to open a highway for those who will preach the Word."[6] Bridgman believed that China's defeat was divinely ordained.

In 1843, the United States sent its envoy, Caleb Cushing, to secure for the United States the same privileges that Great Britain won at the end of the First Opium War under the Treaty of Nanjing.[7] Bridgman and Parker aided Cushing with treaty negotiations. Parker was reluctant to set aside his duties as a missionary-physician but assented to the appointment for "the prospect of having so good an opportunity, thus providentially offered, to promote the great object of my life in China."[8] Like Bridgman, Parker rationalized Western intervention in China in the service of his god.

The resulting Treaty of Wangxia—the first formal treaty between the United States and China—exceeded Parker's expectations by giving Americans the right to erect "hospitals, churches, and cemeteries" in treaty ports. The treaty also eroded China's legal and cultural sovereignty by shielding Americans from criminal prosecution under Chinese law and ending a long-standing prohibition on learning the Chinese language.[9] Bridgman and Parker were central in forging the American link in the chain of "unequal treaties" imposed on China in the nineteenth century.

If these Christian imperialists seem audacious and domineering, however, it is important to remember that they began their careers with feelings of uncertainty and inadequacy. Initially, China loomed in their imagination as a forbidding and hostile land. The challenges of evangelizing in such a faraway land deterred many of them—including not only pioneers of US–China relations like Bridgman and Parker, but also later missionaries like Charles Hartwell who followed them. All contemplated other mission fields where, as Hartwell wrote in his diary, "the immediate prospects seemed so much more encouraging"—in other words, missions that were easier.[10] When Bridgman received the call to China from the American Board of Commissioners for Foreign Missions (ABCFM) in 1829, for example, he admitted that the China mission "was one in which I felt, and long had felt, a deep interest, but had not considered myself as the man for that station; for I had regarded it as one of great importance and responsibility, requiring abilities of the very first order."[11] Remarkably, these pioneers of US missions in China feared that the country would prove too difficult for their skills and backgrounds.

And for good reason. As the ABCFM explained to Bridgman, several difficulties lay ahead. First, and perhaps most significant, was the fact that few had attempted to evangelize China; Bridgman would have to lay the foundation for future missions, including learning the Chinese language. Moreover, the country's territory was vast and its government famously hostile to Christianity and to foreigners. Bridgman would face these obstacles "almost alone," with "few to counsel, to share the responsibility and labor with you, or to sympathize with you in your perplexities."[12] Nevertheless, the ABCFM urged Bridgman to cultivate "a holy enthusiasm" in the thought that there was "no service . . . which opens a wider field, affords opportunities for more varied and painful exertion, or contemplates greater results."[13] The ABCFM's instructions were hardly encouraging.

To prepare, Bridgman read accounts written by other missionaries in China and southeast Asia. He turned specifically to William Milne's *A Retrospect of the First Ten Years of the Protestant Mission to China* (1820), as well as memoirs about Milne by his associate Robert Morrison.[14] Milne's *Retrospect* scarcely assuaged Bridgman's concerns, for Milne candidly acknowledged the disappointing outcomes in the first twelve years of his and Morrison's labors. He admitted that the mission "cannot number many converts—one of those we had, is dead, and the other has lately been imprisoned and beaten for the name of Jesus."[15] The Chinese language was "very difficult;" the climate "not inviting;" and "[the] stern prejudices and persecuting spirit of China continue still unsubdued."[16] On a personal level, the mission had suffered several heartrending losses, including two of Milne's children and his wife, Rachel.[17] Nevertheless, Milne cited the growing number of missionary schools and religious tracts distributed in order to solicit financial support and to attract additional helpers like Bridgman. Before Bridgman departed on October 12, 1829, he made one more visit to Amherst to call on his former professors, though he lamented that "time [was] too short to see the students as I wished to do."[18]

In China, Bridgman, Parker, and their colleagues achieved their greatest successes outside the church. Briefly,[19] Bridgman launched the *Chinese Repository*, a monthly magazine in English that was the world's first journal of Sinology.[20] His *A Brief Account of the United States of America*, written in Chinese, was the first book to describe the United States to a Chinese readership in their native language. Several copies reached Japan where, as Trent Maxey recounts, their descriptions of US political, economic, and social life inspired a young Niijima Jō (class of 1870) to "learn American knowledge" and eventually brought him to Amherst College.[21]

Parker established the Ophthalmic Hospital in Canton in 1835, one of the first in China. In the first three months alone, Parker treated 1,061 patients.[22] Building on this foundation, the same hospital went on to treat seven hundred and forty thousand patients and performed 49,000 operations, between 1855 and 1899, under the leadership of Parker's successor.[23]

Protestant schools, about which William Milne had been so proud, numbered almost seven thousand by 1920 and enrolled some two hundred thousand pupils.[24]

Most importantly, as David Hollinger has argued, "missionary cosmopolitans" like Bridgman and Parker found themselves transformed abroad. They, in turn, transformed the United States by "challenging the provinciality of American public life"[25]

These achievements cannot be divorced from the conditions that missionaries helped impose on China. The belief that China was spiritually desolate and its civilization backward, and the presumption that Christianity was the answer, motivated Bridgman and Parker to join Caleb Cushing's mission to craft a one-sided treaty with China. In the long run, the missionaries' actions undermined the advances they set out to achieve by weakening the Qing government and inflaming antiforeign sentiment.

FROM CHINA (BACK) TO AMHERST: VISITS, LETTERS, COLLECTIONS

Nineteenth-century collegiate cosmopolitans remained connected to Amherst through frequent letter writing and occasional visits to the college. They aimed to energize religiosity and public support for foreign missions and to bolster the educational missions of their institutions by circulating specimens and ideas across the ocean. Amherst's missionary-graduates in China provided it with new research, as well as objects of ethnological and scientific interest. Amherst participated in the European and US extension of "informal empire" over China through collecting, categorizing, and studying Chinese culture and natural history—practicing scientific imperialism that sought to capture evermore "useful" knowledge about the country. However, local conditions often constrained their success.

Missionary visits to Amherst testify to the enduring ties that its former students felt for the college. The outbreak of war between Great Britain and China in July 1840 forced Parker to close his hospital in Canton and return to the United States. Over the next year and a half, Parker met with officials of the ABCFM and the US government, delivered an address about China to a joint session of Congress, attended lectures on the latest medical advances in Philadelphia, traveled throughout Europe, and courted and married Harriet Webster.[26] Amid these important appointments, Parker visited Amherst in late October, even though he had left its halls for Yale University over a decade earlier.[27] While no records remain of Parker's activities at the college during his visit, he likely counseled students who were interested in missionary work and spoke about the opium crisis in China, as he had also done in New Haven, Connecticut.

Charles Hartwell sailed for the United States on May 22, 1877, on furlough from the ABCFM mission in Fuzhou, and arrived in Amherst on July 24, staying for at least five months. Visiting the college allowed Hartwell to check in on his son, also named Charles (class of 1877). Hartwell could also count on the company of an old friend and classmate, Edward "Doc" Hitchcock, the beloved professor of hygiene and physical education. Over the course of his five-month long residence at Amherst, Hartwell participated actively in college life, attending events and socializing with President Seelye and members of the faculty. In October 1877, Hartwell witnessed one of the earliest games of football played at the college, where Amherst defeated Tufts.[28] Not surprisingly, Hartwell also enriched the spiritual life of the college by participating in prayer meetings, preaching sermons, and meeting with students and other youths who sought his counsel. For Hartwell, friends and family offered a continuing connection to Amherst College.

Due to distance, cost, and the demands of mission work, return visits were rare, and missionaries interacted with Amherst primarily through letter writing. Like their visits, these missionary letters reveal the bonds that were forged with Amherst and that reinforced them across time and space. Writing from China on the eve of his twentieth reunion in April 1869, Charles Hartwell asked Doc Hitchcock to convey his greetings to their fellow classmates. "As I cannot be present, I have decided to write you a letter to be read at the meeting, & to send some little mementoes for you to distribute to all, to show that this classmate in China remembers you all & feels an interest in your happiness & welfare," Hartwell wrote.[29] Believing that his friends would "hardly appreciate a sermon in Chinese should I send you a very fine one," Hartwell instead used the letter to recount his experience teaching the Chinese in Fuzhou—whom he called "not generally very musical"—to sing Christian hymns. Along with the letter, Hartwell enclosed copies of translated sheet music, as well as his Chinese calling cards, and invited his American friends to take one of each. He instructed them: "The cards are to be held up endwise as the Chinese usually write perpendicularly from the top to the bottom." In his letters, Charles Hartwell played the role of an early ethnographer. He combined a genuine desire to share the novelty of Chinese cultural practices with his (sometimes) reductive views of Chinese people and his presumption to speak for them.

Missionary letters from China to Amherst were both ethnographic and spiritual. Hartwell concluded his letter to the class of 1849 on a solemn note. "It is very pleasant to me to think how many of us are not only brother classmates, but also brothers in a better sense, brothers in Christ," he wrote. "My prayer is that we all may be such, & may look forward in hope to a more joyful meeting than you now can possibly enjoy in Amherst, where we may together engage in more delightful studies that our college course ever afforded & learn truths in regard to nature & nature's God of which we had then, & have now, but faint conceptions."[30] Hartwell's letter articulates a hierarchy of social relationships in which the men's shared identification as Amherst alumni complemented their identification as fellow Christians. Missionary letters that linked Amherst and China aimed to stoke greater faith and piety (and the financial support these feelings would inspire).

For students, especially those who were members of the Society of Inquiry, missionary letters provided a crucial connection to the wider world. At the society's meetings, students gave reports on various stations in China (probably drawn from reports in missionary magazines) and read letters from missionaries like Bridgman, Josiah Goddard in Ningbo, and Michael Simpson Culbertson in Shanghai.[31] In 1854, the society put in place a plan to regularize this correspondence by assigning various student members to write to foreign missionaries in Amoy, Canton, and Ningbo.[32]

Beyond its spiritual influence, the correspondence of American missionaries in China contributed to the intellectual life of Amherst. In this regard, Amherst mapped to the broader pattern that James A. Field Jr. has observed, regarding the importance of the missionary movement in "contributing to the remarkable nineteenth-century growth of Western knowledge of far places and to the development of a cosmopolitan world culture."[33] For example, missionaries sent publications from abroad, expanding the college's library. In July 1858, Bridgman informed Amherst president William Augustus Stearns that he planned to send "a single copy of the 1st No. of a new journal for the college library."[34] While Bridgman did not specify, it was very likely the *Journal of the Shanghai Literary and Scientific Society*, the first issue of which had been released just one month prior. In addition to this journal, Amherst students could peruse copies of the Bridgman's *Chinese Repository* in the library of the Society of Inquiry.

By sending the journal to Amherst, Bridgman incorporated the college into global circuits of knowledge production, as the Shanghai Literary and Scientific Society soon became affiliated with the Royal Asiatic Society of Great Britain and Ireland. In an address published in the society's journal, Bridgman claimed the prerogative to "discover" native Chinese sources of knowledge, evaluate them according to Western standards, and present them to audiences in Europe and the United States. "In the eyes of the Confucian literati, their beautiful chirography and their classical books are indeed their most precious idols; but, knowing something of their defects, we have no intention of unduly exalting these remarkable productions," Bridgman wrote. "It will, however, be our duty to lay these, as well as whatever treatises they may have produced on the various sciences, all under tribute, and fetch from their store-houses more or less valuable contributions to the noble cause of natural and revealed truth."[35] Importantly, Bridgman dispatched the journal issue to Amherst via the same mission that carried the latest "unequal treaty" with China to officials in Washington, DC. Gunboat diplomacy and Orientalist intellectual impulses made possible the enrichment of early library collections for Chinese studies at Amherst College.

Missionaries also bolstered the college's ethnological and natural history collections by submitting specimens for study. Missionaries remitted "curiosities" from their respective fields to form a museum for the Society of Inquiry. According to the 1838 catalog of the museum, roughly 10 percent of the collection's two hundred and thirty objects were Chinese in origin. A second list in the college's archives (presumably from a later period, though undated) demonstrates that the collection grew to at least 294 total items. By 1857, when the building that housed the collection was destroyed by fire, the society's cabinet of curiosities "had grown to be quite extensive, and idols, implements of various kinds, costumes; in short, a multiplicity of things, illustrating the religious beliefs, the arts and customs of foreign lands, adorned its room."[36] Elijah Bridgman likely sent many of these objects to the Society of Inquiry at Amherst, as he made similar donations to a museum at the Andover Theological Seminary.[37]

The foci of the Society of Inquiry's collection speaks to the attitudes toward China among religious-minded students at Amherst. One significant category of collecting was items related to religious and ritual practices, including tablets and statuettes of Chinese deities, incense sticks and vessels, firecrackers, and funerary money, which the catalog explained were "gilt & silvered papers such as they fold up & burn and say that it is money sent to their deceased relatives for their use in the other world."[38] Illustrating polytheistic and ancestral worship in China not only apprised future missionaries of the religious habits of their prospective converts, but also justified their evangelical interventions against this perceived idolatry.

A second significant category of collecting was clothing. The society came to possess a coat, pantaloons, and patterns for pants and shoes. The catalog called special attention to a "Chinese lady's shoe," presumably a slipper made for bound feet. It is unclear what text accompanied these exhibits to explain their complex histories, usages, and meanings. Without this context, these displays functioned to underscore Chinese culture as exotic and even barbaric.

In addition to these ethnological materials, professors and students at Amherst interested in the natural world counted on missionaries to provide a view into China's flora and fauna. Charles Hartwell had no trouble shipping forty-five species of Chinese ferns to Amherst and to Mount Holyoke Female Seminary (later Mount Holyoke College) in September 1872. However, he found the animal skeletons that his friend Doc Hitchcock requested to be harder to obtain. Hartwell recounted a story from a Chinese boatman about the discovery of a tiger carcass some two hundred miles north of Fuzhou. The $275 price tag for the animal was based almost entirely on the value of the tiger's bones, which, Hartwell explained, the Chinese believe to have great strengthening properties.[39] Hartwell concluded: "You will see . . . you will need to apply to someone else, if you ever wish for the skeleton of a tiger!" Collecting examples of the natural history of China for the benefit of Amherst constituted a form of scientific imperialism. Missionaries, however, had to contend with local desires for these natural resources for traditional uses, checking the ambitions and curiosity of the missionaries and their friends back home.[40] These contestations illuminate the agency of the Chinese in the complex give and take that was always at the heart of Amherst's relationship with China.

THE NEW COLLEGIATE COSMOPOLITANS: THE CHINESE EXCLUSION DEBATE AND OVERSEAS STUDENTS AT AMHERST, 1870S TO 1880S

By the last quarter of the nineteenth century, China was no longer a faraway mission field. Increasingly, it became a domestic-policy issue. Large numbers of Chinese began arriving in the United States around 1850, drawn by the opportunities for work in mining, railroad construction, manufacturing, and other industries. Although many Americans initially praised and welcomed them for their contributions to the development of the US West, these positive reactions soon soured due to racist fears of economic competition and political and social contamination.[41] As the "Chinese Question" became a national one, institutions on the East Coast also became embroiled in the debate over immigration restriction. Amherst was no exception.

The first known visit of a Chinese person to Amherst College was made not by a student, but rather a twenty-one-year-old man named Chen Song who accompanied Peter Parker as his teacher during Parker's return visit to the United States in 1841. A student named Stillman Parker (class of x1845) recalled seeing the pair and was struck by the unfamiliar sight of a Chinese man in western Massachusetts. He recorded his observations about Chen, whom he mistakenly called Chin Lung, in a letter to a friend:

> Dr. Parker and Chin Lung the Chinaman were here last night. The latter was quite a curiosity dressed in the fashion of that country. . . . Don't know how to describe his dress. On his head he wore a close cap something like the one you used to wear but thicker. The clothes around his body were loose. What were they made of I could not tell it being in the evening when I saw him. On his feet he wore sandals with long stockings. Heard him reading in his native language that was quite amusing.[42]

The sight of Chen prompted Stillman Parker to define himself in opposition to the observable differences in their dress and language. Loose clothing, long stockings (on a male figure), and "amusing" speech set off Chen as a "curiosity" so foreign as to be nearly indescribable, and they normalized Parker's own subjectivity.

The Chinese visitor presented himself in a very different light. While he and Peter Parker were in Washington, DC, in February 1841, Chen sat for Auguste Edouart, a French-born silhouette artist. The resulting portrait shows Chen in a declamatory pose, his finger raised, as if to make a point. Chen's clothing, a long jacket that flares at the waist, reflects Stillman Parker's observation that Chen "wore neither coat, pantaloons, or shoes as we do." In fact, his style of dress might have marked him as a woman had it not been for his hair braid, mandated by the Manchu government to be worn by all Chinese men, which runs almost the entire length of Chen's body. With his left hand resting on his hip, Chen projects an air of confidence.[43]

Figure 2. Chin Sung. Auguste Edouart, 1841. Lithograph and cut paper on paper. National Portrait Gallery, Smithsonian Institution; gift of Robert L. McNeil, Jr.

Two inscriptions on the silhouette, apparently by Chen, illustrate Chen's understanding of himself as a cosmopolitan visitor. The first inscription identified the silhouette as "a likeness of Chen Song, who was born in Beijing and came to Yangcheng [Guangzhou] and Macau in Guangdong Province."[44] By proclaiming his connections to China's capital city in the north, as well as its key ports for foreign trade in the south, Chen simultaneously asserted his ties to China's political and commercial spheres and demonstrated his knowledge of its vast territory. In the second inscription, Chen depicted himself as a man of great social and cultural capital: "Often conversing with friends, gazing at the moon, and reciting poetry."[45] As an example of what Mary Louise Pratt calls an autoethnographic text, Chen's inscriptions rejected Stillman Parker's exoticizing characterization of him as an amusing curiosity and presented instead a well-connected and erudite figure.[46]

Chen was the forerunner of a wave of Chinese people coming to the United States beginning around the era of the California Gold Rush (1848–1855). These newcomers sparked a debate over immigration restriction that roiled the nation—including Amherst College—in subsequent decades. College leaders and students took opposing positions that reveal a generational schism over earlier cosmopolitan impulses. In the late 1870s, Congress began considering broad bans on Chinese immigration. One such piece of legislation was the Fifteen Passenger Bill, which Andrew Gyory calls "the first immigration restriction law aimed at a particular nationality ever drafted, debated, and passed by Congress."[47] The bill proposed to limit to fifteen the number of Chinese passengers on any ships to the United States. Violators would be penalized with six months' imprisonment and a $100 fine for each Chinese passenger over that number. The bill passed the House of Representatives on January 28, 1879, without significant debate.

The Fifteen Passenger Bill incensed Julius H. Seelye, president of Amherst since 1877. Seelye believed that the proposed legislation obstructed not only the advancement of the Christian gospel across the world, but also the fair administration of government at home.[48] Seelye, an ordained minister, visited Japan, China, and India in 1872 to 1873 while on leave as a professor of moral and mental philosophy at Amherst. These travels doubtlessly shaped his view that contact with foreign peoples could bring "wild, uncivilized, barbarous, savage people" into "a state of peace and purity and advancing civilization."[49] Furthermore, as Seelye later wrote, "all persons under the government of the United States, of either sex, and whatever their age or race or station, shall be treated by the laws exactly alike."[50] Although Seelye was not an egalitarian in the true sense of the word, he opposed the unjust legislation against Chinese immigrants.

In February 1879, Seelye rallied other college and university presidents against the Fifteen Passenger Bill. He wrote to Boston University president William F. Warren that he had urged president Rutherford B. Hayes to veto the "Chinese Bill" and asked Warren to do the same.[51] Warren told Seelye that his letter "emboldened me to adopt its suggestion, & I have relieved my pent up indignation & grief & shame in as strong a letter as I was able to pen."[52] Samuel C. Bartlett of Dartmouth College and Cyrus D. Foss of Wesleyan University followed suit.[53]

Only Charles W. Eliot of Harvard University declined Seelye's suggestion. Eliot gave two reasons for his decision: he believed there was nothing new he could contribute to the debate in Washington, and he argued that educational leaders would not make persuasive advocates when it came to policy.[54] This was not true for Seelye, who had represented Massachusetts in the US House of Representatives between 1875 and 1877, and whose final months in the House overlapped with the beginning of his presidency at Amherst. The troubling politics of Chinese exclusion offered Seelye the perfect opportunity to combine his evangelical Christian outlook, political experience, and academic position.

Even before Seelye made his objections known to the White House, the Amherst junior class took up the subject in their debate before professor of rhetoric and English literature H. Humphrey Neill, asking: "Ought Chinese immigration to be limited by Congress?"[55] Later that spring, the Alexandrian Society also engaged the topic of Chinese exclusion in their prize debate in April 1879. Four students presented their views on the question, "resolved—that this government should take legislative measures to check further immigration of the Chinese, after notifying the latter government of its intention."[56] Though the specifics of these debates have been lost to time, we might hazard a guess as to their contents by examining debates that took place at similar institutions around the same time.

College newspapers and literary magazines from the 1870s and 1880s suggest that students were generally arrayed against the Chinese. In 1880, for example, a recently graduated Bates College alumnus named Mark Trafton Newton made the case in the *Bates Student* that defenders of Chinese immigration like Seelye were wrong to consider the issue through an economic or religious lens. Instead, Newton classified Chinese immigration as a social question. Applying Charles Darwin's idea of "natural selection" to the problem of immigration, Newton declared, "The real truth is this: it is not always the best that survives. . . . The flowers and vegetables in your garden are better, more useful than the weeds but if left to struggle unassisted, which will finally possess the soil?"[57] Though Newton believed that Chinese immigrants were of an inferior race, he feared they would overrun the United States by their brutish capacity to subsist on less. Other college writings portrayed Chinese immigrants as unscrupulous on one hand and helplessly ignorant about American customs on the other, fueling the exclusionist movement.[58]

Two factors explain why an antebellum graduate of Amherst like Seelye responded to Chinese immigration differently than his students in the 1870s and 1880s. As the chapters in this volume by Gary Kornblith and Richard Teichgraeber III show, in the late nineteenth century, the college moved away from its identity as a missionary-producing institution toward more secular ideas and pursuits. The percentage of Amherst graduates who became missionaries dropped from 32 percent between 1840 to 1865 to only 17 percent between 1866 to 1889.[59] The earlier cosmopolitan outlook of the student body dissipated with this shift.

Additionally, social Darwinism became a pervasive and dominant intellectual force.[60] Popularized by the writings of Herbert Spencer, which first appeared in the United States in the 1860s, social Darwinists applied Charles Darwin's theory of evolution to society. They rejected government regulation and aid, reasoning that if people "are not sufficiently complete to live, they die, and it is best they should die."[61] On the question of race, social Darwinists believed that, as Mark Trafton Newton wrote in the *Bates Student*, admitting Chinese and other immigrants undermined the future prosperity of the United States as an Anglo-Saxon nation.

In the middle of this contentious period, a new group of students assumed the mantle of collegiate cosmopolitanism: students from China who were members of the Chinese Educational Mission (CEM, 1872–1881). The CEM was an early initiative of the Qing government's Self-Strengthening Movement that aspired to cultivate Chinese autonomy from Western expertise. Forty-three Chinese students matriculated at ten US colleges and universities; one of them, He Tingliang, attended Amherst.[62] Born near Canton in 1860, He came to the United States as a twelve-year-old boy and was prepared at Northampton High School and Phillips Andover Academy before enrolling at Amherst as a member of the class of 1883.[63] According to the *Springfield Sunday Republican*, he was "extremely fond of drawing and painting" and a gifted student, and "President Seelye passed many complimentary remarks concerning his achievements while in college."[64]

Unlike the majority of his peers, He pursued a classical course of study.[65] Indeed, the college's focus on this type of instruction partially explains why so few CEM students chose to attend Amherst. As Edward Rhoads observes, a classical curriculum carried "social and intellectual prestige" but had few practical benefits for the technical advances that the Chinese government desired.[66] Sadly, He never had the chance to complete his degree at Amherst. In the summer of 1881, the Qing government ordered the return of all CEM students due to concerns that they were becoming Christianized and were losing touch with Chinese culture.[67] He later completed medical training in Tianjin before serving as a surgeon aboard a gunboat in the First Sino-Japanese War.[68]

Although He was the only CEM student at Amherst, he could count on the company of several others who made their home in the surrounding area. The US Census indicates that twenty-one Chinese lived in Hampshire County in 1880; the large majority of these Chinese residents were CEM students who boarded with white families in Belchertown, Easthampton, and Northampton. (By comparison, there had been only one Chinese resident in Hampshire County in 1870.) Three men named Ah Quen, Ah Wong, and Ah Lee operated a laundry in Northampton, but it is unlikely that He Tingliang interacted with them given their class differences. He may have known of the seventy-five Chinese who arrived in neighboring Berkshire County in 1870 to replace striking workers at Calvin T. Sampson's shoe factory. These shoemakers were, at least in age, his peers: sixty-eight of the seventy-five were under twenty years old when they disembarked at the train station in North Adams, Massachusetts.[69] But unlike He, they were "decidedly peasants."[70] By 1880, when He finished his first year at Amherst, only two out of the original seventy-five remained in North Adams after the expiration of their labor contracts.[71]

His reflections on his time at Amherst have not survived, but those of his contemporary Li Enfu at Yale University show that Chinese students were perfectly aware of the anti-Chinese sentiment swirling around them, and they did not shy away from rebuking it. Li originally entered Yale as a member of the class of 1884 but withdrew along with the rest of the CEM student body in 1881. He reentered Yale in 1884. As one of eight scholarship students selected for the junior exhibition in April 1886, Li gave an address on the Chinese philosopher Mencius. News of his speech drew hostile reactions. At Tufts University, a literary magazine opined: "His offence is rank. The Chinese must go."[72]

But Li had the last word. In his graduating address the following year, Li delivered a scathing critique of anti-Chinese politics. He lay blame for anti-Chinese agitation at the feet of "those men who are determined to get high wages for doing nothing," and he blasted political leaders for nationalizing the issue in order to win over voters in the Pacific states.[73] "When 80,000 offices were at stake, and the hoodlums of California had to be petted, it was not hard... to hoodwink the public with charges against [the Chinese] which are false, or which may be preferred against all immigrants." He also challenged the contradictory logic of the anti-Chinese position: "People ... were staggered at the imminent danger of the Mongolization of America and at the same time found fault with the Chinese for not making the United States their home."[74] Li concluded, "If there is an avenging Deity, (and we believe there is) ... retribution ... is sure to overtake a nation that permits the cold-blooded murder of innocent strangers within its gates to go unpunished?"[75] Sadly for Li and his countrymen, no avenging angel appeared.

CONCLUSION

In the summer of 1905, the Chinese ambassador to the United States arrived in Amherst for a vacation from Washington. Sir Chentung Liang Chen was no stranger to the town. As a CEM student he was known as Liang Pixu and lived in Amherst between 1875 and 1878 while preparing for Phillips Andover Academy. Before he was recalled in 1881, Liang dreamed of studying at Amherst College. The diplomat from China loved this little town in the Connecticut River Valley. "It is difficult to conceive a better spot on earth in which to grow up into manhood than New England," Liang told the *Boston Daily Globe*, "I admire the simplicity and modesty and earnestness of my friends and neighbors here. The family ties, the training that young men get in your preparatory schools and in the smaller colleges such as Amherst, through contact and personal intercourse with the professors and college authorities create conditions for the development of character which cannot be improved upon."[76] Amherst—both the town and the college—loved him back. Liang was made an honorary member of the class of 1885, and in 1903, he received an honorary doctorate of law from the college.[77] This adopted son of Amherst hoped that he could keep relations between the two countries on a cordial footing. Liang said, "We are naturally friendly to the United States."[78]

The life and career of Sir Chentung Liang Chen perfectly encapsulates the layered connections between Amherst and China across the nineteenth century. The Chinese Educational Mission that brought Liang to Amherst had been the Qing Empire's response to the crippling international order that Amherst graduates like Elijah Bridgman and Peter Parker helped to construct decades earlier. Historians have overlooked these links and therefore have not adequately accounted for the significant role that colleges played in US foreign relations in the nineteenth century. Exploring the specific connections between Amherst and China during this period shows that the college shaped the encounters of many of its graduates with China and its people. Amherst inspired them to become foreign missionaries; solicited their donations of research journals, ethnological material, and natural history specimens; and fostered debate about immigration policy. Graduates wrote longingly from China of being with their friends and classmates, and they visited the college while on furlough. Simply put, Amherst mattered immensely in the hearts and in the lives of its graduates who went to China. This sense of identification and the types of connections it engendered—collegiate cosmopolitanism—made Amherst a worldlier institution, and it gave those who went abroad an anchor and a home.

At the same time, collegiate cosmopolitanism enmeshed Amherst in imperial systems of military, cultural, and intellectual domination over China. Xenophobic and racist sentiments tainted the late nineteenth-century perception and treatment of Chinese people in the United States, and the college was only partially successful in recognizing and grappling with these prejudices. As Amherst enters its third century, the history of its relationship with China reminds us that it is not enough to aspire simply to "give light to the world" but to do so justly and with humility.

Notes

1. Robert H. Davis, "Our Relations to China," June 22, 1868, Alumni Biographical Files, Amherst College Archives and Special Collections, Amherst College Library (hereafter ACASC), Amherst College, Amherst, MA.

2. Emily Conroy-Krutz, *Christian Imperialism: Converting the World in the Early American Republic* (Ithaca, NY: Cornell University Press, 2015), 10.

3. Hitchcock Society of Inquiry Records, 1845–1861, Clubs and Societies Collection, Box 22, Folder 2, ACASC, Amherst College, Amherst, MA.

4. According to Kenneth Scott Latourette, the last general edict against Christianity was issued in 1811. See Latourette, *A History of Christian Missions in China* (New York: Macmillan, 1932), ch. 9.

5. Conroy-Krutz, *Christian Imperialism*, 11.

6. "Recent Intelligence," *Missionary Herald* 37, no. 1 (January 1841): 43. Bridgman's letter was dated June 24, 1840.

7. On Cushing's mission, see John Belohlavek, "Race, Progress, and Destiny: Caleb Cushing and the Quest for American Empire," in *Manifest Destiny and Empire: American Antebellum Expansionism*, ed. Robert W. Johannsen, Sam W. Hayes, and Christopher Morris (College Station: Texas A&M University Press, 1997), 21–47; Macabe Keliher, "Anglo-American Rivalry and the Origins of U.S. China Policy," *Diplomatic History* 31, no. 2 (April 2007): 227–57.

8. "Letter from Doct. Parker, August 1, 1844," *Missionary Herald* 41, no. 2 (February 1845): 53.

9. For the text of the treaty, see *Treaty of Peace, Amity, and Commerce, Between the United States of America and the Chinese Empire* (1846[?]), HathiTrust, accessed July 31, 2019, https://catalog.hathitrust.org/Record/011554001.

10. Charles Hartwell, "C. Hartwell Journal (August 15 to December 19, 1850)" n.d., 20, American Board of Commissioners for Foreign Missions Archives, 1810–1961, ABC 67, Houghton Library, Harvard University (hereafter HUHL), Cambridge, MA. It is likely that that Hartwell was referring here to *Memoirs of the Rev. Walter M. Lowrie, Missionary to China*, published in 1849.

11. Eliza J. Gillett Bridgman, ed., *The Pioneer of American Missions in China: The Life and Labors of Elijah Coleman Bridgman* (New York: Anson D. F. Randolph, 1864), 11–12.

12. Bridgman, *Pioneer of American Missions*, 25.

13. Bridgman, 20.

14. Morrison and Milne were the first and second missionaries sent by the London Missionary Society to China, arriving in 1807 and 1813, respectively. It is unclear how deeply Bridgman studied Milne's

and Morrison's writings. Bridgman records in his journal on September 29, 1829, that he "employed my time in Dr. Milne's Retrospect and Dr. Morrison's Life of Milne" while on the steamboat *Benjamin Franklin* to Boston from New York. Bridgman, 15.

15. William Milne, *A Retrospect of the First Ten Years of the Protestant Mission to China* (Malacca, Malaysia: Anglo-Chinese Press, 1820), 293.

16. Milne, *Retrospect*, 294.

17. Milne, 218.

18. Bridgman, *Pioneer of American Missions*, 15.

19. On US missionaries in China, see Dong Wang, *The United States and China: A History from the Eighteenth Century to the Present* (Lanham: Rowman & Littlefield, 2013), 97–120; Daniel H. Bays, *A New History of Christianity in China* (Chichester, UK, and Malden, MA: Wiley-Blackwell, 2012), 41–65; and John Rogers Haddad, *America's First Adventure in China: Trade, Treaties, Opium, and Salvation* (Philadelphia, PA: Temple University Press, 2014), 81–109.

20. Michael C. Lazich, "American Missionaries and the Opium Trade in Nineteenth-Century China," *Journal of World History* 17, no. 2 (June 2006): 199.

21. Arthur Sherburne Hardy, *Life and Letters of Joseph Hardy Neesima* (Boston, MA, and New York: Houghton, Mifflin, 1891), 4. See also Gavin James Campbell, "'We Must Learn Foreign Knowledge': The Transpacific Education of a Samurai Sailor, 1864–1865," *Japanese Journal of American Studies* 25 (2014): 5–24.

22. Chi-Chao Chan, Melissa M. Liu, and James C. Tsai, "The First Western-Style Hospital in China," *Archives of Ophthalmology* 129, no. 6 (2011): 793.

23. Wang, *United States and China*, 111.

24. Wang, 112.

25. David A. Hollinger, *Protestants Abroad: How Missionaries Tried to Change the World but Changed America* (Princeton, NJ: Princeton University Press, 2017), 3.

26. Gerald H. Anderson, "Peter Parker and the Introduction of Western Medicine in China," *Mission Studies* 23, no. 2 (2006): 219–20.

27. Thomas M. Howell (class of 1831) later recalled that Parker left Amherst because he felt that "the Faculty do not notice or appreciate me." Parker supposedly told Howell: "Now mark my word, you will all hear from me and regret that Peter Parker's name is not among the graduates of Amherst College." Quoted in Edward V. Gulick, *Peter Parker and the Opening of China* (Cambridge, MA: Harvard University Press, 1973), 4.

28. Charles Hartwell, "C. Hartwell Journal (1876)," October 14, 1877, American Board of Commissioners for Foreign Missions Archives, 1810–1961, ABC 67, HUHL, Cambridge, MA.

29. Charles Hartwell to Edward Hitchcock, April 9, 1869, Edward and Mary Judson Hitchcock Family Papers, Box 11, Folder 73, ACASC, Amherst College, Amherst, MA.

30. Hartwell to Hitchcock.

31. The records of the Society of Inquiry note the correspondence between missionaries in China and Amherst. For example, Sidney Perkins (class of 1851) read a letter from Goddard at the society's meeting on February 14, 1851, while Edward Baker (class of 1853) read the letter from Culbertson at the March 18, 1853 meeting. See Hitchcock Society of Inquiry Records, 1845–1861.

32. There were two students named Hitchcock at Amherst during the 1853 to 1854 school year: Milan Hubbard Hitchcock (class of 1854) and Charles Henry Hitchcock (class of 1856). The society's roster published in the 1855 *Olio* suggests that it was Charles Henry Hitchcock who received the assignment to correspond with Ball.

33. James A. Field Jr., "Near East Notes and Far East Queries," in *The Missionary Enterprise in China and America*, ed. John K. Fairbank (Cambridge, MA: Harvard University Press, 1974), 43.

34. E. C. Bridgman to William Augustus Stearns, July 13, 1858, Historical Manuscripts Collection, Box 1, Folder 12, ACASC, Amherst College, Amherst, MA.

35. E. C. Bridgman, "Inaugural Address," *Journal of the Shanghai Literary and Scientific Society*, no. 1 (June 1858): 4.

36. George Rugg Cutting, *Student Life at Amherst College* (Amherst, MA: Hatch & Williams, 1871), 60–61.

37. To Andover, Bridgman donated two "Chinese idols" and "a very exact representation of the deformed foot of the Chinese ladies." See Society of Inquiry Respecting Missions (Andover Theological Seminary), *Memoirs of American Missionaries, Formerly Connected with the Society of Inquiry Respecting Missions, in the Andover Theological Seminary: Embracing a History of the Society, Etc.* (Boston, MA: Peirce and Parker, 1833), 365–66.

38. "Catalogue of Articles in the Museum of the Society of Inquiry—A.C. (1838?)," Clubs and Societies Collection, Box 20, Folder 1, ACASC, Amherst College, Amherst, MA.

39. Hartwell to Hitchcock, n.d.

40. As Fa-ti Fan has written, histories of scientific imperialism must account for the "boundary drawing and power negotiations among different groups involved in the activities." In the case of British naturalists in China during the Qing Dynasty, "British investigations of China's natural history had to depend heavily on the Chinese." See Fan, *British Naturalists in Qing China: Science, Empire, and Cultural Encounter* (Cambridge, MA: Harvard University Press, 2004), 2.

41. Erika Lee, *The Making of Asian America: A History* (New York: Simon & Schuster, 2015), 71–75, 90–91.

42. Letter of Stillman Parker, October 31, 1841, Town of Amherst Collection, Box 2, Folder 7, ACASC, Amherst College, Amherst, MA.

43. Andrew Oliver, *Auguste Edouart's Silhouettes of Eminent Americans, 1839–1844* (Charlottesville: University Press of Virginia, 1977), fig. 205. The author thanks Sewell Chan for calling his attention to these silhouettes.

44. Inscription translated by author.

45. Inscription translated by author.

46. Mary Louise Pratt, "Arts of the Contact Zone," *Profession* 91 (1991): 35.

47. Andrew Gyory, *Closing the Gate: Race, Politics, and the Chinese Exclusion Act* (Chapel Hill: University of North Carolina Press, 1998), 138.

48. Lon Kurashige, *Two Faces of Exclusion: The Untold History of Anti-Asian Racism in the United States* (Chapel Hill: University of North Carolina Press, 2016), 28–34.

49. *The Relations of Learning and Religion: Addresses at the Inauguration of Rev. Julius H. Seelye, to the Presidency of Amherst College* (Springfield, MA: Clark W. Bryan, 1877), 23.

50. Julius H. Seelye, *Citizenship: A Book for Classes in Government and Law* (Boston, MA: Ginn, 1894), 58.

51. Julius H. Seelye to William F. Warren, February 17, 1879, William F. Warren Collection, Box 5, Folder 69, Howard Gotlieb Archival Research Center at Boston University, Boston, MA.

52. William F. Warren to Julius H. Seelye, February 18, 1879, Julius Hawley Seelye Papers, Box 3, Folder 21, ACASC, Amherst College, Amherst, MA.

53. Samuel C. Bartlett to Julius H. Seelye, February 19, 1879, Julius Hawley Seelye Papers, Box 3, Folder 18, ACASC, Amherst College, Amherst, MA.

54. Charles W. Eliot to Julius H. Seelye, February 19, 1879, Julius Hawley Seelye Papers, Box 3, Folder 19, ACASC, Amherst College, Amherst, MA.

55. "Locals," *Amherst Student*, February 1, 1879, 90, ACASC, Amherst College, Amherst, MA.

56. "Alexandrian Society II Minutes," April 23, 1879, Clubs and Societies Collection, Box 6, Folder 15, ACASC, Amherst College, Amherst, MA.

57. "The Chinese Question," *Bates Student* 8, no. 7 (September 1880): 110.

58. See, for example, "The Chinese Must Go!" *Argo* 2, no. 8 (October 14, 1882): 105–7.

59. Paul H. Younger Jr., "Terras Irradient: A Study of Amherst College Missionaries in the Near East in the Nineteenth Century" (BA thesis, Amherst College, 1959), 105.

60. Richard Hofstadter, *Social Darwinism in American Thought* (Philadelphia: University of Pennsylvania Press, 1944), 31–50, 170–200.

61. Herbert Spencer, *Social Statics* (New York: D. Appleton, 1865), 415.

62. Of the forty-three CEM students, nearly half (twenty) attended Yale University. The others attended MIT, Rensselaer Polytechnic Institute, Lehigh University, Columbia, Harvard, Lafayette College, Stevens Institute of Technology, and the Worcester County Free Institute of Industrial Science (now Worcester Polytechnic Institute). See Edward J. M. Rhoads, *Stepping Forth into the World: The Chinese Educational Mission to the United States, 1872-81* (Hong Kong: Hong Kong University Press, 2011), 119.

63. "Ho Ting Liang," *Chinese Educational Mission Connections*, accessed December 12, 2018, http://www.cemconnections.org/index.php?option=com_content&task=view&id=80&Itemid=5.

64. "Springfield's Chinese Students," *Springfield Daily Republican*, March 30, 1902, 11.

65. Edward Rhoads notes that twenty-nine out of forty-three CEM students studied science or engineering. This focus on science and engineering was especially strong among those Chinese students who did not attend Yale. Of these twenty-three students, only two, including He Tingliang at Amherst and Ding Chongji at Harvard, studied the classics. Rhoads, *Stepping Forth into the World*, 121.

66. Rhoads, 122.

67. Rhoads, 167–82.

68. "Springfield's Chinese Students."

69. Anthony W. Lee, *A Shoemaker's Story: Being Chiefly about French Canadian Immigrants, Enterprising Photographers, Rascal Yankees, and Chinese Cobblers in a Nineteenth-Century Factory Town* (Princeton, NJ, and Oxford: Princeton University Press, 2008), 5.

70. Lee, *Shoemaker's Story*, 6.

71. Lee, 268–69.

72. Quoted in "Clippin's," *Bowdoin Orient* 16, no. 1 (April 28, 1886): 11.

73. "Graduating Address of Yan Phou Lee, at Yale College: The Other Side of the Chinese Question," *The American Missionary* 41, no. 9 (September 1887): 270.

74. "Graduating Address of Yan Phou Lee," 271.

75. "Graduating Address of Yan Phou Lee," 272–73.

76. "The Chinese Minister Is an Amherst Townsman," *Boston Daily Globe*, July 9, 1905, 32.

77. "Chinese Minister an LL.D.," *New York Times*, June 25, 1903, 5.

78. "The Chinese Minister Is an Amherst Townsman," 32.

"Vesuvius at Home"

Emily Dickinson, Amherst, and Nineteenth-Century Popular Culture

David S. Reynolds

How did Emily Dickinson, one of our greatest poets, emerge from so staid an environment as nineteenth-century Amherst, Massachusetts?

Actually, it was the very staidness of Amherst that produced her explosive literary reaction. Amherst was a religiously orthodox town where dancing and card playing were tabooed, and even a yearly play given by school students raised eyebrows among the pious.[1] The hypersensitive and ever-observant Dickinson reached out omnivorously to the larger popular culture. Through the press and the pulpit, this culture, often zany and sensational, seeped into the ultraconservative environment in the Pioneer Valley of western Massachusetts. It stimulated the active imagination of the outwardly straitlaced but inwardly rebellious Dickinson. What she called her "still—Volcano—Life," her "Vesuvius at Home" where she could take "A Lava step at any time," was projected in poetry whose bizarre images, frequently derived from popular culture, created a boiling magma of imaginative metaphors and rebellious themes that strained mightily against convention.[2]

She was born on December 10, 1830, in a brick house at 280 Main Street, known as the Homestead, that had been built around 1813 by her grandfather, Samuel Fowler Dickinson. Her parents, Edward and Emily Norcross Dickinson, had moved into the western half of the Homestead with their one-year-old son, Austin, earlier in 1830. A sister, Lavinia, arrived in 1833. The family remained at the Homestead until 1840, when Emily was nine. Edward then took his family to live in a clapboard house on North Pleasant Street. In 1855, he repurchased the renovated Homestead, where Emily spent the rest of her life. Emily's brother Austin married her friend Susan Gilbert in 1856; they moved into the Evergreens, a house built for them on the same grounds as the Homestead.

Amherst was Emily Dickinson's world. The initially sociable but increasingly reclusive Dickinson left Amherst rarely and left Massachusetts only once: in 1855 she and her sister traveled to Washington, DC, and Philadelphia.

The Amherst she knew had a rural character.[3] Apart from the busy town center and an area for factories, the town's homes were interspersed with farms, meadows, and forests. The town's common was a hay meadow until 1853, when a local committee on which Austin Dickinson served began improvements that later led to a grass lawn being planted there. At the east end of the common was a distillery that produced over three thousand barrels of apple brandy annually by 1830.[4] In the early nineteenth century, alcohol consumption was astoundingly high in America, and Amherst was no exception. A nineteenth-century historian of Amherst noted, "The minister drank liquor with his deacons, the lawyer with his clients, the doctor with his patients," and liquor was served on all social occasions. The refuse from the distillery streamed through a ravine in the town, giving off odors worsened by the manure and garbage that covered the unpaved streets, which became mud in wet weather and dust in the summer.

Like many New England towns, Amherst had factories. Mills and factories, which ran on waterpower in the era before the wide use of steam power, were common in towns near rivers. Factories in Amherst, with its Mill River and Fort River, produced paper, cloth, yarn, jeans, and carpentry planes. By 1870, the town was the nation's largest manufacturer of straw hats, woven from dried palm leaves imported from Cuba.[5]

Amherst College was the town's intellectual and spiritual hub. In 1821, Samuel Fowler Dickinson participated in founding the college, on ten acres of high land on which were built a four-story building—combining dormitory space and classrooms—and a house for the college president. The college, which offered a full classical and scientific education, was devoted to "the education of pious young men" for the ministry, with the aim of "civilizing and evangelizing the world."[6] Its religious orientation was Calvinistic. The college became a bastion of Calvinism that stood opposed to the Unitarianism of Harvard and Boston.

Emily got strong doses of Calvinism in the First Church of Christ, whose services in its meetinghouse on the corner of South Pleasant Street and Northampton Road she attended with her family until her twenties or thirties, when she stopped going to church. The five preachers who served from 1836 to 1877, several of whom were close to the Dickinson family, venerated Jonathan Edwards, the eighteenth-century theologian of orthodox Calvinism. Their brand of Calvinism, known as New Light, was not as severe as that of Edwards, who had put more emphasis than they on human depravity and God's judgmental wrath.[7] Nonetheless, they retained Edwards's emphasis on the importance of preparing for the afterlife. Other notable followers of Edwards in the Pioneer Valley included Edward Hitchcock, the president of Amherst College, and Mary Lyon, the head of Mount Holyoke Female Seminary. The fact that both colleges accepted Calvinism while requiring close study of science, nature, and the classics reflect the fact that conservative religion did not then conflict with scientific or liberal education.

At least, that's the way things were supposed to be. For Emily, in contrast, education engendered skepticism. She undercut Jonathan Edwards when she wrote jauntily in a letter: "'All Liars shall have their part' — / Jonathan Edwards — / 'And let him that is athirst come' — Jesus."[8] Her point was that Edwards assigned heavenly bliss to God's few, predestined elect, even though could they be utter liars, in contrast to Jesus, who accepted all who reached out him.

For seven years, she attended Amherst Academy. The academy, cofounded by Samuel

Fowler Dickinson in 1816, had a curriculum that included the classics, astronomy, geology, Latin, philosophy, French, logic, rhetoric, and composition. Although the academy's mission was to instill "morality, piety, and religion," Emily emerged from it as a doubter.[9] When in 1847 to 1848 she attended Mount Holyoke Female Seminary, eleven miles across the valley from Amherst in South Hadley, she was not included among students who "professed" (that is, accepted Christ) or "hoped to" profess. Instead, at the beginning of the year, she was one of eighty students who were "without hope," a group that shrank to twenty-nine by the end of the year.[10]

As she matured, her questioning of organized religion became nagging doubt. All of her close family members experienced conversions in the religious revivals that swept through Amherst. She did not. In 1862, she wrote of her family: "They are religious—except me,—and address an Eclipse, every morning—whom they call their 'Father.'"[11] In her poetry, religious faith is a "fine invention"; it "Plucks at a twig of Evidence" with "Much Gesture, from the Pulpit," as "Strong Hallelujahs roll." Such religious "narcotics," she writes, do not dispel doubt, "the Tooth/That nibbles at the soul—."[12]

She loathed the theological sermons of Calvinists, which followed the formulaic tripartite template of text, doctrine (or exposition), and proof (or application), with many numbered subdivisions. When she heard a doctrinal sermon given by the Reverend Julius Seeley, an Amherst College graduate who later taught there and became the college's fifth president, she was terribly bored. She remarked: "Mr. S[eelye] preached in our church last Sabbath upon 'predestination,' but I do not respect 'doctrines,' and did not listen to him."[13]

On the other hand, she warmly embraced what I call *the new religious style*—a sermon style that featured stories, secular illustrations, and humor.[14] In 1853, she went into raptures over an entertainingly anecdotal sermon on Judas and Jesus given by the visiting minister Edwards A. Park, a sermon whose emotional impact she later described: "It was like a mortal story of intimate young men."[15]

She also reportedly went to hear the popular minister Henry Ward Beecher, who in 1851 visited Amherst and gave a lecture, significantly, on "Imagination." Beecher, who had attended Amherst College in the 1830s, was America's foremost pulpit performer. Having rejected the gloomy Calvinism of his childhood, he preached a gospel of love in sermons that were anecdotal rather than theological. Beecher thought that "truth alone is not sufficient" in preaching. He declared, "There be many men who are the light of the pulpit, whose thought is profound, whose learning is universal, but whose offices are unspeakably dull."[16] To combat pulpit boredom, he advocated the use of "rhetorical illustrations," which he said had many important uses, including providing for various classes of hearers, bridging difficult logical places, and holding listeners' attention through variety.[17] Beecher put theory into practice in his colorful sermons at Plymouth Church in Brooklyn. Described by a contemporary as a combination of St. Paul and P. T. Barnum, Beecher drew such large congregations that the directions to his church were to take one of the "Beecher Boats" to Brooklyn and "Follow the crowd."[18]

Dickinson's attraction to the new religious style also influenced her relationship with the Reverend Charles Wadsworth. While visiting Philadelphia in 1855, during her one trip outside of Massachusetts, Emily most likely was taken to hear Wadsworth preach at the

Arch Street Presbyterian Church. It is also known that Wadsworth later visited her at least twice in Amherst, that two volumes of his sermons were given to her, that she probably read many of his other sermons in newspaper reprintings, and that she developed strong feelings toward him. She called him "My Philadelphia," "my dearest earthly friend," her "beloved Clergyman," and "My Clergyman."[19] Whatever Emily's feelings were for Wadsworth, it is notable that in the mid-1850s, just at the moment when she was beginning to write serious poetry, she was deeply moved by a preacher who was one of the antebellum period's foremost innovators in American sermon style.

One newspaper compared Wadsworth to an earlier pulpit innovator, John Summerfield, but stressed that "Wadsworth's style . . . is vastly bolder, his fancy more vivid, and his action more violent. . . . [His topics are] peculiar, and quite out of the usual line"; he is typically "rapid, unique and original, often startling his audience . . . with a seeming paradox."[20] Mark Twain was also struck by the uniqueness of Wadsworth's pulpit manner, noting that he would often "get off a first-rate joke" and then frown when people started laughing. In short, Wadsworth's style was adventurous, anecdotal, and creative, with a tendency to the startling and paradoxical. Emily Dickinson praised his "inscrutable roguery" and seemed to copy his impish style in many poems and in her message to Josiah G. Holland: "Unless we become as Rogues, we cannot enter the Kingdom of Heaven."[21] The jocular familiarity with which she generally treats divine and biblical images doubtless owes much to the new sermon style that Wadsworth perfected.

By aligning herself with several of the most progressive religious stylists of the day, Dickinson was launching a silent rebellion against the doctrinal tradition valued by her father, who, she said, read only "lonely and rigorous books."[22] She once commented that the only way to tell if a poem is good is to ask whether after reading it you feel like the top of your head has been taken off. She applied the same rule to the sermons she attended and the books she read. A religious work, in her eyes, had to possess both striking imagery and a sense of ultimacy; theology or moralizing was secondary to the work's *effect* on feelings and the imagination. For instance, she disdained three Baptist tracts about "pure little lives, loving God, and their parents, and obeying the laws of the land"—dutifully pious stories that, in her words, "dont *bewitch* me any."[23] In contrast, while skeptical of Christian doctrine, she could revel in the Reverend Aaron Colton's "enlivening preaching, . . . his earnest look and gesture, his calls of *now today*."[24] Similarly, she was captivated by "a splendid sermon" from Edwards A. Park, which left the congregation "so still, the buzzing of a fly would have boomed out like a cannon. And when it was all over, and that wonderful man sat down, people stared at each other, and looked as wan and wild, as if they had seen a spirit, and wondered they had not died."[25] The combined imagery here of the fly, death, and religion seems to anticipate Dickinson's famous poem "I heard a Fly buzz—when I died." In both the poem and her letter describing Park's sermon, not theology or Christianity counts but rather the existential impact of a momentous situation.

What the new religious stylists had finally taught Emily Dickinson is that religion could be freely applied to everyday situations and expressed through startling imagery. One of her poetic responses to the new religious style was the redefinition of church, sermons, and worship along quotidian lines. Witness the reduction of religious images to the natural world in the following stanzas:

Some keep the Sabbath going to Church—
I keep it, staying at Home—
With a Bobolink for a Chorister—
And an Orchard, for a Dome— [. . .]

God preaches, a noted Clergyman—
And the sermon is never long
So instead of getting to Heaven, at last—
I'm going, all along.[26]

Not only does this poem shift worship from the church to nature and sing praise to short sermons, but it actually converts God into an entertaining preacher obviously trained in the new sermon style. A similar fusion of the sacred and the secular is visible in the poem that begins "To hear an Oriole sing / May be a common thing— / Or only a divine," in which the last phrase arrests the reader with its offhandedly casual treatment of the holy.[27] Sometimes this casualness is taken to playful extremes, as when she refers to God as "Papa above!" watching down upon a "mouse," who asks for the privilege of living forever "Snug in seraphic Cupboards."[28] Among the many other Dickinson poems that daringly reapply sacred imagery are "These are the days when Birds come back— ," "There's a certain Slant of light," and "Mine—by the Right of the White Election!".[29] In these poems, such images as Holy Communion, sacrament, hymns, and the doctrine of election are detached from their Christian referents and fused with either nature or the human psyche. In still other poems, she displays a jaunty freedom with the Bible, as in "The Bible is an antique Volume," which includes a series of secular reenactments of sacred imagery, such as calling Eden "the ancient Homestead," Satan "the Brigadier," and sin "a distinguished Precipice/Others must resist."[30]

Another fertile seedbed of imagery for Dickinson was temperance literature. After alcohol consumption peaked in Amherst in the 1820s, temperance reform became a strong presence there. When Amherst College was founded, the trustees voted to prohibit students from drinking in town or having alcohol in their rooms.[31] In 1830, Amherst students formed a temperance group whose members pledged not to use ardent spirits, wine, opium, or tobacco.[32] Henry Ward Beecher joined the group when he attended the college, and he went on to advocate temperance from the pulpit.[33] The Amherst South Parish Total Abstinence Society was founded in 1835. Seven years later, the nationwide Washingtonian movement—a society of reformed drunkards that anticipated Alcoholics Anonymous—spread to the town. The South Parish group was renamed the South Amherst Washington Total Abstinence Society, soon joined by the Washington Total Abstinence Society of Amherst East Street and the Washington Total Abstinence Society of North Amherst.[34] In 1848 came the Hampshire County Temperance Union, of which Edward Dickinson became an officer.

Despite all this temperance activity, alcohol production and consumption continued in Amherst. Even with the rise of the Washingtonians in the 1840s, liquor continued to be produced and sold. An Amherst college graduate recalled, "The *trouble*, we came at length to believe, was in the rum places in the village, with fires of hell in full blast." [35] The college's third president, Edward Hitchcock, announced in 1850, "*It were better that the college should go down, than that young men should come here and be ruined by drink places among us*" (italics in original). That year, a prohibition society formed that called for banning of the sale of alcohol in the town.

Aiding in the temperance cause were popular novels, stories, poems, and songs. An increasing proportion of temperance literature, capitalizing on the popularity of sensational fiction, was lurid and violent in its renderings of alcohol's ravages. With the rise of the Washingtonians, who thrilled the public with their graphic anecdotes about battles with the bottle, the temperance movement became riddled with contradictions and ambiguities. Notorious instances of backsliding—particularly that of the Washingtonian leader John Bartholomew Gough who, in 1845, disappeared for a week and then was found in a whorehouse recovering from an alcoholic binge—gave rise to the oxymoronic character of the "intemperate temperance advocate," a staple figure of ridicule in newspapers and popular fiction. George Lippard, in his best-selling reform novel *The Quaker City*, sneered at "intemperate Temperance lecturers," caricaturing them in his portrait of the Reverend F. A. T. Pyne, who declares, "We temperance folks must have some little excitement after we have forsworn intemperance. When we leave off alcohol, we indulge our systems with a little Opium."[36] Likewise, George Thompson in *New-York Life* presents the hypocritical temperance reformer Bob Towline, who boasts that "for over a year I lectured in public, and got drunk in private—glorious times!"[37]

Dickinson may have been exposed to the hypocritical figure of the intemperate temperance advocate through reading popular works or through personal encounters with backsliders; the latter was a likely scenario, since the large majority of those who took the temperance pledge eventually reneged on it. (Is this what Dickinson's editor Millicent Todd Bingham meant when she referred to Dickinson's sister-in-law Susan Gilbert Dickinson as a "superhypocrite" and "a drunkard" despite being an "exquisite housekeeper"?)[38]

Emily was also exposed to what I call *dark reform*—the exposure of vice whose diverting sensationalism overpowered moral lesson.[39] William Bowdoin, the speaker at the Hampshire County temperance meeting Dickinson's father attended in 1851, used images typical of dark temperance. He warned that every glass of alcohol was "a Drink-Offering to the Devil of 36 minutes" of one's life, and he read a dark poem:

The drunkard murders child and wife,—
It matters not a pin
Whether he stabs them with his knife,
Or starves them with his gin.[40]

Dickinson adopted and transformed images and themes of popular temperance reform. In poem #207 ("I taste a liquor never brewed—"), she creatively reworks the popular character of the intemperate temperance reformer. The poem's speaker is a wonderfully fresh avatar of the intemperate temperance advocate. She is both completely drunk and completely temperate. She can exult in her drunkenness because hers is a liquor "never brewed," filling tankards "scooped in Pearl," an image suggesting the pearl-like clarity of the air she loves and the extreme preciousness of her love of nature. She is not the hypocritical intemperate temperance advocate, publicly sober but privately debauched, but the exultantly open one, proclaiming a debauchery that is allied with the highest form of temperance. Dickinson's use of quotation marks in her references to "'Landlords'" who turn drunks out their doors and to alcoholics who "renounce their 'drams'" underscores the fact that she is "quoting," or borrowing, images from temperance writers who used such images. But she uses these images only to transform them. The drunkard being dismissed is a bee that has extracted nectar from a flower. The renouncers of drams are butterflies that are leaving their resting places and fluttering through the air. And the "I" watching this beautiful spectacle only gets more and more drunk for having enjoyed it.

Dickinson's creative toying with temperance images continues in poem #244 ("We—Bee and I—live by the quaffing— "). Once again, the "I" is the transformed intemperate temperance advocate who can openly say that she lives "by quaffing," since her drinking companion is the bee, and her "ale" and "burgundy" are beautiful things of nature. Dickinson again adopts a popular trope by saying she and the bee need not say "all Hock"—a common temperance phrase urging drinkers to pledge ("hock") themselves to sobriety—because life itself "has its Ale."

In the rest of the poem, Dickinson quotes extensively from popular culture. The common temperance trope of the drunken husband who brutalizes his wife is cited in the rhetorical questions "Do we 'get drunk'?" and "Do we 'beat' our 'Wife'?" The dark-reform association of alcohol with death is repeated in the reference to the drunkard "found dead" by a coroner. The taking of the temperance pledge is recalled in the phrase about one who "pledges his." But all of these standard temperance images are couched in paeans to ordinary natural phenomena—bees, clover, nectar, and noontime—that redirect temperance rhetoric toward an affirmation of life's beauty. By manipulating popular temperance imagery, Dickinson joyously expresses her sense of the intoxicating nature of common experience.

Another genre that powerfully influenced Dickinson was popular sensational literature, ranging from the crime-filled penny newspapers that arose in the 1830s to the sensational pamphlet fiction that flooded America in the 1840s and '50s. The antebellum public was fed on an increasingly spicy diet of horror, gore, and perversity in both mass newspapers and the closely allied genres of trial pamphlets and paper-covered adventure novels. Emerson remarked that his fellow citizens spent their time "reading all day murders & railroad accidents" in newspapers.[41] Thoreau, similarly, spoke of the "startling and monstrous events as fill the daily papers."[42]

Stemming from the penny newspapers were sensational pamphlet novels (often called "romances") that featured rollicking adventure and outcasts such as pirates, freebooters, and all kinds of criminals. This action-filled pamphlet fiction, priced cheaply and hawked in street bookstalls, caused increasing alarm among conservative commentators. Surveying popular "Yellow Jacket Literature," one author complained in 1855 that "the popular press is teeming with works" in which "the murderer, robber, pirate, swindler, the grog-shop tippler, the lady of fashion, the accomplished rake and libertine, are meritorious characters, held up in a spirit of pride and levity, and surrounded by a 'halo of emulation.'"[43]

Dickinson was profoundly aware of these seamy dimensions of the American popular mind. It is notable that when she wrote poetry about popular culture, she was preoccupied with its violent, disorienting elements, as in this poem:

> The Popular Heart is a Cannon first—
> Subsequent a Drum—
> Bells for an Auxiliary
> And an Afterward of Rum—
>
> Not a tomorrow to know it's [*sic*] name
> Not a Past to stare—
> Ditches for Realm and a Trip to Jail
> For a Souvenir[44]

Dickinson recognizes here that the "Popular Heart" can be best described in violent images pertaining to war, weapons, drinking, ditches, and prison. The popular culture she perceives is fluid and ever-changing, having been torn from both the future ("Not a Tomorrow to know it's name") and from historical memory ("Nor a Past to stare"). It is associated with the muddy realm of ditches, and it thrives on diverting crime ("a Trip to Jail / For a Souvenir").

She gained exposure to popular sensationalism mainly by reading newspapers. An alarmed essayist, in a piece reprinted in a Northampton paper, denounced the *Springfield Republican* (edited by her friends Josiah G. Holland and Samuel Bowles) because it was following the descent into graphic sensationalism that had been led by the mass newspapers of US cities. In an article titled "The Penny Press," the essayist wrote, reports

> something *startling* every day,—something to draw the attention of the crowds that gather in hotels and bar-rooms or that constantly move through the thoroughfares. . . . Startling disclosures, murders, rapes, butcheries of human beings by war, assassins or casualty, are seized upon with unnatural and indecent avidity; and details not essential for a faithful narration of the facts, but highly relishable to a prurient and depraved appetite, are paraded and made prominent. No matter what the subject—religious or political—moral, social or personal—serious or trivial—all alike are spiced with words that tickle the ears of the b'hoys.[45]

The newspaper in which this reprinted article appeared, the *Hampshire Gazette*, was itself not immune to the craze for sensationalism. It ran pieces with titles like "Shocking Murder in New Jersey," "Fire—Narrow Escape," "A Terrible Accident and Loss of Life," and "The Escape. A Thrilling Historical Narrative."[46] An especially sensational item it featured was a running ad for the Boston Museum, an imitation of P. T. Barnum's museum of freaks and marvels in New York City. Along with novelties like the Feejee Mermaid (actually a monkey's torso sewn to a salmon's tail) and "A Family of Peruvian Mummies," the Boston

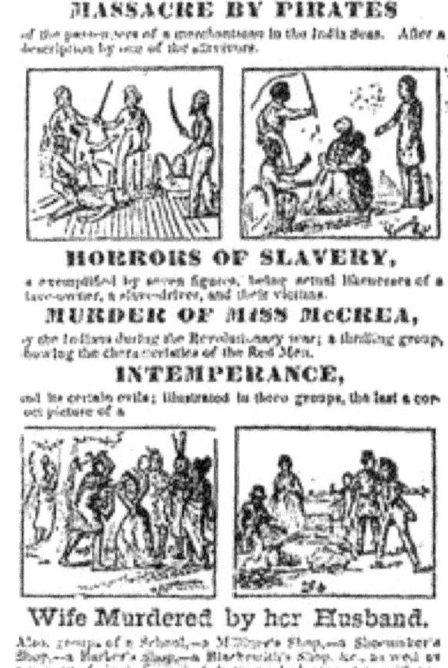

Figure 1. Wax figures: section of an ad for the Boston Museum, *Hampshire Gazette*, January 7, 1851.

Museum had a large exhibit of wax figures that reduced many subjects, from the sacred to the scandalous, to the common level of sensationalism. On display were wax representations of religious scenes ("CHRIST'S LAST SUPPER," "THE CRUCIFIXION," "CHRIST DISPUTING WITH THE DOCTORS"), violent crime ("MASSACRE BY PIRATES," "MURDER OF MISS MACCRAE," "WIFE MURDERED BY HUSBAND"), and Dark Reform ("HORRORS OF SLAVERY," "INTEMPERANCE and its certain evils; illustrated in three groups").[47] The ad was sensational not only in its subject but in its design: it shouted at readers with bolded capitalizations and melodramatic woodcuts (see figure 1).

The increasing space given in American newspapers to crime and tragedy was a source of amused interest to Dickinson. In an 1853 letter to her friend Josiah Holland of the *Springfield Republican*, she declared that the lurid contents of his paper had changed her into a quirky disturber of the peace. "One glimpse of *The Republican*," she wrote, "makes me break things again—I read in it every night. Who writes those funny accidents, where railroads meet each other unexpectedly and gentlemen in factories get their heads cut off quite informally? The author, too, relates them in such a sprightly way, that they are quite attractive."[48] Always hungry for sensational news, she elsewhere thanked her brother Austin for a juicy news clipping about a manslaughter and asked him to send "anything else that's *startling* which you may chance to know—I dont [*sic*] think deaths or murders can ever come amiss in a young woman's journal." Her tone in these letters captures the combined grossness and offhand levity of sensational literature.

The open admission into her consciousness of several popular sensational elements prepared the way for the haunted themes and broken style of her poetry. In a poem written around 1858 (#43), she creates a horrific atmosphere by describing a wooded road haunted by banditti, a wolf, an owl, a serpent, screaming vultures, and beckoning "satyrs fingers." A similar use of sensational images occurs in several other poems, such as these:

I never hear the word "escape"
Without a quicker blood,
A sudden expectation,
A flying attitude![49]

or,

We like a Hairbreadth 'scape
It tingles in the Mind
Far after Act or Accident
Like paragraphs of Wind[50]

Such poems are full of standard sensational images, including hairbreadth escapes, war, guns, murder, and accidents.

She regularly uses the sensational to freshly illuminate themes related to nature, human psychology, and the poetic process. For instance, poem #38 is a kind of "yellow novel" in verse, featuring sensational images of pirates, buried treasure, and murder threats. Dickinson utilizes these common images not to concoct some adventurous plot but to sing praise to the beauty of a sunset:

I never told the buried gold
Upon the hill—that lies—
I saw the sun—his plunder done
Crouch low to guard his prize.

This poem presents the sun as a pirate who leaves on a hill plundered treasure enjoyed by the first-person speaker, who assumes the persona of a hidden onlooker. Creating a mood of excitement, the speaker marvels over the pirate's "wondrous booty" (the sunlight on the hill), consisting of "the fairest ingots / That ever kissed the spade!"

If here her persona is that of an of a pirate's coconspirator, elsewhere it is that of a criminal. In poem #57, she poses as a thief:

I robbed the Woods—
The trusting Woods. [. . .]
I scanned their trinkets curious—
I grasped—I bore away!

Through such pointed redirection of sensational images, Dickinson suggests that criminality is exciting not for its own sake, as a source of mere diversion or fantasy, but for its usefulness as a vehicle for wresting beauty and meaning from everyday experience. In other poems, she poses as the victim, rather than the perpetrator, of crime. In poem #58, for instance, nature is the invasive criminal threatening the speaker, who cries, "A Day! Help! Help! Another Day!"

Dickinson does with sensational literature what she did with religious and temperance rhetoric: she radically personalizes it by redirecting it toward private emotion. Innovatively, she points out that all of us carry within ourselves narratives more exciting than the most sensational popular romances:

> No romance sold unto
> Could so enthrall a Man
> As perusal of
> His Individual One—[51]

Here and elsewhere, she directs sensational images inward, using them as metaphors for the recesses of the psyche. If popular novelists terrified readers with vividly described horrific settings, she took the new step of reminding readers that the scariest rooms lay within. "One need not be a Chamber—to be Haunted—," she writes. "The Brain has Corridors—surpassing / Material place."[52] It's far safer, she continues, to meet at midnight an "External Ghost" or to be chased galloping through an abbey by some would-be assassin than to confront "That Cooler Host, [. . .] one's a'self." The most appalling terrors spring from the fantasies and aggressions lurking within:

> Ourself behind ourself, concealed—
> Should startle most—
> Assassin hid in our Apartment
> Be Horror's least.

Internalizing adventure imagery, she writes in another poem,

> Adventure most unto itself
> The Soul condemned to be—
> Attended by a single hound
> It's own identity.[53]

By finding psychological equivalents of sensationalism, Dickinson delivers messages more horrifying than anything in popular fiction. This becomes clear when we compare images in sensational fiction with similar ones in Dickinson's poem "I felt a Funeral, in my Brain."[54] In the quintessential sensation novel, George Lippard's 1845 best-seller *The Quaker City; Or, the Monks of Monk Hall,* the protagonist, Devil-Bug, has a dystopic dream of the future that begins with a nightmarish vision of "a hazy atmosphere, with coffins floating slowly past, and the stars shining through the eyes of skulls, and the sun pouring his livid light straight downward into a wilderness of new-made graves which extended yawning and dismal over the surface of a boundless plain."[55] Next, Devil-Bug sees the sun assume the shape of a skeleton-head, surrounded by stars, "each star gleaming through the orbless socket of a skull, and the blood-red moon went sailing by, her crescent face, rising above a huge coffin which floated through the livid air like a barque from hell."[56] Presurrealistic in its oddness, Lippard's novel resembles its main setting, Monk Hall, a labyrinthine structure riddled with trap doors that are always opening beneath the reader's feet, sending him tumbling "down, down, down" (in Devil-Bug's oft-repeated words) into another dimension.

Dickinson experiments with a similar range of imagery, involving death, coffins, time/space distortion, and headlong plunges into other dimensions. But by gathering all these Lippardian phenomena in the consciousness of a first-person speaker, she gives them entirely fresh connotations. The fact that the speaker "*felt* a Funeral, in my *Brain*" (my italics) points the poem in two directions simultaneously: first, toward a delineation of an actual funeral service, followed by passage into the afterlife; and second, toward a description of a descent into madness, followed by the collapse of reason. The "I" of the poem, like the personae of several other Dickinson poems, could be recalling her own funeral, with mourners "treading—treading," sitting down at a service, and finally carrying out the coffin, at which point the speaker's soul passes alone into the silent, infinite other world described in the last two verses. At the same time, the "I" could be reliving a terrifying time when it felt as though she were losing her mind. In this light, the last two verses, in which the speaker feels "Wrecked, solitary" as "a Plank in Reason, broke," point to the utter alienation and confusion of the insane person.

The last three lines,

> And I dropped down, and down,
> And hit a World, at every plunge,
> And Finished knowing—then—

bring the poem's two major themes to apt culmination. As a conclusion to a death poem, these lines portray the soul, cast into the unknowable afterlife, hurtling into infinite space and time. As an end to a psychological poem, they suggest the mind plunging without direction toward chaos, until the speaker has "Finished knowing" (i.e., lost the ability to understand anything). On both levels of meaning, the image of dropping "down, and down" and hitting "a World, at every plunge" has far more resonance than does Lippard's account of people falling "down, down, down" through the trap doors of the multilayered Monk Hall. For Dickinson, the explorer of death and the human mind, the downward plunge of the speaker is a frightening tumble into ineffable mysteries.

It is fitting to conclude by considering Dickinson in light of other American women writers, whose best works constituted a literary flowering between 1858 and 1866, the very years that were by far her most productive as a poet.

She had special affinities with the authors of the so-called literature of misery, the genre named and described by Samuel Bowles, the Springfield editor she knew well.[57] If the women authors of the literature of misery sought to establish an artistic middle ground between the effetely conventional and the openly feminist, so Dickinson explicitly rejected the "Dimity Convictions" of traditionalists and the public methods of women's rights activists, while she made the era's boldest quest for specifically artistic exhibitions of woman's power. If the other women writers, such as Fanny Fern and Louisa May Alcott, typically hid behind shifting literary masks, she outdid them all by assuming numerous women's roles in her poems, from the childlike "Daisy" to the regal "Empress."

Dickinson's repeated use of volcano imagery is in the vein of the literature of misery. A basic assumption of this literature is that since women's energies were allowed no viable outlet, they gathered in upon themselves and lay burning inwardly, always threatening to erupt through a placid exterior. The heroines of the literature of misery often looked like sweet moral exemplars but raged inwardly with the ferocity of women victims bent on revenge. This fusion of docile and fiery qualities is summed up by a character in Fanny Fern's *Ruth Hall* (1856), who generalizes: "Whenever—you—see—a—blue-eyed—soft-voiced—gentle—woman, —look—out—for a hurricane. I tell you that placid Ruth is a smouldering volcano."[58] In Lillie Devereux Blake's *Southwold*, the author describes Medora Fielding in a typical moment: "No one could have guessed that the calm indifference of her manner concealed a volcano of rage and scorn."[59]

Dickinson brought full self-consciousness to the use of volcano imagery, recognizing that it applied both to women's lives and to women's literary style. Her sensitivity to these interrelated levels of meaning is powerfully captured in the first lines of the successive verses of poem #517:

> A still—Volcano—Life— [. . .]
> A quiet—Earthquake Style— [. . .]
> The Solemn—Torrid—Symbol—

These oxymoronic lines, which are a highly compressed enactment of the bristling polarities of American women's literature, bring us back to Amherst. Dickinson's poetry, like her life, can be said to have had a constrained explosiveness. Her famous line "My Business is Circumference" suggests her ever-active mind ranging beyond her limited landscape and absorbing the often subversive cultural currents that trickled from without through cracks in the hard shell of Amherst conservativism. When she funneled these currents into the iambic rhythms and simple verse patterns derived from the hymns of her childhood, she produced some of the most startlingly original poetry we have.

Notes

1. Edward Wilton Carpenter, *The History of the Town of Amherst, Massachusetts* (Amherst, MA: Carpenter & Morehouse, 1896), 147–48.

2. E. Dickinson, poems #517, 165, and 1691.Quotations from Dickinson's poetry are from R. W. Franklin, *The Poems of Emily Dickinson* (Cambridge, MA: Harvard University Press, 1998).

3. Some of the information in this paragraph is derived from the excellent website Emily Dickinson Museum: The Homestead and the Evergreens, "Welcome," accessed February 1, 2019, http://www.emilydickinsonmuseum.org/.

4. Carpenter, *History of the Town of Amherst*, 300. The next quotation in this paragraph is on 389.

5. Carpenter, *History of the Town of Amherst*, 292.

6. William Seymour Tyler, *History of Amherst College during Its First Half Century, 1821–1871* (Springfield, MA: Clark W. Bryan, 1873), 42.

7. See Jennifer L. Leader, *Knowing, Seeing, Being: Jonathan Edwards, Emily Dickinson, Marianne Moore, and the American Typological Tradition* (Amherst, MA: University of Massachusetts Press, 2016), 61–77.

8. Thomas H. Johnson, ed., *The Letters of Emily Dickinson* (Cambridge, MA: Harvard University Press, 1986), poem #712..

9. Carpenter, *History of the Town of Amherst*, 155.

10. Vivian R. Pollak, ed., *A Historical Guide to Emily Dickinson* (New York: Oxford University Press, 2004), 34.

11. Johnson, *Letters*, #261.

12. Johnson, #202 and 373.

13. Johnson, #346.

14. David S. Reynolds, *Beneath the American Renaissance: The Subversive Imagination in the Age of Emerson and Melville* (New York: Oxford University Press, [1988] 2011), chpt. 1.

15. Jay Leyda, *The Years and Hours of Emily Dickinson* (New Haven, CT: Yale University Press, 1960), 1, 287.

16. *Oratory: An Oration by Henry Ward Beecher, Delivered . . . in the American Academy of Music, Philadelphia, May 29, 1876* (Philadelphia, PA: National School of Oratory, 1886), 9.

17. For a discussion of Beecher and other preachers, see David S. Reynolds, "From Doctrine to Narrative: The Rise of Pulpit Storytelling in America," *American Quarterly* 32, no. 5 (Winter 1980): 479–98.

18. See Debby Applegate, *The Most Famous Man in America: The Biography of Henry Ward Beecher* (New York: Crown, 2007), 299.

19. Johnson, *Letters*, #750, 766, 790, and 865.

20. "A Pulpit Sketch," *Springfield Republican*, October 22, 1850, reprinted from the *New York Evening Post*. The comment by Mark Twain, quoted in the next sentence, is in Leyda, *Years and Hours*, 112.

21. Johnson, *Letters*, #901 and 715.

22. Johnson, #473.

23. Johnson, #144.

24. Johnson, #144.

25. Johnson, #272.

26. Johnson, #236.

27. Johnson, #402.

28. Johnson, #151.

29. Johnson, #122, 320, and 411.

30. Johnson, #1577.

31. Tyler, *History of Amherst College*, 24.

32. Edward Hitchcock, *Reminiscences of Amherst College, Historical, Scientific, Biographical and Autobiographical* (Northampton, MA: Bridgman & Childs, 1863), 151–52.

33. See Applegate, *Most Famous Man*, esp. 99, 124, 189, and 256.

34. Carpenter, *History of the Town of Amherst*, 391–94.

35. *An Historical Review: One Hundred and Fiftieth Anniversary of the First Church of Christ in Amherst, Massachusetts, November 7, 1889* (Amherst, MA: Press of the Amherst Record, 1890), 77. The quotation in the next sentence is also from this page.

36. George Lippard, *The Quaker City; Or, the Monks of Monk Hall*, ed. David S. Reynolds (Amherst, MA: University of Massachusetts Press, [1845] 1995), 201, 291.

37. George Thompson, *City Crimes; Or, Life in New York and Boston* (New York: William Berry, 1849), 121.

38. Quoted in Richard B. Sewall, *The Life of Emily Dickinson* (Cambridge, MA: Harvard University Press, 1994), 292–93.

39. Reynolds, *Beneath the American Renaissance*, chpt. 2.

40. "Annual Meeting of the Hampshire County Temperance Union," *Hampshire Gazette*, February 25, 1851.

41. Joel Porte, ed., *Emerson in His Journals* (Cambridge, MA: Harvard University Press, 1982), 433.

42. Bradford Torrey and Francis H. Allen, eds., *The Journal of Henry David Thoreau* (New York: Dover, 1962), 267.

43. *Confessions and Experience of a Novel Reader* (Chicago: William Stacy, 1855), 73.

44. Franklin, *Poems of Emily Dickinson*, #1220.

45. "The Penny Press," *Hampshire Gazette*, May 18, 1858.

46. *Hampshire Gazette*, January 11, 1853, February 1, 1853, August 20, 1850, and July 4, 1854.

47. *Hampshire Gazette*, January 7, 1851.

48. Johnson, *Letters*, #264. The next quotation in this paragraph is from Johnson, *Letters*, #114.

49. Johnson, #144.

50. Johnson, #1247.

51. Johnson, #590.

52. Johnson, #407.

53. Johnson, #817.

54. Johnson, #340.

55. Lippard, *The Quaker City*, ed. Reynolds, 370. The next quotation in this paragraph is also from this page.

56. Lippard, *Quaker City*, 370.

57. "When Should We Write," *Springfield Republican*, July 7, 1860.

58. Fanny Fern, *Ruth Hall: A Domestic Tale of the Present Time* (New York: Mason Brothers, 1855), 133.

59. Lillie Devereux Blake, *Southwold: A Novel* (New York: Rudd & Carleton, 1859), 47.

"Fables of Extinction"

Geologist Edward Hitchcock and the Literary Response to Darwin

Jane F. Thrailkill

> I may conclude this chapter by quoting a saying of Professor Agassiz, that whenever a new and startling fact is brought to light in science, people first say, 'it is not true,' then that 'it is contrary to religion,' and lastly, 'that everybody knew it before.'
>
> —CHARLES LYELL, *THE ANTIQUITY OF MAN*[1]

In 2019, the website for Amherst College's Department of Geology celebrated the extraordinary reach of its discipline—"Geology is an interdisciplinary science that encompasses all of the other sciences within it"—while noting that the science's capaciousness places it at the center of contemporary cultural politics: "Geology also encompasses most aspects of environmental science, including contentious topics such as climate change, pollution, resource consumption, and extinction."[2] Looking back one hundred and fifty years to the writings of geology professor Edward Hitchcock, and to Nathaniel Hawthorne's and Emily Dickinson's fables of extinction, one is struck by the persistence of controversy when geological theories meet religious belief. Paradoxically, for the science predicated on studying the ever-changing face of the earth, the old adage applies: *plus ça change, plus c'est la même chose* (the more things change, the more they stay the same).

AMHERST COLLEGE AND NINETEENTH-CENTURY GEOLOGICAL CONTROVERSIES

When Amherst was founded in 1821, most people believed that the Earth's present-day features had been sculpted by the Biblical flood, and that Genesis described actual events that had taken place a mere six thousand years prior. Yet nineteenth-century geologists studying the Earth's layers were beginning to offer evidence for a startling, even distressing, theory: that the Earth was millions of years old, that it had changed dramatically over millen-

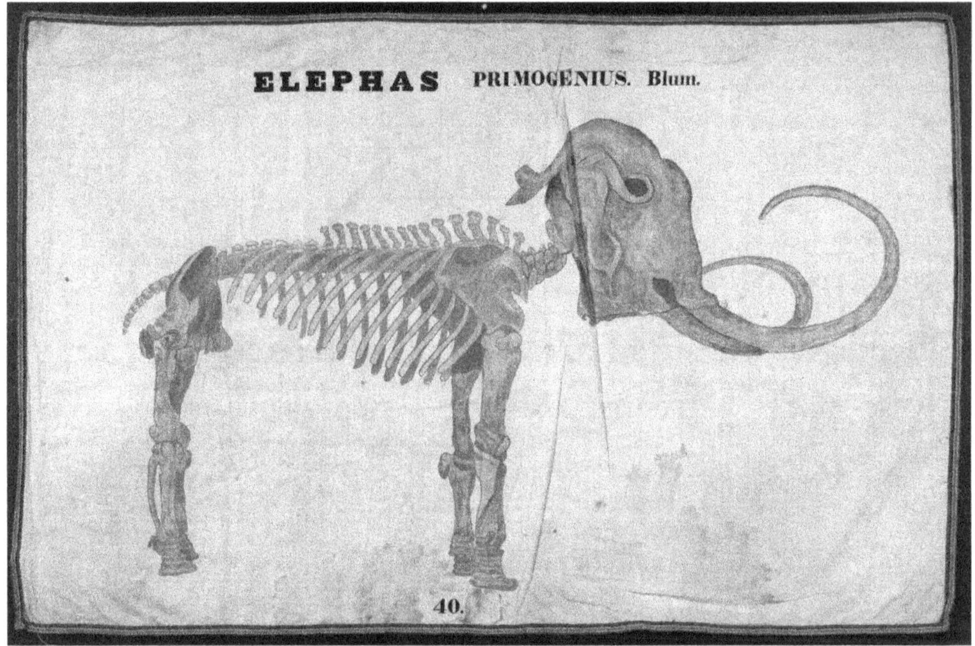

Figure 1. Orra White Hitchcock drawing of a woolly mammoth skeleton: on canvas for use in Edward Hitchcock's classes on geology and natural history. Courtesy of Amherst College Archives and Special Collections, Amherst College, Amherst, MA.

nia, and that these processes of transformation continued into the present. The subtitle of Charles Lyell's *Principles of Geology* (1830–1833) set forth both his theory and his method: "An attempt to explain the former changes of the Earth's surface by reference to causes now in operation." Over the next half century, Charles Darwin would leverage the geological discovery of "deep time" to explain how living beings had evolved over vast stretches of time. *The Origin of Species by Natural Selection*, published in 1859, caused consternation on both sides of the Atlantic, with its account of species transformation and its materialism.

Darwin's most influential critic lived in Massachusetts: Louis Agassiz, the charismatic Harvard zoologist, who organized the specimens in Harvard's Museum of Comparative Zoology (founded 1859) as a monument against Darwin. Yet Darwin's most ardent supporter in the United States, the botanist Asa Gray, was also a Harvard scientist. Pushing back against Agassiz, Gray, in 1860, published a series of positive reviews of *The Origin of Species* in the widely read *Atlantic Monthly*; Gray's book *Darwiniana* (1876) supported the theory of species transmutation and sought to square Darwin's theory with Biblical accounts of human origins.[3]

While the Agassiz-Gray debate consumed Cambridge, ninety miles west, Amherst College was also proving to be an epicenter of geological controversy. In 1877, Edward Hitchcock, son and namesake of the esteemed nineteenth-century geologist, gave an optimistic, proscience speech at the ceremony introducing Julius Hawley Seelye, ordained pastor and professor of mental and moral philosophy, as the new president of Amherst Col-

Figure 2. Edward Hitchcock Sr. (1793–1864), c. 1854. Courtesy of Amherst College Archives and Special Collections, Amherst College, Amherst, MA.

lege. Hitchcock, known as "Doc," was a medical doctor and a beloved professor of hygiene and physical education. Doc's father, Edward Hitchcock Sr., had died a decade earlier, having served on the Amherst faculty from 1825 to 1845 and as its president from 1845 to 1854. Hitchcock Sr. had published almost a dozen textbooks and monographs on topics in natural history, including the widely cited *Religion of Geology and Its Connected Sciences*.[4] Both father and son devoutly believed that science and religion could be happy bedfellows. Doc, in his introductory remarks, noted that a "marked and precious feature" of the college's history is "that, from the very beginning, science and religion, the science even of nature, have been equally emphasized."[5] Hitchcock Sr., in his textbook *Elementary Geology*, urged that "geology furnishes many peculiar proofs of the benevolence of the deity"; the careful study of the Earth makes visible "a perfect unity of design extending through every period of the world's history."[6] Referring to the tumult created by Darwin's 1871 publication *The Descent of Man*, Doc asserted with hope that "in the great conflict that is now upon us, the conflict between science and religion, this institution has nothing to fear."[7]

After the physician had spoken, the pastor took the podium. President Seelye, it quickly became clear, had a very different agenda. "Amherst College was founded by Christian people and for a Christian purpose," he asserted at the start of his inaugural address. In the roughly hour-long speech, the newly installed president used the literary resources of the jeremiad to affirm a declension story, thus countering the progressive narrative built into evolutionary theory: "All the facts of history point backward not to an original savage state," Seelye proclaimed, but rather "to an original golden age of peace and purity. . . . Man became corrupt and degraded instead of being originally such."[8] As Seelye saw it, change for the better came "not by letters, or science" but "by the simple preaching of the gospel, by the story of God's grace."[9] Seelye translated evolution's narrative—present-day humankind's origin in ancestral savagery—into the language of theology, reaffirming Amherst College's Christian mission.

Seelye had a strong advocate on the faculty for his position. The Reverend Enoch F. Burr, lecturer on the scientific evidences of religion from 1869 to 1880, had made a career of refuting Darwin's account of evolution from a scientific perspective. Historian Bert James Loewenberg, in an article identifying myrmidons of anti-Darwinian sentiment in New England, sardonically awards Professor Burr "first honors" as "one of the most influential of all such writers against evolution."[10] Burr tested out his arguments in Amherst College classrooms and published his antievolution lectures as books that were widely praised in religious periodicals. Seelye, in his address, keyed off of Burr's arguments when he highlighted the problems of transformation and contingency, which belie original wholeness: "Nothing in nature rests. Life in unnumbered generations rolling like a flood, light and heat penetrating space in perpetual pulsations, the winds, the waves, the stars sweeping, swelling, circling in ceaseless change, mark the restlessness of nature everywhere. Up and down this realm of things the human thought wanders in its inquiries, seeking rest and finding none."[11] "A Christian college," Seelye urged, "look[s] not at transient but at permanent ends."[12] This tension—between an account of nature in perpetual flux and a vision of changeless, divine perfection—led President Seelye to drop geology courses from Amherst's required curriculum in 1880 (ironically, the same year that Burr stopped teaching at the college).[13]

Hitchcock Sr., writing a generation earlier, had devoted his career to developing arguments that squared the findings of geology with the tenets of Christianity. After graduating from Amherst, Hitchcock Sr. was ordained as a pastor in the Congregational Church of Christ in Conway, Massachusetts, in 1821. Early in his ministry, Hitchcock Sr. felt the draw of natural history, enough to worry that his studies as a naturalist detracted from his pastoral work. He expressed his concern in a letter to Benjamin Silliman, an eminent Yale chemist and geologist:

> As I write this Sabbath evening I take the liberty to propose to you a case of conscience. I have frequently found that my botanical and geological pursuits when zealously attended to, although generally conducive to health, still to have the effect of diminishing [my] spiritual mind and for a time of deadening religious sensibility. . . . Pray tell me if you can the remedy in such a case. Must these pursuits be all together abandoned? Or is there such a thing as pursuing them with a supreme reference to the glory of God?

Silliman swiftly replied that, while "some people think otherwise," he believed the two pursuits were compatible, noting that "both science and literature have been much indebted to clergymen."[14] Hitchcock Sr. clearly took the geologist's words to heart. Three years later, he moved to Amherst with his wife, Orra White Hitchcock, to teach at the college. Orra was an active partner in her husband's pedagogical pursuits, creating over one thousand illustrations of geological, zoological, and botanical subjects. She painted many of her images on large canvas sheets to complement Hitchcock's lectures in Amherst classrooms.

In contrast to President Seelye's later edicts, Professor Hitchcock during his professorship and presidency of Amherst College promoted geology as a science "as essential in education as the kindred branches of Chemistry and Astronomy."[15] In his teaching and research, Hitchcock addressed himself to two fundamental geological concerns, which many theologians had worried were at odds with the Biblical creation: (1) the problem of transformation as it pertained to the fossil record, which seemed to present evidence of species evolution over vast periods of time; and (2) the problem of dust, which seemed to suggest divine forms were materially "recycled." This latter problem focused on the ontology of the material body, which Hitchcock described this way: "Scarcely any truth seems more clearly taught in the Bible than the future resurrection of the body. Yet this doctrine has always been met by a most formidable objection. It is said that the body laid in the grave is ere long decomposed into its elements, which are scattered over the face of the earth, and enter into new combinations, even forming a part of other human bodies."[16] Bodies made in the image of God were perfect, unchanging wholes, yet the actual matter that constituted the body decomposed and entered into new combinations. Hitchcock, writing in the decades before Darwin, resolves the problem of dust through appeal to chemistry, in particular the first law of thermodynamics; the problem of transformation he addresses by appeal to the selfsame process that the great comparative anatomist Georges Cuvier had theorized: extinction.[17]

NATHANIEL HAWTHORNE, GEORGES CUVIER, AND THE ROMANTIC FRAGMENT

Nathaniel Hawthorne was a denizen of Concord rather than Amherst, but he was familiar with both Louis Agassiz and Asa Gray—the three men were members of the Saturday Club, an informal group of writers, scientists, and cultural lights first formed in Boston in 1855.[18] (Agassiz was one of the pallbearers of the novelist's casket, along with Ralph Waldo Emerson, Henry Wadsworth Longfellow, and—surprisingly—Louisa May Alcott.)[19] The scientific topics that occupied Hitchcock—dust and extinction—are at the center of Nathaniel Hawthorne's last completed romance. Appearing in 1859, the same year that Charles Darwin published his theory of species transmutation, Hawthorne's *Transformation* (which appeared in the United States in 1860 as *The Marble Faun*) includes a mythical, verging-on-extinct species: fauns, figured by the character called Donatello. Natural scientists separated living organisms into the categories of *flora* and *fauna*. The faun for Hawthorne is a figure for fauna as such: a term that refers to a species of a particular geological period.

The question of extinction frames *The Marble Faun* from the outset. In the book's preface, Hawthorne wonders if the audience for his work has also been extinguished from the Earth: "Unquestionably, this gentle, kind, benevolent, indulgent, and most beloved and honored Reader did once exist for me . . . But, is he extant now? . . . If I find him at all, it will probably be under some mossy gravestone, inscribed with a half-obliterated name which I shall never recognize."[20] The novelist was right to worry. Readers puzzled over ambiguities of plot and character, prompting Hawthorne in an epilogue to wonder at how science-minded his audience had become, wondering (as they did) "how Cuvier would have classified poor Donatello."[21]

Hawthorne's response to this question, through his meticulous depiction of the relic-filled strata, crypts, and catacombs that underlie the Roman landscape of *The Marble Faun*, situates his only transatlantic novel within geological debates that were being waged from Massachusetts to England and Europe in 1859. Indeed, Hawthorne models his text on the methods of the geologist and the comparative anatomist.

Formally speaking, the work of a religiously oriented geologist approaches that of the romance writer: as D. F. Rauber argues, "The great formal problem of the romantic poet can be stated briefly as the devising of means to embody the infinite in a finite, discrete, and sequential medium."[22] Hitchcock Sr. had organized a well-known cabinet of fossil footprints, placing the suggestive traces of prior life forms into an orderly whole. The aesthetic aspect of geology is vividly apparent in the gorgeous drawings that Orra White Hitchcock made for her husband's classroom and for his textbooks. The professor enlisted her creativity and draftsmanship in *Elementary Geology* (1840), to translate findings from the fossil record into a chart linking excavated matter and the geological record. (Notably, Hitchcock dropped the "Paleontological Chart" from the 1860 edition, concerned it could be misinterpreted as affirming species transmutation.)

Georges Cuvier, who has been called the father of paleontology, was famed for his ability to reconstruct an entire skeleton from the excavation of a single bone. Comparative

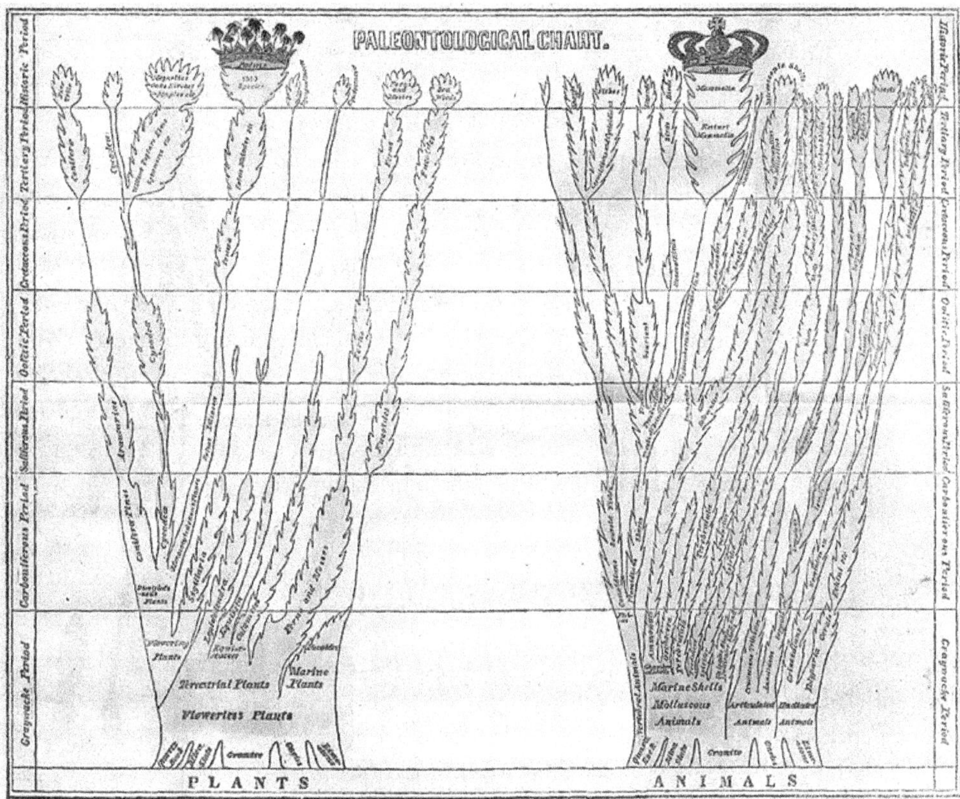

Figure 3. Drawing by Orra White Hitchcock (1796–1863), instructor at Amherst Academy and assistant principal at Deerfield Academy, wife of Edward Hitchcock Sr. Courtesy of Amherst College Archives and Special Collections, Amherst College, Amherst, MA.

anatomy, as practiced by Cuvier, made fine distinctions among bodily structures to situate all organisms, living and fossilized, within an ideal, unchanging order. His most famous work, *The Animal Kingdom*, was published in 1817 and was highly influential on Hitchcock. For anti-Darwinians, catastrophism explained away (seeming) species transformations. Hitchcock puts this point succinctly in 1833: "The more unlike living animals and plants are those found in a fossil state," which can only mean "that there have been several successive creations and extinctions of animals and plants in our globe, before the production of its present organized beings."[23] Pre-1860, extinction seemed to provide a bulwark against evolution's injection of "time's arrow"—to quote Stephen Jay Gould—into the natural world. In the context of natural history, change looked too much like godless evolution; in the context of religion and romance, one entity crumbling and becoming a part of another looked like grim materialism.[24] The romantic fragment became a way of imagining brokenness as mere declension from a perfect whole, one that the painstaking observer could reconstruct into its (imagined) divine wholeness.

In the romantic fragment, theology, geology, and aesthetics are united; through the first law of thermodynamics, chemistry and physics further harmonize these diverse fields of knowledge. This principle of matter was established by 1850, after scientists had observed that the total energy of an isolated system is constant. Energy, they found, could be transformed from one form to another, but it could not be created or destroyed. In 1851, Hitchcock is almost gleeful as he musters chemistry to support the bible's teachings on resurrection. He points to the difficulty, from the perspective of theology, that physical bodies, laid in graves, crumble to dust, thereby losing their shape for the resurrection. Chemistry, he urges, sees the integrity of the body not in matter but in its elemental shape: "The identity of the body consists, not in a sameness of particles, but in the same kinds of elementary matter, combined in the same proportion, and having the same form and structure."[25] With some jubilance, Professor Hitchcock rests his doctrinal case on the wisdom of the sciences: "I am not aware that any successful reply has ever been given to this objection, until chemistry and natural history taught us the true nature of bodily identity."[26] All is not lost, literally: religion, for Hitchcock, could be bolstered by cutting-edge chemistry.

EMILY DICKINSON AT AMHERST ACADEMY: "BIG STUDIES"

While Hitchcock clearly believed he had solved a crucial conundrum, the literary works of the period are more equivocal about questions of bodily transformation. In 1864, the year of Hitchcock's death, Emily Dickinson wrote the following poem that riffs on the question that preoccupied the geologist. "The Chemical conviction / That Nought be lost" is a gorgeous, lyrical encapsulation of the first law of thermodynamics:

> The Chemical conviction
> That Nought be lost
> Enable in Disaster
> My fractured Trust —
>
> The Faces of the Atoms
> If I shall see
> How more the Finished Creatures
> Departed me![27]

Dickinson's biographer Richard Sewall writes that Dickinson, in this lyric, "reduced Hitchcock's long and fervent argument to her own characteristic size—and perhaps with a touch of irony."[28] Her punning on the word "Atoms" aligns the bible's narrative of original perfection (Adam) and the chemistry that is mustered to support a religious viewpoint (atoms, the preserved elemental particles that compose the human form to be resurrected). But as Sewall notes, the effect is comical. Her trust is "fractured," like the bodies disintegrated to dust, and like Hitchcock's weirdly materialistic understanding of resurrection, which affirms bodily wholeness despite disintegration, thus (to Dickinson's ironic eye) twists logic to the breaking point.[29]

Whence this lyrical "conversation" between Emily Dickinson and Doc Hitchcock over natural theology and questions about dust and resurrection? The geologist was a fellow townsman and family friend of the Dickinsons, to be sure, but more important was Hitchcock's role at Amherst Academy, the secondary school that Dickinson attended in the 1840s. (Orra White was the Academy's preceptress before marrying Hitchcock.) Harriet Martineau, in her travels to the United States, records this anecdote from her visit to Amherst in 1835: "[My guide] conducted me into the lecture-room where Professor Hitchcock was lecturing. In front of the lecturer was a large number of students, and on either hand as many as forty or fifty girls. These girls were from a neighboring school [Amherst Academy], and from the houses of the farmers and mechanics of the village.... We found that the admission of girls to such lectures as they could understand (this was on geology) was a practice of some years' standing."[30] Hitchcock designed the science curriculum that inspired the young poet; as Sewall writes, "Coming to Amherst in 1825 from Benjamin Silliman's laboratory at Yale, Hitchcock was largely responsible for attracting science faculty that put Amherst on even terms with Harvard and Yale and opened up such unusual opportunities for students in Amherst Academy."[31] Dickinson herself, in a letter to her friend Abiah Root, bragged about her robust education in scientific subjects: "We have a very fine school. There are 63 scholars. I have four studies. They are Mental Philosophy [Seelye's field of expertise], Geology, Latin, and Botany. How large they sound, don't they? I don't believe you have such big studies."[32]

Science and religion, both encompassing frameworks for making sense of the world's wonders, loomed large for Dickinson during her school years in a town with deep Puritan roots. As she watched the young women around her experience spiritual conversion, she herself confided to Root that "*I* am one of the lingering *bad* ones."[33] Dickinson writes of "this wilderness life of mine," meaning both her affection for the natural world and also her lack of religious conviction.[34] She eschews the Kingdom of Heaven for her household and her garden, writing to Root that "I am yet the Queen of the court, if regalia be dust, and dirt."[35] Dickinson avidly studied Hitchcock's botanical work and, as Joan Kirkby reports, "Edward Hitchcock's *The Religion of Geology*, Minot Savage's *The Religion of Evolution*, and Henry Drummond's *Natural Law in the Spiritual World* [were] all books in the Dickinson family library."[36]

DUST, BONES, AND CATACOMBS

Catastrophism and the first law of thermodynamics excluded time and temporality from the physical sciences. Hawthorne, in turn, drew on geological thinking when he composed *The Marble Faun* under the banner of extinction, dwelling lovingly on categories and things that no longer exist by persistently invoking the ideal of the romantic fragment and the resonant trace (akin to Hitchcock's collection of footprints). But throughout Hawthorne's novel, and in Emily Dickinson's oeuvre, this ideal persistently meets its nemesis: dust. While *The Marble Faun* is explicitly antievolutionary in its figuring of Donatello, the text, in portraying the ruins of Rome and the recycling of bones, nonetheless bears the traces of the very theory that Hawthorne wishes to forestall. Critic Ana Pinto writes of Cuvier that "having established extinction as a scientific fact, he unwittingly introduced the notion of a linear temporality into the natural sciences," which in turn "introduces an irreversible time-arrow into physics, just as evolution had done for biology."[37] Whereas evolution supplanted an idealized nature with a messy, unfinished narrative of adaptation and becoming, the second law of thermodynamics overturned the closed system of the first law by describing the leakiness, waste, and untidiness that attends any transformation of state. The idealized portrait of the Earth depicted by Hitchcock's diagram (see figure 3) was belied by the concept of entropy—a term drawn from the Greek word for *transformation*—and the related idea that the universe was not in a stable state but was in fact cooling. In 1852, Lord Kelvin (the Scottish chemist William Thomson) described "heat death"—that the Earth was destined to become "unfit for the habitation of man." [38] The cultural critic Mark McGurl has crisply described entropy as "the enemy of all organized bodies, the enforcer of temporal unidirectionality."[39]

Hawthorne sets *The Marble Faun* in Rome, the Eternal City, and seeks human existence *sub specie aeternitatis* ("under the auspices of eternity," Baruch Spinoza's term for that which is timeless, unchanging, whole). The narrator waxes poetic over his Cuvier-like ability to compose a cohesive narrative from bits and pieces: "In weaving these mystic utterances into a continuous scene, we undertake a task resembling in its perplexity that of gathering up and piecing together the fragments of a letter which has been torn and scattered to the winds. Many words of deep significance, many entire sentences, and those possibly the most important ones, have flown too far on the winged breeze to be recovered."[40] Rome, with its endless galleries and museums, provides fertile terrain for such acts of recovery. The character of Hilda serves as a copyist, translating artworks salvaged from the Eternal City into tidy images: "If a picture had darkened into an indistinct shadow through time and neglect . . . she seemed to possess the faculty of seeing it in its pristine glory."[41] Like a natural theologian, she is able to discern a timeless conception operative in the dust heap of the material record: "The girl was but a finer instrument, a more exquisitely effective piece of mechanism, by the help of which the spirit of some great departed painter now first achieved his ideal, centuries after his own earthly hand, that other tool, had turned to dust."[42] Studded with the remains of long-dead Christian martyrs, the earth of Rome is written in the *lingua di ossi*: the language of bones.

Yet the novel's optimism about consolidating scattered pieces into a meaningful whole is belied by the narrator's dismay at Rome's disarray, with bones repurposed into architectural structures: "The arched and vaulted walls of the burial recesses are supported by massive pillars and pilasters made of thigh-bones and skulls; the whole material of the structure appears to be of a similar kind; and the knobs and embossed ornaments of this strange architecture are represented by the joints of the spine, and the more delicate tracery by the smaller bones of the human frame."[43] The narrator tries to rescue the scene from grim materialism, urging (in a somewhat forced manner) that while "the greater number are piled up indistinguishably into the architectural design," they cohere into a meaningful form "like many deaths that make up the one glory of a victory."[44] Earlier, jumbled artifacts are mustered as evidence of a Christian city rising up from the decay of Roman blood sport: "Bas-reliefs, the spoil of some far older palace, are set in the surrounding walls, every stone of which has been ravished from the Coliseum, or any other imperial ruin which earlier barbarism had not already levelled with the earth."[45] From one perspective, the story of Rome could be told in progressive layers, with the Christian churches sitting atop pagan strata representing "earlier barbarism." But the narrator can't sustain this idealized (if racist) narrative. Crypts meant to house bones, those ideal fragments that the careful romance writer or comparative anatomist could use to construct a perfect whole, fall prey to the ravages of time: "Between two of the pillars, moreover, stands an old sarcophagus without its lid, and with all its more prominently projecting sculptures broken off; perhaps it once held famous dust, and the bony framework of some historic man, although now only a receptacle for the rubbish of the courtyard, and a half-worn broom."[46] Mark Twain in *Innocents Abroad* (1869) sounded the same note, itemizing the clutter of grisly relics in Milan's cathedral made ludicrous by their disarray: "The priests showed us two of St. Paul's fingers, and one of St. Peter's; a bone of Judas Iscariot, (it was black,) and also bones of all the other disciples; a handkerchief in which the Saviour had left the impression of his face."[47]

The first law of thermodynamics imagined all matter to be accounted for by an ideal equation in which nothing is lost and where the telos of time could be reversed. Doc Hitchcock, in *Elementary Geology*, wrote of the wealth of paleontological knowledge cached in "ossiferous caverns [that] have been used by man as a place of habitation, or more frequently as a place of sepulture. And hence his bones, as well as fragments of pottery, and other relics of a rude people, sometimes are found so mixed with the remains of extinct animals, as to lead to the inference that they were deposited during the same period."[48]

Hitchcock, updating his textbook from 1833 through the publication of Darwin's *Origin of Species*, never wavers in his belief that these "deposits" were the work of a benevolent deity who from time to time saw fit to replace the Earth's species with new ones. The Pioneer Valley itself offered evidence: "It is certainly an interesting thought, that this delightful valley, which now forms so charming a residence for man, once constituted, and for an immense period, the bottom of a tropical ocean." He concludes that "the astonishing change brought about in the course of ages, exalts our conceptions of the wisdom and extent of the plans of the Deity; and leads us to anticipate future changes, whenever those plans require."[49]

In *The Marble Faun*, by contrast, altars to Christian martyrs testify not to divine order but to the inevitability of decay. Candles in a disused chapel had "been extinguished perhaps a half century before," while "the marble vase at the entrance held some hardened mud at the bottom, accruing from the dust that had settled in it during the gradual evaporation of the holy water."[50] Time and again, Rome, in Hawthorne's hands, proves to be entropic, moving inexorably toward chaos; human existence transpires in the novel "sub specie pulveris, under the aspect of dust."[51]

Formally, Hawthorne's last novel itself refused to cohere. Puzzled by myriad holes in the plot and discouraged by its lack of closure, readers and reviewers badgered the author, prompting his first ever addendum to a finished novel. William Dean Howells wrote, "Everybody was reading it, and more or less bewailing its indefinite close," and Ralph Waldo Emerson deemed it "a mere mush."[52] The American edition added a "Conclusion" that somewhat lamely attempted to patch together an ending. Later editions of the British

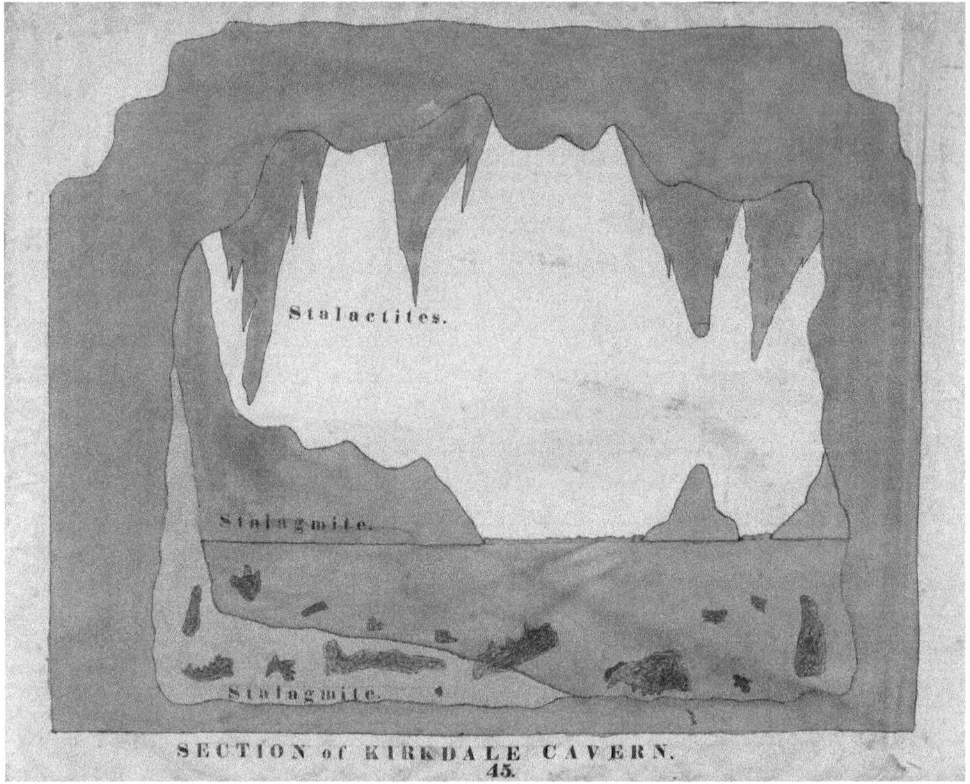

Figure 4. Orra White Hitchcock drawing of Kirkdale Cavern. Courtesy of Amherst College Archives and Special Collections, Amherst College, Amherst, MA.

text included a slightly different addendum, labeled "Postscript." The novel itself came out in pieces, with its staggered publication and changing titles, with the shifty title *Transformation* (for the British edition) replaced by the weightier, marmoreal name *The Marble Faun* for publication in the United States. Indeed, parts of the novel itself were recycled from Hawthorne's notebooks, which his wife Sophia later published in a separate volume.

Emily Dickinson would seem to agree with Hawthorne's agonized capitulation to fragmentation and incompletion.

This Dust, and its Feature—
Accredited—Today—
Will in a second Future—
Cease to identify—

This Mind, and its measure—
A too minute Area
For its enlarged inspection's
Comparison—appear—

This World, and its species
A too concluded show
For its absorbed Attention's
Remotest scrutiny—[53]

For Dickinson, the idea that "This World, and its species" could present a "concluded show" is absurd. The phrase "too minute Area"—a reference to small space—is also a pun, suggesting a small unit of time, as in *two-minute*. Here, Dickinson is startlingly up to date in her geological knowledge, recognizing that, in the context of deep time, human beings were present on the globe for an infinitesimal slice of eternity. Yet Dickinson juxtaposes the smallness of human existence with the scope of the human *imagination* that, modeled in the image of the divine mind, is capable of "enlarged inspection" and "remotest scrutiny." Or, as she wrote in another poem, "The Brain is just the Weight of God—."[54] In a letter dated April 30, 1882, Dickinson dares to make the irreverent remark that "we thought Darwin had thrown 'the Redeemer' away."[55] Randall Fuller speculates that Dickinson is referring to a series of reviews that Asa Gray wrote on *The Origin of Species*, which appeared in the *Atlantic Monthly* in 1860.[56] Dickinson, with characteristic temerity, and Hawthorne, with equally characteristic reluctance, end up siding with a Hutton-inspired geological vision in which individual species emerge, evolve, and become extinct in the vast stretches of unfolding time. They, like Hutton, can discern in Earth's flux nothing resembling a static, idealized whole: just a perpetual unfolding that offers "no vestige of a beginning, no prospect of an end."[57]

CODA: *PLUS ÇA CHANGE*

Flouting President Seelye's 1880 interdict against the teaching of Darwinian evolution, an intrepid Amherst graduate named Benjamin K. Emerson, professor of geology and zoology, continued to bring Darwin's ideas into classrooms at Amherst (and Smith) College—though to a select group, following curricular changes. During Hitchcock's time, geology had been given preeminence in the curriculum. The Amherst course catalogue for 1855 to 1856, under the heading "Plan of Instruction," lists geology first among disciplines taught. By contrast, the catalogue for 1880 to 1881 demotes geology from the core curriculum to an elective, offered only to second-term seniors. In addition, though no other courses in the 1880 to 1881 catalogue had prerequisites, geology and mineralogy did: to take mineralogy, students needed two terms of chemistry, and mineralogy itself was required for a student to take geology.

For the select Amherst seniors who qualified, Professor Emerson's course used James Dwight Dana's *Manual of Geology*. A correspondent of Louis Agassiz, Asa Gray, and Charles Darwin, Dana published the final version of his geology text in 1874, in which "after a prolonged attempt to resist natural selection, [he] at last granted his endorsement."[58] Though it is perhaps not happenstance that the second-term Amherst seniors in 1880, puzzling over course selections, would have found a brand-new elective in the catalogue called Christian Evidence to take alongside—or instead of—geology.

Figure 5. Geology major and Fulbright scholar Olivia Jane Truax, Amherst class of 2016, poses next to a skeleton in the Beneski Museum of Natural History. Courtesy of the Department of Geology, Amherst College, Amherst, MA.

These impediments were short lived. As part of sweeping curricular changes throughout the 1880s, courses offered by the newly formed Department of Mineralogy and Geology became a fixture in the catalogue. In 1899, Professor Emerson became the president of the Geological Society of America, which he helped to found. Moreover, in a lovely poetic rapprochement, Emerson, in 1901, married President Seelye's daughter Anna, though after her father's death (the family are all buried in Amherst at Wildwood Cemetery, which Emily Dickinson's brother Austin helped design). Early in the twentieth century, Frederick Brewster Loomis, a cutting-edge paleontologist who had been a professor in the college's creationist-friendly biology program, became the Hitchcock professor of mineralogy and geology. Loomis's frequent research expeditions yielded some of the Beneski Museum's remarkable specimens, including fossil remains of prehistoric horse- and elephant-like mammals, *Eohippus* and—more famously—mammoths.[59] These, along with Professor Hitchcock's collection of dinosaur footprints, have offered material evidence for Darwin's theories of species transmutation and extinction for generations of Amherst students and visitors.

President Seelye was right, it would appear, to fear the radical worldview that the careful observation-based science of geology—and the equally meticulous eye of the literary artist scrutinizing the natural world—would eventually support. As Gertrude Stein famously described as the cultural absorption of revolutionary new ideas, "For a very long time everybody refuses and then almost without a pause *almost* everybody accepts" (emphasis added).[60] Yet, in 2021, as we celebrate the endurance of Amherst College and honor its longstanding commitment to excellence in the humanities, arts, and sciences, one can't help but note the tiny qualifier in Stein's statement: *almost*. With continued controversies around climate change, evolution, and extinction—not to mention challenges to higher education and to the teaching of the liberal arts—geologists, environmental scientists, and their partners in the expressive arts continue to have our work cut out for us.

Notes

1. The full title of Charles Lyell's book is *The Geological Evidences of The Antiquity of Man; with Remarks on the Theories of The Origin of Species by Variation* (London: John Murray, 1863), accessed December 15, 2018, http://www.gutenberg.org/files/6335/6335-h/6335-h.htm.

2. "About the Department," Department of Geology, Amherst College, accessed January 5, 2019, https://www.amherst.edu/academiclife/departments/geology/about-the-department.

3. For a lively account of the relationship between Asa Gray and Louis Agassiz, which began in 1846 with the two on good terms and then devolved, see Randall Fuller, *The Book that Changed America: How Darwin's Theory of Evolution Ignited a Nation* (New York: Viking Press, 2017), 86–88.

4. Edward Hitchcock, *Religion of Geology and Its Connected Sciences* (Boston, MA: Phillips, Sampson, and Company, 1851).

5. Amherst College, *Addresses at the inauguration of Rev. Julius H. Seelye, to the presidency of Amherst College*, June 27, 1877 (Springfield, MA: Clark Bryan, 1877), 6, https://archive.org/details/addressesat-inaug1920amhe/page/n3.

6. Edward Hitchcock, *Elements of Geology*, 25th ed. (New York: Ivison & Phinney, 1855), 285–88.

7. Amherst College, *Addresses*, 6.

8. Amherst College, 23.

9. Amherst College, 23.

10. Bert James Loewenberg, "The Controversy over Evolution in New England, 1859–1873," *New England Quarterly* 8 (1935): 232–57, 244.

11. Amherst College, *Addresses*, 26-27. It is notable that Seelye's soaring rhetoric as he describes the ceaseless processes of nature echo those of the geologist James Hutton, whose "Theory of the Earth" (published in *Transactions of the Royal Society of Edinburgh* 1, no. 2 [1788]) arrived at the irresistible conclusion that the Earth's history far outstripped conventional religious accounts based on the Christian bible: "The result, therefore, of our present enquiry is, that we find no vestige of a beginning,–no prospect of an end" (304). Charles Darwin built upon the work of geologists, who discovered in the fossil record, a story of transformation over untold centuries. *The Origin of Species* concludes with Darwin's awe at what he called the "grandeur in this view of life": that "whilst this planet has gone cycling on according to the fixed law of gravity, from so simple a beginning endless forms most beautiful and most wonderful have been, and are being, evolved." See Darwin, *The Origin of Species by Means of Natural Selection; or the Preservation of Favoured Races in the Struggle for Life* (London: John Murray, 1859), 490.

12. Amherst College, *Addresses*, 31.

13. "Brief History of Geology at Amherst," Department of Geology, Amherst College, accessed May 14, 2018, https://www.amherst.edu/academiclife/departments/geology/about-the-department/brief-history-about-the-department.

14. Benjamin Silliman, December 4, 1822, Edward and Orra Wright Hitchcock Papers, Amherst College Archives and Special Collections, Amherst College, Amherst, MA.

15. Hitchcock, *Elementary Geology*, viii.

16. Edward Hitchcock, *Reminiscences of Amherst College* (Northampton, MA: Bridgman and Childs, 1863), 8.

17. In *Report on the Geology, Mineralogy, Botany, and Zoology of Massachusetts* (1833), Hitchcock writes about the "creation and extinction of certain huge ferns, sea weeds, zoophytes, and sea monsters, whose relics would be brought to light, not till several thousand years afterwards, by the researches of geologists." See Hitchock, *Report on the Geology* (Amherst, MA: J. S. and C. Adams, 1833), 246.

18. Oliver Wendell Holmes Sr., one of the more verbose members of the Saturday Club, penned a poem honoring its key members: Hawthorne was "The great ROMANCER" and Agassiz "The great PROFESSOR"; see "At the Saturday Club," *Atlantic Monthly* 53 (January 1884): 63–71, 69–70.

19. "Franklin Peirce Discovers the Body of Nathaniel Hawthorne in New Hampshire," New England Historical Society, accessed August 2, 2019, http://www.newenglandhistoricalsociety.com/franklin-pierce-discovers-the-body-of-nathaniel-hawthorne-new-hampshire/.

20. Nathaniel Hawthorne, *The Marble Faun* (New York: Grosset & Dunlap, 1859), iii.

21. Hawthorne, *The Marble Faun*, 375.

22. D. F. Rauber, "The Fragment as Romantic Form," *PMLA* 39 (1940): 229–53, 230.

23. Hitchcock, *Report on the Genealogy*, 245.

24. Stephen Jay Gould, *Time's Arrow, Times Cycle: Myth and Metaphor in the Discovery of Geological Time* (Cambridge, MA: Harvard University Press, 1987).

25. Hitchcock, *Religion of Geology*, 8.

26. Hitchcock, 8.

27. *J* 954, *F* 1070. Citations of Dickinson's poems use the convention of referring to the numbers assigned by the two authoritative collections. *J* refers to Thomas Johnson, ed., *The Poems of Emily Dickinson* (Cambridge, MA: Harvard University Press, 1955); *F* refers to R. W. Franklin, ed., *The Poems of Emily Dickinson* (Cambridge, MA: Harvard University Press, 1998).

28. Richard Benson Sewell, *The Life of Emily Dickinson*, vol. 2 (Cambridge, MA: Harvard University Press, 1974), 346.

29. Hiroko Uno, in contrast to my point, analyzes Dickinson's poetry as simply reflecting Hitchcock's vision; see "'Chemical Conviction': Dickinson, Hitchcock, and the Poetry of Science," *The Emily Dickinson Journal* 7, no. 2 (Fall 1998): 95–101.

30. Quoted in Sewall, *Life of Emily Dickinson*, 347.

31. Sewall, *The Life of Emily Dickinson*, 343.

32. Letter from Emily Dickinson to Abiah Root, May 7, 1845, Emily Dickinson Archive, http://archive.emilydickinson.org/correspondence/aroot/l6.html.

33. Letter from Emily Dickinson to Abiah Root, May 7 and 17, 1850, Emily Dickinson Archive, http://archive.emilydickinson.org/correspondence/aroot/l36.html.

34. Dickinson to Root.

35. Dickinson to Root.

36. Joan Kirkby, "'We thought Darwin had thrown "the Redeemer" away': Darwinizing with Emily Dickinson," *The Emily Dickinson Journal* 19, no. 1 (2010): 1–29, 18.

37. Ana Teixeira Pinto, "Death Wall: Extinction, Entropy, Singularity," e-flux, 2015, accessed March 12, 2016, http://www.e-flux.com/journal/death-wall-extinction-entropy-singularity/.

38. William Thompson, "On a Universal Tendency in Nature to the Dissipation of Mechanical Energy," *Proceedings of the Royal Society of Edinburgh*, April 19, 1852; also published in *Philosophical Magazine* 4, no. 25 (1852): 304–6.

39. Mark McGurl, "A Reply to Wai Chi Dimock," *Critical Inquiry* 39, no. 3 (Spring 2013): 632–38, 633.

40. Hawthorne, *The Marble Faun*, 74.

41. Hawthorne, 48.

42. Hawthorne, 48.

43. Hawthorne, 156.

44. Hawthorne, 156.

45. Hawthorne, 30.

46. Hawthorne, 30.

47. Mark Twain, *Innocents Abroad* (London: Routledge, 1872), 128.

48. Hitchcock, *Elementary Geology*, 143.

49. Hitchcock, *Report on Geology*, 245.

50. Hawthorne, *The Marble Faun*, 225.

51. Michael Marder, *Dust (Object Lessons)* (New York: Bloomsbury, 2016), 33.

52. Quoted in Robert T. Tally Jr., *Poe and the Subversion of American Literature: Satire, Fantasy, Critique* (New York: Bloomsbury, 2014), 142.

53. Dickinson, J 936, F 866A.

54. Dickinson, J 632, F 598.

55. Thomas Johnson and Theodora V. Ward, eds., *The Letters of Emily Dickinson* (Cambridge, MA: Harvard University Press, 1958), letter 750. In *Religion and Literature*, Richard E. Brantley argues that "Darwinism challenged Emily Dickinson to construct a theodicy. For her, evolutionary biology did not mean that there was no God, but that her individual talent, her Charles Darwin-inflected voice of poetic justice, should shift tradition away from justifying, and toward raising skeptical concerns about, the ways of God"; see "The Interrogative Mood of Emily Dickinson's Quarrel with God," *RL* 46, no. 1 (Spring 2014): 157–65, 161.

56. Randall Fuller, *The Book That Changed America: How Darwin's Theory of Evolution Ignited a Nation* (New York: Viking, 2017), 107.

57. James Hutton, "Theory of the Earth," *Transactions of the Royal Society of Edinburgh* 1, no. 2 (1788): 304.

58. Richard Hofstadter, *Social Darwinism in American Thought* (Boston, MA: Beacon Press, 1864), 18.

59. Walter Granger, "Memorial to Frederick Brewster Loomis," *Proceedings of the Geological Society of America for 1937*, June 1938, 173–82.

60. Gertrude Stein, "Composition as Explanation," Poetry Foundation, accessed January 8, 2019, https://www.poetryfoundation.org/articles/69481/composition-as-explanation.

Eclipses, Ecology, and Emily Dickinson

The Todds of Amherst

Julie Dobrow

"He was one of the outstanding astronomers of his time," noted David Peck Todd's obituary in the *New York Times*, "a Professor of Astronomy and Navigation and Director of the observatory at Amherst College for nearly forty years."[1] In the *Amherst Record*, an obituary of his wife, Mabel Loomis Todd, came under the headline "A Friend of Amherst" and mentioned, among other attributes, "for the interests of Amherst College, too, Mrs. Todd was always on the alert." An Amherst alumnus added, "She was so wrought into the fibre [*sic*] of all the old Amherst life in my college days and for many years after," that her death brought with it "a real pang."[2] And the obituary of their only child, Millicent Todd Bingham, firmly situated her as the child of her father, "a professor of astronomy at Amherst College," and her mother, someone who "labored for many years deciphering the letters and poetry illegibly written much earlier by her former Amherst neighbor, Emily Dickinson." This tribute noted that one of Millicent's major life accomplishments was her gift to "Amherst College [of] all of the manuscripts and a daguerreotype, the one known likeness of Emily Dickinson as an adult."[3] In death, as in life, the Todds' affiliations with Amherst College closely aligned with their achievements. As the headlines of their respective obituaries suggested, each of them had made significant contributions to their individual fields, but one of the most salient aspects of their lives was their home in Amherst and their relationships with the college. Indeed, it might be argued that their relationships with the college were part of the glue that bound this small family together, despite the many and varied trying circumstances they encountered, individually and collectively.

DAVID: "PROFESSOR TODD OF THE CLOUDY ECLIPSES"

David Peck Todd's years at the college were marked by notable achievements and significant failures, remarkable publicity for his work and stunning notoriety for it, and personal tumult that roiled his family, the town, and the college, and ultimately resulted in his forced "retirement." His contributions to the college included the development of its nascent astronomy program and the eventual construction of Wilder Observatory, as well as a host of stories about his many peculiarities (such as his penchant for collecting toilet seats from around the world) which might or might not be apocryphal, but to this day are often repeated. More broadly, he made major inroads in astrophotography and became known internationally for his eclipse expeditions. But the professional efforts of his later years and the personal turbulence of his life might have overshadowed his achievements, and these, too, reverberated out from Amherst to the world.

David first came to Amherst College in 1872. He had transferred from Columbia University where he'd started as a precocious fifteen-year-old. David chose to come to Amherst because the college had both a program in astronomy and an observatory. In 1874, during the fall of his senior year, David developed calculations about the Transit of Venus, a rare astronomical event that occurs just twice a century in which the full outline of Venus can be seen as it passes between the sun and Earth. Though he was just an undergraduate, his calculations became widely known and cited by many astronomers of the day. By 1878, he had obtained both an AB and MA from Amherst, and his research on the satellites of Jupiter during the time of their eclipses caught the eye of Simon Newcomb, director of the US Nautical Almanac Office. Newcomb, tasked with developing a standard of astronomical calculations, thought that David's work could be useful in testing his own theories about the change of the rotation period of the Earth.[4] He invited David to join him at the US Naval Observatory, a position David held until 1881, when he came back to Amherst.

David returned to the college as an instructor of astronomy and director of the observatory. He also returned with his young wife, Mabel, whom he married in 1879. The couple left behind, in Washington, DC, with Mabel's parents, their young daughter Millicent, born in 1880. David taught at Amherst until 1917, rising through the academic ranks and serving as secretary of the faculty between 1891 to 1909. One of his lasting contributions to the college was construction of the Wilder Observatory, which opened in 1903 with what at the time was the world's largest Clark refractor telescope (and even in 2020 remains one of the largest).

At the time David returned to Amherst, the college was starting to pivot from its origins in educating young men for the ministry to providing a more secular education with a greater emphasis on professional knowledge production. As the demographics of students at the college began to change, and the funding base supporting Amherst shifted (see Richard F. Teichgraeber III's chapter in this volume), a greater emphasis on science in the curriculum corresponded with David's time on the faculty. In the early twentieth century, Amherst had already earned a spot on lists of institutions responsible for the undergraduate education of significant "American men of science."[5] In a 1911 report that was later widely criticized, the US Bureau of Education ranked Amherst a class 1 institution and in the top forty US institutions in its ability to prepare students for graduate study in the sciences.[6]

And yet, David Todd always felt that his work at Amherst was in constant tension between the college of old, which depended more on theology than science, and what he increasingly saw and felt should be the new directions, an opposition that others around him also felt. Interestingly, even one of Emily Dickinson's poems evocatively utilizes eclipses as a metaphor for this tension between faith and scientifically garnered knowledge:

Figure 1. Professor David Peck Todd. Amherst College Archives and Special Collections.

Eclipses be — predicted —
And Science bows them in —
But do one face us suddenly —
Jehovah's Watch — is wrong.[7]

Much of David's astronomy work in the early years of his career at Amherst focused on the measurement of solar activities of different kinds. His early calculations of the 1874 Transit of Venus led him to be appointed as the "astronomer in charge" at the Mount Lick Observatory the next time a Transit of Venus was to occur, in 1882. David traveled to California and spent two months there, tinkering and setting up and refining photographic equipment. During the 2004 Transit of Venus, astronomers at Lick rediscovered David's stills in storage vaults, which they considered "superb." They digitally animated them, something that would have thrilled David, since he had foreseen that "moving pictures" would be the best way to document certain kinds of astronomical phenomena.[8]

After his work on the Transit of Venus, David turned his attention to other types of solar movement. Although total eclipses of the sun occur every year, the vantage point from which they can best be seen on Earth varies widely. This led David to organize eclipse expeditions that spanned the globe. In all, he led a dozen such expeditions, taking him to five continents and more than thirty countries. Two of the expeditions were specifically known as "Amherst expeditions": the 1896 trek to Japan and the 1901 voyage to the Dutch East Indies (modern-day Indonesia), both funded by Amherst alumnus, railroad magnate, and multimillionaire Arthur Curtiss James, class of 1889. David also chased eclipses in Angola, Brazil, Peru, Libya, and Russia, among other countries. Each of these expeditions required months of planning, hundreds of calculations, and a great deal of fundraising. David shipped enormous telescopes overseas and hired local teams to transport them to remote mountaintops, where they were reassembled. It took David and his team (which sometimes included Mabel and, eventually, Millicent) weeks of arduous travel to arrive at the eclipse destinations. He often needed to invent or modify equipment to meet the local conditions when he arrived.

Many of David's efforts went toward trying to document the path of an eclipse with photographic equipment that could monitor its movement. He worked to invent a mechanism that would enable him to take many exposures rapidly to track an eclipse. David first experimented with this during the 1887 expedition to Japan and refined the apparatus for subsequent expeditions. It's perhaps not surprising that David, who was a fine musician and had once considered a career as a professional organist, came up with the idea to construct an apparatus that would "use air at reduced pressure and was operated by means of a small organ-like, foot powered machine equipped with a perforated paper roll similar to those used on a player piano."[9] Later in life, David believed that this invention was perhaps his most important contribution to astronomy; indeed, today animation and film are considered fundamental methods of capturing the patterns of eclipses. Moreover, in a posthumous tribute, David's former student Charles Hudson, class of 1910, wrote, "How much Dr. Todd's accomplishments influenced Edison and others in the years close to 1893 when this topic was the object of much research [on moving pictures] may never be known. His work was done with glass plates since . . . film was hardly known at the time."[10]

However, for all the ingenuity, long and difficult travel, and endless calculations David put into the eclipse expeditions, almost all of them ended in disappointment when nature intervened and the clouds closed in. After several of these failures, David attempted to inform astronomers along an eclipse's path by telegraph so that more collaborative and coordinated efforts in photographing an eclipse could be made. In recognition of this work, in 1888, Washington and Jefferson College awarded him an honorary doctorate. But the failed eclipse expeditions had long-lasting consequences for David. So consistently was his planning thwarted and so widely was it known, that once, years after his death, a famous British astronomer mentioned to Millicent that her father might better be remembered as "Professor Todd of the Cloudy Eclipses." In his appreciation of David, Charles Hudson suggested, "Perhaps it was the thought of these disappointments, lost opportunities over which he had no control, which, in his last years, unsettled his brilliant mind."[11]

While the eclipse expeditions did not result in the cutting-edge visual record David had envisioned, they still served the function of getting his name—and that of Amherst College—into the newspapers and magazines of the day. Some of these articles were almost certainly written by his wife, whose highly stylized prose and literary flair differed significantly from David's. The series of articles about David's work appearing in the popular press of the day helped him to fund the next expedition and shone light on Amherst College, as well.

Perhaps because of his proven ability to help generate publicity for the college, David was tasked with preparation of the Amherst College exhibit in the 1893 Columbian Exposition in Chicago. In Mabel's recounting of it:

> David's exhibit for Amherst is decidedly the best of the smaller colleges—his divans covered with corduroy, thus utilizing his packing boxes for which an exorbitant storage was charged—are decorative triumphs in their way, with their down pillows of purple and white satin; also his elegant bromide enlargements of buildings and interiors, his faculty and Trustees in frames, his frieze of distinguished graduates, his great seal on purple and white satin. Dr. Storrs and Henry Ward Beecher, General Walker Roswell Hitchcock, Bishop Huntington and Governor Bullock at the entrance, his bookcase of works by the Faculty and the pretty desk with "Amherst Alcove" paper and envelopes headed by the seal—it is all in excellent taste, and refined and attractive, and makes a good "showing" of Amherst.[12]

Around the turn of the twentieth century, some of David Todd's astronomical observations focused on Mars. This work was of interest to the wealthy mill owner and businessman turned astronomer Percival Lowell, who financed two of David's expeditions. Lowell believed that the canals on Mars provided evidence that this planet might host life (and this idea inspired a whole genre of science fiction). Apparently, David came to believe this, as well, for he began to design to send signals to Mars and to receive signals back from the intelligent life he was increasingly convinced lived there. He was an early believer in the utility of airplanes and hot air balloons as ways of providing a higher platform from which his astronomical experiments could occur (he founded the Aero Club at Amherst College—the first such organization in the nation). Though David was certainly not the only scientist attempting to signal Mars—Gugliemo Marconi, for instance, was also experimenting with radio transmissions to the red planet—David's convictions seemed to be more deeply held. David stated in an interview with the *Amherst Student*, "If there is life on Mars, the people [there] ought in the nature of things to surpass us in intelligence. . . . I intend to get up as high and stay up as long as possible [to send signals] up in the rarified atmosphere with nothing to disturb us."[13] And after years of not only publishing academic articles about aspects of astronomy but also cultivating media contacts that would enable him to get his work into the popular press, David found that his attempts to signal "the Martians" drew much media attention. But the coverage wasn't entirely positive. For example, an article in the *New York Times* in 1924, explaining David's development of a machine designed to receive radio signals from Mars, quoted a scientist involved in the analysis of data garnered from "listening in," stating that while he couldn't explain the results, they were "quite likely the . . . results of interference of radio signals" and "a freak we can't explain"—not evidence of the "intelligent life" David suggested.[14] Not surprisingly, David began to face derision from his colleagues. Noted former Amherst professor F. Curtis Canfield, class of 1925, in a somewhat facetious tribute, "His exploits, successful or not, always got headlines in the national press. Amherst had no need of a publicity department with Davy Todd on the faculty."[15]

David's departure from scientific rigor was paired with his apparent departure from sanity. His behavior became increasingly erratic. His attendance at meetings and even his own classes was sporadic. Mabel and Millicent reported his strange sleeping patterns. By 1917, Amherst president Alexander Meiklejohn stated that the board of trustees had granted him an "indefinite" leave of absence. "On the whole, I think it would be better for us, and possibly for you, if your leave of absence were continued," wrote Meiklejohn. "The work in astronomy has not gone well and has been pretty thoroughly out of harmony with the general scheme of instruction."[16]

In the spring of 1917, David and Mabel left Amherst for Florida. There, his behavior devolved further. He spent money lavishly. He sent Millicent on wild errands to find people who did not exist in places that didn't. His sexual infidelities, an issue throughout his life, became more pronounced and less discreet. He periodically disappeared from his home without warning—and without letting anyone know where he was—causing Millicent and her new husband, psychologist Walter Van Dyke Bingham, to go off in desperate search of him. He launched a series of increasingly wild schemes, ranging from his plans to keep the sun from breaking apart (something he was convinced would occur within his lifetime) to finding lost treasure. By 1922, Mabel and Millicent came to the agonizing conclusion that he needed to be institutionalized; between that point and his death in 1939, he was in and out of various mental hospitals, nursing facilities, and asylums.

David Peck Todd's Amherst College career was filled with both significant achievements and significant setbacks. He came to see the destruction of his first office in Walker Hall, which burned to the ground in 1882, as the leitmotif of his life. Millicent later wrote that elemental forces stymied Todd at every turn, "whether fire, which destroyed his calculations, the foundation of his next discovery and building-store of his astronomical reputation, or the cosmos, which rewarded the years of preparations for observing a total eclipse of the sun, each time, by shutting it out."[17] And yet, David Todd's work during the time he was at Amherst College influenced the development of astrophotography in ways he probably saw would become the standard in his field but did not realize during his own lifetime.

MABEL: "A TIRELESS ZEST FOR LIVING"

Mabel Loomis Todd was initially reluctant to come to Amherst. An excellent musician, a talented painter and writer, and an extremely socially engaged person used to the vibrant arts community and society of Washington, DC, Mabel was fearful that the small college town would not yield her as many opportunities as she was used to. But within a few short weeks, Mabel was writing in her journal, "Do you know, I think Amherst in many respects quite ideal. I always did like a college town, with its air of quiet cultivation, and by living in such a one it is possible to continue two things which are otherwise generally not found together—I mean the possibility of living in the country, amid the luxuriance of nature, and yet of having refined and educated society at the same time."[18]

Part of the reason for Mabel's rapid about-face was having made the acquaintance of Susan and Austin Dickinson. Her friendship with members of the Dickinson family, leading citizens of the town with deep ties to the college (Austin's grandfather, Samuel Fowler Dickinson, was one of Amherst's founders, and his father, Edward, had served many years as its treasurer), would lead her into a thirteen-year-long extramarital relationship with Austin (an Amherst alumnus, class of 1850, and treasurer of the college after his father), and introduce her to the poetry of Emily, one of Austin's younger sisters. The Mabel/Austin relationship which has been written about extensively elsewhere, not only quietly incensed the town of Amherst, but also set up a toxic dynamic between the Todd and Dickinson families that had many long-lasting effects, including, ultimately, the division of Emily Dickinson's papers between Amherst College and Harvard University.[19]

Throughout the thirty-six years she lived in Amherst, Mabel was deeply invested in both the college and the community. Faculty wives in the late nineteenth and early twentieth centuries were largely tasked with keeping house and "social obligations [that] required a considerable amount of 'unpaid service,'" like sponsoring receptions, teas, and events of different types.[20] Apart from the social duties she had as a faculty wife, she frequently performed as a pianist or singer at college events. She also taught both music and art at a school developed by Mary E. Stearns (wife of former Amherst College president William Augustus Stearns) that operated out of the president's home, and chaperoned Amherst College dances. Mabel's daughter, Millicent, once related that in 1892, her mother had discovered that "when two Negro boys invited their guests to Commencement," the "Southern boys refused to go to the promenade if the Negro couples were permitted to attend. Having heard this, my mother invited them as our houseguests . . . along with Katherine Garrison, granddaughter of William Lloyd Garrison—and had a reception for them."[21]

Mabel's position as spouse of an Amherst College professor who chased eclipses enabled her to travel the world in a way few people of the late nineteenth century—and even fewer women—were able. She documented her travels to Japan, Tripoli, throughout southeast Asia, Europe, and South America, in articles and in two books. She brought back to Amherst crates filled with artifacts she collected from indigenous cultures, which initially decorated her homes in Amherst and eventually were donated to museums throughout the Northeast. Mabel's role as the spouse of an astronomer meant that she learned a great deal about the field and assisted David in many of his endeavors (indeed, she probably ghostwrote a number of pieces that went under his byline). She also became knowledgeable enough to give talks about aspects of astronomy, wrote a book entitled *Total Eclipses of the Sun*, and cowrote a textbook on astronomy with noted nineteenth century science writer Joel Dorman Steele. When David was asked to prepare an exhibit to represent Amherst College at the 1893 Columbian Exposition, Mabel helped him curate it and presented the college's achievements to the world.

Mabel's many civic contributions to the town of Amherst included her founding of the Amherst Woman's Club in 1893, the development of the Mary Mattoon chapter of the Daughters of the American Revolution (DAR) in 1894, and the establishment of the Amherst Historical Society in 1896. Perhaps less heralded but equally noteworthy were Mabel's contributions to saving areas of forest in Amherst: in 1913, her efforts led to her election as chairperson of the Amherst Forestry Association. Mabel began to purchase land for preservation and wrote widely about it. Her purchase of an island off the Maine coast eventually led to the development of the Hog Island Audubon Camp for adult learners, with the unique, at the time, mission of teaching teachers about environmental education.

Mabel was also involved in efforts that led to the creation of the Everglades National Park. Her daughter wrote of her retrospectively, "Mrs. Todd's love of fine trees sometimes led her into efforts which used up a great deal of time. . . . I sometimes feel that the memorial she would value most would be a forest."[22] Indeed, Millicent would honor her mother by donating eighty acres of land in Pelham that Mabel had purchased to save the trees to Amherst College in 1961.

Lincoln Brower, who, in the early 1960s, was a new young assistant professor of biology at Amherst, was tasked with conducting "ecological studies of the forest and to make these studies a significant part of the curriculum." Years later, Brower, a world-renowned expert on monarch butterflies, recalled, "The forest was hemlock at that time, and I used it for several years as a natural laboratory to study the age distribution of the trees. . . . I remember in my talk [at the dedication ceremony Amherst held] that I mentioned the Amherst College liberal arts way of seeing the World and that we avoided the substitution of activity for thought. I also discussed the concept of the 'private perception of the World' as described by Konrad Lorenz and how the Mabel Todd Forest would help open avenues of better understanding natural history and ecology."[23]

Though Mabel herself aspired to be known most for her writing (during her lifetime, she published over two hundred articles on an astonishing array of topics in the leading magazines and newspapers of the day and wrote or edited a dozen books), she's remembered principally for her work on editing and publicizing the writings of someone else. The irony of being most remembered as Emily Dickinson's first editor would not be lost on Mabel.

After Emily died in 1886 and her sister Lavinia discovered a cache of poems no one knew existed, she became determined to share them with the world. The task eventually came to Mabel, who had recognized the "strange power" of the poetry the first time that Sue Dickinson shared one with her in 1881. After agreeing to this considerable undertaking, Mabel spent the next decade deciphering, editing, publishing, and publicizing the poetry and letters of the reclusive Amherst poet. Aided by abolitionist and leading nineteenth-century literary critic Thomas Wentworth Higginson with the first two volumes of poetry, Mabel's work served to catapult Emily Dickinson to the forefront of America's literary figures. The first several volumes of poetry sold out quickly and garnered excellent reviews. Mabel used her prowess as a public speaker, launching a series of talks about the life and craft of the so-called Amherst myth to promote Dickinson's work—and to increase sales. Though her editing of the poetry has been heavily debated, there is no doubt that without her efforts the world would not know the Emily Dickinson we know today.[24]

Figure 2. Mabel Loomis Todd and Millicent Todd Bingham working on a new edition of *The Letters of Emily Dickinson*, Hog Island, Maine, circa 1930. Todd-Bingham Picture Collection (MS 496E). Manuscripts and Archives, Yale University Library.

Mabel received a total of only $200 for all of her work on editing and publishing Emily's letters and poetry. Lavinia Dickinson claimed copyright of all of Emily's works and refused to share more than a tiny fraction of the profits she realized from their sale. In an effort to "make things more right," Austin wanted to deed Mabel a piece of land he owned, but he died before he actually enacted any paperwork. Though Mabel did follow up and get Lavinia to deed her the land, the one remaining Dickinson sibling reneged and brought a lawsuit against Mabel and David in 1897. When Mabel lost both the lawsuit and an appeal, she decided that she'd had enough dealings with the Dickinsons: she took the remaining unpublished poetry and all of the other Dickinson papers in her possession, put them in a camphorwood chest, and locked them away for three decades. It was only after Austin and Susan's last surviving child, Martha, began publishing her aunt's poetry again in 1914 that Mabel began to think that there would come a point at which she would want to jump back into the Dickinson fray. This didn't happen until the early 1930s, when Mabel decided to try to correct some of the errors she felt Martha Dickinson Bianchi had made in her editions of Emily's poetry and her retelling of her aunt's life. In a series of articles and a reissue of *The Letters of Emily Dickinson* in 1931, Mabel demonstrated to the world that she was still an authority in this area—and a force to contend with.

Writing after her mother's death in 1932, Millicent recounted that a friend of Mabel's had said, "Every outside thing she did came right back to Amherst to be shared here."[25] Many contributions—her civic leadership, her land stewardship, and her artistic, writing, and editing endeavors—were also rooted in Amherst and shared with the world.

MILLICENT: FILIAL RESPONSIBILITIES AND "THE ACCRETION OF THE AGES"

As the only child of Mabel and David Todd, Millicent spent her entire life believing that it was her obligation to finish her parents' unfinished business. This enormous sense of filial responsibility, paired with her repressed but certain knowledge of her parents' lack of fidelity to one another, her growing understanding of her mother's dependencies and her father's mental illness, as well as the extent to which her parents outsourced her upbringing to her grandparents for the majority of the first decade of her life, meant that Millicent grew into adulthood with highly conflicted feelings. Her profound ambivalence about her parents only grew when she saw herself as someone with a completely different moral compass than her mother and when she was forced to confront the increasingly distressing manifestations of her father's mental illness.[26] Though she loved her parents dutifully, she desired nothing more or less than to distance herself from them. This proved to be impossible, and it is clear that much of the trajectory of Millicent's life emanated from and returned to Amherst, and that her most significant professional contributions did as well.

In 1923, Millicent became the first woman to receive a PhD in geology and geography from Harvard. She seemed on target for a successful academic career, teaching at both Columbia University and Sarah Lawrence College and publishing in the field of regional geography until 1929. It was then, with the centenary of Emily Dickinson's birth looming, that Mabel reached out to her daughter and asked for help in preparing a new edition of *The Letters of Emily Dickinson*. Millicent knew that were she to do this, it would tear her away from her own career. Despite her many deep-seated reservations, she agreed. Millicent retooled herself professionally, not only assisting Mabel in a reissue of *Letters* in 1931, but also taking over Mabel's Dickinson work after her death. Millicent edited the remaining unpublished poems that had been stashed away in the camphorwood chest and brought out a new volume of Emily's poetry in 1945. She also wrote three books about Emily Dickinson's life and craft.

One of ongoing sources of anxiety for Millicent throughout most of her adult life was the accumulation of family materials she had been bequeathed, as well as the trunk full of Dickinson poems, letters, and family papers. She felt singularly responsible for dealing with the thousands of pages of the "accretions of the ages," as she referred to them. Millicent was keenly aware that the Dickinson materials in her possession were of particular value. Though Harvard University had acquired a large collection of Dickinson materials and was anxious to obtain Millicent's, as well, she believed that Emily's poems and letters belonged back in the town in which she lived and had written them. And so, in 1946, Millicent reached out to Charles Cole, the newly inaugurated president of Amherst College. She attempted to orchestrate a deal in which Amherst would take not only all of her Dickinson materials but also the eighty acres of land in nearby Pelham and all of her family papers and artifacts as well. After ten years of discussions (including a series of exceedingly difficult negotiations with Harvard, still in pursuit of the Dickinson papers), the Amherst College Board of Trustees agreed to accept Millicent's gifts.[27] The Dickinson papers were catalogued at the Folger Library in Washington, DC, (administered by Amherst College) and shipped to Amherst; Millicent's collection of family papers and artifacts began to be sent to the college and were placed in storage. Her land bequest was finalized in 1961.

Of course, Amherst's newly opened Frost Library was not set up to receive vast quantities of archival materials, and their main interest was in the Dickinson papers. In 1960, President Cole wrote to Millicent that the board of trustees was willing to "release" her from her agreement should she wish to place her family collections elsewhere; fortunately, Yale University, which *was* set up to receive and archive big collections, was willing to accept the vast Bingham/Todd compendia (721 boxes worth). Amherst College retained the Dickinson poems, letters, and documents relating to Mabel and Millicent's editing of them, making the college one of two major repositories of Emily Dickinson's papers and the one with the "largest and most varied holdings."[28]

In the winter of 1957, Millicent received a letter from the board of trustees informing her that she would receive an honorary doctorate of letters from Amherst that spring. She wrote to Charles Cole, "This is not only a very great surprise, it is an equally great honor, which I accept with gratitude and with humility. Please express to them my deep appreciation of an honor which stamps with their approval my long crusade to free the work of Emily from the exclusive claims which in the past have hampered scholars in their study of her poetry."[29] Millicent's most ardent goals had been to ensure that Emily Dickinson's story would be told in the manner she and Mabel thought it needed to be, to publish the remainder of the poems and, most of all, to ensure that future scholars would have access to the

Figure 3. Daguerreotype of Emily Dickinson. Amherst College Archives and Special Collections.

materials. She always believed that Emily's papers belonged in Amherst, and that from Amherst, they could be shared with the world. Millicent would have been most gratified to know that this goal has been realized: in 2012, Amherst College launched an open-access website that contained all of the Dickinson materials they owned.

TO AMHERST, OF AMHERST, ALWAYS

The Todds all so identified with Amherst College that it was part of the moniker by which they identified themselves. David always referred to himself as an Amherst College professor, even when he no longer was. Mabel always chose to be listed as the wife of an Amherst College professor, even though this was hardly her most salient personal or professional characteristic. And Millicent, who had such a conflicted relationship with both of her parents and whose childhood in Amherst was filled with difficult associations that plagued her for her entire life, still felt the connection to Amherst College so keenly that she made one of her life's missions to ensure that the Emily Dickinson papers in her possession would ultimately go to the college.

Though neither Mabel nor David Todd died in Amherst, Millicent made sure that they were both buried in a plot in Amherst's Wildwood Cemetery (a cemetery that, incidentally, Austin Dickinson had helped to create; he is buried with his family down the hill from the Todds). Millicent, who spent the majority of her long life living outside of Amherst, is buried beside her husband in Arlington National Cemetery. Even though she made the decision to have her final resting place far from her parents, Amherst was still very much on Millicent's mind in her last years: she contacted the company in Vermont that had made Mabel and David's tombstones to inquire if it might be possible to make a small slate to lay near her parents, informing anyone who came to pay their respects that, in fact, she was buried almost four hundred miles to the south.[30] The slate was never made. But for Millicent, as for Mabel and David, Amherst would always be a significant part of who she believed herself to be.

It may be that, collectively, one of the Todds' greatest contributions to Amherst College was ensuring that Emily Dickinson's poetry was initially published and, in gifting some of her papers to the College, guaranteeing that the connection between the poet and the college would endure.

Amherst College, as well, was inextricable from the Todds' identity. And their professional contributions, from eclipses to ecology to Emily Dickinson, all of which had roots in Amherst, reverberated out from the Pelham hills to the world.

Notes

1. "Prof. David Todd, Astronomer, Dies," *New York Times*, June 2, 1939, 29.
2. "A Friend of Amherst," *Amherst Record*, November 9, 1932.
3. "Millicent Todd Bingham Dies; Authority on Emily Dickinson," *New York Times*, December 3, 1968, 47.
4. Charles J. Hudson, "David Todd an Appreciation," *Popular Astronomy* 47 (November 1939): 472–77.
5. J. McKeen Cattell, "A Statistical Study of American Men of Science," *Science* 24, no. 621 (November 30, 1906): 658–65.
6. Andy Thomason, "How Did the Federal Government Rate Your College a Century Ago?" *Chronicle of Higher Education*, August 6, 2014, https://www.chronicle.com/blogs/ticker/how-did-the-federal-government-rate-your-college-a-century-ago/83411/.
7. Emily Dickinson, "Sunset at Night – is natural" (poem 415), *The Complete Poems of Emily Dickinson*, ed. Thomas Johnson (Boston, MA: Little Brown, 1960), 198.
8. William Sheehan and Anthony Misch, "Ménage a Trois: David Peck Todd, Mabel Loomis Todd, Austin Dickinson and the Transit of Venus," *Journal for the History of Astronomy* (2004).
9. Sheehan and Misch, "Ménage a Trois," 474.
10. Sheehan and Misch, 475.
11. Millicent Todd Bingham, "Reminiscences," 1963, 2, 44–48, Millicent Todd Bingham Papers (MS 496D), Manuscripts and Archives, Yale University, New Haven, CT; Charles J. Hudson, "David Todd an Appreciation," *Popular Astronomy* 47 (November 1939): 472–77.
12. Mabel Loomis Todd, "Journal," July 23, 1893, Mabel Loomis Todd Papers (MS 496C), Manuscripts and Archives, Yale University, New Haven, CT.
13. *Amherst Student*, May 13,1909.
14. "Seeks Sign from Mars in 30-Foot Radio Film," *New York Times*, August 28, 1924.
15. Curtis Canfield, "An Amherst Astronomer," Chapel Talk, Amherst College, April 13, 1954, Archives and Special Collections, Amherst College, Amherst, MA.
16. Correspondence from Alexander Miekeljohn to David Peck Todd, December 30 1916, David Peck Todd Papers (MS 496B), Manuscripts and Archives, Yale University, New Haven, CT.
17. Todd, "Reminiscences," 44–48.

18. Mabel Loomis Todd, "Journal," October 26, 1881, 3, 46, reel 8, Mabel Loomis Todd Papers (MS 496C), Manuscripts and Archives, Yale University, New Haven, CT.

19. See, for example, Polly Longsworth, *Austin and Mabel: The Amherst Affair and Love Letters of Austin Dickinson and Mabel Loomis Todd* (New York: Farrar, Strauss and Giroux, 1984); Lyndall Gordon, *Lives like Loaded Guns* (New York: Viking, 2010); Julie Dobrow, *After Emily: Two Remarkable Women and the Legacy of America's Greatest Poet* (New York: W. W. Norton, 2018).

20. Amy Mittleman, "Faculty Wives," November 13, 2019, https://www.amymittelman.com/tag/faculty-wives/.

21. Bingham, "Reminiscences," 46–10.

22. Millicent Todd Bingham, *Mabel Loomis Todd: Her Contributions to the Town of Amherst* (New York: George Grady Press, 1935), 19.

23. "The Mabel Loomis Todd Forest," *Atlantic Naturalist* (October–December 1961): 227–31; Lincoln Brower, email correspondence with the author, April 30, 2012.

24. Note that Mabel Loomis Todd and Thomas Wentworth Higginson's editing of Dickinson's poetry has been criticized for its organization thematically; the altering of words or phrases to make the poetry better conform to nineteenth century norms and the naming of poems that bore no titles.

25. Bingham, *Mabel Loomis Todd*, 31.

26. For more information, see Julie Dobrow, *After Emily: Two Remarkable Women and the Legacy of America's Greatest Poet* (New York: W. W. Norton, 2018).

27. For a complete accounting, see Dobrow, *After Emily*.

28. "The Writing College," Amherst College, n.d., https://www.amherst.edu/amherst-story/literary-amherst.

29. Correspondence from Millicent Todd Bingham to Charles Cole, February 4, 1957, President's Office Papers: Charles Cole, 1946–1961, Archives and Special Collections, Amherst College, Amherst, MA.

30. Correspondence from Millicent Todd Bingham to Green Mountain Marble Corporation, June 1953, 8, 159– 88, Millicent Todd Bingham papers (MS (MS 496D), Manuscripts and Archives, Yale University, New Haven, CT.

The "Meiklejohn Affair" Revisited

Amherst and the World in the Early Twentieth Century

Richard F. Teichgraeber III

I

June 19, 1923: In late morning, news that the board of trustees had forced the Amherst College's eighth president, Alexander Meiklejohn (1912–1923), to tender his resignation broke as a national press release from the College Press Bureau. No explanation was offered. Nor was there any mention that the trustees, while forcing Meiklejohn to step down, had agreed to his request not to release two highly critical subcommittee reports on his conduct in office that they believed provided sufficient cause for his removal.

June 20, 1923: The next morning, Amherst's 102nd undergraduate commencement exercises began in College Hall with the announcement that Meiklejohn had been elected an honorary member of the class of 1923. Many of the class's seventy-nine members jeered the trustees as they joined Meiklejohn on stage for the presentation of degrees. Thirteen announced they would refuse to accept their diplomas. "Under current circumstances," one explained on stage, "accepting a degree from the Amherst trustees would be an act of disloyalty to Amherst College." Twelve of the thirteen then walked out, with only the class president remaining behind to lead his classmates out of the exercises. In early afternoon, two faculty members released statements announcing they would tender their resignations in protest. That evening, Meiklejohn used the occasion of an annual alumni dinner for a farewell address in which he casted himself as a martyr to the cause of reform and a victim of conservative alumni, faculty, and trustees who had opposed his efforts and brought him down. In what proved to be the most widely circulated of his remarks, he said: "We have not found out yet how to run colleges. We still have trustees. And I am sure that when we have found out how to run colleges we won't have trustees." Meiklejohn also saw to it that a typewritten copy of his farewell address found its way into the hands of some two dozen newspaper reporters who had been on hand to file stories on the day's events.

June 21–25, 1923: On June 21, almost every metropolitan daily featured a front-page story chronicling events at Amherst the day before. Hundreds of dailies across the country also opened their columns to reports on what the *Boston Globe* called "Amherst's Tempest," many featuring photographs or sketches of Meiklejohn beamed together with the text of news bulletins produced by national wire services. In the absence of an official explanation, editorial writers were free to speculate about the motives and consequences of the board's decision. Some echoed Meiklejohn's fulminating words in even more pointed attacks on the trustees. Some seized on leaked information from the two trustee subcommittee reports, saying that Meiklejohn's administrative incompetence accounted for his demise. Still others observed that, given all that Meiklejohn had done to enhance Amherst's reputation, his leaving defied any exact interpretation. While editorial opinion was divided, most agreed that the Amherst trustees must explain their decision, if only to address widespread suspicion that more than mismanagement was involved, as well as the claim that mismanagement hardly justified dismissal in Meiklejohn's case. On June 25, five more faculty tendered their resignations. (By mid-July, the total would reach nine—roughly 20 percent of the Amherst faculty.)

2

That, to start, is partly to stir interest in once-significant events that today are barely remembered. I also want to draw on them to explain why, after agreeing to address the question of how Amherst and its graduates have engaged the world, I've turned that question around somewhat. "Meiklejohn Affair" operates as a shorthand phrase for events on June 19 and 20 in what follows.

A few years back, I started thinking about the governance of American colleges and universities[1] and found myself intrigued by the Meiklejohn Affair, partly because it was such a highly charged governance controversy, but chiefly because it left a remarkably long paper trail.[2] Earlier students of Amherst's controversy devoted their time to explaining how the trustees decided they had sufficient cause to dismiss a president they knew to be revered by students and admired by educators across the country.[3] But I found myself puzzling about two other aspects of the Meiklejohn Affair. How was it that the trustees settled on the 102nd commencement to send Meiklejohn packing? I also wondered why newspaper coverage and editorial comment lavished on a controversy over governance at Amherst surpassed any on the many similar controversies that came before it. Meiklejohn's was by no means the first case of a president or professor dismissed for conduct deemed unacceptable by trustees. The 1890s, 1900s, and 1910s were littered with them, and several attracted national newspaper coverage.[4] But the Meiklejohn Affair seemed off the charts. It was everywhere I looked. It was headlined front-page news in metropolitan dailies like the *Chicago Daily Tribune* (which reached seven hundred thousand readers) and the *New York Times* (upwards of three hundred thousand), as well as in several hundred smaller dailies like the *Altoona Mirror*, *Star Valley Independent*, *Brownsville Herald*, and *Santa Anna Daily*. What was it about a controversy over Amherst's governance that mattered so much to the outside world?

It took some time to realize that, in looking for answers to these questions, I was examining the Meiklejohn Affair as a national media event. Or, more precisely, Amherst's governance controversy belonged to an era that was almost as media saturated as ours, but also to an era when "media" was restricted almost entirely to some twenty-two thousand-plus daily newspapers, most of which were affiliates of one or more national wire services. Events at Amherst on June 19 and 20 were grist for this huge mill. In time, I made a second discovery that—as a student of academic government—I found of greater interest: it was the trustees' decision to dismiss Meiklejohn during Amherst's 102nd commencement that turned his leaving into a national media event. Had they waited until later in summer—and private correspondence among the trustees makes it quite clear that was their original plan—events at Amherst on June 19 and 20 would not have taken place, and we would not be looking back on a "Meiklejohn Affair" that still needs explaining.

This chapter turns on *the question of what makes Amherst's history worth understanding*. Perhaps at the top of the list should be the myriad ways in which the college and its graduates have engaged the world. But not too far behind, I want to suggest, would be a matter that engaged the world's attention in June 1923: Amherst itself or, as I will refer to it, Amherst's institutional identity.[5] But more about that after I tell how Meiklejohn's leaving got caught in the glare of national publicity.

3

Keep two things in mind. First, a hundred years ago, Amherst commencements were elaborate five-day affairs whose main feature was a variety of alumni reunion events. The 102nd commencement began on Saturday, June 16, with a band-led alumni parade that Alexander Meiklejohn escorted from the town commons to the steps of Johnson Chapel, and ended Wednesday evening, June 20, with a gala alumni dinner where Meiklejohn fired his parting shots at the alumni, faculty, and trustees. Other events included the Alumni Council's then-annual "Lawn Fete" on Tuesday, June 18, where the entire college, residents of the town of Amherst, and other visitors mingled under the Amherst flag, doubtless spending part of their time openly speculating about Meiklejohn's future.[6] By my estimate, some eight hundred alumni and their families attended the 102nd commencement, joined by seventy-nine graduating seniors and their families, two hundred to three hundred townspeople, and seventy or so other visitors of various stripes, the largest percentage of whom were newspaper reporters.[7]

Second, the call to dismiss Meiklejohn in this usually festive setting was not made by the entire board, but by an ad hoc committee of five trustees headed by then board president George A. Plimpton (class of 1876). It is, then, the activities of the so-called Plimpton committee that I recount in this section, because understanding how this ad hoc committee made the call helps to explain not just the origins of events at Amherst on June 19 and 20, but also why so many reporters were on hand to report on them.

The Plimpton committee was created at a board meeting on May 26, the day the trustees first met as a group to discuss the two highly critical subcommittee reports on Meiklejohn that they decided not to release three weeks later. (One concluded that he had been inexcusably careless in handling his personal finances; the other, needlessly contentious in dealing with the faculty.) On May 26, the trustees agreed unanimously that the reports provided sufficient cause to ask for Meiklejohn's resignation. But they reached no agreement about when to ask for it or how to proceed if he refused. Some trustees worried that, given Meiklejohn's position as both president and ex officio trustee, the board was moving into legally uncharted territory. Others insisted that no action be taken without consulting the faculty. Seeing no need for immediate action, however, the board then referred the reports to the new subcommittee headed by Plimpton and directed him to begin making arrangements that would make Meiklejohn's leaving (in Plimpton's words) "as easy as possible for him as much as for the college."[8]

What happened over the course of the next three weeks makes for a very tangled story. Two developments stand out. The first grew out of a meeting in Boston, on Wednesday, June 13, where the Plimpton committee hedged bets for the board by seeking legal counsel on how to proceed with Meiklejohn's dismissal from Harlan Fiske Stone (class of 1894; then dean of the Columbia Law School) and two Boston lawyers familiar with Massachusetts State employment law.[9]

After the meeting, Stone drafted a memorandum that recommended the committee arrange a meeting in Amherst on Saturday, June 16, and there ask three questions of each faculty member individually: Is there "reasonable probability" of establishing "harmonious cooperation" between the president and the majority of the faculty? Do you have "confidence in the President's administration of the college?" And, lastly, and only if the committee was certain that a majority of the faculty would answer "yes,": Do you think it is in the "best interests" of the college for Meiklejohn to resign? With an expected no-confidence vote in hand, Stone continued, next should come "judicious efforts" to secure a voluntary resignation. If that failed, at its scheduled commencement meeting at Amherst on Tuesday, June 19, the board should pass a resolution stating that it was in the "best interest" of the college for Meiklejohn to tender his resignation and then inform him privately that it was in his best interest to answer promptly. And if, after several days passed, a voluntary resignation still was not forthcoming, Stone concluded, "a committee should then be appointed to consider and report to the Board at an early convenient date what further steps should then be taken."[10]

Stone's recommended procedures for interviewing faculty were precisely those that the Plimpton committee came to follow.[11] Why did the rest, which obviously would have pushed the dismissal process well into the summer, go by the board? The morning edition of the June 14, 1923, *Springfield Republican* had much to do with it. Its banner headline announced a "CRISIS AT AMHERST," and beneath it ran a long story by then-young journalist Louis Lyons that explained the origins and significance of Amherst's crisis in considerable detail.[12] "Dreaded rumors have been afloat on Amherst's campus for many days," Lyons began. "The seniors hear that trustees who 11 years ago brought Alexander Meiklejohn to Amherst to instill new educational spirit into a traditional little New England College, are now weary of the long battle their president has had to wage for his liberal ideals in education and that tiring under the strain ... they are now ready to abandon the cause and the man they counted on to make Amherst a living college." Lyons went on to say that, while aware of rumors that Meiklejohn "is to be forced out," faculty did not

THE WEATHER
Fair and Cool Today
Tomorrow, Fair
Details of Weather on Page 2

Springfield Republican

Two Cents

SPRINGFIELD, MASS., THURSDAY, JUNE 14, 1923—EIGHTEEN PAGES

CRISIS AT AMHERST COLLEGE STUDENT COMMITTEE WILL ASK TRUSTEES ABOUT MEIKLEJOHN

OFFERS TREATIES TO MODIFY RULES REGARDING LIQUOR

State Department Would Swap Ship Privileges For 12-Mile Search

SENATE RATIFICATION WOULD BE REQUIRED

Outgrowth of Prolonged Study of Involved Situation Arising From Rum-Smuggling and Court Decision

First Church Would Move To Rear End of Extension But Not Off the Square

Mayor Leonard's Suggestion That Parish Sell to City For $360,000 Declared by Church People to be Wholly Inadequate

CHINA PRESIDENT HELD PRISONER BY MILITARY LEADER

Li Yuan Hung, Fleeing From Capital, Captive Aboard Train at Tientsin

GOVERNMENT AT PEKIN ATTEMPTS TO KEEP ON

American and British Consuls Prevented From Seeing Fugitive Chief, Arrested By Provincial Tuchun

FINDS ONLY SON, LOST 16 YEARS, ON TRIAL FOR MURDER

Unsigned Letter Calls Mother to Courtroom—Coolness of Alleged Slayer, Once Convicted, Broken

Amherst College President Who Is Center of Controversy

DR ALEXANDER MEIKLEJOHN

DISMISSAL REPORT AROUSES STUDENTS TO SHARP ACTION

Vigorous Defense of President Follows Adverse Reports By Faculty Committee—Threat is Seen in Attitude of Seniors and Juniors—Feeling Runs High Over Feared Attack on Progressive Policies—Student Body Strongly Supports President—Prof Hamilton Resigns

LAST STEP-SING HELD AT SMITH

Seniors Give Place to Juniors at Opening Exercises of Commencement Season of 1923

RUHR "ARMISTICE" DISPLEASES PARIS

Purely Question of Berlin Ending Passive Resistance, is Statement—Continued Efforts at London

CALLS ON CONGRESS TO CHECK MURDERS

Federal Control of Firearms Needed, is Finding From Homicide Figures—New England Safest

Motorcyclist Killed When His Machine Topples Over In Front of Automobile

Irwin North of Wilbraham Dies of Crushed Skull After Accident on Upper State Street—Francis Matthews of North Wilbraham Badly Hurt—Motorcycle Overbalanced by Heavy Metal Block—W. B. Whitney, Automobile Driver, Released

WESTERN MASS. MOTORISTS PENALIZED

Registrar Goodwin Suspends Licenses of Many in Springfield District

QUASHES INDICTMENTS OF FRENCH COMMUNISTS

To Die For Sabotage; Terrorism Hits Ruhr

SAYS RED ARMY FED BY FRIENDS

Former British Secret Service Agent Charges American Funds Helping Bolshevist Government

SPORTS

Baseball Results

CONNECTICUT STATE POLICE APPOINTED

COBWEBS GONE; LOST PRISONER REVEALED

MAINE VILLAGERS FLEE FOREST FIRES

Stretch of 25 Miles Along Aroostook Railroad Burning — Inhabitants Barely Escape From Hamlet

NATIONAL GUARD MEN PROMOTED

Col Paul J. Norton Makes Three Lieutenants Captains and Gives Them Command of New Companies

LOCOMOTIVE BROTHERHOOD VICE-PRESIDENT DEAD

FIVE-CENT TROLLY FARE TRIAL FAILS

Figure 1. *Springfield Republican*, June 14, 1923. Amherst Archives and Special Collections, Amherst College, Amherst, MA.

expect "any overt act" from the trustees at the upcoming commencement, and that some of Meiklejohn's faculty supporters also believed there were signs that the trustees "may experience a change of heart." He then, perhaps unaware that all were members of a committee charged with arranging for Meiklejohn's dismissal during the upcoming commencement, identified George Plimpton, Dwight Morrow, and Stanley King by name as trustees that Meiklejohn's supporters were counting on "to lift the problem above personal criticism or political maneuvering and to swing a working majority to a progressive policy for Amherst."

Two days after Lyons's piece appeared, all members of the Plimpton committee gathered at Amherst for what proved to be three days of tense and exhausting meetings that served to ram through Meiklejohn's resignation. The first was a series of individual meetings with faculty on June 16, the day the 102nd commencement began. The last ended around 2 a.m. on June 19, the day before undergraduate commencement exercises. It was at that meeting that Meiklejohn tendered his resignation, but not before he had angrily questioned the competence of the Plimpton committee to judge his case and told its members he would never forgive them.

What should we make of the Plimpton committee? One answer can be pieced together from what committee members later said about themselves: for all the tumult and embarrassment it created, immediate action had been an unavoidable necessity.[13] Or, more precisely, the Plimpton committee believed that its only choice in countering false information and negative publicity generated by Lyons's article was to ram through Meiklejohn's resignation as quickly as possible. Also, because committee members believed (correctly) that Lyons's article had been sourced by Meiklejohn's faculty supporters, they thought that any hesitation would have left the advantage with them, so acting in quick dispatch had also been needed to block their efforts to try his case in the newspaper.

Another answer can be pieced together from dozens of newspaper accounts. Far from blocking Meiklejohn's supporters' efforts to generate more publicity, the Plimpton committee lost control of events and turned the process of dismissing Meiklejohn into a public event—actually, two public events. The first unfolded during the 102nd commencement, where the process of dismissing Meiklejohn affected more than a thousand or so alumni, faculty, and students gathered for the occasion and thereby gave Meiklejohn's leaving great emotional charge and high visibility. While the Plimpton committee's meetings were closed to the public, their time and place (all were held in then Converse Memorial Library) were public knowledge. Ongoing newspaper reports also led many to believe that the Plimpton committee had come only on a fact-finding mission, and so Meiklejohn's fate, therefore, was still an open question. And, finally, on the Amherst campus, the Plimpton committee provided Meiklejohn a public stage on which, for five days, he shuffled between private conversations and meetings with committee members and well-attended events at commencement, and which he effectively seized on to manage own his exit. [14]

The Plimpton committee's activities also played out before a second and vastly larger public: editors, writers, and readers of newspapers across the country. It may be too much to say that in choosing to respond to the Lyons piece as it did, committee members wandered into a mediascape whose workings they did not at all understand.[15] Probably they did not know that in 1923, the number of dailies produced by the country's then-huge newspaper industry had declined slightly from its all-time high of 2,416 five years earlier. But it's clear that they greatly underestimated national interest in their own existence and activities, as well as the possibility of Meiklejohn being dismissed.[16] Exactly how many dailies and weeklies ran stories and editorials about events at Amherst after the publication of Lyons's June 14 piece may be impossible to determine. But we know that the *Springfield Republican* was one of more than eight hundred dailies affiliated with the Associated Press (AP), and that the AP not only beamed various versions of Lyons's explosive June 14 article to its affiliates, it also beamed articles Lyons wrote about Amherst's ongoing controversy each day during the two weeks that followed. Doubtless, it was his widely distributed June 14 piece that also prompted editors of leading northern newspapers to send their own reporters.[17]

4

Tracing the Plimpton committee's misadventures goes a long way toward explaining why the Amherst trustees dismissed Meiklejohn during Amherst's 102nd commencement and why the controversy sparked by its decision attracted unprecedented newspaper coverage. But it has more limited purchase in explaining what the attention of newspapers tells us about Amherst as an institution.

There is no question that much of the national interest in the Meiklejohn Affair can be explained by looking at the particular moment in Amherst's history into which it broke. In the eyes of Meiklejohn's admirers, that moment was defined by what he had accomplished as president. And there is some truth in this. No president before Meiklejohn had imagined Amherst quite as he did in his 1912 inaugural address: "First of all, a place of the mind," a college defined by "great teachers" who were among the "leading minds of their time" and who gave students "an intellectual grasp of the human experience." Nor had any attacked the president's office with the zeal Meiklejohn displayed during his first five years by revising its curriculum and rebuilding its aging faculty with young appointments that compared favorably with those made at Harvard, Columbia, and Chicago. (He also persuaded Robert Frost to join faculty.)

Meiklejohn, at the same time, exerted broad influence in US higher education.[18] And he did so, in part, by eloquently projecting Amherst as a new model of "the liberal college" at a time when universities first had gained dominance in American higher education. Meiklejohn understood that the growth of the US university system had undercut popular belief that a "liberal college" had a distinctive and important role to play. But he rejected the prevailing view that liberal colleges could meet the challenge posed by universities simply by revamping curriculums that now borrowed selectivity from new university-based academic disciplines. In his view, that approach had drawn liberal colleges into an implicit competition they had little chance of winning. The alternative, he insisted, was the "liberal college" that gained new validity by way of a curriculum that introduced students to a common body of knowledge and made them familiar with all the most important branches of knowledge. This cause, he declared, lay "at the very heart of the liberal college."

Figure 2. Alexander Meiklejohn, n.d. Amherst Archives and Special Collections, Amherst College, Amherst, MA.

Little wonder, then, that Meiklejohn's admirers found his dismissal baffling. Or, as his friend (and then-Harvard Law School professor) Felix Frankfurter put it: How could the Amherst trustees not see that because Meiklejohn had conferred "national standing" on Amherst, forcing him to resign was bound to be a matter of "national concern"?

Well, they could and they couldn't. In June 1923, no one was in a position to give a fair assessment of Meiklejohn's presidency. Today, we have access to a documentary record that makes for a considerably more complicated picture. The most generous summary, I think, would be to say that Meiklejohn's successes almost always were accompanied by strain, strain he encountered with old-guard alumni (including several on the faculty) who viewed him as an outsider because he was not an Amherst graduate, strain created by chronic budget deficits that he inherited and left him no choice but to rebuild the faculty by attrition, strain he created with faculty by exercising more discretionary power than either of his two predecessors either claimed or tried to exercise, strain created by his reluctance to accept that he was legally accountable to the trustees for his conduct and that he needed their support to accomplish his purposes.

The list could go on. I draw attention to the strains of Meiklejohn's presidency, however, not to offer my own assessment, but instead to open the way for a different approach to understanding why his leaving attracted so much attention. Frankfurter was quite right in declaring that Meiklejohn's leaving was a "national concern." But, like most of his admirers, he praised Meiklejohn for doing more than he actually accomplished. By which I mean that, if you do some digging in Amherst's history before Meiklejohn arrived, what you discover is that his accomplishments as president did not confer "national standing" on Amherst so much as gave it greater academic substance.[19] Or, put another way, by US standards in the early twentieth century, Amherst already had "national standing" when Meiklejohn arrived, and it was this fact about Amherst as an institution, more than any of his particular achievements, that explains why the world took notice when he left.[20]

To explain in more detail, nine years short of its 1921 centennial, the Amherst Meiklejohn presided over occupied a national landscape of some seven hundred colleges and universities arrayed in all stages of development. It stood out in various ways.[21] Amherst's trustees consisted of a representative cross-section of the nation's cultural and financial elite, including two of the richest men in the United States. Its nationally dispersed graduates—who then totaled 5,132, of whom 3,290 were living—had made Amherst prominent by gaining public distinction substantially out of proportion to their numbers and across a variety of professions.[22] At a time when most US colleges badly needed more students, more faculty, and more money, Amherst had experienced substantial growth. During the presidencies of Merill E. Gates (1890–1899) and George Harris (1899–1912), enrollment had increased from 347 to 462, and the faculty from 32 to 48. Gifts from wealthy donors had helped the endowment grow from $1,225,184 to $2,720, 492 (or $70,3877,371 today).[23] Amherst had also increased its resources by functioning successfully in the orbit of new philanthropic organizations in New York City—especially the Carnegie Foundation for the Advancement of Teaching (CFAT) and John D. Rockefeller's General Education Board (GEB)—whose procedures for distributing grants established standards that were in effect a first national rankings system.[24]

Figure 3. Procession of Amherst students to College Hall; October 1912 inauguration of Alexander Meiklejohn. Amherst Archives and Special Collections, Amherst College, Amherst, MA.

In short, the Amherst Meiklejohn took charge of enjoyed in 1912 remarkable autonomy as well as national recognition shared by no more than twenty or so other US colleges and universities. Funds were not as plentiful as faculty and trustees wanted but more than enough for the college to operate as a freestanding institution. One could say, more precisely, that Amherst was its own self-defined and financially secure community, and that its independence allowed it to engage the world largely on its own terms. One could say, too, that if this was Amherst in 1912, it was an Amherst no one could have imagined at its 1871 semicentennial let alone at its founding in 1821.

Through the 1880s, Amherst had operated as a definitively New England institution. Its students came from New England families headed by ministers, farmers, and teachers, and were educated largely to become ministers and teachers.[25] Its finances were handled in Boston and Worcester by trustees who lived mostly in Massachusetts and whose leadership focused on the goals of achieving financial stability and maintaining the conservative spirit and practices of a de facto Protestant institution—among which were required daily chapel services and presidents who served as pastors of the college church. While Amherst was unusual among "old time" colleges in having a charter that restricted the number of clergymen among its seventeen trustees to seven, up to 1890, all of its presidents were ordained Protestant ministers. Through the 1870s, its faculty consisted almost entirely of Protestant ministers for whom teaching was just one aspect of their respectable clerical careers.[26] Neither Amherst's trustees nor its graduates were wealthy as a group. The college had weathered economic hard times in the 1870s and 1880s, thanks to gifts from a small handful of wealthy donors. The most recent was from Daniel Willis James (partner at the New York City mining company Phelps, Dodge), whose three large gifts would help to increase the endowment from $584,845 to slightly more than $1 million (or $30 million today). Apart from those gifts, however, nothing else going on at Amherst in the 1880s hinted at what lay ahead.

Demographic change began in the 1890s with the arrival of students less rooted in New England culture and—in steadily increasing numbers—from families headed by bankers, businessmen, and lawyers. In the mid-1880s, almost two-thirds of Amherst students came from New England states (mostly Massachusetts). By 1910, it was less than 40 percent.[27] Students were now expected to pursue careers not only in the traditional professions of law, medicine, and the ministry, but also in more lucrative occupations like banking and business. (Of the seventy-five students who graduated in 1895, less than 25 percent intended to be ministers or teachers—in contrast to 50 percent of the seventy-six who graduated in 1879.) By the turn of the century, students also expected whatever careers they pursued to play out in cities like Philadelphia, Baltimore, Chicago, St. Louis, San Francisco, and—above all—New York.

These shifting demographic patterns were not the only changes eroding Amherst's identity as a New England institution. Its identity was also changed by graduates who, in steadily increasing numbers, were nationally dispersed yet remained tied to the college through involvement in a self-organized infrastructure. Established in 1842, the first Society of Alumni initially served to appoint class secretaries, publish class books, coordinate activities of regional and urban alumni associations, and arrange class reunion programs that in time became the centerpiece of Amherst's annual commencements. It also held annual fall meetings at Amherst during the time of fraternity initiations, which, by the turn of the century, attracted almost as many alumni as commencement reunions.[28]

In 1877, with the board's election of Julius A. Seelye (class of 1849) as the first Amherst graduate to serve as president, alumni began to function more directly in day-to-day operations. Seelye initiated the practice of appointing faculty with doctoral degrees from US and German universities. In doing so, he also embraced the practice of professorial inbreeding, appointing Amherst graduates with postgraduate training. During Seelye's fourteen years as president, there were some years when all but one of the faculty were Amherst graduates. As faculty grew in size, the percentage would decline, but very gradually. Of forty-four voting faculty during Meiklejohn's last year as president, twenty-four were Amherst graduates.

Before the establishment of the Alumni Fund in 1906,[29] the alumni as a group were not considered possible sources of endowment donations or capital gifts, and the work of soliciting was left in the hands of the board.[30] Even so, groundwork for anchoring alumni as a key source of ongoing financial support had been laid in the 1870s and 1880s, when (as at other eastern colleges at the same time) graduates who had been members of Amherst's national fraternity chapters raised money on their own to purchase or construct houses in the town of Amherst that served as the first residential fraternity "lodges." Ownership of real estate also involved new alumni responsibilities that included paying mortgages and taxes, seeing that property was properly maintained, and soliciting additional funds to meet mortgage debt.[31]

By the turn of the century, changes in the geographical origins and career choices of Amherst's students were also reflected in the composition of its trustees. Alumni had gained majority status on the board in the mid-1860s and additional power in 1874, when the board revised the charter to provide for alumni-elected trustees designated to succeed five previously elected by the Massachusetts State legislature as they resigned or died. By 1912, the charter-mandated ministerial presence on the board also had shrunk from seven to three, before the provision defining distribution of the clergy was repealed four years later.

There is no question that, as with its students, the watershed decade for Amherst's board was the 1890s. The election of three New York City-based businessmen—George A. Plimpton (class of 1876), Daniel Willis James (1891),[32] and Charles M. Pratt (class of 1879)—marked a critical turning point in Amherst's history even more important than Meiklejohn's appointment as president.[33]

James and Pratt were conduits to two of the largest private fortunes generated by the industrialization of the US economy and the wealth they brought to Amherst—both in the form of endowment donations and of capital gifts—had no precedent. Together, James and Pratt (and family members who either succeeded them as trustees or served Amherst in other ways) were responsible for roughly two-thirds of donations to the college's endowment between the 1880s and 1912. Their capital gifts (especially from the Pratts) also funded much of the construction of eight new buildings added to the campus during those years.

Plimpton allowed Amherst to tap into the nation's industrial wealth in different ways. In New York City, his position as president of Ginn & Co. made him a prominent cultural figure in his own right; at the same time, it allowed him to devote as much time as he wished to soliciting gifts to Amherst and to other cultural and civic institutions where he served as trustee.[34] Elected board president in 1907, Plimpton immediately made his influence felt by soliciting a $75,000 ($2,018,000, today) gift from Andrew Carnegie, filing Amherst's application for enrollment in a new pension plan established by CFAT and requesting a $75,000 matching grant from the GEB). Later, it was also Plimpton who secured matching gifts from the CFAT ($75,000, or $1,059,000 today) and another from the GEB ($300,000, or $4,238,000 today) that helped to launch a national campaign to raise the balance of a targeted $3 million (or $42,383,000 today) Amherst Centennial Gift.[35]

By the time Meiklejohn arrived, eight of Amherst's seventeen trustees lived in metropolitan New York City. The presence on the board of Plimpton, Pratt, and Arthur Curtiss James (class of 1893; elected to succeed his father in 1903), together with the election of New York City corporate lawyer John W. Simpson (class of 1871), had shifted management of the college's finances and fundraising efforts to New York. It also signaled an even larger change in Amherst's identity, because this shift occurred at the same time that the college became more closely connected to New York City by way of two other developments: the first, a steady increase in the number of students enrolled from metropolitan New York City, and the other, several hundred Amherst graduates flocking there to pursue their careers. By 1912, metropolitan New York City had become home to the largest number of students who had graduated from Amherst since the early 1890s, as well as to its largest and most powerful alumni association. The habit of thinking of Amherst as a tradition-bound "New England College" persisted, but the label no longer applied. By 1912, Amherst's center of gravity had moved to New York City.[36]

All that explains how Amherst first staked a claim as a national institution. How does it help us understand what happened during Meiklejohn's years as president and why the world took notice when he left? The short answer is that you cannot fully understand either what Meiklejohn accomplished or why his leaving attracted so much attention without knowing a good deal about fundamental changes in Amherst's institutional identity that occurred during the two decades before he arrived. The longer answer would underline two points. The first is that the large-scale changes that marked Amherst's emergence as a national institution were preparatory to Meiklejohn's election. No one ever had to remind Meiklejohn he was president of Amherst College. But he did not elect himself.[37] Before the turn of the century, it is utterly impossible to imagine any circumstances that might have resulted in Amherst trustees electing him (or someone like him) president.

More telling in understanding why the world took notice when Meiklejohn left is that there were, broadly speaking, two developments that served to enhance Amherst's reputation during Meiklejohn's presidency, with each serving to enhance the college's national standing. Meiklejohn's own efforts to enlarge the college's intellectual and cultural reach certainly were widely noticed, including efforts, which, after World War I ended, were shaped by hopes for social reform that informed progressive assessments of US involvement in the war. These included hiring faculty with settlement house experience, bringing British socialist R. H. Tawney to campus as visiting professor, and fostering the growth of the Intercollegiate Socialist Society and its successor (after 1921) the Student League for Industrial Democracy. In the early 1920s, Meiklejohn also backed a new labor college cosponsored by Amherst and trade unions in nearby Holyoke and Springfield. Faculty appointments he had made in biology and economics joined in this effort.

Of equal significance was the continuing operation of forces that had transformed Amherst before Meiklejohn arrived, the two most important of which were the establishment of the Alumni Council in 1914 and a new generation of alumni leadership on the board. Establishment of the Alumni Council—with representatives elected by twenty-eight alumni associations across the country—signaled a substantive increase in alumni engagement that reached a high point when the council's officers and representatives joined forces with trustees in planning the program of the 1921 centennial and the solicitation of the $3 million Centennial Gift.[38] Its establishment also marked the beginning of a new era in which, by way of the Alumni Council's eight committees, coordinated activity with urban and regional alumni associations, fraternities owned and managed by alumni, and the ever-active prodding of the council's first secretary Frederick S. Allis (class of 1893); alumni as a group came to function as a powerful administrative arm of the college at the same time they became an expected source of substantial annual gifts that would help to pay operating costs.[39]

On the board, where George D. Pratt (class of 1893) would succeed his brother in 1921, the election of Dwight W. Morrow (class of 1895) in 1916 did far more to enhance Amherst's national standing.[40] It also deeply affected the operation of the board for the next fifteen years. After 1920, the finance committee of the board met in Morrow's office in the headquarters of J. P. Morgan & Co. at 23 Wall Street. The board also transferred the college's principal deposit account to J. P. Morgan & Co., and it was there that Morrow took sole responsibility for buying and selling its endowment securities until his early death in 1931. Like Plimpton, Morrow had a close personal understanding of the elite social networks of New York City. After the war ended, he joined forces with Plimpton to become the dominant figures on the board. Few if any important policy decisions were taken without their consultation, and in most cases their opinions determined the timing and outcomes of board deliberations.[41] At a time when Amherst had no development office, and its presidents were not expected to raise money, Morrow and Plimpton acted as a two-man task force for raising capital and endowment gifts.

5

A few things stand out about Meiklejohn's presidency and why his departure attracted so much attention. The first is that, while the Meiklejohn Affair certainly was a deep embarrassment to Amherst, it did no lasting damage to its reputation, and for several reasons. In the long term, the most important was that controversy sparked by Meiklejohn's dismissal never blew open the larger academic community. Meiklejohn himself received many private letters of sympathy and support, but public interest in his case never forced any national academic association—especially neither the Association of American Colleges nor the American Association of University Professors–to come to his rescue or to investigate circumstances surrounding his dismissal.

Three other developments provided more immediate help in restoring Amherst's reputation. First in line was the unexpected the death of Warren G. Harding on August 2, and the immediate succession to the presidency of Calvin Coolidge (class of 1895). Next came the quick and well-publicized refilling of Amherst's depleted faculty with new appointments that included two then-high-profile visitors—Ernest Barker and John Erskine—and the reappointment of Robert Frost.[42] And, finally, when classes resumed in September 1923, it was clear that fears that the Meiklejohn Affair would take a toll on enrollment were misplaced. In 1922 to 1923, Amherst had 523 students; in 1923 to 1924, the number increased to 599; and in 1924 to 1925, it increased to 677. By 1927 to 1928, total enrollment stood at 748, an increase of almost 37 percent.

A final thought: to treat the Meiklejohn Affair as controversy that played out at an institution of high national standing, as I have here, requires a qualification. It will not do to ignore that Amherst remained a de facto Protestant institution during Meiklejohn's presidency, or that through the 1950s, Amherst continued to thrive in a country whose leadership remained overwhelmingly Protestant. In his 1921 centennial address, Meiklejohn declared that Amherst had shed its skin as a New England college and now "belonged to America." It's also true that, under his watch, Amherst left a door partly open for Jews and African Americans during years when discriminatory quotas were established at other colleges and universities in the Northeast. But Meiklejohn also said that Amherst would remain an "Anglo-Saxon college," and he did not tamper with long-standing requirements that included weekday morning chapel exercises and Sunday service in the college church for students not excused (on application to the dean) to attend church services elsewhere with denominations of their choosing.[43] Demographic changes that would make Amherst "belong to America" began—roughly thirty years after Meiklejohn's departure—in the post-World War II decades, with the integration of Jewish Americans into the faculty and student body, and resumed more slowly during the last decades of the twentieth century to include women, African Americans, Asian Americans, Hispanics, and Latinos.[44]

Notes

1. At least three features of US academic governance set it apart from systems elsewhere: (1) by law, boards of trustees (or regents) drawn almost entirely from outside academic life have final say; boards exist elsewhere but are weaker and have more mixed representation; (2) the strong role assigned to a college or university president, who has considerably more power than vice chancellors or rectors who head systems elsewhere, and who also are appointed by the board as full-time executives responsible only to the board; (3) alumni—especially wealthy alumni—have influence found almost nowhere else.

2. Much of the paper trail—including a trove of once confidential board correspondence, memorandums, and reports—can be found in Materials Concerning Alexander Meiklejohn, 1923–48 and Newsclippings Concerning the Resignation of Alexander Meiklejohn, 1923–24, Amherst College Archives and Special Collections, Amherst College, Amherst, MA. My thanks to Mimi Dakin for more than two years of helping me as I've intermittently wandered up and down this paper trail

3. The best of these is Douglas C. Wilson, "The Story in the Meiklejohn Files, Part I," *Amherst* 35 (Fall 1982): 8–15, 28–31; Wilson, "The Story in the Meiklejohn Files, Part II," *Amherst* 36 (Spring 1983): 8–13,53–57, 63–65. Wilson was editor of *Amherst* at the time. He later included his two-part article together with several other essays on Amherst's history for reprinting in Wilson, ed., *Passages of Time: Narratives of the History of Amherst College* (Amherst, MA: Amherst College Press, 2007). Although he mentions the issue only in passing, Wilson was right to observe that the documentary record shows Meiklejohn's left-progressive political views had nothing to do with the trustees' decision to dismiss him.

4. Among the most recent was the highly-publicized dismissal of two professors by Columbia University trustees in September 1917. Both had publicly expressed their opposition to US engagement in World War I. See Carol S. Gruber, *Mars and Minerva: World War I and the Uses of Higher Learning in America* (Baton Rouge: Louisiana University Press, 1975), 187–206. For prominent earlier cases of faculty dismissal by trustees, see Mary O. Furner, *Advocacy and Objectivity: A Crisis in the Professionalization: A Crisis in the Professionalization of American Social Science* (Lexington: University Press of Kentucky, 1975).

5. For colleges and universities, components of institutional identity include: (1) legal (charter), (2) demographic (trustees, students, faculty, and alumni), (3) programmatic (curriculum and extracurriculum), (4) public relations rhetoric and modern-day mission statements, (5) visual (architecture and landscape), (6) financial (endowments, tuition, scholarships, revenue from outside grants and commercial contracts), and (7) associational (ties with other institutions).

6. Doubtless speculation was fueled partly by what Meiklejohn had said at the baccalaureate service that morning. Choosing the parable of the Pharisees as his text, he had launched a thinly veiled attack on the trustees in which he cast himself as the Messiah and the trustees as benighted Pharisees. Alumni prepared to speak for the board—some apparently privy to findings of the withheld subcommittee reports on Meiklejohn's conduct—also helped to stir the pot.

7. It may be impossible to determine exactly how many dailies sent reporters to Amherst, and whether the AP or United Press International sent their own reporters (although that was not uncommon at the time). It is worth noting that the *New York World* (in those days, the city's most respected newspaper) sent the then-young journalist Walter Lippmann to cover events. His long piece in the June 24, 1923, Sunday edition of the *New York World* found its way (in whole or in part) into columns of newspapers in St. Louis, San Francisco, and several other smaller cities.

8. Plimpton to Dwight W. Morrow, May 30, 1923, Dwight W. Morrow Papers, Amherst College Archives and Special Collections, Amherst College, Amherst, MA. Other members of the Plimpton committee were Edward T. Esty (class of 1897), Arthur Gillett (class of 1880), Stanley King (class of 1903), and Dwight Morrow (class of 1895).

9. Harlan Fiske Stone (1872–1946) went on to become US attorney general (1924–1925) and then associate justice (1925–1941) and chief justice (1941–1946) of the US Supreme Court (1925–1941). Stone's nominations to the first two positions were made by Calvin Coolidge while he was the thirtieth US president (1923–1929). Coolidge was elected to the Amherst Board of Trustees in 1921.

10. Stone to Dwight Morrow, June 13, 1923, in Dwight W. Morrow Papers, Amherst College Archives and Special Collections, Amherst College, Amherst, MA.

11. The Amherst faculty vote on the "is it in the best interests-of-the-college for Meiklejohn to resign" question was: 24 yes, 11 no, 1 absent. In June 1923, there were forty-four voting faculty, four of whom were on leave.

12. Louis Lyons (*New York Times*, 1897–1982) went on to become a legendary figure in twentieth-century American journalism, first as a reporter for the *Boston Globe* and later as curator of Harvard University's Nieman Foundation for Journalism. In the early 1920s, daily circulation of the *Springfield Republican* was roughly twenty-one thousand; on Sunday, almost twenty-six thousand.

13. I draw from reports the Plimpton committee filed in March and April 1924, and from Stanley King, "President Meiklejohn's Resignation," typescript ca. 1948, Materials Concerning President Alexander Meiklejohn, 1923–48, Amherst College Archives and Special Collections, Amherst College, Amherst, MA. The tumult sparked by Meiklejohn's dismissal, Dwight Morrow wrote at the time, "is a horrible nightmare to me, but I do not see anything else we could have done." Morrow to Edward T. Esty, June 26, 1923, in Dwight W. Morrow Papers, Amherst College Archives and Special Collections, Amherst College, Amherst, MA.

14. The June 20, 1923, *Boston Daily Globe* article described Amherst's 102nd Commencement as "a week of subterranean maneuvers, of conflicting rumors, of sub-propaganda, of mysteries."

15. On the American newspaper business in the early twentieth century, see Christopher B. Daly, *Covering America: A Narrative History of a Nation's Journalism* (Amherst: University of Massachusetts Press, 2012), 153–216; and Richard A. Schwarzlose, *The Nation's Newsbrokers*, volume 2: *The Rush to Institution from 1865 to 1920* (Evanston, IL: Northwestern University Press), 106–259.

16. In addition to the off-the-charts newspaper coverage it attracted, a second thing that set the Meiklejohn Affair apart from earlier dismissal cases is that the actual day-to-day deliberations of trustees that led to dismissal never before had been the subject of such detailed newspaper coverage. The fact that the doings of the Plimpton committee were such a visible part of the incident sits high on the list of things that made the Meiklejohn Affair such a deep embarrassment to Amherst.

17. Part of the answer to the question of why Meiklejohn's dismissal attracted so much more attention than earlier cases, then, is that in June 1923, not only were there more dailies hungry for stories, more dailies also were affiliated with one or more national wire services that collected and edited stories for distribution via expanded and innovative communications systems. Total newspaper circulation was 27.8 million. Most dailies cost two cents; many households took morning and evening newspapers.

(There were also more than a thousand foreign-language newspapers in the United States in the 1920s.) The slow but steady decline of newspapers—as well as other print-based media such as magazines and books—as the dominant national media began in 1927, when radio first went national.

18. Trained as a philosopher (Cornell, PhD), Alexander Meiklejohn (1872–1964) was a forceful intellectual figure in his own right. When elected Amherst's president, he was appointed to the philosophy department and given the title of professor of logic and metaphysics. He also was a savvy self-promoter. Meiklejohn turned himself into something of a national celebrity, mostly by way of high- profile speeches and magazine articles on the topic of the "liberal college," which he also collected for publication as *The Liberal College*, the first volume in the *Amherst Books* series he launched in 1920.

19. My secondary sources include Claude M. Fuess, *Amherst: The Story of a New England College* (Boston, MA: Little, Brown, 1935); Stanley King, *A History of the Amherst Endowment* (Amherst, MA: Amherst College Press, 1950); King, *Consecrated Eminence: The Story of the Campus and Buildings of Amherst College* (Amherst, MA: Amherst College Press, 1951); George E. Peterson, *The New England College in the Age of the University* (Amherst MA: Amherst College Press, 1963); Thomas de Luc, *Piety and Intellect at Amherst College, 1865–1919* (New York: Arno, 1969); and Theodore Baird, *English at Amherst: A History*, ed. William H. Pritchard (Amherst, MA: Amherst College Press, 2005). I've also mined volumes of the *Amherst Graduates' Quarterly*, 1911–1923.

20. There was ample evidence of Amherst's national standing on hand at Meiklejohn's October 12, 1912, inauguration. In attendance (and robed for parade) were 103 delegates (mostly presidents) from colleges and universities across the country, as well as reporters from several northern newspapers, including the *New York Times*, which, on October 20, reprinted substantial excerpts from Meiklejohn's inaugural address. The whole occasion was "a matter of special note," observed the October 17, 1912, *Springfield Republican*, because of "the fact that at no other inaugural exercises ever held in this century," apart from those at Harvard for its new president Lawrence Lowell in 1909, had there been "so many college presidents in attendance."

21. This is not the place for careful classification of some four hundred and fifty US colleges that existed in the early twentieth century. It is enough to say that many were multipurpose institutions that were "colleges" in name only. A majority were also marginal economic operations with annual incomes under $50,000. In 1900, the modal college enrolled only eighty-three students; before 1920, few colleges reached a faculty size of twenty-five. See Roger L. Geiger, introduction and "The Crisis of the Old Order," in *The American College in the Nineteenth Century*, ed. Roger L. Geiger (Nashville, TN: Vanderbilt University Press, 2000), 1–36, 264–76,

22. There is evidence of various kinds. The 1910 to 1911 *Who's Who in America* found that, among all college graduates in its annual compilation of "distinguished men"—when measured per one thousand living alumnus—Amherst (205/68.3 per 1000) ranked a close third behind Annapolis (235/94) and West Point (221/85). (Harvard had the highest total number: 813/41.2, followed by Yale: 681/42.5.) A much-cited 1906 study on the educational background of 1000 eminent figures in US science found Harvard (106) was the leading source, followed by Yale (52), Michigan (35), Cornell (31), Columbia (28), Johns Hopkins (27), MIT (26), Amherst (23), and Princeton (23). James M. Cattell, *Statistical Study of American Men of Science* (New York: Science Press, 1906). In 1911, the US Bureau of Education made a four-division classification of 344 colleges and universities based on graduates viewed as prepared to pursue master's degrees. Amherst was among fifty-nine in Class I. (The report was surpassed as too controversial.)

23. On a per-student basis—$144,970 today—Amherst's endowment in 1912 probably was the largest among all the "old-time" colleges that had chosen not to transform themselves into universities. Differences in endowment wealth among these colleges was considerable. Amherst's endowment compared

favorably with those of the wealthiest universities at the time. In 1909, Harvard's per-student endowment was $150,806 today; Columbia's was $195,679 today. For university endowment values, see Roger L. Geiger, *To Advance Knowledge: The Growth of American Research Universities, 1900–1940* (New Brunswick, NJ: Transaction, 2006), 276–77.

24. During the Merrill and Gates presidencies, the campus was also transformed by the addition of six buildings to those that identified Amherst as a stately outpost of New England Protestantism. Three were designed by McKim, Mead & White, then the New York City-based masters and chief propagators of Beaux-Arts classicism in the United States. These buildings—especially Fayerweather Laboratory (1892–1894)—gave Amherst a more eclectic architectural identity that now reflected the cosmopolitan tastes of its New York City-based trustees and graduates. McKim, Mead & White later designed Converse Memorial Library (1917) and Morrow Dormitory (1925–1926). (Of the three architects, William Mead [class of 1867] today is remembered more for his administrative than his architectural talents. James K. Smith [class of 1915] joined the firm in the late 1920s, and for the next twenty years served, in effect, as the college's in-house architect, beginning with his design of Moore Laboratory of Science [now Moore Residence Hall].)

25. Between 1821 and 1871, Amherst graduated 1,943 students. Of those, 759 would become ordained Protestant ministers, 79 of whom were missionaries. In 1912, of Amherst's 2,317 living graduates, 634 were in the ministry and 606 in education, 410 were in "commercial pursuits," 364 in law, 144 in medicine, and 62 in journalism or "literature." In the early 1870s, the average graduating class size was 30; in the early 1910s, it was 60.

26. John W. Burgess (class of 1867), who taught at Amherst in the 1870s, later recalled that the college was then "a fitting school for the study of orthodox [Protestant] theology in particular and for law and medicine increasingly"—and not a place of higher learning, so much as a" a place of discipline." Burgess, *Reminiscences of An American Scholar* (New York: Columbia University Press), 147.

27. It would fall to roughly one-third by the mid-1920s. Change in geographical distribution of students occurred mostly as a fall in numbers from Massachusetts and increases from New York City and New Jersey. Between 1906 and 1910, the number from Massachusetts dropped from 170 to 138, while those from New York City increased from 137 to 153, and from New Jersey from 15 to 41. In 1910, the three other states with the largest enrollments were Pennsylvania (27), Illinois (23), and Connecticut (20). Amherst's enrollment in the 1910s could hardly be described as national in geographical scope. But the same holds true for enrollments elsewhere. What made Amherst unusual was that it drew less than 20 percent of its students from within a fifty-mile radius, and only slightly more than 40 percent from within one hundred miles. (Only Williams had a broader geographical reach.) A diverse enrollment in the early twentieth century meant a mix of students from states east of the Mississippi and west of the Ohio rivers.

28. The Society of Alumni's efforts to coordinate the activities of nationally dispersed alumni associations met with limited success. During Meiklejohn's presidency, twenty-eight associations provided solidarity in the form of annual dinners, "smokers"/songfests, and occasional celebrations. But some—especially in New York City and Boston—at times were more than social clubs, serving as settings where alumni criticized the conduct of both the president and trustees, and even proposed policy to the board.

29. It came from the initiative of six graduates, including Talcott Williams (class of 1871, then-editor at the *Philadelphia Press*), but enjoyed limited success before it fell under the control of the Finance Committee of the Alumni Council in 1914. Talcott Williams attended the 102nd commencement, where he headed a panel that reunited past editors of the *Amherst Student* for a discussion of Meiklejohn's presidency and his prospects for staying.

30. Unsolicited gifts were not uncommon, but most were relatively small and made by individuals who wanted to help manage and pay costs of then-student-run activities that ranged from the football team and baseball teams to the glee club and the student council.

31. Founded during the antebellum era, Amherst's fraternities were relatively small and usually gathered in dormitories or in rented rooms. In the late 1910s and 1920s, a new generation of more affluent graduates replaced late-nineteenth-century houses with considerably more expensive, custom-built structures that helped make Amherst something of a New England tourist destination.

32. Daniel Willis James (b. 1832–1904) headed Phelps Dodge & Co., a New York City-based mining company that provided copper wire, sheet copper, brass, and brass wire to domestic and foreign customers. The company operated its own railroads, which transported products from its mines in Arizona and Mexico (where it controlled half of the nation's output). Phelps Dodge was also one of the nation's largest producers of lumber and lumber products.

33. Charles M. Pratt (b. 1855–1935), a director of Standard Oil from 1882–1911, was the eldest son of Charles Pratt (b. 1830–1891) who before him had served as a partner at Standard Oil after John D. Rockefeller bought his prosperous Brooklyn-based kerosene company in 1874. (By the turn of the century, Standard Oil controlled a third of American oil production and captured 70 percent of the world market.) Married twice, Pratt had six sons and two daughters. All of his sons graduated from Amherst; one of his two daughters married Frank L. Babbott Jr. (class of 1913). George D. Pratt (class of 1893) was elected to succeed his brother in 1921.

34. George A. Plimpton (b. 1855–1936) served for twenty-nine years as board president until his death in 1936. In the 1890s, Ginn & Company established itself as the leading publisher of a diverse collection of schoolbooks in the United States. Plimpton helped to open markets in England, Cuba, Puerto Rico, Mexico, and China. (After 1900, one of the company's most profitable activities was standardized tests developed by the College Entrance Examination Board. These nationwide tests were taken by high school students seeking admission to thirty colleges [including Amherst] and universities who also maintained their own high individual standards.) Francis T. Plimpton (class of 1922), George Plimpton's son by his first marriage, would later serve as a trustee. Calvin H. Plimpton (class of 1939), son by his second marriage, was Amherst's president from 1960 to 1971

35. Founded in 1902, the GEB chose to shore up the finances of well-established institutions by awarding grants that had to be matched by funds raised locally, usually by a factor of three or four. The GEB's conditional arrangement effectively coerced colleges and universities to conduct fundraising campaigns and to preserve funds as endowments. Founded in 1905, the CFAT granted funds for professors' pensions. Like the GEB, the CFAT also chose to aid already financially secure institutions (like Amherst). Criteria for eligibility included strict entrance requirements and prohibition of applications from colleges that required a majority of trustees to belong to a particular denomination. Of 421 original applicants, Amherst was one of 52 that the CFAT trustees initially admitted into its pension plan

36. By the turn of the century, the population of New York City (3,437,202) was twice as large as any other US city. Chicago (1,698,575) and Philadelphia (1,293,697) were next in line. (In the world, it was outranked only by London [6,506,954]). By 1920, New York City's population would grow to 5,620,048.

37. There is no evidence that Meiklejohn and the trustees together ever fashioned anything resembling a mission statement or strategic plan. Even so, it's a safe bet that the trustees did not see Meiklejohn's election as a fundamental change. Rather, for the trustees, it was a logical next step in securing Amherst's national standing: hire a professional academic of high standing as president, then charge him with the work of replacing an aging, largely undistinguished faculty with appointments of high academic standing, thereby fashioning an Amherst faculty whose national prominence would mirror that of its graduates. Or something like that

38. It is worth noting that Arthur Curtiss James ($250,000) and seven members of the Pratt family ($541,000) together gave more than 25 percent of the $3 million gift.

39. World War I also marked the emergence of Amherst graduates as a conspicuous force in the nation's political affairs. Dwight Morrow (class of 1895), Harlan Fiske Stone (class of 1894), and Stanley King (class of 1903) were among several who first gained prominence as a result of war service. As secretary of state, Robert Lansing (class of 1886) was the most influential supporter of the entente within Woodrow Wilson's administration. Massachusetts congressman Frederick Gillet (class of 1874; later Speaker of the House) headed a congressional subcommittee with jurisdiction over nearly all appropriations.

40. Dwight W. Morrow (b. 1873–1931) was partner at J. P. Morgan & Co. from 1914 to 1927, US Ambassador to Mexico from 1927 to 1929, and in 1930, he was elected US senator from New Jersey before his early death in 1931. Morrow was both agent and symbol of the large-scale transformations of Amherst's identity that I trace in this chapter. Instrumental in creating the Alumni Council, he also served as president of the New York Alumni Association and chair of the Alumni Fund. As trustee, he headed both the executive committee and the finance committee—the board's two most powerful committees—and chaired the executive committee that organized solicitation of the $3 million 1921 Centennial Gift. Morrow also gave generously to the college—including gifts to fund two endowed faculty chairs and to build a new dormitory named in his honor—and helped to solicit the gift that funded construction of Converse Memorial Library in 1917.

41. Meiklejohn's dismissal by now perhaps is an obvious case in point. It's worth noting that, between 1912 and 1923, Meiklejohn had extensive private correspondence with both Plimpton and Morrow, which opens yet another window on the Meiklejohn Affair: close working relationships between two powerful trustees and a president that bordered on personal friendships and came to ruin with Meiklejohn's dismissal. Letters between Meiklejohn and Morrow tell of several missed opportunities to address some of the conflicts and controversies that led to his dismissal.

42. Correspondence in July and August 1923 shows that Plimpton and Morrow did most of the leg work. Frost had resigned his first appointment in 1920, after a falling-out with Meiklejohn in 1920. He would win the first of his four Pulitzer Prizes in 1924. On Meiklejohn's conflict-ridden dealings with Frost, see William H. Pritchard, *Frost: A Literary Life Reconsidered* (Oxford: Oxford University Press, 1985), 123–29, 131–33, 171–72.

43. Meiklejohn also affirmed that Amherst would retain its identity as a "classical" college, admitting only students who had studied Latin or Greek. Likewise, he continued the practice of recruiting recent alumni with graduate degrees to the Amherst faculty.

44. My thanks to Debby Applegate, Fred Hoxie, and Martha Saxton for helpful comments on earlier drafts of this chapter.

The Amherst Man in the Jazz Age

Debby Applegate

When I first arrived in Amherst in the mid-1980s, with coeducation still new, I was always pleasantly amused whenever I heard the phrase "an Amherst man." My very presence on campus made the term an anachronism, yet I rather liked the idea that we of the Fairest College were recognizable as our own *genus*, slightly set apart from the general run of folk.

Thus, I was vexed to discover while researching a book about Jazz Age New York that among the jaded sophisticates and irreverent wits of Manhattan's literati, the image of the Amherst man was considered shorthand for fellows who were starchy, straitlaced, and laughably earnest. In the long-ago lingo of the hipster, the *genus Ambersticus* was a quintessential "square."

The first place I encountered the Amherst man as punchline was in the 1925 bestseller *Gentlemen Prefer Blondes* by the silent-film screenwriter Anita Loos. *Gentlemen Prefer Blondes* is the fictional diary of Lorelei Lee, a dim but determined gold digger who sets her cap for a wealthy Amherst man named Henry Spofford.

Spoffard is "a very very famous Prespyterian," as Lorelei describes him in her comically poor spelling ("I mean it is unusual to see a gentleman who is such a young gentleman as Mr. Spofford be so Prespyterian because when most gentlemen are 35 years of age their minds nearly always seem to be on something else"), and a silk-stocking reformer, notorious for campaigning against immorality on stage and motion pictures. Or, as Lorelei explains, "Mr. Spoffard spends all of his time looking at things that spoil peoples morals":

> I mean Mr. Spoffard is one of the most famous familys in New York and he is not like most gentlemen who are wealthy, but he works all the time for the good of others. I mean he is the gentleman who always gets his picture in all of the newspapers because he is always senshuring all of the plays that are not good for peoples morals. . . . Mr. Spofford loves to reform people and he loves to senshure everything and he really came over to Europe to look at all the things that Americans come over to Europe to look at, when they really should not look at them but they should look at all of the museums instead.[1]

Spofford's comic flaw is not hypocrisy, however, but a naïve earnestness symbolized by devotion to his alma mater. It provides the laugh line at the climactic moment when Lorelei has finally maneuvered Spofford into proposing marriage:

> So he said that he had gone to Cartiers and after he had looked them all over he had decided that they were not half good enough for me. So then he took a box out of his pocket and I really became intreeged. So then Henry said that when he looked at all of those large size diamonds he really felt that they did not have any sentiment, so he was going to give me his class ring from Amherst College insted. So then I looked at him and looked at him, but I am to full of self controle to say anything at this stage of the game, so I said it was really very sweet of him to be so full of nothing but sentiment.[2]

My next unexpected encounter came in John O'Hara's best-selling novel *BUtterfield 8*, published in 1935. *BUtterfield 8* is the story of Gloria Wandrous, yet another blonde gold digger in Jazz Age New York City, told as tragedy instead of comedy. Again, the Amherst man appears as shorthand in O'Hara's argument that "there can be no symbol of modern youth any more than there can be a symbol of modern middle age." He uses contemporary illustrators to bolster his point. The popular caricatures of flask-toting flappers and racoon-coated college boys drawn by John Held Jr. might be considered "average" by people "who went to East Orange High School and the University of Illinois" and grew up to be like George Babbitt, the small-minded, provincial salesman of Sinclair Lewis's satirical novel *Babbitt*.

By contrast, O'Hara notes, "The average man, Mr. Average Man, Mr. Taxpayer, as drawn by Rollin Kirby looks like the average New York man making more than $5,000 a year":

> He is a man who wears good clothes without ever being a theater-program well-dressed man; it is easy to imagine him going to his dentist, taking his wife to the theater, going back to Amherst for reunion, getting drunk twice a year, having an operation for appendicitis, putting aside the money to send his son to a good prep school, seeing about new spectacles. . . . But no one would call this man a symbol of middle age or American Taxpayer. If he walked along the streets of Syracuse or Wheeling or Terre Haute he would be known as a stranger. He would be picked out as a stranger from a bigger city, and probably picked as a New Yorker. And a Held flapper would have embarrassed any young snob who took her to a Princeton prom.[3]

O'Hara's Amherst man is quite different than Loos's version. He is no longer a wealthy, holier-than-thou do-gooder, yet he is a distinct cut above the materialistic, middle-class Babbitts so excoriated by America's "thinking classes." He is sensible rather than sophisticated, vaguely urban but not really urbane, conventional perhaps but not "common."

For both Loos and O'Hara, invoking Amherst College was clearly intended to *mean something*, to signify a type who would be instantly recognizable to those in the know. So, why did Amherst function as a symbol of the square and respectable in the Jazz Age? And why, over the course of the interwar years, did this popular caricature shift subtly, but decisively, from the priggish Puritan to the bland businessman?

Figure 1. Henry Spoffard, "famous Prespyterian," illustration by Ralph Barton, *Gentlemen Prefer Blondes*, 1925.

THE LOOS VERSION OF THE AMHERST MAN: CHARLES PARKHURST AND WILLIAM TRAVERS JEROME

Let us start with a practical question: Who might Loos have been thinking of when she described the hapless Henry Spofford?

In 1821, the college's founding mission, ably laid out in Gary Kornblith's chapter in this volume, was, in Noah Webster's phrase, "educating for the gospel ministry young men in indigent circumstances, but of hopeful piety and promising talents." Amherst was established as a citadel to defend Calvinism against the Unitarian menace that had already overtaken Harvard. Amherst men were to be evangelical crusaders for Christ, "extending and establishing the Redeemer's empire" on Earth, serving both the good of mankind and the glory of God.[4]

For the first seventy years, that is exactly what the college did, with remarkable success. As Kornblith notes, in those decades, it likely produced more clergymen than any other institution in the United States. Amherst enjoyed a different ethos than Harvard or Yale, where the prerogatives of tradition, wealth, and aristocratic bloodlines dominated. Here, most of the students were from the hardscrabble hill towns of western New England and upstate New York, the pious sons of farmers and parsons, often the first in their families to go to college. Nearly half the students received financial aid, and most supported themselves through odd jobs and school teaching. Their spiritual fervor was so notorious that their Unitarian rivals dubbed it "the priest factory." Temperance societies, where students pledged to renounce hard liquor, were common on many campuses, but Amherst was famous for adopting the radical "cold water" requirement that members also abstain from beer, wine, opium, and tobacco.[5]

At the same time, Amherst was deeply influenced by the new German vision of liberal education, with its emphasis on independent thinking over rote recitation, and scientific observation and experimentation over a priori reasoning. Despite his own heterodox views and suspect status as a Harvard man, Ralph Waldo Emerson was deeply impressed by the intellectual passion of the students when he visited the campus shortly after its founding. The school was "an infant Hercules," Emerson wrote with admiration. "They write and study in sort of fury, which, I think, promises a harvest of attainments."[6]

From the beginning, there was an underlying tension between the college's theological conservatism and its commitment to social progress and independent thinking. The college tended to attract students who combined Romantic literary instincts and fierce evangelical ambition, many of whom devoted their careers to what David Reynolds calls the art of "dark reform—the exposure of vice whose diverting sensationalism overpowered the moral lesson."[7]

So, when Loos was composing her satire, she had many models from which to choose. For most readers in 1925, perhaps the most famous master of dark reform in the United States was the Reverend Charles Parkhurst (class of 1866). As an undergraduate, Parkhurst exemplified the Amherst ideal. A farmer's son, he was indigent, pious, studious, and deeply ambitious for himself and his God. After graduation, he entered the ministry and, in 1880, he was hired to helm the fashionable Madison Square Presbyterian Church in Manhattan.

"Parkhurst was typical of American reformers," as one police historian noted wryly, "combining intense moral indignation and intolerance of opposition with a love for publicity."[8] He was a leader of the Evangelical Alliance, a national association of Protestant churches that were applying spiritual power to urban problems, and a pioneer in what became known as the Social Gospel movement. He earned national fame as the president of the New York Society for the Prevention of Crime in 1891. Horrified by Manhattan's wide-open brothels, saloons, opium dens, and gambling houses, thriving in secret partnership with corrupt politicians and police, Parkhurst mounted a spectacular antivice campaign that made him a hero to both liberal progressives and conservative Christians.

Parkhurst made national headlines when he and two companions donned disguises and spent three weeks posing as customers in Manhattan's red-light districts. They documented in graphic, thrilling detail every sin under the sun, including the *piece d'resistance*: a night in a brothel just three blocks from his Madison Square church, that ended with wild nude dancing and a game of naked leapfrog. The merry sinners of the Tenderloin responded by composing a new twist on a popular tune:

> Dr. Parkhurst on the floor
> Playing leapfrog with a whore,
> Ta-ra-ra-boom-de-ay,
> Ta-ra-ra-boom-de-ay![9]

Around this time, a second Amherst man joined Parkhurst in the spotlight. William Travers Jerome entered in the class of 1883, but left before graduation to study law. The son of a profligate and profane Wall Street financier, Jerome represented a new wave of more urban and secular-minded students. Nonetheless, he shared with Parkhurst that traditional Amherst alloy of personal ambition, a nose for publicity, and a passion to redeem the world. Jerome was a young assistant district attorney in Manhattan during the Parkhurst Crusade. Where Parkhurst brought moral thunder, Jerome brought the hand of law. When Parkhurst's efforts blossomed into what became known as the Lexow Investigation, a sen-

Figure 2. William Travers Jerome, class of 1883, pictured as "Horatius at the bridge," *Puck*, November 1, 1905. Courtesy of the Library of Congress.

sational series of hearings into vice and government corruption, Jerome ran the show. For nearly two years, Jerome directed a public parade of witnesses telling shocking stories of bribery, election fraud, police brutality, and extortion. In 1901, he was elected district attorney, winning international fame for successfully prosecuting the mad millionaire Henry K. Thaw for the jealous murder of the high-society architect Stanford White.

Like many of this new generation, Jerome had little use for the old orthodoxies. He was an enthusiastic drinker and a heavy cigarette smoker who played poker, cursed fluently, and loathed the label of reformer. Nonetheless, his fame as a moral crusader rivaled Parkhurst's, earning him the nickname "New York's Carrie Nation" and "the man with the sledge" after a series of raids where he personally battered down the doors of the city's gambling houses and brothels with axes and dynamite.[10]

Parkhurst's and Jerome's crusades had a lasting impact, inspiring newspaper exposes, scholarship, and clean-up campaigns across the country. Historians consider this a singular moment when evangelical Christians joined with secular-minded progressives to bring an array of badly needed moral and civic reforms to the United States. This powerful alliance between evangelical Christianity and liberal progressivism, that Amherst had done so much to foster, peaked at the end of World War I with passage of the Eighteenth Amendment, forbidding the manufacture, transportation, and sale of alcohol in the United States. It was the crowning victory in the battle for the soul of the nation, heralding the glorious age of virtue for which the college had prayed and labored for nearly a century.

It is one of the ironies of history that this almost unimaginable triumph led to the undoing of the mighty moral reformers. In their spiritual ambition, they overreached. The sheer breadth of the law, its intrusiveness and obvious Protestant bias, its dramatic failures and disastrous consequences, began to sour many people on reformers and their ilk. By the late-1920s, the alliance shattered, split between advocates who focused on social justice and those who concentrated on maintaining traditional values. Men like Parkhurst, who continued to thunder away at vice from his Madison Square pulpit, were denounced as repressed Puritans, prurient censors, and secret hypocrites.[11]

The new ethos of the 1920s was best articulated by the editor H. L. Mencken, whose ultramodern irreverence made him a campus favorite in those years. Mencken could have been describing Parkhurst and Jerome by name:

> Thousands of self-consecrated archangels go roaring from one end of the country to the other, raising the *posse comitatus* against the Rum Demon, or cocaine, or the hobble skirt, or Mormonism, or the cigarette or horseracing, or bucket shops, or vivisection, or divorce, or the army canteen, or profanity, or race suicide, or moving picture shows, or graft, or the negro, or the trusts, or Sunday recreations, or dance halls, or child labor. The management of such crusades is a well-organized and highly remunerative business: it enlists a great multitude of snide preachers and unsuccessful lawyers, and converts them into public characters of the first eminence.... The way he gets his fun is not by stamping out sin, but by giving chase to sinners. He likes to catch a few of them now and then and put them to the torture—but it would give him bitter disappointment if they all came in and surrendered.[12]

THE O'HARA VERSION OF THE AMHERST MAN: CALVIN COOLIDGE AND BRUCE BARTON

Meanwhile, as Amherst's reputation for producing men of piety and propriety was at its peak, the ministry was losing professional status and orthodox Protestantism was loosening its grip on the common civic culture. In its place, the rising industrial and commercial wealth of the late nineteenth and early twentieth century was generating thousands of new jobs in business and law. Although most prestigious Northeastern colleges—including Amherst—did not offer practical, preprofessional courses, college was increasingly seen as necessary to give a boy the polish to mix with men of affairs.

These trends had a direct effect on the college, as Richard Teichgraeber III details in his chapter in this volume. By the time that Calvin Coolidge arrived at Amherst in the fall of 1891, the majority of the student body was no longer drawn from rural New England, and Amherst no longer sent half its graduates into the ministry or education. Most came from large Northeastern and Midwestern cities, especially New York City. They were less likely to be the sons of ministers and small-town tradespeople, and more often the sons of businessmen, lawyers, or doctors who came to college as much to shore up their class status, such as they saw it, as to prepare for a life of service.[13]

Campus life reflected this new orientation. As one student of the time recollected, "It is difficult to explain how thoroughly the undergraduate body, quietly backed up by a number of the faculty, were rebelling against the old religious outlook which placed so much emphasis on evangelism."[14] Students' success was judged not by spiritual or intellectual vigor, observed Claude Fuess (class of 1905), but "by their prowess in athletics, their class offices, their skill in making friends."[15] Sports, especially football, were becoming a passion on campus and among alumni who eagerly followed the Amherst teams in the sporting pages of the urban newspapers. Fraternities had strong influence in the school, with the general approval of the administration. In the 1890s, the grandest campus building, by far, was the new Alpha Delta Phi fraternity house on Pleasant Street, which boasted electricity, a banquet hall, and dorm rooms large enough that a boy could bring his piano from home.

It was increasingly apparent that Amherst's original mission was no longer so compelling, and the type of man it once produced was no longer so admired. In 1912, the trustees sought a new president who could revitalize and reshape the college's mission, choosing Alexander Meiklejohn, a philosophy professor with a reputation as one of the country's most innovative educational thinkers.

"President Meiklejohn came as a reformer," the columnist Walter Lippman wrote. "He came, an alien, openly intending, with the backing of the Trustees to modernize Amherst." He was a type of man unfamiliar to the stodgier folk of Amherst. "The Meiklejohn household is not a Puritan household," observed Lippman succinctly. Nor did he fall into the new mode: "He is not a glad-hander nor, in the college sense, a jolly good fellow."[16]

Meiklejohn set out to transform the college's mandate, retaining the passion for service, social progress, and independent intellectual inquiry, while sloughing off musty orthodoxies and sanctimonious complacencies. "If you don't believe it pays to think, go away, stay away; you're not loyal to Amherst College," he told the boys. "You must be loyal, but don't give us blind loyalty. Open your eyes, try to know and understand, venture. Stand on your own feet, think your own thoughts and then you're an Amherst man."[17]

At first, the new president exceeded expectations, turning the campus into a vibrant intellectual hotbed that pushed students to challenge the conventional pieties of capitalism and society. Meiklejohn took over, in Claude Fuess's words, "a college which was at the moment relatively static, even anemic, and injected into it a renewed vitality."[18]

Meiklejohn's earliest and staunchest foes were among the older professors, many of them alumni and ministers, who detested the new direction of the college. But for those inclined toward the new, Meiklejohn offered an enthralling rebellion against the stultifying culture of Babbitry and Big Business awaiting life after graduation. Amherst in those years, remembered the reporter Lucien Price, was "a refuge from the blatancy, the suburbanity, the family-centric and office-centric universes of American middle-class Plutopolis and Respectaburbia."[19]

Meanwhile, the trustees and alumni were also cultivating a contrasting vision of the Amherst man for the new century. The story begins, yet again, with that ancient rivalry with Harvard.

Frank W. Stearns (class of 1878), a stout, gray-mustachioed merchant and heir to one of Boston's most important dry-goods companies, was counted among the college's most devoted alumni. As one reporter put it, "Amherst is almost an obsession with Frank Stearns."[20] He was increasingly dismayed by Harvard's influence over Massachusetts politics, not to mention that Theodore Roosevelt had been the fourth Harvard man to win the White House. In the spirit of school pride, Stearns and a group of fellow alumni were searching for an Amherst man to groom for the governorship.

In 1915, Calvin Coolidge, of the class of 1895, became that man.

Why Stearns chose Coolidge as their "Representative Man," to borrow Emerson's phrase, was unclear. "Neither wealthy nor poor, neither brilliant nor dull, neither pious nor dissipated, he aroused little comment from teachers or undergraduates," wrote Claude Fuess. "If he had dropped out of Amherst in the spring of 1893, he would hardly have been missed."[21] None of his classmates had marked him out for special success. That honor went to Dwight Morrow, who was voted most likely to be famous, most popular, and class orator. He made good on that prophecy in 1913, when he became a partner at J. P. Morgan, one of the most powerful financial institutions in the world.

Born on the Fourth of July in 1872, Coolidge was the son of a Vermont farmer and storekeeper whose family came to New England in the 1630s. When he arrived freshman year, he embodied the Yankee stereotype, dressed in farm boy finery, with sandy-red hair, narrow blue eyes, a sharp nose, and thin lips that made him look, wisecrackers quipped, like he was weaned on a pickle. When he spoke, which was seldom, it was in the clipped country accent of the Green Mountains. He was shy and awkward, with no idea how to dance or make small talk. To his disappointment, he was not invited to pledge a fraternity until his senior year, when he began to make a name for himself as a debater and orator with a gift for pungent brevity and dry wit.

After graduation, he apprenticed in the Northampton law office of two Amherst alumni and became a country lawyer, living frugally with his wife and sons in a rented two-family home. The young attorney had none of the dash or brilliance of William Travers Jerome, but underneath that cool granite exterior, he burned with political ambition. In his quiet, determined way, he showed a surprising talent for winning office. He began moving up the ranks of the Republican Party, serving as mayor of Northampton, and then entering the Massachusetts State House. He was president of the state senate when Frank Stearns discovered him.

It was Dwight Morrow who first noticed that Coolidge had done surprisingly well for himself, when they met at their fifteenth class reunion. "Coolidge is a very unusual man," observed Morrow, "a strange combination of transcendental philosopher and a practical politician."[22] In 1915, Morrow introduced him to Stearns, who was smitten by this oddly Puritanical politician. He began promoting his new protégé among fellow alumni and Boston bigwigs.

As early as 1916, Stearns was predicting that Coolidge would carry Amherst all the way to the White House, earning him much razzing at alumni get-togethers. But Stearns, remembered one alumnus, "always good natured, yet never losing any chance to spread his gospel, impressed us by his earnestness in spite of ourselves."[23] The merchant personally wrote thousands of letters, buttonholed scores of citizens, and paid to distribute Coolidge's flinty, epigrammatic speeches.

Propelled by their efforts, Coolidge won the Massachusetts governorship in 1918. "For

Figure 3. Calvin Coolidge, class of 1895, as a senior. Courtesy of Amherst College Archives and Special Collections, Amherst College, Amherst, MA.

the past two or three years, when you have talked about Calvin, I have thought you were crazy. I want to say now that I was the one who was crazy," Morrow confessed to Stearns after the inauguration. "I couldn't see the picture. I can now."[24]

Governor Coolidge supported some socially progressive measures like woman suffrage and workplace reforms but held tight to an economic philosophy of low taxes, limited government, and bootstrap individualism. He won national notoriety in 1919 when Massachusetts, along with much of the country, was swept by a series of bitterly fought labor strikes, protests, and riots, stoking fear that the country would fall, like Russia, into the hands of

Figure 4. Frank W. Stearns, class of 1878, in 1923. Courtesy of the Library of Congress.

anticapitalist revolutionaries. When the Boston police walked off the job that summer, the governor fired the rebellious officers, declaring in a terse, widely-publicized statement: "There is no right to strike against the public safety by anybody, anywhere, any time."[25]

In the opinion of his Amherst supporters—if no one else—Coolidge was now perfectly poised to run for president in 1920.

It was around this time that Morrow brought in Bruce Barton (class of 1907). The son of a Congregational minster, he'd planned to follow his father's footsteps, but after graduation, he instead found his way to the new field of advertising. That same year, he established the Madison Avenue ad agency known today as Batten, Barton, Durstine & Osborn (BBDO).

Barton was as peppery as Coolidge was cool, as loquacious as Coolidge was laconic, but they both cultivated the image of a modern thinker grafted onto old-fashioned character. Barton saw himself as adapting the old Amherst ideal for a modern world. "We preachers' sons have an unfair advantage over the rest of the world. Out of about 12,000 names in one of the editions of 'Who's Who' more than 1,000 were names of us," he wrote in April of 1919. "Not all of us make good, of course. A third of us go to the devil; another third float around in between; but the other third rule the world."[26]

Despite his reputation as "Silent Cal," observed the *New Republic*, "no ruler in history ever had such a magnificent propaganda machine."[27] Together they created an ingenious campaign that put Amherst front and center. Barton wrote a series of pamphlets and articles, transforming the governor's deficits into strengths. He presented Coolidge as the quintessential Yankee from a bygone era, a plain-spoken, God-fearing, small-town lawyer who wasted neither words nor money. Not glamorous but steady and trustworthy, a fellow who pays his taxes, goes to the dentist, abhors debt, and minds his own business. In Barton's words: "A man with a vision but not a visionary."[28] Stearns funneled money into the campaign and opened a campaign headquarters in his department store. Morrow provided funds, contacts, and advice from New York City, boasting to a colleague at J. P. Morgan, "The work has all been done by volunteers and the money has been subscribed by Coolidge's Amherst friends."[29]

The cornerstone of this Yankee Cinderella story was Amherst College and the story of Stearns's unwavering belief in his fellow Amherst man. Barton dubbed his inaugural article "The Faith of Frank Stearns: The Story of a Career That Began at Amherst College and Led to the State House." Stearns's devotion, declared Barton, "renews one's courage in the capacity of simple men for unselfish sacrifice. It is a classic of faith."[30]

To the surprise of nearly everyone but the loyal Amherst brethren, Coolidge was nominated for vice president on the ticket with the popular Ohioan Warren G. Harding. They won handily.

By this point, the trustees were increasingly dominated by men of industry, finance, or secular pursuits. After a period of financial strain, they were laboring mightily to keep the college viable and growing, embarking on a massive capital campaign to mark the college's centennial in 1921. They kicked it off by mailing an appeal written by Barton to every alumnus and electing the new vice president a trustee with great fanfare. Within six months, they exceeded their $3 million goal. Meiklejohn, for his part, took a yearlong sabbatical abroad, a decision bound to irritate his critics.

Meiklejohn returned for the Centennial Celebration. But to a jaundiced eye, a spirit of philistinism was vying for control of the campus. Jeffery Amherst (then Viscount Holmesdale, later the fifth Earl Amherst), who journeyed from England to be the guest of honor, described a scene of middle-aged masculine revelry that could have been lifted from Sinclair Lewis's novel.

The first surprise came over bootleg martinis in a private dining room in a skyscraper near Wall Street, hosted by Morrow and several prominent alumni, "a formidable lot of eminent financial gentlemen." Suddenly, in one accord, his hosts rose and began to sing "Lord Jeffery Amherst" in harmony. The Viscount was befuddled:

> What was I expected to do? Sit down? Stand up? Join in–I didn't know the words–or what? I must have looked very silly standing there almost giggling but acutely embarrassed while these distinguished bankers bellowed the song right at me—or so it seemed. I was to hear that song many, many times, so I soon got used to it and easily learned to drink my way through without turning a hair.

The next day, he traveled to Amherst where he stayed with President Meiklejohn and his wife. The Meiklejohns were teetotalers, but the solid citizens of the alumni were gleefully throwing Prohibition to the wind. Every evening before the parties began, the Viscount fortified himself with a slug of olive oil he'd stashed in his room, coating his stomach against their liquid school spirit:

> Class reunions, fraternity get-togethers, old colleagues trying to remember what became of who, when and where, 'The Days When,' which usually ended up in a sea of gin and, of course, the inevitable singing. Alcohol was really necessary, for both sexes and all ages. Without it, it would have been difficult to get into the proper spirit of the whole thing. A large majority sported hip flasks, further supplies were carefully concealed in bedrooms. The richer risked whiskey which costs more but could be very dangerous. Everybody else relied on bootleg or bath tub gin, which after the first paralyzing slug didn't taste all that bad. I was made welcome, almost embarrassingly so, at most of these circuses. Flasks were continuously pressed on me. I was urged to take a gulp from each one. That song was struck up every time I showed myself. But I quickly learned this did not call for any speech or formality, I had only to stand up, swallow my gin and grin. The whole thing was exhausting, intensely enjoyable and for me something utterly new and surprising.[31]

Perhaps it was inevitable that such convivial fellows would grow disenchanted with their high-minded president. Many didn't care for his radical rhetoric on labor and class conflict, his pacifist policies, his welcoming attitude toward minority applicants, and his efforts to minimize athletics and fraternities. (Surely they were shocked by his response to alumni concerns about the poor performance of the college teams. "If you win, you win," he wrote in the *Amherst Graduate Quarterly*. "If you don't win somebody else does. I don't know what more can be said."[32]) The simmering conflict was summed up by the reporter Louis M. Lyons:

> This was a case of a liberal president trying to change a conventional college. He had irritated the New York alumni by trying to restore athletics to the students. He had affronted conservative faculty and Trustees by bringing in liberal, or they said radical, new teachers. His own philosophy was heretical to the local Congregational preachers.

Figure 5. Jeffery Amherst and Vice President Coolidge, Amherst Centennial Celebration, June, 1921. Courtesy of Amherst College Archives and Special Collections, Amherst College, Amherst, MA.

He had married an Italian and extravagant wife, and he tended to run over his budget. All these frictions came to a head that spring.[33]

By 1923, these competing visions had diverged so widely that one or the other must buckle. The enmity of the conservative faculty and Meiklejohn's disregard for both fiscal responsibility and the old guard's sensibilities climaxed during Commencement week. In the middle of the festivities, Meiklejohn was summarily fired.

In his valedictory address at the tension-filled graduation ceremony, the departing president took one last shot at his foes. "America can't think in democratic terms," he declared grimly. "America still thinks in terms of privilege and possession and position and social clubs. America must learn to think in other terms than those, and it has a long task."[34]

Metropolitan journalists flocked to campus over Commencement week to cover the controversy, casting it as the next front in the Jazz Age battles between modernism and old-fogeyism. The college obliged them, with a noisy contingent of students protesting the decision and the older men sedately returning the favor. At the graduation ceremony, wrote Lyons, "I remember Calvin Coolidge in a group of Trustees, turning his back on a group of students applauding Meiklejohn."[35]

To the outside world, the "Meiklejohn Affair" was a symbol of the era's culture wars, a Yankee version of the Scope's Monkey Trial. But beyond the intellectual and social schisms, this conflict hinged on just who the Amherst man should be.

As historian Ernest Earnest put it, "The president was not an Amherst man, and into a close-knit academic community made up largely of alumni of the college he brought other outsiders. In the curriculum he gave prominence to what he called humanistic science, a field still viewed suspiciously by scholars in the older disciplines." One young faculty member informed the readers of the *Nation* that, according to local scuttlebutt, much of the controversy was caused by "the failure of four of the new faculty members to keep their lawn mowed." Nonetheless, Earnest concluded, "Probably a professor of Greek could have left his lawn unmowed with impunity."[36]

If the Amherst man were not to be a cutting-edge intellectual or a holier-than-thou do-gooder, what then would he be? Coolidge and Barton offered the answer.

Two months after the Meiklejohn affair, President Harding died unexpectedly, a deus ex machina worthy of Frank Stearns's prophecy. But even as president, Amherst remained central to Coolidge's persona. "None of Mr. Coolidge's loyalties has found more consistent expression during his White House regime than his fondness for honoring the sons of his Alma Mater," as one journalist observed. Perhaps, proposed another reporter, because nothing got the famously taciturn president talking like old college ties. Besides Supreme Court justice Harlan Stone, Ambassador Dwight Morrow, and secretary of commerce William Whiting (classes of 1894, 1895, and 1896, respectively), he had "two Amherstians on duty" as his personal secretary and general aide de camp, and "even his spiritual needs are ministered to by an Amherst man at the First Congregational Church in Washington DC."[37] His oldest son John enrolled in the class of 1928.

Barton continued to advise Coolidge's reelection campaign in 1924, the same year he wrote the best-seller that would make him a household name. *The Man Nobody Knows* was a retelling of the gospel of Jesus that cast the son of God as a master of "modern salesmanship" and "The Founder of Modern Business": "He picked up twelve men from the bottom ranks of business and forged them into an organization that conquered the world."[38] Barton's Jesus was no nosy prude, no killjoy. "A kill-joy!" Barton protested. "He was the most popular dinner guest in Jerusalem!"[39] The contrast with Parkhurst's generation was stark, but the cleavage between Barton and Meiklejohn was even deeper. "Education is not salesmanship," Meiklejohn famously argued. "No genuine teacher is trying to put something over."[40] To Barton, that was rank heresy: in *his* gospel *everything* was salesmanship.

To no one's surprise this time, Coolidge won his second term by a landslide. As the *Boston Globe* declared, tongue-in-cheek, Frank Stearns "preached the Gospel of Coolidge and the Nation was Converted."[41]

As president, Coolidge implemented tax cuts and protectionist trade policies, and opposed farm subsidies and regulation of the stock market. Benefiting from an unprec-

Figure 6. John Coolidge, class of 1928, as a senior. Courtesy of Alamy.

edented economic boom, the federal budget ran a surplus when he was in office ("I regard a good budget as among the noblest monuments of virtue," he confided to a group of philanthropists).[42] It was only right that the interests of the business community should be looked after, Coolidge declared in the most famous line of his presidency, because "after all, the chief business of the American people is business." (Far fewer remember the final point of that speech: "The chief ideal of the American people is idealism.")[43] Dwight Morrow wisely urged Coolidge to stick with what he considered to be the president's best epigram: "Don't hesitate to be as revolutionary as science. Don't hesitate to be as reactionary as the multiplication table."[44]

"Coolidge," Morrow occasionally remarked, "may possibly be overestimated by the public: he is certainly underestimated by the intellectuals."[45] Political liberals, wisecracking reporters, and self-appointed sophisticates scorned "Silent Cal" as a mental mediocrity who rarely spoke because he had little to say. But among the so-called average Americans invoked by O'Hara—the "silent majority" in Barton's phrase—Coolidge enjoyed vast popularity. Had he chosen to run in 1928, he'd easily have won a third term. Instead, he returned to his modest home in Northampton to write his memoirs. In his final news conference, he declared, "Perhaps one of the most important accomplishments of my administration has been minding my own business."[46]

Frank Stearns's faith was spectacularly rewarded, at least at the outset. Amherst captured the nation's prize plum and expanded the influence of alumni in Washington, DC, and Wall Street. Enrollment at the college soared.

In the long run, however, Stearns and his cabal were hoist by their own potent petard. They cannily made their standard-bearer a defiant anachronism, a symbol of a vanishing America. And Americans loved it. "At a time when Puritanism as a way of life is at its lowest ebb among the people, the people are delighted with a Puritan as their national symbol," Walter Lippmann wrote. "Thus we have attained a Puritanism de luxe in which it is possible to praise the classic virtues while continuing to enjoy all the modern conveniences."[47]

But a man who proudly wore the mantle of the nineteenth century didn't provide much traction for the twentieth. By the end of the Jazz Age, Coolidge and Barton were, as historian Kerry Buckley observes, among the most prominent icons of the era: "Barton, Madison Avenue huckster, booster of a vulgarized Christianity; and Coolidge, dour Vermonter, an accidental president whose laconic manner possessed a reassuring rustic simplicity, but belied by a small-mindedness ill-equipped to deal with the complexities of modern life."[48]

Critics cast them as champions of Mencken's Boobocracy and Sinclair Lewis's Babbittry. Lewis himself lampooned Coolidge's college ties in his 1927 novel *The Man Who Knew Coolidge*, an extended comic monologue delivered by a fictional friend of George Babbitt, who flunked out of Amherst freshman year but boasts of his friendship with the president: "I can remember just's well as if it was yesterday, Cal and me happened to come out of a class together, and I said, 'Well, it's going to be a cold winter,' and he came right back, 'Yep.' Didn't waste a lot of time arguing and discussing! He knew!"[49]

This view was neither fair nor accurate, Mencken insisted after Coolidge's death:

Figure 7. Coolidge campaign button, 1924. Courtesy of Heritage Auctions.

> He was, in truth, almost as unlike the average of his countrymen as if he had been born green. The Americano is an expansive fellow, a back-slapper, full of amiability; Coolidge was reserved and even muriatic. The Americano has a stupendous capacity for believing, and especially for believing in what is palpably not true; Coolidge was, in his fundamental metaphysics, an agnostic. The Americano dreams vast dreams, and is hag-ridden by a demon; Coolidge was not mount but rider, and his steed was a mechanical horse. The Americano, in his normal incarnation, challenges fate at every step and his whole life is a struggle; Coolidge took things as they came.[50]

By Coolidge's death in 1933, the Great Depression and the new appetite for government activism it created had begun to make his "stand-pattism" look like naiveté or, worse yet, willful negligence. It must have been bitter, indeed, for Frank Stearns to watch Coolidge's tart charm evaporate before the exuberant charisma and grand designs of that quintessential Harvard man Franklin Delano Roosevelt.

More puzzling is Amherst's late indifference to its once-favorite son. In 1932, there was talk of him becoming president of the college. Coolidge, with vivid memories of Meiklejohn, dismissed the idea: "No, it is bad enough to have Congress on your hands without having a college faculty."[51] Fifty years later, the only tribute to the thirtieth president was a shabby social dorm, which never struck me as much of a compliment. In the twenty-first century, it was demolished in the name of progress.

Notes

1. Anita Loos, *Gentlemen Prefer Blondes: The Illuminating Diary of a Professional Lady* (New York: Boni & Liveright, 1925), 135–38.

2. Loos, *Gentlemen Prefer Blondes*, 178.

3. John O'Hara, *BUtterfield 8* (New York: Penguin, [1935] 2013), 98–99.

4. Noah Webster, *A Plea for a Miserable World: I. An Address, Delivered at the Laying of the Corner Stone of the Building Erection for the Charity Institution in Amherst, Massachusetts, August 9, 1820* (Boston, MA: Ezra Lincoln, 1820), 7–8.

5. Debby Applegate, *The Most Famous Man in America: The Biography of Henry Ward Beecher* (New York: Doubleday, 2006), 78.

6. Ralph Waldo Emerson, *The Journals and Miscellaneous Notebooks of Ralph Waldo Emerson, 1822–1826*, vol. 2, ed. William H. Gilman and Alfred R. Ferguson (Cambridge, MA: Harvard University Press, 1961), 182–83.

7. See, in this volume, David S. Reynolds, "Emily Dickinson, Amherst, and Nineteenth-Century Popular Culture," 206.

8. Thomas Reppetto, *American Police: The Blue Parade, 1845–1945: A History* (New York: Enigma, 2011), 61.

9. Reppetto, *American Police*, 62.

10. *Summit Record* (Summit, NJ), December 20, 1902, 4; *Courier News* (Bridgewater, NJ), February 14, 1934, 1.

11. This argument is made most thoroughly by John Burnham, *Bad Habits: Drinking, Smoking, Taking Drugs, Gambling, Sexual Misbehavior, and Swearing in American History* (New York: New York University Press, 1994); Peter N. Stearns, *Battleground of Desire: The Struggle for Self-control in Modern America* (New York: New York University Press, 1999); and Andrew Sinclair, *Prohibition, The Era of Excess* (Boston, MA: Little, Brown, 1962), especially chpt. 15.

12. H. L. Mencken, *Mencken's America*, ed. S.T. Joshi (Athens: Ohio University Press, 2004), 25.

13. Bruce Leslie, *Gentlemen and Scholars: College and the Community in the "Age of the University," 1965–1917* (University Park: Pennsylvania State University Press, 1992), 245–47, 258–59; David O. Levine, *American College and the Culture of Aspiration* (Ithaca, NY: Cornell University Press), 118.

14. George E. Peterson, *The New England College in the Age of the University* (Amherst, MA: Amherst College Press, 1964), 132.

15. Claude Fuess, *Amherst: The Story of a New England College* (Boston, MA: Little, Brown, 1935), 275.

16. Walter Lippmann, *Public Persons*, ed. Gilbert A. Harrison (New York: Liveright, [1922] 1976), 67-68, 70.

17. Theodore Baird, *English at Amherst: A History* (Amherst, MA: Amherst College Press, 2005), 171.

18. Claude Fuess, *Stanley King of Amherst* (New York: Columbia University Press, 1955), 137.

19. Lucien Price, *Prophets Unawares: The Romance of an Idea* (New York: The Century Co., 1922), 101.

20. F. Lauriston Bullard, "Calvin Coolidge as Man and Statesman," *Current History* 18 (September 1923): 899.

21. Claude Fuess, *Calvin Coolidge: The Man from Vermont* (Boston, MA: Little, Brown, 1940), 51.

22. Harold Nicolson, *Dwight Morrow* (New York: Harcourt, Brace, 1935), 269.

23. Bruce Barton, "The Faith of Frank Stearns," *Outlook* 126 (September 8, 1920): 61.

24. Fuess, *Calvin Coolidge*, 180.

25. Robert Sobel, *Coolidge: An American Enigma* (Washington, DC: Regnery, 1998), 144.

26. Bruce Barton, "My Thirty-Two Years at School," *American Magazine* 87 (April 1919): 34.

27. Richard M. Fried, *The Man Everybody Knew: Bruce Barton and the Making of Modern America* (Chicago, IL: Ivan R. Dee, 2005), 14.

28. Kerry W. Buckley, "The Man Nobody Knew," in *A Place Called Paradise: Culture and Community in Northampton, Massachusetts, 1654–2004* (Amherst, MA: University of Massachusetts Press, 2004), 475.

29. Buckley, "The Man Nobody Knew," 475.

30. Barton, "The Faith of Frank Stearns," 60.

31. Jeffery John Archer Amherst, *Wandering Abroad: The Autobiography of Jeffery Amherst* (London: Secker & Warburg, 1976), 66–68.

32. Alexander Meiklejohn, "The Athletic Disarmament," *Amherst Graduates' Quarterly* 11 (May 1922), 171–73.

33. Louis M. Lyons, *A Pause to Copy: Memoir of Louis M. Lyons-Journalist* (Bloomington, IN: Xlibris, 2008), 67.

34. Alexander Meiklejohn in James McKeen Cattell, ed., *School and Society* 18 (New York: Society for the Advancement of Education, 1923), 14.

35. Lyons, *A Pause to Copy*, 68.

36. Ernest Earnest, *Academic Procession: An Informal History of the American College, 1636 to 1953*, (Indianapolis, IN: Bobbs-Merrill, 1953), 288.

37. Frederic William Wile, "The Newest Cabinet Member," *The Spur*, October 15, 1928, 42, 8, 48.

38. Barton, *The Man Nobody Knows*, introduction.

39. Bruce Barton, *The Man Nobody Knows: A Discovery of the Real Jesus* (New York: Grosset & Dunlap, 1925), introduction.

40. Alexander Meiklejohn, "Teachers and Controversial Issues," *Harper's Magazine*, issue 177, June 1938, 17.

41. *Boston Globe*, November 9, 1924.

42. Calvin Coolidge, "Discriminating Benevolence: Address delivered over the telephone from the White House to the Federation of Jewish Philanthropic Societies of New York City, assembled at the Hotel Pennsylvania October 26, 1924," Coolidge Foundation, https://www.coolidgefoundation.org/resources/speeches-as-president-1923-1928-13/.

43. Calvin Coolidge, "Address to the American Society of Newspaper Editors, Washington, D.C., January 17, 1925," Teaching American History, http://teachingamericanhistory.org/library/document/the-press-under-a-free-government/.

44. Bruce Barton, "Concerning Calvin Coolidge," *Colliers*, issue 64, November 22, 1919, 28.

45. Nicholson, *Dwight Morrow*, 270.

46. John Whitcomb and Claire Whitcomb, *Real Life at the White House: Two Hundred Years of Daily Life at America's Most Famous Residence* (New York: Routledge, 2000), 286.

47. Walter Lippmann, "Puritanism De Luxe," *Men of Destiny* (New York: Macmillan, 1927), 17.

48. Buckley, "The Man Nobody Knew," 460.

49. Sinclair Lewis, *The Man Who Knew Coolidge: Being the Soul of Lowell Schmaltz, Constructive and Nordic Citizen* (New York: Harcourt, Brace, 1928), 30, 23–24.

50. H. L. Mencken, *Mencken Chrestomathy* (New York: Knopf Doubleday, 2012), 251–52.

51. Fuess, *Calvin Coolidge*, 43.

PART III

Emergencies

"*We* are *and* will *be* forever *Anti-Slavery Men!*"

Student Abolitionists and Subversive Politics at Amherst College, 1833–1841

Michael E. Jirik

Commencement morning of August 26, 1835, began as usual for students, as they arrived at college chapel for morning prayers. After the service, however, Robert C. McNairy, a sophomore from Tennessee, and John L. Ashby, a junior from New Hampshire, confronted each other. The situation turned bloody, as McNairy violently bludgeoned Ashby with a heavy cane. Students and administrators attributed McNairy's attack to southern proslavery animosity toward northern antislavery sentiment. College faculty investigated and concluded that McNairy "violently attack[ed] and cruelly beat a fellow-student, with a heavy cane, thus maiming his person, if not putting his life in jeopardy." He was expelled from the college.[1] The McNairy-Ashby incident, eerily foreshadowing representative Preston Brooks's violent caning of senator Charles Sumner twenty-one years later, was a chapter in a larger conflict over slavery at Amherst College.

Beginning in 1833, a group of Amherst College students organized an antislavery society on campus, which precipitated a significant conflict with faculty.[2] Amherst student abolitionism emerged as white evangelicals were debating the merits of immediate abolition versus colonization. Amherst students took part in these debates, propelling some to activism in abolition where they embraced immediate emancipation and racial equality. Student activism conflicted with the faculty's support of colonization, creating a unique student-faculty confrontation.

Amherst faculty included active leaders in local and state auxiliaries of the American Colonization Society (ACS). They categorically rejected abolitionist ideology and sought to suppress students' abolitionist activism.[3] Faculty efforts, however, had limited success, as students continued to support abolition in spite of faculty restrictions. This chapter shows that the Amherst student antislavery society predated the famous Lane Debates in Ohio in February 1834, signifying student involvement in abolition beyond the famous Lane Rebels.

By the mid-1830s, increasing white reactionary violence against abolitionists, including the murder of the abolitionist editor Elijah Lovejoy, led to the convergence of abolitionist advocacy with assertions for civil liberties, which shaped student activism.[4] Abolitionists argued their activism was protected under the Constitutional provisions of free speech.

Students reorganized an abolition society at Amherst College in the late 1830s, invoking their right to abolitionist activism and forcing faculty to reverse their sanctions. Student abolitionism flourished at the college from 1837 to 1841, at which time students shifted their support from the American Antislavery Society (AASS) to the evangelical, political wing of the movement. While ideological disagreements among abolitionists existed, students represented an expansion in the constituency of the abolitionist rank and file. Abolitionists from all camps comprised a radical social movement for racial equality.[5] The history of student abolition at Amherst College provides a unique window into the history of the abolition movement and student activism.

Historians have often examined controversies over slavery, abolition, and colonization at institutions of higher learning such as Lane Seminary and Oberlin College, presenting these cases as atypical or unique.[6] These histories are tremendously important but overlook the role of students and colleges more generally in the abolition movement.[7]

From its inception in 1821, Amherst College was associated with Congregationalism and the evangelical fervor of the period. The institution aimed "to advance the kingdom of Christ the Redeemer by training many pious youth for the gospel ministry," and its founders believed that Jesus had "opened a way for the restoration and salvation of all men on the condition of repentance towards God."[8] Heman Humphrey, the second president of the college, promoted these ideals and emphasized that each student would receive a "moral education," preparing him for a career as minister or missionary.[9] Students would invoke these same ideals through an abolitionist lens to justify their activism.

Integral to the beliefs of most white evangelicals at Amherst College and in New England more generally in the 1820s, however, was their devotion to the colonization movement.[10] Members of the ACS believed African Americans could never be equal to white Americans and that the removal of free black people would benefit the country socially, politically, and economically. The ACS had a national constituency of white southerners who supported the removal of free blacks but not the end of slavery, as well as white northerners who promoted a gradualist antislavery approach to emancipation, with slaveholders manumitting enslaved people voluntarily. Over time, the cross-sectional support of slaveholders and conservative antislavery members proved debilitating to the organization's platform. Most importantly, the vast majority of African Americans vehemently opposed colonization and refused to comply with its racist scheme of removal. Black opposition to the ACS ultimately transformed abolition into an interracial movement in the 1830s.[11]

Northern white evangelical clergy supported colonization as part of a wider enterprise of benevolent activities. They hoped to remedy what they perceived as public evils, such as the consumption of alcohol, and revive religious piety in the United States. Removing black people from the polity was part of these endeavors. They also infused the ACS with a missionary outlook, hoping to spread Christianity throughout Africa.[12] Their writings and leadership of local colonization organizations show that Amherst College faculty were active colonizationists.

In 1825, professor of rhetoric and oratory Samuel M. Worcester published several essays supporting antislavery measures, culminating in a call for colonization. He believed the ACS was "the most flattering and magnificent" project of benevolence and that emancipation "will be the work of years," perhaps unfolding over "fifty or hundred years." Worcester underpinned his colonizationist arguments with racist ideas, writing that unless structural social changes occur, free blacks "must forever be excluded from a free and indiscriminate participation in the rank and privileges of the white inhabitants" of the United States. He also believed enslaved people needed preparation for freedom and "must be furnished with a residence, where their color shall subject them to no disqualification" as free people.[13] While Worcester opposed slavery, he also opposed racial equality. Worcester and Heman Humphrey collected donations from students and residents of Amherst for the ACS. In 1831, Worcester helped establish the Massachusetts Colonization Society, and in 1832, Humphrey became the president of the Hampshire County Colonization Society.[14] Amherst faculty were important leaders of the ACS at the local and state level, condemning abolitionists as radical agitators and dangerous advocates of a multiracial society.[15] Amherst College became an ACS stronghold.

Along with the advent of the ACS on campus, the 1830s marked a period of rapid growth for the young college. During the college's first decade, enrollment tended to fluctuate between one hundred and thirty and one hundred and fifty students.[16] By 1833, however, a total of two hundred and fifty students matriculated at the school, making it the second largest college in New England. Amherst College historian William Tyler attributed the growth to religious revivals of the Second Great Awakening and the college's mission to foster young ministers and missionaries.[17] The increase in enrollment of white southern students accounted for part of the expansion, changing the demographics of the student body. This, in turn, facilitated the growth of competing ideologies over the question of slavery.

As the student body at Amherst grew, the abolition movement evolved. While black abolitionists and their white allies had been fighting slavery and racial inequality since the Revolutionary Era, opposition to the ACS invigorated abolitionism. African Americans and some white evangelicals together called for immediate emancipation and racial equality. While William Lloyd Garrison famously established the *Liberator* in 1831, his abolitionist newspaper was the product of black abolitionist activism represented in David Walker's *Appeal* (1829) and Samuel Cornish's abolitionist newspaper *Freedom's Journal*. African American subscriptions largely kept Garrison's newspaper afloat. In this context, Garrison emerged as a leader in the movement.[18]

Garrison's arguments had a profound impact on Amherst students. The student periodical, the *Shrine*, reviewed Garrison's anticolonization pamphlet called *Thoughts on African Colonization*. The anonymous reviewer concluded that Garrison's "opinions will have great weight," and encouraged students to consider his arguments.[19] After reading the column, some students began to embrace Garrison's brand of abolition on moral grounds, challenging the faculty's colonizationist ideology. In a debate in the Athenian Society on July 10, 1833, Amherst students explored the competing ideologies. After a heated exchange, the student literary society voted in favor of colonization, as society president Henry Ward Beecher, the son of Lyman Beecher, cast the deciding vote.[20] The outcome of the debate suggests the lingering influence of the faculty and their colonizationist sentiments. In the wake of the victory, students and faculty established an official auxiliary to the ACS on campus.[21]

That the debate even occurred, however, and the decidedly slim margin in favor of colonization indicated abolitionist sentiment was prevalent on campus. After students and faculty organized their ACS auxiliary, eight students resolved to create an abolition society. On July 19, 1833, Samuel Tappan (a distant relative of Arthur and Lewis Tappan), Horace Gray, Thomas Harvey, David Fisk, and Milton Fisher were among the eight students who founded the Amherst Auxiliary Antislavery Society (AAASS), one of the first antislavery societies in western Massachusetts.

Students identified themselves as abolitionists, and the society's constitution affirmed student support for the American Antislavery Society (AASS).[22] The preamble declared, "Slavery is contrary to the precepts of Christianity, dangerous to the liberties of the country, and ought immediately be abolished." Citizens of New England had the right to protest slavery and were morally obligated to do so.[23] Article two of their constitution revealed the radicalism of the students: "Objects of [the] society shall be to endeavor by all means sanctioned by law, humanity, and religion to: effect the abolition of slavery in the United States, improve the character and condition of the free people of color, to inform and correct public opinion in relation to their situation and rights, and to obtain for them equal civil and political rights and privileges with the whites."[24] Students advocated for immediate emancipation. They pledged to reform society and to fight for African Americans' civil and political rights. Members invoked evangelical ideology to justify their convictions. This marked a significant change in the short history of the college, with students for the first time supporting a radical social movement for immediate emancipation and black rights. The constitution addressed positions of leadership, procedures for elections and meetings, and required a membership fee of fifty cents, which funded the correspondences to the parent society and subscriptions to antislavery publications. The student organization would correspond with other antislavery societies[25]

Meeting minutes from 1833 provide a window into the society's early activities. On July 24, members pledged to "enlighten and educate" African Americans who lived nearby and abroad. The next recorded meetings took place on December 4 and 11, where members of the competing antislavery and colonization societies respectfully debated their convictions. Student abolitionists remained opposed to colonization. They believed "repatriation" was an injustice to African Americans because it reinforced racial prejudices and would "weaken the strength of the whole" of the movement.[26] Interest in abolition and AAASS's membership grew on campus from the original eight to upwards of seventy members.[27]

Lecturers from national abolition societies took interest in the student abolitionists at Amherst. Arnold Buffum, the vice president of the New England Antislavery Society, visited the college as part of his lecture circuit that stretched across Massachusetts and greater New England. Buffum's visit and conversations with students encouraged their activism. Buffum later reported that he conversed with "many fine young men" who possessed "correct views and principles upon all important subjects."[28] Amherst student abolitionists were recognized as a significant constituency that underpinned the leading antislavery organizations in the country. Buffum believed Amherst students were important advocates of abolition who would spread the movement, and, as young people, they were the future leaders of the country. Amherst faculty, however, worked to remove organized activity from the college.

External influences, particularly the Lane Controversy, played a decisive role in shaping Amherst faculty's perspective regarding student abolitionism. After the Lane Rebels overtly defied Lyman Beecher and his administration by working with African Americans for racial uplift, Beecher met with college officials from New England and unanimously agreed to quell all antislavery agitation at colleges.[29] The activism of the Lane students convinced Amherst faculty that antislavery agitation could tarnish the school's reputation and disrupt the peace and prosperity of academic institutions. If Amherst became associated with abolition, the school would also lose southern patronage.[30] Faculty believed it was necessary to order the dissolution of both the antislavery and colonization societies.[31]

Meeting minutes from August 11, 1834, suggest that student abolitionists were aware of the growing opposition to their organization. They unanimously approved a resolution stating that members had "no objections to the principles or measures of the Society."[32] The resolution affirmed members' steadfast abolitionist convictions and defended their organization against the possibility of suppression from college leadership. The members continued to hold meetings, but they soon faced the institutional power of the faculty.

In the fall of 1834, President Humphrey formally demanded the dissolution of the campus antislavery and colonization societies. Faculty believed the mission of the institution was not founded on political reform and feared the reputation and success of the college would be endangered if the societies continued unchecked.[33] Colonizationists on campus acquiesced, but an auxiliary to the ACS existed in the Amherst community, where students and faculty could continue their activism.[34] However, student abolitionists did not have the same benefit. The arguments of the faculty were hypocritical, as they had already aligned the college with the inherently political colonization movement. Student abolitionists posed a threat to colonization, and their presence forced faculty to demand that both organizations disband. In this sense, student abolitionist exerted a powerful, subversive influence on Humphrey and the faculty, giving abolition a victory in its own right.

On October 11, 1834, student abolitionists convened at the special request of Humphrey to discuss his recommendation to dissolve the society. After some deliberation, Joseph Haven motioned for the society to "henceforth and forever disband." The motion was discussed "rationally" with a "good degree of interest" but was unanimously voted down, and the members moved to draft a response to the administration's request.[35] At the next meeting, students petitioned Humphrey, refusing to end their organized activities.[36] Over the next four months, a fascinating correspondence unfolded between the faculty and members of the society.

The student abolitionists explained their opposition to the sanction: they could not disband because they morally opposed slavery and were devoted to abolishing it. Representing the students, John E. Farwell wrote of their professors, "We know that they are our guardians, and seek our welfare both for time and eternity" and believe their requests were "made in love." Yet, the young abolitionists could not ignore that over two million of their countrymen were enslaved. They heard "the clanking of their chains" and "their moving pleas for deliverance." The students invoked the golden rule, "do unto others as you would want done to you," to illustrate their commitment to abolition.[37]

Over the course of fifteen months, the students wrote, their membership had increased from eight to over seventy individuals. Their activities consisted of meeting for discussion and prayer for enslaved people, and they resented the indictment that their society was detrimental to the peace of the institution, as they conducted their activities without strife.[38] While student abolitionists acknowledged their ideological opposition to student colonizationists, some members were their "best" and "dearest friends," and they continued to "tenderly love and esteem them."[39]

The students justified abolition by equating it to "the cause of God—the cause of humanity" and demanded their monthly abolitionist prayer meetings continue.[40] Yet, they ultimately deferred to the faculty's judgment, "But if you think the good of the College requires that our body should be dissolved, we pray you to do the work yourselves. Should such be your course with us, we hope to exercise all becoming submission, we will be the very last persons to offer resistance; but-we say it with the kindest feelings-we cannot-No! We cannot be our own destroyer."[41] The student response revealed that faculty retained patriarchal authority over the student body despite the overt challenge student abolitionism posed. The letter ultimately exhibited students' devotion to abolition while unhappily leaving the fate of their organization to the faculty.

Over a month later, students received the faculty verdict. After reviewing the matter, faculty stood by their original decision and believed the college's best interests demanded the organization disband.[42] Yet, in acknowledging the respectful and emotional rhetoric the students employed, the faculty realized the dissolution of the society "would be . . . afflictive" for its members.[43] They proposed that the organization could continue operating if it adhered to specific regulations. It could only meet once a month for prayer, new members could join but soliciting them was prohibited, formal addresses and discussions were banned, and the society was barred from corresponding with other societies and abolitionist editors.[44] The faculty reasoned that those regulations were intended "to guard against Evil internal and external" that would potentially pervade the college.[45] The faculty also maintained their intention was not to influence students' opinion on slavery and would allow civil discussions to continue, but only under their supervision.[46]

This decision signified the influence of the Lane Controversy on the faculty's policy, as they decided to restrict and not completely suppress abolition on campus, hoping to avoid a major conflict with student activists. The faculty provisions would severely limit the activities of the students, reducing them to monthly prayer services. The final sanction prohibiting any communication or subscription to antislavery publications and their editors was especially crippling, as the society subscribed to and read abolitionist publications. Without these connections, members would be forced to operate in isolation.

The AAASS met twice to discuss the faculty's provisions and determine the future of their organization. After serious deliberation, student abolitionists voted unanimously that they could not consciously "as men and Christians" comply with the regulations and forwarded their sentiments to Humphrey.[47]

News of the correspondence between the faculty and students spread rapidly. The *Emancipator* reprinted an article from the *New York Evangelist* of the correspondence between the faculty and the young abolitionists. The editor of the *Emancipator* reported it was "with deep sorrow that we record these proceedings of Amherst College, derogatory to freedom and humanity—No discussion allowed, no communication with the press," and concluded that these events would only "add fuel to the flame."[48] The events surrounding abolition at Amherst College became well known in New England and to the subscribers of antislavery publications. Continued faculty suppression of abolition came close to violating students' civil liberties. The faculty's provisions and unequivocal assurance that slavery could still be debated on campus even if the society dissolved suggested that they were fully aware of the ramifications if they overtly suppressed any antislavery activity.

From the perspective of the students, however, the faculty's regulations were exceptionally strict. After reading the students' response, the faculty replied, announcing that due to the "agitated state of the public mind," the antislavery society at Amherst College "must cease to exist."[49] The following passage from the faculty reveals their awareness of conflicts over abolition at other institutions. They wrote, "It is inexpedient to keep up any organization, under the name of Anti-Slavery, Colonization, or the like, at our Literary & Theological Institutions. This, we believe, is coming to be more & more the settled judgment of the enlightened & pious friends of these Institutions, throughout the country."[50] After following the abolitionist controversy at Lane Seminary, faculty believed disbanding student organizations dealing with slavery would prevent a similar episode at Amherst. The passage shows that faculty believed competing organizations would harm the institution. And they associated abolition as the antithesis to piety and respectability. Nevertheless, faculty conveyed that their confidence in the students' "good principles and good judgment" remained unchanged.[51]

The proceedings of the AASS's subsequent meeting reveal the reactions of students to the faculty ruling. On February 23, 1835, students opened their meeting with prayer for emancipation. It was noted that the meeting was "unusually well-attended," as the fate of their organization was to be decided.[52] After members read the faculty's response, attendees passed several motions that suggested the members would continue their active participation in abolition despite the demise of their formal organization. Members voted: to continue their "monthly subscription," which would be forwarded to the AASS, to "publish the proceedings and communication with faculty," and for the secretary to retrieve from the post office the *Liberator* and *Emancipator* and make them available in his room for those who wanted to read them.[53] The proceedings of this meeting ended with an impassioned resolution: "Whereas we are no longer Anti-Slavery brethren, Resolved that we *are* and *will* be *forever* Anti-Slavery Men!" and the final words, "Brethren, we are no more!"[54]

Student abolitionists continued to actively participate in the abolition movement. They continued their subscriptions and contributions to the AASS, which maintained their connection to the movement and simultaneously defied the faculty's regulations. While students were disappointed their society was dissolved, they refused to allow the faculty's ruling to destroy their morale or dictate their actions. Antislavery sentiment became increasingly prominent on campus over the next two years. The McNairy-Ashby incident occurred just six months after the dissolution of the student antislavery society and proved to be a catalyst for the revival of organized student abolitionism on campus.

Faculty's fear of agitation over the slavery question finally came to fruition and proved the editor of the *Emancipator*'s prophecy. McNairy's attack on Ashby was perceived as a manifestation of proslavery animosity toward abolitionists.[55] Even after the faculty attempted to control student agitation over slavery, they could not isolate the college from the pervasive issue. The McNairy-Ashby incident precipitated a significant shift in students' antislavery sentiments. They believed the episode was a manifestation of the broader proliferation of antiabolitionist violence in Northern states and signified an attempt to suppress antislavery free speech. Some students subsequently began to publicly support antislavery and evoked civil liberties to assert their rights to protest.

Equating abolitionist activism with civil liberties was a growing national trend in the mid-1830s. In response to antiabolition mob violence, abolitionist editors such as Garrison, James Birney, and William Goodell justified their convictions by citing the protection of the constitutional right of freedom of the press. Women abolitionists flooded Congress with antislavery petitions challenging the "gag rule." Abolitionists criticized southern politicians for denying free speech and free press to their citizenry. Southern state legislators actively suppressed antislavery sentiment in southern publications. Abolitionists asserted that they not only attacked slavery, but that the Constitution was on their side and protected their activism.[56]

The surrounding community in Amherst also became more supportive of abolition, marking another local challenge to colonization. On January 20, 1836, abolitionists held the first Hampshire County antislavery convention in Northampton and formed the "Old Hampshire Anti-Slavery Society."[57] The formation of a local antislavery society combined with the violent beating of an Amherst College student for his antislavery views would have a profound impact on the faculty's policies and subsequent revival of organized abolitionism at Amherst College.

In the fall of 1836, a few student abolitionists petitioned the faculty to resume meeting monthly for abolitionist prayer. Surprisingly, the faculty granted the students' request.[58] According to Tyler, the faculty's perspective had changed over the course of fifteen months, as opinions at the college and the surrounding community had become more favorable to abolition.[59] The combination of the McNairy-Ashby incident and the establishment of local antislavery societies likely convinced the faculty that they could no longer suppress a student antislavery organization. Also, faculty fears that antislavery hysteria would plague and cripple the institution seemed to have diminished by the fall of 1836.[60] The student petition demonstrated their continued interest in abolition on campus, despite the fact that antislavery agitation had been banned for over a year. The faculty's approval of the student petition marked a significant change.

For the next year, student abolitionists met monthly to pray for immediate emancipation. Violence toward abolitionists, such as the murder of Elijah Lovejoy for printing his abolitionist newspaper, galvanized the antislavery movement at Amherst College, as students reaffirmed their right to advocate abolition.[61] On November 18, 1837, a small group of students met privately to reinstate the antislavery society on campus.[62] They believed they had a right to organize on campus and maintained it would provide a better medium for action "in the great cause of emancipation."[63] The activists, including Euphraim Allen, Erastus Barnes, and Jesse Bragg, worked to revive the antislavery society on campus. They presented the petition to faculty on December 13, 1837.[64]

Just two days later, students met and Allen read the faculty's response. The faculty "cheerfully granted" the students' request, and the antislavery society at Amherst College was fully revived.[65] The same faculty members and president had completely reversed their decision. This policy change suggests their governing philosophy had been modified out of necessity. Student abolitionist protest, the growth of public support for abolition in the local community, and antiabolitionist violence all affected the faculty's decision.

The students went to work organizing their society. Allen, Barnes, and Bragg drafted a constitution, which aligned it with the original student society. [66] The members also voted to send an account of these events to the *Emancipator* and *Liberator* for publication. In their letter to William Lloyd Garrison, the students revealed that Lovejoy's murder motivated their efforts to reorganize on campus.[67] The remaining meeting minutes follow a procedural pattern. The meetings usually started with prayers for emancipation, members then read addresses exploring the expediency of abolition, followed by debates and votes on resolutions. The society held yearly elections for the positions of president, vice president, secretary, treasurer, and a council of representatives. The abolition society also regularly sent delegates to antislavery conventions in Northampton, Boston, and New York City.[68]

While the revived antislavery society was comparable to the original one in its abolitionist convictions, the new organization had some noteworthy differences. It was much more engaged with questions that confronted the national antislavery movement. For example, the society debated questions such as: Did the Constitution sanction slavery if properly interpreted? Members ultimately decided in the negative.[69] Amherst student abolitionists thus supported a radical abolitionist interpretation of the US Constitution. The society discussed other important questions such as: Was slaveholding always a sin? And: Could abolitionists consistently consume slave produced products? Both were voted in the affirmative. The question of whether or not slaveholders should receive compensation for liberating their slaves was decided in the negative.

Students also collected subscriptions for the abolitionist newspaper *Human Rights*, and they circulated antislavery petitions at the college and surrounding community for Congress.[70] The students at Amherst College were fully immersed in the abolition movement at the local and national levels. Their antislavery interpretation of the Constitution and their involvement in the petition campaigns are particularly significant, as they signified the direction student activism would take in subsequent years.

At a meeting on December 6, 1839, members debated whether or not abolitionism should be brought into formal politics, and members decided in the affirmative.[71] Over the course of the following year, the members of the abolition society began to affiliate with political antislavery organizations. They withdrew the society's affiliation with the Garrisonians and became an auxiliary to the American and Foreign Anti-Slavery Society (AFASS).[72] With this new status, the student abolitionists identified with evangelical abolitionists. The AFASS opposed Garrisonians who supported women's rights and denounced formal political participation and established religion. By siding with the new organization, the Amherst student abolitionists also opposed women's rights and believed in transforming churches to support abolition. After the students joined the AFASS in 1840, they started to meet less frequently.[73] In November 1841, however, the society met three times over the course of a week, when students discussed the expediency of the newly organized Liberty Party as a political abolitionist organization. Members debated the topic at two consecutive meetings and still did not exhaust the issue.[74] A third and final debate was opened to all Amherst students and was well attended.[75] After a lively three-hour discussion, members voted in conjunction with the overall student body to support the Liberty Party. The society secretary recorded the decision "as a *decided triumph* of *Abolition* over slaveocracy in this institution."[76] The entry and the records of the antislavery society at Amherst College end with a poem reading,

> "Slavery rule our sacred land
> We tell thee Southerners never
> Till our Iron Strand, and rocky land
> Are known no more forever."[77]

The last entries in the society's records demonstrate that not only the members of the society, but also the majority of Amherst students, emphatically favored political abolition and third-party politics. By November 1841, student activism made political abolitionism prominent at Amherst College. Members seemingly felt that it was unnecessary to maintain a student organization and became involved in abolitionist politics outside of the college.

The history of student abolition at Amherst College provides an early example of student activism for racial equality at an exclusively white male college. Some Amherst students converted to immediate emancipation and racial equality on religious, moral, and political grounds. Their activism precipitated an ideological conflict with college colonizationists. While initially they were forced to disband their student organization, the implications of their activism and the subversive impact it had on faculty's institutional power marked a victory for student abolitionism. Despite faculty restrictions, Amherst students remained actively involved in the movement and persistently agitated for the right to organize, which bore fruit in the late 1830s. Ultimately, the religious nature of the students' abolitionism led them to support the AFASS and political abolition. Their activism reveals that Amherst students were a crucial, youthful force in the abolitionist rank and file that countered colonization and proslavery supporters. Their support for the Liberty Party and abolition more generally marks a significant precedent in the history of radical student politics. Today's student activists interested in racial justice and equality are the heirs to the legacy of student abolitionist radicalism like that of Amherst students of the 1830s.

Notes

1. William S. Tyler, *History of Amherst College during Its First Half Century 1821–1871* (Springfield, MA: Bryan, 1873), 250–51.

2. "Constitution of the Auxiliary Anti-Slavery Society of Amherst College," *Record of the Amherst Auxiliary Anti-Slavery Society*, July 19, 1833, Anti-Slavery Records 1833–1842, Clubs and Societies Collection, Box 1, Folder 18, Amherst College Archives and Special Collections (hereafter cited as ACASP), Amherst College, Amherst, MA.

3. Tyler, *History of Amherst College*, 246.

4. Leonard Richards, *Gentlemen of Property and Standing: Anti-Abolition Mobs in Jacksonian American* (New York: Oxford University Press, 1970); David Grimsted, *American Mobbing, 1828–1861: Toward Civil War* (New York: Oxford University Press, 1998).

5. Manisha Sinha, *The Slave's Cause: A History of Abolition* (New Haven, CT: Yale University Press, 2016).

6. See, for example, Gilbert H. Barnes, *The Antislavery Impulse, 1830–1844* (New York: Harbinger, 1933), 64–78; Lawrence T. Lesick, *The Lane Rebels: Evangelicalism and Antislavery in Antebellum America* (Metuchen, NJ: Scarecrow Press, 1980); J. Brent Morris, Oberlin, *Hotbed of Abolitionism: College, Community, and the Fight for Freedom and Equality in Antebellum America* (Chapel Hill: University of North Carolina Press, 2014); Carol Lasser and Gary Kornblith, *Elusive Utopia: The Struggle for Equality in Oberlin, Ohio* (Baton Rouge: Louisiana State University Press, 2018); Other important institutional histories include Herman R. Muelder, *Fighters for Freedom: The History of Anti-Slavery Activities of Men and Women Associated with Knox College* (New York: Columbia University Press, 1959); and Melton C. Sernett, *Abolition's Axe: Beriah Green Oneida Institute and the Black Freedom Struggle* (Syracuse, NY: Syracuse University Press, 1986). For a notable exception, see Craig Steven Wilder, *Ebony and Ivy: Race, Slavery, and the Troubled History of America's Universities* (New York: Bloomsbury, 2013), 241–73.

7. Michael E. Jirik, "Abolition and Academe: Struggles for Freedom and Equality at British and American Colleges, 1742–1855" (PhD dissertation, University of Massachusetts Amherst, 2019).

8. Tyler, *History of Amherst College*, 192, 193.

9. Tyler, *History of Amherst College*, 131.

10. Claude Moore Fuess, *Amherst: The Story of a New England College* (Boston, MA: Little, Brown, 1935), 110.

11. Sinha, *The Slave's Cause*, 160–171; Ousmane K. Power-Greene, *Against Wind and Tide: The African American Struggle against the Colonization Movement* (New York: New York University Press, 2014); also see P. J. Staudenraus, *The African Colonization Movement, 1816–1865* (New York: Columbia University Press, 1961).

12. "American Colonization in Massachusetts," *African Repository and Colonial Journal* (hereafter *ARCJ*) 9, no. 7 (September 1833): 219; Staudenraus, *The African Colonization Movement*, 117–35; George M. Fredrickson, *The Black Image in the White Mind: The Debate on Afro-American Character and Destiny, 1817–1914* (New York: Harper and Row, 1971), 6, 7.

13. Samuel M. Worcester, ed., *Essays on Slavery* (Amherst, MA: Carter, 1826), 5–28. Worcester published his essays anonymously as "Vigornious." See David Brion Davis, *From Homicide to Slavery: Studies in American Culture* (New York: Oxford University Press, 1986), 252.

14. "Contributions," *ARCJ* 5, no. 5 (July 1829): 159; "Contributions," *ARCJ* 6, nos. 1 and 8 (March and October 1830): 32, 250; *ARCJ* 7, nos. 1, 6, and 8 (March, August, October 1831): 28, 187; *ARCJ* 8, nos. 8 and 9 (October, November 1832): 282–-83, quoted on 248; "Contributions," *ARCJ* 8, no. 11 (January 1833), 352; Staudenraus, *The African Colonization Movement*, 132-33.

15. Wilder, *Ebony and Ivy*, 266; Fuess, *Amherst*, 110.

16. Tyler, History of Amherst College, 161, 244.

17. Tyler, *History of Amherst College*, 242–44.

18. Sinha, *The Slave's Cause*; 195–227.

19. "Literary Notices," *The Shrine* 1, no. 2 (1832), Student and Alumni Publications Collections, Box 13, ACASP, Amherst College, Amherst, MA.

20. Athenian Society Records, 1831–1846, Box 12, Folder 17, ACASP, Amherst College, Amherst, MA.

21. *ARCJ* 9, no. 7 (September 1833): 216.

22. "Constitution of the Auxiliary," Box 1, Folder 18.

23. "Constitution of the Auxiliary."

24. "Constitution of the Auxiliary," article 2.

25. "Constitution of the Auxiliary," Box 1, Folder 19.

26. Entries of July 24, 1833; December 4, 1833; and December 11, 1833, *Record of the Amherst College Anti-Slavery Society*, Anti-Slavery Records, 1833–1842, Clubs and Societies Collection, ACASP, Amherst College, Amherst, MA.

27. "Constitution of the Auxiliary."

28. Arnold Buffum, "To the Board of Managers of the New England Anti-Slavery Society," *Liberator*, September 14, 1833, 146–47; Richard Newman, *The Transformation of American Abolitionism: Fighting Slavery in the Early Republic* (Chapel Hill: University of North Carolina Press, 2002), 154, 141.

29. Article from the *Boston Courier* reprinted under the subhead "Refuge of Oppression," *Liberator*, July 25 1835, 117; for the events at Lane, see Lesick, *The Lane Rebels*.

30. Wilder, *Ebony and Ivy*, 286; Tyler, *History of Amherst College*, 246.

31. Tyler, 246.

32. Entry of August 11, 1834, ACASP.

33. Tyler, *History of Amherst College*, 246.

34. *ARCJ* 9, no. 7 (September 1833): 216.

35. Entry of October 11, 1834, *Record of the Amherst College Anti-Slavery Society*, ACASP.

36. Entry of October 20, 1834, ACASP.

37. John E. Farwell, Henry G. Pendleton, et al., "Letter to the Faculty of Amherst College," October 21, 1834, *Amherst College Anti-Slavery Society*, ACASP, Amherst College, Amherst, MA.

38. Farwell, Pendleton, et al., "Letter to the Faculty"; Tyler, *History of Amherst College*, 247–48.

39. Farwell, Pendleton, et al., "Letter to the Faculty."

40. Farwell, Pendleton et al.

41. Farwell, Pendleton et al.

42. Faculty of Amherst College, "To the Committee of the Anti-Slavery Society in Amherst College," November 26, 1834, *Amherst College Anti-Slavery Society*, ACASP, Amherst College, Amherst, MA.

43. Faculty, "To the Committee."

44. Faculty, "To the Committee."

45. Faculty, "To the Committee."

46. Faculty, "To the Committee."

47. Entries of December 22, 1834; December 29, 1834, ACASP; William G. Howard, David Andrews, Edward Pritchett, "Letter to the Faculty of Amherst College", January 7, 1835, *Amherst College Anti-Slavery Society*, ACASP, Amherst College, Amherst, MA.

48. *Emancipator*, January 20, 1835; Tyler, *History of Amherst College*, 249.

49. Heman Humphrey, "To the Committee of the Anti-Slavery Society in Amherst College," February 19, 1835, *Amherst College Anti-Slavery Society*, ACASP, Amherst College, Amherst, MA.

50. Humphrey, "To the Committee."
51. Humphrey, "To the Committee."
52. Entry of February 23, 1835, ACASP.
53. February 23, 1835.
54. February 23, 1835.
55. Tyler, *History of Amherst College*, 250; Wilder, *Ebony and Ivy*, 272; Fuess, *Amherst*, 111.
56. Sinha, *The Slave's Cause*, 228–46; Russel B. Nye, *Fettered Freedom: Civil Liberties and the Slavery Controversy, 1830–1860* (Lansing: Michigan State University Press, 1963), 123–27.
57. "Anti-Slavery Convention in Old Hampshire," *Liberator*, February 13, 1836, 25–26.
58. Tyler, *History of Amherst College*, 250; Brigham, "Amherst College," 122.
59. Tyler, 250.
60. Tyler, 250.
61. Wilder, *Ebony and Ivy*, 282.
62. Entry of November 18, 1837, *Amherst College Anti-Slavery Society*, Anti-Slavery Records 1833–1842, Clubs and Societies Collection, Box 1, Folder 20, ACASP.
63. November 18, 1837, ACASP.
64. Entry of November 25, 1837, ACASP.
65. Entry of December 15, 1837, ACASP.
66. Entries of December 19, 1837; December 26, 1837, ACASP.
67. Entry of December 29, 1837, 1837–1841, ACASP; "Amherst College," *Liberator*, February 9, 1838.
68. Entries of December 29, 1837; April 6, 1838; July 13, 1838; August 20, 1838; February 8, 1839; July 12, 1839, ACASP.
69. Entry of February 9, 1838, ACASP.
70. Entries of December 29, 1837; March 9, 1838; April 6, 1838; June 22, 1838; July 13, 1838; October 18, 1838; August 4, 1839, ACASP.
71. Entry of December 6, 1839, ACASP.
72. Entries of April 2, 1840; June 1840; July 14, 1840, ACASP.
73. After the July 14, 1840, vote to align with the AFASS, there is not a record of the society meeting until January 1841.
74. Entries of November 8, 1841; November 12, 1841, ACASP.
75. Entry of November 15, 1841, ACASP.
76. November 15, 1841, ACASP.
77. November 15, 1841, ACASP.

"Some of the Sweetest Christians"

The Wartime Education of Amherst's Boys in Blue

Bruce Laurie

The bombardment of Ft. Sumter in Charleston harbor, South Carolina, on April 12, 1861, by the Army of the Confederate States of America evoked an outbreak of war fever on the normally sedate campus of Amherst College. Students and faculty alike turned from classrooms and lecture halls to the prospect of war. The South had committed treason, broken the sacred bond of union sealed in the hallowed Constitution, and exposed themselves to the full fury of Yankee patriots said to be spoiling for the fight. Five days later, the students received permission to hold an assembly in Johnson Chapel, where college president William A. Stearns sermonized movingly on "truth" and "liberty." Chemistry professor William Smith Clark followed with a somber reading of the Declaration of Independence. The sobered audience joined in a reading of appropriate psalms and then filed out onto the lawn to raise the US flag over the chapel.

The otherwise sleepy town, which had opposed both the War of 1812 and "Mr. Polk's War" on Mexico in 1846, likewise caught the fever with a comparable outburst of patriotism, as porches and storefronts unfurled the national colors. Southern students, whose numbers had grown in recent years, packed their bags and headed home; some students (the numbers are disputed, but anywhere from twenty to thirty) signed an enlistment roster that Clark put on a table outside the chapel and started drilling in anticipation of what lay ahead.

Not everyone was so enthusiastic. One of the dissenting voices came from the brother of a student who presciently predicted that the other slave states would probably follow South Carolina into rebellion, "in which case our difficulties will be still more serious." He added just as presciently that talk of a "quick war" was nonsense; it will be "no boy's play."[1]

This chapter takes a close look at the Amherst students and graduates who joined the Union army or serviced the army on the battlefield. It will spare the reader coverage of the quality of the generals, the minutiae of battlefield tactics, and other matters of military history that have long preoccupied both Civil War buffs and professional historians. I am more interested in exploring the backgrounds and experiences of the Amherst men and boys in uniform, particularly their initial motivations and evolving feelings, not only about

Figure 1. William Smith Clark. Amherst Biographical Records, photographic file. Courtesy of Amherst College Archives and Special Collections, Amherst College, Amherst, MA.

the war but also about slavery, which was the basic cause of the war. As we will see, some of them looked at the conflict through the lens of abolitionism at the start of the conflict. For most of them, however, their religious faith in combination with personal experiences among newly freed slaves decisively changed their views of enslavement—and of African Americans.

When William Smith Clark set up his recruitment table outside Johnson Chapel, the chemistry professor imagined a fighting unit composed exclusively of Amherst boys and men. Soon afterwards, he arranged an audience with governor John Albion Andrew, a radical Republican and war enthusiast who nonetheless politely turned him down. The army, he explained, desperately needed young men from the name colleges for the officer corps who would serve the cause better while spread among the regiments. Perhaps as a courtesy to Clark, a good number were assigned to his Massachusetts 21st Regiment in which he was commissioned as a colonel. A smaller group was assigned to the 27th, but most were directed to scores of fighting units across the North.[2]

Roughly three hundred and forty current and former Amherst College students, including two hundred and forty graduates, served in the Union forces. The classes of 1861 and 1862 contributed more recruits than other annual classes (twenty-seven and thirty-eight, respectively). About fifty more came from the graduating classes of the 1830s and 1840s, and slightly more than one hundred from the classes of the 1850s. Over half of these older graduates became chaplains, physicians, and lesser medical personnel. Nearly one hundred and fifty more were commissioned officers, heavily weighted toward the lower ranks of lieutenants and captains; only ninety-three entered and left as privates.

Perhaps the imbalance between officers and privates explains the comparatively low casualty rate (8 percent versus 15 percent for the Union army as a whole); only forty-two perished, fifteen on the battlefield and the rest from disease, chiefly from various forms of fever. Another forty or so were said to have suffered nonfatal wounds or disease.[3]

Who were these soldiers? Amherst College was founded in 1821 for boys, from what was known at the time as "the country," a holy bulwark against the "tidewater heresies" of the liberal cities.[4] President William A. Stearns declared in 1856, "Scarcely anything in America is more distinctly American than the relation between the colleges and the common people."[5] But not any common people. The college attracted ordinary youths from the villages of New England—not the backwaters or seaports, but more prosperous towns in between; places like Ashfield, Massachusetts, Saxton's River, Vermont, or Bangor, Maine. Of all the soldiers who attended Amherst, very few hailed from the commercial cities of the region—or its industrializing towns. A lad from Chicopee Falls, Massachusetts, was one of the rare children of industrialization. [6]

Why did they sign up? To judge from the memoirs, reminiscences, and correspondence of Amherst College students, there was a mix of motives, the most prominent being a sense of duty and patriotism, the sentiments that initially motivated William Smith Clark. For this reason, time and again, soldiers referred to the enemy as "treasonous rebels," or "rebels," and the war itself as "the rebellion." A good number at the start of the conflict were said to be keen to "have a share in crushing the rebellion."

One of the oldest volunteers was Timothy Robinson Cressy (class of 1828) who became a chaplain. When the war broke out, his father gathered his children around him to explain that their ancestors' military service extended back in an unbroken line to the French and Indian War, so that the "dignity" and duty of the Cressy family had to be maintained.[7] Family pressures also motivated John Perkins Apthorp (class of 1861) who enlisted in the 10th Massachusetts Light Battery, two years after his brother William Lee Apthorp (class of 1859), who fought in the New York 90th Regiment as well as the 34th United States Colored Infantry.[8] These soldiers referred repeatedly to "duty." The Rhode Island schoolteacher

Henry Reuben Piece (class of 1853) told his students as he prepared to leave, "I hold in my hand a strange weapon [a sword given to him by them]. If I fall, I shall fall in the path of duty." He did fall at the battle of New Bern, and he was buried in a mausoleum that he himself had built before he enlisted.[9]

Scholars of "Billy Yank," who stress peer pressure as a motivator, have a point: Amherst students followed the war as closely as merchants followed commodity prices. [10] News of battles and casualties circulated kinetically through the campus. Accounts of deaths brought grief but also provoked signups. A student who, in 1863, reported the tragic death of Frazar Stearns, the son of the president, observed, "The effect of his death cannot be over-estimated." It aroused great "enthusiasm and patriotism," helping to account for the enlistment bulge of that year.[11] Early recruits who had interrupted their schooling to fight and then resumed their studies were greeted with rapt attention. Their war stories unquestionably pushed some students into uniform. Agents from religious groups associated with Christian sects and lay groups also had an effect. A student who heard a talk on campus from a representative of the American Bible Society, fresh from the lower South, was impressed to learn that he had recruited fifteen young women from Mount Holyoke Seminary to go into the region in order to teach "freedmen." He was there to encourage "Christian young men" to follow their example, either as missionaries or soldiers.[12]

The earliest volunteers appear to have been the more eager soldiers, often with excessive brio for the sacred cause. Frazar Stearns had spent a sullen boyhood doubting his faith and badly in need of counseling. He reached out to Edward Dickinson, the father of the poet Emily Dickinson and longtime college treasurer. A distant and seemingly icy figure locally known as "the Squire," Dickinson nursed the boy through his blues with sensitive mentoring. In a touching correspondence, Stearns addressed his surrogate father with the unlikely affectionate nickname of "Eddy."[13] Stearns entered his teenage years agonizing over choosing a suitable career. As he entered Amherst College, he saw the war as the chance to test himself—to settle on something productive. He would become a soldier, perhaps an officer, and in any event, he would be all in. He was reported to be one of the first students to sign up—and one of the first to die. At the battle of New Bern in March of 1862, his face gushing blood from a bullet wound, he "rushed forward with his comrades into the teeth of the enemy's battery." Not long afterwards, he was found "cheering on the men to charge upon the enemy," only to be cut down by Confederate fire.[14] Such foolhardy bravado among Amherst soldiers was not uncommon. David Hill, who enlisted in October 1862, was promoted to captain in January 1863 and saw action in the bloodiest battles in Virginia over the next two years. He commanded the reckless charge into the rows of Confederate riflemen at the battle of Spotsylvania in 1864. As his unit encountered the last line of the enemy, he grabbed the regimental flag dropped by the color guard lying dead in the pits and, pressing forward with colors in hand, screamed at the enemy, "Lay down your arms!" before taking fire that shattered his hand.[15] Hill was fortunate to fight another day. Christopher Pennell was not so fortunate. Pennell, the son of a Berkshire County minister, skewered conflict-averse commanders who held back. At the disastrous battle of Petersburg in July 1864, when his comrades "began to waiver" and "ceased to advance," he seized the flag and rushed headlong into a killing rain of enemy fire.[16]

Figure 2. Frazar Stearns. Amherst biographical records, photographic file. Courtesy of Amherst College Archives and Special Collections, Amherst College, Amherst, MA.

Figure 3. Christopher Pennell. Amherst biographical records, photographic file. Courtesy of Amherst College Archives and Special Collections, Amherst College, Amherst, MA.

Young Pennell would not have been in uniform at all but for his dogged persistence. He had listened intently to Professor Clark's patriotic speech at Johnson Chapel soon after Sumter. He tried to sign up then and there, but at sixteen, he was underage and needed his father's permission. "Our cause is God's cause" he wrote to his father. "It is a sacred duty to fight now. Yield to the South & the blackness of the dark ages will overspread the whole land." He insisted that he needed to fight "the traitors," adding that "the fellows want me to sign" Clark's roster. [17] His father argued that it was a waste of talent for college boys to do the fighting; better to leave the dirty work of the war to the unwashed who would not be missed as much, echoing a common argument among war doubters.[18] Christopher snapped, "I don't like that sentiment. The poor boys that were murdered at Baltimore left families. Do not say they are not missed."[19]

A similar intergenerational drama played out in no less of a place than the Stearns's household. The president was not eager to see Frazar in uniform for fear that he would never return.[20] Frazar proved to be one of the college's very ardent young warriors. He was extremely hard on "political" generals and officers he thought were cowardly or plainly inept, a common feeling among his peers. Freshly in uniform in October 1861, he wrote to his sister that he was "heartsick to be commanded by a Col. who knows no more than—I can express."[21] He spent hours poring over military manuals and recommending measures to improve recruitment. As a junior officer, he strictly enforced minute regulations down to drilling instructions, only to suffer resentment from raw recruits and superior officers alike.[22]

Amherst men were passionate correspondents. They often wrote home to parents, friends, and sweethearts, pining for news from the home front. Christopher Pennell wrote sometimes daily to his parents and the girl he left behind, Sabra Snell, a local young woman with a stern mother with an uncompromising sense of propriety. He had professed his love for her daughter, but Mrs. Snell forbade him to correspond with her for a year in order to test his sincerity. In June 1864, sometime before the expiration of the aching probationary period, he had had enough, writing Mrs. Snell to assure her that he didn't belong to the "class of whining lovers," that his affection for Sabra was true and considered.[23] When Sabra accepted his marriage proposal a month later, he confessed to her that "two sad years, full of apprehension doubt, & unquiet struggles ... [have been] effaced ... & I seem to have suddenly found an eternal fountain of gladness." He closed with the eerie prophecy, "I think it would not be so very hard to die, now."[24]

Pennell and his comrades studiously avoided the rude and rougher features of camp life—drinking, gambling, smoking, bawdy storytelling, and so forth—for more high-minded pursuits. Pennell himself was a voracious reader with catholic tastes, avidly consulting the press and dipping into Greek as well as the American Renaissance novelists and poets. Just before his untimely death, he was deep into *Les Miserables*. [25] His fellow students, Ebenezer Porter Dyer (class of 1861) and Mason W. Tyler (class of 1862) read widely as well. Dyer was fond of John Ruskin, the English art critic cum social philosopher. Tyler reported that he greatly admired *John Halifax*, a Dickensian story about a poor orphan in rural England made good.[26] Not all such breaks from the action, however, were solitary. Tyler reported from the battlefront that his chaplain organized "spelling contests, and we had a debating club that was very well patronized."[27] Many regiments formed bands and choruses, and some boasted talented singers. Frazar Stearns was said to be an accomplished singer who would take to "the woods" and hold forth in a "wonderfully clear and penetrating voice."[28]

Such pastimes proved increasingly important as the war ground on, and the bodies piled up. The early romance of the fight gradually yielded to pervasive war weariness. The loss of a college chum hit especially hard. Mason W. Tyler spent sleepless nights before the bloody battle of Spotsylvania in fear of rebel snipers and awoke one morning to see Yankee bodies "scattered all over the plain." Two of the dead were friends, one of whom he'd known "from boyhood"; another he considered "a brother," whose death left a "feeling of being deserted and left alone."[29] He confessed to a friend, "Oh . . . this cruel war . . . I am sick to death of this [war] business."[30]

Whatever the state of their morale, all soldiers had to reckon with slavery and racism, the nation's sins. As Michael E. Jirik shows in his chapter, the school had a strong antislavery legacy that may have persisted into the 1840s in the form of the Liberty Party, the nation's first political organization devoted to ending slavery. But it's difficult to assess the impact of antislavery sentiment on the students and faculty. None of them mentioned antislavery organizations in their memoirs or letters, nor did they refer to the abolitionist press or any movement luminary. No faculty member identified with the movement or campaigned for it. It's unlikely that student or faculty, devout evangelicals that they were, had much use for William Lloyd Garrison, the father of the American Anti-Slavery Society who was given to anticlerical tirades that accused the northern churches of enabling southern slavery. The American and Foreign Anti-Slavery Society, an understudied abolitionist splinter organized by prelates and lay activists as a counterweight to the Garrisonians in 1839, proved more popular on campus, but little is known of its activities.[31]

Stearns was no friend of abolitionism. The school's third president (1854–1876) had attended Andover Theological Seminary (class of 1831), where he likely fell under the influence of the school's colonizationists, an affiliation that lingered into his presidency and informed his contentious correspondence with his son. The young solider was a fresh recruit in September 1861, when he told his father that he was "troubled" over the fate of his country because of rumors that President Lincoln was considering emancipation. He had thought that the North couldn't succeed without such an audacious step, but after discussing the matter with slaveholders he encountered in Virginia, he'd changed his mind. He was startled to learn that they were "<u>more</u> anxious than <u>myself</u>" over the prospect of emancipation. It was "totally wrong," he reckoned, to declare "a general emancipation" without religious sanction.[32] Though his father often stressed their differences, they were not far apart. "The time for declaring a general act of emancipation," the president wrote back in fall 1861, "has not come yet. Providence cannot be hurried."[33] Two weeks later, he elaborated his doubts: it was not the role of Congress, nor the president, to free the slaves. Emancipation would weaken the North by dividing it. And emancipation would do no good unless the freedmen were armed, a horrifying prospect that raised the haunting question: "[What] would we do with them?" Finally, he reiterated, "I cannot hear God's voice biding us to go any further . . . but when God's providence gives the word . . . I am ready."[34]

Figure 4. William A. Stearns. Amherst biographic records, photographic file. Courtesy of Amherst College Archives and Special Collections, Amherst College, Amherst, MA.

William Stearns's dim view of African Americans was clearly shared by many men in blue. Several Amherst soldiers commented on the pervasive "prejudice" within the ranks, adding that it was especially popular with the Irish and the draftees. It deepened in the wake of the Emancipation Proclamation that effectively changed the conflict from a war for the Union to a war to destroy slavery. This measure further stoked the fires of racism by ordering the formation of African American regiments, a move that many soldiers found particularly offensive, even threatening. Bigoted soldiers made sport of the self-liberated slaves breaking for the refuge of contraband camps or working for the Union army. Some of them invented games designed to make blacks look silly. A regiment stationed in South Carolina came up with the game called "meal feet," in which black men with bound arms and feet were encouraged to dive into barrels filled with meal for a gold coin.[35]

President Stearns's positions through the second year of the conflict aligned with popular opinion in the North more broadly: prowar but against emancipation. Like many Yankees, he appears to have come around on emancipation, if not racial equality, following the enactment of the Emancipation Proclamation. It seems that even with his late and limited evolution, he continued to be more cautious than his students. Though recent scholarship on the politics of Civil War soldiers maintains that they imagined themselves as emancipationists from the start of the war, the evidence is weak for such a sweeping claim.[36] Not that there were no such fighting men; there were some from Amherst College, notably, Christopher Pennell. We have no idea of his political background or the forces that informed his point of view. Possibly, his teachers at Williston Seminary, the Easthampton preparatory school founded by the devout Christian patron Samuel Williston, influenced him, but many other Amherst students studied there as well and graduated without acquiring much of an antislavery spirit. Pennell's only biographer tells us that he was deeply affected by the outburst of religious faith and patriotism at the start of the war. Though the young student had pled his case for enlistment on religious grounds to his father—it was "sacred duty to fight now"—he struck a different note in a plea to his mother.[37] He wrote: "I am a bitter enemy to slavery & to the principle which actuates the South at present. It has been, & is, the desire of my heart . . . by honest means to abolish the system which brings God's curse upon us as a nation. It is slavery which has provoked this treason. An opportunity offers, in crushing treason, to break forever, the power of the slaveholder. I want to have a hand in the business."[38]

We might conclude from this impassioned passage that the Protestantism drilled into Pennell at Williston and then at Amherst did not always promote the conservatism of college president Stearns. This form of Protestantism was a double-edged sword that identified slavery as contrary to the compassionate word of God. It taught that African Americans were not created separately, inherently inferior to white people and condemned to servitude, but of "one blood," the same blood as white people and entitled to the same freedom, if not equality. True Christians were obliged not only to cleanse themselves of sin but also to rid the world of sin so patently manifested in chattel slavery. They did not need to hear from God, as did the college president, to fulfill their mission; they intuited the need to act. In any event, Pennell's parents gave in, and the student interrupted his education in July 1862 after his junior year, resolved to do his part for the Union and for the slaves.

Assigned to the 34th Massachusetts Regiment along with several other Amherst students, Pennell was bored and impatient with the humdrum life of soldiering between combat and the seemingly endless drilling broken by idle time in the encampments. So, he volunteered to command a black regiment. In early 1864, he was commissioned as a lieutenant in the 19th Colored Infantry, his chance to make the difference he had longed for. He was pleased with the commitment of his troops, writing that the "negroes are fast becoming perfect soldiers," that he had "high hopes of success, wherever they send us."[39]

He sometimes fretted over having to repeat himself over and over again, thinking that the lesson had sunk in, only to learn that the men "didn't understand a word of it at all."[40] Nevertheless, he was not discouraged or disheartened, convinced that the men were fully capable of self-improvement. All they needed, he stressed, was "patience," an assessment that comes up repeatedly in the correspondence of other Amherst officers in charge of black regiments.[41]

Pennell puzzled over why he eluded the "difficulties" other young officers in charge of white and black regiments encountered. He puzzled over why the men "under my control seem so attached to me."[42] One reason, it seems, was the respect he showed for his men generally and for his black soldiers in particular, both as individuals and as a group. He had at least two black servants, and in July 1863, he learned that "Speaks," one of the two, had gone missing. He and Speaks had bonded. He had deep knowledge of Speaks's wife and children because he had written to them in his name. Alarmed by Speaks's absence, Pennell went on a "long search for him," finding his body. The next day, he "went up . . . to have a proper inscription put upon [the] head-board of his grave."[43]

Pennell admired Speaks for his loyalty and faithful service. Any number of officers similarly spoke well of their black aides, even as they harbored deep and immovable prejudice against blacks as a race. It was Pennell's soldiering on the ground that deepened his understanding of African Americans and their culture. The key to his more enlightened point of view was his perception of their unusually expressive worship that not a few observers considered a form of primitivism unworthy of proper Christianity.

We get a hint of this through one of Pennell's field officers, Henry G. Thomas (class of 1858), who described the reactions of white and black soldiers just before the battle of Petersburg. Rumors that the high command reversed the original plan of attack, ordering the white units into battle ahead of his black regiment, unnerved the white units. They greeted the news with "consternation," gathering separately to discuss the "strategy" in a utilitarian, matter-of-fact way. The blacks, by contrast, received the change with reverence in the form of a "long silence" in small groups, "studying" and "waiting" like "Quakers for the spirit to move." When the spirit did arrive, "one of the singers would uplift a mighty voice, like a bard of old, in a wild sort of chant." If there was no response, "he would sing it again and again, alternating . . . the words, or more often the music. If this change met with general acceptance . . . one voice after another would chime in; in a rough harmony of three parts . . . ; other groups would join his; and the song became the song of the command." Then as word of the revised plan sunk in, there was "quiet contemplation" until "a heavy voice broke out . . . We-e looks li-ke me-en-a marchin' on, we looks li-ke men-er-war." This was not simply battle preparation; it was mission, a spirited and unifying ritual that defined his soldiers as men and Christians.[44] The carnage at Petersburg, which took down nearly nine hundred men, evoked a poetic moment from Thomas, who applauded the valor and bravery of the black troops as "heroes carved in ebony."[45]

This arresting moment of African American religiosity proved to be the final act that one of Amherst's most intriguing Civil War soldiers would witness. Soon after this incident, young Pennell was cut down by Confederate fire. His adoring comrades paid their respect by leaving his chair in the mess hall empty and his tent vacant. His parents lost their only natural son, Sabra lost her fiancé, and the college lost one of its enlightened young men.[46]

What of the racial education of noncombatants, the large number of Amherst men and boys who never saw action either because their units were not summoned into battle or because they served as medics, chaplains in uniform, or agents of Christian organizations? Shortly after the massacre at Bull Run, a group of ministers organized the Christian Commission (CC) to provide medical services, religious instruction, and consolation to injured troops; it soon ran complexes of clinics and hospitals that may well have ministered to African Americans as well. Next came the Boston Education Commission (BEC), an offshoot of the New England Freedmen's Aid Society formed in early 1862 by a group of Boston patricians. Its gaze fixed on the future, the BEC was designed for the "industrial, social, intellectual, moral, and religious improvement of persons released from slavery in the course of the war for the Union."[47] The men who served the cause in such roles pursued a different path to racial liberalism, a path blazed by their firsthand acquaintance with blacks and slavery—a dimension of the war overlooked by modern historians.

Best known to historians for its work among the freed people on the Sea Islands of South Carolina (which the planters fled at the start of the war, leaving their spreads to their slaves), the BEC deftly exploited the prestige and reach of its Brahmin founders to staff field operations with male students from the first New England colleges as well female students from the region's common schools and academies. The Boston lawyer and BEC stalwart Edward Pierce, who worked closely with Salmon P. Chase, the secretary of the treasury and the most radical member of Lincoln's cabinet, found some Amherst recruits. Ebenezer Porter Dyer (class of 1861), still another son of a pastor (from the seaside village of Hingham, Massachusetts), taught school for a year before he got the call from Pierce, the architect of the Sea Islands experiment, to manage two plantations near Beaufort, South Carolina.

The tangle of private nongovernmental organizations and official bodies like the Freedmen's Bureau have not worn well in the hands of historians, who treat them as stalking horses for modernization working to get former slaves into the fields as soon as possible in order to acclimate them to the rigors of wage labor without depending on state largesse. Self-sufficient field hands, it was believed, would become exemplars of independent free-standing farmers lifted out of dependence on their own merits and primed for the economic transformation of their region. [48]

Even if we concede naiveté behind white uplift programs in the South, it is obvious that the BEC and allied groups helped improve the health, education, and safety of freedmen and women. A paternal hand was a decided improvement over no hand at all—and a neces-

Figure 5. Ebenezer Porter Dyer. Amherst biographical records, class albums, 1861. Courtesy of Amherst College Archives and Special Collections, Amherst College, Amherst, MA.

sity in a region with a history of white supremacy and an abhorrence of emancipation and the more immediate specter of blacks in uniform or in flight from bondage. Civilian snipers and renegade soldiers shot down freemen and women and ganged up for ceremonial lynchings, years before the advent of the Ku Klux Klan.[49] It was in the midst of such perils that noncombatants like Dyer ministered to African Americans. Their experience further reveals the capacity for the moral growth and development of soldiers who, unlike Pennell, enlisted in the Union army as patriots and Christians and not antislavery enthusiasts.

When Pierce tapped Dyer for his stint at Button Hill, in Beaufort, Sout Carolina, the Amherst graduate harbored preconceived notions of African Americans drawn from "Ordway's and Buckley's [minstrel shows]. I expected to find the negroes a happy contented race . . . given to the music and art of personal decoration."[50] He instead learned from his charges who, like their counterparts elsewhere, told Yankee soldiers who would listen of the terrors of slavery—the rule of the lash, tearful family separations, and unbridled sexual exploitation of women. He was horrified to see the "sweating box," a zinc-lined barrel fitted with steam pumps to scald recalcitrant slaves.[51] He grew increasingly sympathetic, not only because of the stories of abuse and mistreatment but also for the freed people's eagerness to learn at a school he set up, called "the Button Hill College for Colored People." It was one of many schools promoted by self-described "Gideonites," Northern-born reformers who descended on the Sea Islands, bibles in hand. Many of them were women teachers from New England with the best of intentions, imbued with the idea that education was the transformative force for a better life in freedom.

Some Yankees like Dyer, who established schools and recruited black soldiers, also bent energies toward economic reform. Dyer was one of the radicalized volunteers who insisted that the field hands, having worked the Sea Islands' fertile soil for free for generations, deserved to be paid for their toil. A sketchy payment scheme he implemented not long after he arrived was part of a more ambitious project of turning the newly freed wageworkers into petty producers, landowners who embodied the dream of free labor ideologues like Dyer himself.[52] He later teamed up with area superintendents—and abolitionists in the civil sphere—to resist the federal government's plan to sell off area plantations to the highest bidders for fear they would fall into the hands of racist entrepreneurs, sealing off hopes of black proprietorship. Dyer and his friends envisioned purchasing the plantations and holding them in trust until it was deemed "expedient" for sale to their field hands.[53] When the superintendents failed to raise enough funds to float their project, Dyer acted on his own, attending a land auction with the intent of organizing his own trust for his workers, only to be edged out by another bidder seemingly less inhibited by Yankee frugality. "Had I considered the subject as much and as carefully as I have since," he reflected in regret, "I should have bought this place, and held it for the colored people, until they could come into possession of it themselves."[54]

Dyer's nearly yearlong stint at Button Hill didn't completely erase his initial impressions of African Americans. He continued to cast a critical eye on the families in his care, complaining of petty theft, dishonesty, and fraught domestic relations. Family quarrels tested his good will, as did frustrating interventions in disputes to adjudicate pilfering. He couldn't help but "wonder," he once wrote in exasperation, whether "some of these people needed the lash."[55] Not long after he started his payment scheme, he introduced a ticketing system to keep track of the field hands' output and curb cheating.[56] He once expressed gratitude for the crafty work of a black spy for the army who was "very intelligent . . . for a negro."[57]

That said, Dyer gradually made his way to higher moral ground. Despite his use of paternalistic and sometimes demeaning terminology, his views reflected the aspirations of the black Sea Islanders. He was confident of their capacity to grow into "a happy, industrious, and law-abiding, free and Christian people."[58] It would not happen overnight, or within the year, he warned; it would take over a "generation," but happen it would if whites had "the courage and patience" to heal the injuries inflicted by centuries of enslavement.[59]

Figure 6. Joseph Allen Leach. Amherst biographical records, class albums, 1861. Courtesy of Amherst College Archives and Special Collections, Amherst College, Amherst, MA.

He left with some disappointments, none greater than losing the bid for the Button Hill plantation, but also with considerable pride. On the eve of his departure, he mused that "several" black children could "read very well. . . . I think their improvement equals that of white children, with the same amount of teaching. The new generation of negroes," he reckoned with characteristic optimism, "will not be like their fathers."[60]

Dyer was scarcely the only Amherst student to learn to despise slavery and think better of its victims. Joseph Allen Leach, a classmate of Dyer, had been assigned to serve in the United States Colored Infantry (USCI) 19th Regiment before being reassigned to a regular combat unit.[61] But his initial role made a huge impression on him—so much so that he appealed to return to it as a chaplain "as soon as I could."[62] He gave no thought to the economic aspects of his mission, for he was not a reformer, only a Christian "called upon" to act as one. He was transformed, however, by witnessing slavery up close in Virginia, writing to one of his professors: "[My] interest and love" for the slave "deepens every day. I went down into one little room of one slave owners [*sic*] quarters and saw 12 or 15 under fourteen years—some as white as your little Willie—no wonder Gods [*sic*] wrath is upon us.—these children were being raised like pigs for the Market—Nothing but blood," he added, "could wipe away so black a stein [*sic*]."[63]

Here was a cardinal sin of the slaveocracy, an unmistakable sign that this particular planter not only succumbed to the imperatives of the market, but he had lost self-control, given in to his baser instincts—instincts that true Christians learned to bridle. Leach contrasted such depravity with the behavior of blacks whom he had converted to the faith, reporting several cases in which black men confessed their love for Jesus. One exclaimed: "Please Father hear me. Please take me. Please give me a new, a clean heart.—; Please save my poor wicked soul." He quizzed another on his "lust" for drink, to learn "no touch dat." What did he do with his "ration?" asked Leach. "Me do nothing," came the reply. "I lets 'em alone." Probing further, he asked if he thought "he was a Christian? Me don't think, I knows," as tears "streamed down his cheeks." He knew he was reborn because "I used to hate what I now love and I loved what—I now hate."[64]

It was a transformative moment for both men, especially for Leach. Much like Pennell, he probed the religious enthusiasm of the benighted African Americans he had grown to respect and love, uncovering "a deep core of conviction" that disclosed "as intelligent views of what it is to serve God as any educated man." He declared them to be "some of the sweetest Christians" he'd ever met.[65]

It isn't possible in this short space to recount the postwar careers of Amherst's Civil War soldiers from the challenges of Reconstruction through the Gilded Age. It is enough to point out that a good number who worked as schoolteachers in the North returned to the South to serve the various Christian organizations that emerged during the war, as well as the Freedmen's Bureau that was formed in its immediate aftermath. Those who entered the service as abolitionists had their convictions confirmed on the slaveholding terrain of the Confederacy. The others, who were more Christian than abolitionist, learned that the stereotypes of African Americans as a race of heathens, doomed to ignorance and dependence, were nonsense. Instead, they found an industrious people eager for self-improvement and, more than that, devout Christians, just as observant as they were. We might think of this shared Christianity as a bridge between the races, a pathway for the men in blue to a more informed understanding of African Americans. The other factor—arguably the critical one—proved to be Amherst soldiers' intimate engagement with self-liberated slaves and those still in bondage who opened their eyes to the human costs of enslavement. Such experiences decisively transformed the college's Christian soldiers from Unionists into advocates for emancipation and, in their more daring dreams, perhaps equality.

Notes

1. E. Harmon to Brother, April 16, 1861, War Materials Collection, Civil War, Folder 2, Amherst College Archives and Special Collections, Amherst College, Amherst, MA. Hereafter WMCCW ACASC. For coverage of the outburst of the patriotic elan on campus following the start of the hostilities that probably prompted Harmon's cautionary note, see *Amherst College Graduates*, August 1917, 235–36. Also see Donald S. Bigelow, "Amherst in Wartime: A Contrast, 1865–1945, *Amherst College Graduations*,1945, 1–9.

2. Edward P. Crowell, *Record of the Graduates and Non-Graduates* of Amherst College in the Services of the Union Army or Navy in the War of the Rebellion (Amherst, MA: Amherst Faculty, 1905), 14, WMCCW ACASC, Amherst College, Amherst, MA; John M. Maki, *William Smith Clark: A Yankee in Hokkaido* (Lanham, MD: Lexington Books, 2002). For Clark's firsthand reportage of his military years, see William, Smith Clark Papers, Archives and Special Collections, W. E. B. Du Bois Library, University of Massachusetts, Amherst.

3. Compiled by the author from Crowell, *Graduates and Non-Graduates* (Sacramento, CA: Creative Media Partners, [1830] 2017).

4. Robert J. Brigham, "A Pious Institution's Reaction to Slavery, 1821–1841" (senior thesis, Amherst College, April 22, 1985), 56, Theses Collection, WMCCW ACASC, Amherst College, Amherst, MA.

5. Quoted in Kanisorn Wongsrichanali, *Northern Honor: College-Educated New Englanders, Honor, Nationalism, and Leadership in the Civil War* (New York: Fordham University Press, 2016), 23.

6. See Crowell, *Graduates and Non-Graduates*, passim; Wongsrichanali, *Northern Honor*, 9. This work points out that of the Amherst College graduates between 1850 and 1865, fully half became clergymen or educators.

7. Crowell, *Graduates and Non-Graduates*, 3. See also, Timothy Robinson Cressy, Alumni Biographical Records, WMCCW ACASC, Amherst College, Amherst, MA, and, W. S. Tyler, *History of Amherst College during Its First Half Century* (Springfield, MA: C. W. Bryon, 1873), 5901–91. It is noteworthy that Cressy early on presided over a congregation that was half white and half black.

8. Crowell, *Graduates and Non-Graduates*, 33 and 40–41.

9. Crowell, 20. Also see Lt. Henry Reuben Pierce, Alumni Biographical Records, WMCCW ACASC, Amherst College, Amherst, MA.

10. The scholarly literature on Union soldiers is too voluminous to treat here in full, but a few of the signal works are Bell Irvin Wiley, *The Life of Billy Yank: The Common Soldier of the Union* (Indianapolis, IN: Bobbs-Merrill, 1951); Gerald F. Linderman, *Embattled Courage: The Experience of Combat in the in the American Civil War* (New York: Free Press, 1987); Reid Mitchell, *Civil War Soldiers: Their Expectations and Experiences* (New York: Viking, 1988); Joseph T. Glatthaar, *Forged in Battle: The Civil War Alliance of Black Soldiers and White Officers* (New York: Free Press, 1990); James M. McPherson, *Why Men Fought in the Civil War* (New York: Oxford University Press, 1997); and Chandra Manning, *What This Cruel War Was Over: Soldiers, Slavery, and the Civil War* (New York: Knopf, 2007).

11. Daniel A. Cohen, "The Life and Death of Lieutenant Pennell: An Exercise in Biographical

Narrative" (senior thesis, Amherst College, 1977), 10, Pennell Papers, Alumni Biographical Records, WMCCW ACASC, Amherst College, Amherst, MA.

12. Edmund Adams Jones in Crowell, *Graduates and Non-Graduates*, 64.

13. F. S. to Edward Dickinson, January 25, 1852, and June 21, 1854, Frazar Stearns Papers, Alumni Biographical Records, WMCCW ACASC, Amherst College, Amherst, MA. The folders in this extensive file haven't been numbered and as a result they could not be cited here. Discriminating readers need to trace the letters by correspondent and date in the various folders.

14. F. S. to Edward Dickinson; Clipping on W. S. Clark, n.d.

15. See David Hill in Crowell, *Graduates and Non-Graduates*, 73–74.

16. See Pennell's obituary, Pennell Papers, Alumni Biographical Records, WMCCW ACASC, Amherst College, Amherst, MA. See also Cohen, "Life and Death of Lieutenant Pennell," 23–25. For tributes to him in the form of clippings, see Pennell Papers, Alumni Biographical Records, WMCCW ACASC, Amherst College, Amherst, MA, passim.

17. C. P. to My Dear Father, April 21, 1861, Pennell Papers, Alumni Biographical Records, WMCCW ACASC, Amherst College, Amherst, MA. See also Cohen "Life and Death of Lieutenant Pennell," 8.

18. Cohen, "Life and Death of Lieutenant Pennell," 8.

19. C. P. to My Dear Father, April 29, 1861, Pennell Papers, Alumni Biographical Records, WMCCW ACASC, Amherst College, Amherst, MA.

20. F. S. to My Dear Father (William A. Stearns), August 28, 1861, and September 30, 1861, Frazar Stearns Papers, Alumni Biographical Records, WMCCW ACASC, Amherst College, Amherst, MA. Also F. S. to My Dear Father (William A. Stearns), October 9, 1861, Frazar Stearns Papers, Alumni Biographical Records, WMCCW ACASC, Amherst College, Amherst, MA.

21. F. S. to Eliza, October 10, 1864, Frazar Stearns Papers, Alumni Biographical Records, WMCCW ACASC, Amherst College, Amherst, MA.

22. F. S. to Eliza, October 22 and 23, 1861, Frazar Stearns Papers, Alumni Biographical Records, WMCCW ACASC, Amherst College, Amherst, MA. Also F. S. to My Dear Father, October 13, 1861, Frazar Stearns Papers, Alumni Biographical Records, WMCCW ACASC, Amherst College, Amherst, MA; clipping, *Hampshire & Franklin Express*, September 15, 1863; C. P to Mrs. Snell, June 11, 1864. Pennell Papers, Alumni Biographical Records, WMCCW ACASC, Amherst College, Amherst, MA.

23. C. P. to Mrs. Snell, June 11, 1864, Pennell Papers, Alumni Biographical Records, WMCCW ACASC, Amherst College, Amherst, MA.

24. C. P. to "Miguonne" (Sabra), July 26, 1864, Pennell Papers, Alumni Biographical Records, WMCCW ACASC, Amherst College, Amherst, MA.. Migounne was his pet name for Sabra but he spelled it variously, sometimes with one *n* and sometimes with two.

25. Cohen, "Life and Death of Lieutenant Pennell," 15–17

26. Mason W. Tyler, *Recollections of the Civil War* (New York: H. P. Putnam's Sons, 1912), 292.

27. Tyler, *Recollections*, 133.

28. Tyler, 134.

29. Tyler, 195.

30. Tyler, 272.

31. Jirik, "We *are* and will be *forever* Anti-Slavery Men".

32. F. S. to Dear Father, September 14 and 20, 1861, Fraser Stearns Papers, Alumni Biographical Records, WMCCW ACASC, Amherst College, Amherst, MA.

33. W. A. S. to F. S., September 17, 1861, Fraser Stearns Papers, Alumni Biographical Records, WMCCW ACASC, Amherst College, Amherst, MA.

34. W. A. S. to F. S., September 30, 1861, Fraser Stearns Papers, Alumni Biographical Records, WMCCW ACASC, Amherst College, Amherst, MA. See also his letters of September 24 and October 2, 1861.

35. Jennifer L. Murphy, "*Life on a Plantation:* Ebenezer Porter Dyer's Civil War Diary" (senior honors thesis, Amherst College, 2008), 44. Ms. Murphy appended excerpts from Dyer's diary to her thesis. Diary entries are cited by year below.

36. Manning, *What This Cruel War.*

37. C. P. to My Dear Father, April 21, 1861, Pennell Papers, Alumni Biographical Records, WMCCW ACASC, Amherst College, Amherst, MA. See also Cohen, "Life and Death of Lieutenant Pennell," 10.

38. C. P. to My Dear Mother, n.d., Pennell Papers, Alumni Biographical Records, WMCCW ACASC, Amherst College, Amherst, MA.

39. C. P. to Dear Madam (Mrs. Snell), January 26, 1864, Pennell Papers, Alumni Biographical Records, WMCCW ACASC, Amherst College, Amherst, MA. See also Cohen, "Life and Death of Lieutenant Stearns," 14.

40. C. P. to Miguonne, July 6, 1864, Pennell Papers, Alumni Biographical Records, WMCCW ACASC, Amherst College, Amherst, MA.

41. On this question of patience, see Bruce Laurie, "Chaotic Freedom in Civil War Louisiana: The Origins of an Iconic Image," *Massachusetts Review*, November 2016.

42. C. P. to Miguonne, July 29, 1864, Pennell Papers, Alumni Biographical Records, WMCCW ACASC, Amherst College, Amherst, MA.

43. C.P. to Miguonne, July 29, 1864, Pennell Papers, Alumni Biographical Records, WMCCW, ACASC, Amherst College, Amherst, Massachusetts..

44. Henry G. Thomas, "The Colored Troops at Petersburg," *Century Magazine*, September 1887, 1–13, Pennell Papers, Alumni Biographical Records, WMCCW ACASC, Amherst College, Amherst, MA. Thomas, still another Amherst graduate, was very much in the mold of Pennell, raising an African American regiment and applauding the general performance of such units. The only information easily accessible on him is Crowell, *Graduates and Non-Graduates*, 33.

45. Crowell, *Graduates and Non-Graduates*, 5.

46. For his obituary and other relevant information, see Pennell in Alumni Biographical Records and Pennell Papers, Alumni Biographical Records, WMCCW ACASC, Amherst College, Amherst, MA, passim.

47. See Willie Lee Rose, *Rehearsal for Reconstruction: The Front Royal Experiment* (Indianapolis, IN: Bobbs-Merrill Company, 1964), 333–35. Rose's coverage of the New England Freedmen's Aid Society, however brief, is one of the few scholarly treatments of this important group.

48. See, for instance, Eric Foner, *Reconstruction: America's Unfinished Revolution, 1863–1877*, 217 and 480.

49. For instance, Laurie, "Chaotic Freedom."

50. Murphy, "Life on a Plantation," 42.

51. Murphy, 42–43.

52. Murphy, 44 and ff.

53. Murphy, 101, 144, and 154–55. Quotation on Dyer, "Civil War Diary," March 12, 1863.

54. Dyer, "Civil War Diary."

55. Dyer, December 2, 1862.

56. Dyer, January 6, 1863.

57. Dyer, October 26, 1862.

58. Murphy, "Life on a Plantation," 32.

59. Murphy, 44.

60. Dyer, "Civil War Diary," May 17, 1863.

61. Crowell, *Graduates and Non-Graduates*, 43. Also see Leach Papers, Alumni Biographical Records, WMCCW ACASC, Amherst College, Amherst, MA.

62. J. A. L. to Professor, June 10, 1864, Leach Papers, Alumni Biographical Records, WMCCW ACASC, Amherst College, Amherst, MA.

63. J. A. L. to Professor.

64. J. A. L. to Professor.

65. J. A. L. to Professor, November 24, 1864.

"Ain't Gonna Pay for War No More"

Taxes, Resistance and Antiwar Activism in the Pioneer Valley and Beyond

Molly Michelmore

In 1972, John Treat and Andrew Von Solis, two Amherst College freshmen, published an article in the *Amherst Student* urging their classmates to break the law. Arguing that "more than 60% of our tax money goes for war—for napalm to burn children, for nuclear weapons, for chemical-biological warfare, for the army to spy on United States citizens," the two urged their fellow Amherst students to limit their "cooperation in paying for this horror" by refusing to pay all federal taxes.[1] Those Amherst students who joined Treat and Von Solis in resisting their federal taxes joined a growing number of Americans using their identity and status as taxpayers to make a variety of political claims; war tax resistance grew in popularity during the Vietnam era. Once the terrain of only a small cadre of dedicated "peacemakers," tax resistance became more commonplace in the late 1960s and early 1970s as antiwar activists and organizations used the practice as a form of both antiwar protest and political mobilization.

War tax resistance was only one avenue through which Amherst College students registered opposition to the US war in Vietnam. As Christian G. Appy's contribution to this volume demonstrates, the Vietnam War, in combination with the black freedom movements, the student movement, and the sexual revolution, convulsed and ultimately transformed Amherst College. The apolitical and self-satisfied college student interested only in "grades, and sex, and sports," that had so disappointed Amherst student John Merson in the early years of the decade, was less in evidence by its end, as Amherst students critically and self-consciously began to engage with the world around them, to "confront the basic issues," and make "this traditional institution pertinent to . . . [their] lives."[2] The history of antiwar protest in general, and war tax resistance in particular, also points to the important, but often unacknowledged, relationships between Amherst the college and Amherst the town. While there were certainly contentious "town-gown" relationships in this period, war tax resisters on campus took their cues from area peace activists at the same time as the presence of Amherst College, not to mention the University of Massachusetts, Smith

College, Mount Holyoke College and, after 1970, Hampshire College, brought potential new activist recruits to the Pioneer Valley.

Amherst College tax resisters were likely influenced by a national organization known as War Tax Resistance (WTR). Founded in 1969, WTR's mission was simple. By telling ordinary citizens how to use their status as taxpayers to register opposition to the ongoing war in Vietnam, WTR would give the right of "conscientious objection" to "all people, not just to those of draft age." Ordinary men and women could "halt and prevent wars" both by "refusing to fight and refusing to pay."[3] WTR also hoped to breathe new life into an antiwar movement whose strategies had so far failed to end the war. As the *Student* reported in April 1970, the nation's "young protestors and reformers had begun to suspect that mass demonstrations are no longer commensurate with present . . . economic, social and political realities." [4] Even as they regularly took part in antiwar protests at nearby Westover Air Force Base, Amherst College students had grown "less concerned about protests beyond the Valley" by the early 1970s.[5] WTR, advocates hoped, would provide citizens with "more concrete avenues of expression, whether electoral or grass-roots community organization."[6]

By 1972, WTR had established over one hundred and eighty educational and political action centers across the country. In a nod to the antitax protests that had preceded the American Revolution, antiwar groups planned "tea bag" tax protests, organized local educational campaigns to show people how to resist taxes, and established "alternative funds" to direct refused tax dollars toward "more constructive purposes."[7] One of the largest and most enduring local WTR centers was Pioneer Valley Tax Resistance (PVTR).

Even before the founding of the national WTR in 1969, Amherst-area citizens experimented with the "possibilities of tax refusal as an effective protest to the war."[8] War tax resistance fit well with the broader political culture of the Pioneer Valley.[9] According to Rob Cox, an archivist at the University of Massachusetts, the people of the Pioneer Valley had long "pursued their own vision of what a just and what an appropriate society is" and organized "around moral issues."[10] Another Valley resident described the area as "one of those magical havens of ultra-progressive politics" thanks to the "five colleges" (the Five College Consortium of the Connecticut River Pioneer Valley of Western Massachusetts: Amherst College, Hampshire College, Mount Holyoke College, Smith College, and the University of Massachusetts Amherst) and its history of "peaceniks and revolutionaries hanging out in the area."[11] "Bringing the war home" through WTR and other forms of antiwar activism brought Amherst College into closer contact with the broader community.

Pacifist organizers in this period joined a host of other activists and organizations from across the ideological spectrum in experimenting with politics that used taxpayer identity to ground and justify claims on the state. These strategies at once reflected the power of the taxpayer as a political identity and helped to constitute taxpaying as an increasingly powerful form of political claims-making. WTR, like other progressive, left-wing, and radical groups, sought to take advantage of the "sense of outrage . . . smoldering in Middle America" in the late 1960s and early 1970s to remake US politics. Where many forms of antiwar activism seemed to only exacerbate the divide between the country's elites—including Amherst College students—and what journalist James Fallows later described as the "boys from Chelsea, thick, dark-haired young men, the white proles of Boston," WTR might bring together, as taxpayers, the antagonists in the era's emerging "class war."[12] Although antitax ideology is often associated with the contemporary right in US politics, the history of war tax resistance brings to light the often forgotten history of progressive tax protest.[13]

Indeed, the rhetoric of taxpayer rights proved almost irresistible in the post-World War II United States, in part thanks to the growth of the federal taxing state during and after the war.[14] It was not until World War II that the majority of Americans came into direct contact with the federal tax system when the Revenue Act of 1942 transformed US income tax from a "class tax" paid by only a small economic elite to a "mass tax," which reached deep into the middle and even working classes. By the end of World War II, the number of federal income taxpayers had grown to 42.6 million, a ten-fold increase from 1939 levels. Federal income tax collections likewise ballooned, reaching $35.1 billion by 1945.[15]

To ensure the success of this new system, the Treasury Department worked hard to create a new "culture of taxpaying," recruiting advertising executives and public-opinion experts to design a campaign to convince millions of Americans to pay their "taxes to beat the Axis."[16] Among these new recruits was Peter Odegard, a Columbia University-educated political scientist who had joined the Amherst College faculty in 1938. Odegard believed that political science and public opinion research could be used to inoculate the public against threats posed by "Nazi, Fascist, Communist and other subversive movements," but only if scholars dedicated themselves to ensuring that the "democratic service state does not degenerate into the totalitarian servile state."[17]

This vision of the role of the political scientist led Odegard into public service. Working first as a consultant to the treasury, he was appointed assistant to secretary Henry Morgenthau in July 1942. From that post, he advocated the "engineering of consent" through public relations techniques.[18] "The average voter," Odegard told an audience in 1936, "is not interested in reams of statistics . . . he is attracted by symbols which catch his eye and hold his interest."[19] A committed New Dealer, Odegard embraced a vision of the liberal state that promised "economic democracy without sacrificing the political liberty that is our most precious heritage."[20] Odegard's primary work was in selling the war bond campaign to retailers and consumers, but this approach shaped the public relations effort to promote and legitimate the income tax. In the end, these efforts to "raise taxes to beat the Axis" linked taxpaying citizenship and the war. Ironically, perhaps, this rhetorical strategy also provided US pacifists and antiwar activists with a new means to register their opposition to the war: tax resistance.

The size and scope of the new federal income tax system, in conjunction with the emergence of a national security state and the anxiety produced by the atomic age, helped to transform tax resistance into a potentially powerful form of conscientious objection. "Peace seekers" recognized that the advent of "push button warfare" would "call for more drafted dollars than drafted men."[21] In 1949, A. J. Muste, a radical clergyman and pacifist, embraced tax refusal as both an act of personal witness and a political strategy. Noting that "the two decisive powers of government . . . are the power to conscript and the power to tax," Muste concluded that the morally consistent pacifist position would be "unquestioningly . . . opposed in principle to paying taxes which went directly and solely to war purposes."[22] Some peace activists also hoped that war tax resistance might prove to be a powerful organizational and political strategy.[23] Because war tax resistance spoke to the shared obligations of taxpayers as citizens, it might prove "an effective device for dramatizing opposition to war." "If one-hundredth of one percent of the people of this country were conscientiously, resolutely, imaginatively, humbly withholding cooperation" from the Internal Revenue Service (IRS), one reasoned, "the prospects for peace would improve immeasurably."[24] For the most part, however, tax resistance remained a form of personal witness rather than a political or organizational tool, and the ranks of tax resisters remained small. By 1962, even the most generous estimates found that "only 300 individuals . . . [were] participating in some form of nonpayment for war."[25]

It took the Vietnam War to popularize war tax resistance. As the United States escalated its involvement in the increasingly costly and unpopular war in Southeast Asia, peace advocates experimented with a variety of ways to bring an end to the war. War tax resisters hoped to leverage the power of taxpayers—whether wealthy suburbanites or college students—to mobilize more people against the war in Vietnam. Antiwar groups targeted "war taxes" as early as 1963. That year, the Committee on Nonviolent Action (CNVA) announced that it could no longer "be an instrument in the collection of a tax from individuals who are conscientiously opposed to paying taxes for war and preparation for war."[26] A year later, folk singer and antiwar activist Joan Baez made headlines when she withheld 60 percent of her income taxes rather than "pay for organized murder."[27] In 1965, after the war had been "Americanized," activists from the CNVA organized a demonstration in front of the IRS building in New York City, to encourage "citizens to refuse to pay all or part of their Federal Income Tax." Connecting the protest to the country's most celebrated tax resister, Henry David Thoreau, the protestors distributed "Thoreau money" to illustrate the phoniness of the "security our defense dollar buys."[28]

President Lyndon B. Johnson refused as long as he could to choose between guns and butter. In 1968, however, with the economic picture deteriorating rapidly, he was forced to accede to budget cutters in Congress by signing the Revenue and Expenditure Control Act of 1968, which paired $6 billion in domestic spending cuts with $10 billion in new taxes.[29] Despite the administration's attempt to frame the new law as an anti-inflationary measure, the press and the public almost always referred to it as the "Vietnam surtax." Enacted less than six months after the Tet Offensive and only three months after Johnson had dropped out of the presidential contest, the new law tied rising tax burdens directly to an increasingly unpopular war, providing antiwar activists with a potentially powerful political and organizing tool.[30]

In February, as Congress considered the White House's tax and budget proposal, twenty Amherst-area activists met at the Unitarian Church on North Pleasant Street to discuss the feasibility of the "withholding of taxes" as a means of protesting the war.[31] Nationally, the passage of the war tax led directly to the formation of the Writers and Editors War Tax Protest, a 528-member group that included James Baldwin, Norman Mailer, William Styron, Betty Friedan, Dr. Benjamin Spock, and urbanist Jane Jacobs.[32] As the war escalated, and in light of the debate over the administration's war tax, mainstream peace groups became more sympathetic to war tax resistance. The American Friends Service Committee (AFSC), which had long opposed war tax resistance, changed its position on the grounds that "the surtax is in fact a war tax imposed to help finance our adventure in Southeast Asia."[33]

The war, and antiwar activism, brought Amherst College students into closer contact with members of the community and with local peace activists. In February 1968, for example, the *Student* reported that the Pioneer Valley Peace Center (PVPC) would hold weekly "evening draft discussions geared toward college students."[34] A week later, the PVPC invited Michael Ferber, a Boston-area peace activist, to address the community on the "implications of joining the Resistance, and the repression that the government and courts" were "presently engaged against the peace movement."[35] In April, in the wake of Martin Luther King Jr.'s assassination, the Students for a Democratic Society (SDS) announced a "Rally for Peace" on the Amherst Town Commons. Leo Marx, of the Amherst College English department, was scheduled to speak to the community on "the possibilities for and necessity of peace." The event marked the beginning of the "Ten Days activities" sponsored by the Smith-Amherst-Holyoke chapters of the SDS, in conjunction with the Valley Peace Center, the Women's International League for Peace and Freedom, and the Faculty Group on Peace and War at the University.[36] The next week, Marx joined civil rights activist Reverend James Bevel at a "rally for Peace in Viet Nam and Freedom at home" on the Amherst town commons. More than two hundred and fifty people attended the rally.[37] At the start of the following school year, members of the Amherst chapter of the SDS expressed interest in "educating the local citizenry in the ideals of the New Left."[38] The Valley Peace Center also advertised "draft workshops" in the pages of the *Amherst Student*.[39]

The election of Richard Nixon, on top of the 1968 surcharge, gave new urgency to war tax resistance. Earlier efforts to "coordinate the various tax campaigns" had failed, and the movement remained relatively small, despite the high-profile actions of a group of committed activists.[40] Hoping to broaden and deepen the movement, and to take advantage of the newly salient power of "taxpayers," made clear by the groundswell of grassroots support for the loophole-closing Tax Reform Act of 1969, the CNVA founded a new organization to coordinate national war tax resistance efforts.[41]

The next year, during the April moratorium, the *Student* reported that Massachusetts antiwar groups had organized "picketing and leafleting at all twenty-one Internal Revenue Service Centers in the state." In Connecticut, students planned to march to the Hartford "IRS Center." In New York City, antiwar protesters had planned a "dramatic gesture . . . against unfair war taxation," including a "Boston Tea Party" in Battery Park, "demonstrations at all IRS centers in the five boroughs," and, after a day of "discussions on the economic impact of the war," a "mass rally in Bryant Park."[42] WTR thus linked student activists, who by virtue of their draft age had a personal stake in ending the war, to the broader public.

War tax resistance depended on and inverted the longstanding relationship between military and fiscal sacrifice established by the World War II-era campaign Odegard had helped to design. The modern American taxing state, rooted in the Second World War, had institutionalized taxpaying as a foundational obligation of national citizenship. But citizenship claims could cut both ways. Where the Treasury Department had, in the past, linked taxpayers' obligation to support the war effort with the "real" sacrifice made by the military, antiwar activists reversed this logic to insist on taxpayers' right to withhold taxes as a legitimate form of protest against an unjust and un-American war. Antiwar activists also saw the relatively democratic nature of taxpaying citizenship as a key to its power as a form of political claims-making. Likening war tax resistance to draft resistance, WTR founder Bradford Lyttle argued that resistance allowed *all* Americans to register their "conscientious objection" to the war. Such direct forms of resistance, antiwar activists argued, were necessary to restore democratic forms of governance and to reverse the damage done by both the Johnson and Nixon administrations to "traditional democratic forms of protest—namely elections and demonstrations."[43]

Tax resistance groups often focused first on the excise tax on telephone service, which many hoped would be a kind of gateway into both tax resistance and the antiwar movement. Unlike income tax resistance, which could be difficult and would expose not only the resister but also her employer to legal jeopardy, resisting the excise tax was relatively easy. As the *Student* informed its readers, "Telephone tax resistance" was "very low risk."[44] According to the War Resisters League, "Every individual with phone service has the clear and effective power to refuse" the excise tax. Because it cost the IRS "more to collect refused tax . . . than the amount of the tax itself," the *Student* assured readers that resisters were unlikely to face any real legal consequences.[45]

Equally important, the telephone tax was closely linked to the "cost of the government's war on Vietnam."[46] Like the 1968 surcharge, the telephone tax was seen as a "clear and uncluttered case of a specific war tax" rather than a "mixed tax," some portion of which would pay for "civilian government."[47] House Ways and Means chairman Wilbur D. Mills's 1966 observation that "the Vietnam operation" made the excise necessary was enough to establish a direct relationship between the war and the phone tax.[48] As the CNVA explained, "We know that revenue for the Vietnam War is revenue for the brutal extermination of thousands of civilians, for the perpetuation of military dictatorship, for napalm and mass bombings, . . . for the indefinite continuation of war." By refusing to foot the bill, American citizens could ensure that this "shall not be <u>our</u> 'operation' <u>our</u> 'bloodbath' or <u>our</u> war."[49]

Telephone tax resistance was a good organizing tool precisely because it was both low-risk and easy. One telephone tax resistance "action bulletin" assured taxpayers that the "government would not be interested in pressing charges" because the IRS did not "desire visibility."[50] Another pointed out that "although there are legal provisions for the enforcement of this tax," there had, as yet, "been no prosecutions."[51] WTR facilitated tax resistance by printing out and distributing "phone tax refusal" cards to explain taxpayers' actions. The cards explained that the "brutal and aggressive war . . . against Vietnam" required the taxpayer to "testify" to his or her "opposition by refusing the pay this tax." These cards served both as a justification for tax refusal and as a low-effort way to recruit future tax resisters by encouraging others to join those who have "decided that it is now necessary to oppose the war tax by refusing the pay the telephone excise tax that helps finance it."[52] Amherst College tax resisters likewise used tax resistance as a way to grow the antiwar movement on campus, and urged interested students to contact them for "information and literature."[53]

Because the telephone tax was "simple, individual and specifically for war," refusing to pay it was a good—and mostly painless—"expression of conscience."[54] Moreover, tax resistance organizations reasoned that if enough people chose to openly refuse to pay the excise tax, it would render the "telephone tax dead" and perhaps "make it impossible" for the federal government "to collect other taxes."[55] Linking tax resistance to the revolutionary spirit of the Boston Tea Party and the nation's founding, war tax resisters insisted, "resistance to unjust taxes has long been a part of the American tradition."[56] The War Resistance League specifically saw telephone tax resistance a means to "initiate hundreds of thousands of people into resistance to the war." By simply "hanging up on the war tax," American citizens might just develop an "appetite for greater risk taking."[57] WTR announced plans to "escalate the number of [phone tax] refusers" to "half million Americans" to "remind Nixon, Agnew and Mitchell that their salaries come out of our pockets."[58] The movement never grew to half a million people. Nevertheless, in 1970, some 28,760 Americans registered their opposition to the war by refusing to pay the phone tax; in 1971, the number of phone tax resisters rose to 56,445.[59] By comparison, that same year, the IRS reported only 1,648 known income tax resisters.[60]

WTR used local groups to "enlist tax refusers" and to use tax resistance as a way to bring more Americans into the antiwar movement. The first "autonomous . . . branches" were established in Boston, Philadelphia, and Chicago.[61] By 1970, the number of centers had climbed to one hundred and sixty. By May 1971, some one hundred and eighty WTR centers had been established. By 1970, WTR's mailing list had grown from twenty-two names to three thousand. While the movement remained relatively small—particularly in terms of income tax resisters—its impact was enough to force the IRS to release new guidelines on how to process "war refusal cases" and to require the "regular monthly reporting of the number of such cases to National IRS."[62] According to *Time* magazine, tax protesters took a "modest pride in the fact that their harassment" had "forced the agency to assign someone at each major center to the position of Viet Nam Protest Coordinator."[63]

War tax resistance as a national movement peaked in 1972. The end of the Vietnam War in 1973 undercut the potential of war tax resistance as the basis for mass mobilization or a renewed progressive politics. WTR and other tax resistance organizations tried to carry the momentum from the Vietnam era into the postwar period, but the results were disappointing. The National WTR ran out of money; many local WTRs, including the relatively large Philadelphia branch, discontinued meetings, eliminated the organization's office, or continued only as a way to lend or give money to "worthy" community organizations through "alternative funds." Leaders in the movement had tried to protect their organizations by making "war tax resistance . . . an entrenched, dynamic and permanent part of American society," but these efforts had been largely unsuccessful.[64]

As the Vietnam War receded into history, the antiwar movement, and the war tax resistance movement it spawned, again became the preserve of a relatively small band of true believers. War tax resistance reemerged in the 1980s, in response to president Ronald Reagan's reinvigoration of the Cold War and the acceleration of the nuclear arms race with the Union of Soviet Socialist Republics. The 1981 decision by the Roman Catholic Archbishop of Seattle, Raymond Hunthausen, to refuse to pay the "war tax" again brought national attention to the connection between war and taxes. Despite Reagan's antitax rhetoric, the IRS actually grew less tolerant of antiwar tax resistance during his tenure. After 1982, many of the techniques war tax resisters had used in the 1960s and 1970s—including claiming fake dependents, taking a "war tax deduction," or using IRS documents to register opposition to war—became subject to new penalties. A new tax law, approved by Congress in 1982, allowed the IRS to fine any taxpayer $500 for submitting "frivolous statements."[65]

Nevertheless, the movement survived, and even thrived, in the Pioneer Valley. One local war tax resister recalled that in the 1980s and 1990s, "there was a higher concentration of war tax resisters" in western Massachusetts "than most places in the country." Wally and Juanita Nelson, who had joined the radical Peacemakers in the 1940s, moved to the area in the 1970s, bringing radical pacifism and tax refusal with them. The Pioneer Valley Tax Resistance (PVTR), which grew out of the Pioneer Valley Study Support Action Group, remained active in the decades after the end of the Vietnam War.[66] Local tax resisters published literature, engaged the local press, organized local "happenings" to educate the public and raise money, and conducted tax resistance clinics. A 1983 brochure, for example, asked, "If you don't believe in war, then why do you pay for it?" Two years later, on the anniversary of the end of World War II, PVTR placed an ad in the *Valley Advocate* urging readers to join the group in "refusing to pay taxes" to ensure "no more Hiroshimas in our name."[67] The advertisement was signed by eighty-two war tax resisters. That same year, the group drafted a "proposal to the national action conference," on the "nonpayment of war taxes" that equated war taxes with "murder and the making of murderers."[68] PVTR continued to offer clinics in war tax resistance. In March 1985, two weeks ahead of the federal tax-filing deadline, PVTR conducted a "Tax Resistance Clinic" at the Jones Library in Amherst and coordinated leafleting in Amherst, Brattleboro, Connecticut, and Greenfield on Monday, April 15.[69] The group continued to host "War Tax Refusal Extravaganzas" for the next decade and a half.

War tax resistance and western Massachusetts returned to the national spotlight in the late 1980s and early 1990s, when the IRS seized and then sold Randy Kehler and Betsy Corner's home in Colrain, Massachusetts, about thirty miles outside of Amherst. Kehler and Corner were war tax resisters and had refused to pay their federal income taxes since the late 1970s. Both had a long history of peace activism. Kehler had served twenty-two months in jail for draft evasion during the Vietnam War. In 1979, he founded the Traprock Peace Center, and two years later, he helped to found a national Nuclear Weapons Freeze Campaign.[70] In 1989, the IRS took possession of the couple's home for the nonpayment of more than $36,000 in back taxes. Rather than leave quietly, Kehler and Corner, as well as their young daughter, stayed in the house. Corner told one reporter, "If it should ever come to physically removing us, we wouldn't cooperate."[71] The government's plans to auction off the house were initially foiled by local and national tax resisters who launched a local pressure campaign to dissuade potential bidders, and submitted their own "bids" in "the form of Nicaraguan currency, goods for the poor, and offers of community service"[72] The War Tax Refusers Support Committee also took out advertisements in local papers, declaring their intent to "nonviolently resist attempts by any buyers to take possession of the home." The campaign worked. With no buyers for the property, the government was forced to buy the home from itself. The success of this effort speaks to the tenacity of the networks of war tax resisters first established in the Vietnam era.

Six months later, in January 1990, the government ordered Corner, Kehler, and their daughter Lillian to vacate their home. When they refused, the Department of Justice (DOJ) filed a civil suit against them. Although Kehler and Corner prepared to challenge the DOJ, in October 1991, a district court judge summarily dismissed the couple's challenge and ordered them to leave the property. When they refused, Kehler was taken into custody by federal marshals for "contempt of court" and sentenced to six months in jail. In response, "affinity groups" of local and national tax resisters occupied the home. According to press reports, supporters "managed to gain entrance through a basement window," allowing more than "a dozen" supporters, "many of whom carried sleeping bags," to enter the house.[73] These affinity groups usually counted "one to two dozen people, some living in the house, and others serving as support persons."[74] Supporters, including such well-known peace activists as David Dellinger and Daniel Ellsberg, came from as "far away as California" and included twelve "affinity groups" from the Pioneer Valley.[75]

In February 1992, the IRS again put the house up for auction; affinity groups mobilized to scuttle the sale a second time, staging a "no bids—not a penny" support rally outside of the Federal Building in Springfield, Massachusetts.[76] This time their efforts failed. Danny Franklin, a part-time police officer from Greenfield, bought the Colrain home—whose market value was probably close to $40,000—for $5,400. The occupation continued, even after Franklin and his fiancée and young daughter took possession of the house in April. Moving into tents around the home, affinity groups kept vigil over the home "twenty four hours a day, seven days a week."[77] Organizers were careful to spell out the "responsibilities of OSC [Occupation Support Committee] People doing Vigil Shifts," encouraging volunteer members to "keep the vigil site and tent area as neat and orderly as possible," to "make sure things are quiet around the vigil by 10:00 p.m," and, under no circumstances, to talk "about the people in the house anywhere near the vigil site."[78] Affinity groups kept up the vigil for more than a year, braving the cold Massachusetts winter in a "small, insulated, moveable structure" the protesters had built to house the "ongoing waves of supporters from all over the country."[79] Then, in June 1993, a federal district court issued an injunction barring Kehler, Corner, and their supporters from the property. Despite the legal risks, most of the protesters maintained their vigil. Over the next few months, more than fifty protesters were arrested. According to one protester, "some people spent time in jail, some found their cases dismissed," and some faced "steep fines and potentially long jail terms."[80]

The standoff between the tax resisters and the new owners of Kehler and Corner's home ended in an out-of-court settlement, what one chronicler described as an "eleventh hour *deus ex machina*" (emphasis in original).[81] Kehler and Corner moved back into their home; they still "refuse to pay taxes that support war and military efforts." In some respects, Kehler and Corner won. They got their home back, the IRS no doubt lost money in prosecuting them, and war tax resistance once again got coverage in national newspapers, including the *New York Times* and the *Washington Post*. The story was even the subject of a feature-length documentary narrated by Martin Sheen.

There is little evidence that Amherst College students took part in the standoff in Colrain. The sixties spirit that had brought together town and college had dissipated by the 1990s. War tax resistance likewise failed to fulfill its advocates' expectations. War tax resistance failed to end the war in Vietnam or check US militarism. Equally important, it had not succeeded in creating a new progressive coalition. WTR activists had joined other progressive organizers, including welfare rights activist and civil rights veterans, in seeing tax politics as a way to rebuild progressive political power. As George Wiley noted, "Elderly and black Vietnam veterans . . . hospital workers, household employees, women, tenants, farm workers, welfare recipients, mineworkers, day care parents, unemployed workers, Chicanos, Blacks, Puerto Ricans, [and] white ethnics" were all *taxpayers*.[82] This shared identity, progressive organizers hoped, could transcend racial, class, and cultural differences to underwrite a new electoral majority. The drama at Colrain—often framed by the press as a revival of the backlash politics of the 1970s that had shattered the Democratic Party and pushed US politics to the right—suggests the failure of this strategy. At least in its public portrayal, the contest between Kehler and Corner, graduates of Harvard and Mount Holyoke, respectively, pitted "liberal elites" and their cultural and social politics against the values and economic interests of working-class families like Danny Franklin's. While this narrative is overly simplified, it is true that the goal of progressive activists to use tax politics to underwrite a new progressive coalition proved elusive.

In the end, tax resistance did not stop the war or stem US militarism. Nor did it provide a lasting basis for a progressive politics. Antiwar protestors thus joined the advocates of women's rights, welfare rights, and racial justice in discovering the limits of tax politics and taxpayer consciousness to effect political and policy changes and disrupt existing hierarchies of power.

Notes

1. Andrew Van Solis and John Treat, "War Tax Resistance Urged," *Amherst Student*, May 1, 1972, 3.

2. "A New Order," *Amherst Student*, February 5, 1968, 2; "Community Power," *Amherst Student*, May 6, 1968, 2.

3. William E. Robinson, "Anti-war Protest at the Crossroads," *Amherst Student*, April 23, 1970, 3.

4. Robinson, "Anti-war Protest."

5. Kim Townsend, *John William Ward: An American Idealist* (Amherst, MA: Amherst College Press, 2014), 64.

6. William E. Robinson, "Anti-war Protest," 3.

7. Bradford Lyttle, "A Summary History of War Tax Resistance and Suggestions for the Future," Swarthmore College Peace Collection, DG 182, PWTR, Box 8, War Tax Resistance Fund—History; and "Philadelphia War Tax Resistance: A Modest Proposal for Life: A New Call to War Tax Resistance," Swarthmore College Peace Collection, PWTR, DG 182, Box 8, Handbook on PWTR, Swathmore College, Swarthmore, PA.

8. Brooke Witing, "Tax Refusal Considered By 20 Area Citizens as Possible Means for Protest of Vietnam War," *Amherst Student*, February 26, 1968, 3.

9. Randy Kehler quoted in Cale Guthrie Weissman, "Growing Up with the War Tax Resisters," *New Republic*, March 3, 2017, https://newrepublic.com/article/141077/growing-war-tax-resisters.

10. Quoted in Weissman, "Growing Up."

11. Weissman.

12. James Fallows, "What Did you Do in the Class War, Daddy?" *Washington Monthly*, October 1975, 5–6, https://web.viu.ca/davies/H323Vietnam/Draft_inequities.1969.htm.

13. By the late 1970s, the US Republican Party had effectively remade itself into the "tax cut party" and had claimed the tax issue as its own. This victory has tended to obscure the importance of tax politics to progressive groups and causes. In addition to WTR, progressives hoped to use public anger toward so-called tax millionaires who exploited loopholes in the tax code to escape paying their "fair share" to anchor a multiracial political coalition. For more on the evolution of the GOP's tax politics, see Issac Martin, *The Permanent Tax Revolt: How the Property Tax Transformed American Politics* (Stanford, CA: Stanford University Press, 2008). For more on the failure of progressive tax politics, see Molly Michelmore, "What Have You Done for Me Lately: The Welfare State, Tax Politics, and the Search for a New Majority, 1968–1980," *Journal of Policy History* 24, no. 2 (2012): 709–40.

14. To be sure, tax resistance predates the second half of the twentieth century. For an overview of the history of war tax resistance, see Molly Michelmore, "Tax Resistance and Pacifism," in *Opposition to War: An Encyclopedia of U.S. Peace and Antiwar Movements in American History*, ed. Mitchell K. Hall (Santa Barbara, CA: ABC-CLIO, 2017).

15. W. Elliot Brownlee, "Tax Regimes, National Crisis, and State-Building in America," in *Funding the Modern American State, 1941–1995*, ed. W. Elliot Brownlee (Washington, DC: Woodrow Wilson Center Press, 1996), 93.

16. Carolyn C. Jones, "Mass-Based Income Taxation: Creating a Taxpaying Culture, 1940–1952," in *Funding the Modern American State, 1941–1995*, ed. Brownlee (Washington, DC: Woodrow Wilson Center Press, 108).

17. "5,000,000 Sought to Aid Democracy," *New York Times*, June 20, 1939, 6; Peter H. Odegard, "The Political Scientist in the Democratic Service State," *Journal of Politics* 2, no. 2 (May 1940): 157.

18. Odegard, "Political Scientist," 164.

19. "Political Oratory Called Meaningless," *New York Times*, October 25, 1936, N10.

20. Odegard, "Political Scientist," 157.

21. Ernest Bromley, "How the Movement on Nonpayment of War Taxes Began," Swarthmore College Peace Collection, Bromley, Box 27, Tax Resistance/Refusal, Handbook on Nonpayment of War Taxes, 1981, Swarthmore College, Swarthmore, PA.

22. A. J. Muste, "Individual Tax refusal, Memorandum," May 1948, Swarthmore College Peace Collection, Bromley, Box 24, Tax Resistance/Refusal, AJ Muste, FOR, Peacemakers, Swarthmore College, Swarthmore, PA.

23. Muste, "Individual Tax refusal, Memorandum."

24. Orval Etter, "Peacemakers and War Taxes," 1950, Swarthmore College Peace Collection, Bromley, Box 27, Tax Resistance/Refusal: Peacemakers—Tax Resistance, 1950–1959, Swarthmore College, Swarthmore, PA.

25. Ernest Bromley, Information Sheet on Nonpayment of Taxes for War: How the Movement Began, March 3, 1962, Swarthmore College Peace Collection, Bromley, Box 27, Tax Resistance/Refusal: Peacemakers—Tax Refusal, 1960–1970, Swarthmore College, Swarthmore, PA.

26. CNVA letter to IRS district director, March 3, 1963, Swarthmore College Peace Collection, DG 17, Committee for Nonviolent Action, Box 22, Projects: IRS Tax Withholding Action, Swarthmore College, Swarthmore, PA.

27. "Joan Baez Again Refuses to Pay Part of Income Taxes," *New York Times*, April 16, 1965, 35.

28. CNVA press release, April 13, 1965, Swarthmore College Peace Collection, DG 17, Committee for Nonviolent Action, Box 22, Projects: IRS Tax Withholding Action, Swarthmore College, Swarthmore, PA.

29. For more on the "agony of the $6 billion" and the passage of the Revenue and Expenditure Control Act of 1968, see Julian Zelizer, *Taxing America: Wilbur D. Mills, Congress, and the State, 1945–1975*

(Cambridge: Cambridge University Press, 1994); and Robert M. Collins, "The Economic Crisis of 1968 and the Waning of the American Century," *American Historical Review* 101, no. 2 (1996): 396–422.

30. By the end of the 1960s, antiwar sentiment was common, even among the silent Americans of middle America. In April 1967, more than two hundred and fifty thousand Americans—most of them "nonradical" and "nonmilitant"—marched against the war in hopes of getting the administration to withdraw American troops from Vietnam. That same month, Martin Luther King Jr. publicly condemned the war effort as "unjust, evil and futile" and cited the "monumental dissent" against the war as a reason to rejoice. See David Farber and Beth Bailey, eds., *The Columbia Guide to America in the 1960s* (New York: Columbia University Press, 2003), 41; and Martin Luther King Jr., "Why I am Opposed to the War in Vietnam," Berkeley Library, University of California, Berkeley, April 30, 1967, http://www.lib.berkeley.edu/MRC/pacificaviet/riversidetranscript.html.

31. Witing, "Tax Refusal Considered."

32. C. Gerald Fraser, "Writers and Editors to Defy Tax in War Protest," *New York Times*, January 31, 1968, 2

33. Memo to AFSC Board of Directors from Stephen Car, September 22, 1967, re: The President's Surtax Proposal, Swarthmore College Peace Collection, PWTR, Box 11, Letters–Tax Refusal, 1969, Swarthmore College, Swarthmore, PA.

34. Richard H. Meeker, "Information on Draft Made Available by Valley Peace Center, ACLU, Others," *Amherst Student*, February 15, 1968, 2.

35. Alan M. Webber, "Elective Politics, Resistance: Alternative Methods of Protest," *Amherst Student*, February 22, 1968, 3.

36. "SDS Plans Rally, Films, Speakers as Part of '10 Days,'" *Amherst Student*, April 18, 1968, 1.

37. Edward Claftin, "Bevel, Former Aid to King, Decries Nationalistic Wars," *Amherst Student*, April 22, 1968, 1.

38. Mark Hall and James Brudney, "150 Attend First SDS Meeting: Issues, Goals, Set-up Discussed."

39. Advertisement, *Amherst Student*, October 7, 1968, 5.

40. "Tax Resistance Project, Memo on Tax Resistance," December 6, 1967, Swarthmore College Peace Collection, Bromley Papers, DG 214, Box 20, Tax Resistance/Refusal: No Tax for War—Correspondence, Swarthmore College, Swarthmore, PA.

41. The Tax Reform Act of 1969 was a relatively progressive tax reform measure that eliminated a variety of loopholes from the tax code and cut taxes for the working and middle classes. The law was a direct result of a public campaign to target and eliminate "tax millionaires" who had exploited the tax code to reduce, or even eliminate, their federal tax liabilities. For more on the Tax Reform Act of 1969, see Molly Michelmore, *Tax and Spend: The Welfare State, Tax Politics, and the Limits of American Liberalism* (Philadelphia: University of Pennsylvania Press, 2011), chpt. 4.

42. Charles Unfug, "Moratorium This Week: Teach-In, Fast," *Amherst Student*, April 15, 1970, 1.

43. Lyttle, "Summary History of War Tax Resistance."

44. Van Solis and Treat, "War Tax Resistance Urged."

45. Van Solis and Treat, "War Tax Resistance Urged."

46. "No Tax for War Committee," WLR flier, February 9, 1968, Swarthmore College Peace Collection, DG 214, Bromley Papers, Box 20, Tax Resistance/Refusal: No Tax for War Committee, Swarthmore College, Swarthmore, PA.

47. FPC Action Bulletin on Telephone Tax Refusal, October 1967, Swarthmore College Peace Collection, PWTR, Box 11, Background: Tax Refusal, Swarthmore College, Swarthmore, PA.

48. Wilbur Mills, "Debate on the Tax Adjustment Act of 1966," *Congressional Record*, February 23, 1966, 3529.

49. "Chicago Workshop in Nonviolence," press release, n.d., Swarthmore College Peace Collection, CNVA, Series 6, Projects, Box 22, Projects: IRS Withholding Action, 1963–1966, Swarthmore College, Swarthmore, PA.

50. FPC Action Bulletin on Telephone Tax Refusal.

51. "Say NO to the War in Vietnam," PWTR flier, Swarthmore College Peace Collection, DG 182, PWTR, Box 8, WTR Clinics and Demonstrations, Swarthmore College, Swarthmore, PA.

52. Reprinted in Calvert, 50.

53. Van Solis and Treat, "War Tax Resistance Urged."

54. FPC Action Bulletin on Telephone Tax Refusal, l.

55. David McReynolds, War Resistance League staff memo, December 1969, Swarthmore College Peace Collection, Philadelphia War Tax Resistance, DG 182, Box 11, War Tax Resistance—National, Swarthmore College, Swarthmore, PA.

56. PWTR, "For Life Liberty, and the Pursuit of Taxes," n.d., Swarthmore College Peace Collection, DG 182, PWTR, Box 11, News from WTR Centers, Swarthmore College, Swarthmore, PA.

57. "Telephone Tax Resistance –A Taxpayers Rebellion," WLR staff document, #1–70, Swarthmore College Peace Collection, DG 182, PWTR, Box 11, WTR National, Swarthmore College, Swarthmore, PA.

58. War Resistance League, flier prepared as part of the Telephone War Tax Resistance–Taxpayers Rebellion, n.d., Swarthmore College Peace Collection, PWTR, Box 11, Wart Tax Resistance–National, Swarthmore College, Swarthmore, PA.

59. "War Tax Protesters," *Time*, June 19, 1972.

60. Kennett Love, "Hanging Up on War," *New York Times*, October 2, 1971, 31. This number *was* significantly higher than 375 income tax resisters reported in 1967.

61. War Tax Resistance, letter, March 3, 1972, Swarthmore College Peace Collection, DG 182, Philadelphia War Tax Resistance, War Tax Resistance–National, Swarthmore College, Swarthmore, PA.

62. Robert Calvert, ed., *Ain't Gonna Pay for War No More* (New York: War Tax Resistance, 1971), 44.

63. "War Tax Protesters," *Time*. The *New York Times* reported the previous year, however, that the IRS saw war tax resisters as an "annoyance more than anything else." See Bill Kovach, "Protest Diverts Telephone Taxes," *New York Times*, February 28, 1971, p7.

64. Lyttle, "Summary History of War Tax."

65. Diane Liederman, "Holyoke Protester Butts Heads with IRS," *Transcript-Telegraph*, January 31, 1985, Swarthmore College Peace Collection, Nelson Papers, Box 18, Series E: Reference Material, Subject: Pioneer Valley War Tax Resistance, Swarthmore College, Swarthmore, PA.

66. "Twenty Years of Pioneer Valley War Tax Refusers," April 12, 1997, Swarthmore College Peace Collection, DG 262, Juanita Morrow Nelson and Wally Nelson Papers, Series C: Juanita and Wally Nelson Together, Box 11, Participation in/involvement with Pioneer Valley War Tax Resisters (Greenfield, Massachusetts), Swarthmore College, Swarthmore, PA.

67. *Valley Advocate*, advertisement, July 17, 1985, Swarthmore College Peace Collection, DG 262, Juanita Morrow Nelson and Wallace F. Nelson Papers, Box 11, Participation In/Involvement in Pioneer Valley Peace Resisters, Swarthmore College, Swarthmore, PA.

68. "Nonpayment of War Taxes," 1985, Swarthmore College Peace Collection, DG 262, Juanita Morrow Nelson and Wallace F. Nelson Papers, Box 18, Pioneer Valley War Tax Resistance, Swarthmore College, Swarthmore, PA.

69. PVTR, "Don't Pay War Taxes," leaflet, Swarthmore College Peace Collection, DG 262, Box 18, Pioneer Valley War Tax Resistance, Swarthmore College, Swarthmore, PA.

70. Randy Kehler "CV," Swarthmore College Peace Collection, DG 262, Series E, Randy Kehler and Betsy Corner (Tax Resisters) and Home in Colrain, Swarthmore College, Swarthmore, PA.

71. Joseph Mallala, "Tax Resisters: IRS to Sell Colrain House to Pay for Taxes," *Recorder*, March 7, 1989, 1.

72. Christopher Daly, "Tax Protests Bring Down a House," *Washington Post*, December 3, 1989, A3.

73. B. J. Roche, "Backers of Tax Resisters Reoccupy Seized Home," December 5, 1991, Swarthmore College Peace Collection, DG 262, Series E, Randall Kehler and Betsy Corner (Tax Resisters) and Home in Colrain, Swarthmore College, Swarthmore, PA.

74. War Tax Refusers Support Committee, "Open Letter to Our Neighbors in Franklin County," March 28, 1992," Swarthmore College Peace Collection, DG 262, Series E, War Tax Refusers/Resisters Support Committee, Swarthmore College, Swarthmore, PA.

75. War Tax Refusers Support Committee; "Colrain Journal: Tax Protest on Military Finds Focus at a House," *New York Times*, March 9, 1992, A8. Ellsberg credited a 1971 meeting with Kehler who had been jailed for draft evasion, with his decision to release the Pentagon Papers.

76. "No Bids–Not a Penny," leaflet, February 2, 1992, Swarthmore College Peace Collection, DG 262, Series E, Randall Kehler and Betsy Corner (Tax Resisters) and Home in Colrain, Swarthmore College, Swarthmore, PA.

77. Betsy Williams, "Following the Courage of One's Convictions," *Pioneer Valley Forum*, Swarthmore College Peace Collection, Nelson Papers, Box 18, Swarthmore College, Swarthmore, PA.

78. "Responsibilities of People Doing Vigil Shifts," n.d., Swarthmore College Peace Collection, DG 262, Series E, Randall Kehler and Betsy Corner (Tax Resisters) and Home in Colrain, Swarthmore College, Swarthmore, PA.

79. Williams, "Following the Courage," 22.

80. Williams, 22.

81. Weissman, "Growing Up with the War Tax Resisters."

82. George Wiley, "Need for a Taxpayer's Uprising," Discussion Draft on Organization, August 29, 1974, WHS, MEJ, File 4: TJP BKGR—State Organizations, California Tax Reform Association.

"A Pervasive and Insistent Disquiet"

Amherst College in the 1960s

Christian G. Appy

When John Merson arrived at Amherst College in 1962 from North Carolina, he quickly found a set of friends who shared his political and social curiosity, particularly Elliott Isenberg and Marshall Bloom. Isenberg started the first Amherst chapter of Students for a Democratic Society (SDS) while Bloom became editor in chief of the *Amherst Student* and later cofounded Liberation News Service, a radical press syndicate, and Montague Farm, a countercultural commune. Merson became president of the student council his junior year and then left Amherst to join the US Marine Corps. He served a tour of combat duty in Vietnam from 1966 to 1967.

In 1962, these freshmen concluded that many classmates "did not care about anything except grades and sex and sports."[1] For Merson, Isenberg, and Bloom, the prevailing student culture seemed apolitical, self-satisfied, and unconscious or uncritical of the white privilege and economic elitism that characterized both the college and the nation. Their view may be exaggerated, but it is certainly true that virtually no one—including the three maverick freshmen--questioned male dominance at the all-male school.

When the decade began, there was not a single woman on the faculty (psychologist Rose Olver arrived in 1962, the sole female professor until 1966). Faculty wives were automatically enrolled in a group called "Ladies of Amherst." As Marietta Pritchard recalls, "People wore hats and white gloves to the formal teas where cucumber sandwiches were served and the college president's best silver service was on display."[2] And throughout the sixties, despite broad social and political ferment, contributors to the *Amherst Student* continued to refer to the students at Mount Holyoke and Smith as "girls" while describing themselves as men. Until 1971, moreover, the college hired women to clean the rooms and make the beds of its students.

The college's most famous professor, historian Henry Steele Commager, exemplified the prevailing liberal complacency of the early years of the decade. A leading public intellectual since the 1930s, Commager had been a strong critic of McCarthyism. He was also an unabashed celebrator of American exceptionalism. In his 1961 article "Do We Have a Class Society?" Commager answered definitively "no." Drawing primarily on nineteenth-century writers like Alexis de Tocqueville and Henry James to prove US classlessness in the mid-twentieth century, Commager rehearsed a familiar argument—the United States had a unique history, distinct from the "Old World," lacking a feudal tradition, inherited nobility, and established church. Born with unprecedented freedoms and opportunities, the United States developed a fluid social system that prevented the rise of fixed or persistent inequalities. "If there is a power elite in the United States," Commager concluded, "perhaps the most interesting thing about it is that anyone with sufficient talent can join.... The rise of the Negro to middle class status is as inevitable as was the rise of the Irish and Italians of earlier generations."[3]

Most Amherst students in the early 1960s not only shared Commager's faith in American exceptionalism, but also believed they were destined to assume a place among the nation's "best and brightest" in law, government, medicine, business, or academic life. Events at Amherst and throughout the world during the 1960s radically challenged all of these assumptions and more. By the latter half of the decade, a rapidly growing number of students (and Commager himself) demanded that the college and the nation confront the flagrant contradictions between their professed ideals and the persistent realities of war, racism, inequality, and academic irrelevance and indifference. The college's history was profoundly altered by the era's political ferment, although many of the most substantive changes—such as coeducation and greater class and racial diversity in the student body—would not be realized until the 1970s and beyond.

However, even in 1962, there were signs of change. Early that fall, Merson and his friends were inspired by H. Stuart Hughes (class of 1937), a Harvard history professor and nuclear disarmament activist who made a number of appearances in the Amherst area while running unsuccessfully as an independent candidate for the Senate. The *Amherst Student* endorsed Hughes, praising his proposal for disarmament with the Soviet Union and a unilateral ban on nuclear testing.[4]

A few weeks later, the Cuban Missile Crisis brought the world to the brink of nuclear war. The *Amherst Student* editors—well to the left of many students in the early sixties—criticized president John F. Kennedy's decision to blockade Cuba as provocative and an "act of war." The paper also posted a prophetic editorial criticism of the faculty: "We deeply regret that most professors have not seen fit to discuss the Cuban situation in their classes. We believe the teacher is responsible for making his discipline relevant to vital current experience."[5]

By 1963, the civil rights movement began to engage a growing number of Amherst students. However, white students like Marshall Bloom dominated organizations like Students for Racial Equality, in part because there were so few African Americans. Until 1968, there were never more than twenty-five black students in an enrollment of roughly twelve hundred. That year, sixteen black students entered— a small number, but enough to provide a larger base for social and organizational identity. As Cuthbert "Tuffy" Simpkins (class of 1969) recalls, "When I got to Amherst [in 1965] there was a weird [unwritten] rule that black students ... wouldn't be more than three to a group.... The burden was on us to integrate." Only in the late sixties, when Simpkins became the first president of the Afro-American Society, did black students feel free to express a collective affinity: "We didn't have to disperse ourselves among everybody. We were just going to sit and enjoy ourselves and be with each other."[6]

During spring break in 1964, Marshall Bloom, inspired by Martin Luther King Jr.'s call for support from northern students and clergy, drove to St. Augustine, Florida, with Amherst College chaplain Lewis Seymour Mudge to challenge Jim Crow and seek to register black voters. Bloom participated in an integrated lunch-counter sit-in and spent five days in St. John's county jail. As Bloom made clear in the articles he wrote about the episode, blacks who participated in such protests sometimes spent six months in jail. Over the next two years, Bloom made several longer trips to the south in support of the civil rights struggle.[7]

At Amherst, Bloom also initiated an exchange program with historically black colleges. According to John Merson, Bloom came up with the idea out of annoyance that the student council considered giving money to the Rugby Club to go to Bermuda for spring training. "Bloom had the idea that if people are going to propose something this stupid and it's going to be taken seriously, why not propose an exchange program." Students from Stillman (Tuscaloosa), LeMoyne (Memphis), and a few other historically black colleges began coming to Amherst during their spring breaks (while Amherst was still in session), and Amherst students went to the southern schools during their break.[8] Innovative as these exchange programs were, they involved a small number of students (fewer than a dozen each year), especially when compared with the more than 125 Amherst athletes who routinely traveled south to train during spring break.[9]

In 1965, attention turned increasingly to Vietnam. For at least the first half of the decade, the majority of Amherst students (as at other colleges and universities) either supported the war in Vietnam or, despite doubts and reservations, were willing to defer to the president on matters of foreign policy. Antiwar protests were relatively small and often challenged aggressively by student counter-protesters. At midnight on April 16, 1965, some one hundred local people (including about twenty-five Amherst students) boarded busses for Washington, DC, to participate in the first major anti-Vietnam War demonstration. As the busses were about to pull out, a group of about ten Amherst students from the nearby Beta Theta Pi fraternity house jumped in front of the busses and formed a chain. SDS president Elliott Isenberg went out to talk with the counter-protesters but returned to announce: "They won't move." At that point, the driver revved the engines and moved forward, slamming the breaks, according to one source, just six inches away from the human barricade. That was enough to scatter the counter-protesters.[10]

Later that year, in October 1965, volunteers of the Committee for Nonviolent Action (CVNA) arrived on campus and set up a display of antiwar literature in a dining hall lobby. During lunch, one student flipped over the CNVA table. At dinner, some students grabbed a stack of antiwar books and pamphlets and burned them in a nearby parking lot. When one of the middle-aged activists went to inspect, students threw water balloons at her and removed air from the peace group's car tires.[11] The students were not punished, only made to apologize and pay thirty-five dollars to cover the costs of the damaged material.[12] In the weeks that followed, a prowar petition signed by 363 Amherst students circulated. It began: "Premature withdrawal from Vietnam would be more immoral than any atrocities of the present war."[13]

In March 1966, some seventy-five Amherst College students (about half of them SDS members) began a hunger strike to protest the US destruction of South Vietnamese crops with chemical defoliants. The action, led by students Roy Chaleff and George Sleeth (both class of 1968) coincided with similar hunger strikes at other institutions, including the University of Massachusetts, Wesleyan University, and Trinity College. Eleven Amherst faculty members issued a statement in support of the strike.[14] One of them, historian N. Gordon Levin, added: "The belief that the triumph of the N.L.F would be a threat to . . . our cherished way of life is to me one of the greatest misconceptions of the 20th Century."[15]

The first Amherst College antiwar protest to gain substantial national attention came at the 1966 commencement. The week before graduation, students learned that the board of trustees had decided to award an honorary degree to secretary of defense Robert McNamara, a major architect of the war since his appointment by President Kennedy in 1961. Thirty-seven of the two hundred and seventy seniors decided to protest the decision by wearing white armbands over their academic robes. Nineteen of them also staged a walkout just before McNamara was to receive his degree. A photograph of the walkout appeared in the *New York Times*, *Life Magazine*, and other publications. Most articles criticized the Amherst demonstration as "foolish and immature" or a "display of boorishness and bad manners." Many writers disapproved of the protesters' long and shaggy hair (just a few years later, their hair length would seem unremarkable, even modest).[16]

A year before the McNamara protest, Amherst junior John Merson left school to join the US Marine Corps. It was a shock to the prowar students on campus who believed Merson was antiwar. He was. After "endless" conversations with Elliott Isenberg and Marshall Bloom, Merson concluded that US intervention was wrong. Yet, as he explained in a memoir, *War Lessons*, he enlisted not out of a commitment to the cause but simply "to prove myself worthy of my father's respect" and because "I had this idea that if I went to war somehow I would come out of it as a stronger person."[17]

While in Vietnam, Merson's most loyal Amherst correspondents were Bloom and Isenberg. Bloom sent him articles and photographs of the McNamara walkout. Merson wrote his father that he found the news "pleasing . . . it showed students in a decidedly political frame of mind, using whatever opportunities might present themselves to give voice to political opinions."[18] Bloom's involvement was "exactly what I would have expected. Marshall had the strongest sense of any of us that we're responsible for our own education. We can't be dictated to."[19]

Merson's Vietnam experience reveals another form of dissent that's not well remembered: the growing opposition of American GIs who came to believe the war they were sent to fight was senseless, futile, and even immoral. The most extreme forms of dissent and disobedience—desertion, mutiny, and the killing ("fragging") of officers—were rare until 1969 and on. However, even in 1967, John Merson and his squad sometimes ignored orders to avoid combat: "I reached a point where I would not go on any patrol in areas where we were either going to kill people that shouldn't be killed or we were gonna get [our own] people killed.[20]

The tipping point for Merson came when his unit was patrolling near the village of

Dai Loc, west of Danang. There had been reports of Vietcong coming down a nearby river. While searching the bank, Merson stripped down and jumped in the water to look for underwater cave entrances. He found an opening just below the water surface that led to an underground room. With this new evidence, the lieutenant ordered two squads to stay by the river all night and shoot anyone they saw coming down the river: "Shortly after midnight, our men on the bank spotted boats coming down the river toward the cave entrance. Waiting until the boats were close, they fired automatic rifles, machine guns, and grenade launchers. . . . None of the boats' occupants survived. All of the people our soldiers had killed were unarmed women, children, and old men, perhaps a total of twenty people."[21] Merson was not a direct part of the killing, but he felt complicit in a massacre that he realized was a predictable result of US policy: "Our rules of engagement called for us to fire on anyone out of his house at night. . . . How little were the victims' lives worth? Little enough that not even an investigation was required. If they meant so little, then what was I doing here? If those lives meant anything at all, then what had I become?"[22]

From that point on, Merson tried to keep his squad out of combat as much as possible by ignoring orders that risked lives, and by volunteering for medical patrols, accompanying a hospital corpsman to villages to offer minor medical treatments.

While Merson was headed to Vietnam, Bloom began a master's program at London School of Economics (LSE).[23] When he returned to the United States in 1967, he and Ray Mungo, former editor of the student paper at Boston University, founded the Liberation News Service. Twice weekly the syndicate distributed articles to four hundred underground and alternative newspapers, a crucial source of information for all the social movements of the era.

The next summer, 1968, Bloom and Mungo moved their operation from New York City to western Massachusetts where Bloom helped found a commune called Montague Farm. Mungo soon went to Vermont to help found Total Loss Farm. They hoped to establish not just countercultural communes to get "back to nature" and "live off the land" (to use the clichés of the communal movement), but to continue political activism.[24] A year later, in 1969, at age twenty-four, Bloom committed suicide. Some friends believed one possible cause was his inability to live an openly gay life—a testament to a liberation struggle still in its infancy.

Yet Montague Farm persisted and retained its reputation for political activism. One resident, Sam Lovejoy, became a major leader of the antinuclear movement. In 1974, in the middle of a winter night, he loosened the turnbuckles on the guy-wires holding up a five hundred-foot weather tower constructed by Northeast Utilities (to collect information for a license to build a twin nuclear power plant in Montague). The tower came crashing down. After turning himself in to the police, Lovejoy defended himself successfully in court and was acquitted (primarily because the prosecution bungled the language of the charge). Eventually Northeast Utilities abandoned the project. Over the next decade, antinuclear protest helped to cancel scores of nuclear plant projects.[25]

When Lovejoy was a senior at Amherst in 1969, the campus was vastly more politicized than it had been just four years earlier. The growth of antiwar opposition at Amherst, as elsewhere in the country, was triggered in part by the looming threat of the draft and the dread of being forced to fight a war that most Americans had concluded was not worth waging. But a broader political transformation was prompted as much by a burgeoning counterculture as by specific events. As students began to question the society's prevailing views about individualism, success, and US exceptionalism, many turned to authors like Herman Hesse, Herbert Marcuse, R. D. Laing, and Ken Kesey for alternative visions and inspiration. Above all, they turned to music and, by the late 1960s and early '70s, marijuana and psychedelic drugs.

For Nick Bromell (class of 1972), author of *Tomorrow Never Knows: Rock and Psychedelics in the 1960s*:

> The primal scene of Amherst in the 1960s was a dorm room—and there were lots of them all over campus—where about six guys gathered in the late afternoon hours to smoke pot and listen to music: Dylan, the Doors, Hendrix, Janice Joplin, Sly, the Beatles, James Brown, the Dead, the Stones.... We listened to this music as if our lives depended on it, as if it gave some kind of sense and order to that turbulent, magical, unrepeatable time we were blessed and cursed to live through. And the thing is, it did.[26]

In the spring of 1969, the campus debated Vietnam, student rights, economic and racial inequality, and the purposes of higher education. These debates took center stage in April, when the faculty agreed to cancel classes and most extracurricular activities for a two-day moratorium on April 28 and 29. The idea for a campus-wide discussion emerged from an English seminar called English and Education, when Jared Kass (class of 1969) asked why they were discussing Keats when a war in Vietnam was still raging. His question prompted such a prolonged and heated debate that it led to the call for a campus-wide discussion. Although a significant portion of professors regarded the proposal as "a sort of spring high jinks," the faculty voted two to one to support it. At least part of the motivation to comply may have stemmed from a concern that radical students would occupy campus buildings (as had occurred at Columbia the prior spring and at Harvard a few weeks earlier).[27]

During the first day of the moratorium, some six hundred Amherst students (about half of those enrolled) joined with one hundred faculty members outside Robert Frost Library for several hours of public discussion. By the end of a four-hour meeting on the second night, the campus agreed to support a range of nonbinding resolutions. Most aimed at giving students a greater voice in the curriculum and governance of the college, but they also included calls to raise the minimum wage for nonacademic employees of the college and to create an admissions policy committed to a "proportional representation of the socio-economic strata of the United States." Support for coeducation also surfaced but gained little traction.[28]

The most significant document produced by the moratorium was a letter to president Richard Nixon drafted by professor of English Leo Marx and dean of the faculty Prosser Gifford. It was, as the letter itself states, approved by an "overwhelming majority of Amherst students, faculty and administration who attended the closing meeting of our days of inquiry." Amherst president Calvin Plimpton had little choice but to agree to send the letter to Nixon over his signature.

The letter, widely cited in national publications, was clearest about one point: the "turmoil among young people" was not "caused by a small minority of students" but reflected a "pervasive and insistent disquiet." Moreover, unrest would continue "until you [President Nixon] and other political leaders of the country address more effectively, massively, and persistently the major social and foreign problems of our society." The letter did not include a specific reference to the Vietnam War but identified "the huge expenditure of national resources for military purposes, the inequities practiced by the present draft system [inequities that most Amherst students benefitted from], the critical needs of America's 23,000,000 poor, [and] the unequal division of our life on racial issues."[29]

The letter was reprinted in full in the *New York Times* and given respectful, front-page coverage.[30] A month later, the *Times* reported on the 1969 commencement and included a photograph of senior Lawrence E. Dilg Jr. playing an electric guitar and singing Dylan's "Sad-Eyed Lady of the Lowlands." Breaking with tradition, the senior class voted to have Dilg offer music rather than a speech. He received a "30-second standing ovation," and "nearly half the class, including six of the nine students graduating summa cum laude, wore red armbands in protest against the Vietnam War. Many raised clenched fists or made a V sign with their fingers and remained silent when the national anthem was played." Open dissent had become a majority experience at Amherst, a dramatic transformation from 1966 when just thirty-seven students wore armbands in protest of Secretary of Defense McNamara.[31]

Efforts to promote racial justice had also escalated by the late 1960s. Even many of the small changes reveal how deeply racism was entrenched at Amherst and the nation. For example, when Harold Wade Jr. arrived at Amherst from Queens in 1964, he was one of only twenty-five African Americans in the student body. In those years, an Amherst a cappella group was still singing "Mississippi Mud," a minstrel song that included the lines: "They keep time by clapping their hands / Just as happy as a cow chewing on a cud / When the darkies beat their feet on the Mississippi mud." Wade told the group to stop performing that song or *their* name would be mud. They did.[32]

Wade went on to help found the Afro-American Society in 1968, the first majority-black organization on campus. After Amherst, he went to Harvard Law School where, in his spare time, he drafted a book called *Black Men of Amherst*. It was published posthumously after Wade's tragic drowning in 1974, a day before his twenty-sixth birthday.[33]

Horace Porter (class of 1972) was one of the young leaders of the Afro-American Society. Porter, the sixth of nine children from a Georgia farm family, had lived as a boy in a small rented house with no electricity or running water. Buoyed by a strong Christian faith, devoted parents, a few important mentors at his segregated high school, and frequent visits to the recently desegregated public library in Columbus, Porter became the only member of his family to attend college.[34] He intended to go to Morehouse in Atlanta but became interested in Amherst after reading *The College Student's Handbook* by Eugene Wilson, dean of admission at Amherst College.[35] Porter became one of twenty-seven African Americans admitted to Amherst the fall of '68 (and one of sixteen who accepted).

Porter took his first trip on an airplane to attend the college he had never seen in a region he had never visited. According to his memoir, *The Making of a Black Scholar*, he arrived at Amherst as a polite, deferential, conservatively dressed, and somewhat intimidated Christian. He quickly became enthralled with the intellectual stimulation of the college; he just as rapidly realized that it was not immune from the specter of racism and exclusion. A white classmate casually used the N-word one night in Porter's freshman dormitory, and another classmate introduced him by saying, "This is my friend Horace from the ghetto."[36]

By the second semester of his freshman year, Porter was among the leaders of the Afro-American Society that had already begun to push the college administration on the creation of a black studies department; increased recruitment, admission, support, and funding of black students; and the establishment of a Black Culture Center. After a few modest steps, many black students believed the college was simply stalling by substituting studies, meetings, and advisory committees for substantive change. When the Board of Trustees met in February, 1969, Porter was among the activists who presented them with a statement denouncing the "glaring deficiencies in the liberal education which Amherst College boasts to provide" along with a set of concrete demands.[37]

What Porter's memoir evokes is not just the growing militancy of Amherst students of color and the justice of their claims (there was, for example, only one African American professor at the college in 1969), but also the sense that growing assertiveness was coupled with doubts and ambivalence.[38] Porter was troubled by the plan to present the demands and walk out without any discussion, particularly because the board included judge William Hastie, the nation's first black federal judge. After the walkout, the protesters sent an apology to Hastie.

The pace of change remained painfully slow, and the Afro-American Society organized one of the most dramatic Amherst protests of the decade. It was announced in the *Amherst Student* on February 18, 1970, with a boldfaced banner headline: BLACKS SEIZE BUILDINGS. At one o'clock in the morning, some two hundred and fifty African American students from Amherst and other area colleges entered four campus buildings (Converse, Frost Library, the Science Center, and College Hall). After successfully and nonviolently demanding that any white students or employees in the buildings leave, the occupiers chained the doors from the inside.[39]

The next morning, President Plimpton agreed to meet a delegation of students at his home. They presented a list of demands, including a major increase in African American enrollment and financial aid, a more robust set of support services, and a black studies department (not just a "program") with a black director. The faculty condemned the building takeovers but called for "substantive negotiations" with the protesters. The occupations had lasted no more than about fifteen hours. The college made no commitment on specific admission goals or financial aid set-asides but did agree to open a black studies department in the fall of 1970.

By contrast with building occupations at Columbia (1968), Harvard (1969), and Cornell (1969), the Amherst action was a relatively polite affair, reflecting, in part, the broader sympathy of the faculty for student dissent and the respect student radicals had for a considerable number of their professors. At Columbia, students occupied a handful of buildings for a week before being violently evicted by New York City police using tear gas and batons.

At Cornell, members of the Afro-American Society took over a building nonviolently but armed themselves after white fraternity members tried to evict them. A photograph of Cornell students carrying rifles became one of the era's iconic images.[40]

Two months after the Amherst occupation, on April 30, 1970, when President Nixon announced his unilateral decision to invade Cambodia, hundreds of schools went on strike, and many shut down for the remainder of the semester. The storm of outrage intensified on May 4, 1970, when national guardsmen killed four students at Kent State University in Ohio.

That night, at 7:00 p.m., the "Amherst Strike Committee" called a college-wide rally in front of Chapin Hall. As people gathered, "Volunteers" by Jefferson Airplane blared from loudspeakers near a makeshift podium: "Look what's happening out in the streets / Got a revolution / Got to revolution." After several student speakers endorsed the strike, professor George Kateb strode toward the microphone. Everyone knew that the brilliant political theorist had been a strong critic of efforts to "politicize" the campus, arguing that it should be a "haven for intellectual development" and not take institutional positions on public affairs. "I don't know any answers," he began, "and I'm not even sure I know the right questions." The crowd fell silent. "My outrage and my dismay have deepened for a very simple and academic reason: Nixon's behavior in Cambodia indicates that the President of the United States now feels he can make any commitment he wants . . . only on extraordinary occasions should the academic community take a stand. I've overcome my very deep scruples about seeing Amherst enter the public arena."[41]

Within an hour of Kateb's short speech, the faculty voted for a resolution, pledging to "join with our students in expressing our outrage" and calling for "the cancellation of all normal activities of the College," to provide time for campus-wide discussions and an "exploration of joint actions of persuasion and protest."[42] Although Amherst students would almost certainly have gone on strike regardless of whether the faculty supported them, Kateb's leadership undoubtedly rallied a considerable number of otherwise reluctant colleagues and students. It also underlines an important aspect of this history: Amherst faculty support for student dissent was deeper than at many other colleges and universities in the nation. In addition to supporting the strike, Amherst professors voted to "formally declare its support for the national movement to end the war in Indochina, to end the vilification of youth by public authorities, and to insure justice and full constitutional freedoms for Americans of all races." At an all-college assembly in Johnson Chapel, professor Leo Marx described the nationwide strikes as "the largest, most comprehensive and militant act by American students and faculty in the history of this Republic."[43]

Some histories have suggested that the Kent State killings and the campus strike movement of 1970 marked the "end of the 1960s" and its social activism. In fact, many important movements were just gaining momentum or had hardly begun—women's liberation, gay and lesbian rights, the environmental movement, the antinuclear movement, disability rights, and more. Nor was protest against the Vietnam War at an end.

Indeed, at Amherst College, the most serious antiwar protests did not occur until 1972, the last full year of US military involvement in the Vietnam War. They were prompted by President Nixon's April 16 announcement that he had ordered a renewal of bombing on

North Vietnam, including the cities of Hanoi and Haiphong. At several all-college meetings, hundreds of students agreed to a two-day voluntary strike to enable participation in protests. One hundred and fifty students fasted for five days and between April 21 and May 11, they participated in fifteen demonstrations at Westover Air Force Base in Chicopee, Massachusetts, blocking traffic into and out of the base, acts for which more than five hundred people were arrested, including a substantial number of Amherst students.[44] Westover was thirty miles from Amherst College and, from campus, you could frequently see and hear gigantic C-5 cargo planes coming and going from Vietnam.

On May 9, Nixon upped the ante by announcing that he had ordered the mining of North Vietnamese waterways and harbors, including Haiphong. Some students called upon the new Amherst president John William Ward (who succeeded Calvin Plimpton in the fall of 1971) to write a letter of protest to President Nixon (like the one sent by Plimpton during the 1969 moratorium).

Although Ward had opposed the war since 1964, had spoken out against it, and had stood in silent antiwar vigils on the town common, he had never participated in a confrontational antiwar demonstration. On May 10, Ward rose to speak at an all-college meeting of eight hundred people. "Write a letter? To whom?" he asked the crowd. And what good would it do? The mines had already been laid: "I do not think words will now change the minds of men in power who make these decisions. . . . I do not care to write letters to the world. Instead, I will, for myself, join in the act of passive civil disobedience at Westover Air Force Base."[45] It may be the only instance in which a college president has ever led his students and faculty in an act of civil disobedience.[46]

Early the next morning, May 11, according to the *New York Times*, "some 1000 students" from area colleges, four hundred from Amherst (along with President Ward and faculty members) sat down in protest at Westover. After they blocked the entrances to the two main gates for nearly two hours, police led or dragged them to busses that drove them to Chicopee jail. Officials were so overwhelmed they postponed the arraignments and sent everyone home.

Ward's antiwar activism, coming in the first year of his presidency, strained his relations with the board of trustees and some college alumni, but perhaps not as much as might have been expected. The alumni office concluded that two-thirds of Amherst graduates defended Ward's participation in the Westover demonstration, with a significant generation gap in attitudes. Among alumni who graduated from the 1930s to the 1950s, a slight majority disapproved of Ward's actions. However, among graduates from the 1960s, an overwhelming 92 percent supported Ward.[47] He would go on to lead the college toward coeducation before leaving Amherst in 1979.

As for historian Henry Steele Commager, his criticisms of the US government in the late 1960s starkly contrasted to early national cheerleading he offered in his 1961 article "Do We Have a Class Society?" The decade seems to have given him a much more acute awareness of the nation's capacity for evil. In the fall of 1972, he published an article called "The Defeat of America," arguing that the nation's moral survival was at stake in Vietnam, and required defeat:

> This is not only a war we cannot win, it is a war we must lose if we are to survive morally. . . . We honor now . . . those Germans who rejected Hitler and his monstrous wars and were martyrs to the cause of freedom and humanity. Why do we find it so hard to accept this elementary lesson of history, that some wars are so deeply immoral that they must be lost, that the war in Vietnam is one of these wars, and that those who resist it are the truest patriots?[48]

That "lesson" had wide support at Amherst College in the early 1970s. But in the decades that followed the Vietnam War, historical memory of the antiwar movement cast it in an increasingly negative and distorted light, a reminder that the transformations of the 1960s were neither so deep nor so enduring as we might imagine.

When I arrived at the college in the fall of 1973, the great majority of my classmates were, like me, white men from upper middle-class families. We had no sooner arrived when one of our classmates, Gerald Penny, an African American from New Orleans, drowned in the Amherst College pool while taking an ill-supervised and antiquated required swimming test.[49] We still ate on china that featured, in purple, an armed colonial-era soldier on horseback—perhaps Lord Jeffery Amherst himself—chasing Native Americans around the rim of the plate. And in November of 1973, the *Amherst Student* ran a lurid, over-the-top column called "Sleazing," offering advice to college men on how to "cash in at slit city." While editors claimed it was a mere satire in support of coeducation, it nonetheless reflected a still rampant culture of predatory sexual behavior.[50]

Yet the "pervasive and insistent disquiet" of the 1960s continued to challenge the college in the decades that followed. It provided the ground on which many changes, great and small, would be built—most dramatically, the strikingly greater diversity of the college's faculty, student body, and curriculum.

Notes

1. John Merson, interview with author, May 27, 2017.

2. Marietta Pritchard's "Life Support" is an unpublished book completed in 2007. The excerpt I'm quoting can be found online at "Amherst in the 1950s and 1960s," Amherst College, n.d., https://www.amherst.edu/academiclife/colloquia/colloquium-seminar-archives/women_teaching/reflections/node/338089; Elizabeth Aries, Rose Olver, and Jane A. Taubman, *Gender Matters: The First Half Century of Women Teaching at Amherst* (Amherst, MA: Amherst College Press, 2014).

3. Henry Steele Commager, "Do We Have a Class Society?" *Virginia Quarterly Review* (Autumn 1961). The essay is reprinted in Alexander Burnham, ed., *We Write for Our Own Time: Selected Essays from Seventy-Five Years of the Virginia Quarterly Review* (Charlottesville, VA: University Press of Virginia, 2000), 131–37. His "familiar argument" can be found, for example, in Louis Hartz, *The Liberal Tradition in America* (New York: Harcourt, Brace and Jovanovich, 1955).

4. *Amherst Student*, September 29, 1962.

5. "Amherst's Silence," *Amherst Student*, October 25, 1962, October 29, 1962 for the criticism of Kennedy. The chairman of the editorial board during the missile crisis was George E. Peterson (class of 1963) and the managing editor was Brooke Gregory (class of 1963).

6. Katherine Whittemore, "His Black History: The Unfinished Story of Harold Wade Jr. '68," *Amherst*, Winter-Spring 2018, 24.

7. Martin Dobrow, "The Shaping of Marshall Bloom at Amherst College in the '60s," *Daily Hampshire Gazette*, May 26, 2016.

8. Merson, interview. Announcements of the exchange programs appear regularly in the *Amherst Student*. See, for example, March 3, 1966. According to John Kroll (class of 1966), the student council once allocated funds for SDS but rescinded the support after some students protested, including Ken Bacon (class of 1966), later a reporter for the *Wall Street Journal* and a spokesman for the Department of Defense. See Kroll, email correspondence with the author, December 28, 2018. According to the *Amherst Student*, April 15, 1965, 3, the student council contributed $135 for a Vietnam War teach-in at the University of Massachusetts, and thirty-five dollars for the publication of a booklet, edited by Leonard Lamm (class of 1966), on student and faculty views of the war.

9. *Amherst Student*, March 17, 1966.

10. See Dan Cochran, "To March, Or Not?" *Amherst Student*, April 18, 1965, 3. Organized by SDS, the demonstration attracted twenty-five thousand people, far more than expected, but still a fraction of the hundreds of thousands who would soon participate in public protest.

11. *Amherst Student*, October 28, 1965.

12. *New York Times*, November 7, 1965. Although there was no punishment, the college president, Calvin Plimpton, did publicly criticize the violent infringement of free speech.

13. *Amherst Student*, November 1, 1965.

14. *New York Times*, March 8, 1966. George Sleeth died in 2005. See "George K. Sleeth '68," Amherst College, n.d., https://www.amherst.edu/amherst-story/magazine/in_memory/1968/georgeksleeth.

15. *Amherst Student*, March 10, 1966. Most of the students fasted for four days, but some continued for a week. During dinner hours, the fasters gathered for discussions of the war. "It drew a larger number of student protestors than have ever been excited by any issue of national politics," claimed Chaleff. And because it focused on the destruction of crops rather than the war itself, it drew a few students who were troubled by the conduct of the war but did not challenge the legitimacy of the war itself. *Amherst Student*, March 14, 1966.

16. "The 145th Commencement," *Amherst Alumni News*, Summer 1966, Marshall Bloom Collection (class of 1966), Box 5, Folder 23, Amherst College Archives and Special Collections, Amherst College, Amherst, MA, contains clippings of the coverage. The *New York Times* coverage by John H. Fenton was evenhanded and made clear that when McNamara answered questions from students and parents prior to the ceremony, "at no time did [the questioning] fall short of good taste." Fenton also quoted Marshall Bloom, saying that his activism was motivated by his love of his college and the country. *New York Times*, June 4, 1966, 1. According to *Time* magazine, when college president Calvin Plimpton read the official citation of the award, his voice broke: "You have displayed an integrity so unquestioned that I am willing to trust my sons to your administration." *Time*, June 17, 1966.

17. John Merson, *War Lessons: How I Fought to Be a Hero and Learned that War Is Terror* (Berkeley, CA: North Atlantic Books, 2008); Merson, interview.

18. Tom Fels, "War Correspondents," *Amherst*, Fall 2009.

19. Merson, interview.

20. Merson.

21. Merson, *War Lessons*, 61–62.

22. Merson, 62–63.

23. Martin Dobrow, "Marshall Bloom's Liberation Search Ended Alone in a Field," *Daily Hampshire Gazette*, May 28, 2016. At the London School of Economics, Bloom was soon elected president of the

Graduate Students Association and led protests against the new LSE director Walter Adams, a supporter of Rhodesian apartheid. During one of these demonstrations, a security guard died of a heart attack, which led to contentious London demonstrations about the radical American—some protesters carried signs saying "Bloom Go Home," others passed out flowers, "A Bloom for Bloom."

24. However, the strains of agricultural life soon made it impossible to sustain the Liberation News Service (especially since the move to Montague Farm left behind, in New York City, a competing faction of the same news syndicate). See Tom Fels, *Buying the Farm: Peace and War on a Sixties Commune* (Amherst, MA: University of Massachusetts Press, 2012); Ray Mungo, *Famous Long Ago: My Life and Hard Times with Liberation News Service, at Total Loss Farm and on the Dharma Trail* (New York: Citadel Press, 1991).

25. Harvey Wasserman, "The Tower that Toppled a Terrible Technology," *The Progressive*, February 27, 2013.

26. Nick Bromell, *Tomorrow Never Knows: Rock and Psychedelics in the 1960s* (Chicago, IL: The University of Chicago Press, 2000); Nick Bromell, interview with the author, January 9, 2019.

27. *Amherst Student*, April 26, 1969. "English and Education" was taught by Kim Townsend, Leo Marx, and William Heath, and attracted students interested in teaching, in part because it would provide an exemption from the draft. According to Townsend, the moratorium grew out of a heated debated sparked by a student named Jared Kass who said he "wanted to know why we were going to talk about Keats when there was a war in Vietnam." Email correspondence with the author, June 3, 2019.

28. *Amherst Student*, May 1, 1969.

29. A full copy of the letter can be found in Immanuel Wallerstein and Paul Starr, eds., *The University Crisis Reader: The Liberal University Under Attack*, vol. 1 (New York: Vintage, 1971), 48–49.

30. "Amherst Warns Nixon on Unrest," *New York Times*, May 3, 1969, 1. The full text of the letter was reprinted on 23.

31. Robert Reinhold, "Folk-Rock Singer Breaks Old Tradition at Amherst," *New York Times*, June 7, 1969, 22.

32. Whittemore, "His Black History," 23

33. Harold Wade Jr., *Black Men of Amherst* (Amherst, MA: Amherst College Press, 1976).

34. Horace A. Porter, *The Making of a Black Scholar: From Georgia to the Ivy League* (Iowa City: University of Iowa Press, 2003).

35. Abraham H. Lass and Eugene S. Wilson, *The College Student's Handbook* (New York: D. White, 1965). The book included a list of books aspiring college students should read. Porter not only read many of the books but initiated a correspondence with Wilson.

36. Porter, *Making of a Black Scholar*, 49.

37. Porter, *Making of a Black Scholar*, 56–57.

38. Porter, *Making of a Black Scholar*, 64.

39. *Amherst Student*, February 18, 1970; Porter, *Making of a Black Scholar*, 64–68.

40. On Columbia University, see Paul Cronin, *A Time to Stir: Columbia '68* (New York: Columbia University Press, 2018); on Harvard, see Roger Rosenblatt, *Coming Apart: A Memoir of the Harvard Wars of 1969* (Boston, MA: Little Brown, 1997); on Cornell, see George Lowery, "A Campus Takeover That Symbolized an Era of Change," *Cornell Chronicle*, April 16, 2009, http://news.cornell.edu/stories/2009/04/campus-takeover-symbolized-era-change.

41. *Amherst Student*, May 7, 1970.

42. Benjamin DeMott, *Surviving the 70s* (New York: E. P. Dutton, 1971), 101–3; *Amherst Student*, May 7, 1970. According to English professor Benjamin Demott, Kateb "galvanized the community. . . . Because he behaved as he did[,] we're in the national movement, committed to the national strike."

43. *Amherst Student*, May 7, 1970. Marx also said the strike was a "profound political act" that exposed the "fundamental and underlying incompatibility between a society devoted to war and racism and imperialism and the principles of higher education for which we all stand."

44. Townsend, *John William Ward*, 95–117; for a slightly different version, see Kim Townsend, "Civil Disobedience: A Question of Institutional Involvement," *Massachusetts Review* 53, no. 4 (Winter 2012): 701–16.

45. Townsend, *John William Ward*, 101–2.

46. James Patrick Brown, "The Disobedience of John William Ward: Myth, Symbol, and Political Praxis in the Vietnam Era," *American Studies* 47, no. 2 (Summer 2006): 5–22.

47. Brown, "Disobedience," 106–7.

48. Henry Steele Commager, "The Defeat of America," *New York Review of Books*, October 5, 1972. The essay is reprinted in Henry Steele Commager, *The Defeat of America: Presidential Power and the National Character* (New York: Simon & Schuster, 1974), 104.

49. Townsend, *John William Ward*, 150–53.

50. Townsend, 93–94.

Contributors

Martha Saxton is professor emerita of history and sexuality and women's and gender studies at Amherst College. She is the author of the recently released *The Widow Washington: The Life of Mary Ball Washington.*

David W. Wills is the John E. Kirkpatrick 1951 professor of religion emeritus at Amherst College.

Gary Kornblith is professor emeritus at Oberlin College, where he taught American history for three decades. His most recent book is *Elusive Utopia: The Struggle for Racial Equality in Oberlin, Ohio,* jointly authored with Carol Lasser.

Trent Maxey teaches Japanese history at Amherst College. He is currently working on a history of twentieth-century Japan through the lens of automobility.

Frederick E. Hoxie is professor emeritus of history, law, and American Indian studies at the University of Illinois Urbana-Champaign. He has received both an undergraduate degree (1969) and an honorary doctoral degree (1994) from Amherst College.

Wendy H. Bergoffen teaches in the American studies department at Amherst College. Her scholarship on American Jewish experience has appeared in *Shofar: An Interdisciplinary Journal of Jewish Studies.*

Nicholas L. Syrett is professor of women, gender, and sexuality studies at the University of Kansas. He is the author of two books: *The Company He Keeps: A History of White College Fraternities* (2009) and *American Child Bride: A History of Minors and Marriage in the United States* (2016).

Matthew Alexander Randolph is a graduate student in history at Stanford University, where he studies the history of the African diaspora in the United States, Latin America, and the Caribbean. At Amherst, he served as historian for the Black Student Union from 2015 to 2016.

Daniel Levinson Wilk is professor of American history at SUNY-Fashion Institute of Technology. He writes about the history of waiters, elevators, and the modern service sector and serves on the board of Remember the Triangle Fire Coalition.

Rick López is professor at Amherst College in history and environmental studies, and chair of Latinx and Latin American studies. He is author of *Crafting Mexico: Intellectuals, Artisans, and the State after the Revolution* (2010) and articles and essays on race, aesthetics, nationalism, and nature in Mexican history. Since 2014, he has served as dean of new students at Amherst College.

K. Ian Shin is assistant professor of history and American culture at the University of Michigan. He is currently completing his first book titled Imperfect Knowledge: Chinese Art and American Power in the Transpacific Progressive Era.

David S. Reynolds is a distinguished professor of American literature and American history at the Graduate Center of the City University of New York. His fifteen books include *Walt Whitman's America*; *John Brown, Abolitionist*; *Waking Giant: America in the Age of Jackson*; *Mightier Than the Sword: "Uncle Tom's Cabin" and the Battle for America*; and *Beneath the American Renaissance: The Subversive Imagination in the Age of Emerson and Melville*.

Jane F. Thrailkill teaches American literature and medical humanities at the University of North Carolina at Chapel Hill and also in the School of Medicine. Her books are *Affecting Fictions: Mind, Body, and Emotion in American Literary Realism* (2007) and *Philosophical Siblings: Varieties of Playful Experience in Alice, William, and Henry James* (forthcoming).

Julie Dobrow is the director of the Center of Interdisciplinary Studies and a professor in the department of child study and human development at Tufts University. Her mother/daughter biography of Mabel Loomis Todd and Millicent Todd Bingham, *After Emily: Two Remarkable Women and the Legacy of America's Greatest Poet*, was published in 2018.

Michael E. Jirik, Ph.D., is a Lecturer in History at the University of Massachusetts Amherst and a Visiting Lecturer in Black Studies and History at Amherst College. He is working on a book manuscript that examines the dynamics of slavery and antislavery at colleges.

Bruce Laurie is professor of history emeritus at the University of Massachusetts Amherst. His books include *Working People of Philadelphia, 1800–1850* (1980); *Artisans into Workers: Labor in Nineteenth-Century America* (1989); *Beyond Garrison: Antislavery and Social Reform* (2005); and *Rebels in Paradise: Sketches of Northampton Abolitionists* (2015).

Richard Teichgraeber III teaches and writes American intellectual history at Tulane University. His most recent book is *Building Culture: Studies in the Intellectual History of Industrializing America* (2010).

Debby Applegate's first book began as a senior thesis in the Amherst College American studies department and was inspired by the statue of Henry Ward Beecher (class of 1934) and her work-study job in the college archives. *The Most Famous Man in America: The Biography of Henry Ward Beecher* won the 2007 Pulitzer Prize for biography. Her next book, on the notorious Jazz Age madam Polly Adler, is forthcoming.

Molly C. Michelmore is an associate professor of History at Washington and Lee University in Lexington, Virginia. Her work investigates the relationship between tax and spending policy and politics in twentieth-century United States. A former congressional staffer and fellow at the Miller Center for Public Affairs, Michelmore's first book, *Tax and Spend: Welfare, Taxes and the Limits of American Liberalism*, was published in 2012.

Christian G. Appy is a professor of history at the University of Massachusetts Amherst. He is the author of *American Reckoning: The Vietnam War and Our National Identity* (2015); *Patriots: The Vietnam War Remembered from All Sides* (2003); and *Working-Class War: American Combat Soldiers and Vietnam* (1993), and the editor of *Cold War Constructions: The Political Culture of United States Imperialism, 1945–1966* (2000). He is currently working on a book about the impact of nuclear weapons on US culture, politics, and foreign policy since World War II.

Acknowledgments

This volume would not exist without the support and enthusiasm of dean Catherine Epstein, president Biddy Martin, the former head of Frost Library Bryn Geffert, and the staff at Frost Library, including Margaret Dakin, Michael Kelly, Rachel Gordon, and Christina Barber. It also is the product of the support of Karen Sanchez-Eppler, Nicola Cortright, John Servos, and others on the board of Amherst College Press. Special thanks to Beth Boukoulos of Amherst College Press and to Amanda Karby of Michigan Publishing. Thanks also to Martha Umphrey and Heather Grimes for our editorial conference. Finally, all the contributors, despite serious time pressures, worked enthusiastically. Some went way beyond their obligations and helped the editor in various ways: my great thanks to Gary Kornblith, Fred Hoxie, Richard Teichgraeber, Christian G. Appy, Bruce Laurie, and Debby Applegate.

CPSIA information can be obtained
at www.ICGtesting.com
Printed in the USA
JSHW021549150422
24907JS00003B/4